ELDER STATESMAN

A BIOGRAPHY OF

J. REUBEN CLARK

BY

D. MICHAEL QUINN

Signature Books • Salt Lake City

"To them of the last wagon" and
to those, like J. Reuben Clark, in loyal opposition.

∞ *Elder Statesman: A Biography of J. Reuben Clark* was printed on acid-free paper and was composed, printed, and bound in the United States of America.

© 2002 Signature Books. All rights reserved.
Signature Books is a registered trademark of Signature Books Publishing, LLC.
www.signaturebooks.com

07   06   05   04   03   02   6   5   4   3   2   1

Library of Congress Cataloging-in-Publication Data
Quinn, D. Michael
   Elder statesman : a biography of J. Reuben Clark / by D. Michael Quinn.
     p. cm.
   Includes bibliographical references and index.
   ISBN 1-56085-155-4
   1. Clark, J. Reuben (Joshua Reuben), 1871-1961. 2. Mormons--United
   States--Biography. I. Title.
BX8695.C287 Q55 2001
289.3'092--dc21
[B]

                                     2001049404

Lettered, clamshell edition by John Lytle

CONTENTS

PREFACE

In July 1993 Brigham Young University Press legally assigned to me "the copyright and publication rights" of "the complete book" titled *J. Reuben Clark: The Church Years*. It emphasized the activities that followed Reuben's years of service as U.S. Undersecretary of State and U.S. ambassador to Mexico. This was my first book, which BYU published ten years earlier. It has long been out of print.

Before the book went to press and after Reuben's children approved a preliminary manuscript, the LDS First Presidency appointed two apostles to give final approval to a revised version before its 1983 publication. BYU administrator Robert K. Thomas relayed "suggested changes" to me in 1982 following his consultations with elders Howard W. Hunter and Thomas S. Monson. So that it could be an officially approved biography, I made numerous deletions and revisions in my first draft.

Recently Francis M. Gibbons published his reactions to the preliminary manuscript I submitted in 1981. He was the secretary to the First Presidency at the time. My book was to be the third in the officially authorized series on J. Reuben Clark.

> When the third manuscript was submitted, President [Marion G.] Romney was offended and visibly upset. I know that because I was present when it was discussed. It was honeycombed with so many questionable anecdotes and quotes and contained so much misleading innuendo as to distort President Clark's role as an Apostle and a Special Witness.
>
> There was serious doubt whether the manuscript would be pub-

lished. It was finally cleared for publication only after numerous items had been changed or deleted. Even then, President Romney had qualms about it. The manuscript as originally submitted probably would have had the approval of the modern warts-and-all school of biography. It is certain, however, it did not meet President Romney's standard of what is appropriate and acceptable in portraying the life of a Prophet.[1]

This perspective is news to me in view of what President Romney's close friend Gordon Burt Affleck told me in 1981-82. As co-trustee of the Clark papers at BYU, Affleck said he read the entire first draft aloud to the nearly blind President Romney who told him he felt it captured the essence of President Clark's personality and church service. And as stated in the preface to my 1983 book, Affleck told me: "President Romney and I want this biography to present him honestly, even if there are controversies." I published that quote while both men were still living and neither disputed it.

President Romney and the two apostles preferred some trimming of quotes and anecdotes that they regarded as sensitive, but they allowed my biography to present the basic controversies of Clark's life and religious experience. Its publication in 1983 introduced readers to his decades of church inactivity before he entered the First Presidency, his near-descent into atheism, his unpopularity with Utah Mormons in the 1930s and 1940s, the widespread resistance to his philosophy about the church's Welfare Program, his being investigated by U.S. intelligence agencies as a possible subversive during World War II, his conflicts with LDS president David O. McKay, and his controversial statements about church administration, doctrinal matters, the fallibility of decisions by the First Presidency and statements by the "living prophet," about academics, politics, Franklin D. Roosevelt, the federal government, Adolf Hitler, Jews, racial matters, and twentieth-century wars and revolutions.

Despite its discussion of these controversies, both Apostle Hunter and Apostle Monson told me they regarded *The Church Years* as "a wonderful biography." This was during individual meetings with me in July–August 1983 following my return from six months in Europe. BYU published the book during my absence. Elder Monson told me that he gave copies of it to all of his children. At this time President Romney was incapacitated and unable to communicate with the public. However, during that summer I received praise from Reuben's children and from Gordon Affleck.

In a published response to the Gibbons essay, LDS historian Lawrence Coates recently noted: "In his condemnation of this kind of history, Gibbons uses such condescending words as the 'warts-and-all school,' who use 'all relevant or irrelevant facts about a person, good or bad, constructive or destructive.'" Coates observed: "When Gibbons uses such condemning labels, he fails to come to grips with the most fundamental issue of whether a book or article rests on sound scholarship. Instead his emotional appeal discredits the messenger in the hope people will not read his message."[2]

Some writers insist that a publication is "balanced" or "objective" only if it corresponds with their own views or with an authority structure's approval. This includes matters of interpretation, as well as decisions about what evidence is appropriate to reveal to readers. Others dismiss any effort at balance or objectivity as philosophically impossible, insisting instead that advocacy is the only "honest" approach for an author. Still others believe it is religiously disloyal for a Mormon to attempt to write balanced history because it allegedly undermines the proselytizing goal of "faith-promoting history." Such views reject the approaches to writing history that I regard as both balanced and preferable to advocacy.[3]

In presenting this biography of J. Reuben Clark, I decided to restore my original draft and to add additional research. While the officially approved version introduced readers to controversies in his life and thought, this unofficial biography fully examines those. However, I have tried to maintain the neutral tone and balance of my comments, interpretations, and narrative.

I have not updated the citations for manuscript collections to reflect more recent processing or cataloging that may have occurred in various archives after my research in the late 1970s. However, if manuscripts are now available in published form or in a more accessible archive, I have changed their citations for the convenience of readers.

In 1988 I resigned as full professor and director of the BYU history department's graduate program due to conflicts with the school's administrators over academic freedom. In a several-month process that began in February 1993, I was eventually excommunicated from the LDS church. In the first official communication to me, LDS leaders listed my recent publications about Mormon history as evidence of my "apostasy" (heresy).[4]

Therefore, some readers may wish to compare this current book with the first draft I wrote in the early 1980s when I was a professor at BYU and an official of the LDS church at a local level. The biography's original note cards are in the collection of my research files at the Beinecke Rare Book and Manuscript Library at Yale University. Those will be available to the public when the collection is fully processed. The biography's first draft and revised drafts of 1981-82 are in my personal papers which will not be available to the public until after my death. However, other existing copies of my first draft may become available in Utah manuscript repositories as they obtain the collections of individuals listed in my introduction as readers of the preliminary version.

I thank Beinecke Library curator George Miles for taking the time to double check variations between the preliminary drafts now at Yale. Also for the patience of double checking the accuracy of certain quotes and bibliographic citations, I am grateful to Alan Barnett, Gary Bergera, Harvard Heath, Walter Jones, Jim Kimball, and Ron Priddis. In addition, I owe special thanks to several persons for the process of transferring my typed manuscript to this printed form: Howard Alan Christy, Connie Disney, and Jani Fleet. With special thanks to Robert Dawidoff, who arranged for the Claremont Colleges to grant me library privileges as a visiting scholar during the first half of the year 2000 and to Walter L. Williams who sponsored my appointment as Affiliated Scholar at the University of Southern California in fall 2000.

As a biographer, I admired many of J. Reuben Clark's views as I became acquainted with them while researching his papers. I was unable to say in the draft written for official approval that I was also appalled by other ideas which he expressed frequently and emphatically.

I state my dissenting biases now. As a lifelong Democrat and left-wing liberal, I disagreed with Clark's Republicanism and conservative political philosophy. As an advocate for an open marketplace of diverse and conflicting ideas (even at BYU), I disagreed with his decades of anti-intellectual emphasis. Although he and fellow travelers regarded *liberal* and *intellectual* as labels of dishonor or disrespect, I have always regarded them as worthy qualities in religious people. I was also extremely offended by his racial attitudes and anti-Semitism. As a self-consciously gay male since the age of twelve, I disagreed with most of what he said about homosexuality. And as the father of my own four children, I grieved that this counselor in the First Presidency publicly announced that sexually active youths were better off dead.

However, as a U.S. veteran of the Vietnam era and as a historian, I had mixed reactions toward his views about war. I understood his distaste for the Mexican Revolution because, from 1910 to 1933, he had to deal with its negative effects on U.S. interests, but as a Chicano I appreciated his expressions of personal affection for the Mexican people. I also understood his disillusionment after disclosures of deception in anti-German propaganda during World War I, the allegations that Britain manipulated the U.S. government into entering this European conflict, and his conclusion that American soldiers who died in 1917-18 "to make the world safe for democracy" had been sacrificed to advance British imperialism. In addition, several military leaders and reputable historians have agreed with his assessment that the Pearl Harbor attack resulted from Roosevelt's goading Japan into firing the first shot so the United States could aid Britain. On the other hand, I regarded Reuben's pro-Hitler statements during the early 1940s as indefensible. His condemnations of American and British wartime atrocities seemed one-sided in view of his silence about atrocities by the Germans and Japanese. Nevertheless, I admired his isolationist consistency in also demanding non-intervention against international Communism during the Cold War despite his fervently anti-Communist views. And I agreed with his statement against U.S. participation in the Indo-China conflict which became the Vietnam War.

From the outset, however, my scholarly perceptions and personal opinions were NOT the emphasis in this biography. I did not regard it as the historian's role to tell readers what to think or what value judgments to make. Nor did I regard it as honest for a biographer to quote his protagonist only when he agreed with his statements or actions. Nor is it appropriate for an author to argue against ideas expressed by the protagonist or to ignore instances where he expressed views that seemed contradictory or when he acted in ways that seemed to contradict previously expressed views. I did believe that it is the biographer's role to explain the context and apparent motivations for a person's acts and words. That also applies to the statements and actions of those who interacted with the protagonist. Those were my views when I began researching this biography in the late 1970s and they remain so today.

Therefore, in my first draft and official biography, I did my best to present J. Reuben Clark's life and ideas from his own perspective. I emphasized what he emphasized. I assumed that many readers who had always agreed with his views and activities would find in the biography even more reasons for admiring him, while many readers who had disagreed with him would find more reasons for criticism. After the book appeared in 1983, those were the kinds of comments I received from readers. His admirers and critics also told me that they were surprised to discover how much more complex he was than they had previously thought. I have maintained the same approach in this expanded, unofficial biography.

D. Michael Quinn

San Cristobal de Las Casas
Chiapas, Mexico
July 1999

Los Angeles, California
January 2001

INTRODUCTION

J. Reuben Clark Jr. (b. 1871) had secular aspirations to be Solicitor General of the U.S. State Department, to be a member of the U.S. Senate, to be ambassador to Mexico, to be Secretary of State, to be U.S. Attorney General, to be a justice of the U.S. Supreme Court. He never aspired to office in the religion of his birth, the Church of Jesus Christ of Latter-day Saints. Yet he became a member of the church's highest quorum, the First Presidency.

A third-generation Mormon, he identified with the LDS church and sought to exemplify its moral precepts in his personal and professional life. But as a civil servant in the U.S. State Department and office of the Attorney General, as an ardent member of the Republican Party, and as a representative of his government in various diplomatic capacities, he thought of himself as Mister Clark or the Honorable J. Reuben Clark rather than as Brother Clark. That changed in April 1933 when he was publicly presented as counselor to the church president.

In fact, prior to 1933 Reuben held such stringent views of the separation of church and state that he felt high church leaders ought to be ineligible for civil office and vice versa. In Mormon terminology, these church leaders are "the Brethren" or the "general authorities" of the church.

His pre-1933 views necessarily circumscribed his religious activities. Although he had been ordained to the LDS office of Seventy, a proselytizing calling, he regarded missionary work as a violation of his position as civil servant in a secular republic. Therefore, he contented himself with setting an example through living a scrupulously honorable life rather than by fulfilling his priesthood role as perpetual missionary in the non-Mormon society where he lived most of his adult life up to age sixty-one.

His lifelong aspirations were shattered when LDS president Heber J. Grant asked him to become his second counselor. Nevertheless, Reuben told his governmental associates that he accepted this calling from the president of his church as he would accept a call to duty from the president of his native republic.

The decades of his life as the Honorable Mr. Clark determined the manner in which he perceived his mission as a religious leader. In his call to the highest echelon of LDS leadership, he could see in himself no outstanding qualifications aside from his activity as an international lawyer, Republican statesman, and diplomat. Therefore, as President Clark, he fulfilled his ecclesiastical position in terms of his previous experience. To have attempted otherwise might only have been a futile effort in personality modification and could also have appeared as a repudiation of his prior experiences. Therefore, from 1933 to his death in 1961, J. Reuben Clark regarded himself as an elder statesman of international law and of the Republican Party who happened to also be serving as a counselor in the LDS First Presidency.

This view of his life's work after 1932 did not conform to his previous insistence on the rigid separation of a man's church service from his political and civil functions. To Reuben, there were compelling reasons of personal faith that seemed to demand this modification. First, any other definition of his church service after 1932 would challenge his deeply felt faith that the LDS president had acted by divine inspiration in selecting him rather than choosing someone with an impressive record of church service. Second, less than a year after President Grant extended this calling to him, American voters gave political power to the kind of leadership and philosophies that Reuben viewed as a threat to all that he believed the United States should represent. This circumstance did not appear as mere coincidence to him but as a confirmation that divine inspiration elevated him to leadership to be a spokesman against this new political and social order. He regarded both the Democratic Party's New Deal and U.S. president Franklin D. Roosevelt as destructive to the nation in which the LDS church was headquartered.

His view of the priorities of his life's career also shaped his view of what a biography ought to emphasize. When the need for such a work was discussed on 9 November 1960, Marion G. Romney recorded that Reuben referred "to things he had done during his life which might be worthy of note." On this occasion, Clark specified that a biography should focus on his contributions in the State Department and other government service. He made no reference to any church service or religious activity as worthy of emphasis. Less than five months before his death, he again discussed this projected biography and seriously questioned the suggestion that one man could complete such a study in even three years. "The trouble is," Reuben wrote in his office diary on 15 May 1961, "my brand has been in too many fires. I have been around too many corrals."

His misgivings were prophetic, for it took several men a number of years to encompass the diversity and complexity of his life. Focusing on his youth, David H. Yarn published the paper-bound *Young Reuben*, which his children felt should be augmented by a more scholarly volume. With emphasis on his secular career that Clark himself preferred, Frank W. Fox wrote the definitive official biography, *J. Reuben Clark: The Public Years*. It was published jointly by Brigham Young University and the LDS church's Deseret Book.

However, the family and trustees of his papers agreed that, despite his modesty about church service, another volume should emphasize that facet of his life. The present biography, therefore, only briefly summarizes his pre-1933 secular career presented so well in Fox's biography. Instead, my biography focuses on J. Reuben Clark's religious life and his experiences as a church leader. Nevertheless, I make necessary references to the secular world to which Reuben was so closely attuned as elder statesman in the church's First Presidency.

Moreover, the nature of his church service requires a departure from a strictly chronological approach. He served as a counselor in the First Presidency for more than twenty-eight years, the longest period of such service in LDS history from 1830 to the present. Where possible, Reuben's diverse activities are in the chapters concerning his service as counselor to each of three presidents from 1933 to 1961. Following this chronological section are several topical chapters where his religious life and thought are best understood through separate discussion.

The nature of his church service shaped this biography's presentation of the latter part of his life. The president of the church has ultimate responsibility for decisions of policy and official action. Although a counselor like Clark oversaw certain areas of general responsibility, final decisions always rested with the LDS presidents. Nevertheless, they expected Reuben to be a vigorous participant in the decision-making process. For example, he often relieved the president of day-to-day oversight of matters that could be delegated to a counselor. He also defended the decisions of "the Church," the administrative vernacular for the First Presidency.

To assess his specific functions and contributions, it is necessary to document the decision-making process from 1933 to 1961. Critically important for such analysis are the verbatim minutes of the First Presidency which were not available to me. Therefore, this biography had to rely on scattered and incomplete references found in such documents as his personal papers and those of his associates. Source availability determined the depth and breadth of this work.

A number of individuals and institutions provided access to documents that were crucial for this study. His children (J. Reuben Clark III, Louise Clark Bennion, Marianne Clark Sharp, and Luacine Clark Fox) generously shared their father with me. The trustees of the J. Reuben Clark Jr. Papers authorized me to research the more than 600 manuscript boxes at Brigham Young University which have since become available to other researchers. Dallin H. Oaks, then BYU's president, permitted me to research the full university archives, which other researchers can examine by request to the current administration. LDS president Spencer W. Kimball and his counselor Marion G. Romney generously granted personal interviews to me and allowed me to research their own diaries from 1941 to 1961. Family representatives of several of Clark's close associates also permitted me to research diaries that were otherwise unavailable to study at the time.

However, the First Presidency's office declined to give access to the historical documents in its vault, as officially requested by President Oaks.

Instead, their secretary directed me to research the relevant manuscripts at the LDS Historical Department where I had already conducted personal research on the church hierarchy for six years as an independent scholar. My already extensive research and the assistance of the above individuals helped to compensate for the lack of access to crucial materials maintained by the First Presidency's secretaries.

In addition to the assistance of the Clark family and trustees, the following persons read and made helpful suggestions about the preliminary draft of this biography: Thomas G. Alexander, James B. Allen, Leonard J. Arrington, Frank W. Fox, Marvin S. Hill, Howard W. Hunter, Gordon A. Madsen, Thomas S. Monson, Robert K. Thomas, and David J. Whittaker. I appreciate and benefitted from their suggestions, but I alone am responsible for the final product.

Compared to the nearly twenty years BYU professor David H. Yarn devoted to editing Clark's massive papers, I expended a relatively small portion of my life for this volume. But during my five years of prolonged absences from home to work at the library, my daughter Lisa assumed I had been "called on a mission." I must express gratitude for the patience and love demonstrated by Jan, Mary, Lisa, Adam, and Moshe Quinn.

Several factors encouraged me to present this eminent church leader in a manner that is both sympathetic and candid. President Clark himself was consistently his own best critic and often referred to his personal achievements and limitations in sermons, correspondence, and conversation. Moreover, when he had views that were controversial, he expressed them publicly as well as privately to Mormons and non-Mormons alike. Marion G. Romney, J. Reuben Clark III, and Gordon Burt Affleck, trustees of the Clark papers, all expressed the firm conviction that my biography should present him candidly as one of the foremost leaders of his generation who also had human limitations and personal challenges.

Specifically, Reuben frequently commented in public and private that he had strong prejudices and views which he expected to be unpopular with many Latter-day Saints. The perspective of history can often see prior controversies in a calmer light, yet this biography may touch on matters that are still sensitive to some readers. J. Reuben Clark was "a towering Church leader who held strong views that were often unpopular," Affleck told me, "but President Romney and I want this biography to present him honestly, even if there are controversies."

In a published statement, Counselor Marion G. Romney of the First Presidency reaffirmed this determination. "I have always hoped that those who would write about J. Reuben Clark Jr. would remember this: To him it mattered little whether he was being praised or criticized; it mattered much, however, whether his course was right and true. Any biographer of President Clark must write the truth about him; to tell more or less than the truth would violate a governing principle of his life."

LDS president Spencer W. Kimball gave me similar encouragement for such an approach to the life of his own cousin. In his personal interview with me, President Kimball was frank in describing the challenges and difficulties Reuben faced in church administration. In addition, the 1977 family biography of President Kimball stands as his approved guideline and hallmark for the writing of sympathetic yet candid biographies of LDS leaders.

Although indebted to the above individuals for their support of historical candor, my attempt to achieve a balance in this biography is based on my own judgments. I should disclose my own belief that the general authorities of the Church of Jesus Christ of Latter-day Saints are called to their positions by divine guidance, and I am confident that they seek to carry out their administrative responsibilities by that inspiration. I also believe in the important truth expressed by President Clark to LDS religion teachers at Brigham Young University, "Yet we must not forget that prophets are mortal men, with men's infirmities" (*Church News*, 31 July 1954, 11). This biography seeks to maintain the balanced viewpoint which he recommended.

CHAPTER 1.

The Waste Places of Zion …
The Rivers of Babylon[1]

O N 1 SEPTEMBER 1871 IN GRANTSVILLE, UTAH, MARY WOOLLEY
Clark gave birth to her first child whom she delighted to name af-
ter her husband, Joshua Reuben. On that day seventy-year-old Brigham
Young presided over the Latter-day Saint church from his stately Beehive
House mansion in the bustling capital of Salt Lake City, only thirty-three
miles from Grantsville. The Mormons had settled twenty-four years ear-
lier in what became Utah. By 1871 they had turned away semi-nomadic
Native Americans[2] and redeemed the untilled land through irrigation.

Fifty years earlier, neither the Mormons as a people nor the LDS
church as an institution existed except in the solitary visions of a New
York farm boy, Joseph Smith Jr. By 1830 he had published a volume of
new scripture and organized a latter-day restoration of the Church of
Christ. He proclaimed himself a prophet who communed directly with
God and angels, who received prophetic inspiration, and who announced
divine revelations.[3]

Despite the First Amendment of the U.S. Constitution, nineteenth-
century Americans could more easily tolerate atheists than accept Mormons as neighbors. Enraged by the clannishness, the political bloc-voting
at election time, the economic solidarity, and the claims for moral and

religious superiority of the Latter-day Saints, anti-Mormons in the United States harassed individual church members and periodically pillaged entire Mormon communities for more than a decade.[4] In 1844 a mob succeeded in killing Joseph Smith at Carthage, Illinois.[5]

His successor, Brigham Young, grimly vowed to take every Mormon who would follow him away from the population centers of the United States to the barren Great Basin of the Far West.[6] For Brigham and tens of thousands of followers, the well-watered, lush, and verdant America east of the Mississippi River was a latter-day Babylon of spiritual jeopardy and captivity.[7] To these Mormon pioneers who "came here [to Utah] willingly, because we were forced to,"[8] the deserts, mountains, and isolated valleys of the Great Basin were a spiritual haven, the latter-day Zion of God.[9] After securely locating the Latter-day Saints in their refuge, President Young never left the Great Basin. He regarded with suspicion any Mormon who voluntarily left Utah to reside east of the continental divide in Babylon.

Reuben's parents exemplified this Mormon withdrawal from the outside world. Mary Louisa Woolley Clark was born in 1848 as her own parents traveled in a wagon train to Utah. Her father was Edwin D. Woolley, a former Quaker, friend of Joseph Smith, business associate of Brigham Young, and a prominent bishop of a Salt Lake City congregation since 1854. Joshua R. Clark, son of a minister in the pacifist German Baptist Brethren ("Dunkards"), came to Utah as a freighter in 1867 and converted to Mormonism five weeks after hearing his first sermon. He became a school teacher in Grantsville where Mary's brother was one of the school trustees. The couple married in July 1870 and made their permanent home in the little town which had a population of 755 that year.[10]

Perhaps because he was a convert, Joshua did not have the same view of national politics as did most Mormons of that time. In 1878 Apostle George Q. Cannon, Utah's delegate to the U.S. House of Representatives, stated: "The Mormons generally on national issues are inclined to be Democrats, and all other things being equal, in the respective candidates of the parties, would vote the Democratic ticket."[11] By contrast, Joshua wrote in 1880 about "the Republican party of which I am a strong advocate." Eleven years later, he wrote, "I feel proud of having the honor of helping to organize the Republican party in Utah."[12] His oldest son would follow his example by being an ardent Republican and being out-of-step for two decades with the political preference of most Mormons.

As Utah struggled to isolate itself from the Babylon of the rest of America, Grantsville effortlessly remained suspended beyond the mainstream of the social and religious life swirling only thirty-three miles away in Salt Lake City. At the edge of a forbidding alkaline waste, the town eked out a marginal existence that kept its population at only 1,240 by 1930. By that time, its native son J. Reuben Clark Jr. was at the pinnacle of his national prominence. He died thirty-one years later when the town stood at barely more than 2,100.[13]

Born and bred in Grantsville, Reuben gravitated to its harsh earthiness. Late in life he liked to escape from the formalities of Salt Lake City to Grantsville where, dressed in overalls, he worked his land and cattle. Brigham Young would have understood this. Devotion to the isolated Mormon village was central to Young's view of the Great Basin as spiritual refuge.

But within Reuben surged talents and ambitions that propelled him out of Grantsville, out of Salt Lake City, out of Utah, out of the provincial West and into the economic and political capitals of the United States, Latin America, and Europe. There—in Babylon—he enthusiastically sought, achieved, and enjoyed an internationally prominent career.[14] His only comparable predecessors, George Q. Cannon of the House of Representatives and Reed Smoot of the U.S. Senate, were LDS apostles who self-consciously served church interests through public office. Moreover, the Mormon electorate voted Cannon and Smoot into national office because they were apostolic candidates with First Presidency endorsement, while national leaders appointed Reuben to high civil office on merit alone.[15]

The Honorable Mr. Clark, whose faith appeared as only a subdued personal trait, functioned in high offices as a secular civil servant. LDS leaders praised his achievements and also periodically encouraged him to neglect church responsibilities in order to participate in the outside world, the world Mormons have always regarded with misgivings. These are

things Brigham Young could not have understood or even imagined possible on the day the Clarks of Grantsville had their firstborn son in 1871.

In most respects, Reuben Jr.'s early life showed no promise of any future fame. The barefoot "Reube," or sometimes "Ruby," was the darling
of his close-knit Mormon parents. Yet they loved him no more than their
other children. Frank W. Fox noted: "When visitors sang their eldest son's
praises, Mary Louisa was apt to snap back, 'We've got nine more just as
good.'"[16] Father Joshua, the family patriarch until his death in 1929, recorded some fond descriptions of his oldest. Nevertheless, he gave similar
emphasis to the achievements of Reuben's brothers and sisters as they followed his journey through the childhood life cycle of a small Mormon
village.[17]

Like a stock actor in a rural drama company, Reuben did what all
Grantsville boys of the 1870s and 1880s experienced. By the age of nine,
he was milking two cows each morning and irrigating the family garden.
By age eleven, he was branding calves and driving cattle from horseback.
By mid-teens, he sheared as many as eleven sheep a day, ploughed the
fields, and sometimes spent several days at a time riding the cattle range.
The Saturday night bath at the Clark home was Reuben's well earned escape from the grime of the fields. Rabbit hunting, fishing, barnyard pranks,
and the occasional party with friends served as spartan diversions from a
daily routine of rural sweat and satisfaction.[18]

Even for barefoot farm boys in isolated Mormon villages, the influence of the LDS church was pervasive. Beyond the pious daily family
prayers and scripture reading that typified Joshua's home were the overlap-
ping commonwealths of church and state. Grantsville, despite its village
size, was the "second town of importance in Tooele County."[19] During
most of Reuben's childhood and youth, the bishop of the ward was Edward Hunter, mayor of Grantsville, who was also the nephew and namesake of the church's Presiding Bishop. Reuben's grandfather Edwin D.
Woolley had introduced Mormonism to the Hunters in Pennsylvania in
the 1840s. In Utah the prominent Woolleys and Hunters maintained personal and business associations.[20]

Like all local leaders of the time,[21] Grantsville's bishop directed the religious, political, economic, and social life of the community. The bishop

decided—or was at least consulted about—every community affair from water rights to dancing parties. The president of the Tooele Stake, which corresponded exactly to the county boundaries of the time, functioned in an identical manner for the Mormon residents of the county. General authorities in Salt Lake City were similar shepherds for the territorial flock but rarely saw Mormons outside the Great Basin. So it was that the Clark family in Grantsville had periodic contact with all the existing echelons of church leadership at least every three months when Tooele Stake held its two-day quarterly conferences.[22]

When Reuben was only nine, one of these stake conferences brought about a convergence of circumstances and personalities that he may have had some knowledge of at the time. They foreshadowed unimagined developments in his life. After his father baptized him on 2 September 1879, the young boy was confirmed a member of the LDS church five days later by Francis M. Lyman, president of the Tooele Stake.[23] In 1877 Brigham Young had asked thirty-seven-year-old Lyman to move from Millard County in west-central Utah to Tooele City. Although county residents may have been disappointed that one of their own was not given this office, Lyman was a gregarious leader and an able speaker who almost immediately won the admiration and devotion of local Mormons.[24]

President Lyman was released in 1880 to become a member of the church's Quorum of Twelve Apostles. The disappointment of Tooele Mormons turned to sullen hostility when the First Presidency announced his replacement at the stake conference of 30 October. The new stake president was not only a non-resident but was shy, withdrawn, and only twenty-three years old. Though LDS president John Taylor came to Tooele for the sole purpose of presenting the young man as the new president, "a goodly number of the saints" refused to vote when Taylor asked them to raise their hands to sustain Heber J. Grant. Even Joseph F. Smith, second counselor in the First Presidency, suggested that "we ought to undo the work that we have done this morning" when Grant declined to bear his testimony because, he said, he did not *know* the gospel was true even though he believed it. Although Grantsville was named for the young man's recently deceased uncle, the Clark family's neighbors told Grant that his appointment as stake president was "an insult."[25] Despite his wholehearted efforts to serve the church, he finally accepted the painful reality that he was generally unpopular among the Latter-day Saints.[26]

Grant's futile effort to win acceptance and the people's grudging support would have been topics of conversation in the Clark family. Grant was more than their stake president. Since childhood he had been a member of the Salt Lake City Thirteenth Ward over which Reuben's grandfather Edwin D. Woolley presided as bishop. Grandfather Woolley attended the Tooele Stake conference and did his best from the pulpit to reassure the people that their new president was a fine choice.[27] Grant felt close enough to the Woolleys in the 1880s to attend their family reunions.[28]

This early convergence of Grant's experience with the Clark family took an added turn in October 1881. As Grant visited the Salt Lake City store of Charles R. Savage, this photographer looked intently at Tooele's unpopular stake president and solemnly told him "that within one year [he] would be a member of the Twelve Apostles."[29] A year and four days later, church president John Taylor announced a revelation appointing Grant to the Quorum of Twelve.[30] Seventeen years after his prophecy, Savage became young Reuben's father-in-law. Reuben would be sixty years old before a haunting significance attached to these seemingly inconsequential intersections of his early life with Grant's.

On summer nights in the 1880s, young Reuben often left the still oppressive heat of his room to make his bed on a haystack.[31] There he could enjoy the stray breezes and gaze at the Milky Way in the cloudless expanse above him. With the languid wonder of youth, he may have noticed that some of the brightest stars shone from dark places far removed from the multitude clustered along the familiar path of the night sky. As he drifted to sleep with the feel of hay on his back, he may have wondered about his future and potential as the image of the stars merged with floating thoughts of the next morning's chores.

His farm boy experiences may have had a universal quality, but his parents noticed a religious intensity in him that was not always characteristic of his peers. When he was nine, his father's diary noted: "The boys sat up late last night and asked a good many questions in relation to the gospel, and what revelation meant. We answered as well as we could do to their understanding."[32] More remarkable than childhood inquiries about doctrine was the fact that, between the ages of fifteen and eighteen, Reuben often attended morning LDS services alone while the rest of the family slept late or visited friends.[33] At the very time of life when many young men resist church attendance, he was remarkably devout.

At fourteen, Reuben gave his first talk at the impromptu request of the bishop at a deacon's quorum meeting. At sixteen, he delivered his maiden sermon, a ten-minute "biographical sketch of our Lord and Saviour Jesus Christ," to the joint meeting of the young men and women of Grantsville.[34] His youthful emphasis on Christology over other possible subjects endured throughout his life, especially during those periods when the Honorable J. Reuben Clark rarely attended church as an adult. The Grantsville bishop ordained him a priest at age seventeen and an elder at eighteen. In March 1890 he was ordained to the office of Seventy by his father Joshua who was one of the local presidents of that quorum.[35]

The Seventies were intended to be "traveling ministers," which meant proselytizing missionaries.[36] In Reuben's case, his ordination coincidentally preceded by only five months his departure from home.

Joshua tried to provide for his eldest son's education by allowing him to read books from the family library, but the young boy was soon rereading the *Young Folk's History of Rome*, the *Child's Natural History*, and Shakespeare's *Complete Works*. He even made several unsuccessful attempts to comprehend Milton's *Paradise Lost*.[37] He attended his father's private school which he found unchallenging. His father, therefore, enrolled him in the tuition grade school at Grantsville's city hall. Even then, Joshua assumed that, with ten children and little money, "a good common school education" would have to be his son's ultimate goal.[38] The father sorely underestimated the eleven-year-old's thirst for formal education, and the next eight years would be a seesaw of frustration for them both.

At the heart of the matter was the fabled Woolley stubbornness which Reuben often acknowledged and described. He said Brigham Young once remarked that if Reuben's grandfather Edwin Woolley "is ever drowned, ... look up-stream, for he always goes against the current."[39] On another occasion, the adult Reuben worked with a non-Mormon whose wife's maiden name was Woolley. The man wondered if she and Reuben were relatives. "Is your wife rather insistent in her opinions?" Reuben asked. "Yes," was the reply. "Does she ever discount her opinions?" No. "If you have a dispute, is she right and you wrong?" When the man answered in the affirmative, Reuben smiled and said, "Yes, we are related."[40] His youthful quest for education displayed his Woolley nature.

His father's diary noted that "Reuben would rather miss his meals than to miss a day from school."[41] He frequently recorded that this determination caused his son to be the only one to leave the house during severe winter storms. Yet the financially strapped father was forced to withdraw his son from the tuition school. Reuben again had to proceed under his father's admittedly inadequate tutorship. After a few tense days of unrecorded turmoil, Joshua wrote: "I concluded to let Reuben go to school another half term. He started again this morning." During some terms he could not attend school at all. After his elementary graduation, he doggedly repeated eighth grade twice more because that was the highest education Grantsville offered and "there was nothing to do." Joshua confided little to his diary of his son's restiveness but did announce the resolution of the conflict in August 1890: "Reuben will go with us to the city in the morning. He will stop in there and go to the Latter-day Saints' College," which offered primarily high school education.[42]

Rural life would remain in Reuben's blood, but the city—first Salt Lake, then New York, then Washington, D.C.—would be foremost in his dreams after he left Grantsville for an education in 1890. His performance in the first midterm examinations at LDS College more than justified the family gamble: one score of 80 percent, four scores in the 90s, and two of 100 percent. Out of a class of seventy-five students, many of whom had better educational opportunities, the barefoot boy from Grantsville was the only student to achieve a score of 100 percent.[43]

Until now his ambitions had been modest but improbable. First, he wanted more than elementary education despite his family's lack of resources. Second, he aimed to distinguish himself in a metropolis despite his provincial background. With a fierce inner drive that even his family could hardly understand, he pushed himself out of the familial nest and into a world where individual comparisons were stark and unremitting.

Reuben found that he was exceptionally competitive and admirably fit. For the first time, he had an external justification for his inner self-confidence. Self-congratulation and boasting were alien to him, but his first youthful foray into the city left him unbloodied and unrivaled among better advantaged colleagues. He asked no favors, only the opportunity to prove himself. The more opportunities he seized, the farther he stretched the boundaries of his origins.

Ultimately, more important than his initial grades was the association he developed with LDS College president James E. Talmage. At twenty-nine, Professor Talmage was "a kind of intellectual whirlwind. Now in geology, now in chemistry, now in medicine, now in biblical scholarship, he swept the horizon before him."[44] With his reputation as a latter-day renaissance man of diverse interests and achievement,[45] Talmage had an extraordinary impact on the young man's emerging intellectual aspirations. Equally important, the British-born, Eastern-educated professor was the boy's first significant exposure to urbane gentility. Reuben later remarked that "[I was] a country boy just entering his twenties, as raw as they make them and they can be made pretty raw, [and] I was blessed by being taken under the immediate tutelage of Dr. Talmage."[46]

He led Reuben through LDS College, through the short-lived "Church University" in Salt Lake City, and then to the University of Utah.[47] Despite his heavy employment schedule as Talmage's assistant, Reuben distinguished himself by completing his teaching credentials and the Bachelor of Science degree in four years, by serving as managing editor of the *University of Utah Chronicle* during his senior year, and by graduating in June 1898 as class valedictorian.[48] Although the mentor was somewhat austere, their relationship was sufficiently close that Professor Talmage solemnized the marriage of Reuben and Luacine A. Savage in the Salt Lake temple on 14 September 1898. This was the first occasion that Talmage performed a temple "sealing for time and eternity."[49]

Beyond providing intellectual expansion and employment opportunities, Talmage had profound influence on the religious attitudes that would govern Reuben's adult life. The professor created the first religious milestone for Reuben in mid-January 1891. It was good that the youth had begun the month with a day of fasting and prayer.[50] Shortly after he returned to LDS College in January for the new term, Talmage informed him that the First Presidency had appointed the professor as curator of the fledgling

Deseret Museum. If Reuben accepted the position as assistant curator, LDS headquarters would regard this service "the same as a mission."[51]

Married or unmarried, all faithful LDS men of the time were expected to fulfill two years of missionary service, often in a foreign land.[52] Reuben even held the proselytizing office of Seventy. Nevertheless, with the blessing of the First Presidency, Talmage offered him the opportunity of secular service for the church instead of a religious mission to gather converts. Hesitating only long enough to consult his father, Reuben accepted the call and its corresponding redefinition of what constitutes service to the church. Talmage inadvertently provided the rationale for Clark's future life as a secular Latter-day Saint.

For a couple of years, Reuben worked at the Deseret Museum. He assisted his mentor in conducting tours, sorting and helping to classify thousands of exhibit specimens, preparing laboratory experiments, as well as other odd jobs. He also did secretarial work.[53]

Along the way, Talmage gave form and organization to Reuben's understanding of LDS doctrine. After the First Presidency asked him to prepare a series of theological lectures on Joseph Smith's Articles of Faith,[54] the professor meticulously organized, explained, and documented LDS doctrine. He submitted his lecture drafts for approval by a reading committee of general authorities, revised his doctrinal expositions as this committee directed, and in 1893 began delivering the lectures and publishing them in full.[55] By eliminating all conflicting or obscure doctrinal pronouncements and by codifying and standardizing doctrines, Talmage, under the direction of the general authorities, established Mormonism's first systematic theology in his book, *The Articles of Faith*.

Reuben was in the middle of this process: "I was with him when he prepared 'The Articles of Faith.' I often jokingly say that I wrote 'The Articles of Faith'—I did—on the typewriter."[56] He typed his mentor's rough drafts and retyped them with the revisions required by the reading committee or by Talmage himself. From the professor's perspective, Reuben was performing a mechanical, secretarial function. In reality, he was Talmage's first convert to the presentation of LDS doctrine in a comprehensive, scripturally documented, internally consistent, logically organized, non-controversial, and easily understood form. Talmage helped define the limits of LDS orthodoxy and his disciple would impose that orthodoxy on church curriculum when he became a member of the First Presidency. (See chapters 7-8.)

Reuben often quipped that his beloved Luacine ("Lute") was his social and religious superior. Although his prolific Woolley kindred were at the upper rungs of Utah society, the Clarks of Grantsville had no illusions about their social or economic standing, especially in the "big city" of Salt Lake. There Luacine's well-known father, Charles Savage, had provided his family with a comfortable living and social fluency as a photographer to the rich and famous. At their wedding reception, "Reuben's family mixed rather stiffly with the visibly prosperous Savages."[57] As regards religious devotion, Reuben held a lifelong belief: "Almost always there is less of the earthly and more of the spiritual in woman than in man."[58] He sought out and married a young woman who fulfilled that expectation. However, Lute's greater devotion to religious observance became a source of increasing tension during the early decades of their marriage.

For the first five years, he struggled to provide Lute with financial security and at least the beginnings of social prestige in the mountains and valleys of Zion. With the help of his father-in-law, Reuben secured his first teaching position in September 1898. At Heber City he launched "one of the first steps toward a public high school" in Wasatch County.[59]

He left Lute at home two days after their marriage to find housing in Heber. After ten days, she decided to go and join him. Biographer Fox observed: "This painful initial separation was only the first hint of what would soon emerge as an abiding theme of the Clark marriage." Lute later wrote of Reuben's departure during their honeymoon, "I did not know it at the time, but this was the beginning of his leaving me, which he has continued ever since."[60]

She missed the familiar life of Salt Lake City but thoroughly enjoyed the Alpine setting of Heber. As an emigre from Salt Lake City society, she became the center of the town's social life: "Well, we danced until ten o'clock, and there being such a small crowd present the party was suddenly dismissed. But we didn't care, as Anna had a sumptuous repast ready for us. We played cards until 11:30 then sat down to an elegant spread." Lute also commented on the first significant church assignment of her husband's life, as well as on her own unaccustomed absence from church service: "Reube's Sunday School class is quite interesting. They are studying the 'Life of Christ.' I am going to try and go: it is quite a change not to teach a class."[61]

Reuben, however, found Heber unfulfilling. His decision to leave at the end of the school year was strangely punctuated by a young girl's pathological fantasy that he had kissed her in the school hallway.[62] But his teaching was not an utter failure since three school principals and a physician eventually emerged from his class of thirteen students.[63]

Back in Salt Lake City, Reuben started the 1899-1900 school year at LDS College teaching Latin, Shakespeare, grammar, rhetoric, and civil government. He soon joined principal Joseph Nelson and four other faculty in a mass resignation due to a salary dispute with the Church Board of Education. This was Reuben's first act of loyal opposition to LDS headquarters. They resigned on Friday and pluckily signed contracts to begin teaching the following Monday at the Salt Lake Business School. The next school year found Reuben in Cedar City as acting principal of the Southern Branch of the State Normal School (for teacher education). However, the Utah legislature rejected his conservative budget request and his reappointment, so he returned to teach at Nelson's Salt Lake Business School. Reuben was beginning to see himself as a vagabond and was miserably frustrated in his desires for further education. He made halfhearted attempts to prepare himself for the bar examination by studying law books at home, but his restive eyes looked beyond the cloister of the Wasatch Range.[64]

The mountains of Utah were also blocking his hopes financially. In November 1901 he wrote George W. Decker, his partner in a coal mine investment, "We had better act quickly and perhaps take what we can get out of it whether it makes us the multi-millionaires we anticipated or not." He estimated their mineral claim was worth a maximum of $5,000, yet offered it to an interested buyer for $8,000. The man would pay no more than $3,500.[65]

According to the expectations of his Mormon family and culture, Reuben had obtained adequate education and had begun a respectable teaching career. Few of his peers wanted more than this. But he concluded that he could achieve his ambitions only outside the Great Basin and out-side Mormon culture. When he expressed that conviction to his wife, her averted eyes told him that she could accept social isolation in a Mormon village more easily than religious isolation in a gentile metropolis. Reuben had tried to find personal fulfillment in all the approved avenues of Zion, including his Sunday School teaching role in every community where he had a secular teaching position. Nonetheless, this all left him as desolate as the alkaline deserts from which his people had carved out tree-lined oases. Ancient Babylon brought remorse to the captive children of Israel, but Reuben felt like a captive in Utah and yearned for the lush opportunities of America's eastern seaboard.

When he at last decided to test the waters of Babylon, he tried to calm his wife's fears and his own guilt by securing the protective sponsorship of church leaders. In November 1902, with the written endorsement of LDS president Joseph F. Smith, he applied for the position of private secretary to Senator-elect Reed Smoot. An LDS apostle, Smoot was starting his first term in Washington, D.C., where Reuben could attend law school at George Washington University. He would never forget nor forgive the in-different coolness with which the senator ignored this church-endorsed application. Ultimately, his friend and co-conspirator in the 1900 affront to the LDS Board of Education made the eastward hopes a reality. Joseph Nelson provided an interest-free loan to finance the trip for Reuben's lit-tle family of pioneers that enabled him to attend Columbia University's law school in New York City.[66]

Before he left in August 1903, he sought a parting benediction from the church's president who set him apart on a "general" mission to be an exemplary Latter-day Saint among the gentiles.[67] Not the usual mission calling, this was the second time that an LDS president defined one of Reuben's secular endeavors as missionary service. Nor was Reuben's so-journ in Babylon typical. Its effect on his personal development was so profound that he later remarked that he had been "reared among the hea-then Gentiles."[68]

On his arrival in New York, he was thirty-two years old, the father of two children, and a Mormon from the American West. His determination to become a lawyer was the only thing he had in common with the

decade-younger Eastern Establishment students he met at the Columbia
Law School. His aspirations had estranged him from his own people in
Utah, but for the next thirty years his Mormon identity created "an intangible but real barrier" between him and those on whom he depended for
the fulfillment of his aspirations.[69] The psalmist had asked: "How shall we
sing the LORD's song in a strange land?" (Ps. 137:4). It was an uncomfortable question for one who was among religious strangers voluntarily, and
Reuben was never entirely satisfied with his own answer.

One approach seemed at least to simplify his encounter. He had a lifetime habit of working long hours, often in the studious retreat of a library.
Not content with the traditional isolation of the law school's cavernous library, he slowly built a personal library in which he could find academic
seclusion even after the school library closed for the night. "The Clarks
have always been noted as late-to-get-up and late-to-go-to-bed," he once
remarked.[70] It was common for him to study in his home library long after
midnight.

His monastic study habits purposely limited his awkward social contact with non-Mormons but also brought him distinction. As one of the
top-ranked students of his class, he joined the editorial staff of the *Columbia Law Review* at the beginning of his junior year. In his senior year, he was
Recent Decisions editor. This provided opportunity for his intense, almost
awesome practice of reading everything he could find about a topic as
preparation for analytical memorandums. His reputation as a brilliant
workaholic led to his employment in the spring of 1905 as a summer research assistant for one of Columbia's law professors, James Brown Scott.
After Scott became Solicitor of the U.S. State Department, he appointed
Reuben as Assistant Solicitor in 1906 following his graduation from law
school. Borrowed from English jurisprudence, the term *solicitor* referred to
the State Department's legal adviser regarding international law.[71]

In addition to Scott's crucial role in introducing him to the State Department, four other Columbia professors had a profound effect on Reuben's views and the career he would pursue. John W. Burgess was founder
of the *Political Science Quarterly*. Harlan Fiske Stone became a member of
the U.S. Supreme Court and its chief justice. Dean Kirchwey was founder
of the American Society of International Law. John Bassett Moore later

became Acting Secretary of State and author of *A Digest of International Law.* In particular, Justice Stone "wrote warm expressions of congratulation" for every advancement Reuben received in international law and diplomacy.[72]

Reuben served in the Solicitor's office for six and a half years. He advanced to full Solicitor and also became virtual Secretary of State in eerie instances when a vacuum of leadership forced him to make policy decisions for the government in crisis situations. He struggled for a time as the unappreciated ghostwriter for Solicitor Scott's published and unpublished memorandums which were highly praised within the Republican administrations of presidents Theodore Roosevelt and William H. Taft. Scott's eccentricities and incompetence taught Reuben to scrutinize everyone regardless of status. It also involved the young assistant in a successful palace intrigue to oust Scott. By the time Reuben became Solicitor in 1910, he had learned indelible lessons about the responsibilities of office and the realities of bureaucratic infighting.[73]

Although he worked in the area of foreign relations with many countries, he gained some of his most significant experience in arbitration, diplomacy, and brinkmanship with regard to Latin America. In particular, the tortuous experience of the Mexican Revolution involved the Solicitor's office in so many ways that Reuben began shaping much of U.S. policy toward Mexico from 1910 to 1913. When the Secretary of State and the Acting Secretary of State were absent from Washington for reasons of business or pleasure, Reuben sometimes had to act on his own authority or make recommendations directly to the U.S. president when crises demanded immediate action. Although much of his work was behind the scenes, the crowning public achievement of his career as Solicitor was his published memorandum *The Right to Protect Citizens in Foreign Countries by Landing Forces.*[74]

The Democratic Party's successful election of Woodrow Wilson as president caused Reuben to leave the State Department in 1913. This ardent Republican thereafter conducted a decade-long private legal practice with offices located in New York City and Washington, D.C. Nonetheless, he did not lose interest in his government's affairs.

Nor did his government lose sight of the valuable former Solicitor.

From 1913 to 1914, he served as general counsel for the American-British Claims Commission. In 1916 the Judge Advocate General of the U.S. Army asked him to accept a special commission as major in the Officers' Reserve Corps so that he could assist in the formulation of a "selective service" program for "conscripting" or "drafting" young men into the American armed forces. He accepted the position, then in 1917 the U.S. Justice Department obtained his reassignment to become Special Assistant to the Attorney General. In 1918 he became executive officer and second-in-command to the Judge Advocate General. Although Reuben declared with embarrassment that he had not merited it, the U.S. government awarded him the Distinguished Service Medal in 1920 for his services in "the Great War," World War I. In his last major service to his government during this period, he was Special Counsel in the difficult negotiations of the Washington Arms Conference of 1921-22. During this decade, he also served as ghostwriter for Judge Advocate General Enoch Crowder, for U.S. Attorney General Thomas W. Gregory, for U.S. Senator William E. Borah, and especially for former Secretary of State and current U.S. Senator Philander Knox in a campaign against United States participation in the League of Nations. In addition to all of this, Reuben maintained a law partnership in Salt Lake City beginning in 1915, even though he was preoccupied in New York as legal counsel for the country's first multinational conglomerate, the American International Corporation (AIC).[75]

Nevertheless, he invested his money in western ventures rather than in the New York Stock Exchange. In the early 1920s, he and his brother Frank "attempted to expand the coal-bearing properties Reuben had once purchased in Cedar City." As noted previously, he had been unable to sell these even at a decent loss in 1901. Biographer Fox continued: "They also considered building a glass plant there and exploiting the high-grade silicone sands of the area. They even jumped into the oil business together, leasing drilling sites at Crown Butte, Montana, with the hope of subleasing them to the oil companies." Instead of reaping a windfall from these long-distance investments, "none of Reuben Clark's enterprises hit the big money; on the contrary, he almost went under. He bought too many properties too soon and too much on credit. Then, banking on the postwar agricultural boom [that he anticipated for the Beehive State after 1918], he laid too much into cash crops of the moment and too little into long-term staples." Utah and the West had failed him again, this time financially. "Reuben had to dig out from the wreckage of a lifetime of dreams."[76]

The ancient Jews languished seventy years among strangers in their Babylonian exile, and the earlier Israelites wandered forty years in the Sinai wilderness to purge themselves of strangers' ways before entering the Promised Land. For nearly thirty years, Reuben discovered how intoxicating his opportunities and successes among the "heathen Gentiles" could be during his self-imposed exile from the Great Basin.

Reuben maintained significant personal, family, professional, economic, and religious ties to what geographers call the Mormon Culture Region centered in Salt Lake City,[77] but he discovered that this sojourn in modern Babylon exacted its own price in his personal life. As a member of the First Presidency, he would later speak about this to an LDS conference of young men. Knowing that many of them would seek their fortunes in the outside world, Clark said, "A great portion of my mature life has been spent away from the Church, away from association with members of the Church, and I have had to live more or less my own spiritual life."[78]

His professional aspirations from 1903 to 1923 required personal adjustments that made his family life unusual, even by the standards of the American East. After she endured the academic widowhood of law school, Luacine expected that their life would resume the normalcy they had known in Utah. Instead, he worked more than six years in the Solicitor's office. She found the heat of the nation's capital insufferable and routinely returned with the children to Utah to spend spring and summer. She wanted Reuben to move to Utah permanently, but each of his professional triumphs diminished her hopes. After he failed to reach Utah in time for the birth of their third child in 1908, he decided to absent himself from the State Department for six weeks to be with her as a sort of penance. When he left again, she endured a few more months of separation and then wrote, "I was just thinking today that when June comes it will be a year since we were together barring the six weeks you were home." She observed, "It seems a pity for you to be alone when you have a family who should be with you," then she announced her intention to join him in Washington, D.C., despite her preference for Utah.[79]

She undoubtedly rejoiced when the Democratic victory in November 1912 required his resignation from the State Department. She hoped he would be satisfied with the laurels of public service he had won and would take up permanent residence in Utah. Instead, he opened law offices in Washington and New York and began staying in Manhattan weekdays during the fall and winter, while visiting Luacine and the children in Washington on weekends. He was absent from them during Lute's annual pilgrimages to Utah from spring to fall for her health and the children's religious education. He rarely visited his Salt Lake City office during this time.[80] His triangular mode of isolation ended when he moved the family to Manhattan early in 1920.

This reunion ended in June when he decided to move the entire family back to Salt Lake City for "political reasons."[81] He wanted to establish a residence from which he could fulfill his aspirations to be a U.S. senator.[82] Now Luacine and the children were in Utah permanently, aside from a five-month residence in Washington during 1921. Reuben spent all but a few weeks a year in New York City from 1921 to 1923. During this time, he and Luacine communed through daily correspondence and weekly long-distance telephone calls.[83]

The strains of this life echoed in Reuben's remarks to LDS women nearly thirty years later: "We of the [male] Priesthood are out in the world. We meet all kinds of conditions. We are engaged in something of a battle from day to day, trying to secure those things which maintain life. We do not have much time with you, nor with the children, and so we must look to you, and do look to you, and we are not disappointed, to build the home and to make it a home."[84]

On those rare occasions when Reuben was with his wife and children during the twenty years following his enrollment at Columbia, theirs was not a typical Mormon home. A teenager during much of the family's residence in the East, his daughter Marianne reminisced: "My father always said, 'Every night should be family home evening.' That was the way our family was. We were always at home. We would have our dinner and then my father would go upstairs and study or work every night of his life. I always remember him working. You just took it for granted. But we could always go up and visit him."[85] Perhaps Reuben's studious isolation during his evenings at home intensified his children's adoration of their father whom they knew had the respect of the world's leaders. Their infrequent association with their father, even at home, gave an unforgettable intensity to those occasions when his children knocked at his open study door. He would immediately set aside his books to answer their inquiries and counsel them. His wife and children cherished having him at home.

Yet as his children grew up, Reuben's "family home evening" was as secular as his life outside the home. The Clark children often met important government officials and heard discussions of their father's equally important work. At the dinner table, he listened with interest to his daughters' talk of boyfriends and school activities. He counseled them to obtain a serious education—preferably at Bryn Mawr rather than any Utah school. After dinner the children listened to the gramophone and played at his feet as he took a short nap: "If a comment or correction was in order, Reuben would duly pronounce it, his eyes still closed, his face immobile."[86]

Isolated from the Mormon Culture Region in an era before church-wide emphasis on family scripture study and family prayers, each of Reuben's children, as he did, lived "more or less my own spiritual life." Even though their father closely monitored their reading, they did not read the Book of Mormon until they attended university. Reuben's father always had daily family prayers, but Reuben's own children could remember such prayers only during their visits to Utah when they were under their grandfather's influence. Even though Reuben wanted his children raised as Latter-day Saints, he postponed their baptisms until the summertime when Luacine took them to Utah, where their grandfather performed the ceremonies without their father's presence.[87] Marianne commented: "We didn't have much formal study of the Church, but it was just in the very air we breathed that we didn't do some things that other people did and that our roots were here in the West. It was just an understood thing."[88] The vicarious religious education of his children was symptomatic of Reuben's drift from the devotion of his youth.

Apostle Reed Smoot had profound influence on Reuben's growing secularism. Unlike Clark, Smoot had been a secular Mormon since his youth. When the First Presidency called him to the Quorum of Twelve in 1900, Smoot was dumfounded and "wondered why he was an apostle."[89] His fellow Mormons shared the wonderment five years later when Senator Smoot publicly testified that he was a lifelong Mormon "but not a very active one," that he had not participated in the LDS temple endowment ceremonies in the twenty-five years since he had unenthusiastically received his own endowment, and that he ignored instructions from the First Presidency to vote in particular ways "because it is none of their business." He made this statement during the U.S. Senate's three-year investigation of his eligibility to remain a senator due to his being an LDS apostle.[90]

For personal and political reasons, Smoot was active in church affairs whenever he was in Utah but demonstrated aloofness in the nation's capital. For many years after he came to Washington in 1903, when Latter-day Saints in the city met together in each other's homes for church services, Smoot attended only the evening services and declined to host them himself until 1910.[91] A little more than a year after his reelection, he decided to open his newly acquired house to church members. Even though there was an average Sunday evening attendance of forty-five to fifty people, he declined to provide priesthood meetings for the men, Relief Society for the women, Mutual Improvement for the youth, or Primary for the children.[92]

As a result, the LDS families in Washington had to fend for themselves religiously. Senator Smoot's LDS secretary usually attended the Bible classes of Associate Justice John M. Harlan.[93] Reuben sent his children to Protestant Sunday School.[94]

Smoot was too preoccupied with his grueling schedule to create more church meetings. He routinely spent his Sunday mornings at work on government business.[95] His Sunday office hours were no secret because he wanted to be known as an effective, seven-days-a-week senator. He often met with government officials on Sundays to prepare the agenda for the coming week.[96]

When not working on Sundays, Apostle Smoot occupied his time with walks through the park, rides in the countryside, visits to the zoo, attendance at the theater, or accompanying other government officials to the services of other religions—anything but LDS services.[97] He sometimes chose secular activities instead of joining his fellow Mormons when they traveled to Baltimore for district conference. By church protocol, he should have presided at these conferences.[98] In addition to this, he persuaded the church president to keep LDS missionaries out of the nation's capital.[99] Reed Smoot's Washington was also Reuben's Washington, and much of the latter's own secularism was a direct response to this secular apostle's travels down the rivers of Babylon.

Shortly after Reuben arrived in the capital, Luacine began lecturing him about church attendance. In October 1906 she wrote, "Above all, quit working on Sundays."[100] He had adopted Smoot's casual approach toward the Sabbath. Worse, when the Smoots began hosting Sunday evening meetings, they "gushingly received" the pro-Smoot Republicans but treated the Democrats and non-supportive Republicans like Reuben with a "forced cordiality [that] was absolutely unchristian."[101] The apostle did not make it easy for Clark to define how he could function as a Mormon in government service while the Senate was trying to expel Smoot because he was a high ranking Mormon leader.

Moreover, Reuben never forgot what he was convinced was an intentional insult when Smoot ignored his application to be his secretary. At best, he felt that Smoot was patronizing. He simply avoided the apostle whenever he could.

His opinion of Smoot poisoned the well of his feelings about church attendance. Until he left the State Department in 1913, Reuben hardly attended LDS meetings at all.[102] When speaking in church during visits to Utah, he avoided religious topics and spoke on subjects such as arbitration treaties or "The Workings of the State Department."[103]

As he began spending more Sundays in New York City and Salt Lake City from 1913 to 1922, he could attend church without the inescapable presence of Apostle Smoot and Reuben's resistance to church activity softened. In 1914 he spoke at LDS meetings on "Present Day Tendencies" and "Causes of the European War." In 1915 and 1916, he even attended Senator Smoot's church meetings and spoke on religious topics: the "Relation Between Material and Spiritual" and "Feed My Sheep."[104]

Nevertheless, Reuben still usually declined to attend priesthood meetings or Sunday School in Manhattan, Brooklyn, or Washington. His typical

Sunday diary entries from 1913 to 1922 were: "July 19—Sunday. Spent the day preparing my memo in Alsop matter ... Nov. 8—Sunday. Spent forenoon with P.C.K. on case ... Sunday—Jan. 3. Carborundum—all day, till 11 p.m. ... Sunday. Munitions all day ... Spent some time on China situation."[105] Reuben continued to mirror Smoot's view that religious aloofness was justifiable for the sake of separation of church and state.

Aside from his personal coolness toward Smoot, the presence of the apostle in the Senate was the catalyst for Reuben's virulent opposition to the church's influence in politics. In 1907 three years of embarrassing testimony and ecclesiastical bloodletting for Mormons ended with the narrow defeat of the effort to unseat Smoot. In March, Reuben wrote a "Why Not?" memorandum: "No Apostle—Presidency of Church, etc. including Presidents of Stakes—shall while holding such office be eligible for election to a political office."[106]

Shortly afterward, he wrote to his father that the LDS church's domination of Utah politics was "un-American," had always caused trouble for the Mormons, and was unnecessary to protect the church or its members. Reuben added that LDS general authorities were "not competent to direct all our activities [and there is] nothing to gain by voting as directed except to increase personal power of leaders."[107]

While discussing "Church (Mormon) interference in politics" with Mathonihah Thomas in 1914, Reuben expressed grudging support for Smoot in the Senate as a fellow Republican. He explained "that a religious leader might also possess the qualifications of learning, wisdom and experience necessary to make him a great civil leader, and therefore entitle him to be listened to in civil matters; but that it was the latter qualifications and not his religious position or [religious] qualifications which gave to him this position, power and right."[108] In 1917 he added that he would not "accept the dictum of an ignoramus."[109]

The public endorsement of the LDS president for Smoot and other candidates was the unspoken context for Reuben's remarks to the Young Men's Republican Club of Salt Lake City in 1923: "In the approaching City election I shall be able to perceive no distinction between a high official of the Mormon Church urging the reelection of one, and a high official of any other Church urging the election of another. Such activity by either official will be wrong."[110] A year earlier President Heber J. Grant had joined with LDS stake presidents and Protestant ministers in endorsing an independent candidate for sheriff. In this election the *Deseret News* had instructed readers how to vote a party ticket and still scratch-vote for the LDS president's choice of the independent candidate.[111]

What is extraordinary about Reuben's venomous statements about church influence in politics is that he was an ardent Republican complaining about LDS general authorities who promoted the Republican Party.[112] The mind boggles to imagine his reaction if the hierarchy had promoted the Democratic Party.

This resistance to such externals as church attendance and LDS influence in politics was symptomatic of his private distancing from strict Mormonism. Crushed under the burden of school debts, unprofitable investments, and maintenance of multiple residences, he began allowing his tithing to lapse "long" before 1906.[113] He did not pay a full 10 percent tithing until 1925.[114] He also regarded the two-year LDS mission as a stultifying interruption for promising young men. In 1912 he successfully interceded with recently appointed apostle James E. Talmage to cancel the mission call of Reuben's brother Frank so that he could continue his engineering profession without interruption.[115]

Like Apostle Smoot, Reuben regarded the temple endowment ceremony as unsatisfying. Despite five years of residence near Utah temples and his periodic visits to Utah, Reuben did not participate in LDS temple ceremonies for more than twenty-five years after the day he received his own endowment. By contrast, his wife Lute attended the temple regularly to receive ordinances as "proxy for those who have died."[116] Reuben also complained about wearing the undergarments required for those who had received the endowment, and he advised the First Presidency to "abolish them."[117] He accurately prophesied that leaders eventually would shorten the sleeves and legs of the wrist-length and ankle-length garments.[118] However, with typical loyalty to his covenants, he continued to wear the required garments even during the oppressive summers of Washington, D.C. Nevertheless, he could not bear to let anyone in Babylon see his temple garments, so he routinely mailed them to Luacine in Utah for laundering.[119]

Although he chafed at many of the external observances of Mormonism, Reuben unflinchingly identified himself with his church when its name was a national epithet. The pressure for him to conceal his Mormon identity was strong enough at Columbia where his religion was academically unfashionable, but the situation was worse when he entered the State Department in 1906. Since the beginning of 1904, newspapers throughout the nation had been filled with sensational headlines and caustic editorials about "the Mormon question" due to the Senate's investigation of Smoot and the practices of the LDS church. With all the detachment of a circus sideshow, Mormon leaders were subjected to relentless cross-examination in the Senate committee's chambers, Mormon doctrines and practices were ridiculed by senators and were caricatured in the press. Most detrimental for Reuben's career, Mormon loyalty to the U.S. government was seriously questioned. Reuben followed the investigation closely, and his copy of the multi-volume testimony transcript is filled with underlinings and marginal notations.[120] Biographer Fox noted, "Indeed, during his first year in the solicitor's office, Reuben lived in constant fear that his Mormonism would come to the attention of superiors and cost him his job."[121]

This experience undoubtedly caused Reuben to leap at the opportunity to exert influence over one of the nation's most influential newspapers. In March 1915 he learned that the *Washington Post*'s owner was willing to sell control of the paper. He immediately wrote Preston D. Richards, his direct liaison with the First Presidency's office:

> Would it not be worth while for President [Joseph F.] Smith to acquire for the [Mormon] people, through subscriptions by trustworthy members, either the control of the paper (as he may think best), or the ownership of a large part of it? I recommend the securing of the control, which I think can be done. Obviously to retain the value which such a medium would have, it would be necessary [that] the interest of our people should not be known.
>
> Would you lay this before President Smith and advise me of the result?[122]

Five days later Richards wrote that the church president and the Presiding Bishop, Charles W. Nibley, were interested enough to ask Reuben to discuss this proposal with Senator Smoot. By then, the *Post*'s owner had changed his mind about selling.[123] During this period Reuben also intervened with friends in the State Department to assist LDS missionaries in foreign countries.[124] These examples demonstrate that he remained a loyal Mormon despite his dissent against the First Presidency's political interventions and despite his various accommodations to living in the Babylon of the East.

Aside from voluntarily proclaiming oneself a Latter-day Saint, the surest means of Mormon identity was observance of the Word of Wisdom: total abstinence from alcohol, tobacco, tea, and coffee. Although he knew that it made him a social pariah in the nation's capital, Reuben strictly observed this. Even though he deeply worried that his Mormon ways would result in his dismissal from government service, he studied alone during coffee breaks in the State Department, declined the obligatory cigars in meetings with diplomats and governmental superiors, and served lemonade to startled dinner guests.[125] There were limits to the accommodations a Latter-day Saint could make in Babylon, and Reuben would neither deny his heritage nor violate its ethical imperatives.

Moreover, Reuben doggedly maintained the simple faith of his youth even when he rigorously questioned certain aspects of Mormonism that he regarded as irritating tangents from the central gospel. On the same occasion in 1914, when he criticized the political actions of LDS leaders, he affirmed, "In other words, I took the position that religion is divine, and therefore not subject generally to human question, alterations, or interferences, and further that the words of those authorized to speak for divinity, must be implicitly accepted, when speaking pursuant to their agency i.e. speaking on religious matters."[126] In his mid-forties, Reuben was expressing the verities of his father Joshua and of his mentor, James E. Talmage.

Reuben's legal practice in New York allowed him the company of his family only on weekends during the winters and not at all during the summers. The resulting loneliness provided too much opportunity for him to pursue the logical consequences of his reservations about the political statements of the LDS church's living prophet whom he had already dismissed as "an ignoramus."

By 1917 he adopted a program of religious inquiry that undermined the verities he had affirmed in 1914. One personal memo began: "If we have truth, [it] cannot be harmed by investigation. If we have not truth, it ought to be harmed." From that premise, he added the observation that scientists and lawyers like himself were neither blindly believing nor very "religious" and that they must refuse to be deceived by others or by their own wishful thinking. "A lawyer must get at facts, he must consider motives—he must tear off the mask and lay bare the countenance, however hideous. The frightful skeleton of truth must always be exposed ... [the lawyer] must make every conclusion pass the fiery ordeal of pitiless reason. If their conclusions cannot stand this test, they are false." When he applied this test "to his religious convictions," he stridently concluded: "What he can himself reason out, according to his standards, he accepts unqualifiedly; whatever cannot stand his tests, he rejects as unfit."[127]

During these religious reflections in 1917, the increasingly introspective Reuben asked himself the questions: "Are we not only entitled, but expected to think for ourselves? Otherwise where does our free agency come in?" His answer was resounding: "If we are blindly to follow some one else we are not free agents. ... That we may as [a] Church determine for ourselves our course of action, is shown by the Manifesto [abandoning polygamy]. We may not probably take an affirmative stand, i.e. adopt something new but we may dispense with something."[128] Perhaps he had never before questioned the assumptions that lay behind the simple faith of his youth and the orderly theology of Talmage. But at mid-life, Reuben proclaimed that there must be no forbidden questions in Mormonism.

The direction toward which his philosophy of religious inquiry led him was indicated in his musings about two essentials: the revelations of Joseph Smith and the LDS belief in progression toward godhood. As he examined the revelations in the Doctrine and Covenants concerning the structure of church government, he wondered to what extent the founding prophet's own reading or experience contributed to what he set down. He asked: "Did he not evolve this out of his own consciousness? Might be interesting to trace the evolution of the Doc. & Cov. with the evolution of the Book of Mormon."[129] When he pondered the Mormon belief in the potential of individuals to attain the godly stature of their Father in Heaven,[130] he was troubled: "Is Space or occupied portions of it divided among various deities—have they great 'spheres of influence'? War of Gods—think of wreck of matter involved—if matter used—or would it be a war of forces?"[131]

Although he regarded these as legitimate doctrinal inquiries, Reuben soon realized that each logical question concerning doctrine led to other questions. Each new question was farther removed from his earlier perceptions and from his ability for rational verification. As he later wrote, "Whenever you push out the circle that circumscribes your knowledge, you merely increase the field of the unknown."[132] By the early 1920s, he came to the quandary he described years later to Cloyd H. Marvin, the non-Mormon president of George Washington University, "For my own part I early came to recognize that for me personally I must either quit rationalizing ... or I must follow the line of my own thinking which would lead me I know not where."[133]

But Reuben recognized where his uncompromising commitment to rational theology was leading him, and he shrank from the abyss. "I came early to appreciate that I could not rationalize a religion for myself, and that to attempt to do so would destroy my faith in God," he later wrote to Marvin. "I have always rather worshiped *facts*," he continued, "and while I thought and read for a while, many of the incidents of life, experiences and circumstances, which led, unaided by the spirit of faith, to the position of the atheist, yet the faith of my fathers led me to abandon all that and to refrain from following it. ... For me there seemed to be no alternative. I could only build up a doubt.—If I were to attempt to rationalize about my life here, and the life to come, I would be drowned in a sea of doubt."[134]

The confidence of Reuben's initial commitment to rational inquiry in religious matters evaporated. He later told the young men of Mormonism that "there came into my life many of the doubts which perhaps creep into yours."[135] He had once believed that in intellectual faith "we may dispense with something." Now he found himself on the brink of dispensing with everything. As he had previously written about LDS doctrine, whatever cannot stand tests, reject as unfit. And so he simply stopped subjecting Mormonism to rational tests.

When he looked for some way to explain his position to others, he discovered an anecdote about Abraham Lincoln. Despite his reputed atheism, this Civil War president justified reading the Bible with the comment: "I have learned to read the Bible. I believe all I can and take the rest on faith." To friends, Reuben related the Lincoln story and added, "Substituting in substance the words 'our Mormon Scriptures,' you will have about my situation." This is what he defined as his testimony of the LDS church and its teachings.[136] Later, as an LDS leader, he recommended this anecdote to a general conference and to individual Mormons.[137] Having once teetered on the brink of atheism, he maintained religious faith as an act of will.

After twenty-two years as a general authority, he would tell his associates at LDS headquarters that he prayed for God's help "to live [so] that I shall never lose the testimony which I have."[138] He had become convinced that no person's faith could withstand uncompromising intellectual inquiry. He concluded that in Babylon, as well as in Zion, the refusal to rationalize one's religious beliefs was the highest manifestation of faith.

Not long after he resolved his crisis of faith in his New York City apartment, Luacine was struggling to resolve her crisis of identity in Salt Lake City. She was in the third year of separation from her husband who was nearly 3,000 miles away. He had returned from the Washington Arms Conference to give a magisterial nod of acquiescence to the efforts of his friends to get him elected U.S. senator from Utah. He wanted the office without having to stoop to campaign for it. He was strangely miffed when the Republican convention in July 1922 steam-rolled over his lackluster availability and gave the party's banner to his well organized Jewish opponent Ernest Bamberger.[139]

It was now 1923. He was in New York, as usual, and his wife was abjectly alone in Salt Lake City. This year became a watershed in their personal lives and in Reuben's religious development.

His life was changed by the loving reproof from the deserts of Zion and by the ruthless currents of Babylon. On 6 January 1923, Luacine reported that their last child, her namesake, was joyfully baptized—like the rest of their children, in her father's absence.[140] Reuben's daily letters poured forth his anticipations that his legal work for the AIC would finally bring them the financial bonanza that would free them from their crushing debts and make all their sacrifices worthwhile. Lute had heard this for twenty years and no longer believed in the dream. On 14 January she reported that their teenage son Reuben III was refusing to attend LDS meetings. She concluded: "While it can't be helped, it seems a pity that our only boy should have to be away from his father when he is going through the most trying period in his life. I hope your work and ambitions are worth the sacrifice."[141]

During the next few months, Lute peppered her daily letters to Reuben with her anxieties and frustrations about their situation. She recounted how she "nearly went to pieces trying to adjust myself" to their prolonged separations. She had finally resigned herself to living that way indefinitely: "If I can't have you, I am trying to adjust myself to living away from you, and I find I am succeeding better than I used to at any rate." Still, it embarrassed her to learn that neighborhood servants assumed she was a widow. In one letter she wrote: "I dreamed I married again last night; don't remember who my husband was. Lovingly Lute." When she told Reuben that she had turned down a church calling, she added, "Does this refinement come from [my] associating with you, or not associating with you?" She asked him "to frame up a nice speech for me to make when I am asked when you are coming home." She expressed fears that he would not be able to visit her for their silver wedding anniversary.[142]

Lute continually expressed her love, confidence, and devotion to Reuben, but finally wrote her deepest concerns in April 1923:

> I don't see why you can't do a little church work where you are. Everyone loves to hear you talk. You would be such a big help if you would take hold. You have been nearly 20 years out of it [except] only in a small way. However, we have thrashed this out before. I have hired you[,] I remember[,] more than once to go to church with me, but now you are of age I will leave your religious training alone, and attend to my own.[143]

He may have flinched when he read that letter, but he seemed so close to making all his dreams and sacrifices worthwhile. He continued his seven-day work schedule for the AIC.[144]

However, internal problems at the AIC were forcing him either to cooperate in unethical transactions or risk losing his job. For him, the outcome was inevitable.[145] As Carl S. Hawkins has written, "J. Reuben Clark was a good Christian while he was an effective lawyer in the professional service of his country and his private clients."[146]

His letter of 12 July 1923 "flabbergasted" Lute with its announcement that he was quitting the AIC and returning home for good. Twenty years in Babylon were at an end. Although he would return in unexpected ways to that world's familiar lushness, he would never again feel the same detachment from his desert Zion. "I have longed for this news and of course was thrilled," Lute wrote, "but when I think of your schemes and what this means to you, I feel I should not rejoice so exceedingly." She added later, "I know your future can't look very rosy to you, but I am sure we won't starve, we can live on love for a while."[147]

After twenty years of detachment from LDS activity, Reuben's first talk after his return to Salt Lake City in 1923 signaled his religious renewal: "The Purpose of Sabbath Meetings."[148] He continued to speak in church on such secular topics as "America's Contribution to World Peace" and "Memorial Day," but during the next six years, he gave more than thirty religious sermons in Salt Lake, New York, and Washington, D.C. Their titles were "Christmas," "Easter," "We Stand for an Individual Testimony of the Divinity of Jesus Christ," "Divine Authority and the Latter-day Saints," "Divinity of Jesus Christ," "The Testimony of John," "Faith," "Genealogy," "Joseph Smith," "Obedience," "Salvation for the Dead," "The Personality of God," "The Book of Mormon," "The Material Age," "The Mission of Motherhood," "The Mormon Pioneer Pilgrimage," "Testimony," "The Free Agency of Man," "Administering to the Sick," "The Crucifixion," and "Do Not Trifle with Your Heritage."[149]

For the first time since he went to Columbia University, Reuben paid full tithing and regularly attended LDS meetings. He was again teaching Sunday School to the adults in Salt Lake City's Twentieth Ward.[150] On 7 June 1925, he was sustained to the general board of the Young Men's Mutual Improvement Association.[151] During 1925 and 1926, the general authorities asked Reuben to lecture to departing missionaries, to talk to tourists at the Sunday morning service in the Salt Lake Tabernacle, and to give a series of sermons on church-owned KSL Radio.[152]

To Fred Morris Dearing, his close friend in the State Department, he wrote: "I thoroughly enjoy living out here in the desert wilderness and while I miss the fleshpots of Egypt and sometimes I am in sad need of a helping from them, I am still quite willing to forgo the mere lucre for the sake of the real life which I am able to live."[153] After twenty years, he was again an active participant in the religion of his youth. He was fifty-four.

In April 1926 a telegram from the State Department summoned him back to Washington for the first of a series of government appointments that would thrust him again into the international limelight. During the first decades of his career, he voluntarily left his Mormon home to seek fulfillment of his aspirations for civil service and wealth. When he chose to leave those aspirations in 1923 and return to the Mormon Culture Region, he assumed that losing a future career in his government's service was the price of his renewed devotion to the interests of his family and his religion. As it turned out, a divine providence decreed that he would no longer need to seek opportunities for position, power, and prestige because these would be thrust upon him throughout the balance of his life. He had been willing to surrender his secular dreams to return to his people, church, and family. His rewards would be greater and more varied than he could have imagined in 1923.

The next seven years of his life were delayed ripples of his 1910-13 plunge into the morass of the Mexican Revolution. It careened through Mexican society with such force that American interests were involved, often disastrously, from the start. Decades later, the shock waves of this first social revolution of the twentieth century continued to jolt the diplomacy of Mexico and its overbearing Colossus of the North, the United States.[154]

From 1926 to 1927, Reuben was first the agent and then the general counsel for the American Agency of the United States-Mexico Mixed Claims Commission. It had the responsibility of settling nearly $1 billion in claims by U.S. citizens for losses suffered during the revolution. He found the bureaucratic maze within this commission as convoluted and tortuous as the claims themselves, and he was less than satisfied with his accomplishments.[155]

But he was dealing with the "possible" rather than the "desirable." Officials in Washington and Mexico City were impressed with his encyclopedic understanding of the issues, particularly the claims of U.S. oil companies against the Mexican government. As a result, from 1927 to

1928, he scurried between Washington and the Spanish-speaking capital to the south as a special adviser to the ambassador to Mexico, Dwight Morrow.[156] In 1928 he also engaged in an unsuccessful campaign to secure for himself the nomination of the Utah Republican Party as candidate for the U.S. Senate.[157]

Two months later, Senator Smoot asked him to interrupt his governmental duties for a last-ditch effort on behalf of Utah's Republican candidates. Reuben's memorandum indicated what he thought of Utah politics, as well as of Apostle Smoot. "Some of the most influential and respectable elements of the Republican Party were in open rebellion there," he wrote, "the ones in rebellion being my friends ... I would not therefore slap my friends in the face by returning to Utah and going against them and [then work] with my enemies (who have been and always will be my enemies)." When he informed the apostle of this decision, Reuben noted that Smoot "adopted a sort of martyr's air, and said if I felt that way he would not ask me to go."[158] Smoot wrote: "Clark backed down [by] making silly excuses and I did not insist upon his going. I was greatly surprised and it will do him no good for the future."[159]

When Reuben was asked to become Undersecretary of State from 1928 to 1929,[160] he was actually irritated at his government's interruption of what he thought would be the conclusion of his work in Mexico. He managed to transcend his administrative routine as Undersecretary by including an incisive analysis as a preface to what Secretary of State Frank B. Kellogg intended to be a routine compilation of statements about the Monroe Doctrine. The result was his crowning publication in the secular world. The *Clark Memorandum on the Monroe Doctrine* defined the limits and abuses of a historic document that had intimidated Latin America more than Europe, to which the Monroe Doctrine was directed.[161] However, Reuben's revisionist view never became "official administrative policy," and within a decade the *Clark Memorandum* was repudiated by Franklin D. Roosevelt's Democratic administration.[162] This was one more reason he disliked FDR.

The Clarks returned to Mexico in 1929 for him to continue his advisory position with Ambassador Morrow.[163] This urbane millionaire

taught Reuben never "to violate Rule Six" which was, "Don't take yourself so damned seriously."[164]

The ambassador's protégé also demonstrated how undiplomatic he
could be if somebody attempted intimidation. An American visitor threatened to ruin Ambassador Morrow's political future if he didn't cooperate.
"While I am not sure exactly how the Ambassador will express himself,"
Reuben replied, "if I were the Ambassador, I would tell you to go to
hell."[165]

When Morrow was preparing to resign to campaign for the U.S. Senate, he wanted Reuben to be his successor as ambassador. However, Reuben's appointment was by no means secure.[166]

At this point, Senator Smoot reminded Reuben why he had disliked
this apostle for twenty-seven years. Susa Young Gates wrote her longtime
friend in July 1930, "I spoke to Reed Smoot a day or two ago about your
being made the Mexican ambassador, and he thought I was talking
through my hat." Upon reading this, Reuben was furious. When he finally
answered her well-intentioned letter in September, he refused even to
write Smoot's name: "There is much I could say—some of it in expletives
and some of it in near profanity."[167] As was true of Reuben's first appointment in the State Department, he didn't need Smoot anyway.

On 3 October 1930 Republican president Herbert Hoover appointed Clark as ambassador to Mexico. That year the United States had
only fifteen full ambassadors throughout the world, and from that date
until February 1933, Reuben represented the crucial interests of his government in a land he had grown to love.[168]

He faced several diplomatic and personal challenges as ambassador.
On the strictly diplomatic side, he had to cope with problems universal to
any embassy, plus disputes about the southwest border of the United States
and American claims resulting from the revolution. His judicious work
with the Mixed Claims Commission, his association with the highly popular Morrow, and his scathing memorandum on the much-despised Monroe Doctrine all helped smooth his ambassadorial relations with Mexican
officials. The city's English-language newspaper also observed that Ambassador Clark "has distinguished himself by a virtue which is not common among diplomats: that of not putting himself forward, of not calling

attention to himself, [but instead] of observing a prudent reserve that has won for him the esteem of all social classes in Mexico."[169]

On the personal side, his modest wealth had been a topic of newspaper discussion, as well as government debate, as to whether he could afford to hold the position. Ambassadors traditionally spent thousands of dollars of their own money to conduct obligatory social diplomacy that exceeded government stipends to embassies. "I seem to have the best advertised poverty in the United States," Reuben wrote sardonically.[170] He solved this matter by spending virtually his entire personal savings on a stringently reduced budget for the embassy.[171] This may have been the reason that Morrow told him, "Clark, you are the least influenced by mere wealth of any man I have ever met." Reuben said that this "was the most flattering compliment I ever had, the one that tickled my vanity most."[172] Other challenges typically involved Reuben's Mormonism.

The first issue was the Word of Wisdom, which received the greatest publicity. Long before the ratification of the Eighteenth Amendment to the Constitution in 1920, Reuben and Luacine had served lemonade to prestigious government guests in Washington. Their choice was awkward, but U.S. officials indulged them. It would have been another matter, however, for Ambassador Clark to require alcohol abstention for diplomatic guests due to his own religious beliefs. Prohibition as a constitutional amendment was his way out. All embassies technically were territories of their respective nations. Therefore, Reuben announced that since Prohibition was the law of the land in the United States, it would be strictly observed within its Mexican embassy. He was apparently the only ambassador who applied such legalism, and he received his share of newspaper criticism. His predecessor had even left $800,000 worth of the finest wines and liquors in the embassy's basement. Nevertheless, from 1930 to 1933, the U.S. embassy in Mexico served dignitaries punch, grape juice, and lemonade rather than port, claret, and scotch.[173]

However, there were limits on the extent to which he could insist on a strict observance of the Word of Wisdom. He could prohibit alcohol on legalistic grounds, and he could politely decline to accept the obligatory cigars in diplomatic exchanges. He certainly could not refuse to allow visitors to smoke. He therefore provided guests with cigars and cigarettes "by the thousands, only to watch the Mexicans pocket them in handfuls because they were American [brands]."[174]

Still more difficult was Reuben's necessary attendance at almost nightly socials as the honored guest of other foreign diplomats and Mexican officials. They routinely provided alcoholic beverages as part of the art of diplomacy. In a letter to his nephew S. Wayne Clark, he described his response to this situation:

> As to the cocktails: When we were in Mexico I usually quietly waved the cocktail aside. However, when so to waive it was too conspicuous I took it, raised it to my lips, held it, and set it down at the first opportunity. ...
>
> ... Coffee came in as usual and I took a cup and took a sip from it and then put it down. On other occasions when it was brought in while I was busy in conversation, I usually took the cup and let it stand by me while I talked, without touching it.
>
> When you are at dinners where coffee is served, or liquors, you can more or less ostentatiously and actor-like turn the coffee cup upside down and ditto with the liquor glasses, accompanied by some loud remark about you being a tee-totaller. This is of course void of all tact and may get you in trouble.[175]

Reuben was not the first Mormon to develop social contacts with government officials. However, he was a pioneer in living the Word of Wisdom in diplomatic situations where social offense could affect the relations between nations.

Another difficulty for the Clarks was the matter of participation in LDS services, which was of delicate diplomatic consequences at the time. Mexico had a long tradition of anti-clericalism and conflicts with the Roman Catholic church. The revolutionary Constitution of 1917 placed draconian restrictions on church prerogatives. Although directed at Catholicism, these measures applied to all religious organizations. Among the supplementary decrees by the presidents of Mexico was one in 1927 which prohibited foreigners from participating in religious propaganda in a church or other public place.[176]

The Clarks came to Mexico as regular church attenders but faced a language barrier and the emotional, sometimes violent issue of church-state conflict. Might there be diplomatic repercussions from attending services of a religion founded on proselytizing by foreign missionaries? On the other hand, native Mexican Mormons knew that Clark was a Latter-day Saint and that he spoke at LDS general conference just prior to assuming his ambassadorial duties. If he declined to participate or speak in LDS services to avoid the suspicion of violating Mexican law, would he offend the Mexican Saints who might think that their representative from LDS headquarters was shunning them? Rather than choose either alternative exclusively, he decided on a middle course.

As ambassador, he navigated between the diplomatic and religious hazards by attending and speaking at LDS services in a limited way. He went with his family to the little Mexican branch on the average of once a month while he was ambassador.[177] To a Mormon in Utah, he wrote, "You ask whether we have any L.D.S. meetings here, in reply to which I wish to say that we have some Indian members who have meetings near here and that occasionally Sister Clark and I go to them, but since they are conducted in Spanish, we do not get much of what is going on."[178] When Reuben did attend, it was usually to speak. On several occasions, he spoke "a few words in Spanish."[179] His wife also tried to talk to the Saints in their native language. Clark's daughter Luacine delighted everyone at church with her fluency in Spanish.[180]

Coping with the language and church-state restrictions was burdensome to Reuben. After attending an LDS meeting across the border in El Paso, Texas, he wrote Lute, "It did seem good however to understand the whole service, to be able to speak at the *service* instead of at a social" (emphasis in original).[181] This referred to the anti-clerical restrictions he had to observe in Mexico.[182]

Still, next to the president of the Mexican Mission, Ambassador Clark was the most important representative of the LDS church in that country. The First Presidency corresponded with him about affairs there. He and the Mexican branch president together selected the site for a future chapel. When the branch honored Reuben at his final departure, "Pres. [Isaias] Juarez arose to speak [and] he was so overcome he could scarcely talk. When he finished he really wept."[183]

Under the circumstances, the Clark family generally spent Sunday as a leisurely respite from the hectic days and nights of the rest of the week. After sleeping late, Lute wrote letters while Reuben rode horseback in a leather riding suit.[184] On Sundays the Clarks occasionally shopped, went canoeing, took rides through the countryside, or toured the ancient pre-Aztec pyramids with Utah visitors. Sometimes they attended concerts, "football" (soccer) games, or the polo club. They also played croquet, cards (acey-deucy), and dominos on the Sabbath, often with non-LDS friends.[185]

As low-keyed as the Clark family's Sunday activities were, they could also be extensive. For example, Lute's diary described one Sunday: "Slept late. Ione and Harold Kidder came to have dinner [i.e., lunch] with [my daughter] Luacine. spent the day here. went to Kidders in the evening. At four thirty we went to a Tea in San Angel to the McGregor Mills. spent some time in the garden. After supper [at night] we entertained 15 guests listening to Movie Actors talking over the Radio—served refreshments."[186] At one of these Sunday socials, Reuben discovered his lifelong love of opera. While in Mexico, Lute wrote her first two articles for the church's Relief Society's magazine.[187]

As was his custom, Reuben also spent many hours in his study, but his thoughts and energies were increasingly on things of the Spirit. To his missionary son, Reuben III, he wrote:

> May the Lord bless you spiritually with a rich outpouring of the gift of the Holy Ghost that there may come to you such spiritual gifts as will aid you in reaching the honest in heart, may he give you faith, humility, wisdom, and cleanliness of spirit; may he bless you mentally that you may have cleanliness of mind, that your understanding may be quickened, your memory strengthened, your mental processes intensified and enlarged that you may comprehend more and more of the Gospel and be able to impart it to others to bring them to a knowledge of the truth.[188]

Ambassador Clark himself was trying to understand "more and more of the Gospel" for the purpose of writing a *magnum opus* on the mission of Christ. He asked his son-in-law Ivor Sharp to send him several studies of the New Testament by conservative biblical scholars.[189] When free of other obligations, the ambassador studied these books in relation to the Standard Works of LDS scripture.[190]

He described the scope of his project in a letter to John A. Widtsoe, his son's supervising mission president and a member of the Quorum of Twelve. Reuben wanted to begin with an analysis of "the philosophy which lies behind John's great Hymn to the Messiah. ... Then I am trying to make rather full discussion of Priesthood ... I am treating the subject by dispensations, tracing the Priesthood line, showing as far as possible the functions and duties of the Priesthood as disclosed by the record of each dispensation. The Mosaic Dispensation is a very large order by itself. There will be more pages and a more elaborate discussion of details than I have seen brought together in one place ... Other subjects besides the Priesthood will be the Godhead, faith, baptism, resurrection, work for the dead, etc."[191] He would never have sufficient time to complete such a massive study. A decade later, Widtsoe would publish, under the Twelve's direction, a study of priesthood along the lines the ambassador had envisioned.

But Apostle Widtsoe and other general authorities were increasingly impressed with Reuben. As early as 1914, LDS publications had heralded him as a "Utah Boy ... who, entirely upon his own merits and in a surprisingly short time, has arisen to a position of international prominence and honor."[192]

The most important of these admirers was Heber J. Grant, who became LDS president in November 1918. Three months earlier, Grant had said he understood that Reuben, for his age, "was the greatest International lawyer in the U.S."[193] A year later, Grant was advocating U.S. participation in the League of Nations but found that this able international lawyer was undermining those efforts. Reuben used his eloquent and masterful talents in anti-League talks to overflow crowds of 10,000 in the Salt Lake Tabernacle and elsewhere. President Grant continued to support the League of Nations but respected Reuben's views.[194] In June 1920 Grant traveled to New York City on business for the Utah-Idaho Sugar Company and stopped at the Clark law office. He asked Reuben for "general friendly advice" about a contract which had already been approved by the church's lawyers.[195]

Although Grant and Clark did not have a close association prior to the 1930s, the LDS president had expressed enough confidence in the younger man that Reuben had the courage to give him unsolicited advice. For example, Reuben was stunned when the First Presidency announced in 1922 that the new mission president in New York City would be Brigham H. Roberts. In 1900 the U.S. House of Representatives had denied Roberts his elected seat because of the plural wives with whom he continued to live.[196] Reuben dashed off an immediate letter of protest to the church president. With typical Woolley bluntness, he wrote: "Now, as I have indicated above, I can understand it may be the purpose [of the First Presidency] to reopen all this old fight and to resubject the people to the consequent persecution ... to induce persecution for the sake of the increased solidarity and spirituality which would follow." He implied that this controversial appointment would handicap the church's "political and financial credit."[197] He shrewdly aimed this last comment at Grant's decades of emphasis on improving the church's credit and business ties with non-Mormon bankers, particularly in the Northeast.[198]

Grant's reply thanked him for this concern and agreed that Roberts might stir up controversy as a mission president in the Northeast. He dryly added that "I can not help but feel that in your enthusiastic interest for the welfare of the Church in that splendid mission you are perhaps a little over exercised about the matter."[199]

Undaunted by the mild rebuff, Reuben was encouraged by the president's sympathetic reception of the unrequested advice. He thereafter prepared drafts of proposed proclamations for general conferences. His draft resolution for the October 1923 conference would, Reuben thought, permanently resolve the question of LDS church interference in politics:

> First:—That from and after this date no member of the First Presidency or the Quorum of the Twelve shall participate in any political discussions or activities of any nature whatsoever, nor seek to exercise either directly or indirectly or publicly or privately any influence or control in any political matters whatsoever ... [excluding] matters of morals or temperance [i.e., alcohol prohibition] ... but in such discussions there shall be no discussion of parties, or their principles, or candidates.
>
> Second, That from and after this date no members of the Quorum

of the First Presidency or of the Quorum of the Twelve shall accept any office or employment of profit or trust under the State or the Federal Government, or under any county, city, or municipality of the state, nor any nomination or appointment for such office.

Third. Any member failing to obey either or both of the two foregoing rules shall by that act forfeit his membership in the Quorum of the First Presidency or in the Quorum of the Twelve respectively and he shall not be again eligible for membership in such Quorums.[200]

He was undoubtedly disappointed that President Grant did not issue such a sweeping proclamation in 1923 or thereafter. Reuben certainly recognized that such a statement would be an implicit apology for previous interventions of the First Presidency in Utah's political life.[201] In addition, if publicly announced, this proclamation would require Apostle Smoot to resign from the Quorum of Twelve or from the U.S. Senate. Since Reuben's proposed statement gave no grandfather clause exemption, he clearly wanted to force Smoot to resign.

Nevertheless, despite his implacable opposition to political activities by the LDS hierarchy, he remained a loyalist for the Republican church leaders in office. In May 1924 he gave the nominating speech for Senator Smoot to be Utah's delegate to the Republican Party's national convention. In so doing, he set aside his personal animosity as well as his opposition to Utah's church-state relationship.[202]

During the next seven years, he continued to attract the interest of President Grant. Reuben researched the legal background of Grant's cherished but unfulfilled plan for providing life insurance to LDS priesthood bearers.[203] He displayed extraordinary skills as an orator in ward sacrament meetings, and the church president told the general conference of April 1926 that Reuben's recent talk on radio was "one of the finest sermons on Priesthood that I have listened to."[204] Reuben's appointment as Undersecretary of State in 1928 and then as ambassador to Mexico brought to Utah and Mormonism the honor of national leaders and positive attention from the nation's finest newspapers and magazines. Grant concluded that Clark was a rank-and-file Latter-day Saint without peer. The president invited him to speak for the first time at a general conference in October 1930 and introduced the new ambassador with the words, "All Utahns are proud of the honor that has come to one of our citizens."[205]

In view of his unparalleled prominence among Utahns, it is not surprising that traditional speculations about new appointments to the apostleship included the ambassador. On 19 May 1931, one of his friends reported the gossip that he was to fill a vacancy in the Twelve. "Not that you wouldn't be a first rate apostle," S. J. Quinney wrote, "but God forbid that your talents be wasted in this direction."[206] With typical bluntness, Reuben answered: "I think there is no more danger of my being named [an apostle] than there is of my flying to the moon. I have never sought or craved church office."[207] There was more substance to the rumor than he dreamed possible.

On the day after the report of this popular speculation, President Grant recorded serious discussion about the ambassador filling the vacancy. The president asked each member of the Twelve to recommend two names as the new apostle, ranked as first and second choice. Of the ten who submitted recommendations, half voted for Reuben—three listed him as first choice and two as second choice. Moreover, he was the first choice of Grant's counselor Charles W. Nibley. Grant himself wrote: "Unless I get the impression otherwise[,] I am unqualifiedly in favor of Brother Clark. Before getting out of bed this morning I was going over the names of fifteen or twenty men, and he stood out prominently as first choice in my judgment. ... In my mind, J. Reuben Clark is one of the outstanding men in the church, intellectually. He is ambassador from the United States at the present time." Grant deferred a final decision until his cousin and first counselor Anthony W. Ivins returned: "On more than one occasion when I have almost made up my mind in favor of some individual my counselor, Brother Ivins, has named some one who pleased me better."[208] After Ivins returned, he suggested deferring the decision until just before the October 1931 conference. At that time, the First Presidency decided to call physics professor Joseph F. Merrill as the new apostle.[209]

On 11 December 1931, another vacancy occurred with the death of Charles W. Nibley, second counselor. Grant's first choice would have been Apostle Smoot. However, six years earlier Grant had decided not to appoint him because "it would not do for [Smoot] to leave the Senate as [he] could do more good there for our people than in any other position."[210] In 1931 Grant still believed that Smoot's most important service was in the Senate. He therefore thought more deeply about his choice for a new counselor.

It had been more than a half century since anyone had been advanced to the First Presidency who was not already a general authority. At that time, Brigham Young chose his son John W. Young for the position. Nineteen years earlier, President Young selected Grant's father-in-law Daniel H. Wells as a counselor in 1857. Wells lacked significant ecclesiastical experience but had been prominent in civil office in Nauvoo and Utah.[211]

Suddenly, as presidents Grant and Ivins renewed one of their aimless discussions about a replacement for Nibley, the church president exclaimed: "I know who we can get. This man Clark, the Ambassador to Mexico." Ivins replied, "You can't get him, Heber, because he is a $100,000.00 a year man." Grant gave a characteristic chuckle and said: "We can ask him."[212]

Just before Christmas 1931, Louise and Marianne were visiting their parents in the embassy. As Louise sorted through the day's mail, she found a letter from the First Presidency. "It's for you from President Grant," she said with merriment. "He is probably asking you to be his counselor." Louise joined in the laughter this seemed to produce in the entire family but then noticed the ashen appearance of her father's face as she handed him the letter. Reuben turned the letter over in his hands, examined the return address, and slowly put it into his coat pocket without opening it. When conversation seemed to lag, he excused himself and went to his study, locking the door.[213]

He felt he already knew the meaning of the letter as he nervously opened the envelope. He refused to believe his feelings because it was not rational to have such thoughts or fears. His eyes quickly skimmed through the usual greetings, the reminder of Counselor Nibley's death, then froze on the words: "After prayerful consideration our minds definitely revert to you as the man whom the Lord desires to fill this vacancy."[214] The rest of the letter became a blur as the ambassador absently brushed his hand across moist cheeks. "Gone were the dreams of a lifetime in law, vanished the ambitions of his life!"[215]

The deaths of his brother, sisters, and father, and even his humiliating political defeats—nothing so devastated Reuben as this letter from the president of his church. For a while, he sat at his desk as if in a daze, then slowly read the letter again and again. As he did, his mind was bombarded with discordant thoughts: "give up my life's work ... thrust aside financial opportunities that promise very large returns ... about to the time when I might begin to garner a real harvest."[216]

After what seemed a lifetime of contemplation in his study, he thought he knew how to respond. His reply took him hours to complete. First, he wrote a long "Memorandum of Explanation" to presidents Grant and Ivins concerning the nature of his assignment in Mexico and the fact that sensitive negotiations were in progress. He expressed fear that President Hoover would consider him a "deserter" if he resigned to become a member of the LDS First Presidency. Then he wrote a cover letter for this memorandum and absentmindedly dated it 19 December 1931, the date of the LDS presidency's letter to him rather than the date of this reply:

> On the other hand, you Brethren must have an enormous amount of work and be in need of help, so much so that you will not care to postpone filling the vacancy for an indefinite time.
>
> In this latter event, I can conceive that, if you think it best not to give opportunity for irritation [to President Hoover and Secretary Stimson] through my leaving before they desire it, you may wish—instead of waiting for me—to fill the vacancy by appointing some one else. If you take this view, I hope you will feel entirely free to act.[217]

It was a supreme example of diplomacy. He had not actually declined the invitation to become a counselor. In fact, he had even expressed gratitude for their confidence in him. Nonetheless, he had presented the situation in terms that would probably cause President Grant to choose another man rather than wait years for the ambassador to complete his work in Mexico.

He felt emotionally drained as he finished his last rereading of the memorandum and letter. Instead of folding the pages, addressing an envelope to the First Presidency, and putting the letter with the next day's outgoing mail, he put his memorandum, his letter, and their letter into a locked drawer without folding them. He felt exhausted and depressed—too depressed to tell even Lute about the First Presidency's letter and his reply. He tried to go through the motions of enjoying Christmas Eve and Christmas Day, but his unexplained gloom infected the whole family. It was the worst Christmas the Clarks ever experienced, yet no one asked what the problem was. They knew the impenetrable silence of the family's "Great Sphinx" too well. Finally, he told Lute. His own feelings had been so somber that he had no anticipation of her joyful reaction to the news. Reuben did not tell her of his memorandum and reply.[218]

On 28 December he took the sheets of paper from the locked drawer, reread them, and laid them to one side of the desk top. He then wrote a different letter to the First Presidency:

> I have never aspired to Church office—its honor and dignity I appreciated, but its responsibilities seemed too grave. I do not now so aspire. If I felt that my personal preferences should now control me, I would ask to be allowed to continue working in the ranks.
>
> But when, as now, a call comes from my superior officers, charged with the responsibility of presiding over the Church and acting under the inspiration of the Lord, then I, responsive to my training and my faith, must answer to the call, not only as a clear duty but as a great privilege.
>
> It is for the Lord to say how and where I shall serve. I trust Him to help me meet the responsibility of my task.
>
> I know, at least in part, my own shortcomings and unworthiness.
>
> I appreciate the honor the call brings to me.

This letter was from Reuben's heart, from the love he held for his heritage. The other letter and memorandum were from his head and his lifelong effort to succeed in a world that could not comprehend him. He placed this letter of acceptance on top of his letter of demurring. Underneath those two was the memorandum outlining why the ambassador should not accept this church calling. He folded them together and mailed the fat envelope to the First Presidency.[219] Now it was out of his hands; it was their decision.

When his letter arrived on 2 January 1932, President Grant was in

California. Counselor Ivins opened the envelope. As soon as he read the reply of 28 December, he telegraphed President Grant: "Party agreeable to our recommendations. Beautiful letter."[220] If Ivins looked at the long memorandum and other cover letter, he probably did little more than skim them. He probably never realized that Reuben had expected them to make a conscious choice between his brief letter of acceptance and his detailed suggestion that they choose someone else as counselor. To Ivins, the other pages probably seemed only background for a "beautiful letter" of acceptance. Reuben would have agreed with that assessment.

The next year was a difficult one for Ambassador Clark. He tried to wrap up negotiations in Mexico while contemplating how and when he would submit his resignation to the U.S. president. At the same time, he had to give whatever comfort he could to an overworked and incomplete First Presidency who wanted him to assume church work as soon as possible. Still another problem involved rumors and second-guessing about his church office and public office.

On 9 January, Reuben wrote President Grant to express his concern about the timing of his resignation. But these were not his worst fears:

> I have gathered from your letters that you wish to announce my appointment at the April Conference, even though I might still be here. I am afraid that the Mexican Government, in its present temper, would not wish to have a high Church official of any Church stationed here as American Ambassador. If they took this attitude, they might ask for my recall, which would be a grave reflection not only upon myself (which might be disregarded) but also upon the United States and upon the Church.[221]

This was sufficient to change the LDS president's plans for a public announcement.

On 3 March 1932, after his return from a trip to Washington and New York, President Grant informed the Quorum of Twelve that he had chosen Reuben as his second counselor. He explained that this appointment could not be announced until he was free of his ambassadorial responsibilities. The next day, Grant wrote Clark that he should leave Mexico with the full approval of the U.S. president and the Secretary of

State. Nothing should be done to bring the "calamity" of Clark's recall as ambassador. This letter relieved Reuben of his anxieties and reassured him that the Quorum of Twelve accepted his appointment.[222]

Apostle Melvin J. Ballard was visiting the ambassador in Mexico when Grant announced the appointment to the Twelve. Since Reuben was telling no one about it, Elder Ballard came to the next meeting of the apostles in complete ignorance of developments. At first, Ballard could not understand why he caused such amusement when "he remarked that he had met a young man in Mexico City who because of his integrity, testimony, power and ability could some day be used in the higher councils."[223]

In letters of 11 March and 20 June 1932, Reuben alerted President Grant to another problem. Utahns were urging him to allow Republican leaders to nominate him for candidacy as governor or U.S. senator. "I do not suppose there is the slightest chance of the Republican Convention nominating me for governor when I am not a candidate for the nomination," Reuben wrote on 20 June, "but if the idea should show signs of life, I hope you can find a way to kill it."[224]

Since his unsuccessful efforts to get his party's nomination in 1928, Reuben had achieved such distinction in government service that not even the divided Republican Party of Utah could have denied him the nomination had he sought it. Accepting the church call in December 1931 had changed everything, even though he could not explain this to his bewildered political supporters in Utah. On 28 August 1932 he wrote Counselor Ivins, begging not to be required to attend October conference lest he be dragged into the election campaign. He added: "Ever since I received the first letter from you Brethren, I have been under a constant strain and, at times, much anxiety lest the course I was following was not the course I should follow. I have constantly prayed about the matter and have had no answer other than a constant feeling that I should finish here fully to guard against my being swayed by personal considerations. ... I am constantly trying to learn what the Lord wants and to do it. Whatever help you Brethren shall give me will be most thankfully received."[225]

The Democratic landslide in the November 1932 election simplified the timing and circumstances of his resignation as ambassador. As a

Republican officeholder, Reuben gracefully departed his diplomatic post just prior to his party's departure from the White House.[226]

He was hard-pressed to be equally adroit in responding to rumors and queries that began as soon as Grant informed the Quorum of Twelve of his call. When a Mormon in New York City congratulated him in April 1932 about his call to the First Presidency, Reuben replied:

> I am obliged to inform you that I have not been so appointed. During the past few months I have been made, by rumor in Utah, Governor of the State, United States Senator from the State, a member of the Quorum of the Twelve, and a Councilor to President Grant. ...
>
> As I recently wrote a friend of mine, I suppose I shall have to wait until I return to the State of Utah in order to work out which, if any, of these various honors may be mine.[227]

As time went by without public announcement, Utah gossip concluded that the church president was delaying because he wanted Senator Smoot as counselor and hoped that he would be defeated in the November election. In the process of protecting Smoot from the political consequences of that rumor, Grant nearly tipped his hand regarding Clark. A statement of 29 October 1932 said that Smoot was not in line for the position of counselor because "selection was made months ago and accepted" by someone else.[228] On 3 November, Grant added that the man "who has accepted is hampered by his business from accepting at this time."[229]

By early 1933, all the rumors pointed to Reuben as the new counselor. However, he could not confirm their truth as long as he was an ambassador and there had been no official announcement.[230] When reporters in Austin, Texas, asked the Clarks on 16 February why they were returning to Salt Lake City, Lute laughed, "To get back to work and make a little money."[231] When asked the question again on their arrival in Salt Lake City, Reuben replied, "I am a candidate for the law business."[232]

On 20 March 1933 Reuben's mind swirled with thoughts and images. He had been baptized shortly before Heber Grant became his stake president. Now he was to meet the LDS president for the first time since agreeing to be his counselor.[233] This year the church's membership was 564,042 in the organized stakes of nine states in the American Far West, with an additional 153,577 Mormons scattered in small branches throughout the rest of the United States and the world.[234]

As Reuben ascended the granite stairs, he thought of his steps from Grantsville to Salt Lake City, to Columbia University, to the State Department, to the U.S. Attorney General's office, to the embassy in Mexico. He looked up at the inscription above the doors he was about to enter: ADMINISTRATION BUILDING OF THE CHURCH OF JESUS CHRIST OF LATTER-DAY SAINTS. He was now sixty-one years old. He thought fleetingly of the steps he had hoped to take to Park Avenue, to the Utah governor's mansion, to the Senate, to the U.S. president's cabinet, perhaps to the Supreme Court. Then Reuben remembered a passage from Dante: "Abandon hope, ye who enter here," smiled to himself, and crossed the portals.[235]

CHAPTER 2.

Differences of Administration[1]

THROUGH THE PUBLICITY OF HIS ACHIEVEMENTS FOR A QUARTER century, J. Reuben Clark was no stranger to church administrators. But the U.S. ambassador was a stranger to church administration when he actively began his duties as a counselor in the First Presidency in 1933. Nearly all of his predecessors had years of service as local presiding officers and general authorities prior to their appointment. By contrast, Reuben remarked, "The bulk of the work which I did in the Church until I was called to my present position was as a teacher in the Sunday Schools."[2] Because he learned his administrative skills in law and government, he seemed to introduce a different style to church administration.

A major difference was his lifelong practice of doing intensive personal research on a question and then preparing a detailed analysis of the matter in a memorandum. Few, if any, of his predecessors did their own research on the subjects about which they had to make decisions. Instead, they delegated this to clerks or secretaries who summarized the information for them. Reuben's departure from that precedent awed his associates. Marion G. Romney observed: "Brother Clark was a student. He never said anything or did anything that he couldn't back up with the authorities. And nobody could ever find a loophole in his presentation." This view was echoed by Spencer W. Kimball.[3] Frank W. Asper wrote about Reuben's administrative style:

For a long time I have watched the way you have decided matters, always carefully dissecting them from every angle and taking a firm stand according to your decision regardless of circumstances or other people's opinions. For this reason, I have come to regard your views as impartial and always built up from solid rock.[4]

The result could be daunting. Oftentimes his memorandum on a topic was dozens of pages long.

When he did not do academic research, he approached every decision with probing questions, a process of verbal interrogation that was a product of his law school training and government service. Although several general authorities held doctoral degrees, he was the first in the church presidency to have a graduate degree. In this highest quorum's history, he was nearly alone in having completed college. All these factors gave tremendous stature to his role as an administrator.

After arriving at decisions slowly, with much research and analysis, he tended to maintain his views rather inflexibly once he came to a conclusion. This tendency sometimes exasperated his wife, Lute,[5] and it was something he acknowledged in himself. He once made an ironic observation to his brother Frank: "We Clarks are a good deal like the Harvard man—you can tell a Harvard man wherever you see him—but you can't tell him much. Even so with us."[6]

His unwillingness to reconsider decisions had possible disadvantages, but it was the product of intensive reflection rather than quick judgment. In fact, he did his best to avoid prejudicial judgment. He once wrote:

The directing of the affairs of the Church is an over-powering responsibility and undertaking. No man can properly approach it except in the deepest humility, with something of an adequate realization of his own limitations, his prejudices, predilections, and human judgment. But every man with Church responsibility must try to cope with and bring under control these elements so far as it is possible for him to do.[7]

With that kind of caution, he arrived at decisions slowly but firmly. It was the stability of his well considered views that caused so many of his associates to use images of "solid rock" in describing him.

Through experience in law and government, he had also developed the trait of expressing himself emphatically. To some extent in correspondence, but especially in verbal communication, he repeated his essential points as many as four times.[8] This was particularly his practice in declining a request: "When you tell people no, you better tell it in emphatic terms; if you say it in a nice way they think you indicate yes."[9] To those in the church who were unaccustomed to such firmness, President Clark's practice of "rarely pulling punches" seemed harsh, especially when combined with his habit of using a gruff tone when engaged in good-natured banter.[10] These were simply administrative approaches that had worked well for him during his years of government service and which he almost unconsciously continued in church administration.

Although he might attribute it to his Woolley ancestry, Reuben's blunt statement of the facts as he perceived them was equally a product of his government service. He had too often seen petty bureaucrats attempt to ingratiate themselves by providing selective information. As a member of the First Presidency, he refused to engage in such practice: "I admonished President Grant that people were prone to say to him what people thought he wanted to hear."[11] Nevertheless, Reuben carefully avoided the pitfall of trying to convert the church president to a particular point of view:

> I have always felt that as a second man it was my duty fully to explain any views that I had on any problem and to make sure they were understood by my Chief, but that there my responsibility ended. It was for the Chief to make up his mind what he wanted to do. It was not my business to try to over-persuade him to do as I thought he should do. I am not sure this is the right attitude, but I am sure it has kept me out of trouble sometimes. At any rate, it has eased off situations that might have led to real difficulties if I had been too insistent.[12]

He was too honest and strong-willed to be a yes-man or cater to anyone's prejudices. Yet he felt a special obligation to avoid usurping the prerogative of the prophet. No matter what the circumstances, Reuben was a strong counselor but not the power behind the throne.

In the decision-making process of the First Presidency, there was not always agreement, as he often told LDS members, but there was loyalty to the final decision of the church president. He told one Mormon that there was often a free discussion of differing views in the First Presidency "before a decision is reached, but everybody supports the decision, whatever his previous views were."[13] Harold B. Lee published Reuben's further explanation:

> When we were discussing some subject the President would turn to each of us and say, "What do you think about this?" or "What is your opinion?" When he asked me I gave it to him straight from the shoulder, as forthrightly as I knew how, even though my opinion was sometimes contrary to his. Then there was the business of resolving our different points of view. But when the President of the Church finally declared, "Brethren, I feel that this should be our decision," President Clark said, "That was the Prophet speaking, and I stopped counseling and accepted without question the decision that he thus announced."[14]

Still, Reuben sometimes expressed his private dissent from decisions of the LDS president. He also publicly stated that the First Presidency could be in error and the church president's statements could be uninspired. (See chapter 7.)

To his brother Frank, Reuben wrote that the process of decision making by the LDS president was not governed by majority rule, and he related an illustrative anecdote about Abraham Lincoln. When Lincoln once called for a vote on a matter, every member of his cabinet voted for it. Lincoln voted against it and declared that the nays won. In like manner, Reuben continued, "the President of the Council therefore declares the decision of the Council."[15]

Members of the presidency themselves were sometimes amused by the turnabouts this policy could produce. When the apostle who opposed the creation of a new stake in a particular place was the one later assigned to help organize this stake, Counselor Henry D. Moyle quipped, "Funny church, isn't it?"[16]

A corollary of that policy was Reuben's consistent practice of dissociating his views from the First Presidency when his statements pertained to matters on which the LDS president had not ruled. He understandably made such a distinction when he expressed partisan political views, but he also did it as a part of routine church administration. For example, when he held a three-hour meeting with individuals "about general conditions and problems at B.Y.U. I made it clear I was not speaking for the Church nor the First Presidency."[17] He realized that it was all too easy for Mormons to assume that any statement by him was "Church policy" or had the specific approval of the president. To guard against inaccurate assumptions of this nature, he carefully distinguished between his independent views and official policies.[18]

Loyal to his superiors, he also respected the prerogatives of his subordinates in church administration. When two men traveled from Logan, Utah, to ask about a particular matter, "I told them that the matter was not one that was immediately under my charge, that it was in the hands of the Executive Committee of the Board of Education, and I would speak to Brother Joseph Fielding Smith about it."[19] Reuben had learned during his first years in the State Department how frustrating it was for a subordinate to have his responsibilities expropriated by a superior. Therefore, he always sought to preserve and respect the principle of delegated authority.

He was absolutely loyal to the "prophets, seers, and revelators" with whom he counseled, but he wanted to prevent extremist views about infallibility that people sometimes propagated. He had direct experience with the give-and-take of decision making, the sometimes necessary reliance on incomplete information, and the human element that exists even in prophets. "We are not infallible in our judgment, and we err," he told the April 1940 conference when announcing a decision of the First Presidency, "but our constant prayer is that the Lord will guide us in our decisions, and we are trying so to live that our minds will be open to His inspiration."[20] He was even more blunt about his own limitations. To LDS critic Frank H. Jonas, he wrote: "I hoped I might escape a charge of insincerity, though I might not hope to escape the charge of ignorance or of inexperience. I have always tried to be honest however much I might be mistaken."[21] A man of intense views, he was disarmingly unpretentious and candid.

He knew the prophets as few know them. He saw how they struggled in faith and prayer to be the mouthpiece of God to his children on earth, and he joined with the rest of the First Presidency in seeking God's inspiration. As he gave full devotion to the LDS president, he expected the same of the Saints. But Reuben wanted LDS loyalty to be untainted by the myth of infallibility.[22]

Still another characteristic of his administrative style was an insistence on expeditious meetings. In government offices and in diplomacy, he had learned that lengthy meetings were usually counterproductive. Elder Romney observed that he conducted administrative meetings "with great despatch and efficiency."[23] Ernest L. Wilkinson simply observed that President Clark "always wanted brief meetings."[24]

An important aspect of his rational approach to decision making was that he tried to think of all possible negative consequences of any proposal under discussion. Taking a worst-case approach to problem solving minimized unpleasant surprises but also tended toward a pessimism which his longest-serving secretary, Rowena J. Miller, described, "In his own life he has felt it wisest to approach problems from the point of view that things may get worse than better, for so approaching you are then prepared for the worst, if the worst comes."[25]

This negativism went hand-in-hand with his practice of intensive research prior to his decisions. It resulted in cautious decision making and implementation. If he felt pressed for a conclusion, he acted swiftly with what information he possessed; but if the urgency was felt only by others, he wanted time to think through all the implications. This conservative approach may have spared him unwise decisions, and its pessimism resulted in many fulfilled prophecies of doom. However, his pessimism also limited innovation and made him resistant to decisions based on optimistic projections from current circumstances. Yet in this conservative way, he could be innovative in both government and church service.

One dimension of his personality that softened his occasional abruptness and forbidding manner was his sense of humor. He was a master of self-deprecation and irony, and he often delighted congregations with his dry humor. Those who worked closely with him knew another side to his humor, as well. He sometimes relieved the tension or boredom of an administrative meeting by indulging in mimicry of specific individuals known to the people present.[26]

Another personality trait affected how he could be approached as an administrator. He had seen too much shallowness in the world to be influenced by flattery, and he had achieved too much success to need praise. "If you do not quit saying so many nice things," he wrote to Apostle Richard R. Lyman, "you will have me believing them one of these days, and that would be a real tragedy."[27] Resistant to praise himself, Reuben had long been appalled at the susceptibility of the Latter-day Saints. In 1931 he complained to Brigham Young University president Franklin S. Harris about how "we repeat complimentary things said of us with so much gusto and smacking of our lips."[28]

Once in the First Presidency, Clark plainly told his fellow Mormons that they were too gullible:

> I wish that we could get over being flattered into almost anything. If any stranger comes among us and tells us how wonderful we are, he pretty nearly owns us. ... You would not think of letting one of our own people suddenly blow into town, boost you a bit, and then carry him around on cushions. These approaches are crude and frequently disingenuous.[29]

Although most of his criticism focused on susceptibility to non-Mormon praise, he knew enough of human nature to realize that church members themselves, consciously or unconsciously, used flattery to ingratiate themselves with LDS leaders. He was near the pinnacle of church authority where that possibility was the greatest and most dangerous. Thus, he refused to accept any praise without a disclaimer.

He lacked previous church administrative experience but often awed his associates in the presiding councils at LDS headquarters. Every church leader has his own strengths, but he brought to the First Presidency an administrative style that was the distillation of twenty-five years of association, service, and negotiation with the highest leaders of business, national government, and international diplomacy. As a shrewd judge of men, President Grant was confident in April 1933 that he "will be a very great help in directing the affairs of the Church."[30] The new counselor did not disappoint him. J. Reuben Clark had distinguished himself as a notable civil servant and he would become an extraordinary LDS leader.

CHAPTER 3.

Three Presiding High Priests[1]
I. Heber J. Grant, 1933-45

A MBASSADOR CLARK WAS MISTAKEN IN ASSUMING THAT HIS POSITION in the First Presidency ended his participation in world affairs. Heber J. Grant selected him as a counselor because of his secular experience, not in spite of it. Grant demonstrated this on the day Reuben made his first visit to the Church Administration Building after returning from Mexico. The LDS president immediately sent him to greet former U.S. president Herbert Hoover in Ogden, Utah.[2]

President Grant knew that his counselor lacked experience in LDS administration. He accurately concluded that the church would obtain unparalleled recognition through the service of a man who had held various government appointments during the administrations of U.S. presidents Theodore Roosevelt, William H. Taft, Woodrow Wilson, Warren G. Harding, Calvin Coolidge, and Herbert Hoover. Reuben felt far more awkward about this than Grant did. After the general conference sustained him as second counselor on 9 April 1933, Clark said:

> Should any of you have hopes about my work in this high office to which I am called, I trust I shall not too much disappoint you. If any of you have misgivings, I can only say that your misgivings can hardly be

greater than my own. I am keenly conscious of my own deficiencies. I come late in life to a new work.[3]

President Grant wanted Reuben to be his counselor in the affairs of the church, but he also wanted him to be an American "elder statesman." Maintaining the esteem of the world's leaders, being the church's spokes- man in civil matters in which Reuben already had the respect of non- Mormons, and serving as the First Presidency's ambassador in secular con- tacts would be possible only because of Reuben's pre-1933 government service. "I think that J. Reuben Clark Jr. is one of the great statesmen of America," Grant wrote. He added, "He is the man of all men who could best occupy the [U.S.] presidential chair in this present crisis in which we are situated."[4]

One current crisis was the Great Depression that caused national un- employment to increase from 3 to 25 percent in three years.[5] Utah's farm income dropped 54 percent while its rate of delinquent farm mortgages rose to 49 percent.[6]

For Republicans and conservative Democrats, another crisis was President Franklin D. Roosevelt's New Deal response to the Depression.[7] To Grant, an even greater problem was that more than half of the Lat- ter-day Saints embraced this Democratic neo-socialism which violated conservative dogmas about laissez-faire economics and the limited role of government. "It is one of the most serious conditions that has confronted me since I became President of the Church," he wrote.[8]

A nominal Democrat at best since becoming LDS president in 1918,[9] Grant privately became a Republican in 1932. Four years later he ex- plained that he "left the Democratic party" when Roosevelt endorsed the repeal of Prohibition.[10] Aside from never forgiving the Democratic pres- ident for making alcohol legal again in the United States, the LDS presi- dent instinctively recoiled from the economic and bureaucratic innova- tions of the New Deal from 1933 onward.

However, the church president's cousin-counselor, Anthony W. Ivins, brought a strongly sympathetic view of the New Deal into the First Pres- idency's deliberations. An ardent member of the Democratic Party throughout his adult life,[11] the first counselor temporarily succeeded in pouring oil on the conservative waters of Grant's political soul.

In extending the call to Clark and in subsequent conversations, the LDS president made it clear that he expected his second counselor to serve the broad interests of the church by means of his government service and contracts. Grant had likewise devoted his life to the LDS church through business associations,[12] and he expected no less of Reuben. Clark described his own view in a letter to J. C. Grey, editor of the *New York Sun*:

> I never had much use for hermits who ran away from the problems of the world out into the desert and merely prayed. That has never seemed to me quite the highest type of human activity. So I must be allowed just a word of defense to say that while I am out in the desert and while I do pray, I am, nevertheless, trying to do a very great deal more.[13]

Since Reuben came to the Mormon hierarchy as a recently retired diplomat, he was able to speak on public matters and act in the advisory civil capacity traditionally reserved for American elder statesmen. He described himself as one of his nation's "elder statesmen," a term LDS publications also applied to him.[14]

While in the First Presidency, he gave formal briefings to the U.S. State Department and testified before the Senate Foreign Relations Committee. The *New York Times* sought his views on diplomatic meetings and federal policies which affected American finances.[15] Men like former U.S. president Hoover, Secretary of State Cordell Hull, future Secretary of State John Foster Dulles, future CIA director Allen Dulles, and George Washington University president Cloyd H. Marvin solicited his advice and opinions.[16] He was the invited speaker at national meetings of the American Bar Association, Boy Scouts of America, Sons of the American Revolution, National Association of County Officials, and many others.[17] The editor of a New York City newspaper best acknowledged his national reputation in soliciting lengthy comments about national policy. William H. Ryan wrote, "Your opinion on this subject should have weight with the People of the Nation."[18]

Just as Reuben was beginning his duties as a counselor, he was pulled in other directions. As an elder statesman, he had been willing to forsake his dreams of flourishing in Babylon for service in Zion, but Babylon was unwilling to forget him. He did not need to seek the role of elder statesman, for representatives of business, government, and politics repeatedly imposed it on him. This required him after 1933 to balance priorities of church service and secular responsibilities. At times he was no more comfortable with the tension between the two than he had been during the twenty years he had devoted himself primarily to secular achievement.

The first distraction occurred barely a week after he was sustained as second counselor in the First Presidency. At 10:30 a.m. on 17 April 1933, a phone call from New York City invited him to join the board of directors for one of America's largest life insurance companies, Equitable Life Assurance Society of the United States. President Clark was accepting his mounting business directorships in Utah as an unavoidable burden of his new position, but this was a thunderbolt from the East. Aside from its compliment to him personally, Reuben could see little to commend his involvement in a company in which the church had no financial interest. It might even appear to Mormons as a competitor to the church-owned Beneficial Life Insurance Company.[19]

The LDS president did not share those misgivings. Grant had been active in the insurance business his entire adult life and highly valued his association with insurance leaders throughout the country.[20] To him, Reuben's presence on the Equitable board was a compliment of national proportions to the First Presidency.

Despite this endorsement, Reuben mulled over all the ramifications in his characteristic fashion and did not telephone his acceptance for six hours.[21] He remained a director of Equitable Life for twenty-five years. Its presidents regarded him so highly that they kept him on the board ten years beyond the age of retirement and ignored his repeated offers to resign. As his successor, Equitable later appointed his close friend and protégé, Apostle Harold B. Lee.[22]

As a new counselor, Reuben launched his 1933 church service in a whirlwind of activity. He spoke at the graduation exercises of the LDS Hospital's school of nursing on 18 May, at the McCune School of Music and Art on 22 May, Utah Agricultural College on 28 May, the University of Idaho at Pocatello on 4 June, and Earlham College, a Quaker school in Indiana, on 12 June. He also gave talks to the Salt Lake County Bar Association, the Provo Chamber of Commerce, and the Los Angeles Chamber of Commerce.[23]

His new position also required close attention to the business activities of the church. Within a matter of weeks, he joined the board of directors of several church-related enterprises: Beneficial Life Insurance Company, Heber J. Grant Co., Hotel Utah, Temple Square Hotel, Utah State National Bank, Utah Home Fire Insurance Company, Utah-Idaho Sugar Company, ZCMI, Zion's Savings Bank, and Zion's Securities Corporation. It was a dizzying pace even for one accustomed to intensive activity.[24]

His 1933 agenda at LDS headquarters was equally diverse. From the end of April to early May, he was working on prepublication editing of conference talks by general authorities.[25] On his own initiative, he drafted a statement against unauthorized polygamy and on 24 May presented it to the rest of the presidency, which issued it as an official statement on 17 June.[26] On 23 June he joined with President Grant in conferring the sealing power on temple workers.[27] On 20 July he presented to the First Presidency a twenty-nine-page recommendation for church relief work.[28] On 28 August he "discussed very briefly with President Grant the subject of Church divorce. I expressed the view we should tighten a bit." Three days later he volunteered to read every instructional manual prior to publication.[29] He had told the church's general conference that he came "late in life to a new work," but he began at full speed.

By this time, the staunchly Democratic views of first counselor Ivins were causing inevitable conflicts with the stridently Republican second counselor. When Clark and Senator Reed Smoot complained to presidents Grant and Ivins on 1 September about the pro-New Deal stance of the Deseret News, Reuben wrote that "a rather sharp difference of opinion developed between President Ivins and myself."[30]

In a First Presidency meeting on 12 September, Ivins urged that the upcoming general conference should endorse President Roosevelt's National Recovery Administration (NRA). Reuben refused to reply but suggested that he would not speak at conference at all if other speakers were going to endorse the NRA.[31] The next day he likewise declined comment at a difficult moment during a meeting of the First Presidency. Ivins announced that since both Grant and Clark loved the American form of government, "we must therefore support the [Roosevelt] Administration." Afterwards, when he was alone with President Grant, Reuben complained that he "was too old to be made a Democrat by Bro Ivins."[32]

Nine days later the U.S. government again extended a call for Reuben's services. On Friday evening, 22 September, a secretary telephoned to request that he meet with President Roosevelt in the next few days. "I said of course I recognized that such a request was a command," and after a three-day train ride, met alone with the U.S. president. FDR asked him to be a delegate to the upcoming Pan-American Conference in Montevideo, Uruguay, because of his expertise in Latin America. Reuben explained that he preferred to be in Salt Lake City because of his church's efforts to organize a relief program. "I said, however, that it had always been my practice that when any National Administration really felt that I could be of service and asked me to help with the belief that I could be of help, rather than with the thought of paying me a compliment, I had always accepted the service." He emphasized his church responsibility, then concluded "that my own situation was such that I would leave the matter this way: That if he really wished me to go to the Conference, I would go though I preferred not to go."[33]

He and FDR had been classmates at Columbia Law School,[34] but they were political antagonists. Reuben found no difficulty in giving this Democratic president ample opportunity to reconsider the invitation. Nevertheless, Roosevelt was an astute judge of his talents and loyalty to government calls. He reaffirmed his request that Reuben go to Montevideo with Secretary of State Hull.[35]

As Clark left the White House, he felt the strain of divided loyalties. The Equitable Life offer had presented no difficult choice. The prestige in financial circles meant nothing to him personally, and he could have easily rejected the opportunity except for President Grant's encouragement to accept. At most, it involved only occasional attendance at directors' meetings in New York City. But now the president of the United States had asked him to accept an assignment that involved a four-month absence from LDS headquarters at the time he hoped to organize a churchwide relief program for thousands of out-of-work Latter-day Saints.

How things had changed since the previous March when he remembered the lines from Dante! The secular world he thought he had given up was now seeking him. He was no longer free even to reject these offers out of hand but felt that he must present all their pros and cons to his "chief," the LDS president.

Grant listened as his telephone call explained the U.S. president's invitation and all of its ramifications. He conferred with Counselor Ivins, and together they proudly encouraged him to accept the government assignment.[36] Reuben returned to Salt Lake City from his White House meeting in time to attend the church's general conference.

During his absence, Ivins had persuaded President Grant to allow the October 1933 conference to virtually endorse Roosevelt's New Deal. Reuben had to grit his teeth when the Democratic counselor urged Latter-day Saints "to get in harmony with the civil officers of the country." Even more so when Democratic apostle Stephen L Richards advocated support of the NRA and urged its critics to support Roosevelt as "in an emergency an army follows its commander." Clark may have choked when Richards continued by saying, "Not infrequently, of late, I have been asked by rather critical people: 'Does the Church believe in the capitalistic system?'" Instead of the resounding affirmation that Reuben would have given, the apostle replied, "My answer has always been: 'The Church has no economic creed that it advocates for the country ... but it sustains the governmental agencies that are set up where it exists, where its members reside.'"[37]

This was barely six months after FDR took office, and Ivins had succeeded in having general conference validate the New Deal's first program, the NRA. Although Francis Gibbons has written that "from the beginning of the New Deal regime, President Grant fought most of its programs,"[38] this did not occur until after the death of his pro-Roosevelt counselor.

Shortly after this general conference, the federal government jolted Reuben with still another request for service. On 13 October 1933 Secretary Hull invited him to help with an organization that was to seek the recovery of more than a billion dollars in defaulted foreign bonds owned by U.S. citizens. Neither Clark nor Grant welcomed this new assignment from the central government. It would involve long absences of the second counselor from Salt Lake City.[39]

Nonetheless, accepting the offer was inevitable. Reuben felt duty-bound unless the LDS president required that he remain under strict adherence to his church obligation. Grant had also committed himself to the proposition that Reuben was as valuable to the interests of the First Presidency in answering government calls to service as he was in LDS administration.[40]

Reuben was unable to attend the initial meeting in Washington but sent a letter of acceptance with a lengthy outline of the benefits of such a proposed organization. The White House included the full text of Reuben's letter in its announcement on 20 October of the formation of the Foreign Bondholders' Protective Council (FBPC). The *New York Times* printed his letter in full.[41] Clark served at the New York offices of FBPC from October 1933 to February 1934 as general counsel, from 1934 to 1938 as its president, from 1938 to 1945 as chairman of the executive committee, to 1953 as director and thereafter as emeritus.[42] A subsequent president of FBPC said that Reuben "was chiefly responsible for laying down the procedures and principles which have ever since governed the Council's work."[43]

Nevertheless, Reuben tried to keep his financial position in perspective. After a few years as president, he wrote to Orval W. Adams, "It is a little bit funny when you think about it, that Marriner [S. Eccles] is head of the Federal Reserve System of the United States; you are head of the American Bankers Association; and myself am head of the biggest dunning agency in the United States, with defaults on over $2,000,000,000." He added: "Anybody would think that we 'Mormons' (I must use the quotes, I fear, in this case) knew something about finance. Two of us, yourself and Marriner, do."[44]

Reuben concluded his 1933 church service with a momentous trip of LDS leaders to the nation's capital. He arranged for FDR to meet in the White House with all members of the First Presidency. With diplomatic astuteness, he included apostles Reed Smoot and Stephen L Richards.

Although Reuben had never liked him,[45] Smoot was Utah's recently de-feated Republican senator. In addition to being Reuben's friend, Apostle Richards was a former Democratic officeholder[46] and had expressed his support of Roosevelt's New Deal at the recent general conference.

After the First Presidency and two apostles met President Roosevelt on 4 November, Reuben helped dedicate Washington's LDS chapel two days later. He then started for the Seventh Pan-American Conference in Montevideo.[47]

As an accredited diplomat of his country, Reuben did not seek to breach the church-state cleavage by imposing religious discussions on others. However, in Rio de Janeiro, "I was flabbergasted at the dinner by having Mrs Rihl say she wanted me to explain Mormonism to her—this coming out of a clear sky."[48]

On Sundays and during the week after finishing his work as a "pleni-potentiary" delegate with Secretary Hull, Reuben studied the New Testa-ment. He read scholarly commentaries on the Gospels and started work on his own parallel version for their accounts of the life of Christ, later published as *Our Lord of the Gospels*. He also made several attempts to think through his remarks for the April 1934 general conference.[49] After the Montevideo Conference, Reuben wrote, "I may have made some friends that will stand me in good stead hereafter.—One can never tell."[50]

When his ship docked at New York Harbor on 15 February 1934, he found that President Grant had been waiting there for him for a month. The next day John Foster Dulles asked him to accept the position as presi-dent of Foreign Bondholders. "I told them I did not know anything about the subject and that in Brazil I had been a veritable Little Red Riding Hood. They insisted. I then asked if they knew my Church job: they said Yes. I explained that when we took such a job we undertook not to take on anything else except with the consent of our associates and that therefore I must consult President Grant." Despite his freely acknowl-edged ignorance of high finance, Reuben's skills as a disarming diplomat and tough administrator had again caught up with him and his church assignment. When he presented this added request to divert his full atten-tion from church work, Grant immediately "said he was for it, though he saw the possibility that the Church [members] might feel I was going on as before and not caring about the Church."⁵¹

Grant was accurate in his prediction that faithful Mormons would criticize Counselor Clark's frequent absences from Utah for non-church activities. It did not seem to matter that Reuben had not sought the assignments and that he fulfilled them only with the repeated encouragement of the church president. "I do hope you can be here more," Lute wrote. "There is quite an under current about your being away."⁵²

The extent of Reuben's absenteeism was precisely tabulated in the First Presidency's daily record of his non-church activities from April 1933 to April 1945. It showed that he had been away from Utah on civil matters for a total of four years, two months, and three weeks during that twelve-year period.⁵³

He was doing what President Grant wanted him to do in bringing prestige to the church, but Reuben felt extremely awkward about these absences. A member of the First Council of Seventy, whose primary responsibility was proselytizing, expressed gratitude for the great work of public relations and missionary work that President Clark was accomplishing by being president of the Foreign Bondholders in New York City. He glumly replied to Samuel O. Bennion: "I may say that I am here only because the Brethren expressed themselves as you have expressed yourself. I sometimes personally question whether it is worth my absence from my home and from my family, as well as from the work there. But, for the present at any rate, following the wishes of the Brethren, I shall continue in this work."⁵⁴

At the same time President Grant encouraged Reuben to accept the FBPC presidency, Utah's Republicans created a more difficult situation by promoting Reuben as a candidate for the Senate. When someone had tried to get him to make a commitment about his political views and future in July 1933, "I said I was out of politics—politically dead." But momentum continued to build in support of his nomination for the 1934 Senate contest. After talking with attorney Ernest Wilkinson about the matter on 21 February, Reuben mused: "I suppose I may be forced to make a decision on this. [As it] looks to me now I can make no effort to get the nomination, but if it comes, they [presidents Grant and Ivins] may wish me to accept it." On 4 March, Reuben learned that Utah Democrat Hugh B. Brown confided to Washington's Mormons "that if I did run, the jig was up with the Demo's."[55] In other words, the Democrats would lose the Utah senatorship if Clark were the Republican candidate. Brown was in a position to know. He became Utah's state chairman of the Democratic Party a month after this remark.[56]

The Senate had been Reuben's ambition.[57] Still, he quashed the 1932 effort to nominate him because he thought his unannounced acceptance of a church office ended any future government service. During his first year in the presidency, however, he discovered repeatedly that Grant was willing for him to accept unsought appointments. Therefore, the prospect of serving as senator now had his renewed interest and hope.

But President Grant had serious misgivings about his counselor becoming a senator. First, Reuben would not simply be shuttling back and forth between Utah and the east coast every few weeks or months. The Senate would require his full-time presence in Washington at least eight months out of the year. When Reuben raised the question on 5 March 1934, Grant "said he felt more or less clear that he needed a counselor, to which I replied that the decision was for him to make."[58] Second was the matter of how Reuben could be First Presidency counselor and a U.S. senator at the same time. Grant told a Mormon advocate of the candidacy "that if Brother Clark were to resign as one of the Presidency they would not care to have him nominated, and certainly it would be counted as Church influence if one of the Presidency were to be running for the senate." Immediately after this 3 April conversation, Grant met with his two counselors. Reuben thrilled him by saying he already "crossed that bridge when he accepted the position as one of the Presidency." He added that he had always been opposed to the idea of a member of the First Presidency or Quorum of Twelve serving in the senate.[59]

Third, Grant feared there was a risk of losing all the prestige Reuben gave to the First Presidency. Utah Mormons had overwhelmingly elected all Democratic candidates in 1932. Voters might now reject his Republican counselor at the polls, which, President Grant wrote, "would be one of the most humiliating things to me that could happen."[60] The prospect seemed closed. On 5 May he told Noble Warrum: "We can't spare him now. There is no likelihood of my changing my mind on this matter." As a non-Mormon and conservative Democrat, Warrum was an anti-New Dealer who continued to urge Grant to allow his counselor to become the Republican candidate.[61]

As the clamor mounted for the 1934 Republican state convention to draft him, Reuben found it impossible to categorically deny the possibility. His pronouncements varied from coy indifference to cryptic encouragements to outward disinclination. On 7 March he told the *Deseret News* that talk of his being named the Republican senatorial candidate was "all news to me. I am not thinking about and am not discussing politics." On 4 April he told the *Salt Lake Tribune* that rumors of his being drafted should not be taken seriously.[62] Nonetheless, after one of his supporters reported the church president's emphatic refusal to let him be the candidate, Reuben replied to Warrum on 21 May, "Perhaps no one can yet tell what the outcome will be."[63]

By early June, prominent non-Mormons and non-Utahns were urging Grant to allow Clark to run. They included Harry Chandler, president and general manager of the *Los Angeles Times*, and Albert A. Tilney, chairman of the board for Bankers Trust Company of New York City.[64]

Reuben decided to be in New York during the convention. He told newspaper reporters, "I cannot, of course, prevent friends from bringing my name into the Utah situation, but I have absolutely nothing to say regarding the matter at this time."[65] This, of course, encouraged his Republican friends to keep promoting his name.

On the eve of departure, he refused to comment about the efforts to secure his nomination. The pro-Clark *Salt Lake Telegram* surmised that "his continued silence regarding his position, is believed to presage acceptance of his nomination if delegates declare for him by acclamation."[66] In response to that report, he sent a telegram from New York City on 17 June to Byron D. Anderson, chairman of the Republican State Committee. It reaffirmed that he was not a candidate for the office and asked his friends to stop their efforts to draft him.[67]

His Anderson letter was a carefully devised document and revealed the extent to which he kept his own counsel. In reviewing his statement, the *Deseret News* proclaimed, "Pres. Clark Refuses to Be Candidate," while the *New York Times* headlined, "Clark Refuses to Run in Utah," and President Grant concluded "that he does not care to be candidate for the Senate, over which I rejoice."[68] All these interpretations were in error, as Reuben stated in a later memorandum.

He had worked over the Anderson statement until nearly 2 a.m. the morning he sent it. Its meaning turned on the implications of the probably too careful wording. "Careless and hasty reading of my Anderson statement left some with an impression, and with others a conviction, that I had by it definitely withdrawn from the race or definitely indicated I would not accept the nomination. The fact that the statement had no such effect or meaning is beside the point; they thought or believed otherwise." He indicated that the crucial passage was, "Being now *actively engaged* in the duties of a high Church office, I do not consider myself available for high office during the existence of *such activity*" (emphasis in original). His private memo unraveled that cryptic wording by saying that he hoped to "set a precedent" of being relieved of his "active Church work in high Church office to take on high civil service."[69] However, his close friend and former law partner Albert E. Bowen complained that "Democrats have chosen to interpret your published telegram as duplicitous, implying that you want the nomination and intend to get it, and have chosen this means of securing it. Of course we all know that is not so."[70] That letter set Reuben's teeth on edge as he ruefully wrote in the memorandum, "When Democrats pointed out the real meaning, Republican friends holding the opposite view further committed themselves."[71]

Few of his friends understood his underlying meaning, but his staunch advocates doggedly "pointed out that the telegram still left the way open for the Republican state convention on July 18 to draft Mr. Clark."[72] That was exactly what Reuben hoped for, but he could not acknowledge this to any of his supporters. He continued to protest weakly against their efforts and their suggestions that he resign from the First Presidency. Yet he added in his letter to J. Parley White, "I agree with you that it might bring trouble on the Party to have myself nominated or anyone else nominated and then have the nomination declined."[73]

Reuben chose Independence Day as the time to reveal to President Grant his full strategy in the 1934 senatorial drama. After expressing "no wish to become the candidate," Reuben said all indications pointed to the Republican convention drafting him anyway. He explained that he had stopped short of "saying that I would not take the nomination even if it were given to me by the Convention" for four reasons. First, it would repudiate his lifelong public affirmation that "civil service when called was the highest civic duty of every patriotic American citizen." Second, it would "merely play into the hands" of persons wishing to charge him or the First Presidency with "Church influence" in politics. Third, his refusal to accept the Republican convention's draft nomination would be blamed as a partisan act of the nominally Democratic Grant and the ardently Democratic Ivins in the First Presidency. Fourth, it would portray the LDS church in the eyes of the nation as defying "the expressed will of one of the great parties" and rejecting the principles of party government under the U.S. Constitution. Reuben expressed regret that "I must either be released or furloughed from my present position" if he were drafted and accepted the nomination for the reasons stated.

He provided the church president with three proposed telegrams. First, his acceptance of the nomination. Second, his telegram asking President Grant to "release me from my duties as your counselor." Third, the proposed telegram from Grant to Clark "to relieve you from your active duties as my counselor for the period of your civic service. This release will take effect this day."[74] As a candidate, Reuben expected to remain technically a member of the First Presidency while being released from participating in any of its activities.

President Grant took this extraordinary letter in stride. He conferred with Ivins and agreed to all of Reuben's proposals, including the text of the three telegrams. Grant concluded his letter of 9 July with the statement, "In view of all the circumstances, if you should be nominated by the convention I shall feel that it is providential and will eventually work out for the best interests of the Church as well as yourself."[75] The church president then reported the correspondence and his decision to the Quorum of Twelve the following day.[76]

When Reuben opened Grant's letter in his New York office on 13 July, it seemed that his lifelong aspirations and dreams were at the threshold of achievement. He had wholeheartedly forsaken his ambition for future government service to accept the church's call in December 1931. Now in a fulfillment of Matthew 10:39, he would receive everything he thought he had given up for service to the church. His impractical belief that the Utah Republican Party should seek him rather than his having to scramble for the nomination had humiliated him in 1922 and 1928.[77] In 1934 there was no force within the party that could deny him the nomination for the U.S. Senate.

With deep gratitude, Reuben wrote to the LDS president on 13 July that his agreement to this proposal "clears the atmosphere and enables me in a measure to see through what has been for myself personally, the most difficult position I have ever faced in my life."[78] It was now only five days away from the Republican convention that everyone expected to stampede to his first-ballot nomination. In addition to Grant's reluctant agreement to release him if successful, five members of the Quorum of Twelve privately urged Republican leaders to draft him.[79] Within a week Reuben would "be released or furloughed" from the First Presidency long enough for the three-and-a-half month campaign and possibly for the six-year term in the U.S. Senate. All he had to do was to wait.

The wait proved too long. Within three days, he changed his mind and decided to abandon the apparently assured realization of his ambitions. He brooded about "his duty to my Church, which many would rank paramount to everything else," but affirmed, "I have never failed to meet any call made upon me. I am therefore not in need of penance service." Although he regarded service to "Party and Country" of equal importance with service to church, he worried about the popular assessment of his loyalty to President Grant. First, there was the published statement that he had delayed starting his service in the First Presidency for more than a year, during which he completed work he regarded as more important. Second was the fact that in the fifteen months he had been a counselor, "I have been absent from Church offices on public or semi-public service about 9 months," which had caused many Latter-day Saints to feel and express criticism. "To have retired from Church work, (by leave of absence, or release, or whatnot)," Reuben wrote, "would inevitably have raised the question, among Church members, as to whether I thought more of personal political ambitions or of my service to my Church. The distinction between service to the Church and service to the Country would be drawn by some Republicans (Churchmen) and no Democrats."[80]

First counselor Ivins was an ardent Democrat who was unwilling to support Reuben's attempted resolution of his church-state obligations in the summer of 1934. According to his son, Ivins made a private long-distance telephone call to Clark shortly after President Grant acquiesced to his accepting a draft nomination. Ivins told Reuben that, despite the president's willingness for a temporary "furlough," his release as a general authority would be final when he began the campaign—even if he lost the election less than four months later.[81]

This would burn Reuben's bridges behind him and leave him to the uncertain political mercies of Utah's electorate, more than half of whom were ardent Democrats. He feared that the remaining voters would be alienated by the apparent reversal of his position as stated in the Anderson telegram and by his exit from the highest quorum of the LDS church in order to seek political office. To a man accustomed to anticipating the worst possibilities in any situation, his euphoria of 13 July evaporated as he thought through the disasters that could follow his acceptance of the Republican nomination.

No one of Reuben's pessimistic viewpoint could be equal to the unbridled optimism required of election candidates. Accepting his dark visions of potential disaster as present reality, Reuben concluded that "my reputation would have inevitably been seriously injured if I had taken the nomination—to the hurt of myself, my family, the Church, more hurt than any of us could unnecessarily take on."[82]

On 16 July his letter of enthused preparation for the Republican convention arrived in the First Presidency's office. At 4:00 p.m. Utah time, he telephoned President Grant long distance with the contrary suggestion that he write a second telegram to Anderson "to the effect that moreover I could not take the nomination if it were tendered to me." To close the door a second time on his life's ambition was hard for Reuben, and he seemed to hope that the church president would talk him out of it. "I wonder how you would feel about that," Reuben suggested brightly, "whether that would be contrary to what you think might be done." President Grant was not about to object to keeping his counselor: "I

would be happy to have you as my Counselor. That is up to you, not me."
Reuben said he would send the telegram "if you feel that way about it."
The president countered: "It is up to you, Brother Clark. I just feel that I
ought not to decide it; it is your affair, not mine." Reuben replied that he
was not asking the president to decide, yet for the second time asked if he
objected to Reuben's refusing the nomination. If he expected Grant to
acquiesce to the importance of accepting the verdict of Republican
Mormons, Reuben underestimated the church president's desire to retain
him as a counselor: "If you send them a telegram that you will not be
available, even if they nominate you, conscience alive, I can not object to
that."[83] That finished Clark's last hope. The LDS president would not object to his declining "the expressed will" of Utah's Republican Party.

Even so, it was after midnight the next morning before Reuben
could bring himself to send the following telegram: "In the event my
name comes before the Republican convention for nomination as United
States Senator I ask you immediately to inform convention that as set out
in my telegram of June 17 to Chairman Anderson I am not a candidate
for the nomination and I am not available for the nomination. Moreover I
should not be able to accept the nomination if it were tendered to me."[84]

Despite some last-minute efforts by Reuben's supporters to draft him
anyway, the convention of 18 July accepted his refusal. The delegates
nominated Don B. Colton who lacked Clark's credentials and ultimately
went down to defeat. The victorious Democrat William H. King was
equally lacking in impressive governmental credentials.[85] Unaware of
how much Reuben preferred to be U.S. senator rather than to be his
counselor, President Grant wrote, "When I learned that Brother Clark
had not been nominated at the Republican Convention, I wired him expressing my pleasure."[86]

With ironic comfort, the once anti-Mormon *Salt Lake Tribune* editorialized at the conclusion of the convention, "The ticket selected, considering the circumstances which prevented the unanimous nomination of J.
Reuben Clark, Jr. for the United States senate, is a good one."[87] This from
a newspaper which had once expressed vociferous opposition to Senator
Smoot because he was an LDS apostle![88] As Reuben wrote, "However unfriendly the *Tribune* may have been in years past it cannot be regarded as

unfriendly now."[89] In Grant's view, this "change from a vile, wicked, lying paper to a splendid newspaper, fair on all questions" was the result of its Roman Catholic publisher John F. Fitzpatrick, "a friend of our people."[90]

In a letter of consolation, Apostle John A. Widtsoe, a Republican, expressed relief that President Clark would not suffer the humiliation of being defeated by Mormon voters in 1934. They were "benefitting by the stream of easy money [and] might vote for existing conditions [of the New Deal] rather than to take a chance on stopping the flow from the open tap in the treasury." Elder Widtsoe expressed grief that the elderly Grant and Ivins were not "as vigorous as in the days gone by, and the problems of this day are the most difficult known to me in my association with the Church." The national situation, Utah's condition, and the Mormon situation added up to one conclusion for Reuben's admirers in Salt Lake City: "We need you here."[91]

As second counselor to the president and only a high priest in 1933-34, Reuben had patiently endured the ecclesiastical supremacy of the Democratic first counselor. Ivins exerted enormous influence on President Grant. But by the time Reuben declined the opportunity in 1934 to cross swords with the New Dealers as a senator, a new day was dawning for the First Presidency. Soon he was able to respond to Apostle Widtsoe's anti-New Deal plea.

Despite the persistent efforts of President Ivins to reconcile Grant to Roosevelt's program, by mid-1934 the church president's own objections were bubbling to the surface. "I am hoping and praying," he wrote in June, "that President Franklin D. Roosevelt and his cabinet are sincere in their efforts to benefit the country by their vast expenditure of money, but I am harassed with doubts."[92] After Ivins died in September 1934, there was no one who could impede Grant's growing conviction that Satan ruled in the White House.

In fact, the LDS president wrote Reuben that "I feel almost that Roosevelt is inspired by the devil himself."[93] Grant eventually could not even speak about the New Deal president without going into a rage. He "pounded the table" and his blood pressure jumped thirty points when talking about FDR.[94] When discussing Roosevelt, on one occasion, he slammed his cane on Franklin J. Murdock's desk and shattered the glass desktop.[95] The only thing that bothered Grant more than Franklin D. Roosevelt was the horrified conclusion that "about half the Latter-day Saints almost worship him."[96] Another 20 percent simply voted for him.

After Ivins's death, President Grant on 4 October 1934 advanced Reuben to first counselor, ordained him an apostle, and made him a member of the Quorum of Twelve Apostles. Therefore, Reuben "would be entitled, if he should outlive the rest of the brethren, to be promoted to the Presidency of the Church,"[97] the succession method since 1844.[98] As former First Presidency secretary Gibbons has written, "Under that principle, upon the death of a Church president, the senior surviving apostle immediately becomes the de facto head of the Church ... in fact, the president of the Church by virtue of his position as the president of the Quorum of the Twelve Apostles."[99]

Ardent Mormon Democrats like James H. Moyle, a former mission president, claimed that as soon as Reuben became first counselor, he launched an all-out campaign against the New Deal. Citing his attacks in general conference addresses, Moyle wrote that "President Clark is largely responsible" for President Grant's "violent" opposition to Roosevelt.[100]

In reality, Reuben only provided eloquent reinforcement to Grant's already entrenched prejudices against the New Deal. It is true that the church president informed the hapless *Deseret News* editor in October 1934 that he was being fired and called him as a mission president in England because "Brother Clark and I had not been pleased with many of his editorials." It did not change Grant's mind when Joseph J. Cannon "insisted that Brother Ivins had endorsed every editorial that he had written."[101] This was seven months after Reuben wrote that he and President Grant "discussed various matters [including the] *Deseret News* editorial policy which neither of us like, and I think I shall tell Joe Cannon so that he may be under no illusions."[102] However, Grant had expressed dissatisfaction with Cannon's pro-Roosevelt political editorials since July 1932, long before Reuben returned from Mexico to join the presidency.[103]

Some also saw an anti-Roosevelt intent in Reuben's warnings to the conferences of October 1934 and April 1935 "that in some states of this Union the issue now seems to be between an ordered, law-governed society and a despotism" and that "there is no room in America for a dictatorship."[104] But these remarks could have easily referred to the elective dictatorships of Mississippi's governor Theodore G. Bilbo and Louisiana's governor Huey Long.[105]

In addition, members of the German-American *Bund* publicly paraded by hundreds at a time in Nazi uniforms from New York to California, and 20,000 Nazi supporters attended one of these rallies in Madison Square Garden.[106] Aside from this public endorsement of German dictator Adolf Hitler, New York City also had organizations of Italian-American Fascists who openly supported Italy's dictator Benito Mussolini.[107]

Nationally, there were millions of political followers of Roman Catholic priest Charles E. Coughlin, whose anti-Semitic radio broadcasts ridiculed America's current form of government and praised dictatorship.[108] For example, Father Coughlin told his American radio audience: "One road leads toward fascism, the other toward Communism. I take the road to fascism."[109] Furthermore, President Clark's conference warnings could have referred to Major General Smedley D. Butler's testimony in 1934 about an alleged plot to establish a military dictatorship in the United States. This involved leaders of the American Legion.[110]

During the economic crisis of the early 1930s, many Americans considered domestic dictatorship as a solution. This option appealed to the era's ultra-conservatives but not to New Dealers or other political liberals.[111]

With Ivins's death, the LDS First Presidency lost its Democratic advocate and made arch-Republican Clark the second-ranking officer of the church. Nevertheless, he was slow to make the frontal assault on the New Deal that many anticipated and almost demanded. When he answered a newspaper reporter's query about the New Deal with the simple statement that he was still an advocate of "constitutional government," the *Salt Lake Tribune* in June 1935 noted that he was finally "breaking a long silence on government affairs."[112]

During the years immediately following his surrender of the Senate nomination, Reuben had quite enough to distract him from any campaign to convert the Latter-day Saints from their New Deal apostasy. First, there were his many weeks in the New York office of the Foreign Bondholders' Protective Council. Then he received an invitation in 1935 from one of the senior partners of J. P. Morgan & Company for him to return to Mexico in the interest of Mexican Eagle Oil, an affiliate of Royal Dutch Shell.

When Reuben wrote the rest of the First Presidency about this offer, he pointed out "the advantage it would be to the Church to have me make such contacts and acquaintances as I have indicated." He then asked whether, "if it appears I can render real service justifying to my own conscience the employment by this company, you would think I ought to accept it." President Grant and his new counselor David O. McKay replied, "Unhesitatingly we recommend that you accept the offer made by the shareholders of the Mexican Eagle Oil Co."[113] Aside from intangible public-relations benefits to the church, Reuben's employment with this international petroleum company brought him the kind of financial windfall he thought he had forever given up by accepting the position in the First Presidency.

With this added employment, Reuben spent much of his time scurrying between Salt Lake City, New York, London, and Mexico City. In addition, he was elected in April 1936 to serve on the Pan-American Union's Commission of Experts on the Codification of International Law. In May 1937 he joined the board of editors for the *American Journal of International Law.*[114]

Church members were generally unaware of President Grant's enthusiastic encouragement of these added secular responsibilities, and the undercurrent of criticism continued about Clark's absences from LDS headquarters. This did not bother Reuben, who knew that his secular activities had the wholehearted blessing of the LDS president. Nonetheless, Luacine fretted about the situation at home: "I saw Pres. Grant on the street. He didn't mention you. In fact people have quit asking when you are coming."[115]

Even the LDS president was criticized by people who preferred the First Presidency to be office-bound. Lute wrote, "Sister [Augusta] Grant was telling us that Golden Kimball said in some ward, I think, that the Lord can't give revelations to Pres. Grant because he does not stay in one place long enough—he travels so much."[116] Grant and Clark shared an expansive view of the First Presidency's role. It would take others a generation to see the LDS church beyond the narrow confines of Salt Lake City.

Occasionally, during this period of frequent travel by presidents Grant and Clark, they participated in joint activities outside Utah. In September 1934 they were with the Mormon Tabernacle Choir at the Chicago World's Fair. In June-July 1935 the two were in Hawaii to organize the Oahu Stake. Joining them on this latter trip were their wives Luacine and Augusta, plus Reuben's long-time friends Preston D. Richards and his wife, Barbara.[117]

> Of this visit to Honolulu, Reuben later wrote to Monte L. Bean: "The hukilau was not too successful on that occasion, but there was an abundance of food at the luau, which went not from 'soup to nuts' but from poi to eels and devil fish. I confess that while I tasted much, I ate little. The entertainment we had, in the production of which the Samoans participated, was very picturesque and highly colorful. I remember one of the acts produced was a Samoan war dance in which there were an abundance of body contortions and some facial contortions that were a bit revolting—it was apparently intended to represent a corpse that died in agony, with his eyes open and his tongue sticking out of his open mouth."[118]

As Reuben returned from Honolulu, he engaged by telegram in the playful banter that characterized the warm relationship he had with his children. On 11 July, Louise and Reuben III telephoned him about some sudden medical problems at home. That same day, they telegraphed him at Los Angeles: "Do not shorten beautiful and delightful pleasure trip just because [of] our paltry sufferings. Would suggest you return home via [Panama] Canal and Europe."[119] Their father was no slouch at repartee and wired back: "Many thanks for your wonderful suggestion, inspired as it was by the utmost unselfishness, high spartan courage, and indomitable fortitude. Sailing soon on Good Ship Life Long Indifference and Gross Parental Neglect."[120] Reuben's keen sense of humor enlivened his family life both in necessary separation and in joyful homecoming.

Not long after their return to Salt Lake City, Reuben began to encourage the LDS president to delegate unessential office responsibilities. Throughout his life, including his first eighteen years as church president, Grant had personally dictated all of his correspondence, official and personal. Originating with the "nervous convulsions" he first experienced in 1882,[121] Grant's insomnia gave him opportunity to record several cylinders of letters on a dictaphone in the pre-dawn hours of the mornings. Nevertheless, it often took him months to answer correspondence.[122] In April 1936 Reuben finally persuaded him to allow the counselor to dictate replies to the personal correspondence. Grant was ecstatic over the results:

> Saturday. [W]as a happier man tonight than I have been for years. Brother Clark started in Thursday answering letters for me without my telling how I wanted him to do it, and I believe in the last two days he has written more than fifty letters, and for the first time in years the drawers in my desk in the President's office, also the papers on my table to the left of my desk have all been disposed of by Brother Clark.
>
> ...I found a piece of paper in his handwriting: "Brother Grant, this is your desk, J.R.C." Certainly, I did not recognize it, and it made me very happy to be so nearly caught up with my personal mail.[123]

Henceforth, Grant routinely had Reuben answer the mail. The church president observed, "I am going to try to think more, work less and have other people do a good share of the work that I have done myself."[124] Reuben had learned administrative delegation from executive officers during thirty years of government service, and he brought those practices to the First Presidency's office.

Another of his administrative reforms was to limit access to the LDS president. Prior to the 1930s, almost anyone could walk into the office and see the president if he was not already in a meeting. On some occasions Grant spent as long as two hours in conversation with Mormons who came to his office without an appointment.[125] "That was changed when President Clark came upon the scene," observed James Moyle, "and the public was fenced out."[126] Moyle's critical appraisal expressed preference for the earlier days of informality. However, by 1935 LDS membership was nearly 600,000 in the stakes of the American West.[127] Just as this made it impossible for the president to read and answer personally all his correspondence, the population growth made it impossible to maintain administrative informality.

The year 1936 also marked the beginning of Reuben's public assault on the Democratic New Deal after three years of virtual silence about national politics. Undoubtedly, he had experienced an inward debate between his thirty-year insistence that general authorities should not speak on political matters and his recognition that Grant expected him to be the spokesman for the First Presidency against the New Deal. Its political and economic philosophies were offensive to both men. By January 1936, Grant was convinced that "Roosevelt is utterly unfit to be reelected President of the United States" and that "he is actually carrying out the Socialist platform instead of the Democratic platform."[128] Again it was an unsought call to civic duty that caused Reuben to become the representative of Utah's anti-New Deal sentiment.

On 5 March 1936 he met in New York City with an emissary of Alfred M. Landon, governor of Kansas and aspirant for the Republican nomination to challenge FDR as president. Governor Landon was "very anxious" for Reuben to attend the national convention in June as a delegate-at-large from Utah to assist in writing the Republican Party's platform.[129] In his letter to Counselor McKay, also an ardent Republican,[130] Reuben asked the First Presidency to decide whether he should accept the offer. He added:

> The possible developments and implications of my participating in the Convention and in the nomination, if he be nominated, might be that I would be asked to take an active part in the campaign itself, possibly not alone as an adviser, but as a speaker and in the event of the election of the Governor, I might possibly be asked to take some responsible position in the Administration.[131]

He was being modest. Landon had offered to appoint him as Secretary of State in the event of defeating Roosevelt.[132] A few weeks after this March meeting, Reuben publicly endorsed Landon.[133]

The LDS president may have shuddered at this new prospect of losing Clark in order for him to serve in public office. However, in the two years since the 1934 Senate problem, Grant's opposition to the New Deal had intensified. He encouraged his counselor to join Landon's forces. The LDS counselor helped the Republicans write their platform and witnessed Landon's nomination. He conferred with the candidate in Topeka in July, after which Reuben announced to reporters gathered in the First Presidency's office, "Governor Alf M. Landon of Kansas will make a great president."[134]

More than half of the American Latter-day Saints disagreed with his assessment. Reuben's friend Albert Bowen reported that Utah Mormons were saying that "you are working with one of the vilest political men in the country—[George] Wilson—and you are nothing but a Dictator." After Lute learned of that report, she spent a sleepless night: "Hearing people criticize you is new to me, so I guess it got me."[135]

Reuben continued to work for Landon's campaign outside Utah, but a letter from his brother Ted in Grantsville underscored the tense political and religious situation in Utah: "I am fully convinced that if you go on the stump here among the Saints that much of that respect and good feeling towards you will change, as it has to all the other [LDS] leaders who have done it. If I have any influence at all with you, I want to say don't do it. You can't afford to. Many of your own side will lose confidence if you do."[136]

His brother's words echoed his own pre-1933 convictions against the hierarchy's political activities. He declined a request six days later from the Republican National Committee that he give twelve speeches for Landon in Utah because "I would harden this situation and solidify opposition rather than gain votes."[137] He gave speeches for Landon and against the New Deal in Idaho, California, Arizona, Texas, and Colorado but not in Utah.[138]

President Grant, however, was impatient with a situation that seemed to ignore his desire to convert the Latter-day Saints from their New Deal devotion. Aware of this growing frustration, Reuben presented an anti-New Deal editorial for approval by the church president who "seemed to be so anxious to say something regarding the New Deal." Grant suggested publishing it as a signed statement of the First Presidency, but Reuben prevailed on him to let it appear in the *Deseret News* on 31 October as an unsigned, front-page editorial entitled, "The Constitution."[139]

Without naming Franklin D. Roosevelt, Reuben's editorial accused the U.S. president of knowingly promoting unconstitutional laws and advocating Communism. By contrast, he noted that the "other candidate [Landon] has declared he stands for the Constitution and for the American system of government which it sets up." The newspaper repeated the editorial in full on the second page.[140]

On the eve of the 1936 presidential election, this threw the vast majority of Latter-day Saints into a rage. National newspapers and Mormon New Dealers had already concluded that the First Presidency's April 1936 announcement of a churchwide relief program was actually intended to undermine and supplant the New Deal's relief programs.[141] The Utah political atmosphere was so emotionally charged that nine years later James Moyle still remembered this *Deseret News* editorial as a sensational act. Formerly Utah's Democratic chairman, Moyle was a New Deal officer.[142]

Of the letters sent to the First Presidency about the editorial, 71 percent criticized it, assumed that the First Presidency authorized its publication, and guessed that Reuben had written it. Although the minority in favor of the editorial described it as courageous and inspired, New Deal Mormons saw it differently. An Idaho Mormon wrote that it "is very prejudiced, misleading, and a wilful misinterpretation of the views and ambitions of one of the greatest presidents our country has ever had." A young returned missionary concluded that Clark was the author and wrote President Grant that it "was a blatant insult to the voting intelligence of every Latter-day Saint." The entire presidency of a local elders quorum in Utah County asked, "Is the Deseret News owned by our church or does the Hearst interests own a part?" A stake high councilman in Utah County wrote, "It's things like this that creates mistrust and ends in apostasy." A ward bishop wrote, "It's an insult to the L.D.S. people." A New York Mormon called the editorial unbelievable "effrontery." An LDS judge and former Utah legislator wrote, "I am not any more a Communist than you are and neither [is] Franklin Delano Roosevelt, nor are we any more Communists than J. Reuben Clark." Another wrote that it was with difficulty that he restrained a meeting of 200 Latter-day Saints in Salt Lake City from issuing an open condemnation of the article. An elder in Sanpete County wrote that the editorial "makes it hard for some of us to sustain as prophets, seers and revelators, wholeheartedly men who will stoop to such political practice ... even below the standards of the most unscrupulous politician in its method." Two of Cache County's commissioners and two others jointly canceled their subscriptions to the newspaper because the editorial "is detrimental to the best interests of the citizens of this state as well as to your paper itself." All of these LDS critics signed their full names.[143]

The letters represented the sentiments of most Utah Mormons. More than 1,200 Latter-day Saints canceled their subscriptions to the *Deseret News* on account of this editorial. A few days after its publication, 69.3 percent of Utah's vote went to Roosevelt and the Democratic Party's New Deal.[144]

Not all Democratic Mormons remained angry for long about the pre-election editorial of 1936. For example, eighteen months later, local bishop Marion G. Romney visited the church president: "He [Romney] told me that he was very much perturbed over the editorial that was published before the last election when Roosevelt was reelected, being an official in the Democratic party, that it was a hard blow." However, Romney said he had "prayed to the Lord, and he never got anything straighter than that that editorial was just what ought to be published." Grant concluded, "I am delighted when I find that a bishop's church comes first and foremost with him, and that his politics has not warped his judgment spiritually."[145] That was the church president's account of their meeting.

Romney wrote that Grant said: "I know they charge President Clark with this editorial, but President Clark told me not to publish it. He said they would say, 'You are using the paper for political purposes.' He told me just what would happen, and it did happen. But I put the editorial on the front page of the News over his objections. The people criticized him, but when they criticized him, they were criticizing me; and when they were criticizing me, they were criticizing the Lord."[146]

Landon's landslide defeat in November 1936 ended Reuben's hopes of becoming Secretary of State. His sister Esther also feared that the pervasive criticism in the wake of the election might result in his release from the First Presidency.[147]

Such criticism might have given pause to a man of lesser mettle.

"Speaking personally," Reuben told the next general priesthood meeting, "I am more or less accustomed to criticism. Not a little of my life has been spent in public office ... and practically without exception, I have found this criticism to come from men whose selfishness was not being served by the way in which I was attempting to carry out and perform the duties of my office." He concluded by observing that "criticism seems to be an inescapable accompaniment of the doing of righteousness, strange as that may seem."[148] Six months later he told another general priesthood meeting that he was unaffected by any criticism as long as he knew he was doing what President Grant wanted and as long as he himself felt he was "doing my best in the Lord's work."[149]

Reuben directed these pointed remarks to priesthood conferences because he knew that his critics included elders quorum presidents, bishops, high councilmen, stake presidents, and mission presidents.[150] Yet he classified his critics as New Dealers, the Communists, "the emigre Jews," the previous three groups' "friends and their converts," as well as the greedy and selfish, skeptics, apostates, "near apostates," economists, and "politicos."[151] He also told a general conference that he tossed anonymous letters into the wastebasket without reading them and likewise disposed of "signed scurrilous letters."[152]

To the contrary, his personal papers indicate that he read and kept most, if not all, letters of criticism—both anonymous and signed.[153] "One cannot harbor the spirit which you have put into your anonymous and other letters, and that you have expressed to me personally," he wrote to a former mission president, "without suffering grave injury. I say this in all kindliness and without any personal rancor whatever."[154]

Reuben may also have accepted one anonymous verdict that "in all the history of the Church there has never been an official more generally disliked than he is."[155] At any rate, he often began his sermons with an anticipation of rejection. "What I shall have to say tonight will probably be not too popular," he told a general priesthood meeting; "I shall try to say it in as sweet a way as I can."[156] He felt such disdain for his Mormon critics that "he did not care much" when a sympathetic stake president commented that church members "did not know me and so misunderstood and misrepresented me."[157] He later told his non-LDS friend Fred Morris

Dearing that his critics were "sons of Belial (s.o.b., initially but euphoniously given as the sons of Belial in place of the shorter word at the end)." He added, "I am not forgetting them, even though I forgive them."[158]

Part of the reason for his hostility toward Mormon critics was that they were equally critical of Heber J. Grant to whom Reuben felt all true Latter-day Saints owed complete loyalty. "The word constantly comes back to us," he told the General Welfare Committee, "that some of our general boards and members are not loyal to President Grant. ... I am tired of the way people speak about him. I don't believe you would ever have gotten along if you hadn't been loyal to the Presidency of the Church."[159]

Throughout his service as counselor, Reuben dismissed Mormon criticism as disloyal, self-serving, and unworthy of reflective examination. This assessment coexisted with his lifelong affirmation that faithful Mormons had the right to disagree with their leadership. Likewise, Counselor Clark sometimes expressed his own dissent against decisions of the LDS president.

On occasion, however, he was disarmed by the soul-searching reservations of a genuine admirer. "I am sorry," he wrote to LDS mission president Lee B. Valentine, "that on a few occasions I have given you some difficulty in following along with me, and all I can say is that maybe you are right and I am wrong."[160] Aside from that rare hypothetical reflection, Reuben gave no ground to his critics.

After the stinging failure to dissuade Latter-day Saints from voting for the New Deal in 1936, the First Presidency was preoccupied with promoting the church's relief program at home and abroad. Although Reuben had authored the first comprehensive statement of the program's philosophy and organization in 1933, his responsibilities with FBPC in New York City prevented his close supervision of the Church Security Program, later renamed the Welfare Program, until the 1940s.[161]

Nevertheless, while in Manhattan he was able to have direct influence on the national publicity given to the church program. *Time* magazine covered the announcement and initial steps of the Welfare Program and included this LDS effort in a motion picture news digest called the *March of Time*. While in New York City, Reuben corrected some misconceptions in the scripting and filming of this newsreel. "I have impressed upon them that President Grant was a business man of large experience, and was not the clerical type at all," Reuben wrote to the rest of the First Presidency. "The scenario as I first saw it had one 'shot' of him retiring to a room for [prayerful] communion and reflection. The script stated something of the sort. I told them that was not President Grant; that we did not do our Church work in that style."[162] Even though LDS members might also have had similar assumptions about the devotional style of routine decision making in the First Presidency's office, Reuben did not want to romanticize the president's businesslike deliberations.

With the refinements he was able to persuade Time, Inc., to bring to their newsreel, the First Presidency was quite pleased with it. Motion picture theaters screened it throughout America early in 1937. Reuben's children were ecstatic. "I saw the March of Time, and Popsy, old dear, you stole the show," his daughter Luacine wrote. "I clapped loudly and vociferously [in the theater], for weren't you my Pa? ... The voice sounds exactly like yours, so if a solitary tear accompanied by a soulful sniff and a choked sob was wrung forth from your beauteous, plump and slightly nutty daughter, who was to blame?"[163]

While President Clark concentrated on the Welfare Program, President Grant continued to be preoccupied with challenging the New Deal. Prior to general conference in April 1937, he confided that he was severely tempted to instruct "every Latter-day Saint in the name of the Lord" to "rise up and rebel against Roosevelt's administration."[164] He asked God's inspiration to guide him and his counselors "in all that we do to overturn the [U.S.] President's attempt to pack the Supreme Court of the United States." But then he remembered the overwhelming support of FDR among the Mormons, and he further prayed to "not offend true Latter-day Saints, but that our labors in this regard may touch the hearts of honest Latter-day Saints and change them."[165] To his dying day, Grant was bewildered that the majority of devoted Latter-day Saints supported what he regarded as a satanic political power. Also to his dying day, the LDS president yearned to give Mormons an ultimatum to reject Roosevelt and the New Deal.

Grant's Republican counselors shared his suspicions about the New Deal, yet acted as restraints on his hopes to force a choice between the charisma of Roosevelt and the authority of the First Presidency. After April 1937 conference, he reported to Counselor McKay that an LDS member in Las Vegas wondered if it was not time for the Lord to have the First Presidency openly attack the New Deal. Grant told his second counselor, "I have sometimes thought the same thing, but we don't seem to be a unit, and until we are I guess it is wise to let things alone." Rather than accepting this implied request for McKay to cease his restraint, the second counselor replied that "there will come a more opportune time than the present."[166]

Although first counselor Clark became a member of the Republican National Committee in December 1937,[167] he joined McKay in preventing an official church denunciation of the New Deal. Reuben confided to Utah's governor, "I had never stirred up President Grant to take any action which he took, and that I had tried studiously to avoid doing anything that was really political."[168] Reuben was the most qualified member of the LDS presidency to criticize the political philosophy and programs of the New Deal. When he did speak out, it was at Grant's prodding.

In more than sixty-one years as a general authority, Grant's closest associates were Joseph F. Smith and Anthony W. Ivins.[169] Reuben was probably next in his affections and esteem. The president felt awe for his international reputation, his administrative skills, and his eloquence of speech and writing. Grant was also overwhelmed by his absolute loyalty and his eagerness to promote the president while remaining in the background himself. When Reuben prepared a major address for the LDS president to deliver as his own, Grant responded in June 1937, "Your memorial speech was one of the finest I think that has ever been delivered." He added: "Once during the reading the tears came into my eyes, and it was a little awkward for me to read. I have never received more compliments for an address than for that which you prepared." Grant changed the wording of the text from first person to third person to give subtle credit to the man who was satisfied to remain unacknowledged to others. He confided to his diary, "I will just say that I thank the Lord for J. Reuben Clark Jr. as one of my counselors and for the wonderful address that I was able to read."[170]

As Reuben began reducing his commitments with the bondholders' council in 1938, he spent more time with the First Presidency and other general authorities. In August 1938 he became president of the church-owned radio station KSL[171] and also began exercising more direct oversight of the Welfare Program.[172] In May 1940 Lute wrote a letter to Reuben in New York City which may have led to still further reductions of his non-Utah activities: "I know no news—am staying home as a lonely wife should—and as I always do."[173] By the end of that year, he was meeting with the Welfare Committee as often as McKay, and by 1943 he was the only member of the First Presidency at most of the committee's meetings.[174]

With Reuben's more frequent presence in Salt Lake City, Grant in December 1938 increased the regular meetings of the First Presidency to three times a week.[175] Among the myriad of administrative problems they discussed was the frequent change of bishops. Reuben concluded that the rate of change was unnecessary and informed a special meeting of priesthood leaders: "Last year we installed approximately two hundred bishops in the Church, which is twenty per cent, roughly, of the Church bishoprics ... At that rate we would change bishops every five years and that is too often. A bishop can hardly get his feet under him in five years." He criticized stake presidents for requesting a change just to get rid of a disagreeable personality: "You will have to live with your bishops as others may have to live with you."[176] The smiles and chuckles that attended this remark were indicative of President Clark's use of humor to ease corrective counsel.

Aside from reinforcing instructions, Reuben's humor made his criticisms delightfully memorable. During remarks about the importance of performing vicarious temple work, he told the bishops, "I feel quite sure that the person who goes into the temple session and sleeps through the ceremony is not gaining very much himself." He convulsed the meeting by adding: "It is almost like work for the dead being done by the dead."[177]

But European developments were beyond the amelioration of humor. The stability of Europe, where the church had hundreds of American-born missionaries and tens of thousands of native-born members, had deteriorated steadily since Adolf Hitler's National Socialist German Workers Party came to power in 1933. Hitler brought Germany out of more than a decade of postwar chaos, but one price of the Nazi revitalization of Germany was the creation of a bellicose empire. Hitler rearmed Germany in 1935 in repudiation of the Versailles Treaty, remilitarized the Rhineland in 1936, militarily occupied Austria in 1938, obtained a negotiated seizure of the Sudetenland portion of Czechoslovakia under threat of war that same year, and militarily seized the rest of Czechoslovakia in March 1939. The following month, Nazi Germany's ally, Fascist Italy, invaded Albania. Hitler's often-stated next conquest was Poland. On 24 August, Germany and its arch-enemy Russia publicly signed a nonaggression pact which secretly divided continental Europe into Nazi and Soviet spheres of influence and conquest. Now Europe was poised on the brink of war. All that was necessary was a German invasion that would bring Great Britain and France to the aid of Poland, an ally by tradition and treaty.[178]

The entire First Presidency viewed these events with anxiety, but President Grant deferred to Reuben's judgment. Their principal concern was the best policy to pursue concerning the American missionaries in continental Europe. When the continent seemed on the brink of war in September 1938, the First Presidency sent word through the U.S. ambassador for all American missionaries in Germany to evacuate immediately to the Netherlands and Denmark. When the Munich Pact at the end of September seemed to resolve the crisis, missionaries gradually returned to Germany.[179]

Reuben continued to monitor European developments through the news media and his personal contacts in the State Department. By 21 July 1939, he felt the situation demanded preparations for closing the German missions. In a meeting of the First Presidency, "I raised the question as to whether or not we wished to continue to send missionaries to Germany, pointing out that in case of war it might be a question of getting our missionaries out of Germany [or] having them thrown in concentration camps, with all the horrors that that entails." Presidents Grant and McKay agreed with this assessment and decided to stop sending new missionaries to Germany.[180]

As representatives of Hitler and Josif Stalin signed the nonaggression pact, Reuben concluded that the lives of American missionaries would be forfeited by any delay in evacuation. He flew into action on 24 August, arranging with the State Department for visas and then cabling the German mission presidents to evacuate all missionaries immediately to Holland or Denmark.[181] Counselor McKay had left that morning for "Oregon and Washington [state] on a visit."[182] In his absence, Clark and Grant worked with their secretary Joseph Anderson until midnight making hectic arrangements for "our missionaries to get out of Germany and France at once."[183]

Reuben had not faced such life-and-death decisions since his days at the State Department when the Mexican Revolution erupted. His timing of the evacuation of 150 missionaries in Germany could not have been more precise. Apostle Joseph Fielding Smith and his wife Jessie were touring Europe at the time. When they reached the mission headquarters in Frankfurt on 25 August, "things were surely popping. Phone calls, telegrams, and cablegrams, and everyone busy packing."[184] The same frenzy was occurring in Berlin where Thomas E. McKay was mission president. He was the brother of Counselor McKay.[185]

The West German Mission president arrived by air from Hanover on the plane's last civilian flight before its diversion to military activity on the Polish border. Barely an hour after Apostle Smith and his wife crossed the border into Holland on 26 August, the Dutch prohibited further entries. This stranded two mission presidents, their families, and most LDS missionaries. The Nazis immediately stopped all civilian telegraph and telephone service and announced the suspension of civilian railroad passage after 27 August. Amid the chaos of war mobilization, all foreigners and many native Germans, especially Jews, were making frantic efforts to flee the country. Dozens of LDS missionaries could neither be reached nor accounted for by the two mission presidents before they left for Denmark. Nevertheless, by the evening of 28 August, all but one missionary were out of Germany and Poland, and the last escaped the country the next day. As these American Mormons were preparing for passage to the United States, Hitler's forces invaded Poland on 1 September. World War II had begun.[186]

However, Reuben continued to be more concerned about the domestic threat of the New Deal than he was about Nazi victories in Europe. His eloquent speeches against the New Deal brought him greater attention among Utahns, as well as among national Republican leaders. After he gave the keynote address at a national insurance meeting in New York City as a replacement for the invited speaker, President Grant wrote, "I feel that it was providential that he went to New York because he made a speech that will be of value to the nation, whereas if I had gone, I could have made a speech that would of been of some value to the Church, but nothing to compare with the worldwide benefits of Brother Clark's address."[187] This was not simply a provincial assessment of Reuben's influence as an elder statesman. The national press regularly reported the content of his talks at the semiannual LDS general conferences and his addresses at annual meetings of business groups.[188]

Much to Reuben's chagrin, his public visibility caused many of his friends in Utah and throughout the nation to try to resurrect his long-dead political aspirations. When he learned in May 1938 that Republican leaders in Congress wanted him to become a candidate for U.S. senator, he replied that he preferred to live in Utah, had no desire to go to the Senate, and had no intention of becoming a candidate. He did not absolutely foreclose the possibility, however: "I then said I wished to make this reservation, (merely because I could not definitely see into the future), that if the circumstances changed and it did seem really to be more or less imperative that I run—A situation which I felt very confident would not arise as a practical matter, that as a theoretical matter it was a possible situation—that then I might change my determination, but that I had no present intention whatever of becoming a candidate."[189] He was again leaving the door to elective office slightly open, but the contingency never materialized to make it "imperative."

Nevertheless, a local political leader tried to encourage him to run for the U.S. Senate in 1940. "I said nothing doing, and I did not want any talk of drafting me, either."[190] People were still urging him to seek the position in the mid-1940s. With resigned finality, he replied to J. H. Gipson, president of Caxton Printers, "As I look at Washington now and see how almost everything that is done is at variance with all of the convictions that I have, I am sure that if I were there I should become nothing but an unheeded nuisance."[191] To another advocate of his senatorial candidacy, Reuben added wryly: "I can not imagine any worse punishment than to have to live in Washington. It would be worse than having to live in New York."[192]

Just as he could no longer take seriously any talk of his becoming a senator in the 1940s, he dismissed more expansive suggestions. Since the mid-1930s, Harry Chandler, owner of the *Los Angeles Times,* had repeatedly urged him to become a candidate for the U.S. presidency.[193] The persistence of such appeals is one measure of the esteem that secular leaders continued to hold for Reuben long after he gave up a civil career for church service.

By 1940 the church president's physical disability made it difficult for Reuben to consider prolonged absences from Salt Lake City. He had tried to preserve Grant's aging vitality by convincing him to delegate more. In April 1938 he gave instructions to a closed meeting of general authorities, welfare workers, stake presidents, and bishops that they should avoid taxing the president's energies. "If he knew I was saying this, I suppose I would be reprimanded," Reuben confided, "but he is not supposed to know and I am not going to tell him; and if he hears about it I will know somebody has told."[194] In November of that year, Grant was confined to his bed for more than ten days, but he refused to relax his pace of work. During a visit to Los Angeles in February 1940, the eighty-three-year-old president suffered a stroke that paralyzed the left side of his body, disfigured the left side of his face, and severely impaired his speech.[195]

In the dark days of these initial symptoms, Reuben asked for instructions. Grant gamely replied that "he would live as long as the Lord wanted him to live and lead the church." He then expressed confidence that he would outlive the two apostles next in line as his successors, Rudger Clawson and Reed Smoot.[196] Grant was prophetic, for he outlived Apostle Clawson by nearly two years and Apostle Smoot by more than four years.[197]

Grant's fierce determination enabled him within several months to overcome the worst of the initial symptoms, yet residual effects remained for five years. For two and a half years, he was able to walk only by dragging his left leg. He regained his speech but it remained deliberate and slow. He was able to come to the office only a couple of hours a day at best, and he was virtually bedridden during the mid-1940s.[198] Although his mind remained alert until a few days before his death, he was the first church president to be physically incapacitated for an extended period of time.

Grant's physical debility was compounded by the absences of second counselor McKay. At the very time of the church president's stroke, McKay was seriously ill with a lung ailment that kept him at home for several weeks. He had periodic health problems thereafter.[199] In addition, McKay loved to visit with church members at stake conferences and other meetings, and he was often absent from Salt Lake City.[200] "President Grant has been threatened by a cold," Reuben wrote to explain why he would not be able to visit his daughter Louise in New York City. "He is down again this morning, and President McKay is away until Monday and I do not like to leave the place here alone even for a day."[201]

From 1940 to 1945, Reuben was often the only member of the First Presidency at the office for weeks or months at a time. By August 1942 now-general authority Marion Romney observed, "President Clark probably has as great a load to carry as any man in the Church ever had, as he must supply the vigorous leadership to the Church when he is only a counselor."[202]

Reuben noted the gravity of this challenge. On 15 February 1940 he wrote to the absent Grant and McKay:

> No matter how crowded a house may be with people nor how busy one may be with the affairs of the day, one is always lonesome when the head of the house and a helpmeet [are] away. So, I must confess to a good deal of loneliness as I jostle around in these big shoes where I so often feel the need of the wisdom which you brethren could bring.
>
> However, the most of my life has been spent not in command but as an assistant, more or less far down the scale, to those who were in command, and during that rather long experience I have learned how to post-pone action on matters of real importance, and hope I have some skill also out of this experience in determining what is important and what is not. I am aiming in my work here to make no determination on matters of major policy or importance. I hope this will give you a measure of a restful sense of security that I shall at least try not to do anything that you could not approve of. ...

I hope you are not worrying about me. During many years of rather intensive work I have learned reasonably how to take my rest under strain and stress, and am doing the best I can to be careful now so that I can continue to be around. I am feeling very well indeed. I am sensible, I think, of the responsibility which rests upon me, but at the same time I am always remembering Rule 6, the nubbin of which was, you will remember, "Don't take yourself so d----- seriously." ...

From the little I know of the situation of each of you, this is not a matter of days and perhaps not of weeks. I ask you to take the full time necessary; a relapse for either one of you might be a very serious thing.

In the meantime I shall try to carry on as best I know how. I shall try to make as few major decisions as possible and reduce my mistakes to a minimum, though mistakes I shall of course make because we, most of us, make mistakes.[203]

This administrative philosophy was a way of life for Reuben from 1940 to 1945. President Grant was most often confined at home while Counselor McKay was sometimes also absent from the office due to ill health or other reasons. With an iron loyalty to the LDS president, Reuben had a healthy awareness of the potential of this situation for self-aggrandizement. He consistently worked to keep himself subordinate to the absent president and to coordinate with the absent second counselor.

He used several administrative strategies to avoid any unnecessary accretion of power to himself in the 1940s. When someone tried to get him to made a decision for the First Presidency on his own authority, he said that the "First Presidency must decide, that I could not."[204] He visited President Grant at home several times a week to inform him of matters discussed in administrative meetings at headquarters and to present matters for approval prior to any implementation.[205] If Reuben conducted major business without Grant's advanced approval, he quickly announced the fact to the president: "I apologized for not consulting him before K.S.L. stockholders meeting—told him about putting Ivor Sharp on Board of Directors; told him of condition of company."[206] Sharp was Reuben's son-in-law.

Reuben was also scrupulous in his efforts to include the second counselor in the decision making of the 1940s even though Clark himself was most often the initial contact for all decisions. When McKay was home sick, Reuben telephoned him for consultation prior to decisions.[207] When people tried to get him to make decisions about matters within the delegated responsibility of the absent second counselor, he told them to make arrangements to see McKay themselves.[208] Reuben often conferred with the co-counselor prior to presenting a matter for the president's approval.[209] However, if Reuben had conferred first with Grant, he reported to the second counselor at the next opportunity.[210] Even after he had presented Grant with the consensus of opinion on important matters discussed at the weekly meeting of the apostles, the two "decided to await return of Pres McKay."[211] At the very time circumstances in church leadership allowed Clark to be the power behind the throne, or virtually the throne itself, he consistently subordinated his administrative powers.

As Frank W. Fox observed of Reuben's government service: "He was a self-effacing man. He worked most happily behind the stage. On any number of occasions, he turned his back contemptuously on administrative opportunities. He had no taste whatever for power and prestige. Yet powerful and prestigious responsibilities were constantly being thrust upon him, and he found himself grudgingly obliged to accept them."[212]

Although Grant was ailing physically, Reuben found it necessary as late as the 1940s to exercise a restraining influence on the president's vehement anti-Roosevelt feelings. FDR was seeking an unprecedented third term as U.S. president and Grant was determined that Utah would not help him achieve it. In July 1940 the LDS president toyed with the idea of publishing an inflammatory anti-Roosevelt editorial in the *Deseret News*, "even if we should lose a hundred or five hundred subscribers ... [and] no matter how many people might be almost ready to apostatize."[213]

On 7 August, Grant decided that he wanted to issue a statement, signed by all the general authorities, against Roosevelt's third term. He would do so if he could get "within a half dozen" of unanimous approval from the LDS hierarchy. He first obtained the acquiescence of the Presiding Bishopric and then gave copies of the anti-Roosevelt publication *Smoke Screen* to any apostle who balked at the idea. By mid-October he planned to mail the official, ecclesiastically unprecedented political statement to all LDS stake presidents just prior to the election.[214]

At this point Reuben decided that he needed to defuse this potentially explosive situation in church-state relations. On 13 October he worked on a political statement "so as to have something ready if matter became imperative, due to Pres. Grant's feelings."[215] He presented this to the president as an unsigned editorial for the *Deseret News*. It argued against Roosevelt's third term. Clark told the LDS president that he had consulted with political leaders who thought the intended statement by all the general authorities would cause great problems without much hope of changing votes. Grant reluctantly deferred to his first counselor's assessment with the comment, "I suppose that temporarily at least[,] I will abandon my pet desire to have the Presidency, the Twelve, the Seventies and the Presiding Bishopric publish a card [i.e., official notice] that we hope and pray that Roosevelt will be defeated."[216]

Reuben undoubtedly would have preferred that the *Deseret News* not publish any election-eve document that could be construed as attempted "church influence" on voters. Nonetheless, in his often-stated desire not "to try to over-persuade" the LDS president,[217] he regarded the editorial in the church newspaper as preferable to issuing a disastrously partisan edict signed by all general authorities.

On 31 October the *Deseret News* published an unsigned "Church and State" editorial, which argued that church leaders had the civil right to speak out on political issues. The next day the LDS newspaper printed Reuben's unsigned editorial, "The Third Term Principle," which asserted the Constitutional danger of electing a president to more than two terms.[218] Mormon voters were unimpressed by the logic of either, and 62.3 percent of Utah's votes helped elect Roosevelt to his third term.[219]

Despite all the pre-election evidence of FDR's overwhelming support, Grant was "dumbfounded" at the Democratic president's 1940 re-election.[220] In this same contest, primarily Mormon voters elected Herbert B. Maw to the first of his two terms as Utah's Democratic governor. "Leader of the liberal, pro-FDR wing of the party," Maw defeated conservative Democrat Henry D. Moyle for the nomination.[221] Son of James H. Moyle, Henry was already one of Reuben's closest associates at LDS headquarters.

At the same time Reuben was navigating Utah's troubled political waters, he conducted preliminary services in Idaho for one of the most important spiritual endeavors of the church. On 19 October 1940 he presided at the cornerstone laying for the Idaho Falls temple. Grant was too ill to attend the services so counselors Clark and McKay officiated in his absence. Before McKay laid the cornerstone, Reuben gave the principal address, saying that "our whole philosophy as a Church and a people is bound up in the building of temples." He continued: "We are the greatest people of temple builders, taking our interpretation of the word temple, that has ever walked on the face of the earth." After his remarks, McKay laid the southeast cornerstone and offered the prayer.[222]

As Reuben began the second year of trying to coordinate the First Presidency's decisions with an often bedridden president, he reflected on a similar situation in the Quorum of Twelve. Younger apostles had to carry the added burdens of travel and administration that were impossible for their very elderly colleagues. On 19 February 1941 he discussed with the second counselor the possibility of appointing some assistants to the Quorum of Twelve. First Presidency secretary Gibbons later described this as "the most far-reaching organizational initiative" of Grant's administration, unequaled in importance from the time of the prophet Joseph Smith until October 1975.[223]

After counselors Clark and McKay discussed this proposal with the church president, Grant told the Quorum of Twelve on 13 March, "The First Presidency feel that five men should be ordained to the Apostleship, but not to be set apart as members of the Council of the Twelve ... on account of the growth of the Church and the further fact that some of the Brethren are advanced in years and some not in good health." The apostles approved this innovation, but Joseph Fielding Smith objected that there was no scriptural authority for ordaining added apostles, even though there was administrative precedent. He and three other apostles urged that the men be high priests only, but with delegated authority to do all necessary work.[224]

On 14 March the Twelve's president, Rudger Clawson, told the First Presidency that the apostles were willing to accept whatever definition the presidency gave to the new assistants. On that same day, Reuben noted that the First Presidency "tentatively agreed on group of High Priests—

in lieu of other plan."[225] On 15 March, however, "President Grant said he had not changed his opinion that we should call these brethren apostles and ordain them Apostles, but not make them members of the Twelve; they are to be sent out to do the same work as the Twelve do in the Stakes of Zion."[226]

The final result occurred on 6 April. President Grant deferred to the minority view of the Twelve's four members. The general conference sustained Harold B. Lee to fill a vacancy in the Quorum of Twelve and five high priests as Assistants to the Twelve.[227] Elder Lee and one of these new assistants, Marion G. Romney, would soon become Reuben's closest associates and protégés at LDS headquarters.[228]

As Reuben contemplated the growth of LDS membership geographically, he suggested another innovation in March 1941. He "pointed out that increasingly few—proportionately—of our people came to Conference: that few saw one Conference pamphlet: that few sermons were printed in our ordinary magazines: that few took the Deseret News: that the old time method of Presidents of Stakes and bishops returning and giving accounts was largely in discard and so few people really know what went on at Conference." To correct that situation in a growing Mormon population, he suggested to President Grant that the stake presidents in Los Angeles, southern Idaho, southern Utah, and northern Arizona rent auditoriums large enough to accommodate expected attendance. A closed-circuit radio broadcast could transmit all general conference sessions to these areas where the reception of the church's radio station, KSL, was not adequate. Moreover, in the rural areas of KSL coverage, Reuben suggested that a radio be placed in the chapels so that those who did not have home radios could listen to the general conference. The president enthusiastically accepted this recommendation, and the April 1941 conference began this use of broadcast media.[229] As a personal consideration for the bedridden president, Reuben also arranged for KSL to provide a private line to Grant's residence so that he could listen to all the proceedings of the June MIA conference.[230]

In July, Clark discussed another proposed innovation with newly appointed Apostle Lee. "President Clark unfolded some of his ideas relative to what he called then a simplification of the present Church programs."[231]

This was not a random thought nor the first time he gave it serious atten-tion. More than a year earlier, he presented a "Memorandum of Sugges-tions" about the matter to a private meeting he called for the heads of all auxiliaries, including the genealogical program. He proposed that they co-ordinate and streamline their activities and instructional manuals.[232]

During the 1940s nothing came of his proposal for simplifying the auxiliary programs. This was due to four factors. First, there was adminis-trative inertia among the auxiliary leaders who protected their preroga-tives. Second, the ill health of President Grant made it difficult, if not impossible, even to consider launching such a far-reaching restructuring of the church's various programs. Third, Reuben himself was preoccu-pied with other matters that had higher priority for him. The fourth fac-tor was George Albert Smith's direct opposition to altering the traditional activities and authority of the auxiliaries. Smith became president of the Twelve in 1943 and Grant's successor two years later.

Nevertheless, after this 1941 conversation, "the concepts sunk deep into the fertile mind of Harold B. Lee." He implemented the idea twenty years later under the banner of Church Correlation.[233]

Gibbons referred to this as "the revolutionary correlation program."[234] Whether or not he specifically opposed the simplification proposal, Presi-dent Grant did not accept every suggestion for change. He rejected Clark's recommendation for the *Deseret News* to publish a Sunday edition, a prac-tice that began temporarily three years after Grant's death.[235]

One event prevented 1941 from simply merging in memory with other years for Reuben and his family. The placid Sunday of 7 December was shattered by the news of a surprise bombing attack on the U.S. Navy's fleet anchored at Pearl Harbor, Hawaii.[236] More than a year earlier, Reu-ben had written his brother Gordon, "I am not fearing Japan, although they may lick our navy in the first conflict." He added, "Whether Japan will attack us or we attack Japan I do not know."[237]

When news of the Japanese attack interrupted all radio broadcasts in Salt Lake City about 1:00 p.m., Reuben felt a cold terror. His beloved son-in-law Mervyn Bennion, Louise's husband, was stationed at Pearl Harbor as captain of the battleship *West Virginia*. When unconfirmed re-ports flashed across the radio that the air raid sank his ship, Reuben immediately sent a telegram to his cousin Ralph E. Woolley, president of the Hawaiian Mission. It asked about the safety of the missionaries and Hawaiian Saints and also about the *West Virginia.* For three days the Clarks lived in a limbo of hope and despair until they received official word that Mervyn had died on the bridge of his ship.[238]

Reuben "showed deep emotion as he spoke of the death of his son-in-law" whom he loved as a son. He had expected Mervyn Bennion to become a member of the Quorum of Twelve Apostles.[239] Like December 1931, Reuben would always remember this December with special poignancy.

Through 1942 he continued to insist that attention be given to the LDS president or to the First Presidency as a unit rather than solely to him. Out of necessity, he was performing a yeoman's service but did not feel he deserved special attention. On 6 April, "President Clark read a long Address of the First Presidency," wrote Grant. "We approved and signed it, but he wrote it, and it was a very fine address. I was perfectly willing that he should take the credit of preparing it, but he insisted that it was the Address of all three of us, and that it would not be right for him to sign his name to it."[240] Reuben also wrote nearly all of the First Presidency message of 3 October but again declined the president's offer to show him as its author.[241]

This selfless devotion may have led President Grant to confer the temple's highest ordinance on Reuben and Luacine after more than a decade of declining to authorize the "second anointing" for anyone. Apostle George F. Richards, president of the Salt Lake temple, had frequently sought Grant's permission to renew the ordinance, especially for general authorities who had not received it. On 24 December, Grant signed the Clarks' recommends for entrance into the temple's "Holy of Holies." No greater Christmas gift was possible.[242]

Reuben initiated still more innovations in 1943. On 6 February, Grant wrote, "President Clark asked me what I would think of holding regional priesthood meetings in our temples, the priesthood meetings to be held by the First Presidency and the Council of the Twelve with the attendance of the priesthood of the region." The LDS president readily agreed to hold solemn assemblies in the temples, the first such meetings for decades.[243] After several years of research, Reuben presented the First Presidency a comprehensive reorganization of church financial operations. The Quorum of Twelve ratified this financial plan in April 1943.[244]

As a part of Reuben's effort to restrain Grant's emotional reactions to the New Deal, he advised against the president's intention in 1943 to censor the contents of James H. Moyle's memoirs about Utah's Democratic Party. Grant agreed "to have Brother Joseph Anderson [my secretary] near me if I decided to have a talk with Brother Moyle with the understanding that he would occasionally kick my foot so that I would not get excited. [President Clark] doesn't want my blood pressure to go too high."[245]

Despite all of Reuben's efforts to minimize the pressures on Grant, by 1943 the president's determination to continue working had sapped his energies and eroded his temporary recovery from the 1940 stroke. He was too weak to speak at any general conference after April 1942. A year later he was unable to attend the important weekly meetings of the presidency and Quorum of Twelve in the Salt Lake temple. "President Heber J. Grant has not met with the brethren in a meeting on Thursday for many weeks," wrote Apostle Joseph Fielding Smith in June 1943. "He is confined to his home most of the time, but is keen on many matters, especially everything financial."[246]

On 1 July, Grant's diary stated, "There is nothing of any great moment." He commented that his counselors were opening and answering all the mail. Secretary Anderson gave a brief verbal summary of letters before Grant signed them. For the period of 1 July to 31 December, Anderson wrote the following: "President Grant did not dictate his journal for this period. He was still convalescing from an illness of nearly four years ago. He comes to the office nearly every day for a short time and signs the mail that had been prepared by his Counselors for the First Presidency, also missionary calls and letters pertaining to missionary work."[247] A later secretary in the First Presidency's office, A. Hamer Reiser, commented that during the 1940s, "J. Reuben Clark was the de facto President of the Church, and President Grant not only knew it but allowed it."[248]

Still, Grant's weakened condition was not critical nor did it demand the ever-present attention of the first counselor. During this same period,

Reuben visited "a dozen stakes and missions of the Church in Canada, and the Pacific Northwest and Idaho." He traveled to Chicago to speak at a national convention of insurance executives.[249]

His schedule remained busy in 1944. In January he successfully promoted the organization of a "reading committee to read all stuff put out by us—whether by Twelve or by Dept. of Education, or for use by our Priesthood quorums or auxiliaries." In February he gave an important address on public policy to the Los Angeles Bar Association. In March he attended the organization of a stake in his native Grantsville. From then to May, he helped resolve a problem with the U.S. military's draft boards concerning deferments for members of ward bishoprics.[250]

For personal reasons, the year 1944 was particularly difficult. Although he continued his varied responsibilities of church oversight, he was grieved by his wife's terminal illness that began in the spring. When Reuben, Harold B. Lee, and Marion G. Romney prepared to give a priesthood administration to her on the morning of 5 July, "he seemed very broke and was filled with emotions as he tried to talk about her." Although Lute continued to "waste away," Reuben bore testimony that her pain, which had previously required drugs, stopped on the morning elders Lee and Romney administered to her. By the end of July, he was resigned to the passing of his beloved wife.[251] She died on the morning of 2 August. Apostle Lee visited Reuben at home and commented, "It is a wonderful experience to stand in the presence of a great man bowed in sorrow."[252]

Reuben would always have the tenderest feelings about Lute—her memory and her passing. Thirteen years later he wrote to a non-Mormon friend whose wife had recently died:

> I therefore know something of your problems that will come from the loss of the loving tenderness of a wife with [her] concern over yourself, of the intellectual and spiritual intimacies which were an incident to your lives together, and of the thousand and one little absences that will come daily to you because she is not there to share them with you.
>
> Fortunately for me my faith has taught me that the separation will be but temporary, and that my time coming, I shall join her when we

shall go forward together in a resumption of a cherished relationship that shall last for the eternities to come. I found solace and comfort for the present moments in seeking the consolation and resignation which our Heavenly Father can and will give.

This was the comfort he extended to Irving S. Olds, chairman of U.S. Steel Corporation.[253] Reuben had not often displayed his love for his wife of forty-six years, nor the magnitude of his loss in her passing.

His public image was of an immensely controlled man responding skillfully to the unyielding demands of church and community service. In August the president of the Western Pacific Railroad, headquartered in San Francisco, asked Reuben to become a director of the company. President Grant urged him to accept the offer, even though Reuben wondered whether the interests of the church really demanded such added responsibility.[254] In September, John Foster Dulles asked President Clark's opinion concerning international law and the authority of the U.S. president as commander-in-chief.[255]

In the fall of 1944 Reuben oversaw the redefining of the responsibilities of the presiding quorums. In October he "raised with [Grant] the question of Presiding Bishopric [instead of the presidency] ordaining and setting apart Bishoprics of wards." He noted that McKay and the Twelve also "felt it would be better if this ordinance was performed by members of the Council and the Assistants," to which the president assented. In November, Reuben presided at a meeting with a committee of the Twelve concerning the First Council of Seventy. They decided not to ordain the Seventy's presidents as high priests and not to sustain them ahead of the Assistants to the Twelve.[256]

During 1944 Reuben seemed to lose physical vitality from the combined strain of compensating for President Grant's absence, plus shouldering the grief of Lute's last illness. In an unusual departure from his robust health, he suffered digestive disorders in January that kept him at home for three days. He was sick for four days with a cold in March and was down with the flu from 27 September to 1 October. In November he openly indicated his physical weariness when the Twelve's president, George Albert Smith, suggested that all the general authorities participate in a special proxy endowment session on Grant's birthday. Reuben replied: "I counseled against asking the Brethren to go to the Temple on Pres. Grant's birthday. I said so far as I was concerned, I must for the present time at least, husband my strength."[257]

Judicious about preserving his own strength amid the demands of the presidency's office, Reuben was increasingly concerned about Heber J. Grant. On 1 February 1945 he "expressed some anxiety" about the president's weakening condition.[258] He continued to meet weekly with Grant to present matters for approval and to administer to him. Grant's prolonged ill health and the advanced age of members of the Twelve were becoming matters of general concern by the spring. In March, mission president Hugh B. Brown told Reuben that there was "a very great deal of talk and dissatisfaction in the Church." Reuben gamely suggested "that it might be over my speeches." Brown replied that the dissatisfaction was about the debilitating old age of "so many of us of the General Authorities."[259]

The April 1945 conference also confronted Reuben with a delicate question of propriety in reorganizing the general presidency of the Relief Society. He and Counselor McKay notified Belle S. Spafford on 4 April that she was to be advanced from second counselor to president of the church's women's organization. The next day she met with Reuben to present her choice of counselors. The interview began humorously when Sister Spafford said she understood from a conversation with the retiring president that her calling was for a five-year period. Reuben looked at her over the rims of his glasses and quipped, "Sister, you may not last that long!" But he greeted with momentary silence her choice of his own daughter Marianne as one of her counselors. This was only two years after Reuben had advanced her husband to the KSL board of directors. "Now, Sister Spafford," he intoned with emphasis, "you'd better think again about that. She's my daughter, and you'd better think again about that." He was determined to avoid any suggestion that he gave preferential advancement to his children. He was taken aback by Spafford's protest that Marianne should not be discriminated against simply because of her relationship to him. Reuben was torn between his parental pride for a daugh-

ter's achievements and his legalistic sense of administrative propriety concerning nepotism. He told her again, "Well, you think about it."[260]

Spafford thought it over and remained firm about her recommendation in a meeting several hours later. Therefore, the general conference of
6 April sustained Marianne Clark Sharp as first counselor in the Relief
Society's general presidency.[261] To preserve Reuben's rigid sense of administrative propriety, all official letters between father and daughter were
very formal. She addressed him as "Dear President Clark" and signed her
full name, while he addressed his letters to "Dear Sister Sharp" and signed
his full name.[262]

Despite Grant's absence, the general conference included a formal
message from him, read by Secretary Anderson.[263] Apostle Lee noted,
"The Conference sessions were highlighted by a message from Pres.
Grant, that obviously had been carefully edited by Pres. Clark and Pres.
McKay."[264]

On 12 April 1945 Franklin D. Roosevelt's death heralded the end of
what Heber J. Grant had defined as "one of the most serious conditions"
he had faced as LDS president. His reaction to the display of grief by
Latter-day Saints at the passing of their New Deal champion was probably similar to Apostle Joseph Fielding Smith's tart observation, "There are
some of us who have felt that it is really an act of providence."[265] Apostle
Smith, a lifelong Republican, had opposed Roosevelt and his Supreme
Court appointees as "noted for radical views on government."[266]

Likewise, Reuben repeated a story about his cousin meeting a group
of Salt Lake Mormons who mourned FDR's death. They wondered why
the Lord would take this president whom they so needed. With typical
Woolley bluntness, Reuben's cousin said, "The Lord gave the people of
the United States four elections in order to get rid of him, that they failed
to do so in these four elections, so He held an election of His own and
cast one vote, and then took him away." Reuben really enjoyed this
anecdote.[267]

The surrender of Nazi Germany on 8 May heralded the end of what
Grant regarded as the second greatest tragedy in his long presidency—
World War II. As if the resolution of these two great issues relieved his pres-
sing burdens, the LDS prophet's physical condition rapidly deteriorated.

As Grant's death seemed imminent, Reuben prepared for the orderly transition of authority to the president of the Quorum of Twelve. This was complicated because George Albert Smith was visiting the eastern states. On 14 May, Clark informed the next senior apostle George F. Richards of the president's precarious condition. If Elder Smith were still out of town when he died, Reuben said, Elder Richards "would have to take over."[268] President Grant died that day.

When the apostles met in the temple the next day, Reuben entered the meeting with no thought of clinging to the previous twelve years of his supreme status. "President Clark had gone way down the row and was standing between Charles A. Callis and Albert E. Bowen. That was his place of seniority." However, George F. Richards said it was "rather awkward" to see the former counselors no longer in a presiding role and asked Reuben to "take charge of this meeting."[269]

By the time of President Grant's funeral on 18 May, George Albert Smith had returned to the city. He began the funeral services by announcing that Reuben, no longer a member of the now-disorganized First Presidency, would conduct the services. Spencer W. Kimball, then a junior member of the Twelve, described his reaction to Reuben's demeanor in his first post-1933 public meeting as a subordinate to eight apostles:

> Then when Pres. Clark announced the speakers he said "'President' George Albert Smith will now address us" etc. [T]hen *"Elder David O. McKay of the Council of the Twelve Apostles* will address you" then *"Elder J. Reuben Clark Jr. of the Council of the Twelve Apostles* will address you." Such humility!!! Such power!!! Such honor!!! (Most any where else in the world that I know of, there would have been evidence of ambition, envy, jealousy, ill feeling). It is the work of the Lord. These are truly great and inspired and "called" men of God who have been leading the Church through the declining days and months and years of Pres. Grant's presidency.[270]

Reuben had been in the secular world and had experienced its honors, its opportunities, and its conflicts. The man who had called him away from that world into church service as an elder statesman was now dead.

Perhaps only a few of the Latter-day Saints in 1945 fully appreciated the fact that they were witnessing the passing of the last of twentieth-century Mormonism's pioneer leaders. These prophets and apostles had devoted their lives to alignment, rather than confrontation, with non-Mormon society. In 1945 Mormons were a minority in a sometimes bemused but no longer hostile United States. LDS leaders might still take potshots at the political philosophies and policies of the national administration, but they were part of the "loyal opposition" of millions of diverse Americans in a republic.[271] It was a different world from the nineteenth century and a different kind of Mormonism.[272]

Reuben had been at the pinnacle of LDS leadership during the culmination of this process in the presidency of Heber J. Grant. Now the United States had begun its permanent commitment to international relations while the church was about to begin its own acceleration into internationalism. President Grant had set J. Reuben Clark's course of service as an elder statesman in the First Presidency. It now remained for his presidential successors to steer the course of church leadership and to decide what functions Reuben would serve at the helm.

CHAPTER 4.

Three Presiding High Priests[1]
II. George Albert Smith, 1945-51

W HEN THIRTEEN YEARS OLD, GEORGE ALBERT SMITH RECEIVED A
blessing from a local patriarch who prophesied that the young
man would become an apostle. He attained this office at age thirty-three.
The blessing also stated that Smith's church service would excel that of
any of his family. His grandfather had served as first counselor to Brigham
Young. The patriarch added that he would become a "prophet in the
midst of the sons of Zion."[2]

That prophesy was fulfilled on 21 May 1945 when fourteen apostles
and the church's patriarch assembled in an upper room of the Salt Lake
temple. On motion of George F. Richards, the second-ranking apostle in
seniority, a unanimous vote sustained seventy-five-year-old George Albert Smith as the eighth president of the LDS church. On that occasion
President Smith chose J. Reuben Clark as his first counselor and David O.
McKay as second. In a practice extending back to 1889, this preserved the
positions of the counselors in the previous First Presidency.[3]

For those who resented Reuben's criticisms of the New Deal, there
was hope that a new president would limit his power and alleged self-
aggrandizement. Clark's influence, especially during the last five years of
Heber J. Grant's life, had been misunderstood. One Mormon wrote the
new president: "If the Lord ever chose a man to do a special work, He has

selected you to put a curb on J. Reuben Clark and he certainly needs a curb and a sharp one." C. N. Lund continued by describing him as selfish, arrogant, unkind, and heartless. He gave President Smith a double-edged compliment: "You are a man with a heart and with human sympathy. Everybody loves you. I think you do not have an enemy in the whole world—and I think Pres. Clark does not have one true genuine devoted friend."[4]

To some observers, President Smith literally put his counselor "in his place" by moving him down the hall to a different office space. Because Grant was rarely able to be at work from 1940 to 1945, he had asked Reuben to occupy the church president's room while the president took a smaller one.[5] The *Church News* reported in June 1945 that President Smith had reclaimed the president's room.[6] This seemed, even to some devout church members, that he had symbolically curtailed Reuben's alleged preeminence.[7]

Actually, he had not wanted even the suggestion of preeminence. He felt profoundly relieved to be free of his five-year burden of carrying the major load of the First Presidency's office. To his close friend, Apostle Harold B. Lee, Reuben "expressed himself as being at ease now with a third man to make decisions and to be responsible for them."[8] To non-LDS associate James Grafton Rogers, he frankly stated in June 1945, "I have less responsibility because the new President, George Albert Smith, is reasonably well and therefore able to take the responsibility."[9]

Biographer Merlo J. Pusey noted that President Smith "came to rely heavily upon his first counselor, and their relations were extremely close. Before making any important decision he wanted to know 'what Reuben thinks.'"[10] In fact, he would unassumingly walk from his own office down the hall to Reuben's room to ask advice. His first counselor had to remind him: "President Smith, you don't come to me, I come to you. You are the president and I am the counselor. When you want me, you call me."[11] As Pusey observed, Counselor Clark "never overstepped his authority."[12]

However, barely a month after the installation of the new president, Reuben had cause for concern. On 27 June, George Albert was too tired to join the rest of the general authorities in a temple session commemorating the martyrdom of Joseph and Hyrum Smith.[13] Fatigue in a septuagenarian was not unusual. Nevertheless, the work strain and Smith's occasional comments about "tired nerves" were disturbing echoes of earlier health problems. In fact, Reuben's greatest challenge was his effort to shield the president from pressures that could cause him to relapse into a breakdown.

The severity of President Smith's previous health problems required Reuben to give first priority to preserving his medical stability. Assistant church historian Preston Nibley commented that, as a young apostle, George Albert Smith "had exhausted his supply of nervous energy."[14] Due to overwork and a frail physical constitution, he had suffered from January 1909 to mid-1913 with what was described in his diary as a "general collapse," by a physician as "nervous prostration," by a biographer as "nervous collapse," by Reed Smoot as "mental trouble," and by President Grant as a "nervous ... breakdown." The medical term was neurasthenia.[15]

By whatever name, the symptoms seemed to emanate from the stress of church service. In their worst manifestation, these symptoms left him unable to fulfill his responsibilities or do anything else. Attributing the onset of these symptoms in 1909 to his work load the previous year, Apostle Smith's condition had deteriorated to the point that he perspired, trembled, had "a nervous chill," and had to sit down after speaking to a general conference for only three minutes. He was barely thirty-nine. His withdrawal from public life became so intense that beginning in November 1909, "I remained in bed until about the 1st of May [1910] when I had my clothes brought to me and [I] dressed for the first time in over five months." In the fall of 1910, he voluntarily entered Gray's Sanitarium of Salt Lake City for ten weeks "to take a course of treatment for my nerves." With much recuperation and later seclusion in Ocean Park, California, by mid-1913 Smith was finally able to resume active service as an apostle.[16]

He seemed to be able to cope with the physical and nervous strain of church service from 1913 until 1930. At that time, President Grant feared that the apostle was heading for another breakdown because he "is getting very nervous."[17] For the next three years, Smith seemed to be teetering on the ragged edge of a collapse, indicated in his self-descriptions: "a condition of nervousness that was most distressing," "My nerves were run down," "My nerves very much unstrung," "Why am I so nervous?" "My

1 1 0 • ELDER STATESMAN

nerves are nearly gone but am holding on the best I know how," and "I was appointed to Alpine Stake Conference but my nerves are trembling so I have been excused."[18]

Twelve years after that last comment, George Albert Smith received the office of ultimate responsibility and therefore of greatest stress in the church. In view of his breakdown of 1909-13 and his near relapse of the 1930s, nothing was more important for the church from 1945 to 1951 than preserving his emotional and physical health. Only eighteen months younger than Smith, the robust and healthy Reuben regarded him as elderly and frail.

The first counselor was therefore determined to spare the president from as much intense activity as possible. When President Smith's son-in-law Robert Murray Stewart expressed gratitude, Reuben replied:

> I assure you that I am happy to help President Smith in his work in whatever way I can. I do not feel in so doing that I am conferring any favor upon him, because it is my duty to him and to the Lord to do what I can to assist him in his great work and responsibility, and I have never considered that I needed to be thanked for doing my plain duty.[19]

Reuben was not as successful in this effort as he wished. "I was trying to do all I could to help him," he explained to the president's daughter Emily Smith Stewart, "but [found] that in some respects he was difficult to help." As an example, he noted that George Albert disliked being away from the office on any day, including holidays. He insisted on reading all incoming and outgoing correspondence, a practice that Reuben had persuaded President Grant to abandon. "I observed that if her father could get confidence in us [his counselors], it would save him a good deal of labor."[20] He likewise told the president's brother Winslow Farr Smith that "it was too bad he [George Albert] could not feel to rely upon himself [Clark] and Pres. McKay in the matter of handling the correspondence."[21]

Reuben and Emily discussed how her father delighted in meeting with individual Mormons. Clark had succeeded in instituting careful screening of walk-ins during Grant's administration,[22] but President Smith wanted an open-door policy. "He loved them and they loved him," Reuben acknowledged. However, these visits sapped the president's energies and diverted his time from administrative concerns in a growing church population. The daughter and counselor eventually agreed that during general conferences "they could have somebody stationed at the house to sort of keep people away," a person Reuben referred to as "a guard and filter."[23] He confided these observations to Emily because he knew she had more influence with her father than anyone else did. "I thought maybe she might get something over to him."[24]

In fact, it was Emily Smith Stewart's influence on her father that constituted an especially sensitive challenge for President Clark. As early as 1932, she had persuaded her father to defy the rest of the Quorum of Twelve and the First Presidency. This involved their wish to release her from the general board of the Primary children's organization. After a year of persistent opposition from her father,[25] President Grant wrote on 23 March 1933: "I felt almost as though I didn't want to join in a prayer circle with Brother George Albert Smith while he takes the position that he does. I know how hard it is for parents to judge of their own."[26] Grant made that observation three days after Reuben began his full-time duties as counselor. This was one of the first things the new counselor learned about the internal dynamics of the Mormon hierarchy.

After Apostle Smith's wife died in 1937, he remained a widower and lived with his oldest daughter, Emily. He welcomed her presence as a needed support.[27] Reuben could understand his emotional ties to her following the death of Sister Smith. Since 1944 Reuben himself had been a widower who felt mutual dependence on, and support from, his own widowed daughter Louise, who now shared the Clark residence at 80 D Street. The similarities of their bereavements and familial residences made it far easier for the first counselor to cope with the administrative dimensions of President Smith's dependence on Emily.

Nevertheless, as a junior member of the Twelve, Apostle Spencer W. Kimball sensed that Reuben had to work against the influence which Emily exerted while her father was president.[28] Having served as an assistant secretary in the First Presidency's office, A. Hamer Reiser confirmed that Smith's reliance on his strong-willed daughter was an undercurrent throughout his presidency.[29] This was a difficult administrative situation for Reuben as first counselor.

For example, her influence was not always subtle. As Francis M. Gibbons observed: "The elder girl, Emily, was so active and aggressive and filled with self-confidence, it was said of her later that had she been a boy, she surely would have risen to the presidency of General Motors or some other major enterprise."[30] On one occasion George Albert telephoned from his home to give instructions to Reuben, who noted, "As the conversation progressed he said Emily was sitting by him and I could hear her prompt him."[31] In view of the earlier Primary controversy, Reuben knew he could not directly challenge Emily. He could not even discuss with President Smith any concerns about the degree to which he deferred to her rather than to his own counselors.

Instead, the counselor discussed this "family situation" with Winslow, the president's brother who had long been critical of his niece's influence. Reuben said that as counselor, he was "trying to help the situation, and to protect Pres. Smith against any possible criticism."[32]

George Albert Smith also had different views of the secular role of the First Presidency than his predecessor did. He eventually asked his counselor to provide an accounting of his non-church activities during the previous twelve years. From 10:00 to 11:45 a.m. on 3 August 1945, "I made a very comprehensive, though relatively brief explanation," Reuben wrote. He related the circumstances of his entry into the presidency, as well as President Grant's encouragement for him to take on such activities as the Foreign Bondholders' Protective Council. He mentioned "the KSL situation at the time I took over, explaining the infelicities of that situation and telling him of the growth of the institution."[33]

Reuben asked his secretary, Rowena Miller, to prepare a detailed twelve-year summary. President Smith was apparently perturbed to find that he had spent more than a third of his time away from Utah in secular engagements. He therefore asked him to further curtail his already diminished non-church activities.[34] As a result, Reuben resigned from the executive committee of Foreign Bondholders in 1945 and limited his previous commitments to occasional attendance at the directors' meetings of FBPC and Equitable Life in New York City and of Western Pacific Railroad in San Francisco.[35]

Nevertheless, like his predecessor, George Albert Smith was impressed by the extent to which non-Mormons outside Utah continued to seek the wisdom of his seventy-four-year-old first counselor. Therefore, he allowed Reuben to continue as an elder statesman in such capacities as a member of the Commission of Experts on Codification of International Law. Clark was the invited speaker in November 1945 at the annual meeting of the National Industrial Conference board in New York City and at the Chicago meeting of the Insurance Agency Management Association in November 1947. From 1948 onward, he was a trustee of the Foundation for Economic Education at Irvington-on-Hudson, New York. He served as a trustee for the Theodore Roosevelt Memorial Association of New York City from 1950 on.[36] Although George Albert was a different personality and president from Heber J., both men recognized the unique contributions their counselor gave to the church and to the country.

Not that Reuben hesitated to decline secular appointments. He suggested that a lower-ranking general authority accept his own invitation to serve on the board of a Utah cancer organization because "the moment we got on one [charitable organization] we have to get on others, or by refusing [we] make them mad."[37] He also declined the invitation of U.S. Secretary of State Dean Acheson to attend the signing of the North Atlantic Treaty,[38] but then Reuben was unalterably opposed to the formation of NATO. (See chapter 9.)

Less than two months after presidents Smith and Clark discussed the latter's secular activities, Reuben participated for the first time in dedicating a new temple. He had given the address at the cornerstone laying in Idaho Falls and was to now give his first major dedicatory address. On 23 September 1945, "he said that he believed that with the people that morning in this House of the Lord were those who have gone on before. He said he believed that Joseph Smith, the prophet of the Lord, was rejoicing with us and he said also that he was sure President Heber J. Grant was there also."[39] After President Smith gave the prayer in the first session, Reuben read the prayer at subsequent sessions on 24–25 September. All three members of the First Presidency alternated in giving keynote addresses and reading the dedicatory prayer.

However, only presidents Smith and McKay led the "Hosannah Shout" in each session.[40] Reuben had never before participated in this ritualized chant. In view of the decades he had avoided LDS temple ordinances before 1933, he may have felt uncomfortable about it. President Smith certainly offered him the opportunity, but in 1945 this ceremony was led by the two who had previously participated as apostles in dedicating temples in Hawaii, Canada, and Arizona.

Although President Smith resisted delegating his heavy responsibilities, his health seemed to be holding up, which was a relief to Reuben. The president presided at all sessions of the October 1945 general conference. He traveled with his two counselors to attend the Long Beach (California) stake conference in February 1946. He attended all the general sessions of the April 1946 conference but decided to rest at home rather than attend the evening meeting for bishops. This became the occasion for some of Reuben's self-deprecating humor. "I am what Elder Lee (I think it was) last night referred to as a 'destitute,'" he said as he began his remarks to the bishops. "President Smith was to talk to you tonight but he is unable to be here, and this is the result."[41]

Reuben also took occasion at this meeting to make his bluntest public statement against a new development in general conferences: reading talks from prepared texts. He usually gave secular talks from prepared texts, but very rarely prepared sermons in advance except for handwritten notes on small scraps of paper.[42] Three years earlier he had warned his protégé Harold B. Lee that prepared conference addresses tended to be "abrupt and out of harmony." He urged this junior apostle to join him and other general authorities "to use our influence to get others to desist from the practice of reading their talks."[43] Apostle Joseph Fielding Smith was equally opposed to the practice. He wrote concerning general conference, "Prepared speeches made days in advance, perhaps weeks, do not breathe the spirit of the occasion."[44]

The trend was moving inexorably toward prepared texts because of media broadcasts. Nevertheless, Reuben was adamant in his opposition. To the bishops, President Clark said in April 1946: "I listened with great interest and delight, as I always do, to Brother Hinckley. He gave us a great sermon, and what I am now going to say I say as a compliment to Brother Hinckley." However, his next words were really directed to other general authorities in attendance: "I hope he will never read another speech. You read well, Brother Hinckley, but you are a speaker. That is the way with many others who read what they could better speak."[45] To the end of his life, Reuben still privately urged other general authorities to stop reading their talks.[46] The tide of media packaging of LDS general conferences was against him in this respect, but he was accustomed to swimming upstream.

Another area where he resisted the trend was in LDS youth programs. He learned that the general leaders of the Young Men's and Young Women's programs thought he was opposed to them. He replied that, although he supported them, "they were in a rut; that the young people wanted religion; that we overemphasized amusement, making it an end in itself rather than a means to an end."[47] Nevertheless, the Mutual Improvement Association continued to conduct extensive athletic, camping, speech, drama, dance, singing, and other recreational and cultural activities.[48] To President Clark, this seemed to subordinate the religious instruction that was also part of the program. Yet George Albert Smith had been a promoter of youth activities as general superintendent of the YMMIA and as a member of the National Executive Council of the Boy Scouts of America. When Smith urged a meeting of the Expenditures Committee in November 1946 to allocate more funds for the youth programs, "Pres. Clark said he thought it was time we were teaching our young people to work rather than to play."[49]

Neither Smith nor McKay shared Reuben's jaundiced view of youth programs. Not until Harold B. Lee entered the First Presidency as a counselor and then as president were the annual all-church athletic and dance competitions relegated to local and diminished status. Likewise, as a member of the presidency, Lee disbanded the autonomy of youth organizations and put all auxiliaries directly under priesthood administration.[50] This was part of Reuben's administrative legacy that he did not live to see.

President Clark also maintained an inflexible position with regard to church expenses. He tried to eliminate expenditures he thought were incompatible with the sacrifices of Latter-day Saints who paid tithing. He demonstrated this parsimony in a comic-opera situation that occurred in May 1947. He walked into the First Presidency's office one morning and found delivery men from ZCMI installing a large Persian rug. Its invoice was $12,000. No one—President Clark, President McKay, the financial secretary to the First Presidency, or the church purchasing agent—had knowledge of the rug or who had authorized its purchase. ZCMI's president was likewise uninformed. President Smith remembered only that somebody had made a reference to it.[51]

Finally, President Clark learned that Emily Smith Stewart had arranged for its purchase and delivery. Three more rugs, invoiced respectively at $2,675, $7,000, and $12,000, were scheduled to be installed as well. One was for the Quorum of Twelve's room, though none of the Twelve had advance knowledge of this either.[52]

Reuben was beside himself by the time he learned the full circumstances. However, with coolness born of decades in administration, he was able to tell the president "that in my judgment we had no right to spend the tithing of the people for these expensive rugs and furnishing of these offices." Meanwhile, President Smith had received approving comments from several general authorities about the beauty of the handwoven rug already on the floor. He added that his family's Persian carpets lasted indefinitely. Reuben stared for a while in silence at the ornate, intricately handcrafted rug and then commented that with the passage of time, people might want to redecorate. That would waste the initial purchase price despite the rug's long life. "I also told him that while I did not pretend to have any taste in the matter, I did not think that the rug was a suitable rug for that room, the colors were not good, brighter colors were needed." President Clark suggested that if their office needed new floor covering, they could get good quality wall-to-wall carpeting.[53]

The next day President Smith repeated his praise for the rug now lying on the floor of the First Presidency's office, but he agreed to leave the final decision "to us folks here." Reuben immediately replied that he would cancel the order for the $33,675 worth of rugs and send back the one that had already been delivered.[54]

The matter did not end there. Two years later ZCMI delivered to the First Presidency's office another oriental rug—this time invoiced at $3,800. Again, Emily had ordered it "without authorization by the Committee on Expenditures," which included the First Presidency and several apostles. Although the ZCMI salesman was to receive a 1 percent commission, Emily saw special significance in the fact that she had examined the rug and approved its purchase. She announced the next day that President Smith wanted her to have part of the commission. By this time, Reuben had resigned himself to the fact that one way or another the First Presidency's office was going to get an oriental rug, but he drew the line at the idea of a split commission. He prevailed on the church president to allow the salesman his full $38.00. His daughter's compensation would be the pleasure of seeing her chosen rug in place of the otherwise drab coverings in the presidency's office.[55]

In all of his conversations with President Smith about the rugs, Reuben was careful to oppose them on the basis of his well-known parsimony. He made no reference to Emily's initiative in ordering $37,475 of luxurious furnishings on behalf of the First Presidency during America's postwar economic uncertainty. Nor did he emphasize by way of criticism the obvious fact that no one in the hierarchical or administrative line of authority, with the possible exception of President Smith, had been consulted or informed. These were symptoms of the larger administrative "family problem" involving Emily. In the spirit of an Abraham Lincoln anecdote, Counselor Clark decided to plow around the obstacle rather than try to uproot it.[56]

In the post–World War II economic situation, Reuben had already observed in February 1947 that the church Welfare Program "may be moving into a very critical period." A year earlier, the LDS church had begun sending supplies to war-ravaged Europe, and President Clark regarded the U.S. economy as unpredictable. He wanted to decentralize the Welfare Program and "no longer bid against the government in taking people off relief."[57]

The New Deal seemed to have lost much of its appeal to Mormons and non-Mormons alike. The LDS program would need to adapt to the post-Depression and postwar economic and political circumstances. Reuben worried that too rapid restructuring might cause comment. In June 1947 he advised Harold B. Lee and Marion G. Romney "to urge caution in the development of the Welfare Program, lest we upset the president."[58] The attitude of one Clark protégé was evident in the fall of 1947 when President Smith vetoed "our proposed simplification program" that Reuben had first advocated seven years earlier. Elder Lee wanted to expand the program's centralized uniformity to the church at large. He ridiculed the church president's views as merely "sentimental objections."[59]

At another conference of ward bishops, Reuben commented on 3 October 1947 about the church's new role in providing international assistance. He observed that one of the presiding officers thought the First Presidency and the Welfare Program were acting too slowly in shipping goods to Europe and that, as a businessman, he knew better how to make such shipments. He had therefore sent some goods on his own. President Clark observed that the shipment still had not arrived, though due months ago. His next comment convulsed the bishops with laughter: "If you will pardon me, I might say maybe we are not as dumb as we look."[60] As a speaker Reuben was able to move from humorous aside to the most profoundly serious admonition.

Three days later President Clark gave an address in general conference that was possibly his most moving, intensely personal, and artistic sermon. Later published as *To Them of the Last Wagon*, he gave this "Tribute to Pioneers" in the centennial year of their arrival in Utah. He intended his address to challenge two popular practices that were especially obvious in 1947: first, the incessant adulation of prominent leaders rather than the common folk of pioneering, and, second, a tendency to bask in the reflected glory of one's ancestors. He began by expressing reverence and tribute to "those souls in name unknown, unremembered, unhonored in the pages of history." On the second theme, he concluded by saying: "We may claim no honor, no reward, no respect, nor special position or recognition, no credit because of what our fathers were or what they wrought. We stand upon our own feet in our own shoes. There is no aristocracy in this Church."[61] Elder Lee applauded this criticism of "some *name* families in the church,"[62] but Reuben was swimming against the main current of the pioneer centennial. His sermon was also far more than a statement against elitism among Utah Mormons.

At another level, this October 1947 sermon was a prime example of Reuben's eloquence:

> So through dust and dirt, dirt and dust, during the long hours, the longer days—that grew into weeks and then into months, they crept

along till, passing down through its portals, the valley welcomed them to rest and home. The cattle dropped to their sides, wearied almost to death; nor moved they without goading, for they too sensed they had come to the journey's end.

That evening was the last of the great trek, the mightiest trek that history records since Israel's flight from Egypt, and as the sun sank below the mountain peaks of the west and the eastern crags were bathed in an amethyst glow that was a living light, while the western mountainsides were clothed in shadows of the rich blue of the deep sea, they of the last wagon, and of the wagon before them, and of the one before that, and so to the very front wagon of the train, these all sank to their knees in the joy of their souls, thanking God that at last they were in Zion.[63]

One of the reasons that Elder Romney and others compared President Clark with Winston Churchill was a perceived similarity in their masterful use of the English language. Likewise, Mormons saw a favorable comparison in the keen perceptions of government by the LDS counselor and the British prime minister.[64]

Henry D. Moyle commented that when Reuben gave a talk, "not another man in the Church could have duplicated it."[65] President Smith wrote, "It is a beautiful talk and beautifully delivered, as only President Clark can do it."[66] In the judgment of many, J. Reuben Clark was the most eloquent speaker in the church.

His 1947 address had a more personal dimension as well. He had long recognized the unpopularity of many of his views among the Latter-day Saints, particularly when he felt it necessary to chastise them. He had publicly expressed disdain for his critics. He also knew that many church members regarded him as aloof, even though he had their interests at heart. He used his tribute to the average Mormon pioneer as a means of communicating to the present Latter-day Saints an awareness that he understood their occasional estrangement from "the Brethren who sometimes seemed so far away ... [from] the last wagon, [where] not always could they see the Brethren way out in front, and the blue heaven was often shut out from their sight by heavy, dense clouds of the earth." Using the pioneer exodus as a symbol for his own exhortations to current Mormons, Reuben observed: "So corrective counsel, sometimes strong reproof, was the rule, because the wagon must not delay the whole train. But yet in that last wagon there was devotion and loyalty and integrity, and above and beyond everything else, faith in the Brethren and in God's power and goodness."[67] He appreciated the underlying bedrock of faith in the LDS members he chastised. His sermon was a quiet expression of hope that they understood his compassion for them.

In January 1948 he began a series of KSL-Radio lectures on Sunday evenings that lasted more than six months. His announced theme was "On the Way to Immortality and Eternal Life," and his intention was to give a detailed outline of LDS doctrine. The lectures were published a year later in book form. Most of them emphasized scriptural justification for Mormon doctrines, with citations to scholarly sources. As he outlined the LDS belief in a separate identity for God the Father and His son, Jesus, Reuben's prose became emotionally expressive and lyrical, transcending the style of the rest of the lectures:

> Then, on the cross, when the lees of life were ebbing away, and mortal strength had almost gone, he cried out in the words pre-voiced by the inspired Psalmist a full millennium before, "My God, my God, why hast thou forsaken me?" So questioned the Son of the Father as the darkness of mortal death blinded his eyes.
>
> All these are not the outcries in prayer of a mighty soul in divine agony to an immense, formless, impersonal, spiritual essence, without body, without parts, without passions. These are the heart outpourings of a loving Son, weighted with the sins of men, to a divine Father, who knew, who suffered when the Son suffered, who loved his Only Begotten as only God can love; a Father who had mercy; a Father in whose image and likeness the Son was; a Father who could speak and answer back, who could give aid and succor to a Son in distress as He had done time and time again during the Son's mission on earth.[68]

Since childhood Reuben had been most eloquent when speaking of the Savior, and this passage stands in stark contrast to the more didactic, proof-text style in the rest of his lectures.

In fact, he prefaced his published presentation with the warning that "the book is not light reading. Perhaps much of it will be tedious and dull." But he commended it to all Christians because he sought to demonstrate through scripture and historical scholarship the errors of traditional Christianity and the correctness of the latter-day restoration.[69]

An unexpected incident gave to these radio lectures and their publication a decidedly anti-Catholic thrust that Reuben had not originally intended. Monsignor Duane G. Hunt, the Roman Catholic bishop of Utah, was at the same time giving Sunday radio talks over the LDS church-owned KSL. He infuriated President Clark by speaking on the primacy of the pope and defending the Holy See at Rome as the temporal repository of apostolic succession from the apostle Peter. Reuben regarded this as a rebuttal to his own talks and a frontal assault on Mormonism. "Bishop Hunt seemed to have declared war," he said.[70] Twelve years earlier Hunt had published a book in rebuttal to articles in the LDS women's magazine about Catholicism.[71]

President Clark now explained to his friend John F. Fitzpatrick, the Catholic publisher of the *Salt Lake Tribune*, that Monsignor Hunt's remarks demanded an answer. He began, "With reference to the conduct of the Bishop, I said to John that I could not but reflect on what might be the situation if we went to Rome and applied for time over the Vatican station and they gave us the time for nothing (John raised his eyebrows) and then we proceeded to lambast the Catholic Church over their own station on the time which they had given to us."[72] Fitzpatrick reported to the bishop that the First Presidency felt he had opened a propaganda war against them on their own radio station. Monsignor Hunt replied: "Oh, God forbid. Do you mean that?" He insisted that he had no intention of "getting into any radio argument with the Church here."[73]

However, it did not take much to unleash Reuben's anti-Catholic views.[74] Three years earlier in a conversation with Apostle Mark E. Petersen, a protégé,[75] "I told him I wondered whether or not this Communist who had just turned Catholic had not been acting as a stool pigeon for the Catholics all these years."[76]

In 1948 he was convinced that Hunt had fired the first shot of a sectarian battle. Reuben's radio talks therefore soon included criticism of papal primacy and infallibility, praise for Catholic heretics as true saints, and discourses against Catholic corruptions of morality, authority, doctrine, and liturgy. Moreover, when Reuben published *On the Way to Immortality and Eternal Life* a year later, he added a 220-page appendix about Roman Catholic indulgences, hagiolatry, relics, images, Mariolatry, and simony.[77]

Utah's non-Catholics responded favorably to his public anti-Catholic crusade. At midnight after one of these broadcasts, a Protestant telephoned the Clark home to say "he did not agree with all the theology but Pres. Clark certainly handed the Catholics one."[78] After Reuben's conference address on "The Church of the Devil," Apostle Lee wrote: "He described the nature of the evil so accurately as well as their methods that everyone who thinks would know he was referring to the Catholic Ch[urch]."[79] Although the other two members of the First Presidency made no specific comment, presidents Smith and McKay privately expressed anti-Catholic views as intense as Reuben's.[80]

A review of his book in the Unitarian press observed, "While sharply critical of the practices of the Roman Catholic Church, he is singularly free of carping and bigoted criticism." It concluded that the "book is worthy of careful study by Unitarians, because it reveals the personality and the faith of one of the outstanding religious leaders in America today." Not surprisingly, the *Church News* reprinted this.[81] This review was equally important in showing that Clark's national status had not dimmed.

As for the Catholics of Utah, they tried to shrug off these attacks. Monsignor Hunt continued to give KSL radio broadcasts affirming papal infallibility.[82] Because the LDS church owned KSL and Clark himself was its president,[83] the continued broadcast of a Catholic viewpoint is a measure of the tolerance that existed between contending religions in Mormon-dominated Utah.

Reuben did not limit his penetrating gaze to the structure and evolution of Roman Catholicism. He saw disturbing implications in the accelerating growth and complexity of the LDS church. On 12 June, when he was spending a Saturday in the presidency's office, he jotted in his office diary two of his nagging fears about the direction in which he saw the LDS church moving: "1. Appraising Church activities by business asset-liability procedures." Within this brief statement are the following issues: Can spiritual development and achievement be measured statistically, or will the use of statistical measures of success and failure in church activities actually undermine spirituality by glorifying external piety? Yet should church funds continue to be spent to support statistically unproductive proselyting areas or administrative programs for which there are only isolated claims for rich spiritual development? Could efficiency become the end rather than spirituality? His next notation was:

> 2. Church activities widening so much in scope and variety in fields where Church leaders have little training and experience, so that non-leaders are able to suggest better means and methods than leaders, all of which breaks down influence of Church leadership.[84]

He had personally experienced the dramatic increase of bureaucracy in the U.S. State Department from 1906 to 1929, and he was now witnessing the rise of a bureaucracy at LDS headquarters. He saw that the increased influence of bureaucrats and technocrats was inevitable in a church of geometric growth.

What were the implications of the increased dependence of prophets, seers, and revelators upon specialists in decision making? Could presiding quorums inadvertently surrender their autonomy to bureaucrats? Would the situation be remedied by calling technocrats to be general authorities? He perceived the problems in embryo but saw no easy solutions.[85] He instinctively resisted the administrative developments he so briefly described, and he knew those disturbing tendencies would increase with greater church population. He decided on a watch-and-warn policy that would characterize his private administrative counsel during the last decade of his life.

But in 1948 he was trying to cope with a more immediate problem that centered on the workaholic disposition of President Smith. The only success Reuben had achieved in getting him to delegate his heavy burdens and reduce his stress was that the president retained the services of D. Arthur Haycock as a private secretary.[86]

Nonetheless, Smith still drove himself mercilessly. Moreover, he could not tolerate any hint of relaxation by the other hard-pressed general authorities. In February 1948 Reuben canceled Elder Lee's conference assignment in Idaho because of icy roads. Smith countermanded the instructions and told Lee to drive to Idaho: "President Clark called later to say that he had done everything he could to discourage such an ill-advised trip." While on the trip, Elder Lee barely escaped serious injury when his car skidded on ice and went off the road.[87]

At the last temple meeting of the First Presidency and apostles in July 1948, prior to their designated vacation period, Reuben urged the brethren to take "a real rest" and to decline speaking requests. President Smith immediately responded by instructing "the brethren that they ought to be constantly available throughout the vacation period and not to expect to make it a full vacation."[88] Counselor Clark maintained a respectful silence but feared that President Smith would drive himself into the physical and emotional collapse he had previously experienced.

By the fall of 1948, Smith's condition was frighteningly close to repeating his earlier breakdown. On 6 October his diary stated, "My nerves are giving me some discomfort as a result of exhaustion." His condition gradually worsened until he recorded in January 1949 that he remained at home in bed "with tired nerves." Reuben dreaded a return of his 1909-13 incapacity and of the administrative conditions of 1940-45. The counselor grimly remained at his post as the president's condition worsened. On 20 January 1949 Smith was admitted to a Los Angeles hospital, from which he was discharged on 8 February. He recuperated in Laguna Beach, California, until early March. Despite this rest, he was not able to attend all the sessions of general conference in April.[89]

A week later Emily gave her father and Reuben more reason for nervous anxiety. On 13 April she confided to President Clark that some years ago she had joined the American Committee for the Protection of Foreign Born, the Anti-Fascist-Refugee Committee, and the National Council of American-Soviet Friendship. She did this at the urging of Utah's Episcopal bishop Arthur W. Moulton whom she and her father had long befriended and joined with in community activities.[90] Now, as America was plunging into anti-Communist hysteria,[91] she discovered that Moulton was "consciously mixed up with some Communist organizations." The three she belonged to were all on the U.S. Attorney General's list of subversive groups. "I tried to be very cautious about any observations I made," Reuben wrote, "but I did tell her that I have never trusted Bishop Moulton, and that I had indicated to her father that I did not, but that I thought her father had not paid too much attention to what I had said."[92]

In fact, Reuben had been very blunt two years earlier about the Episcopal leader. "Bp. Moulton was one of those who joined in the protest against the deporting of the communist leader, [Gerhart] Eisler. Pres. Clark said he was not telling him what to do, but he would be fearful of any organization with him [Moulton] as the leading spirit."[93]

Emily asked what she should do now. Reuben advised her to inform her father of the situation to avoid further difficulty and then to trust that their mutual friend, John Fitzpatrick of the *Tribune,* would protect her and President Smith from any embarrassing publicity. Most important, Reuben advised them both to let matters rest "and not get excited."[94] In view of his attitudes toward American Communism, his response was very restrained. (See chapter 8.)

Reuben had previously reassured President Smith's brother that he and Counselor McKay would jointly relieve the president as much as they could from the burdens of the office.[95] However, in April 1949 McKay went to California to assist his wife in her recovery from an illness.[96] On 3 May, Reuben wrote to one of his associates in Foreign Bondholders, A. Helen Morgan:

> I cannot tell when I can get East again. The situation here gets a little more difficult and confining all the time. Just when I can take time away from the office I do not know. I do not mean by this that I am "*the* indispensable man," but so long as one has a job[,] one has to do one's best to do it, which is my situation at the moment. President Smith is able to spend only two or three hours a day at the office, and that leaves a situation where I have to be here more than I otherwise would.[97] [emphasis in original]

Two days later President Smith's physician informed him that there was "nothing organically wrong" with him. Nevertheless, he remained in bed instead of attending the temple meeting of the First Presidency and the apostles.[98]

It reminded Reuben of the beginning of President Grant's incapacitation. Now the first counselor was nearly seventy-eight years old himself and uncertain that he could indefinitely shoulder the burdens of the First Presidency's office as he had previously. If he did not carefully maintain his own strength and that of President McKay, they might soon join President Smith in nervous exhaustion.

On 15 July 1949 Reuben acted with a sudden resolve that typically sprang from long contemplation. Counselor McKay noted: "While I was dictating to Clare [Middlemiss], President Clark came in. Said that he wanted to talk to me about *vacations*; that he felt [we] should both go on a vacation, and that it should be settled here and now." Reuben gave the second counselor first choice. They decided on 8-22 August for McKay and 22 August-5 September for Reuben.[99] It was his first vacation since he joined the First Presidency in 1933. He remarked to his former secretary VaLois South Chipman that it was "one of the fewer than half dozen I think I have had since I went into the State Department in 1906."[100]

Unlike presidents Smith and McKay, Reuben had always had an iron constitution that justified his own workaholic ways. However, if he was going to succeed in persuading them to preserve their strength in between emergencies, then he would have to take time off as well. Besides, a vacation was not a bad idea for a seventy-eighth birthday present.

Although he resisted some of Reuben's solicitous attempts to ease his burdens, President Smith felt both admiration and affection for his first counselor. When he learned that the Grantsville First Ward was to be dedicated on 9 October 1949, he wanted to join in honoring the place of his counselor's birth and ranching operations. On that Sunday, Smith and his daughters Emily and Edith left the Stewart home, picked up secretary Haycock, and drove to Clark's ranch house in Grantsville. There they met with the stake presidency and ward bishopric and ate a lunch prepared by Reuben's daughter Louise. Smith took a nap at the ranch and attended the chapel's dedication services.[101]

By now, President Smith was trying to reduce the tension he was under and to rest a little more. Yet the strains of his office caused further deterioration in his health. Ten days after the pleasant visit to the Clark ranch, his younger daughter Edith Smith Elliott telephoned the Church

Administration Building. Her father would not be in the office due to "a dose of nerves," she told Reuben.[102]

For months President Smith had tried to ease his administrative burdens. For example, he had begun consulting alone with Reuben prior to the meetings of the entire First Presidency. This allowed the formal meetings to conclude in half an hour.[103] But this also amounted to an exclusion of second counselor McKay.

However, Smith was having difficulty being in the office even for half an hour. At home in December, he wrote: "At 5:00 President Clark came in to say that he was holding two or three important matters which he wished to go over with me for my opinion."[104] Reuben had again adopted strategies to insure the administrative preeminence of an ailing president.

From 12 January to 27 February 1950, President Smith was in Laguna Beach "to rest my nerves." He returned to California for that same purpose in March and stayed at the beach ten days. From 30 July to 29 August, he was absent in Hawaii, a trip primarily for recuperative purposes.[105] Added to these absences from Utah, there were days when he rested at home or was able to be in the First Presidency's office only a few hours at a time.

Reuben shouldered the added burdens of the office without complaint but described the adjustments necessary in his life when he wrote non–LDS friend A. Helen Morgan and her husband, Archer:

> The fact is, I am usually at work by eight o'clock in the morning and I normally am constantly at the office until 5:30 and sometimes nearly six, and am here every Saturday. In the night time I usually rest until perhaps nine and then do some work at home. Even then I have great difficulty in keeping anywhere near up on my day to day tasks. I have almost entirely given up any social life beyond the great blessing which is mine in having my children clustered about me [in homes in the Salt Lake City "avenues"], all but Reuben [III at BYU in Provo], and they come in and visit me practically every evening for a few minutes. I cannot conceive of any greater blessing than this that could come to me.[106]

He wanted to do even more to help President Smith, but the church president continued to read and dictate correspondence even during recuperative absences.[107] President Clark knew that this was taxing on the president but tried not to nag.

He made whatever adjustments necessary in his own routine to accommodate President Smith's failing health, frequent absences, and diminishing attention span. Under these circumstances, it exasperated Reuben beyond words when he stepped in a hole on the way home from the Salt Lake Twentieth Ward on 18 September. Injuring his head, ankle, and knee in the fall, he had to remain at home for four days.[108] He returned as soon as he could to full activity.

Reuben realized that George Albert's insistence on monitoring even trivial activities in the office was more than a reflection of lifelong hypertension. It was also a manifestation of an unexpressed fear of surrendering the unsurrenderable, the responsibility of being president of the high priesthood, a duty he felt deeply.

By 1950 the church's growth was demanding careful attention to new approaches and a reexamination of former policies. In a letter to church member Monte L. Bean on 26 September, Reuben suggested one such innovation that soon became a new policy of the church. This saved an enormous amount in expenditures for new chapels by building them "so as to house *wards* instead of *a ward* in such buildings."[109] In this case, his famous parsimony blended well with the needs of a growing population. Still, he did not want to disturb the ailing president by urging too many innovations.

Nor did the first counselor wish to embarrass President Smith by correcting him when the distractions of illness and old age slowed his comprehension or caused forgetfulness. Yet there were occasions when Reuben decided that "the Order of the Priesthood" required his intervention. Such was the case when the First Presidency and Quorum of Twelve ordained Delbert L. Stapley an apostle and set apart David O. McKay as president of the Twelve on 5 October. "Pres. Clark corrected the President when he failed to confer the keys of authority on Bro. Stapley and wondered if it was enough to merely set Pres. McKay apart without the formal bestowal of [the] keys of authority."[110]

After President Smith attended all sessions of the October general conference, his health began to falter so much that he had to delegate most of his responsibilities. On 20 October he fainted at the dinner table and "remained at home for seven weeks convalescing from the fatigue that had overtaken him."[111] On 24 October he consented to having presidents Clark and McKay sign routine letters. He reserved "only the more important and policy matters for the signature of three, thus husbanding my strength." In the next few months, Reuben needed to consult with the president more frequently at his home. Smith's last visit to the office was on 9 January 1951. On 3 February he was hospitalized.[112]

On 14 February the senior counselor and church president expressed their deepest feelings to each other about the situation facing the First Presidency:

> [President Smith:] It has been suggested to me that I go to some other part of the country and try to get better. I have felt that the headquarters of the work of the Lord was here. Most of the financial interests of the Church are controlled from here, and I have thought we ought to have men in charge so that in the event of the sickness of the President they could carry on. If the President is sick, things would go forward any how ...
>
> President Clark: I have done all I can and will do all I can to carry on. I have a real affection for you. I have no desire except to help you and help carry on the Lord's work.

Following those words, the president asked that his counselor administer to him with the assistance of Smith's relatives and Secretary Haycock.[113] Everyone realized that his health was nearing a crisis.

At his own request, President Smith left the hospital on 24 February to begin constant medical care at home. Reuben visited him at least every other day and administered to him by request. From 26 February onward, the president's twenty-four-hour nurses often described his mental condition as "very confused, very nervous," "disoriented," or "irrational." Yet President Smith continued to try to review decisions of the First Presidency. Finally on 13 March, his physician "ordered that nothing be brought to him for decision." On 30 March, Haycock reported that the president was "completely disoriented." The prospect of this continuing much longer was terrible to contemplate. He suffered a stroke, a partial recovery, and then a relapse. The end seemed only a matter of days away.[114]

When his counselors visited on 2 April, President Smith "did not even remember them."[115] McKay wrote in his diary: "I realized that possibly the end was not far off. It came as quite a shock to my nervous system, for I fully sensed then what his passing means."[116] Although Reuben was first counselor, second counselor McKay ranked next in apostolic seniority and was therefore successor to the president in the event of his death.

Reuben made daily visits and stayed at the president's bedside from 1:30 to 4:30 p.m. on 4 April. Three hours later presidents Clark and McKay rushed back to comfort the now-departed president's loved ones.[117] A gentle, loving spirit had found rest from the cares of the church to which he had too rigorously devoted his life's energies.

As senior apostle, David O. McKay was now president of the LDS church even prior to the formal sustaining vote and organization of a new presidency. Secretary Gibbons wrote: "George Albert Smith passed away quietly at 7:27 P.M. At that moment the burden of Church leadership shifted to the capable shoulders of David Oman McKay."[118]

President Clark displayed the same deference to apostolic ranking as he had at Grant's death. When the fourteen members of the Quorum of Twelve met in the temple on 6 April to prepare for the funeral and general conference, Reuben immediately took his place in seniority as the sixth apostle. When President McKay asked for Reuben's assistance in planning the funeral, the former first counselor replied to the former second counselor: "You don't need to feel you need to honor me, Brethren. I know my place and I am happy." When the general authorities entered the Tabernacle an hour later for the first day of the annual general conference, Reuben took his place with the others without presuming to have any special function in the conference. President McKay asked him to leave his seat and join him in presiding at the first session and to conduct the second session on 6 April. Reuben "made it beautifully clear that he conducted it by delegation, not by right when he said: 'I conduct this Conference by courtesy,' and never before did that word COURTESY mean so much," wrote Elder Kimball, then of the Quorum of Twelve. He added: "Brother Clark is magnificent!!"[119]

CHAPTER 5.

Three Presiding High Priests[1]
III. David O. McKay, 1951-61

W HILE AT THE UNIVERSITY OF UTAH IN THE 1890S, J. REUBEN Clark became acquainted with David O. McKay, whose future wife, Emma Ray Riggs, graduated with Reuben in 1898. McKay became a member of the Quorum of Twelve about the time that Reuben began serving in the U.S. State Department. In 1908 Lute wrote, "I also met Apostle McKay who said many nice things about you, and wished to be remembered to you."[2]

When Heber J. Grant asked Ambassador Clark to be his counselor in 1933, Reuben held the proselytizing office of Seventy. When he began his active service with the First Presidency in 1933, Grant ordained him a high priest. At that time, Apostle McKay was seventh in seniority among the Twelve. That included President Grant and first counselor Anthony W. Ivins. After the Ivins funeral in September 1934, Grant said that he wanted to select Apostle McKay as a counselor. Reuben replied, "I am very glad; he is the man that I had thought of and would like."[3]

The general conference in October sustained Reuben as a new member of the Quorum of Twelve and then as first counselor in the First Presidency, with Apostle McKay as second counselor. Elder McKay remarked: "I have known President Clark since my school days in the

131

University of Utah. I admired him then. I considered him one of the choicest young men I had ever seen or had ever known. ... I love him as a friend, and to be associated with him now in this high quorum, the highest in the Church, makes me feel very happy and thankful, but also very humble."[4] The association of these two men was one of the most extraordinary in LDS administrative history.

David O. McKay and J. Reuben Clark served together for twenty-seven years, from October 1934 to October 1961. Theirs was the longest presidential association in LDS history. The nearest competitors were Brigham Young and Heber C. Kimball, with twenty-one years together.[5] Aside from its longevity, the Clark-McKay experience was also the first instance of someone serving as co-counselor and then with a man as counselor to him as LDS president.[6] The Clark-McKay association is therefore among the most significant in Mormon history. It certainly was the most important association for Reuben during his experience in three presidencies.

There were several similarities between Clark and McKay. A week after Reuben's second birthday, David was born in Huntsville, Utah, a town with a population only 300 greater than Grantsville. Both boys grew up with a love of farm life that they maintained throughout their lives by continuing to keep farms in their respective birthplaces. Both became general authorities as outsiders, having been away from the mainstream of the business, economic, social, and ecclesiastical life of Utah's cities. Neither had enough LDS presiding experience to be a high priest prior to appointment as general authorities; both held the proselytizing office of Seventy at their appointment.[7] The two were also among the few general authorities in the first century of Utah history who were not closely related by kinship or marriage to other church leaders when they entered full-time service.[8] Both became general authorities at times of great stress for the church: McKay during the difficult days of the U.S. Senate's investigation of Reed Smoot, and Clark during the Great Depression. Both were active Republicans, even though Reuben was the only one to hold a national post.[9] Both were ardent anti-Communists and both supported Senator Joseph R. McCarthy's anti-Communist crusade. (See chapter 8.)

Despite these similarities, the two were vastly different in personality and administrative style. Marion G. Romney once observed that Clark and McKay were men "of an entirely different type ... a balanced pair of counselors."[10] Their differences are crucial for understanding their twenty-seven years of service together because they were members of the First Presidency in counterpoise. From 1934 to 1951, the administrative balance between the two men was in favor of President Clark due to his position as first counselor. From 1951 to 1961, the balance tipped toward President McKay due to his position as LDS president. During his own subsequent service in the First Presidency, Romney characterized the differences between these two. He observed that McKay was a gentle poet-philosopher whereas Clark was a determined administrator-legalist.[11]

This difference characterized their religious discourse. When President Clark quoted secular writers in sermons, he usually cited authorities in the law and political science, only occasionally citing literary sources. President McKay quoted Robert Burns, John Dryden, Oliver Goldsmith, Thomas Gray, Heinrich Heine, James Russell Lowell, Joaquin Miller, Alexander Pope, Jean-Jacques Rousseau, John Ruskin, Sir Walter Scott, William Shakespeare, Herbert Spencer, William Makepeace Thackeray, and John Greenleaf Whittier. McKay also quoted his own poetry.[12]

McKay was a liberal arts teacher when Reuben was experiencing the rigors of Columbia University Law School. After 1906 Apostle McKay developed his administrative style in the congenial atmosphere of Sunday School administration while Reuben honed his skills in the combative practice of law, government, and diplomacy. Everyone acknowledged Clark's administrative strengths, but another tough administrator, Ernest L. Wilkinson, observed that "President McKay is a great spiritual leader but he is not an executive."[13] First Presidency secretary Francis Gibbons echoed that observation by writing that "President McKay was, in a sense, the antithesis of the traditional 'organization man.'"[14]

Although both men valued spirituality, McKay tended to give it pre-eminence in church administration. By contrast, Reuben tended to subordinate spirituality to rational examination.

McKay had sought "spiritual manifestations" since his childhood. "Heavenly beings were real from my babyhood on," and he heard audible voices of deity throughout life. He participated in charismatic church meetings where some saw angels and others saw a halo around his head. He witnessed the phenomenon of non-English-speaking listeners understanding his sermons without benefit of translation. He had at least one vision of the Savior, raised a dead child to life, and healed a blind man. Starting the year after he became a counselor, LDS books publicized these incidents.[15]

On the other hand, President Clark shared Grant's suspicion of "overly spiritual" people. Five years before becoming a counselor, Reuben wrote in 1928: "Men with great testimony of healings, of visions, of dreams, of tongues—lose the faith. I do not wish for, nor seek, the testimonies of the flesh. To me they would be of the earth[—]earthy. I wish the testimony of the spirit."[16] Likewise, President Grant said: "I have never prayed to see the Savior, I know of men—Apostles—who have seen the Savior more than once. I have prayed to the Lord for the inspiration of His Spirit to guide me, and I have told him that I have seen so many men fall because of some great manifestation to them, they felt their importance, their greatness."[17]

As a counselor in the presidency, Reuben continued to express this personal disdain for "Divine interposition," as he called it.[18] When stake patriarch Ira C. Fletcher inquired about his special witness of Jesus Christ, President Clark frankly replied, "If you mean circumstances as to when I saw with my eyes the Savior, or heard with my ears His voice, I will have to say to you in all honesty I never had that experience, I never have sought it."[19] As a counselor, Reuben publicly acknowledged that it was possible to receive such a testimony "from the senses, the eye, the ear, the touch," but he regarded such faith as "uncertain." He preferred "the testimony of the Spirit."[20]

Therefore, he urged Latter-day Saints to "listen to the still, small voice" in their decisions,[21] yet for him this process was one of rational experimentation. In a letter to his non-LDS friend Mrs. Francis Huntington-Wilson, he wrote that "spiritual knowledge may be gained through reading, observation, and conduct of experiments—experiments in right living, right thinking, and a complete and whole-hearted search for truth, spiritual truth."[22]

His testimony had passed through a fiery ordeal more than a decade before he entered the First Presidency, and he kept his faith simple. Although he believed implicitly in divine inspiration—particularly for the LDS president—Reuben tended to be cautious in ascribing divinity to his own moments of inspiration. He wrote to another non-LDS friend, Cloyd H. Marvin:

> Occasionally I have the experience of seeming to have a ray of light strike through my mind that, like a lightning flash, illumines for the fraction of a second, some infinite truth, but it is gone so quickly that it leaves only an impression, like a lightning flash of a landscape that I would like to study. But I try not to let these things mislead me in my thinking. I try to hang to hard facts.[23]

He wrote this after serving in the First Presidency for twenty-two years.

President McKay's easy acceptance of personal impressions and Clark's preference for studious examination led to major differences in decision making. For example, when the Salt Lake temple presidency wanted approval for microfilming temple records in 1939, Reuben "became rather unpleasant" in demanding whether full investigation had been conducted prior to deciding in favor of this. By contrast, he noted, "I think President McKay rather favored going ahead with the photographing and doing the investigating afterwards."[24]

Reuben always demanded thorough research prior to a decision, while McKay was willing, even eager, to make immediate decisions based on his own impressions. This continued to separate their administrative approaches throughout their twenty-seven-year association. Thus, Romney and Spencer W. Kimball would stand in awe of Clark's thorough research, in which "nobody could ever find a loophole."[25] By contrast, assistant secretary A. Hamer Reiser described McKay as "an impetuous man."[26] Apostle Harold B. Lee also commented, "As usual, Pres. McKay had taken snap judgment."[27]

The different ways in which the two arrived at decisions also affected the permanence of their decisions. Because Reuben arrived at conclusions methodically, he almost never changed his mind. By contrast, McKay's preference for "investigating afterwards" inevitably led him to reconsider, even to the point of vacillation. "Explained the bill to President McKay," ran an entry in Reuben's office diary for 1947, "and his reaction was rather instantaneous and negative, that he felt we ought to keep out of it, then when [McKay] thought into the thing[,] he ~~backed down~~ seemed to feel differently."[28] Secretary Reiser also commented about "some of his difficulty in getting President McKay to make categorical decisions."[29]

The differences widened even further with respect to how McKay and Clark reacted to outside influence. Reuben had been involved in administrative battlefields in the State Department, in law, and in international diplomacy. He did not question his decisions or modify them because of criticism and attempted flattery. After several years in the First Presidency, he wrote to LDS professor Milton R. Merrill, "I have learned to accept criticism, opprobrium, and even hate without too much disturbance."[30] An admirer praised him for making decisions in spite of attempts by others to influence him.[31]

On the other hand, David O. McKay had virtually no experience with combative administration. He loved intimate association with crowds and individuals, treasured close fellowship with the Latter-day Saints, basked in adulation, and shrank from criticism. Secretary Gibbons acknowledged that McKay liked his "celebrity status," and wanted "to be recognized, lauded, and lionized."[32]

For those same reasons, McKay was vulnerable to flattery by those seeking to influence his judgment. Because he made impromptu decisions, whoever could get to him first with loving words was likely to receive his support for reasonable requests. BYU president Wilkinson said that Wendell Mendenhall obtained his appointment as chairman of the church's Building Committee "through ingratiating himself with President McKay."[33] He also observed that, "the peace loving soul that he [McKay] is, it is very difficult for him to make decisions, regardless of their merits, where there is violent objection."[34]

Another personality difference had profound significance. Reuben, at heart, was an unreconstructed pessimist who "felt it wisest to approach problems from the point of view that things may get worse than better."[35] His view of humanity was summed up by this comment: "So far behind us as we can reach with history, tradition, or myth, there are in man the same selfishness, envy, avarice, cruelty, ambition, domination, love, and hate, that exists in him today, no other or different."[36] By contrast, McKay was an unshakable optimist who assumed that the worst of conditions would improve, that favorable conditions would become even better, and that human nature was basically good. As a comparison to Reuben's view, he observed, "Man is a spiritual Being, and at some period of his life everyone is possessed with an irresistible desire to know his relationship to the Infinite."[37]

These fundamental differences regarding the idea of progress and human nature affected how the two men planned for the church. Reuben favored slow growth and cautious, parsimonious expenditure of church funds. McKay favored expansive growth and liberal expenditures.

As administrators, they also had differing conceptions of the national and international character of Mormonism. Thirty years of training and experience before 1933 predisposed Reuben to see everything in terms of U.S. nationalism. His conception of secular and religious neutrality in time of war was a reflection of his idealistic view of the mission of America and of Americans, including the Latter-day Saints. Moreover, all his activities and sermons as elder statesman in the First Presidency were based on the assumption that Mormonism's most important issues were within the United States. Reuben never studied or visited a foreign country except in the interests of the USA. Even his general conference talks about the international church assumed that all his listeners and readers were Americans.

In contrast to Reuben's religious nationalism, McKay was a lifelong internationalist in his view of the church. His patriarchal blessing as a thirteen-year-old boy promised that he would "assist in gathering scattered Israel." He served a proselytizing mission among the people of Great Britain from 1897 to 1899. He toured the missions and prospective missions in the South Pacific, Asia, the Near East, and Europe from 1920 to 1921. From 1922 to 1924, he served as president of the European Mission and revisited the Near East in 1924. He also visited the far-flung members of the church outside the intermountain West as often as he could.[38] In the general conference of April 1927, he said: "Most earnestly do I hope that we shall never lose the great conviction that the world is our field of activity."[39] This difference of emphasis regarding internationalism and their respectively conservative and expansive views of the activities of the church caused the two leaders to approach decisions in divergent ways.

The administrative and philosophical counterpoise of Clark and McKay was observed by both Mormons and non-Mormons who had dealings with LDS headquarters. After his interviews with twenty-one influential Utahns, including LDS administrator Adam S. Bennion, Apostle Mark E. Petersen, and President George Albert Smith, non-LDS writer John Gunther observed, "A counterweight to Clark to some extent is the benign old second counselor, David O. McKay, a middle-roader."[40]

Moreover, for various personal, philosophical, and administrative reasons, most church administrators from 1934 to 1961 tended to align themselves either with Clark or McKay. As president, Spencer W. Kimball later observed that the popular division of general authorities and administrators into "Clark men" and "McKay men" could easily be exaggerated. However, he verified that there was a gravitation either toward Clark's leadership and philosophy or toward McKay's. Kimball further observed, "There was no serious division, but President Clark supported President McKay despite his non-agreement with President McKay's policies."[41]

Secretary Gibbons described Clark's mentorship at LDS headquarters: "In the process, he became the mentor and the father figure of a powerful group of younger leaders, Harold B. Lee, Henry D. Moyle, and Marion G. Romney, whom in private he often referred to affectionately as 'kids.' Beyond this trio of disciples, all of whom ultimately became members of the First Presidency, was a host of other leaders or administrative personnel who regarded President Clark almost with awe and who sought to emulate him. His counsel was listened to with avid interest, and his words were quoted as having almost scriptural authority."[42]

In addition to a nearly identical assessment by Reuben's children, two other LDS administrators specified those who strongly aligned themselves with either Clark or McKay. Gordon Burt Affleck, the church's purchasing agent and a self-described "Clark man," and A. Hamer Reiser, the First Presidency's assistant secretary and a self-described "McKay man," both said that Clark's closest supporters and protégés were Ezra Taft Benson, Albert E. Bowen, Charles A. Callis, Matthew Cowley, Spencer W.

Kimball, Harold B. Lee, Henry D. Moyle, Mark E. Petersen, LeGrand Richards, Marion G. Romney, Joseph Fielding Smith, and John A. Widtsoe, all of the Quorum of Twelve Apostles; Gordon B. Hinckley and Nicholas G. Smith of the Assistants to the Twelve; and Joseph L. Wirthlin of the Presiding Bishopric. President McKay's closest supporters and protégés, according to Affleck and Reiser, were Adam S. Bennion, Hugh B. Brown, and Stephen L Richards of the Quorum of Twelve; Alvin R. Dyer, Thomas E. McKay, and N. Eldon Tanner of the Assistants to the Twelve; Marion D. Hanks of the First Council of Seventy; and Thorpe B. Isaacson of the Presiding Bishopric. Despite such personal alignments, all these general authorities were loyal to both members of the presidency.[43] Some regarded as Clark men became closely aligned with McKay after he became LDS president. That was especially true of Ezra Taft Benson and Henry D. Moyle.[44]

Elder Brown was an example of the less-than-iron-clad distinction between McKay men and Clark men.[45] He was clearly a McKay man in his devotion to the liberal arts, his softer administrative style, his favorable view of militarism, his favorable view of the nature of humanity, his general optimism, and his disinclination to emphasize religious orthodoxy for either teachers or students. Nonetheless, "he remarked that President Clark was his mentor in law and religion, but not in politics." Brown had been Reuben's law partner in Utah for four years. As an extension of his work with this law firm, Brown joined his legal mentor in a private LDS study group that included three ardent Clark men: Bowen, Lee, and Romney. Their participation continued for years after Brown left Reuben's law firm.[46]

This dual mentorship was also true of Elder Hinckley, who has been LDS church president since 1995.[47] He worked closely with Reuben since preparing the first churchwide budget in 1938 at Clark's request.[48] He also helped prepare one of the counselor's books for publication.[49] Hinckley's official biographer notes that "President Clark had been solicitous of Gordon during his formative years at Church headquarters, and over the years the two had spent many hours together." Nevertheless, even if Reuben and his protégés regarded Hinckley as a "Clark man," from 1935 to 1959 Hinckley privately regarded Stephen L Richards as "his mentor." Richards was McKay's closest friend and most like-minded associate in the hierarchy, and Clark had numerous differences with Richards. Moreover, Hinckley began serving as a general authority only three years before Clark's death. Thus, he had a more extensive administrative relationship with the longer-lived McKay, "the gracious and commanding figure with whom [Hinckley] had enjoyed a marvelous personal association."[50]

On certain issues, Reuben had profound disputes with some of those whom his family and closest associates regarded as Clark men. He and John Widtsoe sometimes clashed about what Clark regarded as extremist views concerning food, and for decades they were on opposite sides over the Higher Criticism of biblical scholarship. Likewise, Reuben did not share Joseph Fielding Smith's dogmatic approach toward LDS scriptures, which led to their significant disagreement about organic evolution. (See chapter 7.)

Nonetheless, as President Kimball described, there tended to be a natural gravitation of like-minded general authorities toward one of the two men Apostle Romney described as "of an entirely different type ... a balanced pair of counselors." This extended beyond LDS administration into social activities.

Aside from gatherings to which all members of a quorum were invited, the strongest Clark men tended to socialize among themselves. With their wives and close family members, President Clark and protégés Lee, Moyle, and Romney often gathered together or as the only general authorities in attendance at larger social functions.[51] When these four invited other authorities to a private social, they usually included only other Clark men and their wives. The McKay-men exceptions were Brown, at meetings of the above-mentioned study group of Clark men, and Isaacson, who apparently attended such a social only one time.[52] Bishop Isaacson's inclusion was partly because he closely supported the Welfare Program and partly in response to the few occasions when he held socials at his own home and invited Clark and his other closest allies in the hierarchy.[53] The near segregation of Clark's protégés from McKay men in private socializing was a reflection of their administrative coalitions.

In spite of personal and administrative differences, there was always a cordial relationship between McKay and Clark. As counselors, they addressed and signed their letters to each other in the familiar "David" and "Reuben," although the former often addressed the first counselor in the more formal "President Clark." More enthusiastic for entertainment and cultural events, McKay often sent complimentary tickets for activities to Reuben and his family.[54]

Moreover, he continually fretted about McKay's health and his tendency to abbreviate recuperation from frequent surgeries and illnesses. "I hope you will take care of yourself and that your strength will rapidly return," Reuben wrote after the co-counselor had been periodically ill in 1938. "Among the many bits of wisdom I have dropped at your feet, mostly to be trodden upon, do not forget this one: You cannot do a full day's work at the office and then a full day's work on the farm in the same twenty-four hours."[55] On other occasions, such as April and May 1938, March 1940, July 1945, November 1946, and April 1950, Reuben felt that the second counselor was too ill to resume regular activities and virtually ordered him to stay away from the office for recuperation. McKay's typical reaction at these times was, "I'll have to admit that I am weaker than I thought I would be."[56]

Clark's presence in the office while McKay was absent actually reversed the situation that had existed during the first few years after McKay entered the presidency. At that time, Reuben was most often in New York City on business for the Foreign Bondholders. When President Grant started a three-week California vacation in January 1935, for example, Lute wrote to Reuben in New York City, "Poor Bro. McKay—I suppose you are hard at work at your office." In the fall of that year, she reported to Reuben that his secretary, VaLois South, "said when Pres. Grant is away, Bro. McKay goes to Ogden to look after his potato crop—so Bro. [Joseph] Anderson [the secretary] is in charge much of the time."[57] Because Reuben thrived on office work, whether in Washington, New York, or Salt Lake City, he probably needed Lute's comments to help him realize the extent to which administrative isolation burdened the second counselor who loved crowds and traveling.

His regret about McKay's often solitary vigil at headquarters in the 1930s turned into a vague sense of guilt as he also considered the financial disparities between the two counselors. McKay had never made much money as a school teacher or college administrator, was often in debt, and relied almost exclusively on his "allowance" as a general authority.[58] In addition to his own church stipend in the 1930s, Clark received $15,000 annually as president of FBPC. He garnered a fee of $108,000 from the work he did for the Mexican Eagle Oil Company.[59] In the Great Depression, this was a huge amount of money—easily equal to the wealth of a millionaire in today's purchasing power. All this came to Reuben while he was away from LDS headquarters on non-church business.

He could not in good conscience allow the second counselor to remain virtually alone in the office without added compensation. Beginning 17 February 1936, the first counselor wrote a series of personal checks to McKay for a total amount of $14,089 that year. Reuben called it a gift of "respect and affection."[60] This accurately described the personal feelings of the two men toward each other.

Nevertheless, disagreements bubbled to the surface during Grant's administration. Shortly before entering the First Presidency in 1934, Apostle McKay expressed concern "with the highly conservative attitude of J. Reuben Clark" in a two-hour interview with LDS member Joseph A. Geddes.[61] During the periods Reuben was in New York City, McKay may also have been irked by the fact that some Mormons, including Grant's son-in-law Robert L. Judd, preferred to await Reuben's return rather than consult McKay.[62]

Disagreement surfaced publicly regarding U.S. participation in World War II. As a fervent nationalist and isolationist, Reuben was appalled in 1940 to learn that McKay "was so pro-ally he is ready to go to war, almost—probably not so much pro-ally as anti-Hitler." Reuben reported this "division of opinion" to President Grant, who agreed with his position.[63] Two years later *Time* magazine reported a "disagreement in the First Presidency itself" from comments the counselors made during general conference.[64]

While the United States was in the midst of war with Nazi Germany,[65] Reuben drafted a statement which condemned "hate-driven militarists" and urged the immediate offer of a negotiated end to hostilities. He created a furor when he read this as a statement of the First Presidency at the general conference on 3 October 1942.[66] The next day, second counselor McKay made an impassioned sermon which catalogued the "fiendish" conduct of the Nazis and their Axis allies and categorically stated "that peace cannot come until the mad gangsters ... are defeated and branded as murderers, and their false aims repudiated."[67] When Mormons asked Reuben about the diametrical opposition between the second counselor's talk and the previous statement, he tersely replied: "While at our conference I read the Message of the First Presidency, it was not my message but the message of all the members of the Presidency, who all approved and signed it. The address President McKay made the following day was his own address."[68]

Reuben did everything he could during Grant's incapacitation after 1940 to honor Counselor McKay's line of responsibility and to never exclude him. But this difficult administrative situation added to the strains of philosophical and administrative differences between the two.

Clark later told Elder Kimball that difficulties in the relationship of the two counselors began surfacing during the last years of President Grant's life.[69] In apparent reference to this, Apostle Lee recorded in May 1943 that Reuben "discussed the problems that are arising as a new president of the Church looms. Was impressed by Pres. Clark's great humility."[70]

Secretary Reiser later observed that part of the inner-office problem was that Elder McKay was a "stickler for protocol." According to Reiser, he always resented being a subordinate to Reuben. When they were sustained as counselors, Reuben was a still a high priest yet was made first counselor because of his prior service as second counselor. McKay felt that he himself should have been first counselor because of his nearly thirty years in the Quorum of Twelve.[71] It did not matter to him that Clark was ordained an apostle when McKay became second counselor. Nor did it matter to him that there was ample precedent for appointing a man as first counselor who had lesser ecclesiastical experience or status than the second counselor.[72] McKay still felt that the position should be based on apostolic seniority.[73]

Reuben had not created the circumstances of his own church service, and he was confident that any misunderstanding between him and the second counselor could be resolved in the spirit of brotherhood. He wrote in June 1944, "Had conference with D.O.M. we ironed out some differences."[74] But to McKay, the issues were not simply misunderstandings or a matter of ill will. The difficulty involved fundamental differences of perspective in which the views of the counselor with twenty-seven more years of experience as a general authority were subordinated because of being second counselor. That problem could not be resolved through discussion.

Counselor McKay's resentments undoubtedly increased during the administration of George Albert Smith from 1945 to 1951. Smith preferred to seek Reuben's advice and felt closer to him than to McKay. Biographer Merlo Pusey observed, "George Albert came to rely heavily upon his first counselor, and their relations were extremely close." By contrast, Smith's "relations with his second counselor [McKay] were less intimate."[75] McKay was sensitive enough to recognize the disparity between the president's formal cordiality with him versus Smith's warmly dependent relationship with Clark.

In addition, when Smith's health declined, Reuben shortened the presidency's formal meetings to thirty minutes by deciding all agenda items with the LDS president in advance. This left McKay to attend *pro forma* meetings in which his views didn't matter since the other two had already made up their minds about every item on the agenda. (See chapter 4.)

The issue might have seemed resolved when President Smith died in 1951, leaving Elder McKay as senior apostle and automatic president of the church.[76] But President McKay brooded about the upcoming reorganization of the First Presidency and his choice of counselors. It was generally expected that he would advance his closest friend among the authorities, Apostle Stephen L Richards, but everyone expected him to be second counselor.[77]

McKay knew that was the expectation of others, but he could not endure the thought of putting his closest friend in the same situation he himself had endured for sixteen and a half years. Richards had more than seventeen years of seniority over Clark as an apostle. Moreover, Richards shared President McKay's administrative expansiveness, optimism, and other views which were foreign to Reuben.

McKay shrank from the prospect of having the administratively somber Clark continue to have ascendance over a counselor who shared the church president's views. Finally he prayerfully made a decision that he explained to a church educator who was critical of Reuben's negativism: "How do you think I have gotten along with him? If I ever had any inspiration it was when I selected Stephen L Richards as my first counselor, against all precedent."[78] For sixteen years he had been subordinate counselor to Clark, but as Secretary Gibbons wrote, "their roles of domination and subordination had been reversed."[79] Now McKay was in charge.

He waited as long as he could to confide his decision about the change of counselors. For the first time since McKay himself was sustained an apostle in 1906, a general conference convened on the church's anniversary date of 6 April without presenting the authorities for a sustaining vote. The morning session of 8 April also passed without the presentation of officers, and only one day of conference remained in which to reorganize the First Presidency. To delay longer would cause comment, but McKay first had to inform Reuben of the change. Then he had to ask the Twelve for their sustaining vote. By noon on 8 April, President McKay knew he could not postpone the action any longer.

As she always did, Louise brought some sandwiches to her father's office to eat alone with him during the recess between conference sessions. They had just begun eating at 12:30 when President McKay knocked at the door. He seemed flustered by Louise's presence and asked Reuben to come to his office. A few minutes later, he re-entered his office, avoiding his daughter's puzzled look as he said he wanted to eat alone and take a nap. She knew better than to ask what was the matter. His cheerfulness had turned into an icy inwardness that filled her with gloom.[80]

For a few minutes after Louise quietly shut the door behind her, Reuben stared thoughtfully at the door and mentally pictured the nearby office of the man who was now LDS president. They had served together in the First Presidency for nearly seventeen years, during which time they had loyally counseled two presidents and had supported each other. Reuben's mind stumbled over the thought: Even though we have differed in our views, could President McKay actually doubt my loyalty? Immediately his own words to the priesthood meeting the night before rushed upon him. "And so I come back to my theme song in all of these meetings: We must have unity," he had said. "We must work together. We must submerge our individual likes and dislikes."[81] President McKay had said something to him about seniority of apostleship as the reason for the change in counselor position, but it seemed to Reuben like a distinction without a difference.

In the world of government where Reuben had received his administrative training, a shift of a man's position from first to second assistant was a stark demotion. In all the history of the church LDS hierarchy, he thought, never before had a counselor in any quorum been changed from first to second. Nor could he think of a single instance in a ward or stake where such a thing had happened.

He had never aspired to church office, but Reuben had pride in the fact that he had faithfully and vigorously fulfilled the office of first counselor since 1934. No matter what public explanations were given, how could church members regard his demotion to second counselor as anything other than the severest administrative censure possible—short of his complete release from the First Presidency?

His thoughts drifted back through the years. He seemed to see his beloved Lute and the strain in her face from all their separations and their sacrifices for a career he eventually surrendered for church service. All that had now come to this. He suddenly remembered the letter he once wrote Lute about a diplomat who was retiring. "The poor old 'dodo' (with respect) weeps whenever he thinks of leaving the service. He is one of the nicest old ladies I have ever met," he had written caustically. Then he had added the reflection, "But as we get older we all get more tearful—so I suppose it is something to be looked forward to."[82] Now he thanked God silently that Lute had not lived to see this general conference, and then he gave vent to unaccustomed emotion in the solitude of his office. He was nearly eighty and the next decade would be difficult.

President McKay asked all members of the Twelve to meet in the temple at 4:30 following the afternoon session of conference on 8 April 1951. As everyone anticipated, he began the business of this special meeting by explaining the need to reorganize the First Presidency. Joseph Fielding Smith, second apostle in seniority, immediately moved that David O. McKay be sustained formally as president of the church. The motion was seconded by Stephen L Richards, third in seniority, and unanimously voted in the affirmative by the assembled apostles.[83] As Secretary Gibbons has written, "He then dropped an unexpected bombshell by nominating Stephen L Richards as First Counselor and J. Reuben Clark as Second Counselor."[84]

Elder Kimball described the reaction of the apostles:

> I was stunned when he explained that he had chosen Elder Richards first, Pres. Clark having served as first counselor for long years to President Grant and Pres. Smith. I looked around and found the other brethren stunned. It was hard to understand. I knew Elder Richards had been a close and lifelong friend [of President McKay] but I was not prepared for this. ... All the others of the Twelve seemed to be alike stunned. We had been wholly unprepared for this shock. Pres. Clark had stood and accepted this call and in this order like a god. What a man! What fortitude! What courage and self control! What self mastery! How could any mortal take a blow like that and stand? But he did.

After the assembled men unanimously voted to sustain President McKay's choice and ordering of counselors, Kimball recorded that the rest left their room in the temple in unaccustomed silence: "Not until we started down the steps of the temple did I come to realize that I was not alone in my bewilderment and devastation." The apostles "walked back to the office building numb. The other brethren from Bro. Lee down came together at the corner of the building and commiserated together ... our hearts were breaking for that elder stalwart who for two regimes had carried the major load."[85] Apostle Benson wrote in his diary, "There was expressed a feeling 'It will kill Brother Clark' and also 'The people will not be reconciled.'"[86]

That evening several members of the Twelve paid unannounced visits to the Clark home to commiserate directly with Reuben. He "assured us that he would never do anything to cause a break between the Twelve and Pres. McKay and would try his best to be a good counselor, despite the humiliation that was inescapable."[87] Clark's reassurance about not causing a split was significant. It reflected the loyalty he saw in his protégés and the severity of dissent they had expressed against the new president's decision.

Reuben began the morning of 9 April with an earnest prayer that the Lord would sustain him through a difficult experience. Not even his own children knew that he would be demoted at the solemn assembly which would sustain the new First Presidency.[88] Added to the burden of that change in his life and his fears of the effect it might have on them, Reuben had to bear one further burden this morning.

President McKay asked him to present the names of the new First Presidency and other officers for the sustaining vote. Thousands of people in the Salt Lake Tabernacle and tens of thousands of television and radio listeners would be able to detect the slightest trace of emotion in his voice as he announced his altered position in the presidency. All these circumstances added up to an electrifying moment. His daughter Marianne later wrote:

> Your calm, judicious manner with no hesitancy, no tremor, and without rancor, greatly increased the spirit of solemnity. I guess most everyone believed that you had made a mistake as you read the second name, but no one who did not know, could have imagined that there was the slightest personal connection between you and what you were saying. ...[89]

President McKay then explained that apostolic seniority, rather than "any rift," was the reason for the change in Elder Clark's status, which he insisted was not a demotion.[90] He called on him, as the newly sustained second counselor, to speak before the new first counselor.

Reuben's words at this moment have been quoted without understanding the truly dramatic circumstances of their utterance: "In the service of the Lord, it is not where you serve but how. In the Church of Jesus Christ of Latter-day Saints, one takes the place to which one is duly called, which place one neither seeks nor declines."[91]

Apostle Kimball wrote: "The congregation was breathless. ... [and] there were many tears throughout the great congregation. ... No one could tell if Pres. Clark carried any scars or injuries. ... No complaint, no self-pity[—]neither in act nor attitude. He accepted it. He proclaimed the majesty of the Church." Kimball added that on this day Reuben "did more in his perfect reactions perhaps to establish in the minds of this people the true spirit of subjection of the individual to the good of the work, more than could be done in thousands of sermons."[92] Secretary Anderson wrote that President Clark spoke "with a courage that has seldom been equaled, I am sure, in Church administration."[93]

Elder Romney, then an Assistant to the Twelve, summed up these events in his diary:

> I remember that President Clark said to me on one occasion, "My boy, you always keep your eye on the president of the Church, and if he asks you to do anything which is wrong and you do it because of your loyalty to him,[94] the Lord will bless you for it."
>
> I know President Clark will be vindicated ... and I do not believe the Lord will let him down. His performance in this conference in [his] taking what most people consider a demotion and [in his] presenting the authorities in the solemn assembly, has endeared him in the hearts of the people more than anything he has ever done. It must be that he is being tempered for a greater glory. Perhaps some of the rest of us must be trained to step down gracefully, and President Clark is the only man great enough to give us a demonstration of how to do it.[95]

On this day Reuben maintained his rock-like stability and strength while he also characteristically tried to moderate the adulation of his admirers. After the conference session, Apostle Kimball took the hand of his first cousin and expressed heartfelt admiration for what he described as a great demonstration of self-mastery. President Clark told him, "It wasn't easy."[96]

Beyond the general authorities, others had mixed reactions to this reorganization. The response tended to reflect the divergent attitudes among Latter-day Saints and non-Mormons about Reuben's political influence and statements. Newspaper columnist Drew Pearson, who interviewed prominent Utahns including J. Bracken Lee about "my old friend Reuben Clark," published this assessment: "Today, at the age of 80, Clark is the most reactionary apostle in the Mormon church—so reactionary that when McKay became president he promptly demoted Clark from his place as No. 1 counselor."[97]

By contrast, one of Reuben's Mormon admirers reported that, in his travels throughout Utah, people asked "why Pres. Clark had to take a back seat. He wanted Pres. Clark to know that people throughout the State, Mormons and non-Mormons, do not approve of the movement [i.e., President McKay's action]; he does not either, and as a non-Mormon told him yesterday, he said the Presidency of the Church is slipping, [and he] does not like to see the way things have gone."[98]

Secretary Reiser, a self-described "McKay man," also commented on the negative response. It "was interpreted by some people as a demotion for President Clark, and there was some flurry about it among the people, some gossip developed, and there was some uneasiness. Some people were critical and even vocalized their criticism."[99] John K. Edmunds, then president of the Chicago Stake and later president of the Salt Lake temple, said: "I heard a lot of brethren talk about that remark. Some of them wondered how President Clark could continue in the Presidency and wondered if he would resign his position in the Church and so on. ... People felt that he was being demoted."[100] However, when Alma Sonne, an Assistant to the Twelve, heard anyone criticize this "selection of Stephen L Richards as first counselor ahead of J. Reuben Clark, Alma always stoutly defended President McKay's choice."[101]

Those who applauded or decried Clark's subordination generally looked at it in terms of political influence or ecclesiastical status—tokens of power. There were others who felt only the crushing personal dimension of the event. Reuben had worried about the effects it might have on his family, but he underestimated the strength he had given them. Marianne expressed the feelings of all of his children in a letter she wrote him on 19 April:

> Of course I felt stunned and heartsick and kept questioning in my mind as to how such a thing could come to you following your years of devoted service to the Lord. As I thought of it during that day these words kept coming to me and comforting me, "For whom the Lord loveth he chasteneth." (Not that I feel to ascribe the secondary action to the Lord). Still I know that it is suffering and sorrow which give us wisdom and understanding, and that the Lord's purposes are never thwarted. Also that good triumphs and returns to the giver.
>
> Never before that day, with all my love and appreciation for your

great and noble soul and of your achievements, have I felt so proud to have you for my father. ...

To me this experience through which we are passing is the greatest lesson which you have taught us, an example which should encourage and sustain us always and bind us closer together in the eternal family unit, coming on top of your wonderful teachings.

I believe your spirit grew to a new height that day—perhaps one to which you might never have attained without this experience.[102]

As for Reuben himself, he masked his inner feelings whenever friends expressed resentment about the change.

On one occasion his emotions nearly overtook him as he defended President McKay. Two days after the solemn assembly, he answered one person by relating an incident when he was new in the hierarchy and had complained to President Ivins about someone's faults. Ivins responded that he would accept all of the person's failings if he could have the person's virtues. After recording this defense of McKay, Reuben added a note to his office diary: "I was happy that I got through without any blubbering. The Lord blessed me."[103]

Initially, he told non-LDS friend A. Helen Morgan that he was unsure whether or not his responsibilities would diminish now that he was a second counselor.[104] A major question in the minds of many was whether the president would relieve him of supervising the Welfare Program. There was an unusually large attendance at the next meeting of the Welfare Committee on 13 April. Romney observed: "The brethren and sisters evidently came to see what would happen under the new administration. President Clark took charge as usual." The protégé learned later in the day that McKay had asked Reuben "to proceed as usual in the welfare work."[105] Moreover, although the church presidents had served as chairmen of the "This Is the Place" Monument Commission since 1937, McKay declined to accept the governor's invitation to become its chairman in 1951. Instead, he recommended Clark for the appointment.[106]

Reuben was pleased with these decisions, yet the former first counselor refused to allow the new counselor to defer to him. To begin with, Clark had a long-standing friendship with Richards, who was "among the very oldest acquaintances and friends that I have in Salt Lake City."

Reuben had written in 1949 that of his friends, "none is more staunch" than Apostle Richards.[107] For his part, Richards felt awkward about the situation for the first few months.

As first counselor, Richards tried to honor Clark's previous position. When President McKay was unable to attend the weekly temple meeting of the presidency and apostles on 3 May 1951, Richards seemed willing to let Reuben conduct the council meeting due to his years of experience. Clark insisted that as second counselor he should take the lead only when both McKay and Richards were absent.[108] A month later he publicly stated this principle at the conference of the Mutual Improvement Associations. President McKay was unable to attend the opening session of the conference. At this first public meeting where the newly sustained counselors presided in the absence of the church president, President Richards again deferred to the second counselor. Reuben immediately corrected any impression this incident might cause to those who witnessed it:

> I think with his [Richards's] permission I ought to say a word. In his well-known kindness and consideration and courtesy, he said to me before he began, did I wish him to go forward, and I said "Yes," but I do not want you young people to get any erroneous idea from that. He is the presiding officer of this conference in the absence of President McKay. He does not need to consult me, though he graciously did so.[109]

As deeply as he was hurt by his subordination in 1951, Reuben refused to allow the slightest hint that any of the prerogatives of the first counselor's position remained with him. His demonstration of that principle so deeply impressed one of the local MIA leaders in attendance that twenty-three years later the man described it as "the most beautiful example I've ever seen in Church procedure."[110] Unflinching loyalty to the order of the church was more important to President Clark than any personal consideration.

Nevertheless, he firmly believed that integrity to one's personal beliefs was synonymous with loyalty to a superior, and he continued to state his views frankly to the new LDS president. Although presidents McKay and Richards were enthusiastic supporters of youth activity programs, Reuben told the apostles in June of his disdain for the effort "to continually further recreational activities."[111] He also soon found himself in disagreement with the united position of McKay and Richards on church expenditures. Reuben told the first counselor in August: "If you two brethren feel that way, of course I will go along with you. I am not going to stand out. If you feel that way, I will go along."[112]

However, it would be an overstatement to say that presidents McKay and Clark always disagreed or that presidents McKay and Richards always agreed. For example, regarding President George Albert Smith's choice of a counselor in the Presiding Bishopric, Reuben confided in 1946 that "both he and Pres. McKay [second counselor] were opposed to the man nominated and that he was of the opinion that a powerful minority could be mustered in the Council" against Smith's decision. Likewise, in a 1947 temple meeting, there was "a rather heated discussion with Stephen L. Richards and Joseph Fielding Smith on one side, and Pres. Clark and Pres. McKay on the other."[113] Still, that was not the most common alignment.

Perhaps to a greater degree than McKay had anticipated, it was obvious that he and Counselor Richards were of one mind, whereas Clark often saw things differently. The fundamental differences after April 1951 were consistently resolved in the same manner. Reuben stated his reservations and then loyally sustained the authority and decision of the president. As he informed the First Presidency's secretaries on one occasion, "I know who the President of the Church is, I know what his authority is, I know what he wants and that is what he shall have, even if I don't like it."[114] Reuben was implacable both in his bluntness and in his loyalty. Since his initial appointment to the hierarchy, he had informed rank-and-file Mormons, as well as non-Mormons, that such was the church's procedure. In January 1952 Elder Romney observed that "his loyalty to the President is inspiring."[115]

Nevertheless, President McKay's personality made it difficult for him to acknowledge loyal opposition within his presidency. Even to the knowing Quorum of Twelve, he often stated, "I assure you there is unity in the Quorum of the First Presidency."[116] By contrast, President Clark informed individual apostles "that 'compliance' was not 'unity.'"[117]

Considering McKay's sensitivity to public image, one can imagine his acute embarrassment about publicity less than a year after his installment.

Nationally syndicated newspaper columnist and radio personality Drew Pearson reported in February 1952 that the "new president of the Mormon church is kindly, elder statesman David O. McKay ... Opposing him is J. Reuben Clark."[118]

Reuben was typically unruffled by this public observation. When a secretary read the article to the church president, Reuben "laughed and told him to pay no attention to what Pearson said." This was easy to do locally because "the Utah papers did not publish it."[119] Like similar blackouts in local newspapers, Reuben may have arranged this through consultation with compliant editors and publishers like John Fitzpatrick. (See chapter 4.)

However, Reuben must have been especially irked that Pearson twisted the knife by calling McKay an elder statesman. Everyone knew that this was Clark's unquestioned role as former U.S. ambassador and former Undersecretary of State, while the new church president had no similar service.

Reuben had resigned himself to his diminished status and dismissed with cavalier disdain any public comments about tension within the presidency. However, for ten years after the 1951 reorganization, he brooded about potential reversals and actual reversals of his treasured achievements in LDS administration. Suddenly unsure about the permanence of his contributions to the church, he became increasingly defensive of his protégés and programs. As a result, he became suspicious of innovations promoted by President McKay and the other counselor.

Elder Romney observed that "Brother Lee and Brother Moyle and I were the ones who were under Brother Clark's tutelage."[120] Therefore, Reuben fretted that President McKay might diminish his three closest protégés administratively as he had diminished him. He rejoiced in October 1951 when McKay advanced Romney from assistant to full membership in the Quorum of Twelve, where elders Lee and Moyle were already serving.[121] The position had been vacant since April.

Advancing Reuben's acknowledged protégé had the effect of denying the assumptions and rumors that the president was intentionally reducing the counselor's influence. There is no known evidence indicating that the months of negative comments about Clark's demotion played a role in McKay's choice of Romney as the new apostle. However, in view of the new president's own sensitivities, this widespread criticism may have been a factor.

Reuben continued to worry about the relations between President McKay and the Clark men. Not long before the Drew Pearson incident, Apostle Lee told the Grantsville Stake conference that he esteemed Reuben "above any other man." Clark warned Lee privately that the remark "might have some repercussions, as well it might be repeated by those wishing to make trouble."[122] Likewise, recently appointed apostle Romney's attitudes made him vulnerable to criticism "by those wishing to make trouble." The same month that Lee implicitly ranked Reuben above the others in the presidency, Romney wrote that Clark "is the greatest man that I ever associated with," which he repeated a month later.[123] McKay was the church's president, but Reuben's protégés indicated whom they valued most.

Apostle Lee later observed that his mentor's sensitivities to the president's attitudes were such that even "a little incident" could cause Reuben to feel "worried." An example was the council meeting when Elder Lee routinely selected a hymn, announced the number twice to the assembled presidency and apostles, yet "Pres. McKay disregarded it and without comment announced an entirely different song." Clark regarded that as an intentional slight.[124]

In fact, there was some basis for Reuben's concern that President McKay resented his close association with Elder Lee. For example, Reuben bluntly told BYU president Ernest Wilkinson that because of his youthful vigor, "Brother Lee stood a good chance of being a President of the Church."[125] Clark often reminded Lee of this likelihood and, in Lee's words, once "told me some things which he felt I should know for future reference regarding some of the brethren."[126] On one occasion Wilkinson told McKay that "it looked to me like Brother Lee had been talking to President Clark. He [McKay] commented, 'That's obvious.'"[127] Secretary Gibbons noted: "President Clark occasionally used Elder Lee to float ideas in committee meetings, which ideas he did not want to have seen as originating with him. ... In addition, he used him occasionally to pass on words of 'counsel' to some of the Brethren, or to headquarters personnel, in cases where it was felt inappropriate for such to come directly from him."[128] McKay's "that's obvious" comment showed that he resented Lee's role as Clark's proxy.

Reuben's concern for the status of his protégés was intensified by a situation in the office of the president. Clare Middlemiss had been McKay's private secretary since 1935. In 1949 she stated, "I have devoted my whole life to President McKay—I want nothing more."[129] After McKay became president, Middlemiss became a power in her own right. Functioning as an executive secretary, she also had her own secretary.[130] Gibbons noted that Middlemiss "draft[ed] suggested answers to letters for the Prophet's consideration before he had even read the correspondence."[131]

Her domination was sufficient to result in the uncomfortable transfer of D. Arthur Haycock out of the office and out of LDS headquarters. Secretary to the former church president, Haycock and Reuben were close friends.[132] General authorities informed U.S. Senator Frank E. Moss that "one of the problems we have is that Miss Middlemiss runs the office of President McKay and often calls in his name to order things done."[133] Of far greater concern to Reuben was what one McKay biographer called "the watchful diligence of the hovering Clare Middlemiss."[134] She wielded virtually absolute power in granting and denying access to the president and thereby became a crucial factor in church administration.

"One of the most constant frustrations I have at the Church Office Building (I am not alone in this)," wrote Wilkinson, "is that of trying to get to see President McKay through his secretary." At this time Wilkinson was chancellor of church schools and president of BYU.[135] When Reiser became assistant secretary to the First Presidency, he observed her activities in disbelief. For example, she denied some members of the Quorum of Twelve access to the president at times when he was available for consultation. By contrast, she allowed instant access for favored authorities and administrators who were ecclesiastically subordinate to the excluded apostles.[136]

Personal access was administratively crucial because President McKay often made on-the-spot decisions. Therefore, both general authorities and lesser administrators made "end runs" around official meetings in order to obtain his personal approval where it might otherwise need the sanction of a council.[137]

As Gibbons acknowledged, the administrative power of Middlemiss "created some unintentional problems" involving "the historic difference between line and staff personnel."[138] In other words, she rivaled the authority of the church president's counselors.

Moreover, because access to the president required a convivial relationship with both him and his secretary, flattery became the administrative lubricant of the McKay administration.[139] Reuben had trained his protégés to abhor flattery, and he understandably worried about the fact that it was McKay men whom Clare tended to give immediate access and Clark men whom she tended to postpone. As for Clark himself, Middlemiss could not have denied him access even if she had wanted to.

McKay achieved the administrative equivalent of this by denying his counselor the opportunity to raise a dissenting voice. For example, in May 1951 McKay and Wilkinson wanted to invite former U.S. president Herbert Hoover to speak at the BYU commencement ceremony for graduating students. Two other invited speakers had declined. Wilkinson suggested that Reuben extend this invitation to his close friend, but he vigorously opposed this as a third-choice insult to the former U.S. president. When McKay learned of Clark's reaction, he instructed Wilkinson to ask Hoover himself. Reuben did not learn of this until a month later—after Hoover declined.[140]

Within two years, he was informing general authorities and community leaders of his exclusion from decision making. "President McKay has never said anything to me about it," he replied in March 1953 when asked about decisions the presidency was announcing about educational and financial matters. Reuben made a similar statement in July.[141] In December 1956 he learned about a decision of "the First Presidency" by reading about it in the *Salt Lake Tribune*. President McKay explained to a community leader that "I had not taken my associates into my confidence on this matter until I knew where we stood."[142] When a church member asked about a financial matter a month later, Reuben replied: "I don't know very much about it. The discussions that have been had about this have only casually come to my notice and I think they were conducted primarily by President McKay."[143] To some extent this was David O. McKay's unique administrative style during his entire service as president. It also indicated the extent to which he tried to avoid receiving counsel that was contrary to his own judgment.

From 1951 to 1959, however, it was difficult to exclude Reuben's contrary advice from deliberations. During these years, he was usually at his desk while President McKay was touring missions for weeks at a time. The *Deseret News* aptly noted in July 1952 that "President Stephen L Richards and President J. Reuben Clark Jr., who have carried on the heavy burdens of the office of the First Presidency, were glad to see their President back."[144] More important, because of repeated illnesses and hospitalizations of the other two, Reuben was "by all means the most vigorous of the three and the most productive."[145] Midway during this eight-year period, he wrote, "I am having a difficult time to go through an increasing pile of work."[146]

Aside from occasionally excluding Reuben altogether from administrative decisions, President McKay more often neutralized his dissonant counselor by forging an administrative juggernaut with first counselor Richards. For example, if Clark objected to the philosophy or content of a proposed statement, presidents McKay and Richards dropped the subject for the balance of the meeting. After Reuben left the room, they then asked a secretary to type the statement in final form, which they presented to him with their two signatures already in place. Further comment was unthinkable at that point and Reuben silently accepted the inevitable: "I therefore attached my signature."[147] In council meetings with other general authorities and lesser administrators, presidents McKay and Richards "over-ruled" Clark's contrary views.[148] Even when he presided alone at the presidency's office in the absence of the other two, McKay circumvented him by declining to give instructions and authority to act in their absence.[149]

Aside from being outflanked administratively from 1951 to 1959, Reuben was fighting a rearguard action to protect his most prized achievement, the Welfare Plan. Since 1937 he had felt that Democratic apostle Richards disagreed with the distinctly anti-government philosophy of the program. He noted that Elder Richards seemed to prefer to "leave the money side of relief to the Government (State and Federal) while the Church confined itself to spiritual and character rehabilitation."[150]

Less than a year after he was demoted, Reuben concluded that the Welfare Plan was under siege. By February 1952, the two counselors were giving opposite instructions to leaders in Canada about Mormons accepting government gratuities.[151] This was essentially a conflict between Clark's nationalism and the internationalism of presidents McKay and Richards. The latter two expressed an evaluation of Reuben's intended letter to Canadian Mormons on this subject:

> President Richards further said: "I just feel that we do not have to do things like that when we can leave people to act for themselves, and while we cannot individually approve of everything governments do, I think the policy as outlined in [President Clark's] letter would lead us to take objection to what governments all over the world are doing. We, the Church, are world-wide, and it makes so many people feel that they are not in good standing because they are not fully following the counsel of our brethren."
>
> [President McKay] answered: "That is true, and they do not like to go against our counsel, and as you say, when they do, they feel they are out of harmony."
>
> Brother Richards then said: "We cannot regulate the affairs of all governments, and I wonder if the time has not come when we can say that we express no official view; that we leave it to the people for determination themselves."
>
> [President McKay] remarked at this point that "We believe in being subject to kings, presidents, rulers and in obeying, honoring, and sustaining the law."
>
> President Richards stated that "there is nothing in the law (Canadian) that prevents us from teaching family solidarity, and from advocating those high principles of our Gospel, but when it comes to interfering with the policies of the government, I doubt that it is our function."[152]

Aside from this challenge to his philosophy on charitable assistance, Reuben told his protégés in the Quorum of Twelve in March 1952 "that Pres. Richards was putting the Welfare Program on rather shaky ground in a very adroit way with the fear expressed that we might become competitive with industry, etc., etc."[153] Two months later Apostle Romney "was greatly disturbed over a report from Thorpe Isaacson that Pres. McKay had made some derogatory statements about the Welfare Program."[154]

In Reuben's view, the first counselor was also undermining his role in the program. In a presidency meeting in November 1952, Richards opposed his continued attendance at the biweekly Welfare Committee meetings he had attended for twelve years.[155] Reuben stopped attending for one month. He and his Welfare associates wondered if he was to be deprived of all responsibility for the program.[156]

After this brief interruption, Clark resumed supervision of the Welfare Plan yet maintained a siege mentality about it until his death. In July 1953 he warned Apostle Lee to postpone its expansion to avoid "adverse reactions from the President." He advised very careful implementation of the program's existing activities "in order to avoid any possible diminishing of welfare developments from their present state."[157]

He was also miffed in 1955 that Elder Richards disapproved of the Welfare Committee officially sponsoring a luncheon for a civil defense convention in Salt Lake City. Therefore, "Pres. Clark later arranged with Bp. Thorpe B. Isaacson and Carl Buehner [of the Presiding Bishopric] to pay for the dinner out of their own pockets."[158]

By 1957 Reuben and his protégés were expressing alarm about the potential loss of the program. In March he confided to Apostle Romney that he was "not [being] kept advised in detail of what is to be done there."[159] Four days later Apostle Lee reported that the Welfare Committee held "a stormy meeting with the First Presidency," meaning President McKay and first counselor Richards.[160] Lee viewed this as "the same antagonisms against the program which were common back in 1936 when the program began," but now he was uncertain whether it would survive.[161] In October, Reuben wrote of the "growing uncertainty in Church about welfare; Brethren talking both ways."[162] In December 1957 he privately advised his protégées "not to press for important decision[s] which might bring an impasse from the First Presidency and thus lose much that we have gained in the welfare program."[163] Again his warning about "an impasse from the First Presidency" referred to the fact that he was overridden by presidents McKay and Richards.

Although the Welfare Program remained outwardly vital to the church, Reuben and his associates believed that they had lost a war of attrition. "When President Clark passed away there was no one at the top vigorously pushing it," remarked Elder Romney. The latter admitted that he did a "very unwise thing" on one occasion by telling McKay: "There hasn't been a general conference address on welfare since you became President."[164] The perception of opposition to the program made its defense Clark's major preoccupation after 1951.

He also found himself in the unfamiliar position as a conservative voice in a more liberal First Presidency. Ever the statesman, he drafted a First Presidency message for Christmas 1953 that proposed to lecture the people of the world on their responsibilities. Presidents McKay and Richards discarded it because "some outside of the Church might look on it as arrogance."[165] As a parallel to their disagreement about the Welfare Program in relation to government programs, President Richards advocated that BYU accept federal grants. Reuben condemned this as "socialistic," but "as usual, President McKay was very much influenced by President Richards, although instinctively his feelings were otherwise."[166] In the public eye, Reuben continued to be a vigorous leader and eloquent spokesman, but administratively he was in checkmate.

His protégés also saw evidence of deep division between him and the first counselor. During a temple meeting in February 1955, Reuben's colleagues recommended that his *Our Lord of the Gospels* be the instructional manual for the next year's Melchizedek priesthood quorums. Apostle Lee wrote, "Characteristically, Pres. Stephen L. Richards voiced objections on the grounds of the expense involved, but everyone, I think, sensed the fact that his objections were deeper and later he voiced his feelings to Henry Moyle, but without any logical reason, which leads to the conclusion that he objects just because the book was written by Pres. Clark."[167] When Elder Lee raised the question again a month later, "there was evidence that the opposition was fully primed against Pres. Clark's book for some reason." Afterwards Reuben "quietly" told him, "It's alright—I'll still be around in three years from now."[168] Three years later his book was adopted as the instructional manual.[169]

Although some expected these tensions to poison the feelings between the two counselors, quite the opposite was true. LDS administrator Gordon Affleck knew of their administrative conflicts and assumed that "they nearly hated each other." Instead, he discovered that they shared a deep respect and affection which they expressed publicly and privately.[170] For example, Apostle Romney wrote in April 1955: "I don't remember seeing a time when Brother Clark and Brother Richards seemed so friendly. It was a delight to be in their presence."[171]

The three strong-willed members of the First Presidency shared times of hilarity as well. The *Salt Lake Tribune* captured such a moment in its photograph of the cornerstone ceremony for the Relief Society's headquarters. In presenting a copy of this photograph, Reuben explained: "With embarrassing apologies for so much levity on a solemn occasion. The masons were sort of removing the excess mortar we three had spread on too thick; Pres. Richards observed: 'The fault of all amateurs is to spread it on too thick.'"[172] And a loving brother could not have been more solicitous than Reuben when presidents McKay and Richards were ill.[173]

Moreover, despite Clark's personal demand for consistency, he loyally defended McKay's agonizing vacillations during the so-called "Ricks College controversy." President McKay eventually defined this as "the most important matter that he had had to decide as President."[174] His own emphasis justifies an extended examination of it and Reuben's role in the controversy.

On the surface the issue was simple: whether to keep church-supported Ricks College in the town of Rexburg, Idaho, where the school was founded at the turn of the century. The alternative was to move it to the city of Idaho Falls where the church had more members and a temple. Complicating this question was the understandable personal, historical, financial, and religious commitment of the Rexburg people for keeping the college despite whatever advantages might exist for moving it elsewhere.[175]

When Rexburg citizens expressed concern about rumors that the First Presidency was considering the move, President McKay impulsively replied on 17 March 1954, "Rest assured there will be no change in Ricks College."[176] Characteristically he sent this private message "without clearing with his Counselors."[177] However, Reuben's name appeared as the co-signer on McKay's follow-up telegram in July which reaffirmed, "The college is not going to be moved from Rexburg."[178] The president committed himself before the Church Board of Education could begin an intended investigation of the merits.[179] This provided grist for years of bitter controversy that peppered LDS councils and erupted into the public press.

Early in 1957 President McKay joined with his counselors and the board of education in carefully considering the circumstances of maintaining the school at Rexburg or moving it to Idaho Falls. In April they began an unforeseen cycle of controversy by voting to endorse a move. After announcing this decision to college, church, and community leaders in Rexburg, most general authorities were stunned to finally learn that President McKay had committed himself against such a move three years earlier. By now, he was convinced that the evidence supported the need for a move, and he was appalled by the bitter attacks from Rexburg leaders who blamed Church Commissioner of Education and BYU president Wilkinson for this.[180] In the face of this uproar, President McKay reversed himself again and decided that the church would build a separate junior college in Idaho Falls. This was the formal decision during his meeting on 1 July with Reuben and the executive committee of the board of education.[181]

Ten days later McKay met alone with Rexburg leaders, told them of the decision to keep Ricks in Rexburg, but also promised them that the church would not build a competing junior college in Idaho Falls. This worsened the situation by yet again privately reversing a decision made in council.[182]

The Church Board of Education and McKay's counselors learned about this by reading it in the newspaper. Wilkinson privately said that he would resign as commissioner in protest if it were not a church calling. Counselor Richards said that President McKay's published explanation was "the silliest thing I ever heard," and he was "quite incensed that President McKay had quoted him as being in favor of the decision." To the contrary, McKay had merely telephoned his decision to Richards without opportunity for discussion.[183] Yet President McKay assured Rexburg's leaders that "he had talked by telephone with President Stephen L. Richards, who was then at his summer home at Hebgen Lake and that he was in full accord with the action taken."[184] As for Reuben, he simply counseled Commissioner Wilkinson "not to be precipitate in making any decision, but to move slowly in the situation." But as the Rexburg newspapers mounted an increasingly vitriolic campaign against Wilkinson, the counselor suggested that he file a lawsuit against them.[185]

In the midst of this controversy, Wilkinson expressed frustration during a private meeting with Reuben in April 1958. Without naming McKay, Wilkinson complained "that I sometimes, in accordance with decisions, would cross certain bridges and then have the bridges torn out by the brethren through changing their minds and that I had been left stranded." Reuben acknowledged that such reversals "couldn't be justified."[186]

By autumn the advocates and opponents had begun a pitched battle to manipulate President McKay. Wilkinson assembled a convincing battery of data that overwhelmingly supported the move to Idaho Falls. This painstaking and thorough research was all that was needed to convince the legal minds of presidents Richards and Clark. In a meeting at the McKay home on 31 October, the First Presidency decided to move Ricks College to Idaho Falls. The president asked that this decision be presented for approval by the Quorum of Twelve and then the Church Board Education.[187]

Apostles Romney and Brown announced the unanimous decision of all three church councils to a special priesthood meeting of shocked Rexburg leaders.[188] Wilkinson saw the following lesson:

> There is one moral to the Ricks transfer, namely that if one is right (as I was sure I was) one should not hesitate to question the decision of the President of the Church (President McKay had formerly decided to leave Ricks at Rexburg) as long as it is done properly. With the strong support of President Richards, who knows how to handle President McKay, we finally got this serious mistake rectified.[189]

However, the angry Rexburg leaders were equally convinced that they were right. They also felt they were justified in questioning President McKay, his counselors, the Twelve, and the board of education. They likewise thought they knew "how to handle President McKay."

The stake president was astute enough to approach the church president with loving flattery while trying to drive a wedge between him and his counselors:

> President McKay: Why don't you want to meet the [First] Presidency?
>
> President [T——]: They seem to be rebuking me to the point where I don't want to take it any longer. You have been so kind and lovable, but the other brethren seem to make me feel that I have lost the track.[190]

With a carrot-and-stick technique of persuasion, he and other Rexburg Mormons alternated flattery with hardball. They wrote personal letters to McKay and made statements to the newspaper that "hammered home constantly" that he had publicly committed himself not to move Ricks College. They accused him of breaking his word, which a local historian concluded was an intentional tactic to "hurt President McKay."[191]

Throughout the increasingly bitter controversy, Reuben adamantly defended President McKay. In a meeting of the full presidency with Ricks College administrators on 15 November 1958, one man insisted that their fervent prayers had been answered by the Lord and that the answer was contrary to the current position of the First Presidency. Reuben fumed: "You know, we prayed about it, too, and after all[,] ours were the prayers that counted in this situation and not his individual prayers, that we had the whole Church to consider."[192]

By February 1959 the issue had escalated into a fever pitch of animosity. "President McKay felt that he needed to be sustained in some way" and persuaded Wilkinson to publish an argumentative pamphlet, *Ricks College: A Statement*, despite Wilkinson's apprehension that such a publication might widen the controversy.[193] Sure enough, the citizens of Rexburg replied with the vitriolic *Dr. Wilkinson's Role in the Proposal to Move Ricks College.*[194]

In a two-hour meeting of the First Presidency with the Rexburg stake presidency on 10 February, Reuben unleashed the full power of his lifelong loyalty to the president:

> President Clark made this statement, "May I ask a question? This of

course we will agree with is a Church matter, but this Committee of 1000 has appealed to the people of the United States. Am I right about that?

Brother [T——]: "That is right."

President Clark: "That is wholly contrary to the discipline of the Church. ...

May I put one question to you? When you go on your knees to pray, do you pray that the Lord will guide and direct the Prophet, Seer, and Revelator to change his mind, is that your prayer? ... I have wondered as I have known of your position, I have wondered what I would say if I got down on my knees to change a decision of the First Presidency."

Brother [T——]: "We have never asked the Lord for that."

President Clark: "But you have treated it as if no decision had been made."[195]

Four days afterwards the First Presidency published a condemnation of the Rexburg publication in the *Church News* and reaffirmed the decision to move Ricks College.[196]

But the Rexburg people would not relent. They kept pressure on McKay to reconsider the matter.[197] They reaffirmed their determination immediately after the First Presidency's February statement.[198] Four months later Wilkinson asked Reuben if McKay would agree to meet with these lobbyists again and reopen the deliberations. He replied: "I don't know. The President is failing fast."[199] Despite the strength of his loyalty to the president's decision, Reuben knew how much McKay needed to feel everyone's love and how deeply the criticisms by Rexburg's Latter-day Saints tormented him.

In this regard, Reuben and his like-minded associates harbored intense feelings against Rexburg's stake president. Clark said that the leader's behavior "was a slap against the First Presidency."[200] Romney predicted that "because of the extremes to which he had gone [this stake president] would die a very discredited man, and for all practical purposes [be] out of the Church."[201]

President McKay's ability to resist the alternating intimidation and flattery of the Rexburg people lasted another year. When he reversed himself for the last time concerning this "most important matter that he had had to decide as President," he said that his counselors were the real source of the problem:

> He said he had made a mistake when his two counselors (Presidents Richards and Clark) had talked him into announcing that it would be moved to Idaho Falls. He told me that he was home ill at the time they came and obtained his consent. It was apparent to me that he thought he had been imposed upon by his counselors.[202]

When he reported his decision to the Quorum of Twelve on 30 June 1960, McKay said: "All indications favor going to Idaho Falls," yet he felt the school should remain in Rexburg. Henry D. Moyle's response on that occasion reflected the views of all those present:

> I agree with President [of the Twelve, Joseph Fielding] Smith that there is only one course that we can pursue, and that is to sustain you, President McKay, in whatever your inspiration directs you to do, and as far as I am concerned I hope and pray that whatever course is taken[,] that it will bring peace and satisfaction to your soul, and eliminate from you the feelings of uncertainty that you have had about it up to date.[203]

Ricks College remained in Rexburg and Wilkinson remained chancellor of LDS schools. Reuben remained unshaken in his rock-like loyalty to President McKay, whom he respected too much to manipulate or "over-persuade."[204]

Even though Clark saw himself as administratively diminished, relatively good health enabled him to continue his varied activities. He remained a director of church-affiliated corporations and of Equitable Life and Western Pacific. He received an honorary doctor of law degree from BYU in 1952. He published his decades of New Testament research in two volumes, *Our Lord of the Gospels* in 1954 and *Why the King James Version?* in 1956. His speeches at university commencements and general conferences continued to appear in pamphlet form. He gave major addresses before such diverse groups as the American Society of Beet Technologists, the Utah Farm Bureau Federation, and the Utah Cattlemen's Association.[205]

A representative of the church's publishing company, Thomas S.

Monson, who was then in his mid-twenties, consulted frequently with the aged counselor about the publication of *Our Lord of the Gospels.* In one meeting Reuben asked him to read aloud some of the miracles from Luke: "President Clark removed from his pocket a handkerchief and wiped the tears from his eyes. He commented, 'As we grow older, tears come more frequently.'"[206]

As an octogenarian, President Clark continued his energetic contributions to the church's growth. Aside from dedicating chapels and two welfare buildings, he participated in the groundbreaking, cornerstone laying, and dedication of the Los Angeles temple.[207] He remained a dynamic influence in several church councils and general boards.

In 1953 he made a far-sighted proposal to restructure priesthood governance. This was an expansion of his idea twenty years earlier for regional administration of the Welfare Program. He now proposed that the church's increased growth justified a regional priesthood council for total administration. Not until fourteen years later was his proposal implemented by the creation of regional representatives of the Twelve, a fulfillment that President Clark did not live to see.[208]

In November 1958 he wrote to Fred Morris Dearing, his closest associate from his days in the State Department fifty years earlier:

> I feel fortunately for myself, and I hope reasonably so for some others, that my whole life was changed almost a quarter of a century ago since which time my thought and my writing have turned primarily to matters religious. It has been a great thing for me, Fred, to have the course of my thought change. I think it has kept me from falling into some of the incidents of normal old age.[209]

Reuben had been an energetic member of the First Presidency for as long as many members of the church could remember. He continued to awe his associates by the vigor of his mind and body.

Nevertheless, events within the circle of his dearest friends and loved ones had caused him to think increasingly of the ravages of mortality and the impermanence of life. In February 1952 he wrote a melancholy letter to his non-LDS friend A. Helen Morgan describing the events of the previous month. The death of a dear friend's mother was followed a few days later by the death of the friend, Preston D. Richards. Then in a cascade came the deaths of Reuben's sister-in-law, his daughter-in-law's mother, his former bishop, his unborn great-grandchild through miscarriage, and his "very dear friend" Joseph F. Merrill of the Twelve. Six months later another granddaughter was partially paralyzed by polio.[210]

Reuben also noticed that with each birthday in his eighties the celebrations were increasingly more dramatic as if in anticipation of his passing. This was particularly true on his eighty-fourth birthday in 1955. He was feted by a special equestrian show at the Salt Lake County Fairgrounds and given this eulogistic tribute by Apostle Lee as the inscription for an oil portrait:

> In him are superbly blended a quality of faith which transcends reason, an indomitable courage of decision no matter the odds, a high sense of honor and devotion to duty, a keenness of perception which approaches spiritual seership, an intellect to challenge the converse of the mightiest, and yet a tenderness in his nature which prompts a genuine consideration and sorrow for the unfortunate as though their afflictions were his own.[211]

His associates and family would begin to notice with disappointment that he was starting to give in to a sentiment he expressed two years earlier, "I am, unfortunately, reaching the place where all of my future is behind me."[212] They inadvertently contributed to this conclusion by their fervently expressed living eulogies and appreciations that he was still alive. However, with typically sardonic humor, Reuben told his friends, "Give me a little more taffy while I am with you, and a little less epitaphy when I am gone."[213]

In 1956 his family were understandably upset when he fell in the shower while visiting with stake president Howard W. Hunter in California. This resulted in a broken rib and a cut on his forehead.[214] The accident was the first sign of unsteadiness in his legs which would eventually put him in a wheelchair.

The melancholy undercurrent in his last decade of life was also partly the result of his odd-man-out relationship in the McKay presidency. Without mentioning his feelings about his lessened status, Reuben told a secretary in the First Presidency's office that he enjoyed the personal associations there but that his position was one of "the accidents of life." He added in this letter to LaRue Sneff, "I think there are few duties which will count for much in the Hereafter."[215] He undoubtedly expected to die as second counselor. But the year 1959 brought unexpected changes.

President Richards had been periodically ill with coronary ailments, and his sudden death in May 1959 created a vacancy in the presidency. His death devastated David O. McKay, with whom he shared "a David-and-Jonathan friendship."[216] On 20 May, McKay wrote: "The regular meeting of the First Presidency—*the first without my dear friend, companion, and advisor*—President Stephen L. I could not believe that he had gone, and kept looking for him to come in" (emphasis in original).[217]

Aside from its personal dimension, the first counselor's death had an important effect on the McKay administration. Wilkinson wrote:

> President Richards has been a great strength in the Presidency of the Church and will be missed sorely by President McKay who relied completely on him. He undoubtedly had more influence under President McKay's administration than any other man save President McKay himself and he was responsible for many of the decisions of President McKay.[218]

McKay and Richards had usually been of a different mind from Counselor Clark, but now the prospects were very different.

Gibbons noted, "Although there was great need for the vacancy to be filled promptly, President McKay, mourning the loss of his friend, did not act for more than three weeks."[219] As he surveyed the Quorum of Twelve for a possible replacement, he confronted the Clark-men reality. The six senior members of the Twelve were either Reuben's acknowledged protégés or were closer to his philosophy than they were to the church president's. In addition, President McKay had justified demoting Reuben by appointing a counselor with more seniority. But to apply the seniority argument in 1959, he would have to call Joseph Fielding Smith as first counselor. They had almost as many personal and philosophical differences as McKay and Clark. (See chapter 7.)

On 12 June, McKay responded to the need by calling Reuben as his first counselor and Henry D. Moyle as his second. Apostle Lee thought it was "almost too good to be true" for Reuben to be elevated to his former position and one of his acknowledged protégés to be made second counselor.[220]

However, there were elements in the situation that foreshadowed future difficulties. McKay asked Moyle to be second counselor without consulting Clark, whom he informed after the fact.[221] More important, for the past several years, Moyle, a Democrat and fiscal liberal, had increasingly manifested support for expansive church expenditures advocated by President McKay and opposed by Clark.[222] Nevertheless, Reuben and his close associates rejoiced in the developments of June 1959.

Whereas Reuben had muted his unhappiness when he was demoted, he made no effort to conceal his happiness now that the situation was reversed. He frequently told others that his reappointment in 1959 was a "promotion."[223] He told the MIA conference in June: "President McKay has appointed me again as a First Counselor in the Presidency of the Church. I am grateful beyond expression for the confidence that implies, grateful for the respect, also, and for the affection which I am sure lay behind it." He left it to his listeners and to readers of the *Church News* to draw their own conclusions about the inverse implication of his previous demotion.[224]

Although he had lived long enough to resume the office of first counselor, that same year marked the steady deterioration of his health. Throughout the early 1950s, he had been troubled with frequent colds and flu, and from January to March 1959, he was at home with illness.[225] For six weeks in July-August, he was again nearly incapacitated at home with what his physician allowed him to believe was "nerves and fatigue and also edema."[226] The doctor confided to others "that most of his heart had gone and he gave him only another year."[227] In November, Reuben had another relapse caused by thrombosis. Four months later he had a brief case of Bell's Palsy on the left side of his face.[228] His physician, family, and friends concealed from him their fear that he could die at any time. This succeeded in uplifting his evaluation of his general health.

There was one ailment that no one could conceal from him and which ultimately eroded Reuben's will to live. Increasingly his legs were unable to support his large frame and body weight. Although he maintained a lifelong enjoyment of such delicacies as pecans, gorgonzola cheese, and lobster Newburg,[229] he had struggled since the age of thirty to avoid obesity. He ate moderately, skipped breakfast altogether, and sometimes missed lunch as well only to find himself gaining more weight.[230]

As early as 1957, the combination of his great weight, arthritis, and other weaknesses incident to old age created such difficulty in walking that he installed a small elevator in his home.[231] By June 1959 he could not walk up steps without assistance,[232] and in November could "hardly stand" at all.[233] This weakness soon extended to other extremities: "My fingers are becoming all thumbs so I have difficulty sometimes dressing myself in the morning."[234]

For a man accustomed to good health and bearing others' burdens, his physical decline caused him to become morose. His traditionally good-natured, humorous comments about himself were now bitingly gloomy: "Today I called the telephone company ... I was curious what the fellow on the other end looked like and whether he was as ugly as I am."[235]

His physical misery and wounded pride spilled over into relationships. At a meeting of BYU's board of trustees in June 1959, "Brother [Clyde] Sandgren went over to point out to him the place on the agenda at which we had arrive[d], but President Clark, with his independence, pushed Brother Sandgren away, stating, 'I can find it myself. I don't need any help.'"[236] Beginning in November, Apostle Romney observed that Reuben was increasingly "testy," "sharp and firm" with his closest associates.[237] Shortly afterward he began telling others that U.S. Secretary of Agriculture Ezra Taft Benson "was doing more to destroy the small farmer than anyone else had done."[238] Apostle Benson regarded Clark as his political mentor "and close friend."[239]

The recently reappointed first counselor also had little confidence in the accelerated baptism program that his protégé Moyle was promoting. Reuben warned that "we should not become too engrossed in the number of baptisms to the expense of actual conversions."[240] Apostle and future president Kimball said that Clark was opposed to the "kiddie baptism program" as it existed in England, Scotland, North and South Carolina, the Gulf States, and elsewhere from 1959 onward. But his cousin, he said, was weak in health and influence and therefore unable to stop the mass baptisms of youths promoted by Counselor Moyle.[241]

In addition to their disagreements about church finances and rapid baptisms, Moyle acquiesced in denying his former mentor the opportunity to continue functioning as an elder statesmen in the First Presidency. Reuben's secretary, Rowena Miller, pointedly noted in November 1959 that "Pres. Clark was not invited to go with them" when presidents McKay and Moyle met with the Czech ambassador.[242] By contrast, eight months later Elder Romney sought his mentor's advice "about how I should deal with the Chilean Ambassador."[243]

Various tensions with the second counselor served as the background for Reuben's speech in March 1960 to a meeting of mission presidents. President Moyle presided over the church's missionary program. He told them that Moyle "was kind enough to feel it would not be amiss, [if I spoke]—I think he had in his mind[—]if I said the right things."[244] That was Reuben's trademark humor, now with a cutting edge. Six months later, two of his like-minded associates in the Twelve, Joseph Fielding Smith and Harold B. Lee, openly criticized Moyle's "accelerated missionary program," saying that "baptisms were being made so fast that conversions would not be permanent."[245]

Meeting with the Twelve in June 1960, the ailing counselor irritably criticized Elder Lee for not visiting him at home. Lee replied that he hadn't been asked to stop by. Reuben shouted, "I don't have to ask you!" Lee wrote that "Pres. Clark's outburst of temper" had "marred" this otherwise "pleasant meeting in the temple."[246]

Reuben missed the opening sessions of October 1960 conference because of his difficulty in walking. He wept openly for the first time in the presence of David O. McKay.[247] When he attended the morning session of 9 October and took faltering steps to the pulpit with the aid of President McKay, "the people were breathless." He gave what would be his last public sermon.[248] Sandwiched between humorous comments about his physical decline, President Clark declared, "I renew to you this morning the testimony I have given to you for over a quarter of a century, I believe [at] every conference, a testimony that God lives, that Jesus is his

Son and is the Christ, a testimony that the Father and the Son appeared to the Prophet."[249]

From this time forward, Reuben attended no public meetings. He went to fewer and fewer of the regular First Presidency meetings and temple meetings with the Twelve. He became dependent on his daughter Louise, his friend Gordon Affleck, and Secretary Reiser to push his wheelchair when he left home.

He shed tears again in meeting with Apostle Romney, who observed on 27 October, "He feels like he's unwanted and useless."[250] The next day Apostle Lee wrote that he "is still in a very depressed state and has apparently ruled himself out of much future activity. He seems obsessed by the idea that a man in his 90th year has nothing to which he can look forward."[251] Reuben restated this whenever Lee visited him.[252] When elders Lee, Moyle, and Romney visited his home to discuss Welfare Program matters, they found he was interested only in arranging for his funeral, death bequests, and biography.[253]

His gloom about his own condition began to be mirrored in an almost unrelenting pessimism about the condition of the church. In meetings of the board of education, he accused President Wilkinson of being "money mad," and he opposed any expansion of the BYU campus because it might be destroyed in warfare.[254] He likewise opposed the expanding financial expenditures, the explosive growth of the building program, and the banking and investment policies approved by President McKay and second counselor Moyle. He called these "dangerous trends" and a "critical condition."[255]

Occasionally, Reuben was the lone dissenting vote in administrative meetings. At these times "President McKay simply asked for another vote to make it unanimous." Then "President Clark voted in the affirmative." Because he was "too negative on too many matters," the church president ignored "much of his advice."[256]

Reuben often said he was grateful that he never became a senator during the New Deal years as he had once hoped. "His views would have been so out of date with the prevailing philosophy that he would have been known as a common scold" and would have become "an unheeded nuisance."[257] Sadly this is how he regarded his last years as a member of the First Presidency.

President McKay always had difficulty coping with Reuben's contrary views. Clark's frequent absences from presidency meetings after 1959 allowed the church president greater ability in excluding his dissenting counselor from decision making. This exclusion was nearly total during the remaining years of the reinstated counselor. "I don't have any influence in the Church any more," he told non-LDS governor J. Bracken Lee.[258] In retrospect, First Presidency counselor Hugh B. Brown observed:

> Well, he was being severely tried by the fact that the President was making a number of decisions without referring to him in any way, and that hurt him. He felt that his advice, his counsel should have been sought. Not always followed but at least considered.[259]

He had always included McKay in the decision-making process during the years when McKay was second counselor and absent from the office due to illness. Reuben felt crushed that similar consideration was not extended to him.

He never understood that it was as painful for McKay to receive his emphatic dissent as it was for Reuben to be denied the opportunity to express it. BYU's president wrote that McKay "smilingly approved" when Wilkinson referred to President Clark as one of the church's "calamity howlers" and that McKay in October 1960 "complimented me for resisting his counselors."[260] By November 1960 Apostle Lee observed that Reuben was brooding "over matters about which he is not kept too well informed."[261] Nevertheless, when President and Sister McKay visited the counselor at home two weeks later, "he seemed very appreciative of our call."[262]

In January 1961 Reuben referred disparagingly to "the diarrhetic effusions from my mouth and from my pen." He informed U.S. Senator Wallace F. Bennett, "I have thus far refrained from authorizing anybody to publish [a collection of] my so-called addresses or speeches or talks, thinking that they were better to be left until after I am laid away." This was in response to Elder Benson's suggestion that he publish them.[263] The caustic self-description was symptomatic of Reuben's mood at this time, but for years he had rejected every suggestion that he publish an anthology of his talks.[264]

In February he wrote, "The difference between ripened-age and rotten age is pretty narrow."[265] By then, he had to be "carried by chair up the steps to the Church offices when he is able to come, and also up the steps of the Temple when he is able to attend the Thursday meetings."[266] In April he told the meeting of the First Presidency and apostles that "we surely would not know what he was going through and that he was not praying for continuation of [his] life."[267] Two weeks later he told them: "Brethren, I am still able to crawl around ... It is hard to have led the life I have led in activity in various positions, and then to have to give all that up."[268]

As Affleck and Reiser pushed his wheelchair, he often told them: "Old age is a sonofabitch!" He even said this to a young man he had just met in the Church Administration Building.[269]

By May, Reuben seemed to wonder if he would be forgotten by people generally. He wrote that he was "irritated today" after talking in the First Presidency's office with some visitors who "met an old man that they did not know anything about."[270] A week later BYU's president visited him at home and commented, "From my contacts with him it is quite obvious that he is not being consulted on current Church policy."[271]

Reuben was so unhappy about his physical condition and his virtual exclusion from decision making that he exerted himself to attend a meeting of the First Presidency on 14 June for the express purpose of offering his resignation. Despite their many differences, President McKay would not even consider such an action:

> Let me tell you, you are not going to be relieved of your position. We are going to call in another man to do work that we need done, but we are not going to release you of any position. You are the first counselor in the First Presidency, and you will remain that, so you need not be worried. We shall call in the necessary help. The Lord bless you! The work will go on, and you come whenever you can. There is no embarrassment to us.

Undeterred by these supportive words, Reuben replied, "You do whatever you think best, and if that means relieving me, it will be all right."[272] The next day he told the temple council meeting with the apostles that "he had nothing special to report. He said he was sitting around considerably," then added that "idleness is not happiness."[273] On 22 June he renewed his offer to be released and then burst into tears when President McKay again reassured him that he wanted him to remain as counselor.[274]

The man President McKay chose to take up the slack in Reuben's absence was Hugh B. Brown. A member of the Twelve since 1958, he was coincidentally the general authority who spoke immediately after Clark's last public sermon at the 1960 conference.[275] On 22 June 1961 McKay announced to the apostles that he was calling Elder Brown as a special counselor. Apostles Lee and Brown immediately went to the Clark home where Reuben "wept like the dickens." Nevertheless, he reassured Brown that his appointment was in accord with Clark's own advice to President McKay.[276] Now Reuben was functionally, though not officially, replaced in the First Presidency.

For Reuben, the remaining three months of his life were simply a burdensome wait for the release of death. By July he was forgetful, morose, listless, and nearly non-communicative. Early in the month, Apostle Romney visited him and observed: "He sits in his study in his parlor alone most of the time. It is a sad thing to see him and talk to him—a man of mighty power intellectually and spiritually, gradually breaking down." Two weeks later Romney commented: "He seemed very depressed; his mind wandered considerably. I tried half a dozen approaches, but couldn't get him interested in any subject. He didn't care to make more than a comment or two on any of them. He was not interested in what I had to say."[277] Elders Lee, Romney, Moyle, Smith, and Petersen, and friend Affleck, among other close associates, visited President Clark at home and periodically administered priesthood blessings to him.[278] His family, friends, and colleagues, including President McKay, celebrated with him a quiet ninetieth birthday.[279]

His life was in its ebbtide when the church was moving forward to its general conference. One of the last visits by a church authority was that of David O. McKay on 23 September to discuss upcoming business connected with the conference.

His devoted daughter, Louise (Mrs. Mervyn Bennion) answered the door and took me to President Clark who was in his wheelchair with a shawl around his shoulders. With tears in his eyes he listened to the matters that I presented to him, and gave his approval of the proposals made. I could see that it would be impossible for him to be with us at our Conference meetings. This was my last conference with him in this mortal life. He did not pay much attention to the details. He said, "Whatever you Brethren have decided, I approve."

We went back even to our schooldays. We remembered that he and Sister McKay graduated together from the University of Utah. ...

President Clark was very emotional as he recalled the schooldays, and particularly the 27 years that we have stood shoulder to shoulder in the First Presidency. We caressed and bade each other goodbye. I left the house with a heavy heart. ...[280]

It was a conclusion of quiet drama for an unparalleled personal and administrative association. The elder statesman and the gentle philosopher had come to final terms. Three days later Reuben was incapacitated by a stroke from which he never recovered. This prevented his receiving other visitors who wished to share farewells.[281]

His name was presented for the sustaining vote of the church membership at conference for the last time. His daughter Luacine "telephoned President McKay on behalf of the family and expressed their gratitude for his kindness in not replacing President Clark."[282]

Reuben died peacefully in the early afternoon of 6 October 1961. It came as he had expressed in the poem "When I Would Pass."

> When the light on the eastern cliffs
> Sweeps upward to be lost in dusk
> And the rich glow of living amethyst
> Fades into the steel grey
> Of twilight, and then darkness, the realm
> Where day dies and fecund dawn is born,
> The herald of the sun-lit day to come,—
> Then I would pass,
> Silently, in peace.[283]

Whether by youth or recent conversion, more than half of the 1.8 million Latter-day Saints throughout the world in 1961 had no recollection of a First Presidency without J. Reuben Clark.[284] In one way or another, his influence touched every LDS leader who was then living. Among the immediate reactions to his death, perhaps the most appropriate was that of Marion G. Romney: "For him it is a relief and a release from frustration. He has been a mighty man, a great 'Prophet Statesman.' Surely he has gone to a great reward."[285]

CHAPTER 6.

Ministering to the Saints[1]

MOST OF J. REUBEN CLARK'S CHURCH SERVICE INVOLVED PUBLIC speaking and high-level administration. He tended to keep himself aloof from the intensive personal ministry of local officers. As a counselor in the First Presidency, "I felt myself that the problems of the Church were sufficient to absorb our energies, and that the individual problems ought to be left for others." This was a logical and prudent use of time and energy, but he also felt a responsibility "to work for others, to give to others, to relive human suffering, to keep people as reasonably happy as we can."[2] Although he tried to fulfill that service primarily as an exponent and administrator, he also extended himself in a limited ministry.

He received the office of Seventy when he was eighteen but never regarded himself as a successful missionary.[3] First, he never served a full-time mission. Second, as a civil servant he avoided imposing religious discussions on non-Mormons among whom he lived and worked. He was content to allow his Mormon identity and ethical living to accomplish a work of passive proselytizing. He seldom brought up religion but did not hesitate to answer inquiries from non-Mormon friends about LDS beliefs.

When orchestra maestro Leopold Stokowski visited Mexico City in 1931, he asked Ambassador Clark to explain the basis of Mormonism. Stokowski later remarked, "I am not a religious man, I am a musician, yet the religious ideas expressed to me by Mr. Clark appealed to me as being eminently good, beautiful and true."[4]

Never a forceful missionary, Reuben more actively promoted LDS teachings among his non-Mormon friends after he became a general authority. While in Buenos Aires, he performed his "first baptism" on 5 September 1936 for a "brother-in-law of Richard Evans." Fifteen years later, he noted that the man was an active LDS member living in Chicago. Still, Reuben did not consider his first baptism to be a conversion story. He had merely performed the ordinance without having taught the gospel to this person.[5]

Reuben's infrequent efforts at proselytizing individuals were nonetheless impressive. To Reeve Schley, an Episcopalian who was vice president of Chase Manhattan National Bank and director of fourteen other major corporations, he wrote in 1941:

> I notice that you [said you] have no thought of joining the Church. On my part I have no thought that I am converting you. I thank you for the compliment to me personally regarding my mode of life.
> I am not sure that I agree with you that "it is scarcely worth while for two busy men to enter into a discussion of theology." I am not sure that if theology be given the field and importance it claims, there is very much else in the world worth a real discussion between two honest men, however busy they may be.

Despite his innocent disclaimer, he then outlined in detail to Schley the LDS gospel and his convictions about it.[6] After entering the First Presidency, he occasionally sent unsolicited copies of the Book of Mormon and other LDS publications to associates in the State Department and the business world. During the last decade of his life, he maintained a regular religious dialogue by mail with Cloyd H. Marvin, president of George Washington University.[7]

Nevertheless, President Clark was as suspicious of overly enthusiastic missionary work as he was of any other enthusiasm. In 1943 someone told him that the canning operations of Salt Lake City's Welfare Square included non-members as a public relations activity to make non-Mormons "feel good toward us." He replied: "We are not here to make people feel good. We are here to do our work and preach the gospel."[8]

Aside from his jaundiced view of public-relations proselytizing, he also opposed superficial conversions. A non-Mormon friend in Salt Lake City wrote in 1948 that his children wanted him to join the church, that he had attended services with them, had grown fond of the ward's bishop, had met several times with missionaries, had read "a good deal" of the Book of Mormon, but had not decided whether he should join. Reuben's reply was immediate:

> Do not join our Church merely to please your son. Do not join un-less you have what we call a testimony, which is a burning realization that Joseph Smith was a prophet, that through him the Lord restored the Gos-pel and His Priesthood, and that this work was divinely set up and is di-vinely led. If you were to join on any other basis than this, unhappiness would be your lot, and things probably would arise which would result in your separation from the Church, which would be unsatisfactory for you and for us.[9]

The man's letter could have been a "golden opportunity" to urge him to follow his inclinations and join the church. But even the prospect of a ready convert could not quench Reuben's lifelong disdain for emotional-ism and quick decisions.

Nine years later he wrote mission president D. Arthur Haycock, "With reference to the chart which you enclosed, I wish to congratulate you upon the tremendous growth you have made in your baptisms." He added: "I hope your conversions at least approximate your baptisms. Little side reports that drift into me indicate that that is not always the fact in the missions."[10] To Reuben, a sharp growth in convert baptisms was cause for scrutiny, not celebration. For that reason, he opposed the accelerated "baseball baptisms" that his former protégé Henry D. Moyle promoted worldwide during the last two years of Reuben's life.[11]

Until he was seventy-six years old, Reuben was convinced that his own missionary efforts had utterly failed. However, during October 1947 conference, a young married woman from California surprised him by saying she converted after reading some of his published explanations of

LDS teachings. He replied that she was his "first and only convert, then."[12] A few years later, he "was utterly amazed" to learn that a married couple converted after hearing him explain LDS tenets to a gathering of newspaper journalists. His missionary efforts had been so passive most of his life and so selective later that he told a missionary meeting in 1956, "In spite of that kind of missionary labor (President McKay, I might as well unburden the whole thing here)—I have at least three converts to my credit, who came in and told me so."[13]

Although he never claimed he had the gift of healing, and, in fact, was suspicious of anyone claiming such a gift, he frequently demonstrated faith in the potential to invoke God's healing through priesthood administrations. In the mid-1920s, a young couple moved into the Salt Lake Twentieth Ward where Reuben taught the Gospel Doctrine class. The young man became ill and his wife asked Reuben to administer to him. After doing so, he took the woman aside "and told her to get a doctor as soon as she could, that her husband had a bad case of appendicitis." Even though the attending physician had no clear diagnosis of the young man's difficulty, the couple went to the hospital for tests, where it was determined that the man did have appendicitis. The doctor who performed the emergency surgery "said he ought to be dead, but he recovered."[14] On another occasion, President Clark administered to a young woman who had Hodgkin's disease and was pregnant with her first child. Her physicians had told her she could not survive this childbirth. He later commented: "The Lord listened to our prayers on that occasion when I administered to her, and she has not only had a child but several others, her family now numbers nine. Again I say, the Lord can do wonders."[15] Moreover, Apostle Spencer W. Kimball described it as "a miracle" when Reuben administered to him for his loss of speech which was restored to him immediately after the blessing.[16]

In some instances he administered for the peaceful release of the dying, not to heal them. On 25 July 1939 he and Heber J. Grant visited Apostle Melvin J. Ballard who had leukemia and brain hemorrhages. Reuben wrote: "Sister Ballard sent out word that she would like Brother Grant to dedicate him to the Lord. As we walked in, Brother Grant said he could not do it, and asked me to officiate." Grant explained: "I do not think he recognized us. His eyes glared, and I felt that I just could not utter a prayer dedicating him to the Lord. He is the first man that I nominated to be an apostle, and I asked Brother Clark to comply with the request of the family." Reuben wrote: "I asked the Lord that if his time had come and he was to pass on, that he be taken in peace and not have to suffer and struggle. I did not dedicate him to the Lord." President Grant concluded, "I was impressed by his putting a good, strong *if* in his prayer."[17] Elder Ballard died five days later.[18]

Twenty years later President Clark told a general priesthood meeting that in administering to the sick or when making any request in prayer, everyone should pray "even as Christ prayed in the Garden," saying, "Nevertheless, not my will, but thine be done."[19] For example, in administering to Apostle Harold B. Lee's father, Reuben "blessed him to get well, unless his time had come to go." Samuel M. Lee died two days later.[20]

Reuben merged rationality with faith as he performed the healing ordinance. Marion G. Romney wrote in his diary: "He gave Ida a blessing. It was an extraordinary blessing, calm, sure, appropriate, comforting. He has a great mind, well-trained, perfect faith, and great strength."[21]

As he spoke with people about priesthood administrations, he absolutely refused to let them think the healing occurred because he was the one performing the ceremony. "I want you to understand this," he told the wife of a general authority as he was about to administer to her, "that in and of myself I have no power to heal you, but I have faith that the Lord can do it and we will ask the Lord to bless you."[22] A woman came to him for a blessing because he was a member of the First Presidency, even though she had received an administration from Elder LeGrand Richards of the Twelve. Reuben quietly observed that "there was no more spiritual man than Brother Richards."[23]

Clark's frequent counsel to accept the will of the Lord in physical difficulties met a severe test during the polio epidemic of 1952. A member of his own family was stricken with that disease, but he stated to the priesthood session of October conference that year:

> When physicians tell you that little can be done, that they know nothing about the disease, I tell you, you fall back awfully fast on the

Lord, in humility, [and] having lived reasonably righteously, the Lord will hear us. ... then, it being his will and in his wisdom, he gives us the blessings we ask for, for ourselves and for our loved ones.

Then in a spontaneous expression of compassion, President Clark told the conference he had learned that the son of Tabernacle organist Roy M. Darley had contracted polio. Reuben prayed, "May the Lord bless and heal his little one." He later learned that the child had a high fever up until the time of the priesthood meeting, after which the boy's temperature returned to normal.[24]

Reuben felt special compassion for Latter-day Saints when death came to their loved ones despite priesthood administrations, despite promises of patriarchal blessings for long life, and despite the youth and potential of the deceased. He once wrote a two-page, single-spaced, typed letter to a grieving widow who could not understand the precipitous deaths of her husband and his brother:

> Personally, I am not sure that the time of our going, certainly if our lives are righteous, is of any particular importance in the Great Plan, or to the individual, nor is the manner of our going of any importance; it may be by disease, long and lingering, by tragic suffering to the one passing and to his loved one; it may be by sudden failure of the heart, or a blood clot in the brain, or it may be by accident. The method makes little difference. ...
>
> It is my prayer that the Lord will bless you and give you a surcease to worrying and pondering about matters concerning which the Lord has given us no distinct revelation, and that you may be able to travel forward in faith, relying on the Lord's kindness, mercy, and justice.[25]

He was not simply stating platitudes, a practice alien to his very nature, but expressed his deepest convictions. He had suffered through the deaths— lingering and precipitous—of his parents, his brother, sisters, wife, son-in-law, and many other loved ones. "Why is a good man taken and an evil one left? This is an inscrutable problem," he wrote to Romania Hyde Woolley.[26] He told non-LDS friends that he found comfort in the gospel of Jesus Christ that "makes things bearable."[27]

Knowing the grief of death in his own experience, he could not take

lightly the grief of others. When Apostle George F. Richards grew faint
the day after his wife's funeral in 1946, Reuben embraced him.[28] When a
young man was killed in a freak accident at the Hotel Utah in 1949, he
looked up the young man's membership record so that he could ask the
ward bishop to comfort the fellow's parents.[29] To the widow of his LDS
associate William E. Ryberg, he wrote in 1950: "I hope you will allow me
to express to you my deepest sympathy for the great loss and resulting sorrow which has come to you. I know the burden you bear and the grief
that afflicts you, for I, too, have endured."[30] When some young girls were
killed by lightning during an outing in Idaho in 1951, he suggested that
the general presidency of the Young Women's organization send flowers
and a personal letter of condolence to each of the parents.[31]

In June 1952 an automobile struck a little girl in front of the Salt Lake
Twentieth Ward chapel where President Clark was attending an evening
meeting. Dressed in a white summer suit, he rushed to the scene of the accident and took "that little, bleeding child into his arms" until medical assistance arrived.[32]

He became accustomed to giving religious counsel about sickness
and death, but his limited experience in church administration often left
him unprepared for other realities. In July 1933 he had his first experience
with what he called "religious cranks." A man sent him the "word of the
Lord" which condemned him for being "a man of the world, and not of
the Holy Priesthood," and "disfellowshipped" him for not resigning from
the First Presidency.[33] In 1938 a man congratulated Reuben on his conference talk, then asked for "five thousand Dollars to finance a book's
publication exposing crime which is synonymous with sin."[34] The pa-
thetic instability of such people cropped up in another letter: "You
wouldn't want to see me in an insane asylum, would you?" the Mormon
exclaimed, then asked Reuben to tell two men to go to hell and concluded with a request for $12,000.[35]

Even Mormons who were mentally stable could make bizarre requests. In 1945 a woman telephoned "to ask whether or not it were wise
to invest in real estate." On this same day, a man visited Reuben's office to
ask whether to sell a house. During the next several years, LDS men and
women pestered him with similar questions about their personal finances.

Remarkably, he took time to counsel with them: "We talked various investments, but I gave no advice."[36] One woman asked President Clark to help complete her income tax forms.[37] Another visited the presidency's office in 1949 to learn how to patent and sell "a sanitary toilet seat cover she had invented." On the same day as that visit, a BYU sophomore asked Reuben if he should transfer to the University of Utah.[38]

While he patiently allowed church members to impose on his time with odd requests, he showed little patience for rank-and-file Mormons who tried to give him advice about LDS policy. To one member whom he labeled a "crank," Reuben wrote, "I never knew a section hand who did not know better how to run the railroad than the railroad president knew how to run it."[39] He replied with equal sarcasm when George H. Brimhall Jr. attempted to instruct him about the operation of old age pensions, which Reuben had publicly condemned. (See chapter 12.) He did not tell these letter-writers that prior to becoming a general authority, he himself had mailed unsolicited advice to the LDS president, who likewise disregarded it.

Reuben grew to resent such demands on his time. He strongly urged other general authorities to spend less time counseling. To Apostle Kimball, he wrote, "I may be all wrong about this—but I do not conceive that trying to straighten up the petty difficulties of petty people, not always 'with all their buttons,' as people now say, is a primary duty for the Church."[40]

Nevertheless, Reuben hesitated to turn away anyone who came for counsel. In 1951 a man went to him for advice about business affairs:

> Pres. Clark said that he could not come to one of the Brethren with the thought that they had revelations for people who want advice; the Lord can do it and sometimes He does do it, but generally he gives us our free agency to work out our own affairs, that he would be glad to talk to him, but he was a poor man to come to, [and] had had no real experience in business affairs.

The man still persisted in asking for Reuben's advice.[41]

Nor would Reuben indicate impatience over the time consumed by such interviews. It was not uncommon for him to spend forty-five minutes or longer with someone who sought a listening ear.[42] In view of his private feelings against the hierarchy's involvement in such counseling, this was extraordinary. But it was an echo of his pre-hierarchy approach in Mexico: "Reserved and yet accessible, the ambassador was ready to talk to anyone."[43]

Although he tended to be a legalist, he took a different approach in ministering to Latter-day Saints. This is best indicated by the blessing he gave his brother Samuel when ordaining him a bishop in 1941:

> We bless you, dear brother, with the spirit of fatherhood, that you may be able to be a father to all the members of your Ward. We bless you that you may be able to put out from your heart every feeling but one of affection and kindness to every man, woman, and child in your Ward.[44]

A decade later he gave similar advice to Thomas S. Monson: "Knowing that I was a newly appointed bishop presiding over a difficult ward, he [President Clark] emphasized the need for me to know my people, to understand their circumstances, and to minister to their needs."[45]

Toward opponents, Reuben could deliver blistering condemnations; to his closest associates in church administration, he could be unnervingly blunt. But in personal counseling, he spoke with restraint, compassion, and the openness of a loving father. To priesthood leaders, he said:

> We always like to try to make a rule and then to fit everything into the rule, and having made one ruling under a given set of circumstances we try to make the same sort of ruling under every other like set of circumstances. Now, brethren, I don't believe you can do that where you are dealing with the spiritual side and that is the most important side in all that we are trying to do.[46]

Throughout his varied experiences in the secular world, Reuben found both complexity and diversity in people's motives, actions, attitudes, abilities, weaknesses, and vulnerabilities. As one of the highest leaders of the church, he felt he could not righteously ignore such diversity among those who struggled to be Saints. "I fear that some of us are going to be greatly surprised," he once wrote, "to see in the Celestial Kingdom a number of people that we would have assigned to a far lesser Kingdom."[47]

Reuben was particularly concerned about the tradition of categorizing lapsed Mormons as "inactive" or "apostate." Although he used these terms himself, he tried to encourage others to recognize that the words described a condition that might not be permanent. "Do not go to them and approach them on the basis that they are lost or on the basis that they are criminal," he warned bishops in 1948.[48]

He told the bishops the following year, "Occasionally you will find in the Church the greatest good coming from putting in [ward positions] men even before they have reformed." He quoted the words of an inactive Mormon when asked to be the new bishop of a ward, "Hell, I do not even know how to pray." Reuben added: "But he did. We all know how to pray. This man became a great bishop."[49]

Some people failed to understand that Reuben was capable of compassion. They saw him only as the statesman, only as the Republican loyalist, only as the vigorous administrator, only as the self-sufficient scholar, only as the legalist and constitutionalist. As Bruce C. Hafen has observed, "For all his tough-mindedness and high standards, J. Reuben Clark's attitudes toward other people were sensitive, humane and the very opposite of elitist."[50]

"President Clark was a kind, thoughtful, generous man and a congenial companion," Elder Romney observed. "I don't know anyone who was more thoughtful of us who worked under his direction. Whenever one of us was absent because of illness, he daily inquired concerning our welfare. He was ever solicitous about our safety as we traveled."[51]

Clark's compassion extended to administrative situations involving those who were far down the chain of command. In 1939 the First Presidency decided to release Joseph S. Peery after long service as a Temple Square tour guide in what was then called the Temple Block Mission. Reuben was troubled about what to say to him and how this release might affect him. The president of the mission "said he was sure it would practically kill Brother Peery to be released." That settled the matter for Reuben. "I said I thought that if it were going to have any such effect upon Brother Peery as Brother [Joseph J.] Cannon suggested, that we ought not to release Brother Peery, as his services had been too great and too devoted to warrant any such procedure." He recommended against even making a suggestion that might disturb "the peace of mind of Brother Peery."[52]

Reuben also wrote letters of encouragement and pleaded for spiritual renewal of other Mormons. He spoke of "more sorrow than I can express to you" to church members who had discarded their testimonies.[53] Even for "apostates" who came to his office with "blasphemous" words and arrogant attitudes, "I tried to talk calmly and kindly but straight-forwardly."[54]

As another example, most "inactives" did not refrain from using coffee, tea, alcohol, and tobacco as required by LDS leaders in the twentieth century.[55] Reuben urged the active Mormons to keep their outward observance in perspective. "I hope I will not be misunderstood," he told the bishops, "for I am a thorough believer in the Word of Wisdom, but I should like to say that the use of tea and coffee and tobacco is not the worst offense in the world."[56] Likewise, with reference to the location of the Word of Wisdom in Section 89 of the Doctrine and Covenants,[57] he criticized "the 89ers—Word of Wisdomers" who made tea, coffee, tobacco, and alcohol more significant than "Lying, Stealing, Cheating, hating, backbiting, character ruining, and defaming [gossip]."[58]

Moreover, he opposed what he regarded as extremist nutritional views. For example, he criticized an unnamed "sister," apparently Leah D. Widtsoe, who had told "the wives of the authorities" at one of their socials that "they should not eat citrus fruits or drink milk." In exasperation, Reuben said that if such talk continued, "pretty soon we would not be eating anything."[59]

He could also be harsh in his public instructions concerning sexual conduct and morality.[60] As early as 1941, he told young men and women that it was "the law of this Church" to prefer to bury a young Latter-day Saint rather than for the youth to be sexually unchaste. The church's newspaper printed this on its front page.[61] In his published remarks to young women in 1946, he said that he did not trust his own daughters, himself, or anyone else in matters of sexuality.[62] In his published remarks to general priesthood meeting in 1949, he warned, "A wise and pure boy or girl, one that wishes to be clean, will not 'pet,' nor 'neck,' nor 'love-play,' nor practice any other undue physical indiscretions."[63] He told bishops in

1950 that it "is not healthy" for a young man and woman to dance together all evening.[64]

As early as 1951, his published remarks to a general priesthood meeting apparently alluded to homosexuality when he criticized men for walking around nude in gymnasiums.[65] By this time he had asked Gordon Affleck to organize a surveillance for possible homosexuals in the steam room of the church-owned Deseret Gymnasium.[66]

In 1952 the *Relief Society Magazine* published President Clark's warning to LDS women against "self-pollution" and "carnal knowledge with beasts." He told them that birth defects occur because "way back beyond the reaches of our memories or our knowledge, some mother or some father committed a wrong which passes down."[67] His daughter Marianne Sharp was the magazine's editor.

At this 1952 meeting of LDS women, he also warned that "homosexuals are today exercising great influence" in American society. He asked these women, "I wonder if you girls have ever reflected on the thought that was in the mind of the man who first began to praise you for your boyish figures."[68] In 1954 he specifically warned males at general conference against "that filthy crime of homosexuality."[69] In 1960 he wrote of a "serious 'homo' situation at B.Y.U.,"[70] reflected in surveys over a twenty-year period which showed that 10 percent of the male students admitted to having homoerotic experiences.[71]

Despite such explicit references to sexual misconduct, Reuben opposed any form of sex education. He told the general priesthood meeting in 1949:

> Parents are grasping at straws in an effort to hold their children. The cry is raised that the Church needs a book on sex. But what should such a book tell? Already the schools have taught sex facts *ad nauseam*. All their teachings have but torn away the modesty that once clothed sex; their discussions tend to make, and sometimes seem to make, sex animals of our boys and girls. The teachings do little but arouse curiosity for experience. It is said these courses tell enough about the generation of human beings to enable the youth, largely, to escape parenthood. Books are written, courses are given about courtship and marriage. To what point? ...
>
> A word on chastity can be given in one sentence, two words: Be

chaste! That tells everything. You do not need to know all the details of the reproductive processes, in order to keep clean. Be chaste because God commanded it. That is all there is to it.[72]

There was one particular philosophy of sex education that he especially condemned in his 1951 address, "the doctrine that the sex urge is like the urge for food and drink, [a teaching that] is born of Satan, and the man or woman who teaches it, is Satan-inspired."[73]

Mormons responded to President Clark's condemnations. A woman who had committed adultery twenty-seven years before, and who had since that time "done nothing but sorrow and repent for her misdeeds," sought his counsel; likewise, a male applicant for church employment "who had committed sexual transgression as a youth."[74]

Reuben spoke so harshly to prevent the chaste from succumbing to temptation. But he also realized that his words might crush the hearts of those who had already committed transgression. In his copy of Gibbon's *Decline and Fall of the Roman Empire,* he penned the following marginal note, "Because in our weakness we cannot live the lofty moral and spiritual life of the gospel is no argument that such a life is not desirable or that it is not the life prescribed by the Master."[75] His use of the word *cannot,* rather than *choose not to,* is significant because throughout his life he wrote private notations with legalistic precision. In this case he seemed to be saying that there are some humans who do not have the ability to reach the lofty standards of the church.

Despite the obligation he felt to condemn sin in the strongest possible terms, he peached the entreaty: "All you repentant transgressors come, partake of God's all-wise divine justice and of his boundless, infinite mercy and love. To transgressors, yet unrepentant, the Lord calls."[76]

Reuben raised a strident voice against sins of all kinds yet spoke healing words privately to transgressors. Concerning a teacher at a church school who had engaged in homosexual intimacy for several years, the man's stake president "enquired about whether he should be handled churchwise [i.e., through disfellowshipment or excommunication, and] I said thus far we had done no more than drop them from positions they held."[77] Visited by a woman who had committed adultery twenty years before but had lived "a good, clean life" since that time, President Clark said: "Where transgression has been in secret, the essential thing is repentance."[78]

To former apostle Richard R. Lyman, who was publicly excommunicated for violating church rules of sexual conduct, President Clark wrote:

> With reference to the other matter to which you refer, it is a consolation to know that however much we who are here may err in our judgment and decisions, nevertheless the Lord knows all and in the Hereafter He will see that all wrongs are righted and all proper restorations accomplished.
>
> My own formula with reference to these matters I have often expressed as follows: I believe that the Lord will bestow upon us all the rewards that it is possible for Him to bestow, having in mind in connection with His infinite mercy and love and charity, the absolute demands of justice. On the other hand, I think that He would impose the least penalty for our errors and misdoings that it is possible to impose, having in mind His love, charity, and forgiveness, that the demands of justice absolutely require.[79]

These words had special significance because, as Lyman assumed, Reuben had made the decision to investigate and discipline him.[80]

A few years later, however, Reuben was simply baffled to learn of the situation in an LDS ward not far from Salt Lake City.

> It appears that the Bishop has been making love to the wife of one of his counselors; that one of his counselors has been making love to the wife of the other counselor, and that the counselor not involved in these two observations has been making love to some third party. None of the men were straight in the situation and the only woman who was straight was the wife of the bishop, who has five children and [is] about to have another.

He did not have a ready answer when the stake president asked what he should do. Ignoring the situation seemed impossible, yet excommunicating the ward's entire bishopric and two of their wives would have a devastating effect on the local members. "I told President P—— that they would have to decide what they wished to do down there, and I said they must have in mind the effect which the situation would have on the young people of the ward, that that was the prime consideration."[81]

In matters of legal justice, Reuben could also urge the broadest leniency. He once petitioned the chief of the Los Angeles Probation Department to grant probation to a Latter-day Saint convicted of perjury. Even though the man had taken "no active part in Church work, he has always been a man of profound religious convictions" and had been a devoted husband and father.[82]

Concerning suicide, President Clark said "that the idea was to be as comforting to the family as possible, [which] in cases of suicide had double grief." He authorized LDS funerals for suicides, including burial in temple clothes, "on the theory that no person in his right mind would commit suicide, and as he was not in his right mind there was no crime involved."[83] He kept in mind the legal dimensions of justice, but always reminded himself and others not to lose sight of the human dimensions of compassion.

He sometimes commented publicly on the relationships between the male-only priesthood of the church and its women's auxiliary, the Relief Society. He instructed local bishops in 1947:

> I want to say a word about the Relief Society. Most of you brethren, I am sure, are married, and if your homes are happy ones, as I assume they are, you know that your wives expect some kind of consideration. If she has earned a little money ... [she] should not relish the idea of your going into her purse and taking her money and using it for some expense of your own. It will not work, as probably some of us have found.
>
> Now the Relief Society Presidency and the Relief Society [members] are the mothers of the Ward. I have heard of cases where the Relief Society had considerable money—a lot of money for the Relief Society (I heard of one case where the Relief Society of a Ward had $1,000), and when the Bishop started to build a meeting house he went and took the $1,000.00. Now the meeting house is your business, Bishops, and I suggest you try to get the money some other way than by appropriating it,—I could call it by some other names (laughter) [from the audience], than by appropriating the Relief Society funds.
>
> My home has been a Relief Society home all of my life, and I know something of the work that is entailed and done by the Relief Society in

trying to get a little money. Now they ought to help [you], and they will help. I am amazed at the way the Relief Society has harkened to the brethren of the priesthood. If we thought as much of the priesthood as most of our sisters do, it would be a better world. Let us not impose upon them.[84]

Throughout Reuben's life, the Relief Society of each ward or branch collected, maintained, and expended its own funds independently. When Apostle Lee entered the First Presidency a decade after his mentor's death, he ended the financial independence of the women's organization.[85] Beginning in 1946, the two men had sharply disagreed about what Elder Lee called "the old traditional Relief Society aloofness."[86]

President Clark also took frequent opportunity to give counsel about marriage. To the anxious mother of a young girl who wanted to marry a non-Mormon, he reminisced about his own worries that his daughters might marry a non-Mormon. He added:

> Quite obviously, measures of force are out of the question, even if they were wise, and they usually are not. If you could get her to put off her marriage for a period, then get her back into active Church work, it might make your problem easier.[87]

When an LDS woman asked if she would be guilty of sin by marrying outside the church, he replied, "There is no sin in honorable marriage," and reminded her that the basis of a happy marriage should be mutual love. He added that converting her intended husband to the church would contribute to their happiness.[88]

He extended this emphasis on love and honorable marriage to the question of whether first cousins should marry. Although Utah law prohibited such marriages in the twentieth century as incest, several general authorities had married first cousins during the nineteenth century and had fathered children with these wives. For example, Presidents Brigham Young, Lorenzo Snow, and Joseph F. Smith had married first cousins.[89]

In 1941 Reuben wrote to a woman in Provo:

> Your letter of the first of June came to me this morning, in which you ask certain questions concerning the marriage of cousins, the

question arising because of the fact that your daughter wishes to marry her cousin.

There is no rule of the Church against the marriage of cousins. The State of Utah does not permit first cousins to marry. I am advised that the law of California does permit them to marry. I know of cases where cousins have gone to California to marry.

After couples have been legally married, they may then be sealed in the Temple for eternity, even though they be cousins.

On the question as to the wisdom biologically of cousins marrying, I offer no suggestions. In olden times marriage of far closer relationships than that took place. It is my understanding that for many, many generations, indeed for thousands of years, the Jews have married cousins. It would seem to me that the questions must be answered by the parties themselves.

I am sure that you will upon reflection agree with me that to advise any couple (free from disease and who are mentally normal) not to have children after marriage is a very serious matter.[90]

And that is where Reuben ended this letter, signing it "Faithfully yours." He obviously rejected the option of asking married cousins not to have children. The first cousins in this case followed his not-too-subtle advice on how to circumvent Utah's law against incest. They traveled to California for a civil marriage, "were later sealed in the Salt Lake Temple," and had three children.[91]

His reference to marriages between relatives closer than first cousin may indicate that he had seen the First Presidency's nineteenth-century minutes and correspondence about this matter. Brigham Young authorized his secretary, George D. Watt, to marry Watt's half-sister, and this brother-sister couple had three children.[92]

In 1947 another young couple visited President Clark in Grantsville to ask that he perform their marriage. The young woman toured his home, verbally admired its construction and conveniences, and told her fiancé how nice it would be for them to have such a home. After listening to her tell the young man how she expected things to be, Reuben interjected: "Sister, I have been seventy-five years building this home. Don't you expect this young man of yours to build it for you next year."[93]

Reuben stressed the necessity for consideration and equality within a marriage. He expressed this humorously to an audience of young people when he praised LDS women: "When we are by ourselves, we men admit that we are not good without them. (laughter) We do not dare admit that before them because they know it already."[94] To a relative, Reuben expressed his earnest convictions about domination of a marriage partner:

> In the first place, there will not be happiness in any household, true happiness, if there be not love, true love, accompanied by trust and consideration and courtesy. ...
>
> In the next place, there cannot be true happiness nor peace nor the Spirit that should be in a home where either the man or the woman assumes or tries to assume a dominant spirit to the point that what the dominant party wants is always right, no matter what it is, which, of course, means that the dominant party assumes [that] what I will call the entire household wisdom resides in the dominant party. That is almost never true.[95]

Beyond his private counsel, he publicly advised LDS men to respect the dignity and rights of their wives.[96]

Yet he had little enthusiasm for those who bemoaned the second-class status of women and who urged measures for "greater equality" for women. When a young unmarried man expressed dissatisfaction to him about the inequality of women's position in the home, "Pres. Clark rather smiled and said he would find out after he was married more about this 'inequality.'"[97]

When a new bride wrote about her employment, civic activities, and her career plans, Reuben wrote an immediate reply of "deep anxiety." He said: "I, of course, come from a very old vintage, where the thought was that it was the woman's place to make the home and the husband's place to earn the living. There were, of course, always exceptions to this rule, but there should be some reason for it [to be] wholly acceptable to both."[98] His secretary, Rowena Miller, wrote: "President Clark is of the opinion that a mother's first duty is to her children and that they should not be neglected in behalf of the performance of any other duty."[99] He resisted any effort to alter in theory or practice the traditional position of women as housewives and mothers, in which he perceived no inequality.

Nevertheless, he was well aware that his own Republican Party's national platforms since 1940 had called for an amendment to the U.S. Constitution "providing for equal rights for men and women."[100] He regarded such an amendment unnecessary and dangerously innovative. But he also expressed a calm reassurance to the general conference of April 1944 that the Constitution's purpose was to protect minorities. Whenever "that inspired document" is amended as prescribed by the Constitution itself, he assured the congregation, "it will be an amendment that the Lord will approve."[101] He rested secure in his faith that God would safeguard both the divinely established institution of marriage and the divinely inspired Constitution.

He therefore resisted any hint of hysteric opposition to the bills and amendments concerning equal rights for women. On 25 January 1950 the U.S. Senate voted for an Equal Rights Amendment.[102] On that day the general presidency of the Relief Society offered to oppose "the bill for equal rights for women. Pres. Clark suggested they keep out of it; there will be some of the women who will think it is a fine thing."[103]

He publicly proclaimed that "motherhood is the highest type of service of which we mortals know"[104] and expressed disapproval of efforts to restrict birth. Nevertheless, he recognized that special circumstances might require modification of this general recommendation. To a woman who favored government programs encouraging birth control:

> I told her that so far as I knew the Church had never officially taken a position upon the question of birth control though all of our teachings were against it. ...
>
> I stated that we had a belief in the free agency of man and that that belief forbade us to attempt to coerce people. I stated that in this view the question of birth control was left for determination to each individual man and wife, who would, however, if the matter came up, be reminded of the principles of the Church that govern such matters.[105]

Aside from the question of free agency, Reuben also recognized that the medical welfare of the mother governed the matter of birth control.

He made this clear when a mother of five children asked if she should be sterilized after two physicians recommended it. President Clark said that he would advise her as "if she were my own wife or my own daughter." If she had the opinion of the two best physicians available to her, and if she herself felt that their recommendation to be sterilized was the best course of action, then "I would tell the wife or the daughter that she do as the doctors advised."[106]

He applied this pragmatic approach to abortion, even though he and the First Presidency shared a general abhorrence of it.[107] He recognized that there were circumstances where an abortion might be necessary due to the emotional-physical health of the pregnant woman or the medical condition of the unborn fetus. For example, a woman sought his counsel on behalf of herself and several other pregnant women who had contracted German measles. Concerning this inquiry:

> I told her she should seek the advice of her physician [concerning an abortion], getting such advice and counsel as she can, and also seek the Lord in prayer. She said that in such cases the hearing of the child may be affected, or the child may even be Mongoloid [i.e., Down's Syndrome]. I suggested that she might wish to get the advice of two or three doctors in the matter.[108]

Such questions were fundamental to society and the gospel. Despite his own preference for unrestricted birth, he counseled that special circumstances might allow a departure from the general rule to "multiply and replenish the earth." In his view, decisions about birth control or abortion required consultation with competent medical authorities, earnest prayer, and mutual agreement between husband and wife. Significantly he never said that LDS members should consult their priesthood leaders about using birth control or having an abortion.

He rejoiced so greatly in his own children and their devotion to church that he felt an immediate concern for the upbringing of all LDS children. Although he firmly believed that husband and wife must both be involved in parenting children, he reminded men that practical circumstances focused the parenting function on the mothers:

Now, brethren, at best we are somewhat clumsy at leading and directing our children. We are away from home, of necessity, a great part of the time, our thoughts are along other lines, we have to battle for our existence, for the livelihood of our families. ... And so to the sisters of the Church ... we must primarily look for the rearing of our children.[109]

As a result, whenever he spoke to women's groups, he invariably praised their efforts, burdens, and accomplishments in child rearing.

Occasionally, Reuben believed that fathers deserved special praise. To David A. Broadbent, he wrote:

I doubt if there be anybody in the Church who has a better record, or even an equivalent one,—to rear a family of fourteen [children], all of whom marry in the Temple, all of whom have college degrees, and all of whom are living as good members of the Church.[110]

Nevertheless, as previously quoted, Reuben recognized "good people" might not believe in Mormonism, nor attend LDS services, nor live the Word of Wisdom, nor marry in a temple, nor always live the church's precepts of ethics and morality. He also recognized that even such righteous fathers as Adam, Noah, and Jacob in the Bible, and Lehi in the Book of Mormon had children who were wayward or left the faith. This also occurred among children of modern apostles and prophets.

He specifically countered the criticism of some people that children of LDS leaders strayed because their parents were preoccupied with church service. He repeated an anecdote of J. Golden Kimball:

Brother Kimball said well, he spent a good deal of time preaching the Gospel, doing the Lord's work, and if his family went astray he was sorry, but he said, "I get some consolation out of the fact that when I go around and see the people, I think the Lord has not done too good a job Himself."

After the laughter died down from this story, he spoke with utmost seriousness to local bishops: "Do what you can to save the young people in your own homes."[111]

Indeed, despite his preoccupation with church administration, President Clark was deeply concerned about the spiritual welfare and present happiness of the Latter-day Saints. Even his attention to procedures and programs was a manifestation of his interest in the children, youth, husbands, wives, widows, poor, infirm, and elderly of Zion. He conducted his personal ministry in his own way and according to his own talents. This service was a product of his lifelong sense of identity with the Latter-day Saints and his feeling of responsibility to them.

CHAPTER 7.

By Study and Also by Faith[1]

THROUGHOUT HIS LIFE, J. REUBEN CLARK HAD AMBIVALENT ATTI-
tudes about the interplay between the life of the mind and the life
of faith. He treasured the world of "facts" but recognized their insuffi-
ciency as a way of life. He was an avid reader and researcher but was convinced that a total commitment to intellectual inquiry led inevitably to
atheism. He urged the primacy of faith but was uncomfortable with overly
spiritual people. He expected others to consider his pleas to abandon their
inadequate secular and religious positions, but he declined to read anything that was contrary to his own views. He was appalled by the confidence of the ignorant and suspicious of the smugness of the intellectual.
He was a living exemplar of higher education but preferred limited education in LDS colleges and at Brigham Young University. He defended total
freedom of thought but frequently decided that censorship was necessary.
He relied on the scriptures for doctrine but resisted doctrinal dogmatism.
Prior to becoming a general authority, he had rejected unquestioning
obedience to decisions of the LDS president. As a First Presidency counselor, he urged unquestioning obedience to the prophet, while reminding
everyone that the church president could also be mistaken. As a private
person and as a member of the First Presidency, he sought a conservative
balance between the imperatives of reason and revelation.

People often referred to his brilliant intellect, but he felt uncomfortable with the description. As a freshman member of the State Department in 1906, he wondered if such praise was really a form of mockery. His wife, Lute, replied: "I believe you get a wrong idea of the things people say about you. I sincerely think they are all meant." Then she added, "Never mind, Honey, you can't help being bright; only don't get the big head."[2] After he became a member of the First Presidency, many Mormons expressed awe at his knowledge. Others leveled anti-intellectual criticism at him. His sister Esther reported in 1940 that a young man told a ward Sunday School class that "Pres. Clark knows too much for one person." She commented, "I guess he thinks there should be a more even distribution of brains."[3]

Part of his discomfort with the popular view of him as a gigantic intellect was his recognition that he was not a Renaissance man of learning. For example, he tried to make his personal library a self-contained collection of "the greatest minds of all history that have left records, both in the religious and the secular worlds."[4] BYU president Ernest L. Wilkinson described it as Reuben's "famous library (certainly, there is none other like it between Chicago and the West Coast)."[5] Nevertheless, his library and his personal research focused primarily on international law, Communism, politics, Constitutionalism, biblical studies, religion, Judaism, and LDS scripture. He never claimed extensive understanding in other areas of knowledge.[6]

Even when he published a book that distilled his years of research into the Higher Criticism of the Bible and the importance of the King James Version (KJV), he admitted that ignorance of biblical languages and lack of rigorous training in the field left him very much a novice.[7] When those at Deseret Book Company chided him for being overly modest, Reuben sent his secretary, Rowena Miller, to his library "for copies of the books [he had cited] to show what scholarship was."[8]

However, this modesty was combined with his lifelong self-confidence as a researcher. When University of Utah president A. Ray Olpin congratulated him on his book's research, President Clark replied: "I did not get it by socializing."[9]

Nevertheless, he readily admitted that he did not have an insatiable thirst for knowledge, even in those areas in which he was vitally interested. One of his "fundamental rules" was "that I never read anything that I know is going to make me mad, unless I have to read it. To this rule I have added another, which is applicable here: I read only as time permits materials which merely support my own views." This stunned fellow lawyer Wilkinson to whom he wrote this explanation, "You do not have to get very far down in any article before you can tell whether or not the fellow is writing or saying something that is generally along the line of your own beliefs."[10] More often he did not bother to read publications before dismissing their significance.[11]

Thus, he could draft a two-page list of general criticisms about Fawn M. Brodie's biography of Joseph Smith and write a proposed review of the book even though he had not read it. In this letter to his brother Frank, Reuben explained that he circulated his proposed review among trusted friends "who have read the book." They told him that his sight-unseen evaluation "more or less characterizes the whole treatment" in Brodie's *No Man Knows My History*. For example, his proposed review stated:

> While the book seems popularly to be appraised as a chronicle of new and hitherto unpublished documents giving a true picture of the Prophet Joseph, the fact is it is almost wholly a rehash of charges against the Prophet that began to be made over a hundred years ago, which, being then discarded, were buried as base falsehoods. Since then they have from time to time been dug up and paraded again, only to be reburied because again found false. They are now dug up again and re-paraded from motives that are quite apparent from the book itself. ... There is very little material used or cited that has not been already published. The book has a veneer of pseudo-scholarship.

That was a remarkable set of observations by someone who had not actually read the book he was formally reviewing.[12]

When he authorized Apostle Mark E. Petersen, his protégé, "to publish the review of the Brodie Book" in May 1946,[13] it now had dozens of brief quotes from the book. This more-than-two-page anonymous "Appraisal of the So-Called Brodie Book" in the *Church News* had Reuben's often-used "so-called" in its title, his legalistic references to evidence, much of his phrasing, as well as his comparison of her approach with that of a biblical scholar. However, the review's quotes demonstrate that there were additions by someone who had actually consulted this controversial biography.[14] Reuben might have made these additions himself but, due to his above "rule" for reading, it is more likely that one of his trusted friends "who have read the book" provided them for publication.

Even after receiving favorable comments from an associate he had asked to read and evaluate another book, he could still confidently dismiss it as insignificant without reading it himself. Concerning Sterling M. McMurrin's *Philosophical Foundations of Mormon Theology,* the First Presidency's assistant secretary, A. Hamer Reiser, informed Reuben: "In fact, I finished the reading feeling that he has done rather well by Mormonism. He made me aware, with increased clarity and conviction, of a quality in the Gospel, as we teach it, which transcends the philosophies of men ... [which has] a sturdy independence and substance of its own, which deserves the respect of thoughtful people." Reuben referred to Reiser's evaluation in writing to the president of the University of Utah, which had published the book. In this letter to Olpin, he dismissed McMurrin's analysis in this way: "I am not worrying about the mysteries, and the little I am able to do, which is very small, I try to do with the one idea of building up our simple faith. A lot of people are troubled about a lot of things about which they know nothing."[15]

In shunning the designation *intellectual,* Reuben was not simply being modest but was acknowledging fundamental limitations. First, as already noted, he would not consider views that were contrary to his own. Second, he had difficulty comprehending abstract ideas even though he was a master of researching and categorizing mountains of facts and concrete data. "I can hardly get through a couple of verses of Paul and not get lost," he once wrote to BYU religion professor Sidney B. Sperry. "I know this is my fault, because Paul's logic and reasoning are all too subtle and refined for me. I can do a little better with Peter."[16] He gave up trying to understand the writings of Mary Baker Eddy because he found her ideas of Christian Science "entirely beyond the powers of my mind and my reasoning powers."[17] Secretary Rowena Miller observed that he likewise shunned discussion of Asian religions because "they involved an understanding of abstractions that he, personally, did not understand."[18]

Beyond religious abstractions, he had difficulty comprehending complex secular thought. When the president of Equitable Life sent him a copy of a speech, Reuben replied that he nearly drowned trying to understand it, "but I sort of held my breath and struggled to the top." He concluded his letter to Thomas I. Parkinson, "I accept your conclusions whether or not I fully understand the reasons, and I congratulate you on another fine speech."[19]

Despite the brilliance of his mind and speech, J. Reuben Clark shrank from the complex and abstract. After his crisis of faith in the 1920s, he manifested little of what is called intellectual curiosity. Likewise he felt a lifelong estrangement from those he referred to as "so-called intellectuals" and "so-called liberals."[20]

In fact, his distrust of Mormon intellectuals was a result of his own spiritual-intellectual crisis in earlier life. In the attempt to rationalize and intellectualize the LDS gospel, he found himself heading toward absolute skepticism. In letters to non-LDS friend Cloyd Marvin, he said that he avoided atheism only by refusing to question fundamental gospel principles.[21] He expressed to the Latter-day Saints his gratitude that he had the "sixth sense" that "enables him to believe in Mormonism."[22] He assumed that his own experience had universal application and told a general conference, "I have come to feel that there is none who can safely rationalize."[23]

He would probably have agreed immediately with a subsequent Pulitzer Prize-winning book that there is an essential difference between a "mental technician" and an "intellectual."[24] Reuben was a mental technician and would have understood why 92 percent of surveyed Mormons who held Ph.D. degrees did not list him among "the five most eminent intellectuals in Mormon history."[25]

Likewise, when a man asked him to identify which LDS leader after Joseph Smith contributed most to the intellectual life of the church, he replied, "I am not sure that I can see in what way the answer to the question would materially help us in solving the problems of daily life, which, after all, is the prime consideration in any study of the Gospel."[26] He often told LDS members that he kept his faith simple.

A significant example was his attitude toward proving the historicity of the Book of Mormon.[27] During the intellectual inquiries of his earlier life, he had once written that it "might be interesting to trace ... the evolution of the Book of Mormon." He had written this while commenting about a published revelation of Joseph Smith, "Did he not evolve this out of his own consciousness?"[28] Because this religious inquiry had led him to the brink of atheism, he now avoided such questions like the plague.

As First Presidency counselor, he approached the Book of Mormon only from an orthodox perspective. In 1946 he wrote, "While I doubt if any discoveries will ever be made which will enable us to say this definitely proves the Book of Mormon is true, nevertheless, I know that there are very, very many evidences in the ruins of Mexico and Central and South America that go to sustain the truthfulness of the book." Archaeological evidence was an obvious approach, but he suggested another in this same letter to J. Willard Marriott:

> It has been my feeling that if someone, who could get the confidence of the Indians, could get out among them, he would find in their [oral] traditions other and better evidences as to the accuracy and truthfulness of the Book of Mormon than will be found even in the ruins. But that would be a work practically of a lifetime by someone who would be willing to put up with all the inconveniences of living among the Indians, of gaining their confidence, and of practically becoming one of them, and that is a big order.[29]

For the next decade, Reuben continued to say that it was important to investigate archaeological parallels, yet repeated that these would always be inconclusive.[30] Eventually, he regarded the oral traditions of Native Americans as inconclusive as well. For example, he wrote to Thomas Stuart Ferguson, founder of the New World Archaeological Foundation: "It will be necessary to be most careful to see that these traditions of the Indians are not the result of the early teachings of the Catholic priests." However, 450 years after European conquest, Reuben regarded such verification as an impossibility because an Indian "would not be able to distinguish between what a real tradition was and what was a tradition in his own mind."[31] Thus, while he viewed Meso-American archaeology and folklore as significant, he regarded a spiritual testimony of the Book of Mormon as sufficient.

As a general authority, he adopted a double-edged educational philosophy. He regarded all highly educated people, particularly intellectuals, as atheists in embryo. He therefore insisted that, to justify their existence, LDS educational institutions must provide the rudiments of college education within a religious atmosphere that gave priority to faith and diminished intellectuality. Even prior to entering the hierarchy, he voiced this concern to BYU president Franklin S. Harris. This was in response to Harris's talk in praise of the higher educational backgrounds of some LDS leaders.[32]

In 1938 President Clark stated his educational philosophy explicitly to church educators in the Aspen Grove talk, "The Chartered Course of the Church in Education":

> You do not have to sneak up behind this spiritually experienced youth and whisper religion in his ears; you can come right out, face to face, and talk with him. You do not need to disguise religious truths with a cloak of worldly things; you can bring these truths to him openly, in their natural guise.[33]

In succeeding decades, LDS leaders have often quoted and referred to this talk. For example, a later acting president of the Twelve, Boyd K. Packer, regarded it as the "measuring rod for religious views, philosophies, and teachings."[34] Appointed a general authority just days before Reuben's death, Elder Packer printed the full text of this talk in his own *Teach Ye Diligently.*[35]

By contrast, after listening to Clark deliver these instructions, one teacher had a different view. Sterling McMurrin condemned the Aspen Grove talk as a "notorious address" which said that "there is to be no freedom in matters pertaining to religion and morals."[36] With respect to "academic freedom," McMurrin accurately interpreted Reuben's talk and general views.

As an outgrowth of this emphasis, President Clark became the prime mover in 1944 to establish at BYU what he called a "School of Theology," a "post-graduate school in gospel," or a "divinity school."[37] As expressed in a First Presidency letter he formulated, this postgraduate program would be "only for the purpose of developing and demonstrating the truth of the Restored Gospel and the falsity of the other religions of the world, and thereby up build the faith and knowledge of post-graduate scholars."[38] When this program evolved during the 1950s into a traditional graduate school with degrees in secular fields, he opposed this intellectualizing development.[39] The other members of the First Presidency outvoted him.

Reuben voiced his dissatisfaction to President Wilkinson:

> I assume that I am an apostate, that I am no friend of higher learning, that I am just a low-down ignoramus, but in that ignorance I want to say to you that I am not at all concerned with the relative fewness of our attendance at the Y who are graduate students. In this ignorance of mine, I have a feeling that the mission of the Brigham Young University is not to make Ph.D.s or M.A.s, but to distribute among as wide a number as possible the ordinary collegiate work leading to Bachelor Degrees and to instill into the students a knowledge of the Gospel and a testimony of its truthfulness.[40]

He was never reconciled to the enlarged enrollments and educational programs at this church school. He consistently opposed the physical, academic, and financial expansion of BYU that occurred during the last years of his life.[41]

Nevertheless, he simultaneously chafed against what he perceived as mental laziness and conformity among Latter-day Saints. In 1947 he wrote, "Too many of our people have quit thinking—Politically—Socially—Spiritually."[42]

For example, he believed that the intelligent thinking of a community is both expressed and encouraged by its newspapers. In 1936 he said, "I am most anxious to make our paper [the *Deseret News*] do for our Church what *The Christian Science Monitor* has done for the Christian Science Church."[43] However, his hopes in this regard were unrealized throughout his life. Twenty years later Wilkinson, a member of the *Deseret News* board of directors, despaired that they would ever achieve the goal of getting "into the News of some of the qualities of the Christian Science Monitor." He explained that the rest of the *News* board failed in its "duty to raise the standards of its readers rather than just give them what they want; such as funnies [i.e., comic strips] and pages of sports news."[44]

Moreover, President Clark was not absolute in his warnings against intellectualizing the gospel and delving into its mysteries. He regarded those efforts as legitimate, even if they were dangerous. In writing a 1941 response to a philosophical treatise by N. L. Nelson, he observed at the outset, "You have thought deeply and it seems to me, in the main, logically, about many fundamental matters, most of which I assume would be classified as 'mysteries,' [for] which you have thought the little we are told through to a conclusion." Reuben concluded his six-page, single-spaced, typed analysis of Nelson's manuscript with the words, "Praying that the Lord will bless you in your labors of strong, vigorous, creative thinking."[45]

So there were limits to the pressures he was willing to exert against Mormon intellectuals. When Apostle Petersen asked for permission to excommunicate those he suspected of having disloyal and apostate attitudes, "Pres. Clark cautioned that they ought to be careful about the insubordination or disloyalty question, because they ought to be permitted to think, you can't throw a man off for thinking."[46]

At its most extreme, the insistence on spiritual and mental conformity in the church resulted in what Reuben classified sarcastically as "the Celestial Kingdomers." These Latter-day Saints accept "only those who believe and act as they do: They have narrow rules; narrow principles. The Prescriptions of the Talmud are of their kind of thinking. They cut off men who do not follow them."[47] This restated Brigham Young's sentiment: "It floods my heart with sorrow to see so many Elders of Israel who wish everybody to come to their standard and be measured by their measure. Every man must be just so long, to fit their iron bedstead, or be cut off to the right length."[48]

Rejection of religious narrowness led Reuben to tolerate the views of some with whom he might otherwise disagree. A few years before his own call to the hierarchy, he advised his missionary son, Reuben III, "The philosophy of the Gospel is so deep and many sided, its truths are so far reaching [that] it is never safe to dogmatize, even about the most elemental principles, such as faith."[49] In his official capacity, he advised LDS members: "We ought not, therefore, to get discouraged because somebody sees a revelation in a different light from the way in which we see it. We are entitled to our opinion; the other man is entitled to his opinion, but the revelation stands until God changes it in the regular way."[50]

Even though "the revelation stands," President Clark regarded written revelations as guidelines for the prophets, who then exercise their freedom and common sense. He told a temple meeting of the First Presidency and Quorum of Twelve that "the Lord gave these general instructions, and the brethren more or less floundered about within broad limits as to the details of the situation which they set up." In church administration, he did not regard written revelations as ironclad limitations.[51]

Because he disliked religious dogmatism, Reuben was able to be remarkably noncommittal when asked about deeper aspects of doctrine. This was especially true concerning the nature of God. To one inquirer, he wrote that "it does not make any difference to your service nor to mine, whether God is progressing or whether He has come to a stand-still."[52]

Even though the official position of the First Presidency was to classify the "Adam-God theory" as heresy and to deny that Brigham Young had advocated it,[53] Reuben adopted a less strident approach. To someone who inquired about it, he replied, "It is my understanding, which may be erroneous, that the Brethren have always differed as to that doctrine—even in Brother Brigham's time."[54] To an advocate of the doctrine, he wrote, "I understand that in the days of President Young, this controversy raged with considerable fury, but I believe with no casualties and with no one winning a decision." He concluded: "I am equally sure that none of us can understand it because we are dealing with matters of infinity and we are only finite. The Lord has not revealed these mysteries to us."[55]

This non-committal approach was undoubtedly influenced by the statement which was in Reuben's copy of *Discourses of Brigham Young*: "It is as much my right to differ from other men, as it is theirs to differ from me, in points of doctrine and principle, when our minds cannot at once arrive at the same conclusion."[56] Utah's pioneer prophet emphasized that there could be loyal opposition within the LDS church and even affirmed that it was the *right* of faithful Mormons to disagree with the church president's doctrinal pronouncements. This may have provided the context for Reuben's seemingly contradictory views about LDS loyalty and about dissent from the doctrinal statements of living prophets in the twentieth century.

Even in religious disputes about which he had pronounced personal opinions, he avoided setting himself as the arbiter of what was possible for God. For example, he had deep prejudices against Roman Catholicism and publicly condemned Mariolatry, the adoration of the Virgin Mary.[57] Nevertheless, he was unwilling to denounce reported visions of Mary as false or devilish. In one of the most famous of these reported experiences, a fifty-year-old Mexican Indian saw a vision on 9 December 1531. The result was the "cult" of Our Lady of Guadalupe.[58] Reuben wrote his reaction to this story in a letter to Joseph T. Bentley, president of a Mexican mission:

> I have always had a natural interest in the story of Juan Diego and the "visitation" to him of the Virgin Mary. I have always been a little more tolerant toward the concept of some sort of vision on the part of Juan Diego, or somebody else, because, though the Spaniards were trying to set up a Christian concept and practice that we know to have been false, nevertheless that concept, whatever it was, was far ahead of the cannibalistic worship of sacrifice which the Aztecs held. I have always felt that perhaps the Lord permitted something in order to add an appeal to the Mexican mind that was not embraced in the concepts which the Spaniards were trying to give of Christianity. However, this is my own idea.[59]

His acceptance of the possibility of such a vision may have been linked with the transition in his attitudes toward the Mexican people. (See chapter 10.)

To young missionaries who might be tempted to give authoritative answers to obscure or unimportant doctrinal questions, he advised them to answer simply "I do not know."[60] He followed his own counsel. When a guide at Temple Square "wanted to know when the spirit entered the body and whether the still-born child had a spirit—Pres. Clark sent word that that is one of the mysteries."[61] When a church member asked about the fate of "the Sons of Perdition," he merely observed that he was "trying never to become one."[62] With good humor and an emphasis on the importance of simple faith, he sidestepped doctrinal speculations that others felt compelled to embrace or battle against.

When Apostle Harold B. Lee asked whether the gift of the Holy Ghost existed in the days of Adam, "Pres. Clark said he did not know."[63] He answered likewise when a church member asked if amputees will be resurrected with their limbs fully restored, then added, "and I do not know to what I could direct you to get an answer."[64] He apparently chose not to refer this Mormon to Apostle Joseph Fielding Smith's confident answer to this question five years earlier in the church's magazine. Prior to Reuben's correspondence about this matter, general authority Bruce R. McConkie had reprinted Smith's answer as one of the *Doctrines of Salvation*.[65] Although Reuben's children regarded Elder Smith as a Clark man because the two were like-minded in many ways, these two leaders clashed over doctrinal dogmatism.

After declining to make an inflexible pronouncement about a doctrine he considered debatable, Reuben told one church member that there were other general authorities who "would probably be happy to give you the advantage of their opinions."[66] In view of his objections to their published expressions of dogmatism, his comment undoubtedly referred to Smith and McConkie.

In fact, Reuben regarded it as a serious problem when other general authorities seemed eager to make authoritative pronouncements. He tried to discourage BYU administrator Harvey L. Taylor from publishing current talks of general authorities to the student body "upon important matters" because "some matters have come to my attention where the Brethren not only differ among themselves, but where they differ with the First Presidency."[67] He told Apostle Petersen of his own opposition to answering doctrinal questions in print because "the First Presidency receives some pretty tough questions sometimes; and they don't always agree in the Quorum."[68] Three weeks later he again told Petersen that "the First Presidency have so many questions coming up they have to side step. ... [and] what he [JRC] is fearful of is religious [doctrinal] questions, and suggested that in view of what Pres. [George Albert] Smith said, they confine their religious questions [in the *Church News*] very narrowly, and for the present at any rate do not discuss any doctrinal question."[69]

One such difference surfaced in May 1953 between President Clark and Elder McConkie, at that time a member of the First Council of Seventy. The *Church News* published Reuben's talk to BYU students wherein he stated that in the premortal state Satan and Christ presented two different plans for the conduct of mortality and that Christ's plan was chosen. By contrast, the church's *Improvement Era* published in the same month an article wherein McConkie stated that such a claim for two plans "does not conform to the revealed word."[70] When a puzzled member of the church asked about this contradiction, Clark answered that "the difference may be merely one of interpretation." His secretary, Rowena Miller, explained that he "sees no reason for changing his own views nor his nomenclature. As long as he remembers, there have always been two Plans spoken of."[71]

He devoted far more space to commenting on a fundamental disagreement between himself and a senior member of the Quorum of Twelve. Since the 1930s, Apostle Joseph Fielding Smith had been locked in a controversy concerning his scripturally fundamentalist denunciation of organic evolution. The apostle had criticized the willingness of other general authorities to advance evolution as God's method of creation.[72] Reuben himself had questioned the consistency of scientific theory in a 1915 sermon, "Evolution," but since 1924 had made occasional statements in public and private that the method of creation was unimportant.[73] As first counselor in the church presidency, he intended to make that point specifically in a major address to the Relief Society in 1946. He sent an advance draft of the talk to Elder Smith, who wrote a detailed critique of the talk's references to the creation.

In a lengthy reply to Smith, President Clark observed, "Much of your argument loses significance when we cease to give highly technical meaning to general terms." He continued his letter:

> You seem to think I reject the scriptures, or some of them. I do not intend to do so, but obviously I am no more bound by your interpretation of them than you are by mine. ...

You observe, "Reason teaches us that the Lord worked during the creation *on his own time.*" The point has no significance to my subject, but reason does not teach me that. Reason teaches me that in the infinite, finite time of any measure has little if any importance or value. Indeed, from our mortal point of view, there probably is no *time* as we know it, in eternity, either simple or in multiple. [emphasis in original]

The periods of temporal creation are of no importance to my subject.

You quote from Section 77 of the Doctrine and Covenants. I do not get from that section the meaning you give it.

Apparently the basic difference between us is this: you do not accept the scriptural record as given in historical sequence; I do. ...

Now, as to what the earlier brethren have said—where they have declared themselves as speaking under inspiration and by the authority of the Lord, I bow to what they say. But where they express views based on their own understanding and interpretation, then none of us are foreclosed from exercising our own reasoning powers, inadequate though they may be; but the earlier views do not foreclose us from thinking. This is particularly true, where we come to interpreting their interpretations.[74]

Having said this much in rebuttal, Reuben defused their private controversy by omitting from the text of his talk the words which most offended Apostle Smith: "So far as the record goes, the temporal creation in which Adam took part might have worked through one million or many millions of years."[75]

He was willing to let the matter rest without public comment until 1954 when Smith made a public issue of the conflict between his own scriptural views and the scientific theories of creation. The First Presidency had instructed him in 1931 to "leave Geology, Biology, Archaeology and Anthropology, no one of which has to do with the salvation of the souls of mankind, to scientific research, while we magnify our calling in the realm of the Church." Nonetheless twenty-three years later, the apostle published a book attacking scientific theories of evolution as inconsistent with LDS faith. By that time, all members of the First Presidency who had instructed him to stop his anti-evolution campaign were dead, all of the scientifically trained apostles with whom he had waged a quiet controversy had passed on, and Elder Smith himself was next in line to be LDS president.[76] He anticipated that his book would create some controversy when it went on sale in April 1954, and he wrote the following inscription in the copy of *Man: His Origin and Destiny* that he gave to Reuben: "Hoping that you can tolerate a part of this if not all."[77]

President Clark had outlined in the 1946 letter his difficulty with the inflexible doctrinal assumptions of the apostle toward organic evolution. Now Elder Smith was publishing them to the world as though they were the authoritative statements of the church. Reuben decided to counter this in an indirect manner.

More than two months after publication of the book, he gave an address to LDS religion teachers at BYU about the physical attributes of the human body. Concerning early biological development, he said that "man, monkey, elephant, turtle, snake, are of one kind, indistinguishable," and commented that the human embryo "develops and matures upon some principle of 'evolution.'"[78]

Whether or not Apostle Smith regarded this as a challenge, four days later he gave a talk to the same group of teachers in which he promoted his book as the doctrinal answer to evolutionary theory. He told the educators that LDS doctrine refuted such other scientific views as the assertion that the sun was gradually cooling in temperature. On 28 June he gave a second talk to LDS educators in which he gave a detailed doctrinal denunciation of evolution and geologic time.[79]

Reuben did not want to challenge Smith's dogmatic rejection of evolution in the way other general authorities did in the 1930s. They had published contrasting views on the specific topics that Joseph Fielding Smith addressed.[80] Nevertheless, President Clark did want to clearly establish an essential principle of church doctrine.

Nine days after Smith's second anti-evolution talk, Reuben spoke to this same group of LDS educators about "adventurous expeditions of the brethren into these highly speculative principles and doctrines." In such cases, he noted, honest differences of interpretation were possible. He commented that sometimes general authorities and other prominent priesthood leaders had spoken "out of turn" about matters in which the revelations of the Lord were not conclusive and about which the LDS president had not declared the official doctrine of the church. He observed that these leaders still declared their doctrinal views "with an assured certainty that might deceive the uniformed and unwary." This remarkable address continued to demonstrate the main theme:

> When any man, except the President of the Church, undertakes to proclaim one unsettled doctrine, as among two or more doctrines in dispute, as the settled doctrine of the Church, we may know that he is not "moved upon by the Holy Ghost," unless he is acting under the authority of the President.[81]

Although he did not refer to specifics, President Clark knew that Elder Smith had not published *Man: His Origin and Destiny* with the authorization of the church president. In fact, David O. McKay decided with his counselors to deny requests that the book be used as a text in LDS seminaries and institutes.[82]

President Wilkinson wrote, "The conflict between President McKay and President Smith was on a question of doctrine [organic evolution] which, to my mind and the mind of President J. Reuben Clark, Jr., was entirely irrelevant to the Church."[83] McKay dismissed the significance of *Man: His Origin and Destiny* in letters to rank-and-file members. The earliest explained that "the Church has not approved of the book; and that so far as evolution is concerned, the Church has not made any ruling regarding it, and that no man has been authorized to speak for the Church on it."[84]

Reuben would have preferred that the apostle had never published this anti-evolution book,[85] but he did not make any effort to challenge it directly or to restrict its availability to the public. The views both men expressed in 1954 entered the LDS marketplace of ideas with relatively equal success. Elder Smith's book went through several printings, while President Clark's talk, "When Are Church Leader's Words Entitled to Claim of Scripture?" was published in the *Church News* in 1954, republished in pamphlet form by the LDS Department of Seminaries and Institutes in 1966, and included in the lesson manual for Melchizedek priesthood quorums in 1969. Ten years later, *Dialogue: A Journal of Mormon Thought* reprinted it, followed shortly thereafter by a BYU reprint.[86]

On occasion, however, President Clark was willing to employ censorship because he wanted to avoid the spiritual equivalent of shouting "Fire!" in a crowded theater. To counter what he regarded as the long-standing infusion of liberal theology in LDS lesson manuals, he urged the establishment of a "Literature Censorship Committee" in 1940.[87] He formulated the purposes of the subsequently designated Committee on Publications in a 1944 letter he drafted for the First Presidency:

> The function of this Committee is to pass upon and approve all materials, other than those that are purely secular, to be used by our Church Priesthood, Educational, Auxiliary, and Missionary organizations in their work of instructing members of the Church in the principles of the Gospel and in leading others to a knowledge of the Truth. ...
>
> To meet such required standards for use by Church organizations, such materials must:
>
> 1. Clearly set forth or be fully consistent with the principles of the restored Gospel.
>
> 2. Be wholly free from any taint of sectarianism and also of all theories and conclusions destructive of faith in the simple truths of the Restored Gospel, and especially be free from the teachings of the so-called "higher criticism." Worldly knowledge and speculation have their place; but they must yield to revealed truth.
>
> 3. Be so framed and written as affirmatively to breed faith and not raise doubts. "Rationalizing" may be most destructive of faith. That the Finite cannot fully explain the Infinite casts no doubt upon the Infinite. Truth, not error, must be stressed.
>
> 4. Be so built in form and substance as to lead to definite conclusions that accord with the principles of the Restored Gospel which conclusions must be expressed and not left to possible deduction by the students. When truth is involved there is no place for student preference or choice. Youth must be taught that truth cannot be blinked or put aside, it must be accepted.
>
> 5. Be filled with a spirit of deepest reverence. They should give no place for the slightest levity. They should be so written that those who teach from and by them will so understand.
>
> 6. Be so organized and written that the matter may be effectively taught by men and women untrained in teaching without the back-

ground equipment given by such fields of learning as psychology, pedagogy, philosophy and ethics. The great bulk of our teachers are in the untrained group.[88]

This directive was a distillation of his often-expressed views about LDS instructional materials. The philosophy, even the words, he used in drafting this letter became the charter of what was later known as Church Correlation.[89]

Although President Clark wanted everything in LDS instructional manuals to "breed faith and not raise doubts," his preferences for the public image of Mormonism varied. Sometimes he made bald-faced admissions to newspaper reporters. At other times he suppressed embarrassing information.

Aside from his well-known frankness in talking with church members about himself and problems in LDS administration, he could be equally candid with non-Mormons. When reporters for Time, Inc. assumed in 1936 that President Grant went "to a room for [prayerful] communion and reflection" before making administrative decisions, Reuben replied "that we did not do our Church work in that style."[90] When a representative of *Look* asked him in 1942 about church divorces, he replied: "Our divorces are piling up, we are influenced by the same waves of emotion and sociological elements as affect the whole country. We are just all mixed up, but I think that still our divorce rate is lower than the average."[91] When a reporter for the *Wall Street Journal* asked in 1943 if there had been divine instructions to "the Church leaders regarding the post-war world," he replied, "I am not aware that any such revelations or visions have been received by any of the leaders."[92]

On the other hand, Clark was willing to use his influence against Utah writers who presented Mormonism in what he regarded as an unfavorable light. In 1949 he used an intermediary to urge the Guggenheim Foundation to drop its support of Dale L. Morgan's projected multi-volume history of Mormonism. Otherwise "the Guggenheim Foundation and the Guggenheim interests [would come] into ill repute in this area."[93] This referred to the Guggenheim investment in the Kennecott Copper Mine.[94] Four years earlier Reuben may have similarly encouraged the LDS president to write a letter to Apostle John A. Widtsoe "in regard to a forthcoming book by Miss Maurine Whipple, uncomplimentary to the Church and the State, and asking him to take up the matter with the Governor and the officials of the two counties named in the book." This involved her book, *This Is the Place: Utah,* by New York publisher Alfred Knopf.[95]

In 1951 he successfully interceded with representatives of the motion picture industry to cancel a projected film on the 1857 Mountain Meadows Massacre. Warner Brothers studio was basing the movie on Juanita Brooks's scholarly study published by Stanford University.[96] She had already complained in print that "President Clark had decided that they [the affidavits regarding the massacre] should not be made available ... The most difficult thing to understand about all this is not so much the refusal to show the affidavits as the consistent and repeated refusal to discuss the question."[97] As Reuben wrote in 1951 to express his unwillingness to discuss a subject about which he already disagreed, "it is a waste of lather to shave an ass."[98]

However, it was not possible to control the national press. "Your article is hopelessly inadequate and almost completely distortional of Mormon life," he wrote in a 1954 letter to *Life* magazine's assistant publisher, Hud Stoddard. In this letter, which he ultimately decided not to send, he vented his frustration with the media:

> I am looking forward to the time (I may not live to see it) when someone will come from some of your magazines who, first, knows something about the Mormons, and secondly, who will try to tell the truth about us and fairly report us in word and picture. We Mormons are not grotesque[—]either in our appearance or our living. We are not freaks. We are not ignoramuses and the records of educational and scientific activities and achievements of America will show this. We are not priest-ridden.[99]

In other cases where the agency of individual Mormons conflicted with President Clark's sense of propriety, he declined to use his powers to impose censorship. At the same time, he left no uncertainty about his expectation of self-censorship. The best example of this occurred in 1957 when he learned that BYU professor James R. Clark was planning to publish an article about the defunct and little-understood Council of Fifty in LDS history. Reuben tried to dissuade his nephew by saying that the fact of their family relationship would make it appear to members of the church that the article had President Clark's approval. He told Professor Clark, "You are telling a lot of things you don't know anything about" and that "I don't think any good Churchman should do it," that "I think it is unwise." Yet when his nephew asked if he was specifically telling him to discontinue the project, Reuben replied: "I think you should not touch it, but you can if you want. I am not going to tell you not to do it, but I think you will make a mistake if you do it."[100]

In 1958 Professor Clark published the first-ever article about the theocratic Council of Fifty.[101] This did not harm his church status nor his reputation at headquarters. With the permission of the LDS president, he subsequently edited a multivolume publication of First Presidency messages and official statements.[102]

The principle of personal freedom was too important an issue to J. Reuben Clark for him to use his administrative powers against ordinary members of the church who chose to write and publish things he preferred left alone.[103] Nonetheless, he was more willing to consider the suppression of publications by general authorities if he felt they were inadvertently creating problems for the church.

His earliest comments about such matters involved the writings of Apostle Widtsoe and his wife, Leah, a granddaughter of Brigham Young. In 1944 Reuben opposed her intention to include chocolate and cocoa in a discussion of the "Word of Wisdom" in a church magazine for children. Concerning a 1947 meeting, Apostle Lee wrote: "John A. Widtsoe and Pres. Clark clashed on the subject of whole wheat bread. Bro. Widtsoe, in an insinuating manner, told Bro. Clark that if he were informed he would know the importance of whole wheat bread, to which Pres. Clark replied that others, who were as equally informed as he (Bro. Widtsoe), disagreed with him."[104]

In October 1948 Apostle Albert E. Bowen referred to Widtsoe's complaints that the church newspaper advertised cola drinks. Because of their caffeine, Widtsoe regarded them as a violation of the Word of Wisdom, which prohibited coffee and tea. President Clark wrote, "I said John and Leah had stirred up more trouble with their dietary ideas than any one else and that except for my affection for them I would have urged the Brethren to restrict their activities."[105]

His reaction was so negative because of another incident involving the Widtsoes earlier that same year. Their book on the Word of Wisdom was cited as the first footnote in a physician's article in the *Improvement Era,* which began, "Excessive use of refined sugar in the United States has become a serious nutritional problem." This eight-page scholarly article created a public relations problem for the church's sugar company, of which Reuben was an executive director.[106] Aside from Widtsoe's book serving as the inspiration for this article, he was coeditor of the magazine and may have encouraged the author to write this. Reuben therefore commissioned another author to write a refutation. "Pres. Clark suggested that he make no reference to the previous one in the Era, but cite the authorities and the results of experiments on the value of sugar as a food."[107]

When a committee headed by Apostle Widtsoe published a *Year Book of Facts and Statistics* in 1949, President Clark suggested to LDS president George Albert Smith that "this booklet contained some information that would be better not circulated." As a result, the president asked Widtsoe to withdraw it from circulation.[108]

First counselor Stephen L Richards and Apostle Petersen recommended in 1955 against reprinting a 1921 article about the temple's ordinances by the now deceased Widtsoe. Reuben agreed that the article should not be reprinted. But as second counselor, he disagreed with their proposal to publish it in altered form: "I did not think we were justified in re-writing articles that had been prepared by men who were dead."[109]

In the matter of restricting the publications of general authorities, Reuben became most involved with the writings of Elder McConkie. In December 1955 Salt Lake publisher Bookcraft advertised an upcoming McConkie publication, *Sound Doctrine: The Journal of Discourses Series.* The First Presidency had future advertisements withdrawn.[110] After Reuben read 150 pages of the first manuscript volume of this projected series, he recommended that the First Presidency stop its publication altogether. He explained his reasons to Elder McConkie in person:

I said [to him that] I assumed that he would not print, that is, was not proposing to print the sermons of the other [deceased] brethren, that is, the early brethren, on such matters as the Adam-God theory, so-called, and the sermons on plural marriage. He said that was his idea. I said that I personally[,] and I thought the other brethren [of the current First Presidency] agreed with me, felt it would be unwise to issue a Journal of Discourses with those sermons omitted[—]inasmuch as that would give the [Fundamentalist] cultists an opportunity for attack which might increase our present difficulties instead of mollifying them. ...

I mentioned the fact that the title he had given to the collection "Sound Doctrine," implied that there was other doctrine [in the *Journal of Discourses*] that was unsound and that perhaps it would not be wise to give forth that implication. He seemed to agree with that idea. ...

I said I felt that we were having a great many books published now by some of the leading Brethren; that these books did not always express all the sentiment of the other Brethren, at least some of them, and might be contrary to it; he admitted that.

I also called attention to the fact that it would have been better if he had conferred with the Brethren before he began the printing of his book, instead of afterward, and he admitted that that was a mistake which he had made.

Clark expressed the hope that he "should not suffer any undue loss" financially by ceasing publication of *Sound Doctrine*.[111] Because it had been advertised in advance, Elder McConkie's unauthorized book never reached the bookstores.

The First Presidency thought they had resolved Elder McConkie's misunderstandings about publishing books for LDS readers. However, the question thrust itself on Reuben again less than three years later. In mid-1958 Bookcraft suddenly released thousands of copies of Elder Mc-Conkie's 776-page book, *Mormon Doctrine*. This volume announced the author's position as a general authority and the author's preface described the book as the "first extensive compendium of the whole gospel." He noted that the scriptures were "the chief source of authority quoted" and that any interpretations were "from such recognized doctrinal authorities as Joseph Smith, Brigham Young, Joseph F. Smith, Orson Pratt, John Taylor, and Joseph Fielding Smith."[112]

Although the implication of the title and preface was that this was an authoritative and comprehensive statement of LDS doctrine, the author had not informed the First Presidency or even fellow members of the First Council of Seventy that he intended to publish it. His own father-in-law, "Joseph Fielding Smith[,] did not know anything about it until it was published."[113] By keeping his upcoming book a secret, he successfully prevented the hierarchy from again stopping publication.[114] This clearly contradicted his previous acknowledgment that it was "a mistake which he had made" in not "conferr[ing] with the Brethren before he began the printing of his book," *Sound Doctrine*.

All of this violated every rule President Clark had observed in his own publications about LDS topics. For example, he did not publish his decades of biblical study without the specific and repeated permission from the church president. (See chapter 8.) Even then, the first words of *Why the King James Version?* were: "For this book I alone am responsible. It is not a Church publication."[115]

Reuben needed only to see the title page and read a few pages of Elder McConkie's *Mormon Doctrine* to cause him to bring the matter to President McKay's immediate attention. "I was urgent in saying I did it only because I felt he must know," he wrote. "I was sure we had to do something because this book would raise more trouble than anything we had had in the Church for a long while."[116]

After some delay in deciding what to do about this runaway bestseller, the First Presidency appointed apostles Petersen and Marion G. Romney to scrutinize the content of the book.[117] As protégés of President Clark, both reviewers shared his disdain for doctrinal dogmatism. Elder Petersen found "errors and misstatements" on nearly every page, and Elder Romney wrote a letter to the president summarizing areas needing deletion or revision.[118]

McKay arrived at the conclusion which Reuben had decided at the outset. In a statement to the author's father-in-law and the rest of the Twelve, the church president said "that Brother McConkie's book is not approved as an authoritative book, and that it should not be republished, even if the errors (some 1,067 of them) are corrected."[119]

The president retreated from the First Presidency's initial decision that *Mormon Doctrine* "should be repudiated." McKay decided against requiring McConkie to make a public apology because "it might lessen his influence" as a general authority.[120] Instead, the president simply decided to write private letters denying that it was "an official publication of the Church."[121]

However, five years after Clark died, President McKay reconsidered the decision to prevent further publication of the book. By then, Joseph Fielding Smith was his assistant counselor. The president decided to allow his counselor's son-in-law to publish a revised and expanded edition.[122] In fulfillment of Reuben's worst fears, the dogmatic *Mormon Doctrine* gained the stature among many Latter-day Saints as the authoritative expression of official doctrine.[123]

In all of Reuben's attitudes toward the relationship of intellect, scripture, doctrine, and faith, there were three fundamentals: his unwavering testimony, his insistence on freedom of intellect, and his loyalty to the role of the church president as prophet of God. He told the general conference of April 1949: "The priesthood never compels. God himself does not compel the intellect, nor does he attempt to overthrow it." In a second sermon to that same conference, he added: "I bear my testimony that I know that God lives, that Jesus is the Christ and the first fruits of the resurrection. I know that the gospel and the Priesthood were restored through the Prophet Joseph." To him, all other considerations were secondary to that testimony.[124]

For example, he said that Mormons should not expect democratic rights in the LDS church. He told the general conference of 1945, "We are democratic in our concepts of the Church, but we are not a democracy; we are a kingdom, the Church and kingdom of God on earth."[125] He later explained this to a missionary meeting: "I hope Brother [Mark E.] Petersen will pardon me—but this is not a democracy; this is not a republic; this is a kingdom of God. The President of the Church is his premier, if you will, his agent, his possessor of the keys. Our free agency which we have does not make us any more nor less than subjects of the Kingdom and subjects we are,—not citizens, Brother Mark."[126] As a reflection of his suspicions about intellectuals, Reuben affirmed that only the LDS president "has the right to rationalize"[127] and that only he "has any right to change or modify or extend any revelation of the Lord."[128]

He assured the general priesthood meeting in October 1946 that the Latter-day Saints could always follow the LDS prophet who will never lead them astray: "The Lord has never permitted it and He never will, because that would be an act of deceit of which He is incapable."[129] However, like others who have expressed this view, President Clark did not explain how this was consistent with the founding prophet's published revelation providing for the excommunication of the church president. His sermon also contradicted other official statements that the prophet is capable of apostasy and can lead the Saints astray.[130] As stated in Reuben's copy of *Discourses of Brigham Young*, "I would beseech and pray the people to live so that if I do not magnify my office and calling, you will burn me by your faith and good works, and I shall be removed."[131]

In fact, Reuben had already told the general conference of April 1940 that the First Presidency "is not infallible in our judgment, and we err."[132] He reminded the membership in April 1949 that the LDS president "was a prophet only when he spoke with the spirit of prophecy," paraphrasing a statement by founder Joseph Smith.[133] Reuben instructed LDS educators in 1954 that "even the President of the Church has not always spoken under the direction of the Holy Ghost." As in his earlier talk to general conference, he told the religion faculty that it was only by diligent study, earnest prayer, and faithful listening to the promptings of the Holy Ghost whereby a person could know when the LDS president or any other general authority was acting according to the will of God.[134]

This was his restatement of published sermons by an earlier prophet. Reuben's copy of *Discourses of Brigham Young* proclaimed: "I am more afraid that this people have so much confidence in their leaders that they will not inquire for themselves of God whether they are led by him. I am fearful they settle down in a state of blind self-security, trusting their eternal destiny in the hands of their leaders with a reckless confidence that in itself would thwart the purposes of God in their salvation."[135] Young further warned against what he had heard from some members: "'I do not depend upon any inherent goodness of my own,' say they, 'to introduce me into the kingdom of glory, but I depend upon you, brother Joseph, upon you, brother Brigham ... I believe your judgment is superior to mine, and consequently I let you judge for me.'" Rather than praising their faith in the living prophet, Young warned them: "Now those men, or those women, who know no more about the power of God, and the influences of the Holy Spirit, than to be led entirely by another person, suspending their own understanding, and pinning their faith upon another's sleeve, will never be capable of entering into the celestial glory, to be crowned as they anticipate; they will never be capable of becoming Gods."[136]

As stated at the beginning, J. Reuben Clark sought a conservative balance between the imperatives of reason and revelation. The issues were sometimes difficult to resolve, but he did the best he could as both church spokesman and church administrator.

CHAPTER 8.

Mark Them Which Cause
Divisions and Offenses[1]

PRESIDENT CLARK EXPRESSED A CERTAIN AMOUNT OF TOLERATION for LDS members who had "disloyal thoughts" and probed doctrinal mysteries he thought should be left alone. However, he was an unrelenting critic and administrative opponent of those who violated the priesthood "rule and order of the Church"[2] or who taught things that undermined what he perceived as the simple, orthodox gospel of Christ. He did not see himself as a witch-hunter or Grand Inquisitor and publicly condemned the historical policy of Roman Catholicism to "attack and follow up all heretics."[3]

Nevertheless, he firmly believed that he could not discharge his responsibilities without raising a warning voice. To remain silent would contribute to the spiritual destruction of the people he served. Thus, he tirelessly devoted himself to warning Mormons generally and LDS administrators specifically about the dangers he perceived and the enemies he recognized. He directed much of this effort to religious heterodoxy and apostasy but also gave great attention to Constitutionalism, Communism, and Utah politics.

Fundamental to his campaign against Mormon heterodoxy was his conviction that the church was vulnerable to the same kind of apostasy that occurred in early Christianity. He voiced this publicly during the October 1944 general conference:

> I want to say to you brethren, and I am not professing any spirit of seership or prophecy, I am only going on the lessons which history has taught me, but I tell you we are beginning to follow along the course of the early Christian church. So long as that church was persecuted from without, it prospered, but when it began to be polluted from within, the church began to wither.[4]

A year later he warned the general conference to beware of two elements of early apostasy—the introduction of specified dress in church administration and the accretion of pageantry in church ceremonies.[5] "The creeping in of pagan rituals, rites, and ceremonies in the early Church," he told Gordon B. Hinckley in 1948, was the kind of problem "we ourselves must fight in the Church today, and I thought it was a good thing to make that clear."[6]

In 1950 Reuben warned local bishops that one of the first signs of spiritual decay among early Christians was their desire for the praise and acceptance of nonbelievers. Then he asked darkly, "Do any of you brethren know anything about such a tendency as that?"[7] In early 1952 he informed the general priesthood meeting, "There is a startling parallel between the course that is coming in to us today and the course that was in the early Church, so startling that one becomes fearful." He specifically warned against the little groups of dissenters which were presently inconsequential but which might one day overwhelm the church as they previously did the early Christian church.[8]

Because he anticipated parallels between early Christianity and a latter-day apostasy, he focused attention on three groups: the devoted and well-meaning Mormons who incorporated secular scholarship within the gospel; teachers in the Church Educational System, particularly at the church's main school, Brigham Young University; and those who constituted what he regarded as the only significant schismatic movement in his experience—the men and women who continued to advocate and practice polygamy contrary to twentieth-century LDS policy.

Convinced that efforts to reconcile Greek philosophy with Christ's teachings had corrupted the early Christian church,[9] he found a similar tendency in efforts to reconcile the gospel with the Higher Criticism of the Bible by secular scholars. With antecedents extending to the sixteenth century, Higher Criticism developed in the nineteenth century. This included scholarly analysis of scripture, with an emphasis on the reliability of ancient texts and the transmission and construction of their narratives, their literary style, and their historical context.[10] Many biblical critics were believing Jews and Christians, but there were also atheists among these scholars. That fact, plus Higher Criticism's revisions of traditional assumptions, caused all biblical literalists and various religious leaders to brand it as an atheistic attack on Judeo-Christian religion.[11]

Other general authorities disagreed with him, but Reuben was adamant in rejecting the scholarly analysis of the Bible. In so doing, he aligned Mormonism with some of the attitudes characteristic of evangelicals and Protestant fundamentalists.[12] To understand his rejection of biblical scholarship from the 1930s onward, it is important to remember that he regarded his own near-descent into atheism from 1917 to the early 1920s as an inevitable result of his questioning how the texts of Mormon scriptures "evolved."

Before moving to Salt Lake City, he had already begun a decades-long disagreement with Apostle John A. Widtsoe about this scholarly analysis of the Bible. In his 1930 book *In Search of Truth*, Widtsoe wrote, "Higher criticism is not feared by Latter-day Saints." He added, "To Latter-day Saints there can be no objection to the careful and critical study of the scriptures, ancient or modern, provided only that it be an honest study—a search for truth."[13] Widtsoe was one of Reuben's respected friends, but the ambassador wrote a 1930 letter that was not subtle in its implied criticism of how the apostle had approached Higher Criticism:

> However, I come to deplore the fact that some of our "literatti" as I call them, do not spend more time on the philosophy of the gospel as revealed in ancient and modern times, and less on the pagan philosophy of ancient times and the near-pagan philosophy of modern times.[14]

From the 1920s to 1930s, First Presidency counselors Charles W. Penrose and Anthony W. Ivins joined Widtsoe in encouraging biblical Higher Criticism.[15]

Five months after Reuben entered the First Presidency, the *Church News* began publishing articles about the potential of Higher Criticism for Book of Mormon study. On 16 September 1933 the second full-page article, written by religion instructors Sidney B. Sperry and H. Grant Vest, presented "the Problem of Isaiah in the Book of Mormon." Clark's reaction to this is not documented but can be surmised from his statements before and after 1933. Probably because of Ivins's influence, Reuben was either unable or unwilling to stop the *Church News* series. It continued with "The Synoptic Problem in Its Relation to Modern Revelation" on 30 September and "The Johannine Problem in Its Relation to Modern Revelation" on 7 October.[16]

Although he had written negatively about the topic since 1930, Reuben first read an example of it in 1934. He dismissed a book by Charles A. Briggs as "impudently cocksure, and yet so shallow and so unscientific so far as his consideration of evidence goes." He concluded, "If all higher criticism is of this sort, it surely is worth little."[17] This Protestant author's work resulted in a sensational heresy trial.[18]

By contrast, Apostle Widtsoe published a 1940 article in the church periodical wherein he described the Higher Critics as "lovers of the Bible." He said they were trying to "purify the text" and that their "avowed objective is not to discredit the Bible, but to discover truth." He tempered his praise with caution: "The purpose of Higher Criticism may be acceptable; but its limitations must ever be kept in mind ... theories are forever changing."[19]

Reuben could not accept even a partial endorsement of such biblical scholarship. He was appalled that a member of the Quorum of Twelve would give any encouragement to teachers who were already incorporating Higher Criticism into their instruction.

In 1943 Widtsoe republished his endorsement of the new scholarly approach to Bible studies in a book by Salt Lake publisher Bookcraft,[20] and Clark, now first counselor, prepared an administrative counterattack. On 19 April he informed Milton Bennion, superintendent of all church Sunday School instruction:

Furthermore, the tenets of the "higher critics" do not agree with the fundamental doctrines and teachings of the Church; their doctrines are, in practically every case, calculated to destroy the simple faith of our people; the theories of the "higher criticism" cannot be taught with sufficient thoroughness to youth, or even grownups, to enable those to whom they are taught either to judge of their falsity or, if convinced of their falsity, to explain the same to others. I therefore venture to suggest that all such teachings as this should be completely eliminated from our Church institutions. ...

There is abundant evidence that those who are preparing the lessons for our Church institutions have something of a knowledge of sectarian scholarship, which they seem rather fond, if not proud, to display; but there is almost nothing to indicate that they have ever really delved into our own Church history or doctrines.[21]

Widtsoe would have learned about these instructions indirectly. That was not the case a year later when Reuben achieved the final consolidation of his position.

He drafted a letter signed by the First Presidency in August 1944. It instructed the Committee on Publications that "paganistic theories and tenets of the so-called 'higher criticism' have not been without their influence [in LDS publications]; none of these have a place in our Church. They should be wholly eliminated from our literature." Widtsoe was a member of the committee which received this instruction.[22] By means of this 1944 statement, Reuben effectively silenced the only general authority who had publicly given a cautious hearing for scholarly analysis of scripture. He thereby also neutralized the previous statements of this apostle.

However, this First Presidency statement did not silence two other general authorities who had doctoral training. Without publishing their views, Apostle Joseph F. Merrill and Seventy's president Levi Edgar Young continued to encourage Latter-day Saints to explore Higher Criticism.[23]

Reuben had previously maintained public silence about the topic as long as Apostle Widtsoe's endorsements had continued without challenge from the LDS president. But after President Grant signed the 1944 letter, Reuben took frequent opportunity to be the church spokesman in this area. In June 1945 he used a college baccalaureate as the vehicle for a massive assault. He aligned Higher Criticism with Nazism, Bolshevism, and Fascism as enemies of Christianity, calling it a "sinister school of thought," "pettifogging scholarship," an "attack upon God and Christianity," and atheistic in all its manifestations.[24] Despite the fact that many of the twentieth century's biblical scholars were believing Christians and church attenders, he described them as "atheistic scholars" in a subsequent general conference address.[25] He placed biblical scholarship in a stark either/or context in which "they are wrong and we are right." He declined to argue the merits of their work because "it is a waste of lather to shave an ass."[26]

In 1946 Clark indicated the extent to which he had ignored biblical scholars in his previous seventeen years of intensive study about the Bible.[27] He "talked to Bro. [Mark E.] Petersen about the word Jehovah and asked if he could find anything to show that the Lord is the Jehovah in the Bible."[28] In asking this question, Reuben was apparently unaware of the origin of the word "LORD," which appears throughout the King James Version (KJV) of the Old Testament. The English translators used LORD to stand for the four Hebrew letters, the Tetragrammaton, traditionally transliterated into English as JHVH or Jehovah.[29]

Reuben regarded most scholarly analysis of the Bible as an effort to deny its divine origin, and he refused to take even one step down a path he was convinced would ultimately lead to a rejection of divine inspiration. In 1953 he advised LDS youth not to use the word *love* in rendering the *charity* passages of I Corinthians 13 "as the modernists would have us."[30] He devoted his main address of April 1954 general conference to attacking Higher Criticism and the Revised Standard Version (RSV) of the Bible.[31] This was all preliminary to his final statement on the matter, the 473-page *Why the King James Version?* which he published in 1956 after twenty-five years of painstaking research.[32]

Clark defended the KJV as if it were more than a biblical translation but was *the* Bible. He used scholarly sources to argue that supremacy. Philip L. Barlow, an LDS editor of the *Journal for the Scientific Study of Religion,* has noted that Reuben's book "appropriated most Protestant arguments for the KJV, linked them to uniquely Mormon concerns, and in the process made subsequent LDS spokesmen dependent on his logic."[33]

During the years of his public campaign against biblical scholarship, he was pleased at the support by most of the apostles but was disappointed that David O. McKay did not share his repudiation of Higher Criticism. The LDS president acquiesced to his request to address the 1954 conference on the matter. However, when he asked for authorization to publish *Why the King James Version?*, President McKay replied "that he thought we ought to be a little bit careful about criticizing the Revised Version." The president observed that the RSV more accurately translated some passages than did the "Authorized Version" (KJV). Likewise, the revised translation substituted easily understood modern terms for the KJV's antiquated English that often confused current readers. Reuben countered with the observation that President McKay would probably not wish to rewrite the plays of Shakespeare for the same purpose. The LDS president agreed. At one point in the conversation, Reuben exclaimed, "We cannot give up the Authorized Version!" He repeatedly asked if McKay objected to his publishing *Why the King James Version?* Each time, the president said that he did not object. When Reuben again asked the same question as the president was leaving, McKay turned and said, "Go ahead and print your book."[34]

Reuben felt understandable elation at being able to publish what he called his "magnus opus."[35] Nonetheless, his March 1958 letter to Cloyd Marvin, president of George Washington University, expressed disappointment that few of his fellow Mormons shared the intensity of his views about biblical scholarship:

> Contrary to your kindly prediction, I have not had many comments on the book. My own fellow communicants who are of the scholarly class, concluded, (I am sure with one or two exceptions) that I knew nothing of what I was talking about and so paid little attention to the book.[36]

It was a bittersweet conclusion to his effort to defend the purity of the gospel against inroads by latter-day paganism, but Reuben was always more interested in bearing witness than counting converts.

This was underscored for him five months later when BYU president Ernest L. Wilkinson sent him a religion professor's assessment of Reuben's separately published harmony of the four Gospel accounts of Jesus' life. Professor Eldin Ricks wrote: "Inasmuch as all of the material in *Our Lord of the Gospels* may be found in the New Testament, one cannot help but wonder why Melchizedek priesthood holders should purchase President Clark's book, as many have done, unless it be to profit by the very interesting and highly plausible sequence of events that he has set forth. The least that can be said is that a distortion of his arrangement cannot help but confuse the user." This was similar to the objections previously expressed by first counselor Stephen L Richards who had initially prevented the adoption of Reuben's book as a priesthood manual. In response to Wilkinson, Clark wrote with both restraint and irony, "Thank you so much for your kind note and be good enough if you will, to thank Brother Ricks for making the analysis, which I find is very interesting."[37]

Despite his public campaign for the KJV, Reuben privately advocated that the church produce its own English translation of the Bible. In a remarkable conversation at the Clark home with LDS scholar Hugh Nibley, Reuben said "that the Bible should be gone over and studied with reference to the ancient manuscripts such as Aleph, Vaticanus, Alexandrinus, Bezae, etc., etc., so that we might have our own translation. That the Revision made by the Prophet Joseph was never completed and therefore, I felt we could not safely rely on it. The study and revision [if done now] would give us a text upon which we could rely as a translation of the manuscripts."[38] Thus, the KJV did not need to be the only acceptable Bible in English as long as the differing translation was produced by LDS scholars whom Clark trusted. Contrary to all his public statements and writings, he believed that Mormons could have a better English "translation of the manuscripts" than the KJV.

There were also some questions about the New Testament that intrigued scholars but simply did not interest Reuben. "Personally, I have never made any attempt to analyze or reach conclusions as to the authorship of the books of the New Testament," he wrote. "It is my faith that they are true accounts—as to who was the actual writer of them is a matter of small consequence to me."[39]

Nevertheless, because he was convinced that many LDS teachers had yielded to the enticement of Higher Criticism, Reuben exerted unrelenting administrative pressure against these "modernists" within the Church Educational System. He expressed this concern in August 1933 when he "volunteered to read every Manual next year before it was printed." He said that the authors of LDS instructional manuals constituted a "group of radicals."[40]

He began the assault in a March 1934 letter to presidents Grant and Ivins. He recommended that every prospective seminary teacher of LDS high school students be "first carefully examined as to his beliefs." He urged the establishment of a board of inquiry, including a lawyer "to see that the facts are learned, and at least one non-college man," to determine: "Is the B.Y.U. through its teaching corps—whether in the Department of Education or elsewhere—teaching false doctrine."[41] Four years later he announced this publicly in his Aspen Grove talk, "The Chartered Course of the Church In Education":

> For any Latter-day Saint psychologist, chemist, physicist, geologist, archaeologist, or any other scientist, to explain away, or misinterpret, or evade or elude, or most of all, to repudiate or to deny, the great fundamental doctrines of the Church in which he professes to believe, is to give the lie to his intellect, to lose his self-respect, to bring sorrow to his friends, to break the hearts and bring shame to his parents, to besmirch the Church and its members, and to forfeit the respect and honor of those whom he has sought, by his course, to win as friends and helpers.

He emphasized that LDS teachers "are not to teach the philosophies of the world, ancient or modern, pagan or Christian."[42]

In reviewing a New Testament manual in 1940, he wrote: "This book is seemingly based upon the idea that it is quite all right to develop the creeds and dogmas of the sectarian world but all wrong to develop our doctrines on gospel truths. ... The course [text] shows not a little bookish familiarity with secular treatises, but none with our own literature."[43] He continued to question the faith of LDS educators throughout Grant's administration. In 1946 he informed successor George Albert Smith that "we had a number of teachers that were so imbued with modern trends and high[er] criticism that it was not possible for them to teach the Gospel as we understand it."[44]

To some extent, Reuben simply assumed that those with a Ph.D. degree were untrustworthy. He commended Irvin Hull as one of the exceptions: "I am most grateful for yourself and for a few others who, having their Ph.D.'s, still are able to hold the Gospel in its simplicity."[45] His assumption about the perilous condition of LDS education was reinforced by evidence of secular scholarship in church manuals. He likewise found evidence of secularism and alleged lack of faith in BYU professors, reported to him privately by students and faculty whom he trusted.[46]

He expressed anxiety to his protégé Marion G. Romney in 1959 about "the so-called liberals at Brigham Young University."[47] A year later he told President Wilkinson: "You have got some members of the faculty who are destroying the faith of our students. You ought to get rid of them."[48]

Many of the intellectuals and Ph.D.s in the Church Educational System, at BYU, and throughout the church felt that their faith and devotion to the church were unjustly questioned. Many within the new majority of college-educated American Mormons also chafed against what they perceived as anti-intellectualism in LDS leaders.[49] But the fact remained that in the eyes of Clark and his like-minded associates, it was faith, not intellectuality, that was on the defensive.

Long before he became interested in Higher Criticism or LDS education, Reuben began a lifelong battle against those who entered into new plural marriages after the church's "Manifesto" of September 1890. Few developments in Mormon history have been as complex as polygamy. After it was officially announced in 1852, some 60-75 percent of Mormon men declined to ever enter into plural marriage as sanctioned by the published revelations, even though they regarded those documents as divine. During the 1880s the First Presidency continued to promote new plural marriages in defiance of congressional laws, U.S. presidential proclamations, Supreme Court decisions, disfranchisement of polygamists, arrest warrants, fugitive exile, imprisonment, and federal confiscation of church-owned property and funds. By contrast, in the 1930s the LDS church actively suppressed polygamy by means of loyalty oaths, surveil-

lance techniques, blacklisting, excommunications, and support of legislation harsher than the federal government ever enacted against pre-1890
polygamists.[50]

Between the polarities of this extraordinary transition were two periods when LDS leaders moved in different directions simultaneously.
From 1880 to 1890 the leaders publicly and privately insisted on the impossibility of abandoning plural marriage while some contemplated and
experimented with ways of compromising or terminating the practice.
From 1890 to 1910 the hierarchy publicly and privately insisted that the
Manifesto had ended sexual cohabitation with plural wives married prior
to 1890 and that it prohibited new plural marriages anywhere in the
world. During the same time, however, some of the same general authorities privately advocated polygamous cohabitation and new marriages. As
I have previously written, "The Manifesto inherited ambiguity, was created in ambiguity, and produced ambiguity."[51] Throughout most of his
adult life, Reuben was affected personally and administratively by this
transition.

Polygamy had been common in the Woolley family, on Reuben's
mother's side, but his father remained a monogamist for twenty years before the Manifesto of 1890. In that document LDS president Wilford
Woodruff officially announced, "I now publicly declare that my advice to
the Latter-day Saints is to refrain from contracting any marriage forbidden by the laws of the land."[52] On the basis of this and subsequent assurances by the First Presidency, the U.S. government ended its campaign
against the LDS church and granted statehood to Utah in 1896. Latter-day Saints then began their occasionally rocky path toward full acceptance and general admiration by the American public.[53]

The greatest single obstacle to this transition was the reemergence of
polygamy as a national issue between 1898 and 1910. Part of the problem
was the fact that a majority of Mormon polygamists continued to cohabit
with their plural wives. This included most members of the First Presidency and Quorum of Twelve. As a result, from 1899 to 1906 there were
criminal indictments against President Lorenzo Snow, second counselor
Joseph F. Smith, and Apostle Heber J. Grant for illegal cohabitation and/or
adultery.[54] More serious for the public image of the church was the fact

that the First Presidency had acquiesced in the performance of new plural marriages.[55]

The number of post-1890 plural marriages was about a tenth of the pre-1890 number for a similar time period.[56] In 1907 the First Presidency dismissed these post-Manifesto marriages as "sporadic cases" which "have been so few."[57] By contrast, First Presidency secretary Francis M. Gibbons wrote that "a comparatively large number of polygamous marriages had been performed after the Manifesto."[58] Whether regarded as few or many, the first public disclosure of post-1890 polygamy caused acute embarrassment to the church.

If Reuben was initially unaware of the involvement of fellow Mormons and his not-too-distant kin and in-laws in new polygamy, he got a rude awakening while at Columbia University. The U.S. Senate's investigation of Reed Smoot from 1904 to 1907 created headlines nationally. Four printed volumes of official testimony indicated that several members of the Quorum of Twelve had entered into and performed new polygamous marriages after 1890. If the sensational newspaper reports didn't convince Reuben, family members soon verified that Apostle John W. Taylor, husband of Reuben's first cousin Janette "Nettie" M. Woolley married two plural wives in Utah in 1901. Reuben's first cousin Mary E. Woolley became the plural wife of a church patriarch in a ceremony performed in Salt Lake City in 1900. His aunt Fannie Woolley became the wife of a stake president in a polygamous ceremony in Colorado in 1902. Senate testimony also indicated that the bishop of Reuben's Grantsville ward, James L. Wrathall, secretly married the ward's Primary president in 1900 and lived with her in Utah.[59] These were obvious violations of the church's Manifesto as well as of state laws.

Even the fact that many post-1890 marriages occurred in Mexico did not help the situation. Mexican law also specifically prohibited polygamy, including cohabitation with plural wives married in other countries.[60] These disclosures humiliated Mormons like Reuben who had assumed that the Manifesto was an inflexible document which ended the polygamy question for all time.

His legalism and preference for consistency recoiled at the specter of new polygamy coexisting with repeated denials by the First Presidency. As an innocent bystander to the controversy swirling around the Senate investigation, Reuben was in a particularly agonizing situation once he became Assistant Solicitor for the State Department in 1906. As one of the nation's highest legal advisers, he could not look on post-Manifesto polygamy with the least degree of allowance. It offended his religious principles, not to mention violating state and international laws.

He therefore welcomed President Joseph F. Smith's official pronouncement of April 1904 that polygamists would be subject to excommunication. Reuben also felt grim satisfaction at the announcement two years later that apostles John W. Taylor and Matthias F. Cowley had been forced to resign for violating this "Second Manifesto."[61]

But even this was not enough to salve Reuben's personal humiliation as a "modern" Mormon or redeem the church's honor. In March 1907 he wrote a memorandum "vehemently" urging the excommunication of all "who have married [polygamously] since the Manifesto."[62] If such action were applied to all plural marriages between the 1890 Manifesto and the so-called "Second Manifesto" of 1904, the excommunicants would have included Reuben's first cousin, aunt, and bishop.[63] Post-Manifesto polygamists included 25 percent of the stake presidents, 18 percent of the mission presidents, 11 percent of the counselors to stake presidents, and a lesser percentage of ward bishoprics in 1904. Moreover, an inquisition would have been awkward for 50 percent of the general authorities who had either sanctioned, performed, or entered into new marriages during that fourteen-year period.[64]

If Reuben did not fully realize the ecclesiastical carnage that would result from wholesale excommunication, Apostle-Senator Reed Smoot had a better estimate. He knew enough of it not to insist on Reuben's draconian solution. Instead, Smoot advised the First Presidency that all men who had married new wives from September 1890 to 1904 should be immediately released from presiding offices in the church.[65] This would redeem the church in the eyes of the U.S. government, the American people, and Mormons who were offended by the disclosures. President Smith initially refused to allow such "a wholesale action" but finally acquiesced to the gradual release of some of these men.[66]

In 1906 Reuben expressed profound relief when his post-1890 polygamist neighbor was released as bishop of the Grantsville Ward.[67] He had to swallow his legalism when he learned that Wrathall moved his plural wife back to Grantsville in 1907 and then served on the stake high council from 1907 to 1925 and in the presidency of the stake high priest's quorum from 1925 to his death. Although the plural wife continued to live in Grantsville until 1934, her husband died a few months before Reuben entered the First Presidency in 1933.[68] This spared Reuben the embarrassment of having evidence of post-Manifesto polygamy literally in his own back yard while he was a member of the First Presidency.

He and the other general authorities had to face a far more difficult challenge than the generally benign resolution of polygamous marriages performed from September 1890 to 1904. Certain Mormons would not stop performing and entering into new marriages despite the concerted opposition of the First Presidency and Quorum of Twelve after 1906. LDS headquarters learned in 1910 that local patriarch Judson Tolman had been performing marriages since the 1904 declaration. Therefore, the First Presidency issued instructions at October 1910 conference for all stake presidents and bishops to excommunicate any person "who advises, counsels or entices any person to contract a plural marriage ... as well as those who solemnize such marriages, or those who enter into such unlawful unions."[69]

But polygamy would not down. In 1914 Reuben was stunned to learn that John W. Woolley, a temple worker and patriarch, had been performing such marriages. This resulted in the excommunication of Reuben's eighty-two-year-old uncle,[70] who continued to perform marriages.[71] In the First Presidency's office, Reuben's secretary, VaLois South, was a daughter of one of these post-1914 polygamists.[72]

His first cousin Lorin C. Woolley was the primary advocate for Patriarch Woolley's right to perform marriages despite the opposition of the current LDS president. Lorin's argument was that President John Taylor allegedly gave John W. Woolley supreme authority in 1886 to continue the practice of plural marriage, no matter what the church itself might eventually do. Lorin said that he too was one of those who received this authority directly from President Taylor.[73]

Reuben was proud of his Woolley ancestry and relations but felt saddened that the name was so prominently associated with the defiant practice of polygamy. Rarely in Utah during the period in question, he had not known much about the arguments of those who continued performing post-1904 polygamy. He gathered that they based their authority on previous authorization. This was a topic that had not yet been addressed in church pronouncements.[74]

Therefore, as a rank-and-file Mormon, he sent his own proposed statement to the First Presidency in the hope that they would announce it to the October 1923 general conference:

> Resolved that the Church of Jesus Christ of Latter Day Saints, in solemn conference assembled, hereby reaffirms the rule and order of the Church as it has always heretofore existed and as it does now exist, namely that all delegated keys, powers, and/or authorities cease and determine, and become of no force, value, or efficacy whatsoever, upon the death of the person making the delegation thereof, and that all ordinances, sealings, bindings, promises, or other acts whatsoever made, done or performed under and pursuant to such delegated keys, powers, and/or authorities and made, done, or performed after the death of the person who made the delegation, are null, void, and of no efficacy or effect whatsoever ...[75]

He thus sidestepped the historical issue of whether or not any LDS president prior to Grant had authorized the performance of plural marriages after 1890. Instead, Reuben argued that any such delegated authority ended with the death of the president involved.

President Grant was so outraged by those who continued to perform and contract plural marriages that he gave little notice to the lawyer's unsolicited legalisms. He was particularly furious that Reuben's cousin Lorin was circulating stories that seemed to have no basis in fact. Instead of issuing Reuben's proposed declaration in October 1923, President Grant privately dismissed Lorin Woolley as a pathological liar. This led to Woolley's excommunication in January 1924 for "pernicious falsehood."[76]

By the time Reuben entered the First Presidency, his cousin was the guiding light of the vanguard of polygamists who waited for the opportunity to "set the House of God in order."[77] In April 1933 President Grant read "one of the circulars from Jesse B. Stone in which there were a number of statements made by Lorin Woolley, some of which I know to be absolutely false."[78]

Ever active to give legitimacy to his claims, Lorin spent the last year of his life telling his followers that J. Reuben Clark had been associated in various ways with the activities and claims of the Woolley schism. One of their excommunicated followers asked for verification of these stories that Lorin told from April 1933 to his death in September 1934. Reuben set the record straight:

> 1. Did John W. Woolley or Lorin C. Woolley ever represent to you that they both or either of them held the keys of the Priesthood and the fullness of the Apostolic Authority?
>
> Answer: Lorin C. Woolley, the son of John W. Woolley, may have made some such statement. I do not recall. If he did, I never believed it. Uncle John Woolley never made any statement to me about it.
>
> Did you ever accept these men as having this authority and then later feel that you had made a mistake and that such authority rests with the President of the Church?
>
> Answer: No.
>
> 2. Were you ever counseled by either of these men to remain in the government service and to not accept the position of counselor in the First Presidency of the Church?
>
> Answer: No.
>
> 3. Were you ever called or asked by either John W. Woolley or Lorin Woolley to hold an office in the Kingdom of God Organization, which organization is separate and distinct from the Church, which was organized in this dispensation by the Prophet Joseph Smith, and perpetuated at least in part through the administration of President Joseph F. Smith? This organization has sometimes been called the "Council of Fifty."
>
> 3a. If you were called to this position, did you accept this call to the Kingdom Organization and then later repudiate it?
>
> Answer: No such request was ever made nor mentioned.
>
> 4. Have you ever had a plural wife sealed to you by either John W. Woolley or Lorin C. Woolley or anyone else?
>
> Answer: As to the first part of this question—No. With reference to the other part of the question, it is none of your affair, but it happens here, also, that the answer is—No.

5. Have you ever had a plural wife sealed to you who was a Lamanite [Native American] lady, even a princess, and whom you later abandoned?

Answer: No.

6. If John W. Woolley or Lorin C. Woolley did not represent to you that they held the Keys to Priesthood, did they ever tell you that they had been set apart by President John Taylor to keep plural marriage alive in the earth?

Answer: I have no recollection of any such statement; if so, I did not accept it.

7. Did Lorin C. Woolley or his father ever tell you about the eight-hour meeting of 1886 wherein President John Taylor received a revelation in relation to plural marriage in which the Lord said, "I have not revoked this law (meaning plural marriage) nor will I for it is everlasting and those who will enter into my glory must obey the conditions thereof?"

Answer: I have no recollection of any such interview.[79]

Because of the wild stories Lorin Woolley circulated, President Clark concluded that "whether he knew he was falsifying I did not know, but he did not tell the truth."[80] As I have previously written, "Amid the sectarian warfare involving Mormon polygamy, truth has often simply been a negotiable commodity."[81]

Of far greater worry to LDS authorities than Woolley's veracity were their periodic discoveries of new marriages among the Mormons decades after the Second Manifesto of 1904. President Grant had been making "angry" pronouncements against renegade polygamists for years.[82] Almost as soon as Reuben entered the church hierarchy, the president encouraged him to bring his talents to that battle. Grant gave him the first orientation on 25 April 1933, spending the better part of the morning telling Clark about the manner in which four members of the Quorum of Twelve entered into plural marriages after 1890 and performed them for others after the Manifesto.[83] Within a month, on his own initiative,[84] Reuben drafted the longest denunciation the LDS church has ever officially published. It was fourteen printed pages.

As approved and issued by the First Presidency on 17 June, this "Official Statement" went far beyond previous messages that had simply denied post-1890 plural marriage as a matter of church policy. As drafted by Clark, this circular combined for the first time various historical, legalistic, ecclesiastical, and doctrinal denials of the legitimacy of polygamy after 1890. He summarized U.S. legal actions, gave a doctrinal justification for the 1890 Manifesto, referred to the 1891 petition for federal amnesty signed by the First Presidency and Quorum of Twelve, reminded readers that the federal government granted Utah statehood in 1896 upon the provision of perpetual abandonment of plural marriage, and noted that the Utah constitution incorporated that provision. The statement relegated the performance of plural marriages from 1890 to 1904 as actions of "a few misguided members of the Church, some of whom had been signers of the petition praying for amnesty." Adopting the legalistic argument of Reuben's unused 1923 proposal, the First Presidency then denounced as "pretended" the claim that church president Taylor had a revelation in September 1886, insisting that the church archives held no such record or corroboration of any such revelation. The presidency dismissed the alleged authority to continue plural marriage as "illegal and void" and condemned "the corrupt, adulterous practices of the members of this secret, and (by reputation) oathbound organization" of Mormon fundamentalists as a modern version of the satanic Gadianton Robbers of the Book of Mormon.[85] To his State Department friend William Dennis, Reuben explained that the First Presidency issued the statement against polygamy "because some carnally-minded old birds are saying the Church is not in earnest about the matter, and were winking at the situation."[86]

To those in the church who had always opposed new plural marriages, the 1933 statement seemed to be exactly what had long been needed. As written by Clark, the denunciation was a comprehensive, legalistic, and uncompromising denial of priesthood claims by Lorin Woolley and his followers. The First Presidency instructed that the document be read in its entirety during a general meeting of every LDS congregation.[87]

Unfortunately, this 1933 proclamation was an uncomfortable echo of a situation Reuben had created while in the State Department. In 1912 Solicitor Clark had inadvertently transformed the civil unrest of Mexico "from a sandlot revolt into a full-blown rebellion" by issuing a bellicose statement.[88] Clark later realized that his 1933 document was fatally flawed and that it transformed a ragtag collection of polygamist sympathizers, who valued their church affiliation, into a cohesive movement of true schismatics. They thereafter rejected LDS leaders, militantly proselytized, and for the first time in the twentieth century became an actual threat to church stability.

The most fatal flaw of the First Presidency's 1933 statement was that its historical arguments either sidestepped or denied verifiable facts about Mormon polygamy. With the hindsight of a dozen years, President Clark confided to a member of the Quorum of Twelve "that one of the reasons why the so-called 'Fundamentalists' had made such inroads among our young people was because we had failed to teach them the truth."[89]

While the 1933 pronouncement stated that authorized plural marriages could not be performed after the Manifesto, this flew in the teeth of widespread knowledge that from September 1890 to April 1904 members of the First Presidency and Quorum of Twelve had authorized and performed such marriages in Mexico, Canada, and the United States, as well as aboard ship.[90] Moreover, it was also well known that Reuben's co-counselor in 1933, Anthony W. Ivins, had performed dozens of plural marriages from 1897 to 1904 in Mexico. Most of these were solemnized only on receipt of written authorization from the First Presidency.[91] Decades later President Spencer W. Kimball approved his own biography which acknowledged his father-in-law's polygamous marriage: "There was little or no stigma on polygamy entered into in Mexico after the Manifesto."[92]

One crucial element in the 1933 statement of presidents Grant, Ivins, and Clark was its denial of the existence of John Taylor's revelation of September 1886. Reuben's wording took great pains to classify this revelation as pretended and spurious because it was never presented to a presiding council of the church and because the archives "contain no record of any such revelation, nor any evidence justifying a belief that any such revelation was ever given." In fact, this 1886 revelation was discussed in meetings of the Quorum of Twelve and First Presidency in 1890 and 1892 at which Grant was in attendance. Aside from accounts in personal diaries, official minutes of those meetings were recorded in the First Presidency's office journal, which was in the presidency's vault in 1933, as it is today. In 1909 assistant church historian Joseph Fielding Smith copied the 1886 revelation "from the original manuscript" for the archives. During 1911 this revelation was again discussed in meetings of the Twelve at which Grant was again in attendance.[93]

The 1933 statement denied important facts known to many polygamous and non-polygamous Latter-day Saints. For example, there were thousands of children of those who were married by First Presidency authority from 1890 to 1904.[94] By its very appearance of comprehensiveness, Reuben's statement diminished the credibility of the First Presidency denials and increased the credibility of the Mormon fundamentalist arguments for continuing polygamy.[95]

Related to the first flaw, the statement made no distinction between the validity of plural marriages from 1890 to 1904 and those performed thereafter. If the First Presidency had acknowledged the new marriages that had been authorized between 1890 and the Second Manifesto, it could have affirmed that the same authority which once allowed those now forbade any such future marriages. Lacking this distinction, the statement enabled Mormon fundamentalists to argue with the unwitting blessing of the First Presidency that plural marriages in the 1930s were as valid as those performed from September 1890 to 1904. That was crucial for those who knew about the ceremonies performed for nearly fourteen years after the first public disavowal of the practice.

In other words, the rigorous legalism of the First Presidency statement was doomed by its underlying explanation that was historically untrue.[96] The document allowed the conclusion that polygamous marriages performed in 1933 by Lorin Woolley were as valid as the polygamy performed in 1903 by Anthony W. Ivins. Under these circumstances, Reuben's otherwise valid attacks on Woolley's priesthood claim were pointless.

Several factors indicate that this 1933 statement galvanized the loosely affiliated polygamy sympathizers into a vigorous schism, the fundamentalists. Even though many of the sympathizers were bitter about Grant's April 1931 statement, polygamist leader Joseph W. Musser had written, "I sustain Prest. Grant and the Brethren before the Lord and pray for their guidance and welfare, but I cannot subscribe to the denunciation of the principle of Celestial Marriage." By contrast, a week following the publication of the First Presidency's 1933 statement, Musser wrote that "they have exceeded the limit" and that he prayed for God's vengeance to descend on them. Within a few months, he was telling groups of polygamy sympathizers that they "were beyond the authority of any of the General Authorities, not one of whom, (Gen. Authorities) was qualified to preside over such Saints, for they had, by their public utterances or acquiescence repudiated the Patriarchal Order of Marriage."[97]

Up until 1933, pro-polygamy Mormons consciously avoided a schismatic mimicry of any of the ecclesiastical activities of the LDS church. Instead, they simply went about quietly performing and living plural marriage. Aside from a dozen or so Sunday devotional and testimony meetings in the 1922-23 period, most polygamy sympathizers, including those who had been excommunicated, attended no organized meetings of polygamists. Instead, they attended the regular LDS meetings of their resident wards. In stark contrast, from 1933 onward, many stopped attending LDS services and began organizing and attending polygamist Sunday School and sacrament, priesthood, and Relief Society meetings. Fundamentalists began performing their own baptisms, confirmations, and ordinations of boys and men to a priesthood that duplicated the structure of the LDS church. Even those who continued attending LDS meetings also attended fundamentalist services.[98]

The 1933 statement was also directly responsible for a virtual explosion of fundamentalist propaganda. By contrast, during the previous decade, the appearance of pro-polygamy tracts was sporadic.[99] Musser began his prolific career as a fundamentalist publisher in June 1933 as a direct response to the presidency's statement. B. Harvey Allred, married to a plural wife in 1903 by Anthony W. Ivins under authority of the First Presidency, was so outraged that he wrote a book in 1934 "to refute [the] statement of Church leaders of June 17, 1933." Fundamentalists began in 1933 to mail thousands of tracts to all local LDS leaders. From 1935 onward, fundamentalists published a pro-polygamist magazine, *Truth*.[100]

Worst of all, from the point of view of President Clark and his associates, 1933 witnessed the transformation of polygamists from virtual stagnation to vigorous growth. Shortly after the death of Lorin C. Woolley, his heir-apparent, Joseph Leslie Broadbent, told a group of followers that the growth of the movement had been a "losing game" until 1933. "Since then there has been continued advancement among those looking for truth."[101]

The increased propaganda was partly responsible for this rejuvenation, yet the polygamist publications multiplied because of the First Presidency statement. The LDS church's public stance was itself the single most important factor in the success of the Mormon fundamentalists.

By trafficking in half-truths, the First Presidency's 1933 statement unintentionally gave credibility to Mormon fundamentalist claims that were otherwise indefensible. Those who knew about the authorized plural marriages up until 1904 were the most vulnerable. They knew that much of what the fundamentalists were saying was historically true, and so it became easier to accept the rest of fundamentalist propaganda since much of what the First Presidency had said was historically false.[102]

For defensive reasons, neither general authorities nor fundamentalists wanted to give credit to LDS headquarters for the rise of the schism. Nevertheless, with his typical candor, President Clark said in 1945 that the polygamous fundamentalists had success with Latter-day Saints "because we had failed to teach them the truth."[103]

Perhaps this attitude was the reason Reuben did not oppose a proposed biography of John W. Taylor. This apostle was dropped from the Twelve for post-Manifesto polygamy. "They wanted to know what I would think of Samuel W. Taylor writing a biography of their father. I said he was a very colorful character, but a biography would involve considerable difficulties, of which they knew."[104] That simple observation was in remarkable contrast to his opposition to the historical writings of Fawn M. Brodie, Maurine Whipple, Juanita Brooks, Dale L. Morgan, and his own nephew James R. Clark.

He demonstrated personal candor when speaking with the daughter of LDS bishop Heber Bennion who had married his only plural wives after the Manifesto. Apostle Cowley performed these marriages in 1901 and 1902, both in Salt Lake City. In 1920 Bennion began publishing pro-polygamy tracts that were critical of LDS policy.[105] Mary Bennion Powell told President Clark that polygamy brought "misery and unhappiness" and asked why her father and other Mormons had lived it. "I told her because the Lord told us to," Reuben answered. She replied: "Is that all?" His response: "Well, that is sufficient." When she reemphasized the unhappiness in polygamous families, Clark said that "in the long view, looking into eternity," plural marriage brought happiness. She disagreed again, and he concluded, "Well, sister, evidently you have made up your mind about this matter, so I think you will have to work it out yourself."[106]

However, President Grant had not given Reuben a mandate to proclaim the hidden history of past polygamy. His assignment was to suppress current polygamy, and Reuben went at it with a vengeance. The First Presidency statement was just a prelude.

It was not a new idea to require suspected polygamist sympathizers to sign a loyalty oath. That was the 1921 innovation of Apostle George F. Richards, who applied the oath to temple workers.[107] However, Reuben had experience in overseeing the Justice Department's activities against suspected subversives during World War I.[108] This predisposed him to favor a churchwide loyalty oath in the mid-1930s for those suspected of supporting new polygamy.

Filled with his legalistic phrasing, this document required the signer to "solemnly declare and affirm that I, without any mental reservation whatever, support the Presidency and Apostles of the Church; that I repudiate any intimation that any one of the Presidency or Apostles of the Church is living a double life ... that I denounce the practice and advocacy of plural marriage ... and that I myself am not living in such alleged marriage relationship." Refusal to sign was grounds for excommunication.[109] In 1934 a brief summary of this oath became one of the questions asked of every Mormon during the annual interview to verify their worthiness for a temple recommend.[110]

One problem with the loyalty oath was its requirement to deny living in plural marriage. This made life more difficult for more than a hundred faithful Mormons who were still living in polygamous marriages performed by apostles between 1890 and 1904. The wives included members of LDS auxiliary general boards, plus ward or stake presidencies of the Primary, Relief Society, and Young Women's auxiliaries. Their pre-1904 polygamous husbands now included middle-aged and elderly temple presidents, stake presidents, stake patriarchs, high councilmen, temple workers, bishops, and a BYU department chairman. Only three of these men married an additional plural wife after 1904, and none of them were involved with the fundamentalist movement.[111] In addition, dozens of couples who married in polygamy *before* the 1890 Manifesto were also alive in the mid-1930s and vulnerable to the uncompromising require-ments of the loyalty oath.[112]

In an effort to focus the church campaign more directly against fun-damentalists, in 1938 President Clark began commissioning loyal priest-hood leaders to conduct surveillance on people attending meetings at residences of known schismatics. In Salt Lake City, he appointed local bishop Fred E. H. Curtis to supervise several trusted men. They moni-tored those who entered these meetings, copied license plate numbers, and obtained the car owners' names from Utah's department of motor ve-hicles. Clark coordinated with the Presiding Bishop's office to forward the names to local bishops and stake presidents to take action against the in-criminated persons.[113] When the surveillance supervisor was released as ward bishop, Reuben "told him the First Presidency had not released him from his work with uncovering the adulteryites." Curtis continued to su-pervise that work for several years. His surveillance area included Ogden, Utah.[114]

Reuben's oversight of this quiet campaign to ferret out Mormon fundamentalists was not without frustration. Fundamentalists discovered the surveillance almost immediately in 1938.[115] In August 1939 Musser published an open letter identifying Clark as the one responsible for "clearing the community of polygamous teachings and living."[116] Al-though he was receiving separate lists of fundamentalists from Salt Lake City's police department in 1940, that source of information ended in 1941 when a new chief assigned the detectives to other work.[117] The First Presidency also found that bishops and stake presidents were reluctant to convene excommunication courts against people who were implicated by these surveillance techniques. In reporting this "considerable trouble with Bishops and Stake Presidents," the surveillance supervisor noted that "this group is growing by leaps and bounds and the attendance of young people is astounding."[118]

Unruffled by these frustrations, President Clark simply intensified his anti-polygamy campaign in the 1940s. As another way of identifying proto-fundamentalists, he authorized temple presidents to select trusted men and women to infiltrate the ranks of temple workers "to watch and report to the First Presidency what they found to be going on in such matters."[119] At the same time, he encouraged the director of Salt Lake City's public library to exclude Mormon fundamentalist literature from its holdings. He asked the city's postmaster to prohibit the mailing of fundamentalist publications.[120] At a meeting of the First Presidency with Salt Lake County's stake presidents, one local leader suggested that the district attorney "was a good Latter-day Saint and would persecute [sic] the 'new polyg's' criminally if it were deemed wise." In response, Reuben urged that criminal prosecution should begin as soon as possible.[121]

It was through the church's intense surveillance that President Clark learned the astonishing news that a member of the Quorum of Twelve was keeping company with a woman other than his legal wife. Worse still, this woman had previously been the post-1904 polygamist wife of another man. In mid-October 1943 Reuben took Apostle Harold B. Lee into his confidence about the problem and asked him to begin a secret inquiry. On 2 November, Reuben informed Apostle Joseph Fielding Smith and asked the two men to begin nighttime surveillance of their fellow apostle. Not until a week later did Reuben inform the Twelve's president, George Albert Smith. At Clark's direction, Lee and Smith joined with the Salt Lake City police in forcibly entering the residence where the apostle and the woman were spending the night.[122] The result was that on 12 November, the Twelve excommunicated Apostle Richard R. Lyman.[123]

Among the tragedies involved in this situation was a bitter irony. Since 1934 men and women had been excommunicated because they refused to "repudiate any intimation that any one of the Presidency or Apostles of the Church is living a double life," while in fact a member of the Twelve had been living "a double life" of secret polygamy since 1925.[124] The fundamentalist press pointed out this contradiction.[125] President Clark himself worried for the next several years that former Apostle Lyman might actually join the fundamentalist movement.[126]

Reuben had to accept this crushing setback plus his frustration with the resistance of local bishops and stake presidents against the anti-fundamentalist campaign. Despite his own quiet dissatisfaction about the lack of complete candor at LDS headquarters about polygamy's history, he pressed on with his efforts to oppose fundamentalist polygamy. Ten months after Lyman's excommunication, former bishop Curtis testified in criminal court about his years of tracking suspected polygamists.[127]

After the arrest of these polygamists, but before the criminal trial, their lawyer telephoned President Clark at home with an offer to withhold testimony embarrassing to the church. The attorney said he would do so if the First Presidency stopped supporting this prosecution of the polygamists. There followed a discussion about the legal terms *malum in se* (intrinsically bad) versus *malum in prohibitum* (bad because it is prohibited), during which Reuben rebuffed the attorney's offer:

> As he talked he tried to draw some distinction between malum prohibitum and malum in se. I said: "Well, in the eyes of the law and disregarding entirely [any] religious considerations, the pre-Manifesto people were guilty of adultery and so are these people guilty of adultery." I asked him whether adultery was malum in se or malum prohibitum, to which he replied "I won't answer," to which I replied, "You *have* answered."
>
> As the conversation progressed I said, "Well, there is nothing the Church can do about it under any circumstances. We cannot go down and ask that this indictment be quashed."[128]

On this occasion and subsequently, Reuben denied that he had instigated any legal actions against the fundamentalists. In 1951 he even declined to furnish evidence against the polygamists to a detective agency representing Arizona's attorney general.[129] However, he encouraged Latter-day Saints to report what they knew about current polygamists to the civil authorities, and he monitored the progress of criminal court cases involving them.[130]

"During the final days of preparations" for the famous police raid in 1953 against the fundamentalist town of Short Creek, Arizona's governor "made daily contact with a Church leader, usually Apostle Delbert L. Stapley, to keep the Church posted on every step of the process."[131] Governor Howard Pyle gave President Clark a ten-day advance notice of the raid, which was planned for Sunday, 26 July. Reuben classified this document as "Ultra Confidential."[132] The Arizona police arrested the entire population of the polygamous commune in a raid that *Time* magazine said had "the ponderous secrecy of an elephant sneaking across a skating rink."[133]

Contrary to the expectations of Arizona's governor and the First Presidency, there was a national backlash of sympathy for these polygamist families.[134] Therefore, Reuben took care to arrange for news blackouts in the *Deseret News* and *Salt Lake Tribune* of stories that could give favorable publicity to these fundamentalists.[135]

Since World War I, Reuben had believed that social and political upheavals resulted from conspiracies by small groups of dedicated revolutionaries.[136] As an LDS leader, he was constantly watchful for evidence of subversion and treachery among the Saints. The polygamist revolt of Mormon fundamentalism was by far the longest-standing preoccupation of his scrutiny. He felt that it was almost impossible for an LDS member to be loyal to the twentieth-century church after the person became entangled in the theological, psychosexual, and familial web of renegade polygamy. Of later origin, but equal intensity, was his assault on Higher Criticism in particular and higher education in general. As one who had abandoned intellectualism to preserve his own faith, he regarded complex religious inquiry as an addiction that usually led to overdose of intellectualism and death of faith. He was an unrelenting critic of LDS teachers and writers who did not share that view. Superimposed on his other concerns was his conviction that the LDS church was subject to the same centrifugal pressures and corrupting influences as early Christianity.

As a member of the First Presidency for twenty-eight years, Reuben considered himself a watchman on the tower (Ezek. 3:17) whose sight and weapons were directed within the fortress rather than outside it. That also applied to his statements and activities about matters that some might regard as beyond the sphere of religion: the U.S. Constitution, Communism, and Utah politics.

As a young man in the State Department, he had regarded the Constitutional restraints of the Senate on foreign affairs as an irritating handicap.[137] But as he matured, his reverence for the U.S. Constitution grew. "Taught from my infancy that this constitution of ours was inspired and that the free institutions which it creates and perpetuates are God-given," Reuben told an audience in 1919, "I am a member of that class which has a firm and unshakable determination to guard our institutions and our constitution at all cost; that believes that ours is the greatest and best government upon the face of the earth."[138] At general conferences he often said that "to me the Constitution is a part of my religion. In its place it is just as much a part of my religion as any other part."[139] The foundation for his Constitutional views were LDS revelations in which God expressed approval of this crucial document of 1787 (D&C 101:77, 80).[140]

However, Reuben did not regard the divinely instituted Constitution as static. As he explained to Elder ElRay L. Christiansen, the Constitution provided for change through amendments. He gave special praise to "those Amendments which had to do with the destruction of slavery and the enfranchising of the colored man."[141] He reassured a general conference that God would approve any amendment that was adopted in the way the Constitution prescribed.[142]

In fact, he believed that the problems of modern capitalism required new amendments. Although he cherished America's free-enterprise system, he regarded employers and corporations as greedy and "rapacious" in their exploitation of workers.[143] One result of this view, as the *Deseret News* informed Reuben's Mormon readers, was that "my sympathies have always been, and now are, with the laboring man in his unequal struggle with capital."[144] He supported the existence of labor unions: "I am not against unions properly managed. I think that capital with its selfishness, sometimes to the nth degree[,] has forced employees to join unions, to get together for mutual protection, for actual existence."[145] He publicly restated this: "Personally, I am a firm believer in American unions, operated under our free institutions and constitutional guarantees; I think unions have a proper, and at times, necessary function in putting capital and labor on an equal footing. But no real American can approve and support the labor racketeer, sabotage, force and intimidation, the closed shop, and like un-American abuses of true American unionism."[146] A balance between extremes was what he advocated.

The second result of his regarding industrial capitalism and corporate management as "selfish" and "rapacious" was that there was a need for Constitutional revision concerning the role of workers in the modern industrial world:

> The Constitution was framed to provide for a government over what was essentially a non-industrial world. The great bulk of the people were engaged in agricultural pursuits. ...
>
> From that simple social setup we are moving into one that is entirely different. In the first system most men might and could and [did] work for themselves. In this industrial world ... the bulk of the people are entering into a situation of employer and employee. ...
>
> The employer is the corporation, a single, soulless concept, managed by a relatively few officers and management; the employee [is] a great group of hundreds or thousands who are the workmen. Inevitably this new world calls for some new rules and regulations if men are to be protected against one another, employer against employee, and the employee against the employer. ...
>
> Human liberty against the political despot, tyrant, or what-not, was gained but slowly over the centuries, without any predetermined pattern or plan. It may be that the new relationships that arise, indeed that are part of our new industrial world, will have to be worked out in the same way, yet if the problem was envisaged and studied it might be that an easier, quicker and less costly solution could be found.[147]

He also favored Constitutional amendments to provide a 25 percent limit to taxation and a six-year, single term for the service of the U.S. president.[148] As Elder Romney observed, "Although he was passionately patriotic and loyal to the Constitution, President Clark did not think it was perfect."[149]

Nevertheless, he made a clear distinction between those who revered the Constitution, seeking to amend it to adapt to necessary conditions, and those he regarded as Constitutional "defamers." The latter, in his view, wanted to discard the Constitution and the government it provided in order to establish a new social and political order that he condemned as "despotism."[150] As part of his opposition to the Democratic Party's New Deal, Reuben warned in the 1930s and 1940s that the national government seemed to be moving dangerously beyond the Constitution. He told LDS general conference:

> You and I have heard all our lives that the time may come when the Constitution may hang by a thread. I do not know whether it is a thread or a small rope by which it now hangs, but I do know that whether it shall live or die is now in the balance.[151]

He saw little, if any, improvement in the Constitutional situation during the last twenty years of his life. But he did not "grow despondent" because his faith was that the Lord would not allow the Constitution "to be thrown down, but that on the contrary, that He would cause it to be preserved."[152] He believed that the LDS gospel and church would always support the Constitution and its principles.

Yet he was wary of Mormons who suggested that the elders of Israel would one day save the Constitution by military intervention or force of arms. In 1949 his secretary, Rowena Miller, wrote, "President Clark wishes me to acknowledge your letter and to say that he has never felt that the Church would save the Constitution by armed force."[153] Nearly eight years later he instructed the general conference: "The Constitution will never reach its destiny through force. ... God never planted his Spirit, his truth, in the hearts of men from the point of a bayonet."[154]

Reuben's reverence for Constitutional principles and his abhorrence of violence and social upheaval were the foundations for his decades of speaking against Marxism and Communism. True to his policy of avoiding disagreeable reading, he never devoted much time to studying Marxism as a philosophy or Communism as a social system in the Soviet Union or elsewhere. In 1949 he wrote fellow conservative Ernest Wilkinson, an anti-New Deal Democrat, "I am sorry to say that you have an exaggerated notion about what I have done in the matter of studying Communism, because I have done practically nothing at it except for a most casual reading, so I cannot supply you with any bibliography."[155] He may have given the topic "a most casual reading," but his private library contained more than 700 publications about Communism.[156]

He foresaw the dangers that Marxists, Communists, and V. I. Lenin represented for world order,[157] and by the early 1900s he was collecting their publications.[158] Reuben privately expressed concern about their influence in July 1915, two years before the Russian Revolution.[159] He was horrified by its chain of events: the successful Bolshevik Revolution of October 1917, the slaughter of the Czarist family and anti-Bolsheviks during the ensuing civil war, the radical transformation of property and power in the USSR, the ruthless suppression of all dissent and diversity, and the crusading zeal of the Communists.[160] Only one thing caused him greater alarm: among both intellectuals and industrial workers in Europe and the United States, there was evidence of sympathy for the Russian Revolution and of support for the Marxist ideology underpinning it.[161] Therefore, as early as 1919, he publicly "began my crusade against Communism."[162]

However, he spoke against Communism only during periods when he held no civil office. He was out of government service when the Russian Revolution occurred. Thereafter he was notably silent whenever he held positions in the State Department or diplomatic corps.

Moreover, all of this must be understood within the context of his emphasis on the right of revolution and of national self-determination. As biographer Frank W. Fox observed, "Nothing set Reuben apart from other conservatives more clearly than his attitude toward the right of revolution."[163] In a 1913 memorandum to the U.S. president, Reuben asked: "Is the United States prepared to say what form of government shall exist in every other country in the world? Is it prepared to say that no people shall rise up and throw off a despotic power, or correct intolerable evils, by force of arms?"[164] As much as he was appalled by bloodbaths like the French and Russian revolutions, Reuben regarded these upheavals as the people's right.

After obtaining a copy of *Discourses of Brigham Young*, if not earlier, he seems to have been aware that Utah's pioneer prophet considered violent revolution the divine right of every country's citizens: "When misuse of power has reached a certain stage, the divinity that is within the people asserts its right and they free themselves from the power of despotism."[165]

In fact, in a 1920 talk to the residents of Salt Lake City, Reuben called this the "Divine Right of revolution" and asked, "And who are we to presume to challenge this right of a people to adjust its wrongs by revolution?"[166] This obviously referred to the Bolshevik Revolution and government, against which the United States had sent a military force in an undeclared war of 1918-20. Shortly before he made this statement, some of these 14,000 American servicemen were publishing descriptions of their ineffective war against the Russian "Reds."[167]

In view of his condemnations of Communism and the Bolsheviks during the previous decade, his 1929 conversation with two Soviet diplomats was extraordinarily revealing. "I told them I was not frightened of their communism," he began. "I considered that the Russian people had a perfect right to have any sort of government they wished; that the kind of government which they had [Stalinist] was their business and not mine; that I would regard it as most improper and unfriendly for my government to send propagandists to persuade the Russian people that theirs was a bad form of government, and that ours should be adopted instead thereof."[168] Although he served as Undersecretary of State at the time, his remarks were not constrained by diplomacy. For the previous twelve years, the U.S. government had refused to recognize the Soviet Union,[169] and these men had no diplomatic status that Reuben needed to honor or placate. His words on this occasion starkly demonstrated his personal convictions about the right of revolution and the legitimacy of any *status quo* which followed it.

Nonetheless, after becoming a counselor to the LDS president, he intensified his campaign against American acceptance of Communism. This was consistent with both his international views and his own nationalism. He had no objection to the form of government that Russia or Germany or Indo-China might choose, but he exercised his right as an American citizen to denounce any "drifting" of his own country toward Communism.[170] "He thinks that we are being Sovietized by design," wrote Elder Romney.[171] This reflected Reuben's negative views of U.S. president Franklin D. Roosevelt and his Democratic Party's New Deal.

Before his appointment, the First Presidency had not officially commented on Communism. Reuben believed that it was essential to make an official statement because he was convinced that Latter-day Saints were affiliating with Communism in one way or another. As early as 1934, he expressed concern about an LDS member "who has been bitten by this modern communistic bug, and as I have repeatedly observed I have never seen any of them get over it after they have been infected."[172]

Therefore, he drafted the message which President Grant and his counselors issued as a "Warning to Church Members" on 3 July 1936:

> With great regret we learn from credible sources, governmental and otherwise, that a few Church members are joining, directly or indirectly, the Communists and are taking part in their activities.
>
> Since Communism, established, would destroy our American Constitutional government, to support Communism is treasonable to our free institutions, and no patriotic American citizen may become either a Communist or supporter of Communism.
>
> Communism being thus hostile to loyal American citizenship and incompatible with true Church membership, of necessity no loyal American citizen and no faithful Church member can be a Communist.[173]

This was the first time the LDS Presidency had officially attacked a legal political party in the United States. The Communist Party had appeared on the election ballots of various states since 1922 and on the Utah ballot since 1928. A total of 936 Utah voters supported it in the 1932 election.[174] Clark knew that the Communist Party of the United States of America (CPUSA) was a legal organization because he obtained published copies of its election platforms from 1928 onward.[175]

Two weeks after the First Presidency's declaration, he opposed the request of Earl Browder, the American Communist Party's candidate for U.S. president, to speak at the Salt Lake Tabernacle. Reuben also recommended to second counselor McKay that the American Legion go to Salt Lake City's Liberty Park in uniform and "with staves (picks and ax-handles) to attend the Rally" of the Communist Party there.[176]

This led to the First Presidency's review of surveillance reports. On 27 July 1936, five days after Reuben's letter, Seventy's president and general manager of the *Deseret News* Samuel O. Bennion reported that he had assigned two reporters, "who are new, and not known in Salt Lake City," to infiltrate local Communist Party meetings. Not for investigative journalism, their observations went to the First Presidency.[177] Beginning the same month, Lester Wire, a Roman Catholic and chief of Salt Lake City's "subversive detail" of detectives, was also sending the First Presidency reports of surveillance and infiltration of Communist meetings in the city. This transfer of confidential reports was undoubtedly authorized by police chief Harry L. Finch, a Mormon.[178]

In the November election, only 279 Utahns voted for the Communist Party's presidential candidate. The Communist vote had plunged almost 78 percent in Utah while nationally it declined only 22 percent.[179] The drop in support was consistent with the national pattern in the massive reelection of President Franklin D. Roosevelt in 1936, but Utah's greater decline may have been influenced by the First Presidency's statement. However, because the number of Communist voters in Utah was so small to begin with, the difference in rates of decline may be insignificant.

One of the LDS infiltrators spoke directly to Reuben in 1939. "He said that at the meetings which he had attended of the Communist Party they had advocated mass assassinations ... and that high up among those who were to be first taken were the Church Authorities, all of whom were to be murdered." Clark listened with interest but without any evidence of panic: "I suggested that he go back to see Governor [Charles R.] Mabey and explain the whole thing to him."[180] Until 1940, Detective Wire continued to provide Communist surveillance information to the First Presidency either directly or through an ardent anti-Communist and Mormon, Jeremiah Stokes.[181] Upon receiving one of these surveillance reports in April 1940, Counselor McKay wrote, "Communist rats are working here in the United States and are gnawing at the very vitals of our government, and I wish every one of them could be sent to Russia where he belongs."[182] This indicated the degree to which he shared Reuben's viewpoint.

The transfer of police reports ended the following month when Utah's Communist Party newspaper exposed the activity. "In Salt Lake City, for several years past, the situation has been so silly that one member of the city police force, Detective Lester Wire, has occupied himself with compiling a list of alleged communists, which he has taken, from time to time, not to his official superiors but to a messiah anointed by busybodies to save Utah from the Bolsheviks." Reuben apparently regarded the latter phrase as a reference to himself and kept this article in his personal library.[183]

This sharing of intelligence information between LDS headquarters and law enforcement agencies has continued to the present.[184] It is another administrative legacy of J. Reuben Clark.

He also made repeated statements against viewing the church's practice of the United Order as compatible with Communism. The First Presidency's 1936 statement affirmed:

> To our Church members we say: Communism is not the United Order, and bears only the most superficial resemblance thereto; Communism is based upon intolerance and force, the United Order upon love and freedom of conscience and action; Communism involves forceful despoliation and confiscation, the United Order voluntary consecration and sacrifice.[185]

This uncompromising statement apparently did not resolve the difficulty.

At the October 1942 general conference, Reuben condemned the idea of "communism being merely the forerunner, so to speak, of a reestablishment of the United Order. I am informed that ex-bishops, and indeed, [current] bishops, who belong to communistic organizations, are preaching this doctrine."[186] A year later he told a meeting of LDS bishops, "Now there are some here who will not like what I am going to say, but I repeat what I said today: Communism is Satan's counterfeit for the United Order, that is all there is to it."[187]

He wrote to former French Mission president Edgar B. Brossard in 1944: "But it is not Fascism that I am fearing. The world has dealt with Fascism since the beginning of time. It is Communism that is the real danger, except that a lot of these fellows have not the courage to denounce Communism because of Russia."[188] The reason was that in 1944 Communist Russia was a military ally of the United States in war against Nazi Germany. He later amplified his view publicly:

> There is this difference between Nazism and Communism—the first leaves [i.e., allows] private property and individualism, however

much appropriated and curtailed to meet the immediate crisis; the second destroys both private property and individualism, making the state all-pervading, all-absorbing, a god of human mind.[189]

As political systems, he regarded Nazism as the lesser of two European evils from 1933 to 1945. This was one reason for the relative tolerance he expressed for Adolf Hitler and Nazi Germany. (See chapter 9.) Another reason was his previously noted emphasis on national self-determination. As biographer Fox observed, President Clark believed "that the German form of government, revolutionary though it [Nazism] may be, was nobody's business but Germany's."[190]

Reuben was never reconciled to the World War II alliance of the United States and the Soviet Union against Nazi Germany because this seemed to imply a grudging acceptance of the Communist system.[191] "I have harped on the general tenor of communism until people think I am 'screwy' on the subject," he wrote to Utah political scientist Frank H. Jonas in 1943, "but I have never been more earnest, and I think, never more right, than in my position on this matter." He was insistent because Americans "are being communized at something of a fast pace."[192]

In 1946, probably with Counselor Clark's encouragement, the presidency of George Albert Smith renewed the decade-earlier interest of Grant's presidency in obtaining lists of Mormon Communists. In August the First Presidency wrote U.S. Senator Elbert D. Thomas, a faithful Mormon, asking if he could obtain for them a copy of a Senate committee's secret "list of the Communists of the United States." With icy formality, Thomas replied in September, "The Communist Party records in the states where the Communist Party is organized in America are open as are the Democratic and Republican Party lists." He reminded the First Presidency that it was the responsibility of FBI director J. Edgar Hoover to keep track of suspected subversives.[193] As evidence that Reuben was the driving force behind the 1946 letter, eight years later he asked his secretary, Rowena Miller, to write a similar request to Utah's Senator Wallace F. Bennett for the "names of persons or organizations that have been cited as subversive."[194]

In 1947 Reuben also asked Mark E. Petersen to get the names of "the professors and businessmen who might be sponsoring this concert" by African-American singer Paul Robeson at the University of Utah. Clark explained that the concert's general sponsor, American Youth for Democracy, "is a communist organization." When Elder Petersen gave him a list, "Pres. Clark thought there were more people backing the Robeson concert than were listed on the note given him. Bro. Petersen will have it checked into."[195]

Reuben was anxious that no Latter-day Saint be identified in any degree with Communist terminology or become too knowledgeable about its philosophy or be sympathetic to the Soviet Union. "Because of the connotation given to the name through the communists," he opposed using the term "youth conference" in the church's Mutual Improvement Associations.[196] In a letter to LDS political scientist G. Homer Durham, he explained that he opposed publishing much about what Communists actually believed because "you do not build virtue in the home by picturing the allurements of a house of prostitution."[197] For the same reason, he did not want LDS youth or young adults to travel to the Soviet Union.[198] After all, they might become infected with what he called the "poison-plague" of "Communism in Russia."[199]

Despite his own campaign against Communism, President Clark had mixed feelings about the American anti-Communist movement. On the one hand, he himself tended to blur, if not eliminate, any distinctions among Marxists, Communists, revolutionaries, anti-democratic socialists, pro-democracy socialists, and New Dealers.[200] For example, he told Durham that scientist Albert Einstein, a Jewish refugee from Nazi Germany, "is at heart a socialist, if not a communist."[201] He accused news columnist Drew Pearson and his LDS assistant, Jack Anderson, of being proto-Communists because "the things for which Pearson stood and for which he [Anderson] stood were things that inevitably led to communism, if followed through."[202] Likewise, Reuben wrote to one inquirer, "As to how you will recognize a communist, I can only say that if you will listen to them talk and find them advocating communistic principles, they are probably communists."[203]

Like respected conservative columnist William F. Buckley, he also praised the intent of U.S. Senator Joseph R. McCarthy's anti-Communist campaign.[204] Reuben purchased the senator's publications[205] and used his own administrative power to stop *Deseret News* editorials critical of Mc-Carthy's tactics.[206] President McKay likewise supported Senator McCarthy and later told the apostles about "the farce that is going on now in Washington between McCarthy and the Army [in televised hearings]. Undoubtedly, the Communistic influence is being exerted there to lessen the influence of men who would ferret out the enemies in the high places of our government."[207]

On the other hand, Reuben acknowledged that fervent anti-Communists were sometimes guilty of character assassination. He himself had been classed as a fellow traveler with Communists because he opposed NATO.[208] After Henry C. Dworshak was similarly accused, Reuben comforted this U.S. senator by saying, "I have always understood that you lay over on the right side of the communistic line, which is the farthest away you can get from the communist party."[209] Thus, when McCarthyism struck at someone he knew and trusted, Clark renewed his opposition to the wartime hysteria of pointing "an irresponsible finger of unsupported suspicion."[210]

He was especially leery of those he regarded as extremists among the Mormon anti-Communists. Even though Jeremiah Stokes was the first LDS member to become an anti-Communist pamphleteer,[211] Reuben declined in 1945 to aid him in any way in distributing his literature.[212] He warned his son Reuben III that Stokes was "intensely anti-communist" and to "be awfully careful in using his stuff."[213]

Likewise, despite the encouragement of his LDS friend Harold Bennett, Clark in 1946 declined even to meet a Mormon who was trying to form an anti-Communist organization. Reuben's secretary, Rowena Miller, wrote in his office diary: "He says everybody passes the buck to Pres. Clark, [and] wants to know what he [JRC] is doing before joining him [the anti-Communist]. Pres. Clark feels he cannot be used as a front to get this man going, so does not feel he can spend time with him."[214] When California stake president Hugh C. Smith sent him a stridently anti-Communist national publication in 1954, President Clark responded, "I am always troubled to know how much reliance can be placed in this kind of literature."[215]

However, he agreed with Apostle Ezra Taft Benson, U.S. Secretary of Agriculture from 1953 to 1961, on two essentials. First, that the Communist menace in America was real. Second, that anti-Communists who were stable and wise should be supported.[216] As Reuben wrote in 1947 to Sumner Gerard, an officer of the Committee for Constitutional Government, "I assure you that I am in sympathy with all effective measures that are calculated to bring home to the American people the blessings of free government which they now possess and the dangers of the dictatorship which now casts its shadow on us."[217]

With the permission of President George Albert Smith, Reuben became a trustee in 1948 of the New York-based Foundation for Economic Education (FEE).[218] This organization published pamphlets like *Where Karl Marx Went Wrong.*[219] Reuben's personal library had several of its publications including *Morals and the Welfare State, Planned Chaos,* and a criticism of the United Nations.[220] Its monthly publication, *The Freeman,* contained such articles as "UN Versus US," "The Collectivist Menace," and "Not Victories for Communism."[221] Aside from buying books about Marxism and Communism since the early 1900s, Clark had been collecting publications against socialist "collectivism" since the 1930s.[222] Becoming an officer of a conservative foundation was a natural extension of his apprehensiveness about these matters. He persuaded church-affiliated businesses to contribute to the FEE.

This led to the following conversation in August 1949 with Jack Anderson of the *Washington Post.* Anderson said:

> We have uncovered a lobbying outfit in Washington known as "Foundation for Economic Education." They are breaking the federal laws. They claim tax exemption as an educational institution, although they are actually a lobbying organization. I have the word of several congressmen on that. ... I got hold of a confidential list of substantial donors which included ... Utah-Idaho Sugar Company, Beneficial Life Insurance Company, Z.C.M.I. and other Church-owned or controlled institutions.
>
> I have made the investigation, and it has been necessary for me to write the story, but because of my membership in the Church I have left

out the organizations owned or controlled by the Church. I would, however, like to discuss the matter with President Smith.

At the end of this entry, Reuben noted, "I told Brother Jack Anderson
that I would present the facts to President Smith and advise him later as to
the possibility of an interview."[223]

Clark described the meeting with Anderson in a letter to Leonard E.
Read, president of the FEE: "That whether or not our method of procedure was taxable or nontaxable was another question, and that if we had to
pay taxes I would want to pay the tax and continue our propaganda."
Reuben added that Anderson had "objected to the use of Church funds
in support of the Foundation. I told him the Church had advanced no
funds. Well, they were funds that came from Church owned and controlled businesses, he said. I told him that was true in part, but not wholly
true."[224]

Despite his continued role as national director of America's oldest
pacifist organization, the American Peace Society, Reuben told a church
member in 1950, "*Peace organizations*: a number of them are communisti-
cally led." In part, this may have reflected his exasperation that fellow director Alger Hiss was publicly accused of being a Soviet spy in August
1948. The American Peace Society's magazine did not remove Hiss from
its published list of directors until the spring of 1949.[225]

Clark also instructed the *Deseret News* in 1951 to promote local meetings of "the anti-Communist 'crusade.'" He said "the bishops would do
well to have called this matter to the attention of their congregations."[226]

Despite the First Presidency's statement that "no faithful Church
member can be a Communist," Reuben did not support the excommunication of LDS Communists. In 1952 Apostle Petersen wanted to instruct
a stake president to excommunicate a man who belonged to the American Communist Party. Clark joined with President McKay and Counselor
Richards in replying, "As you will appreciate, it would not be feasible to
excommunicate this man for being a Communist."[227] Even though Mc-
Kay and Clark expressed ardently anti-Communist views, they did not
want to punish LDS members who disagreed with the First Presidency's
public statements.

Nor did President Clark accept the claim of some anti-Communists that fluoridating a city's water supply was a Communist plot.[228] In answer to one Mormon who said in 1955 that "it is against our freedom to have fluoridation," Reuben reminded him that "chlorine was put in our water" without ill effects.[229]

Nevertheless, he continued to encourage what he perceived as wise anti-Communist speeches and books. He wrote LDS author W. Cleon Skousen in 1958, "I thank you for the superscription in your book and I am happy if anything that I ever said came to be of service to you in this tremendous undertaking." He added that Skousen's *The Naked Communist* was "very entertainingly written."[230]

Following Reuben's October 1959 conference address against Marxism, presidency secretary Joseph Anderson reported the counselor's earnest concerns:

> President Clark wishes me to say that he did not expect Marxian sympathizers, whatever their particular Marxist cult might be, to approve of what he said; but he hopes that Latter-day Saint Marxist cultists will give sober, prayerful thought to the whole problem before abandoning truth for error.[231]

Six weeks before Reuben's death, the LDS president responded to the comment of "Elder Benson and others of the Brethren" who said that a stake president "has been a little extreme in his efforts to combat" Communism. President McKay replied that "we must be careful about condemning any efforts that are anti-Communistic because Communism is a real danger in our country."[232] This was a subject about which he and Counselor Clark had always agreed.

Because Reuben regarded the Democratic New Deal as anti-Constitutional and pro-Communist, he became even more ardently Republican upon entering the First Presidency. In a draft of one talk, he wrote, "The Republican Party was born to save the Union; it has lived that it might save our Constitution with its free institutions."[233] By 1940 even local Republican leaders regarded him as the virtual head of the party in Utah despite his disclaimer "that I had no such place, in fact nor in thought."[234]

For nearly two decades, without his asking, county and state Republican leaders, candidates, and officeholders met with him in the Church Administration Building to seek political counsel and support. Anti-New Deal Democrats did likewise. In particular, prospective candidates or their advocates repeatedly attempted to obtain Reuben's official endorsement.[235] He sought to remain noncommittal and explained "that the Church could not undertake to pick candidates, but after the candidates were picked, our interest in the general welfare would lead us to try to exercise such persuasion as we properly might to get the best men elected."[236]

It was a particular challenge when elected officials—both Republicans and conservative Democrats—asked President Clark about the course they ought to pursue in a specific matter. In 1939 he stated some broad principles which governed his approach to such situations for the rest of his service in the First Presidency:

> We were in a position where we could not keep our mouths closed and then condemn them for what they did or did not do. I observed that of course we were in a position to indicate, for example, that we thought they ought to do all they could to lower taxes; to decrease State employees instead of to increase them; to avoid radical labor legislation; to avoid all Communistic legislation; to have the existing sabotage law stand unchanged, unamended, in the interest of labor, etc., etc.[237]

He likewise gave advice about legislation and political matters to LDS officeholders in California, Idaho, Utah, and Wyoming either in person or by telephone.[238]

By the 1940s Reuben also adopted the policy of referring nearly all political inquirers and matters to three trusted associates. Questions of financing Republican candidates and causes went to Orval W. Adams, president of the church-owned Zion's First National Bank. Reuben sent Republicans to Apostle Lee, Democrats to Henry D. Moyle, chairman of the General Welfare Committee since 1938 and member of the Twelve since 1947.[239] Clark explained the nature of this delegation to one inquirer, "I suggested that he see Brothers Lee or Moyle, or both of them; that while they were not undertaking to guide the Church in politics, nevertheless we had determined that they should interview people so that we would only get one expression or explanation."[240]

The First Presidency also wanted to be informed about the progress of bills in the Utah legislature, sometimes for lobbying purposes but sometimes not. In 1943 Reuben described a meeting with his friend Gordon Affleck, a local bishop and the church's purchasing agent: "Asked him to keep track of legislation in the Legislature and report to us but we did not intend to use him for lobbying. He expressed gratitude for the latter, [and] said he would be happy to do the former."[241]

In 1948 President Clark emphasized that the church had not attempted to influence Utah's governor: "So far as I knew President Grant had never, since I have been here, sought to interfere with the running of the State Government, never having made any requests of the Governor, so far as I recollected and of which I knew." He added that during the administrations of Grant and George Albert Smith, "I personally had never made any requests of the Governor and that I had, so far as I remember it, called only one matter to the attention of the Governor, and that was recently and had to do with the chaplaincy of the State Prison."[242]

A minority of church members still wanted Reuben to be more politically assertive. In September 1949 he explained to J. H. Gipson, "It is not possible for me in my position, wisely to take an active part in politics, but my heart is right, and such things as I may do, I shall do to try to get safe and sound policies into our government."[243]

Among the political things he undertook was to arrange for private financial assistance in times of political need. In November 1949 he enlisted the aid of Adams of Zion's bank and Harold Bennett of ZCMI to get last-minute contributions for a city commissioner's election: "Pres. Clark suggested $1,000."[244]

Because he usually avoided using his church position to influence politics, he wrote a bristling reply to Drew Pearson's nationally syndicated article in November 1950. Pearson had described him as Utah's Republican boss who had unseated a U.S. senator for supporting the New Deal. Reuben wrote:

> In view of this background I think probably you would be glad to

know that you are almost completely misinformed regarding my work and position here in Utah. For years I have taken no part whatever in politics, and while I have let my personal views be known about various matters political, I have no reason to believe that they have had any particular influence. I believe I know who some of the persons are who have talked with you to the building up of a bogie-Clark who has no existence except in their imaginations. I took no part in the recent campaign. I believe if I had taken part there might have been more "lame ducks" than there were. Senator [Elbert D.] Thomas was defeated because people were tired of him and of the things for which he stood. I did not defeat him.[245]

Ardently pro-FDR, Thomas had "originated and introduced significant New Deal legislation" during eighteen years as Utah's senator. He "was largely responsible for the creation of" such well-known programs as the Civilian Conservation Corps (CCC) and the National Science Foundation (NSF).[246] Reuben publicly condemned such "alphabetical bureaus" of the federal government.[247] In addition, after 1939 Thomas advocated that the United States join Britain against Nazi Germany,[248] and he was a founding member of the Emergency Conference to Save the Jewish People of Europe from the Nazis.[249] President Clark opposed both proposals. (See chapters 9, 10.)

During the same year as his complaint to Pearson, however, Reuben demonstrated that he could say and do divergent things concerning Utah's politics. After meeting with Adams to discuss the details of an upcoming political talk in May 1950, "Pres. Clark said he wanted to be in a position to say that what has been said has been without his knowledge and consent."[250] In other words, he wanted to maintain plausible denial.[251]

This was certainly the case when the U.S. Secretary of Agriculture wanted to use the tabernacle in Logan, Utah, for a political speech in July 1950. Reuben gave specific instructions to Thorpe B. Isaacson, then a counselor in the Presiding Bishopric, to make "a personal suggestion" to the four stake presidents of Logan to "keep the Church out of it" by declining to allow the Democratic speaker to use the Logan Tabernacle. Instead, they were to offer him a school house. Four days later a Mormon telephoned Reuben's secretary, Rowena Miller, to complain that "use of the Tabernacle for Secretary of Agr. [Charles F.] Brannan had been with-drawn after all arrangements had been made and rental fees paid, and it was being stated that Pres. Clark was the authority for this action, and that if the situation were not altered it would hit national news." In one of her rare first-person entries in his office diary, she noted, "President Clark told me that he had had nothing whatever to do with the matter, had not talked with anyone at *Brigham City* concerning the question, and told me I could quote him on that which I later did when Arthur Gaeth called me about four o'clock."[252] Formerly a mission president, Gaeth made the same complaint to George Albert Smith. The LDS president wrote: "President Clark said that he had nothing whatsoever to do with the mat-ter; and so I called President McKay. He had not spoken to anyone and neither had I." Smith then informed the Logan stake president that the First Presidency had no involvement in the incident.[253] In this case, Reu-ben extended plausible denial to how he answered the church president's inquiry about this matter.

Likewise, in 1951 Reuben seemed to say and do contrary things si-multaneously. During his hour-long conversation with a Utah legislator in June, "I made it perfectly clear time and again that I was not trying to bring Church influence to bear on him, or tell him what to do, but that if I were in his place I would consider very carefully before I went contrary to the wishes of a President of the Church."[254]

In fact, six months earlier President Clark had coordinated an exten-sive lobbying effort in the Utah legislature by two apostles representing the major political parties. In January 1951 Elder Moyle obtained his ap-proval to hire two attorneys to draft bills for cooperative LDS legislators to introduce. The next month elders Albert E. Bowen, Matthew Cowley, Lee, Moyle, and Petersen had private meetings at the Church Administra-tion Building with both Republican and Democratic legislators.[255] These five apostles were all "Clark men."

In 1953-54 general authorities made an abortive effort to influence Utah's vote on reapportioning the legislature. Apostle Moyle said pri-vately, "Brethren, don't you realize that if this proposal is passed that the Church will control twenty-six of twenty-nine [state] senators."[256] In the pattern Reuben had established in the early 1940s, Democrat Moyle and

Republican Lee jointly lobbied the legislators of their respective parties. The two reported back to Clark and then to President McKay.[257] When asked privately by legislators about the First Presidency's views "about the proposed reapportionment," President Clark typically replied in March 1953 that "Brother Moyle and Lee were handling these matters."[258] Nevertheless, Utah's primarily Mormon electorate defeated this reapportionment proposal by 142,972 votes to 80,044—mainly because President McKay had publicly declined to take responsibility for the political activities of the two apostles.[259]

As a result, Reuben advised his two protégés to take precautions in their political meetings with McKay. He instructed Apostle Lee to "be silent on politics because of past experiences and to document for future reference my [Lee's] notes on the meetings with[,] and the instructions we had received from[,] Pres. McKay on the Junior College and Reapportionment referendum because of insidious inferences which still persist to the effect that Brother Moyle and I [Lee] were responsible for the distribution of literature on these issues, without authorization."[260] Reuben was clearly unhappy that President McKay had used plausible denial to undercut the credibility of the counselor's protégés in political lobbying.

Despite his ardent Republicanism, Reuben also opposed one-party rule—even by the GOP. In 1956 he expressed his view that "a Democratic Congress, as a brake on a Republican administration, during these critical times, was not a bad arrangement. ... It will be irritating to the President [Eisenhower] at times, but it will also be safe."[261] This applied to Utah politics as well. The state Democratic convention nominated a "good man in each place," he wrote his non-LDS friend A. Helen Morgan that same year, "and if they are successful in becoming our officers they will, I am sure, give us a good administration."[262] He was as good as his word, and privately persuaded Apostle Moyle to abandon his intention "to institute some political activities intended to defeat the Democratic candidate."[263] Ever the Republican, Reuben was ever more the Constitutionalist with an abiding trust in the "checks and balances" of power.[264] He had an equally abiding suspicion of the evils in one-party rule and in popular election mandates for the chief executive.

Throughout his life he was pragmatic about Republican candidates. For instance, his relative Roland Rich Woolley wrote to complain about the nomination of California native, Richard M. Nixon, as the 1960 candidate for the U.S. presidency. "I do not recall that California has been conspicuous for her statesmen in the past," Reuben replied. "Why be fussy now?"[265] In this election President McKay created controversy among faithful Mormons by publicly endorsing Nixon's unsuccessful candidacy against Democrat John F. Kennedy.[266]

In only one respect did President Clark maintain a close political consultation with an elected official in Utah. This was his well-known association with Governor J. Bracken Lee, a non-Mormon who was politically independent and anti-New Deal.[267] Lee frankly expressed to other political leaders his own view of Utah politics::

> Gov. Lee: I said to them you are never going to have any success in Utah unless you let the leaders of the Church give you some advice. You better make it a point to talk with the Church officials to find out if they are going along with it or not.

Reuben undoubtedly appreciated this comment. He had his secretary transcribe it verbatim.[268]

Nearly every contact between the Utah governor and the church's elder statesman was at Governor Lee's initiative.[269] When the First Presidency counselor did initiate a meeting, he began by saying, "I told him that I appreciated that it was almost impossible for a man to divest himself of his position in a matter about which he talks, but so far as it was possible to do so, I was divesting myself of my [church] position, and was coming to him merely as an American citizen."[270] Oftentimes Reuben declined to contact the governor when various LDS administrators urged him to do so. As he explained, "To ask the Governor for favors would put us in a position where if he asked us for favors we could not well refuse."[271]

One time President Clark felt duty-bound to contact J. Bracken Lee when it was rumored that the governor would veto the Utah legislature's Sunday-closing bill. Apostles Lee and Moyle had lobbied the Mormon legislators on the matter for two years,[272] but the governor regarded this as discrimination against Jews and Seventh-day Adventists.[273] When Governor Lee argued that these people should have the right to observe their own Sabbath and then conduct business on Sundays, Reuben countered, "Suppose you had a group of harlots come in and object to any restrictions you might place on them." He concluded his rare effort at direct lobbying with the statement that "it seems to me that in matters affecting, as we think this does, the religious and moral welfare of a community, I am wondering if the minority, where there is no legal right, whether the minority should control."[274] The governor, like other listeners of President Clark's political counsel for nearly three decades, did not accept the warning voice. In response, Reuben may have written the blistering editorial in the *Deseret News* urging Mormon legislators to consider only "the great majority of Utah's citizens" and override the governor. Instead, the Mormon-dominated legislature sustained his veto.[275]

Reuben did not complain directly to Governor Lee. As he said five months later when he thought President McKay was pressuring the governor about another matter, "You can't hit a man over the head and expect him to do you a favor."[276]

Although disappointed at any rejection of his earnest counsel or warnings, Reuben felt that he had fulfilled his responsibility by energetically expressing his views. He was often amused by those who tried to put one kind of label or another onto his efforts. He told the priesthood meeting at April 1935 conference that "in Wall Street I am known as a radical; at home as a sort of man-eating conservative."[277] Seventeen years later he publicly defined himself since many others had failed to label him accurately:

> I am pro-Constitution, pro-Government, as it was established under the Constitution, pro-free institutions, as they have been developed under and through the Constitution, pro-liberty, pro-freedom, pro-full and complete independence and sovereignty, pro-local self-government, and pro-everything else that has made us the free country we had grown to be in the first 130 years of our national existence.
>
> It necessarily follows that I am anti-internationalist, anti-interventionist, anti-meddlesome-busybodiness in our international affairs. In the

domestic field, I am anti-socialist, anti-Communist, anti-Welfare State. I am what the kindlier ones of all these latter people with whom I am denying any association or sympathy, would call a rabid reactionary (I am not, in fact, that).[278]

To that list, one must appropriately and necessarily add that J. Reuben Clark was a watchman on the tower of Zion. He raised a warning voice to the Latter-day Saints about dangers he perceived in religious and secular spheres. In that capacity, he often found it necessary to "mark them which cause divisions and offenses."

Young J. Reuben Clark Jr. *Courtesy Special Collections, J. Willard Marriott Library, University of Utah*

Reuben's hometown of Grantsville, Utah. *Courtesy Utah State Historical Society*

James E. Talmage,
Reuben's academic mentor
in the 1890s. *Courtesy
Utah State Historical
Society*

Reed Smoot.
Although Reuben disliked
him, this apostle-senator was
Reuben's role model as a
secular Mormon from
1903 onward.

Major Clark
during World War I.
Courtesy Marriott Library

J. Reuben Clark's family about 1919. Marianne, Lute, and Louise; Reuben III and Luacine. *Courtesy Marriott Library*

Undersecretary
of State Clark, 1928–29.
*Courtesy Utah State
Historical Society*

Ambassador Clark with Mexican president Ortiz Rubio in 1930. *Courtesy Marriott Library*

When Reuben entered the Church Administration Building in March 1933 to commence his activities as counselor in the LDS First Presidency, he thought of this passage from Dante: "Abandon hope, ye who enter here." *Courtesy Utah State Historical Society*

First counselor Anthony W. Ivins (an apostle for nearly 26 years), President Heber J. Grant, and second counselor Clark (newly ordained high priest) in April 1933. *Courtesy Marriott Library*

The Council Room of the First Presidency (chairs at far right) and Quorum of Twelve Apostles. The altar in the center is for the "true order of prayer." When not away from Utah for secular activities, Reuben attended the Thursday "temple council meeting" here. *Photograph by Reuben's father-in-law, Charles R. Savage*

U.S. delegation to the Seventh Pan-American Conference, Montevideo, Uruguay, 1933. Sophonisba Breckinridge, Ambassador Alexander W. Weddell, Secretary of State Cordell Hull, J. Reuben Clark, J. Butler Wright, and Spruill Braden. *Courtesy Utah State Historical Society*

First counselor Clark (newly ordained apostle), President Grant, and second counselor David O. McKay (an apostle for twenty-eight years) in October 1934. *Courtesy Utah State Historical Society*

Honolulu, Hawaii, 1935: Reuben, Luacine Savage Clark, Heber J. Grant, Augusta Winters Grant, Preston D. Richards, and Barbara Howell Richards (front row). *Courtesy Marriott Library*

Presiding Bishop
Sylvester Q. Cannon,
a Utah officer of the New
Deal, was the chief oppo-
nent of Counselor Clark's
philosophy of church wel-
fare from 1933 to 1938.
*Courtesy Utah State
Historical Society*

Clark's protégés in the LDS Welfare Program: Henry D. Moyle, Harold B. Lee,
and Marion G. Romney. *Courtesy Marriott Library*

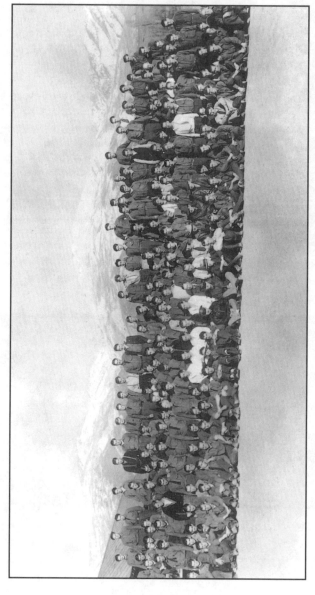

Utah's Civilian Conservation Corps (CCC) during the Great Depression. This was one of the Democratic Party's New Deal "alphabetical bureaus" which Clark condemned. Utah's participation in the CCC was twice the national average. *Courtesy Utah State Historical Society*

The grain silo at Welfare Square, Salt Lake City, a monumental symbol of Counselor Clark's Welfare Plan. *Courtesy Marriott Library*

Lute and Reuben in London in 1937. Four years later Reuben publicly announced that England "is neither a democracy nor a republic" in response to those who wanted the U.S. to aid England against Nazi Germany. *Courtesy Marriott Library*

Das deutsche Kriegerdenkmal in der Salzseestadt, Utah.

"Wer aus seiner Heimat scheidet, ist sich selten bewußt, was er alles aufgibt; er merkt es vielleicht erst dann, wenn die Erinnerung daran eine Freude seines späteren Lebens wird . . ." "Erst im Auslande lernt man den Reiz des Heimatdialekts genießen, erst in der Fremde erkennt man, was das Vaterland ist."

Gustav Freytag, Soll und Haben.

German–American Mormons at the German War Memorial in Salt Lake City, 1938. A month after Adolf Hitler began World War II, Clark asked the LDS general conference to remember that many faithful Mormons were pro-Germany. *Courtesy Marriott Library*

Reuben's son-in-law Mervyn Bennion was captain of the battleship *West Virginia* and was killed during the Japanese attack on Pearl Harbor on 7 December 1941. *Courtesy Utah State Historical Society*

Japanese-American families arriving at Utah's Camp Topaz. In November 1942 Reuben successfully opposed the federal government's plan to release them to Utah's cities for the duration of World War II. Instead, these west coast Asian Americans remained incarcerated until 1946. *Courtesy Utah State Historical Society*

First counselor Clark, President George Albert Smith, and second counselor McKay in May 1945. *Courtesy Utah State Historical Society*

Emily Smith Stewart's influence on her father, President George Albert Smith, was a challenge for Counselor Clark from 1945 to 1951. Stewart was a member of the LDS general Primary board in the 1920s and early 1930s. *Courtesy Manuscripts Division, University of Utah Libraries*

Reuben in his private library at 80 D Street in Salt Lake City's Avenues district. He described his library as a collection of "the greatest minds ... that have left records, both in the religious and the secular worlds." *Courtesy Utah State Historical Society*

America Forever

★ ★ ★ ★ ★

ZIONIST WAR-MONGERING

in the

U. S. A.

★ ★ ★ ★ ★

A Documented Primer
for the
GULLIBLE GOYIM

★ ★ ★ ★ ★

June 1948 issue

★ ★ ★ ★ ★

"Am I therefore become your enemy,
because I tell you the truth?"
Galatians 4:16

★ ★ ★ ★ ★

by
MARILYN R. ALLEN
P. O. Box 2243
Salt Lake City
Utah

Reuben had two copies
of this pamphlet in his
personal library along
with multiple copies of
the anti-Semitic *Protocols
of the Elders of Zion.*
Courtesy Marriott Library

In 1948 President Clark reassured Mormons that the LDS Hospital segregated Negro blood from that of white people "to protect the purity of the blood streams of the people of this Church." *Courtesy Utah State Historical Society*

While Reuben served as its vice president, the Hotel Utah employed African Americans as servants but prevented them from residing or dining there. He wrote in 1949, "Since they are not entitled to the Priesthood, the Church discourages social intercourse with the Negro race." *Courtesy Utah State Historical Society*

First counselor Stephen L Richards, President McKay, and second counselor
Clark (newly demoted) in April 1951. *Courtesy Utah State Historical Society*

The administrative
power of secretary Clare
Middlemiss on President
McKay was a challenge
for Counselor Clark.
*Courtesy Utah State
Historical Society*

A polygamist family at Short Creek, Arizona, after the husband and father had been jailed in the 1953 police raid. For the previous twenty years, Reuben had promoted church surveillance, civil restrictions, and criminal prosecutions against Mormon fundamentalists. *Courtesy Utah State Historical Society*

Director J. Reuben Clark with officers of Western Pacific Railroad, headquartered in San Francisco. In 1956 he advised the railroad not to admit Jews to its board of directors. *Courtesy Utah State Historical Society*

Joseph Fielding Smith was president of the Quorum of Twelve when he published *Man: His Origin and Destiny* in 1954. Of their disagreement concerning organic evolution, President Clark wrote, "You seem to think I reject the scriptures, or some of them. I do not intend to do so, but obviously I am no more bound by your interpretation of them than you are by mine."

Bruce R. McConkie, Seventy's president and son-in-law of Apostle Joseph Fielding Smith, published the 1958 *Mormon Doctrine*, which President Clark predicted "would raise more trouble than anything we had had in the Church in a long while." *Courtesy Utah State Historical Society*

J. Reuben Clark Jr. in later life. He died in 1961.
Courtesy Utah State Historical Society

CHAPTER 9.

They That Take the Sword

J. REUBEN CLARK'S ATTITUDES ABOUT WAR, MILITARISM, AND PACI-
fism were a reflection of his religious background and the circumstances of the world in which he lived. Prior to his own young manhood,
Mormonism had exercised selective pacifism. Until 1898 the church
ignored the dictates of secular authorities in matters of warfare, and Mormons became militarists or remained pacifists according to the instructions of the LDS president.[1]

Reuben's personal heritage was likewise ambivalent. His paternal
grandfather was a "Dunkard" (a pacifist sect), but his father served in the
Union Army during the Civil War. His maternal grandfather was a pacifist Quaker who converted to Mormonism and then sent his sons to fight
against U.S. troops during the Utah War of 1857-58.[2]

In his own life, Reuben witnessed U.S. participation in the Spanish-
American War, the Philippine Campaign against pro-independence Fili-
pinos who opposed American colonialism, the "Great War" (World War
I), the Russian civil war, World War II, the Korean War, and the "Cold
War" with the Soviet Union. Mormons, including his close relatives, were
involved directly or indirectly in all these conflicts. He lived long enough
to fear World War III and to comment on the early stages of the Vietnam
War.

As a young man, he tended to favor militarism. In the hysteria and popular clamor that drove the U.S. government to war with Spain in 1898, only the earnest entreaties of his parents and fiancée, Luacine, kept him from volunteering. In a letter to his parents, he said he felt like a coward for not joining the Utah volunteers, writing "the matter has been with me a struggle between love and duty. I should have enlisted at the first call had it not been for the wishes of yourselves and another to whom I feel my consideration is due." These were his thoughts about the struggle that thrust the United States into international prominence through defeating Spain and acquiring its colonies in the Pacific and Caribbean. This cost less than 2,500 U.S. deaths.[3]

Reuben accepted the position of director of the American Peace Society in 1912 as an extension of his membership in the American Society for Judicial Settlement of International Disputes (ASJSID).[4] However, he had little real sympathy for pacifism, which he regarded as impractical and dangerous.

As a succession of unintended events and consequences thrust Europe into the Great War in August 1914, Reuben saw the conflict in absolute terms. He believed England and her allies represented God-given democracy. Germany and its Central Power alliance were the "hordes of Satan" representing the monarchies of barbarism.[5] By 1915 he expressed earnest wishes for England's victory and stretched his legalism in writing briefs that defended the British naval blockade as simply "extralegal." He argued that the sale of U.S. munitions to England and France did not violate American neutrality in the least.[6] As a Republican loyalist, he expressed lifelong contempt for Democratic president Woodrow Wilson, yet in April 1917 he wholeheartedly accepted the president's message to Congress that entry into "the European War" was necessary because "the world must be made safe for democracy."[7] As he had failed to do in the Spanish-American War, Reuben demonstrated his conviction by entering the ranks of the military. He received the commission of major in the Judge Advocate General.[8]

As Europe stumbled into war in 1914 and America followed suit less than three years later,[9] Reuben regarded pacifists as intolerable. In May he informed Theodore Marburg of the ASJSID that he wanted to resign as a director of its peace auxiliary. He dissented from its pacifist policies and propaganda three months before European diplomacy collapsed into war. He again suggested resigning in his December 1914 letter to Arthur Deering Call, executive director of the American Peace Society, because it opposed peacetime enlargement of the U.S. army and navy. Within two weeks Reuben was condemning his "peace-at-any-price colleagues." In 1916 he formally resigned from the Peace Society's board of directors.[10]

In March 1917 he denounced pacifism in a letter to Marburg:

> The older I get, the more I see, the more experience I obtain, the more I become convinced that the peace propaganda and the present peace propagandists are both equally impractical and illusory, as also inimical to the interests of this nation. If we get into war, as seems now all but inevitable, we shall have to put some of them in jail, and personally I should like to begin with Mr. Bryan.[11]

This referred to William Jennings Bryan, the Democrat who resigned as U.S. Secretary of State to protest President Wilson's alleged efforts to provoke war with Germany. At the time of Reuben's letter, Bryan was continuing his pacifist campaign against presidential policies.[12]

A month later the United States declared war on Imperial Germany and became a military ally of the British Empire. Later renamed World War I, the Great War or European War resulted in more than 116,000 American deaths.[13]

In his special assignment to the U.S. Attorney General's office during World War I, Reuben revisited his previously stated wish to jail pacifists. On the one hand, he supported the imprisonment of thousands of German and Austrian nationals and urged that the legal restrictions on "enemy aliens" in the United States be applied to women as well as men. Nevertheless, Major Clark was appalled at anti-German hysteria and the legal repression of American citizens who were war critics: "I shall be no party to hounding any man or woman to jail or to the gallows, merely because some one whispers a criminal accusation or levels against him an irresponsible finger of unsupported suspicion."[14]

For twenty years after the Armistice of November 1918 ended the European bloodshed, he continued to work for sane militarism and to reject pacifism. He attacked the League of Nations provision in the Treaty of Versailles and the treaty itself in ghostwritten talks for U.S. Senator Philander Knox. In 1919 Reuben told a crowd of 10,000 people in the Salt Lake Tabernacle that the United States should reject the League and refuse to compromise national sovereignty. He argued that Americans would "waste the strength God has given us" by joining "in petty squabbles over a few rods of miserable European blood-sodden soil."[15] A group of Mormons in favor of the treaty publicly denounced Reuben's talk as "pro-German" and "traitorous."[16] Such accusations would echo about him during the Second World War.

Most Americans assumed that all U.S. troops were leaving Europe after the 1918 Armistice, but until 1920 there were 14,000 still in Russia waging an undeclared war to overthrow the Bolshevik Communist government. This effort failed.[17] Despite his anti-Communist views, Reuben publicly criticized the idea of trying to reverse the outcome of the Russian Revolution or any other revolution. (See chapter 8.)

In 1921-22 he served as special counsel for the State Department in the Washington Arms Conference. He fully supported its aim of reducing the possibility of war by treaty provisions that limited naval armaments. This would reduce the kind of arms race that contributed to the recent European war.[18]

In May 1923 he became chairman of the New York Committee for the Outlawry of War.[19] This was a reversal of his emphatic views barely a year earlier. "A treaty outlawing war would only handicap the 'righteous' nations," he had argued in a 1922 memorandum, "never the 'criminal.'" Biographer Frank Fox explained that Reuben thought that outlawing war would prevent "punishing criminal nations and deterring their future misdeeds." Therefore, in Reuben's words, "war is a necessary factor in human progress."[20] An extraordinary statement by any standard.

However, with the enthusiasm of a convert, in March 1924 he defended his new role in outlawing war. He denied that he was a pacifist or utopian dreamer:

> But, as I said in my last letter, ours is not a pacifist movement. We do not proceed toward peace along the path of disarmament; we expect

disarmament through the riddance of war, rather than riddance of war through disarmament.

... The main thing, however, is that it will be difficult or impossible to start a war when once we have so re-ordered the world, and international wars have become as unlawful as domestic wars of revolution. These latter cannot be prevented but as they proceed in the teeth of the law, they are rare and are illegal and criminal.[21]

With such convictions, it is not surprising that he endorsed the 1928 Kellogg-Briand Treaty, or Pact of Paris, which outlawed war.[22] Ten years later he dismissed this treaty, and by implication his own 1923-24 activities as "poetic pseudo-Messianic dreams of universal peace."[23] He had readopted his pre-1923 views about the futility of trying to "re-order" the world.

Consistent with his position in the two decades after World War I was his refusal in 1930 to become a director of the American Peace Society.[24] By the time he entered the First Presidency in April 1933, it seemed that his attitudes toward militarism, warfare, and pacifism had solidified. Yet during his nearly thirty years in the Mormon hierarchy, his pronouncements signaled a transformation that varied from subtle shifts of emphasis to complete reversals.

Whereas he had previously opposed alliances and interventions if he thought they served no vital U.S. interest, he eventually opposed even those where vital American interests were involved. He continued to affirm that wars of one kind or another were inevitable, but no longer did he believe that there were any "just" wars.[25] He became convinced that war was irredeemably corrupting and absolutely evil. Before 1933 he saw scheming militarists only in foreign nations, but thereafter, he became convinced that the most dangerous military plotters were in the U.S. Joint Chiefs of Staff. In his earlier life, he had ridiculed pacifists and toyed with the idea of jailing conscientious objectors. As a member of the First Presidency, he became an unmistakable pacifist and gave what encouragement he could to conscientious objectors during wartime. In a reversal of his views during World War I, he became pro-German and anti-English during World War II. Although he continued to battle against domestic

Communism in America, during the post-1945 Cold War he urged the United States to stop its efforts to contain international Communism.[26] Instead, he recommended that America enter into diplomatic and military accommodation with the Soviet Union. Most remarkable of all, he thought it was preferable for all of Asia to become Communist rather than to have American soldiers fighting there.

In the eyes of most Europeans and Americans during the 1930s and 1940s, Adolf Hitler and his Nazi Germany were the fiends of Europe.[27] However, Reuben had mixed views about Hitler and his National Socialist German Workers Party.[28] On the one hand, he described Hitler's 1934 purge-trials of fellow Nazis as "an assassination tribunal."[29] Prior to his first visit to Nazi Germany, Reuben wrote: "The German authorities have, I am very sure, kept all of the bad of Kaiserism (probably jettisoning much of the good); at any rate, they seem to have kept their criminal methods."[30] After his second visit, he told a general priesthood meeting that "there are things about it that to me are detestable."[31] This criticism was compatible with the anti-Nazi evaluations of most contemporaries and historians.

Nevertheless, his views did not imply total repudiation. His complex reactions paralleled the views of Charles A. Lindbergh, America's national hero of the 1920s and 1930s. What a biographer has written of Lindbergh almost exactly describes Reuben's response to Nazi Germany:

> Despite his world-wide travels, he had never visited Germany before the summer of 1936. Neither he nor his wife spoke or read the German language. He never met Adolf Hitler, and he never embraced Hitler's National Socialism. He disapproved of much that occurred in Nazi Germany. At the same time, however, he admired the German efficiency, spirit, and scientific achievement and technological accomplishments. To a degree he began to "understand" and sympathize with certain German attitudes and actions in the 1930s, even when he did not approve of them.[32]

President Clark had a personal interest in the Lindberghs. Aside from being the wife of the pioneering aviator of the *Spirit of St. Louis*, Anne Morrow Lindbergh was the daughter of Reuben's ambassadorial mentor,

Dwight Morrow. She "was convinced that the Nazis were not to blame for their brutal aggressions."[33]

Although his attitudes were close to those of the Lindberghs, especially Charles, Reuben saw Nazi Germany through the perspective of his long experience in diplomacy and international law. And he had to confront Nazi realities in terms of his administrative concerns about the Latter-day Saints who lived there: "By 1930, Germany had 12,000 Mormons, more than any [other] country in the world except the United States."[34]

Since 1919 he had regarded the Versailles Treaty as a vengeful and an unjust punishment of Germany for all of Europe's mistakes.[35] After Hitler announced that, contrary to the treaty, he was remilitarizing Germany, Reuben told U.S. Senator Hiram W. Johnson that "Germany wrote at least the head note to a great new chapter in European history," adding that he could not blame Hitler for scrapping the Versailles Treaty.[36] By then Reuben had already acquired English versions of Hitler's triumphal speeches as translated by a Nazi publisher.[37]

As early as December 1933, more than eight months after Reuben began his service in the First Presidency, the LDS church signaled its effort to seek accommodation with the Nazi regime. In an article, "Mormonism in the New Germany," the Church Section of the *Deseret News* enthusiastically emphasized the parallels "between the Church and some of the ideas and policies of the National Socialists." First, the Nazis introduced a "Fast Sunday." Second, "it is a very well known fact that Hitler observes a form of living which 'Mormons' term the 'Word of Wisdom.'" Finally, "due to the importance given to the racial question [by Nazis], and the almost necessity of proving that one's grandmother was not a Jewess," there was no longer any official resistance against genealogical research by German Mormons who "now have received letters of encouragement complimenting them for their patriotism."[38]

Published at LDS headquarters, the Church Section, later the *Church News,* used powerful visual symbols to demonstrate Mormon support for the Nazi regime. In January 1936 it published a photograph of an LDS basketball team giving the Nazi *Sieg Heil* victory salute. The following July it published a photograph of Apostle Joseph F. Merrill seated in front of the swastika banner of the Nazi Party during the Berlin conference of the Mutual Improvement Association for Mormon youths. In August 1937 there was a similar photo of LDS president Heber J. Grant seated in front of the swastika banner at the MIA conference in Frankfurt.[39] Visually, the message was that LDS leaders and young German males supported the Nazis. In other instances, Reuben was quick to criticize subtle messages that he disapproved of in the church newspaper's photographs and he immediately prohibited the repetition of such illustrations. (See chapter 10.) By contrast, the repeated publication of pro-Nazi photos in the *Deseret News* indicated that he did not oppose them.

When he was on business for the Foreign Bondholders' Protective Council, President Clark visited Berlin for six days in August 1937, then again for a few days the following year. He was favorably impressed with living conditions there. During each visit, he met with LDS mission leaders and Reichsbank president Hjalmar Schacht.[40] At this time Schacht was also "the central figure in National Socialist rearmament."[41]

In view of his frequently stated opposition to the control or regulation of business by the central government,[42] Reuben was also impressed by newspaper reports that "Hitler Champions Business Freedom."[43] Years later he said that at least Nazism allowed "private property and individualism" whereas Communism did not.[44]

In 1937 Clark returned to Utah about the same time as Berlin's mission president, Roy A. Welker, who stated: "The Nazi regime in Germany is characterized by marked orderliness and both the government and the people are strongly opposed to war. ... Nazi dislike of Jews and hatred of Communism are at the root of most propaganda against that nation."[45] In other words, this LDS mission leader claimed that Jews and Communists were responsible for the published criticisms of the Nazis. Welker had undoubtedly expressed these views when President Clark met with him.

During Welker's presidency in Berlin, his wife gave administrative advice to the head of the Nazi women's organization. In turn, Sister Welker's friendly association with this high-ranking woman "helped the Church a great deal."[46] At one point the mission president's wife obtained Hitler's personal approval for the narcissus flower as the symbol for German girls in the LDS church's Bee Hive program.[47]

After Reuben's second visit to Nazi Germany, he reported its condition in a First Presidency meeting in July 1938. He included in his outline some praise: "Germany's chin is up, No direct attack on religion, Young people's standard—what would Fuehrer do?"[48]

His comment about the Nazi approach toward religion was odd for several reasons. First, it contradicted his 1934 letter about "forbidding them to worship except as they direct, just as the Governments are doing in Russia and Germany."[49] Second, his 1938 assessment contradicted the *Deseret News* front-page articles during the previous five years concerning Nazi policies against Jews and Judaism.[50] His personal library already contained three books about this.[51]

Third, his words in the First Presidency's meeting contradicted the Berlin mission president's statement to general conference in 1937 that the Nazis had banned "something like thirty-four small religious denominations."[52] Reuben's library had a related 1938 article about the general "plight of religion" in Nazi Germany.[53]

However, President Welker had quickly added that Hitler "has said that the Mormon people are doing the German government no harm and he wants them let alone."[54] This was apparently Reuben's only interest in the religious situation in Germany as he described it nine months later to the presidency.

In his report to Grant and McKay, Reuben added his own observation that there was widespread support of Hitler among German members of the church.[55] This was the context of his plea to the general conference of October 1938: "Let us not make a great body of the membership of our Church feel that they are outcasts from us because of the acts of their governments."[56]

The Twelfth Article of Faith encourages Mormons to be loyal to whatever system of government they live in.[57] President Clark could see no benefit to the German Saints if American Mormons or church leaders criticized the Nazi government. As early as September 1933, the LDS mission president in Berlin, Oliver H. Budge, informed the *Gestapo* (secret police) that Mormons "teach that the present party in power, and the laws governing the country, be supported by the church."[58]

Clark's pro-German sentiments were also a direct reflection of his hostility toward England during this same period. He had both British and German ancestry, but by the late 1930s had adopted several anti-British views. First, British propaganda had painted a false picture of the Germans during World War I and of the war itself. Second, the English government had exploited U.S. neutrality and trade after 1914 to link the United States with Britain and force American intervention. Third, Britain and France were ultimately responsible for the rise of Nazi Germany because of their punishment of the conquered nation. Fourth, British propaganda after 1933 was painting a false picture of the Nazis in order to justify a war to protect the British empire against a resurgent Germany. Fifth, the English government and Anglophiles in the United States were doing everything possible to obtain another military alliance of Britain and America in order to pursue war. Though controversial, these were the same conclusions of many other diplomats, historians, journalists, political scientists, and "average" Americans.[59]

Worse, in 1928 a naval intelligence officer publicly disclosed that the British Admiralty in 1915 had intentionally exposed the civilian ship *Lusitania* and its American passengers to German submarines. According to some, this was intended to force the United States to enter World War I as Britain's ally.[60] For decades the U.S. government concealed the cargo manifests which showed that the *Lusitania* was transporting munitions and weapons when it was struck by a torpedo that killed hundreds of Americans.[61] This somber perspective on U.S. entry into the European war of 1914-18 increased anti-British feeling among those who wanted to isolate their country from Europe's conflicts of the 1930s.

Reuben did not hesitate to announce his suspicions about the British, despite the fact that there was overwhelming pro-British sentiment at the time. When a general authority condemned Nazi territorial acquisitions in the general priesthood meeting of April 1938, President Clark asked the conference: "Has Great Britain ever seen anything lying loose that she did not pick up? France is in no better position. So, brethren, let us be quiet at any rate about this matter."[62]

As the European situation steadily deteriorated, Reuben saw Americans generally, including most Latter-day Saints, adopting what he considered a lopsided support of Britain. He felt it imperative, as a former diplomat and current member of the First Presidency, to argue for true neutrality. In the October 1938 conference, his general priesthood address warned against accepting propaganda from Europe.[63] His intent was to attack British propaganda, but his generally pro-British listeners probably assumed that he was questioning the truthfulness of Nazi propaganda.[64]

In November he warned that U.S. president Roosevelt was trying to get the United States into a war.[65] At that time, the only European conflict was the Spanish Civil War. It reinforced Reuben's conviction that the wars of the 1930s were simply conflicts between empires and aspiring empires.[66]

In the Spanish Civil War, the Catholic church and Nazi Germany supported Francisco Franco's Fascist revolutionaries while the Soviet Union supported the besieged, constitutional government of the Spanish Republic. In this conflict's many foreshadowings of World War II, defending democracy meant accepting anti-democratic Russia as a military ally. Three thousand Americans chose to travel to Spain on their own to fight on the side of the anti-Fascist Spanish forces, yet half the soldiers in this Abraham Lincoln Brigade were members of the American Communist Party. Before the civil war ended in 1939, a special unit of the German air force had introduced saturation-bombing of Spanish towns and cities.[67] After the first year of this war, President Clark announced, "I am afraid that what is happening in Spain is but a forecasting shadow of what may be looked for in the next great war."[68]

In May 1939 the *Church News* promoted Reuben's views about Nazi Germany by publishing a letter from the secretary of the East German Mission, headquartered in Berlin. "Every Mormon missionary in Germany is fairly walking on air, head high" because of an article in the *Volkischer Beobachter,* which he called the "official organ of the government and the [Nazi] party." The article by mission president Alfred C. Rees described Mormonism, but the mission secretary's introduction in the *Church News* gave Utah readers a defense of Hitler's regime: "Among the many erroneous and unfounded impressions which seem to have gained ground at home, and which we believe are completely exploded through the appearance of this article: That Germany is being 'paganized.' That the word 'God' does not appear in the public press. That all religions are taboo. That Christianity is frowned upon."[69] It is unknown whether

Reuben was consulted in advance about this article, but it supported his evaluation a year earlier that the Nazi regime made "no direct attack on religion." The article also reinforced his often-stated rejection of anti-Nazi propaganda.

A month after the commencement of the Second World War in September 1939, Reuben wrote a First Presidency statement that condemned war in general.[70] He told the October conference that this was an "unholy war" and that Latter-day Saints should expect "deceit, lying, subterfuge, treachery, and savagery" on all sides.[71] He reminded another LDS conference that World War II was an "unrighteous cause" that "began as a war for empire" to determine which nation would dominate Europe.[72] He explained that in this "unrighteous war," Great Britain was trying to preserve its own empire and Nazi Germany was seeking empire.[73] Such statements were a direct assault against the claim that Britain and France had justifiably declared war to combat Nazi aggression.[74]

He also warned people to disregard most of the anti-Nazi reports in the newspapers. He regarded them as exaggerations and false propaganda.[75] This echoed the published statements of Berlin's mission president in 1937 and the mission secretary in mid-1939.

A month after the German invasion of Poland, Reuben told the general conference of October 1939 that Americans should remember:

> There are in the Church tens of thousands of faithful members, and in the [U.S.] nation millions of loyal citizens, whose choice would be, because of their German ancestry, that Germany should become the dominant power of Europe, and following that, perhaps of the world.[76]

Pro-British Mormons were appalled that Clark would express no objection to Nazi Germany becoming the world's "dominant power." His comments did resonate with Utah's population of German Americans, who were pro-Nazi.

Mindful of his role as elder statesman, Reuben provided government leaders with copies of the First Presidency's 1939 statement on war and U.S. neutrality. He also furnished them with copies of his own general conference talks on these subjects.[77] At October 1939 conference, he warned that American participation in World War II would not bring prosperity. Instead, "there would follow the greatest depression in all history."[78]

In April 1940 an American serviceman died in the German air raids on Norway, a neutral country prior to the Nazi invasion. Serving as military attaché in the U.S. embassy, he was the first U.S. serviceman to be killed by German forces.[79]

In May and June, President Clark may have been the anonymous author of two isolationist letters that were published by the *Salt Lake Tribune,* whose publisher was his friend John F. Fitzpatrick. They reflected Reuben's views and used his phrasing. In the May letter, "An American" wrote: "I don't know whether the German [military] moves are justified or not. I can only say that European problems can only be solved by Europeans. ... And those who conspire to involve us in the European war are guilty of continental treason." In June "One American" wrote that "little harm will result from the possible English capitulation to Germany."[80] In a subsequent protest against U.S. military policies, Clark described himself as "one American citizen."[81]

On 9 July he warned the Young Republicans of Utah that Roosevelt "seemed to be trying to get Japan to go to war with us" as a backdoor way of entering the European conflict.[82] His words would eventually seem prophetic and haunting.

It did no good when Latter-day Saints expressed to him their conviction that Britain must be victorious against Nazism for the benefit of the rest of the world. Reuben merely countered: "The Germans appear to have the idea that they are fighting for their lives. And of course England and France, not Germany, declared this war."[83] He wrote this rebuttal to Amy Brown Lyman, general president of the LDS Relief Society, on 15 July 1940, a month after France surrendered and the Nazi army entered Paris.[84]

He warned the October general conference that "by all the rules and principles by which nations have governed their conduct in the past, the United States has already committed several hostile acts [against Nazi Germany] and we are in fact now at war."[85] Years later American historians and intelligence officers agreed that from early 1940 to December

1941, President Roosevelt was directing U.S. armed forces in an undeclared war against Nazi Germany.[86]

At the end of October 1940, Reuben wrote his brother Gordon, "I have never been afraid of Hitler." He explained that the Nazi "empire" would not outlive Hitler and would never "bring any great force across an ocean three thousand miles wide to reach us."[87] He wrote this while the armies of Germany and Fascist Italy were in control of nearly all of continental Europe from Poland westward to the border of Spain, a neutral but pro-Nazi dictatorship.[88] In his view, the United States had no vested interest for participating in this war.

As more people urged U.S. intervention to rescue Britain, Reuben became bolder in his opposition. In February 1941 he used a Lincoln Day speech in Boise, Idaho, as a vehicle for lashing out against intervention as a means to preserve democracy. He began by observing that Britain "is neither a democracy nor a republic." He recounted the horrors of a century of early relationships between Britain and America: "British emissaries had encouraged if not indeed incited the Indians to raid, burn, scalp, murder our frontiersmen in our border settlements." In addition, the British violated treaties with the United States, illegally seized U.S. vessels, forcibly removed American seamen on the high seas, blockaded Atlantic ports, wantonly burned Washington, D.C., during the War of 1812, exerted cruel oppression against the Irish and forced their emigration, and engaged in numerous other disputes which climaxed during the U.S. Civil War. Concerning that conflict, "France and England were in feeling and attitude hostile to the Union and did all they could to help the Confederacy. Yet we were fighting for human freedom and the preservation of a government whose free institutions guaranteed it." In a thinly disguised parallel to England's situation in 1941, he added: "We did not ask Britain to help us; we only asked her to be neutral."[89]

This public attack on the proposal to aid Britain caused isolationists and antiwar leaders to solicit his assistance. Leaders of the nationally organized America First Committee asked his support in their effort to stop American aid. Reuben declined to affiliate with the organization. He said he would restrict his activity to public statements, with this comment: "I think a little reflection will show you why this seems to be wisdom."[90]

There was a predictable backlash to President Clark's speech. One church member accused him of stirring up "old hatreds," observing that "you sounded more like an apostle of the creed of these murderous butchers, the Huns, than an apostle of the L.D.S. church." Another asked, "Why didn't you tell about the bombing of Amsterdam by those wonderful Germans you seem to admire so much?"[91] She said that his talk would be resented by all Latter-day Saints in Britain, Canada, Australia, and New Zealand because they "are Britishers first and Mormons second." "I hope you are ashamed of yourself. You should be!" were the words of another Mormon. "Dozens of people have said the same thing: 'What will non-Mormons think about an apostle of the Church of Jesus Christ preaching this hatred of the British?'" All of these LDS critics signed their full names in their letters.[92]

Reuben was unruffled by such criticism. With a certain amount of satisfaction, he wrote John Bassett Moore, formerly an Acting Secretary of State: "I pretty well stirred up all the Anglophiles in this area."[93] Beth Smith Jarman observed in her analysis of Utah isolationism during this period, "Anglophobia was an important facet of American isolationism generally."[94]

In cinema newsreels and newspaper photos, the world was seeing the awesome brutality of the Nazi *Blitzkrieg* across nearly all of Europe,[95] yet Reuben continued to defend the Nazis. In April 1941 he wrote, "Looking at the long range of history one can find no nation who has been more acquisitive in the matter of territory than has Great Britain; no nation has been more ruthless, not even Germany, than has Great Britain when she took over the Boers of South Africa."[96]

He was so favorably impressed by his visits to Nazi Germany in 1937 and 1938 that his positive evaluations of Hitler were undeterred by subsequent events. After N. L. Nelson wrote a book against Hitler,[97] President Clark criticized this LDS author:

> He [Hitler] was to the Germans as a voice crying in the wilderness, and offering to lead them out of the economic and political bondage in which the Treaty of Versailles left them. ...
>
> ... I should like you to excuse my warning you against your

assuming as truth most of the criticism you see leveled against Hitler and his regime in Germany. ... Hitler is undoubtedly bad from our American point of view, but I think the Germans like him.[98]

Clark wrote this in June 1941 after the Nazi absorption of Austria and Czechoslovakia, bombardment of England, invasion of Russia, and subjugation of Italy, Poland, Norway, Denmark, Holland, Belgium, Luxemburg, France, Hungary, Romania, Bulgaria, Yugoslavia, Albania, and Greece. By this time, Nazi-Fascist forces were also in control of North Africa's French Morocco, Algeria, Tunisia, Libya, Sudan, Abyssinia (Ethiopia), and Somalia. Nearly surrounded, British forces in Egypt were the only barrier to the Suez Canal and Nazi access to Saudi Arabia's oil. In addition, to avoid invasion, neutral Switzerland and Sweden were contributing to Nazi finances and war industry. Neutral Liechtenstein furnished soldiers for a German SS military unit.[99]

Reuben also knew that his assessment of Hitler's popularity did not apply to the millions of Jews and anti-Hitler Germans who had been sent to Nazi concentration camps. His private library contained a 1933 account by a survivor of the "Nazi murder camp of Dachau," plus a 1934 narrative by a survivor of another "torture camp" in Germany.[100] In a 1939 meeting of the First Presidency, he had spoken of German "concentration camps, with all the horrors that that entails."[101] Prior to his June 1941 letter, the Deseret News had also reported mass executions in Nazi concentration camps.[102]

Criticism of Reuben intensified in August 1941 when he joined former U.S. president Hoover and fourteen other Republican leaders in a national appeal against intervention on Britain's behalf. They asked that the "American people should insistently demand that Congress put a stop to step-by-step projections of the United States into undeclared war." They affirmed that World War II was "not a world conflict between tyranny and freedom" and insisted "that American lives should be sacrificed only for American independence or to prevent invasion of the Western Hemisphere."[103]

Clark was among those prominent Americans who used every conceivable argument against the Roosevelt administration's open support of

Great Britain's war efforts.[104] Beth Jarman wrote that he "was Utah's leading spokesman for the isolationist cause."[105]

Among the responses he received was one from a "Former Admirer" who said that it was the unanimous opinion of his high priest quorum that Reuben sounded like one of the "appeasers" or "fifth columnists" of pro-Nazi subversives. "If I did not think that subconsciously you are revengeful I should sign this letter," this church member wrote.[106] Likewise, the San Francisco Press Club editorialized, "Clark denies he's pro-Hitler, but says Red victory would be a calamity for civilization as he knows it, so he's preaching *Heilsolationism* with Hoover."[107] This linked the word *isolationism* and the Nazi victory slogan *Sieg Heil*.[108] But Reuben was undeterred. His confidence that he had taken the right stand was bolstered in September when President Roosevelt authorized U.S. ships to "fire first" when approached by German warships or submarines in the Atlantic.[109]

At October general conference, Reuben warned about "the effort to take our boys across the Water" to participate in World War II.[110] He ignored the fact that many American and Canadian Mormons already were crossing the Atlantic as volunteers in Britain's war.[111] "We are in the midst of the greatest exhibition of propaganda that the world has ever seen, and all directed toward one end," he said.[112]

He wrote a First Presidency letter on 11 October that informed the director of the U.S. Defense Bond program, "We do not believe that aggression should be carried on in the name and under the false cloak of defense." President Grant noted, "I thank the Lord that President Clark is capable of writing such a fine letter."[113] Although Reuben did not use the word "aggression" to describe Germany's actions from 1939 to 1941, he used that term to describe U.S. efforts to prevent the Nazi conquest of Britain.

At the end of October with an acid pen, he suggested to one of the editors of the *New York Sun* that the best way to end European warfare was to transport all the British to Canada and the United States.[114] He wrote this four months after Germany, without provocation, had launched a surprise invasion of the neutral USSR. By the time of Reuben's October letter, the Nazis seemed close to conquering Communist Russia.[115] As previously noted, he thought that "Red victory would be a calamity for civilization" if this Nazi invasion failed.

Clark's mixed feelings came to the surface again in November 1941 as the federal government was turning Utah into a wartime economy as part of the U.S. support of Britain.[116] On the one hand, he angrily condemned Roosevelt's administration as "a group of men who had no concern for the future of our people," having made Salt Lake City "the center of one of the most heavily fortified areas in the United States—Fort Douglas on the east, the Ordnance Plant west of the city, the bombing fields out west of Tooele, and now the government is talking of putting $24,000,000 in igloos for the storing of ammunition near the airport."[117] On the other hand, he acknowledged a week later "that we could hardly as a Church urge engagement in war activities—yet we needed employment for our people and we did not want riff-raff here" if Mormons didn't take the war-related jobs and outside workers had to be imported.[118]

Prior to the U.S. entry into World War II, the FBI suspected many Utah Mormons of being "Hitlerites." In 1940 Reuben acknowledged "the sympathy of our members" for Germany, commenting that the First Presidency made an effort "to keep our people (Germans) in line."[119] Nevertheless, in November 1941 he admitted trying to "suppress" the anti-Nazi writings, speeches, and activities of Arthur Gaeth, the former LDS mission president in Czechoslovakia.[120]

Most of those who opposed intervention from 1939 to 1941 reversed themselves after 7 December 1941 when Japanese forces attacked the U.S. territory of Hawaii.[121] Imperial Japan was an Axis ally of Nazi Germany.[122] After nearly every ship in the Pacific Fleet was sunk or crippled at Pearl Harbor, these former isolationists supported U.S. entry into the war, the most prominent among them being Charles Lindbergh.[123]

Nevertheless, Reuben remained implacably opposed to U.S. involvement. Instead of regarding the Pearl Harbor attack as justification for war, he stated publicly and privately that Roosevelt had goaded Germany and Japan into attacking the United States to provide a reason to declare war on behalf of Britain.[124] This was also Lindbergh's view.[125] On 12 December 1941, probably influenced by Reuben's comments, President Grant wrote, "I blame the war on President Franklin D. Roosevelt."[126]

They arrived at this conclusion without knowing that Roosevelt had told his Secretary of War on 25 November that "the Japanese are notorious for making an attack without warning." Secretary Henry L. Stimson next wrote, "The question was how we should maneuver them into the position of firing the first shot without allowing too much danger to ourselves."[127]

President Clark continued to regard U.S. participation in World War II as criminal—even after Pearl Harbor. As Harold B. Lee wrote: "He denounced the present war as needless and the coming slaughter of our boys as a crime and that the war could not close [i.e., end] until this nation [the United States] had been humbled[—]possibly by great sorrows or by hunger when there might be required a policing of our homes by Priesthood quorums to defend them from thieving marauders."[128] Even for a pessimist, this was a morose view of the consequences of conducting warfare on the other side of the world.

Within days after his son-in-law Mervyn Bennion died in the Pearl Harbor attack, Reuben wrote a proposed First Presidency message addressed "To the Fathers and Mothers, Sons and Daughters of the Church Throughout the World." It was in extraordinary contrast to the war fever that gripped the United States after 7 December 1941:

> We have seen and we shall see these young men go out with commissions to kill their fellow men. Every lofty instinct of their souls and ours has cried out and will still cry out against this mission of destruction. It is not the Master's way. It is the jungle law of the beasts. ...
>
> For they who die have neither the option nor the power to determine whether their country's cause is true or false.

This version of the message remained unused.[129] Counselor David O. McKay had long favored a U.S. declaration of war against Nazi Germany.[130] Moreover, President Grant undoubtedly regarded Reuben's statement as unwise after the Japanese killed thousands of Americans in the U.S. territories of Hawaii, Guam, the Philippines, and Wake Island. A firestorm of criticism would have been the likely result of publishing such anti-military views at that time—within days of the Pearl Harbor attack.[131]

Instead, the First Presidency settled on a toned-down "Greeting" on 13 December, which urged soldiers throughout the world to avoid "cruelty, hate, and murder."[132] Reuben put the sentiments of his unused editorial into a statement for the following general conference.[133]

He exerted his antiwar feelings in another way on 17 December. The First Presidency sent a "Dear Brethren" letter to Utah's members of Congress, asking them to vote against "a new proposal to reduce the Selective Service age below its present level, possibly down to eighteen years."[134] In addition, when the general conference in April 1942 adopted an official statement on war, Grant wrote, "President Clark read a long Address of the First Presidency. We approved and signed it, but he wrote it."[135]

Reuben's usual pessimism combined with his abhorrence of American intervention in Europe to make him a wartime prophet of doom. In a letter to Henry C. Dworshak, then a member of the U.S. House of Representatives, he wrote that the United States would "come out of this war hated by practically the whole world, including Britain."[136] In the summer of 1942, Reuben thought that Britain and Russia would soon be forced to capitulate to Germany. In such a case, Germany would assess its war debts "against Britain (since it must not be forgotten that Britain and France declared and opened this war) and, of course, whatever the indemnity might be[,] Britain would expect us [the United States] to pay it." He wrote this to one of his former State Department friends, William Cullen Dennis, who was then president of a Quaker college.[137]

At the autumn general conference, Reuben announced the full text of a First Presidency message condemning "hate-driven militarists" and urging the Allies to agree to a negotiated peace.[138] At this time, Dwight D. Eisenhower was commander of all U.S. troops in Europe.[139] Of this statement, President Grant again noted that "Brother Clark practically wrote it all."[140]

Shortly before the start of Russia's counteroffensive and nearly two years before the Allied invasion of France, Reuben's October 1942 general conference proposal would have left Nazi Germany in control of nearly all of continental Europe east of Spain and west of the Soviet Union. Second counselor McKay followed Clark's reading of the First Presidency statement with his own conference address that demanded the

Allied military's pursuit of a total defeat of the Nazis.[141] As Reuben's administrative subordinate, Counselor McKay had obviously signed the First Presidency statement in reluctant compliance instead of harmonious agreement. After conference, rank-and-file members criticized the ghost-written First Presidency message for advocating "a stalemate peace."[142] It was not an exaggeration when *Time* magazine described this conflict within the church leadership and identified President Clark as "a last-ditch isolationist."[143]

Even as Allied victory in North Africa became a reality in late 1942,[144] Reuben was convinced that defeat of the Axis powers would lead to war between Britain and the United States. In January and April 1943, he wrote former president Hoover that it "will require more statesmanship than we have seen in the last ten years to avoid a clash within the next quarter of a century between the United States and Britain."[145]

Two months later Clark wrote that he was plagued by the "ghost that haunts me most." He feared that the United States was so corrupt that it would collapse before it could defeat Japan in the Pacific where the U.S. had vital interests. By contrast, this June 1943 letter expressed no concern about Nazi Germany controlling most of Europe: "We ought to cease worrying about Europe; they can stew in their own juice without materially affecting us."[146] As clear evidence of Reuben's continued conflict with the second counselor about the Nazis, McKay told the October 1943 general conference that "there is now no alternative but to push relentlessly forward until the murderous dictators are apprehended, and their ruthless power and subversive doctrines forever overcome."[147]

Reuben was obiously worried that the American Communist Party was making the same demand: "Open the Second Front Now! Smash Hitler and Crush the Axis!" A second front in western Europe would help the Soviet Union triumph militarily, a prospect Reuben regarded as a "calamity."[148]

Therefore, in February 1944 he gave a talk which proclaimed, "We must have a peace based on justice rather than might."[149] Prior to the Allied invasion of northern France, and while the Soviet army was still engaged in driving Nazi forces from Russian soil,[150] Reuben's peace proposal would have left most of Europe in Hitler's control. Nonetheless, his public statements on this matter had wide circulation throughout the United States.

In April the *New York Sun* reported that Clark was among several men recommended to form a treaty conference to arrange for "a peace magnanimous and just."[151] Two months before the D-Day invasion of France, a "magnanimous" treaty would have preserved most of Nazi Germany's territorial gains. The cease-fire involved in such treaty negotiations would allow Hitler to complete the annihilation of all of Europe's Jews—which readers of the *Deseret News* already knew was a Nazi goal.[152]

Like other Americans, J. Reuben Clark expressed "loyal opposition" to the war.[153] On 1 November 1944 he denounced "our present war" for its "needless sacrifice of some of the finest lives we have in America." He wrote this shortly after U.S. troops captured Aachen, the first German city surrendered by the Nazis.[154]

In view of Clark's consistent hostility toward U.S. participation in World War II, it is not surprising that he used his administrative influence to limit any LDS support for America's war effort. When asked whether the First Presidency ought to allow LDS members to work in munitions plants, he replied that "we as Christians should be against war." He acquiesced in allowing Latter-day Saints their own choice in the matter as "the lesser of the two evils."[155] He then used every argument he could muster in a six-page, single-spaced, typed letter to Secretary of War Stimson lobbying against added munitions plants or military installations in Utah.[156] He grudgingly allowed the FBI to have the names of returned missionaries who could furnish information about "towns and cities in Axis countries." However, he absolutely refused to allow returned missionaries to act as spies in the countries where they had served.[157]

After 1941 President Clark authorized a less than 1 percent increase in the war bonds owned by church institutions. He refused to cooperate in providing church payroll deductions for war bonds.[158] He told a government war bond representative in 1944 that the church's participation had been "liberal," adding, "I know we have been criticized ... [but] the Church will not take over the responsibility of financing this war and in this area."[159] His exasperation was understandable since the First Presidency's financial secretary, Frank Evans, had reported in March 1942 that "the total of such bonds held by all Church institutions— Church owned or controlled—amounts to nearly twenty million dollars." Later that summer Reuben had authorized the purchase of $150,000 more in war bonds.[160] The federal government wanted the church to buy more, but he refused. Nevertheless, he did not prevent the church's youth programs from organizing girls and boys to solicit individual purchases of war bonds.[161]

He was especially watchful to prevent LDS participation in what he regarded as military propaganda. In April 1944 he refused the military's request for him to be photographed with an LDS woman serving in the Women's Army Corps (WAC) because he said the First Presidency opposed women serving in the armed forces.[162] In August the Mormon Tabernacle Choir president agreed to provide background music for a war bond promotional movie featuring images of U.S. troops landing on the beaches of Europe. A member of the Presiding Bishopric and the president of the Twelve had already given their approval. Nonetheless, Reuben canceled the arrangement because "it is most improper for our Tabernacle Choir to be singing a background while our boys were going in and being blown to pieces."[163]

He was even more emphatic when asked if the choir would participate in a V-Day celebration of victory. He declined the invitation to speak, disapproved the use of the choir, and prohibited use of the Tabernacle. He suggested that the organizers use the state's capitol rotunda instead.[164]

His jaundiced perceptions about World War II caused him to reverse his view of pacifism. While he was previously hostile toward pacifist organizations, in June 1939 he accepted membership in the American Peace Society. He commented that he would not be able to be very active but said he was "happy to be numbered among you, and to add my bit in sane movements for peace."[165] As First Presidency secretary Francis M. Gibbons wrote, by 1941 Reuben "harbored deep-felt pacifist views."[166]

Although the First Presidency had urged Latter-day Saints since 1898 to follow their governments in matters of military service and war,[167] President Clark now wished that the church was strictly pacifist. In June 1942 he told Quaker college president Dennis "that your Church is wise in its stand against war."[168] In June 1943 he told the secretary of the Society of Friends in Philadelphia that he was "in deep sympathy" with their view of war. He confided to another Quaker in California that he had repudiated his earlier acceptance of defensive war and become as ardently pacifistic as his Quaker and Dunkard ancestors. He added that "it is very difficult for me to act in accordance with my ideas on what seems to be wisdom in this terrible situation."[169] That seemed to refer to the constraints of his church position that prevented him from more actively opposing participation in the war.

Nevertheless, he declared for the public record his own personal repudiation of offensive and defensive warfare. Since the beginning of World War II, he had served on the American Peace Society national advisory council. In November 1944 he became a member of its national board of directors. From then until his death, its official publication, *World Affairs*, listed him as a director.[170]

His status as a statesman, high church officer, and one of the Mountain West's most prominent citizens combined to give his antiwar sentiments a sinister cast in the eyes of some observers. In 1943 he published a talk he gave to insurance executives in Chicago about the conduct of the war, the federal government's plans for postwar America, and the character of the FDR administration.[171] A Salt Lake City Mormon publicly denounced this speech as "the most reactionary, critical and near seditious ever delivered in any country during war time." C. N. Lund expressed astonishment that President Clark would say such things during World War II when he seemed to be "almost welcoming enemy victory." "Had Brigham Young made such a speech during the Civil War, with tenfold more justification than at present, history might have written him down as a traitor," Lund wrote.[172] By contrast, influential executives outside Utah praised the talk.[173]

Reuben undoubtedly regarded his wartime critics as comic relief to the tragedy of what was occurring around the world. After all, these were the people he dismissed as "Anglophiles" and "hate-driven militarists."

He might have been less cavalier if he had known that the FBI and military intelligence agents took a dim view of such antigovernment and antiwar pronouncements. He had been alerted as early as 1940 that the

FBI was keeping tabs on Utah's "Hitlerites," and he expressed puzzlement that the informant had singled him out for this disclosure.[174] Yet it was well known that, in contrast to his frequent and strident criticisms of Roosevelt and the federal government, he rarely criticized Hitler and the Nazi government. From 1935 to 1943, he privately defended Hitler and his wartime conquests—an unusual position for a pacifist.

By 1943 an undercover investigator of fascism in the United States reported in a best-selling book that "a nest of pro-Axis Americans was functioning quietly" in Salt Lake City. Writing under the name John Roy Carlson, author Arthur Derounian identified his pro-Nazi contacts in Utah, all of whom were Latter-day Saints.[175]

In the paranoia about loyalty that attends war, it is not surprising that U.S. naval intelligence agents were making reports in 1942 about Reuben's public statements on pacifism and against the war. By 1943 the FBI's interrogation of suspected subversives in Utah revealed his private encouragement of their antiwar views.[176] Moreover, the Church Administration Building was only two miles from the army's Fort Douglas, and it is therefore likely that army intelligence personnel also conducted secret inquiries about him. Prior to my research for this biography, the army destroyed its investigative files on U.S. civilians.[177]

Nevertheless, Reuben was unintimidated by any critic. He probably would not have altered any of his pronouncements even had he known about the suspicious interest of U.S. intelligence agencies. He certainly would have regarded this as yet another example of wartime's "irresponsible finger of unsupported suspicion."[178]

The hostility he felt toward war put him in an awkward position as a member of the First Presidency. Its official position was to praise the heroism and patriotism of any soldier in service to country. But despite his powerful prejudices against it, he did not give specific counsel to avoid or refuse conscription. After the Pearl Harbor attack, LDS members asked whether their sons should enlist or wait to be drafted. He told these anxious parents that the only virtue in enlisting was the ability to choose one's service. He advised them that "there was no dishonor or disgrace" in waiting to be inducted.[179]

He was more candid with his own family. In March 1942 he wrote that he "shall feel a little better" if his brother Frank's son stayed out of military service altogether. In November he told another nephew, S. Wayne Clark, that the indifference and "actual opposition" of many Americans to World War II was the result of "the fact that there is a considerable portion of our people who do not believe that we should be in this war."[180]

The church president approved a letter in January 1943 stating that "the Church leaves this matter of conscientious objecting to war to the individual."[181] There was no reference to the option of pacifism in the First Presidency's prior statement of 1942,[182] so Reuben undoubtedly suggested this clarification.

In April 1943 an American Mormon in Colonia Juarez, Mexico, asked whether he should send his sons, who were technically Mexican citizens, on LDS missions or let them enter the U.S. military. President Clark replied that he would send them on missions.[183]

In November a young LDS elder asked him a question that put into sharp focus the difficulty of Latter-day Saints for whom he was the silent mentor of pacifism. "Can I feel that my Church understands and recognizes the validity of my being a conscientious objector," the young man asked, "or am I repudiated, as a matter of Church policy, in my stand?" Perhaps never before had Reuben seen the agonizing personal dimension of the tension between the gospel imperative for pacifism and the acquiescence of LDS policy for militarism. He told the young man that the church had no policy regarding conscientious objection and that it did not censure Latter-day Saints who chose that path.[184]

The First Presidency had stated in March 1942 that it would not assist draft evaders by calling them on proselytizing missions. Nonetheless, Reuben worked to obtain draft deferments for members of ward bishoprics. He also resisted the suggestion in 1944 that the First Presidency initiate investigations of possible draft evasion by missionaries and members of bishoprics.[185]

In May 1944 he faced a new challenge when informed by the field secretary of the National Service Board for Religious Objectors that the government had interred several Latter-day Saints in "camps" for conscientious objectors (COs). They had declined military service and refused to perform alternate service having any real contribution to the conduct of the war. President Clark replied that he himself had adopted the pacifism of his ancestors.[186]

From this time onward, he sympathetically monitored the status of these Mormon COs. Representatives of the "Peace Churches" provided financial support to them during their internment and kept Reuben informed of their status. After the war, he arranged for LDS headquarters to refund the Peace Churches all costs for having maintained "our boys" in these "CO camps."[187] He probably drafted the letter in which he and the LDS president complained that the pacifists "were apparently treated to all intents and purposes as were prisoners of war."[188] This reflected a concern that he had as early as the First World War.[189]

When everyone else in America and Utah prepared to hail the victorious American soldiers as returning heroes, Reuben sounded a more somber note in his conference addresses of October 1944 and April 1945:

> But some [American veterans] are coming back wounded in spirit and in mind by hate, by revenge, by a willingness to kill, and sometimes by a will to kill, wounded and corrupted under compulsion in thoughts and acts and concepts which have never entered our minds and hearts. ...
>
> These boys out in the field have placed before them constantly, achievements and the value of achievement in the destruction of human life. The thing for which they now receive praise, the things for which they work to get commendation, are unknown to us in our lives of peace.

He urged Latter-day Saints to be mindful of the brutalizing influence of the war on soldiers. He asked the general conference to give "our best effort and best thought" in helping the returning veterans make the difficult transition to a world where all life is valued and violence is abhorred.[190]

He was sympathetic and cautiously supportive of conscientious objectors, but the tragedy of those who did not escape the war's horrors "has shaken me to the very roots ... and grieve[s] me beyond expression."[191] World War II left up to 60 million dead and 80 percent devastation of many cities in Japan and continental Europe. For its limited population, the LDS church suffered heavy losses. Utah's 1,450 military deaths were above the national average.[192] At the war's end, a total of 5,714 Mormons in U.S. uniform "were killed, wounded, or missing in action."[193] In addition, 600 LDS members in Germany perished in the warfare along with hundreds of other non-U.S. Mormons in Britain, continental Europe, the Pacific islands, and the British empire.[194]

Even after the war and contemplation of its losses, Reuben's view of Nazi Germany did not seem to change. He condemned the postwar Nuremburg trials of Nazi leaders[195] and never commented on the Nazi extermination of Europe's Jews. He did write that during World War II the United States and England attempted "virtually to destroy the German people, a loss which is not only fiendish in its conception but in its execution. There is no people in the world to replace the German people."[196] In reading through more than 600 boxes of his personal papers, I found no similar criticisms of Japanese or German conduct during World War II. The only books in his private library about the war criminals of Germany and Japan were gifts to him, not books he purchased.[197]

Moreover, his condemnation of the effort "to destroy the German people" did not include German Jews because his emphasis since the 1930s was on those whom he described as "Aryan natives."[198] While *Aryan* had previously meant a speaker of an Indo-European language, Reuben adopted the well-known Nazi usage for non-Jews of "superior" racial origins (Germanic, Nordic, Anglo-Saxon). He used *Aryan* in this way despite the fact that his private library had two "anti-Fascist" publications which condemned such use of the word. He probably gave little attention to this criticism because both books were issued by American Communist publishers.[199]

The primary casualty of World War II, over which he grieved for the rest of his life without consolation, was America's saturation bombing of German cities and its use of atomic bombs against the Japanese people. He regarded that last act as America's betrayal of its God, of its moral mission to the world, and of the human race.

Two days after the atomic bomb devastated Hiroshima in August 1945, and a day before its use against Nagasaki, Reuben wrote an editorial for the *Deseret News* saying that the United States had perverted scientific truth, betrayed God's trust, and used the atom bomb without justification. He made those judgments in spite of his acknowledgment that the A-bomb saved countless American lives by avoiding a prolonged ground war with Japan. He then drafted a chilling prediction as a consequence of the bomb's use by the United States against civilians:

> Its use to kill will become the aim and practice of all nations. Some-time our children's children will have it turned against them, that they, too, may be exterminated, annihilated. When that time comes they will have no moral weapon against it, for we, their ancestors, will have cursed humanity by its first use; they may [also] have no physical weapon to combat it. And humanity may be as depraved and Christian virtue as dead then as now. Our posterity must pay the penalty, to the last farthing.[200]

He did not publish that prophetic editorial, but at the service of all churches of Salt Lake City on 4 September 1945, he stated the essential elements of the editorial. He toned down the reference to future use against the United States to read: "It *can* be turned against us."[201] Convinced that a future enemy would drop atomic bombs on cities of the United States, he warned the Latter-day Saints to prepare themselves for the total disruption that nuclear holocaust would cause in America.[202]

Shortly after the bombs fell on Japan, Reuben began urging the First Presidency to build underground, bomb-proof storage areas for the irreplaceable records of the church. Thirteen years later the LDS president agreed to begin work on such a project.[203] The result was the Little Cottonwood Canyon granite vaults which were constructed to withstand "a hydrogen or atomic bomb."[204]

In a talk to the LDS Sunday School conference of June 1946, President Clark returned to a favorite theme to give subtle praise to pacifists. "My ancestors on one side were Quakers. On the other side they were Dunkards—a closely affiliated group. During this war, they, with others, have been called the Peace Churches." Then he announced that he declined to "talk about the subject of the evening," which was a program celebrating the bravery of American soldiers and the outcome of World War II.[205]

He was so convinced of the unrighteousness of the Second World War and the futility of its losses that he could hardly conceal his bitterness. When one Latter-day Saint sent him the Roll of Honor of family members who had served in the U.S. armed forces during the war, Reuben thanked him for the gift but commented, "I could say something about the real 'Cause' for which they served and for which some died, but I refrain."[206]

He acknowledged that several general authorities "felt that it [the atomic bomb] was given to us by the Lord to insure our victory."[207] But he continued his own unqualified condemnation of its use on Japan. Furthermore, he denounced American military and political leaders for preparing to engage in nuclear war.

His most extensive LDS talk on this topic was at the general conference of October 1946. First, he condemned the American military for killing 250,000 German civilians in its two-day bombing of the non-militarized city of Dresden. Then he told the congregation that the United States committed "the crowning savagery of the war" by using atomic bombs against Japanese "men, women, and children, and cripples." He expressed amazement that there was not a general protest in the United States against this, "but that it actually drew from the nation at large a general approval of this fiendish butchery." He said that "God will not forgive us" for celebrating the means of such wholesale slaughter and continuing to research even more efficient weapons of destruction. He concluded with a bitter, emotional protest:

> And, as one American citizen of one hundred thirty millions, as one in one billion population of the world, I protest with all of the energy I possess against this fiendish activity, and as an American citizen, I call upon our government and its agencies to see that these unholy experimentations are stopped, and that somehow we get into the minds of our war-minded general staff and its satellites, and into the general staffs of all the world, a proper respect for human life.[208]

His outrage grew when former president Hoover informed him that the minutes of the 1945 decision showed that U.S. president Harry S. Truman ordered the use of atomic bombs despite knowing about the imminent collapse of Japan's war effort.[209]

Therefore, a month after Hoover's disclosure, Reuben prepared the editorial, "Day of Atonement," which condemned the wanton character of the bombing. "After Japan was on her knees, beaten into submission, ready to surrender," he wrote, U.S. military leaders prevailed on the commander-in-chief to exterminate "helpless men, women, and children, the aged and the decrepit, the sick, all non-combatants." Thus, he concluded, "Man lapsed back to the standards of the dark ages."[210]

He later expressed to a general conference welfare meeting his ultimate condemnation. Concerning the nuclear weapons which the United States had used and was continuing to develop, "I had this terrible thought come into my mind—maybe it would have been a good thing if we had had the intelligence annihilated that has brought this terrible, up to the present time, curse upon humanity."[211]

His total repudiation of the purposes, conduct, and outcome of World War II determined his reactions to the post-1945 world. He condemned America's international supremacy and its Cold War with Russia's Soviet Union.

The first item of his postwar agenda began while U.S. troops were still fighting in Europe and the Pacific. On 2 February 1945 Apostle Mark E. Petersen informed him that both the Utah legislature and Congress were in favor of "legislation providing for compulsory military training after the war."[212] As a director of a pacifist organization, Reuben was outraged by the proposal to conscript American youth in peacetime. Three days later he wrote a proposed message for the First Presidency, which amounted to a frontal assault against the U.S. military:

> 1. A great standing army has always led to a destruction of liberties and the establishment of tyranny ...
>
> 2. A great standing army, with its war-minded controls, always looks for opportunities for use of the army, and military influence is always exerted to that end.
>
> 3. A great standing army has the effect of making the whole nation war-minded. It makes a nation truculent, overbearing, and imperialistic, all provocative of war.[213]

Clark was the only twentieth-century LDS leader to refer to the United States as "imperialistic."[214] The First Presidency, at his urging, instructed Elder Petersen to use this unpublished statement to lobby Utah's legislators against the draft.[215] This was the opposite of Reuben's support for enlarging the peacetime American military in 1914.[216]

As local and national support grew for retaining the draft, the First Presidency in June 1945 counseled Mormons in Congress to oppose it. Apostle Lee wrote: "Pres. Clark served notice that he proposed to force the brethren to take a stand for or against the resolution except to repel invasion or imminent national danger. He expressed his opinion that the Church of Jesus Christ could not consistently take any other position."[217] This same month Reuben confided to his Quaker friends that the church would soon issue a statement to that effect.[218]

In December a three-page letter went to all "members of the Utah delegation in Congress, as well as to the Congressional delegations from other states in which a considerable number of the members of the Church reside." The First Presidency's letter gave seventeen arguments and concluded that "we have the honor respectfully to urge that you do your utmost to defeat any plan designed to bring about the compulsory military service of our citizenry."[219] After nearly a year of privately lobbying elected officials, the First Presidency published the statement against "universal compulsory military service." It followed the general outline of Reuben's February 1945 memorandum but with a softened emphasis.[220]

In January 1947 he also came to the aid of a Mormon who had been a conscientious objector to World War II. A local draft board tried to prevent him from serving a full-time mission after his release from the CO camp more than a year after the war's end. Reuben did what he could to intercede on the young man's behalf.[221]

Even after the post-1945 hostility between America and the USSR resulted in the Cold War and Russia's development of nuclear weapons, he continued to assault the U.S. military. In September 1947 President George Albert Smith seemed willing to encourage LDS youth to enter the National Guard. Reuben objected that such an action "would be going back on our position taken on Universal Military Service."[222] Two months later he gave a talk to insurance executives in Chicago that was published as a pamphlet by the *Deseret News*. He warned:

> Furthermore, I regret to say, indeed I am almost ashamed to say, that at the moment, our military branches seem in almost complete control of our own government. They appear to dominate Congress, and under the circumstances, we may assume they are in sufficient control of our foreign relations to be able to set the international scene. ... We are not justified in doubting, on the facts we have, that we of the United States are, for the first time in our history, under a real threat from our military arm, and if the plans of the militarists carry, we shall become as thoroughly militarized as was Germany at her best, or worst.[223]

As the Cold War intensified, he warned his church associates to be on guard against any steps toward "a military dictatorship" in America.[224]

In this light, it is not surprising that he informed U.S. Senator Arthur H. Vandenberg in December 1947 that the military veterans of Utah "will go to jail" rather than serve in another war.[225] In March 1948 Reuben was unperturbed that a U.S. army general blamed the church for Utah having the lowest rate of National Guard training in the nation.[226]

A month later Reuben equated service in the U.S. armed forces with murder. He warned the general priesthood meeting of April 1948, "You cannot fill the hearts of man with murder and then have a normal world." He explained that this "is one reason why the Church has taken the position it has taken regarding compulsory military training." He next condemned those who accepted continued militarism after World War II: "How many of us brethren are really horrified by the thought of the indiscriminate, wholesale slaughter of men, women and children—the old, the decrepit, the diseased; or are we sitting back and saying, 'Let's get at it first.' How far away is the spirit of murder from the hearts of those of us who take no thought in it?"[227] Eleven years later he informed a prospective instructor of the Air Force ROTC program at BYU "that he, personally, would not like to have on his conscience the destruction of one human life, however justified, to say nothing of the destruction of hundreds of thousands that might be involved in the use of the H-bomb."[228]

In his opposition to America's continued development of nuclear weapons, Reuben knew that he had adopted the same position advocated in Communist propaganda.[229] However, that did not deter him.

With such views, it is remarkable, almost inconceivable, that he allowed himself to be photographed in the cockpit of a jet fighter. He did so even though he hated flying and had tried to persuade all general authorities to use trains rather than planes.[230] This photograph occurred because Apostle Joseph Fielding Smith, next in line to be LDS church president, loved flying in military jets. A biographer describes the incident:

> So, when the president of the Twelve took up flying in jets, President Clark launched a campaign to get him to stop. While he was reluctant to order his apostolic senior, President Smith, to cease and desist as he had done with his protégé, President Clark hinted that he ought to give it up. It was then that Elder Smith sought to turn the tables and convince President Clark of the safety and the joys of jetting. How he did it remains a mystery, but two years after President Smith began to fly in jets, he persuaded President Clark to accompany him to the airport to at least check the plane out.

Somehow Elder Smith persuaded him to go for a ride in the military jet. This was only the second time in his life that Reuben had been a passenger in any aircraft.[231]

Despite his lifelong opposition to Marxism and Communism, Reuben joined the minority of pre-1941 isolationists who opposed America's Cold War efforts to stop the spread of international Communism.[232] In April 1947 he opposed military aid to Greece and Turkey in their campaigns against Communist insurgents.[233] In October he refused to join all other former U.S. ambassadors in signing a public appeal for Secretary of State George C. Marshall to give military and economic aid to China in the face of Mao Tse-tung's Communist victory.[234] Aside from his emphasis on nonintervention, Reuben saw this as fulfillment of his warning two years earlier about the United States becoming "Santa Claus to the World."[235]

In April 1949 he was the only former or current U.S. ambassador to object to ratification of the North Atlantic Treaty. The resulting organization, NATO, was designed to protect western Europe and North America from Communist aggression. A supporter of NATO testified before the U.S. Senate Foreign Relations Committee that J. Reuben Clark was among the "well-meaning but impractical pacifists, pseudo-liberals, rabid isolationists and, of course, the Communist party with its assorted fronts" who opposed NATO.[236]

Reuben undoubtedly felt grim amusement at the irony that American super-patriots had accused him of being a Nazi sympathizer during World War II and now accused him of being a fellow traveler with the Communists. In reality, he was a consistently patriotic American who opposed international intervention by the United States against any presumed evil. Undeterred by critics, he delivered a major address against NATO in Salt Lake City in August.[237]

He became even more emphatic shortly after the United States agreed to join the United Nations in a "police action" against Communist North Korea for invading South Korea.[238] The Korean War would eventually kill nearly 37,000 Americans.[239] In June 1950 President Clark gave the following advice to his cousin about the U.S. army reserves, "Get out of the d--- thing as soon as you can."[240]

In December 1950 a Utah bishop asked Reuben to speak to two young men in his ward "regarding their attitude as conscientious objectors." The bishop apparently expected him to instruct the boys to support the Korean War against Communist expansion. Instead, he replied, "I would not undertake to advise them; that whether or not they were really conscientious objectors and whether or not they wished to plead that in connection with military service, was a matter wholly for their determination."[241]

Predictably, he was equally anxious that the United States get out of the United Nations because "all they do is send our boys to Korea."[242] His private library had various publications warning about the possibility of World War III by such a path,[243] and he published his opposition to the Korean War.[244]

He regarded the philosophy and conduct of the United Nations as identical with the League of Nations which he had opposed since the end of the First World War.[245] Rather than being an instrument of international arbitration, cooperation, and peace, the United Nations, in Reuben's eyes, eroded U.S. sovereignty and required U.S. intervention in international conflicts.[246]

When the U.N. charter was announced in 1945, he wrote a sixty-two-page, double-spaced, typed critique of the document. He addressed this to the editor of the *Deseret News,* with the comment: "Acceding to your request I am submitting to you a few general observations upon some of the more obvious and important factors of the San Francisco Charter. I have not attempted to make anything but a more or less cursory analysis."[247] Although the LDS newspaper was always responsive to First Presidency requests, it could not publish a sixty-two-page document in its regular columns. Reuben told rank-and-file Mormons about this treatise, but by the end of 1945 he had concluded that it might never be printed.[248] The most of it that he ever published was an excerpt in his 1952 *Our Dwindling Sovereignty.*[249] His official explanation for his memorandum not being published was that "the Church had avoided taking any stand pro or con on the United Nations because our people were on both sides of the question."[250] BYU eventually printed the full text twenty-six years after his death.[251]

However, there was another more significant reason that his anti-U.N. memorandum was not published. From 1945 until Reuben's death, LDS presidents Smith and McKay had greater hope for the United Nations than he did. President Smith's daughter Emily Stewart was on the Utah Council for the United Nations,[252] and she had significant influence on her father. President McKay had positive views toward the ideals and achievements of the United Nations.[253] Reuben assumed that Counselor Stephen L Richards "would be more favorably inclined toward the United Nations than he was."[254]

In fact, shortly after becoming first counselor, Richards expressed concern about articles against the United Nations. Written by the son of Apostle Albert E. Bowen, a Clark man,[255] the series of four anti-U.N. articles appeared in the *Relief Society Magazine.* Its editor was Reuben's daughter, Marianne Sharp. "President Richards said that the United Nations is a highly controversial political issue. Sister Sharp said they had been aware of that, and so they had approached it from the standpoint of the dangers to the Constitution, and had thought that by tying it to the Constitution they would avoid that. Pres. Richards thought that many would not be sufficiently discriminating to recognize that."[256] One can imagine Reuben's amusement when he learned of his daughter's reply to President Richards.[257]

To a like-minded friend, A. Helen Morgan, a non-Mormon, Reuben did not mince words on the topic. "The sooner we get out of the U.N. the better off we will be, but there are an awful lot of people who still are blinded by the brilliant rainbows which the pro-U.N. people can produce."[258] By extension, he regarded LDS presidents Smith and McKay as "blinded" by such propaganda.

One of the arguments for U.S. participation in the United Nations was that America's power in the post-1945 world seemed to require it.[259] This was the reasoning of most political scientists, whom President Clark dismissed as "that class of individual you must tell how to run the world before criticizing it."[260] He undoubtedly agreed with the title of a book in his private library: *U.N. Is U.S. Cancer.*[261]

However, David O. McKay's ascension to the office of LDS president in 1951 greatly diminished Reuben's freedom to express his opposition to the Cold War. McKay was a lifelong internationalist whose disagreement with Clark over American participation in World War II was a matter of public comment and discussion.[262] As church president, McKay affirmed his views to a non-Mormon that "the Church was militantly opposed to the godless atheism of communism and would not hesitate to oppose force with force if it became necessary."[263]

Though he knew of Reuben's opposition to war generally and the Korean War specifically, in June 1952 President McKay assigned his counselor to speak to LDS young men in support of military service. Clark began his talk by commenting that "I would not want to spend two years in the service." He referred to his sympathy with the pacifist view of his Quaker ancestors and said, "I loathe war, and all that goes with it." Then he dutifully went on to address his assigned topic, "Two Years in the Service Can Be Profitable."[264]

His approach to military service against international Communism as making the best of a loathsome situation was hardly the endorsement of the Cold War that the church president wanted. A month later "Pres.

Clark was considerably concerned over the quoted statement of Pres. McKay to the effect that 'the only way to deal with Russia was by force, which was the only language they knew.'"[265]

As the Korean War continued for another year, Reuben became more open about his opposition to the church president's endorsement of the conflict. In April 1953 President McKay approved the government's request for a general authority to be photographed with silent-film actress "Mary Pickford to advertise the bond drive." McKay asked him to do this. "President Clark said he did not wish to do it," so the president asked another presiding officer to fill in for his dissenting counselor.[266]

Ray C. Hillam and David M. Andrews have observed that "President McKay saw the Korean War as a justified effort to contain the spread of communism; President Clark viewed the war as unconstitutional. Both condemned communism with vigor, but they often disagreed on American foreign policy and techniques of containment."[267] In deference to President McKay, Reuben gave little publicity to his conviction that the United States should enter into a diplomatic and military accommodation with the Soviet Union. Likewise, he did not publicize his view that it might be preferable for all of Asia to become Communist.

However, in 1947 he did publicly express hope that the United States and the Soviet Union would "reach a mutual live-and-let-live understanding."[268] Throughout the 1950s, he privately condemned the policy of the U.S. government toward the USSR. For example, he wrote, "I have felt and still feel that our military 'over-lords' want a war and want it quick."[269] After McKay became president, Reuben stated this sentiment only privately. In 1951 he expressed the hope "to see if something could not be worked out in a friendly way, with the Russians."[270] Four years later he expressed this to Apostle Ezra Taft Benson, then U.S. Secretary of Agriculture, as "to make an arrangement with Russia."[271] He repeated this in letters to Alfred M. Landon, former governor of Kansas and former candidate for the U.S. presidency.[272]

Clark told general conference of his alarm at Soviet premier Nikita Khrushchev's boast that the USSR would "bury" the United States. But instead of advocating increased defense spending or militarism, he simply warned the Latter-day Saints against becoming Communists.[273]

Reuben privately replied in 1954 to the question of what the United States should do concerning French Indo-China, soon to be partitioned into the independent countries of Laos, Cambodia, North Vietnam, and South Vietnam. His private library had a 1933 book about Communist tactics in the region.[274] Twenty-one years later, Reuben wrote U.S. Senator Dworshak that the area was not worth American blood, then added:

> Finally, while unalterably opposed to Communism, I can imagine that an enlightened Communism may be a whole lot better than a decrepit, deficient, corrupt colonial government. I rather feel that that principle could be applied to very much of the situation in the whole Far East. We enlightened, Democratic governments of Western Europe and America have never conducted ourselves in such a way as to endear ourselves to the great Asiatic populations. We have sown the wind; we may reap the whirl-wind.
>
> In my personal view, our greatest danger and greatest handicap is the concept, not yet more than half-expressed, sometimes, perhaps, not even fully recognized, that we are destined to dictate to and rule the world, though we have not enough sense to rule ourselves wisely. That is the first step towards the ultimate decay that led to the downfall of Rome, that is carrying forward Britain, France, Italy, and, of course, Russia.[275]

This 1954 letter was consistent with his decades-earlier affirmation that the Russian people had every right to engage in the Bolshevik Revolution and to accept Leninist-Stalinist Communism as their form of government. His willingness for Vietnam and the rest of Asia to become Communist was contrary to the U.S. government's commitment to "contain" its spread at any cost.[276]

Most significantly, U.S. president Eisenhower was convinced that "possibly 80 per cent of the [Vietnamese] population would have voted for the Communist Ho Chi Minh" if given the opportunity. Therefore, from 1954 onward, the Eisenhower administration's policy was to delay free elections as long as possible. Instead, the U.S. government provided military aid to South Vietnam's pro-American dictatorship against Communist insurgents ("Viet Cong") who were denied the ability to vote for reunification with Communist North Vietnam.[277] By contrast, President

Clark affirmed that people had the right to violent revolution if they were denied the option of peacefully choosing their form of government— even if their choice was the Marxist Communism that he despised.

He had no illusions about the prospects in Vietnam nor about American policy toward the area. During a visit to the State Department in the summer of 1958, he asked "about the Far East." Afterward he wrote his non-LDS friend Fred Morris Dearing about this meeting with government policy makers: "First, that they only told us about the things they wanted us to know about; second, that about those things they only told us what they thought we ought to know; and third, that they lied whenever it seemed convenient."[278]

In 1959 Salt Lake City's newspapers printed front-page articles about the first U.S. servicemen killed in Vietnam, which had 1,500 military "advisors" at that time.[279] Reuben lived long enough to know of American deaths in a region he had said was "not worth spending our blood for."[280] But he was in physical decline and devoted his remaining energy toward condemning what he regarded as disturbing developments at LDS headquarters. (See chapter 5.)

By his 1961 death, the United States had accelerated its plunge into the morass of the Vietnam War.[281] The conflict claimed 58,000 American lives before South Vietnam finally fell to the Communists and was militarily united with North Vietnam. There were up to 2 million Vietnamese wartime deaths, mostly civilians.[282] These were the consequences of refusing to allow a democratic vote to decide whether to unite peacefully with Communist North Vietnam.

President Clark had often publicly expressed his conviction about the absolute futility of war. He often spoke about the evils of American participation in World War II after the Pearl Harbor attack. In view of such sermons from 1939 to 1946, it is unlikely that he would have remained silent had he lived to see the media's coverage of the saturation bombing of North Vietnamese cities, public execution of suspected Viet Cong operatives by South Vietnamese officers, burning of pro-Communist villages by U.S. soldiers, post-massacre photos from the village of My Lai, the Phoenix Program of U.S. personnel torturing and murdering South Vietnamese civilians regarded as pro-Communist (with military quotas for "eliminating" up to 1,500 each month), propaganda parades of American prisoners of war, plus the daily television images of young Americans dying in Vietnam and domestic protests against the war.[283] But ill health and death had stilled the voice of Mormonism's extraordinary twentieth-century peace advocate.

Less than five years after Reuben's death, Utah banker and financier Marriner S. Eccles publicly condemned America's military activities in Vietnam: "We are there as an aggressor in violation of our treaty obligations under the United Nations' charter."[284] LDS scholar and BYU professor Hugh Nibley also publicly condemned the war.[285]

Likewise, about 10 percent of LDS youth opposed the war, sometimes becoming conscientious objectors, draft dodgers, or refugees to Canada.[286] Because there was no comparable spokesman among general authorities against war after Clark,[287] these young Mormons could only turn to his published statements against war.[288] They did not have access to his unpublished statements supporting conscientious objectors and opposing their imprisonment.

Still, President Clark had a message of comfort for the 90 percent of Mormon youth who supported U.S. participation in Vietnam, who served as soldiers there, who surrendered their universal love of humankind there, who survived Viet Cong and North Vietnamese prisons, who were horribly wounded there, who died there, or who suffered emotional damage there. Two years after Reuben rejected the idea of sending Americans to Indo-China, he told a post commander of the American Legion:

> I honor greatly men who make the last sacrifice for a Cause which they know and in which they believe.—In major part such was the position of those who died that our Government might be born. But I think I honor more those who at the behest of their Government, in the matter of pure patriotism give their lives for a Cause which they do not understand and which perhaps is not understood by those who called them to the Colors.[289]

This melancholy comfort also applied to all whose loved ones were casualties of war.

CHAPTER 10.

All Nations, and Kindreds, and People, and Tongues

DURING J. REUBEN CLARK'S LIFE FROM 1871 TO 1961, HE WIT-nessed enormous changes in the attitudes and conduct of Western society, the United States, and the LDS church toward the races and eth-nic peoples of the world. During the period of his childhood to young manhood, few political leaders, religious teachers, moral philosophers, or ordinary citizens of the Western world questioned the superiority of the Caucasian, or "white," race and the inferiority of darker-skinned races and peoples. This world view gave justification to racial segregation, to laws against interracial marriage ("miscegenation"), and to Western colo-nialism in Africa, Asia, the Middle East, Latin America, and the Pacific.[1]

Although the United States has always been a land of immigrants, by the 1880s the native-born Americans who descended from North Euro-pean immigrants had added one further distinction to humanity. The mil-lions of "new immigrants" after 1870 were "undesirables" because they were primarily Roman Catholics, Jews, Asians, Slavic East Europeans, or swarthy South Europeans. Even though many Hungarians, Poles, Rus-sians, Bulgarians, Romanians, Balkan Muslims, and Italians were as blue-eyed and blondish as the stereotypical Scandinavian or German, they were regarded as inferior due to their cultural and linguistic differences from even brown-eyed, dark-haired people in the North European countries east of Poland, west of Spain, and north of Italy. In the United States before the 1930s, the authors, newspaper editors, college professors, government leaders, and church ministers were predominantly of British or Germanic extraction. Few Jews were admitted to the ranks of these pre-1930 opinion-makers. Therefore, the educated and religious culture of white America reflected Anglo-German attitudes toward race, ethnicity, and culture.[2]

Throughout two-thirds of Reuben's life, those attitudes flourished from the cities to the hamlets of America. During the years of his service in the First Presidency, such attitudes and the practices they fostered began crumbling. He reflected his time and society, as well as their transitions with regard to the peoples of the world.

In rural Utah, young Reuben's experience with aliens was limited to Mormon immigrants from northern Europe. He had virtually no personal contact with anyone outside of what he called the "pure white race."[3] Still, this LDS youth had the full endowment of racism characteristic of late nineteenth-century America. This included *xenophobia,* a fear and dislike of people who are different from one's own group, and *nativism,* a preference for native-born Americans.[4]

His father recorded that the University of Utah audience gave a wild ovation when Reuben's 1898 valedictory talk made the thundering statement: "America must cease to be the cess-pool into which shall drain the foul sewage of Europe."[5] This reflected the prevelant hostility of the native-born of the 1890s toward new immigrants from eastern and southern Europe.

Although he moved to cosmopolitan New York City at age thirty-two, this did not teach Reuben egalitarianism (acceptance of all humans on an equal basis). His associates at Columbia University Law School included the champions of eugenics, a then-popular theory about human "breeding." Eugenics emphasized the racial superiority of people who were Anglo-Saxon (English-Germanic).[6]

However, his experiences at Columbia and in the State Department convinced him of the necessity for justice in the relationships of all races and peoples. In a 1942 letter to former U.S. president Herbert Hoover,

Reuben said that the British and Americans were primarily responsible for the "color-hate" that was dominant and which had antagonized the colonial peoples of the world, especially the Japanese. Then he added:

> In saying this I would not wish to be understood as advocating the mixation of the races. I am wholly against this. I believe in a pure white race, but I believe in justice to the colored races, a justice they have not heretofore had, and [I] feel that justice to them is indispensable to a peaceful world.[7]

In his mature life, particularly during his service in the First Presidency, he merged the racial attitudes of his youth with the training of his legal and diplomatic careers.

His experiences with Mexican people provided the first catalyst for altering his racial and ethnic views. From 1910 to 1913, and periodically thereafter, he had been enmeshed in the legal and diplomatic aspects of the Mexican Revolution, with its social chaos, shifting loyalties, political assassinations, human suffering, economic losses, and atrocities.[8] This added to his xenophobic indoctrination and resulted in a pronounced dislike for Mexicans, whom he had never met except in formal interchanges with emissaries to Washington. Nearly twenty years after his first visit to Mexico, he admitted to an LDS priesthood conference: "I went with a great prejudice against the Mexican people." But he studied "the history of the people, their oppression—they were downtrodden and had been for 400 years under the heel of despotism." More important, he associated with Mexican Mormons, and the result was a melting away of his negative prejudices during his diplomatic service in Mexico from 1927 to 1933.[9]

Three years after he entered the First Presidency, most of the native Mexican Mormons became involved in a nationalist schism against LDS headquarters. Flourishing for a decade, the Mexican Schism, or "Third Convention," demanded the right to choose native Mexicans as mission president, local leaders, and missionaries.[10] Because the Third Conventionists often justified their actions by quoting Reuben's statements to them while he had been ambassador, he drafted a First Presidency letter to the schizmatics in 1936:

President Clark has repeatedly pointed out to you the great responsibility that rests upon you as a people; he has told you that you should fit yourselves to carry on missionary work in Mexico and not only in Mexico, but also among the others of the descendants of [the Book of Mormon's] Lehi throughout the whole western continent. This does not mean, and President Clark has so stated, that this should be done through an independent organization of your own, nor that you should direct this work as from a central organization. President Clark has always known and had in mind, and his statements have been in accord therewith, that the Church organization must stand as it is and that you should carry on under that Church organization.[11]

He left to others the challenge of resolving this situation, but he demonstrated his effort to balance ethnic conciliation with his lifelong emphasis on loyalty. In 1944 he wrote a 113-page memorandum about the Third Convention.[12] Two years later George Albert Smith began the process of reconciliation by visiting Mexico and allowing the schismatics to speak directly with an LDS president for the first time.[13]

Eight years after he had last been in Mexico, President Clark wistfully spoke of his desire "to visit again that beautiful land and have some association at least with that soft voiced and generally gentle people."[14] Twenty years after leaving this Latin country, he wrote to Isaias Juarez, "I shall never forget that super excellent *mole de gallina* which we used to have at your mother's home. I have never eaten any other *mole* that was equal to hers." He concluded the letter, "I will be glad if you will remember me to the saints there and say that I still hope sometime to come to Mexico and see them all again."[15]

Reuben was especially concerned about Anglo-American Mormons intimidating Latino Saints. When LDS authorities discussed incorporating the Mexican branches of the American Southwest into the regularly organized stakes of the area, "Pres. Clark felt a bit apprehensive about turning the Mexicans over to these cold-blooded Americans."[16] The Mexicans represented the most complete reversal of his earlier attitudes toward peoples and races.

Likewise, he praised Apostle Spencer W. Kimball's activism on behalf of Native American Indians:

Your work in the cause of the Lamanites is, of course, outstanding. I am happy that in your service in that field you are able to shut your eyes against many of the disadvantages and problems which are incident thereto, and which are too much before the eyes of many of the rest of us.[17]

In praising his first cousin's emphasis, Reuben deftly acknowledged that some of the apostles were somewhat negative about it. Kimball's biography verified this.[18] In an interview Kimball added that Counselor Stephen L Richards gave only grudging support to the church Indian program.[19] This may have been another area of tension after Richards supplanted Reuben as first counselor.

It was especially significant that President Clark did not romanticize the historical process of establishing Utah's Zion on native lands. He reminded LDS members in the Salt Lake Tabernacle that Americans had "gained the most of the land which we possess, including that on which we stand, by conquest ... I loathe conquest, I loathe oppression."[20]

Yet he remained a nationalist concerning U.S. relations with Latin America's Hispanic, Brazilian, Latino-African, and indigenous peoples. When Alfred M. Landon became a U.S. delegate for the Pan-American Conference, Reuben wrote in 1938: "I hope you will be spared the experience which I had [in 1933] at Montevideo—that of sitting and hearing the United States libeled and slandered and thrown into the gutter by the Latin-Americans. The three or four hours which I had of that when I was at the last conference is quite sufficient to last me the rest of my life."[21] A year later he also gave Hamilton Fish Armstrong, editor of *Foreign Affairs,* a vitriolic assessment of Latin America's uselessness to the United States.[22]

Years before his service as an ambassador, Reuben's opinion of the Japanese had already gone through a transition. He was always uncomfortable with Japan's military strength because the U.S. acquisition of colonies in the western Pacific during 1898-1900 had added America to that island nation's competitors for regional resources and power. Biographer Frank W. Fox noted that he "fretted over the 'yellow peril'" and expressed his share of "Nipponophobia," or fear of Japan.[23] But he was as good as his word about the need for justice toward the Japanese. In 1913 he represented Japan's embassy in legally challenging a California law which discriminated against Japanese residents.[24] In fact, his relations with Japan in international law and diplomacy were mutually agreeable. He seriously considered accepting an offer to serve the Japanese imperial government in an advisory capacity.[25] Fox observed that "the forces of the twentieth century were inevitably at work on Reuben, too. He performed legal work for the Japanese and grudgingly came to respect them."[26]

While in the First Presidency, Clark's attitude toward the Japanese was extraordinary because of the dramatic way in which Japan affected his own life. The Nipponophobia of many Americans seemed vindicated on 7 December 1941 when the Japanese launched a surprise attack on the U.S. fleet anchored at Pearl Harbor, Hawaii.[27] His son-in-law Mervyn Bennion died as one of the first casualties, and the grief of his loss never left the aged church leader.

Yet Reuben neither felt nor manifested any bitterness toward the Japanese. Even before the Pearl Harbor attack, but especially during World War II, the headlines of the LDS church newspaper frequently used the derogatory word "Jap."[28] This reflected the speech of most non-Asian Americans during this time. By contrast, he almost never used the term— even in corresponding or speaking with those who did.[29] I found only one occasion when he used the word "Japs"—when it appeared on both sides of a transcribed telephone conversation with Harvey H. Bundy, special assistant to the Secretary of War.[30]

In 1942 Reuben also said that "personally I had no antipathy toward the Japanese" when telling a government official that he opposed a "relocation center" in Utah for Japanese immigrants and American-born Nisei who were being involuntarily removed from the West Coast.[31] His disapproval did not stop the federal government from confining Japanese-American citizens in the Utah relocation center, Topaz.[32] However, in this November 1942 conversation, he stridently opposed the federal government's proposal to release Japanese-American families from their incarceration if they would settle in Utah during the balance of the war. Apparently without consulting LDS president Heber J. Grant or second counselor David O. McKay in advance of his statement, Reuben told the War Relocation Authority's representative that "we did not want the war to leave us with a Japanese problem in this State [of Utah]; we preferred no Japanese."[33]

As Utah's elder statesman, Clark's opposition may have been the deciding factor in the federal government's decision not to release law-abiding Japanese Americans from these barbed-wire camps in early 1943. Their incarceration continued until after the war's end—nearly three more years—despite the fact that these West Coast Americans had demonstrated overwhelming loyalty to the U.S. government which had imprisoned them.[34]

His cousin, Apostle Kimball, observed that he never heard Reuben utter a word of antagonism toward the Japanese.[35] Rather than celebrating Japan's defeat in 1945, President Clark publicly condemned the United States for using atomic bombs against Japanese "men, women, and children, and cripples."[36]

While he felt no recrimination against the Japanese for the death of his son-in-law, he opposed marriage between Caucasians and Asians. A young LDS serviceman in Hawaii wrote in August 1945 that he wanted to marry a Japanese-American girl who had just completed a full-time mission there. Although the two young people shared the LDS gospel in common, President Clark wrote the young man a three-and-a-half-page, single-spaced, typed letter. It echoed the racial concepts of eugenics that he had learned at Columbia forty years earlier:

> Your race excells in one line of activity, her race in another, and I am not prepared to say which is the better, though, of course, I do prefer my own race, but that is not because I regard her race as inferior. ... So that, personally, I have nothing but kindness for the [Japanese] race and am free from race prejudice. ...
>
> The experience of the human race shows that the mixation of races so different as are the Anglo-Saxon and the Japanese, is frequently not healthy, either biologically, temperamentally, or as a matter of character. Too frequently the worst elements of character in each of the races is brought out in the progeny. This, I believe, is a biological fact. I am not talking about the worst of the characters of the two individuals that mate, but of the characters of the two races.[37]

The young man listened to this advice, married "a white girl," and raised a happy family. Into the 1950s Reuben sent copies of this letter to parents whose sons were considering marrying Asian girls.[38]

In this regard, Chieko N. Okazaki, a Japanese-American resident of Salt Lake City, described her experiences with racial discrimination from the 1950s to the early 1960s. Decades later, as counselor in the Relief Society general presidency, she noted: "A Japanese person could not be sealed to a Caucasian in the Salt Lake Temple at that time because of state law. We could not buy life insurance and could not insure our cars." She added, "We had difficulty buying a home."[39] Utah law not only prohibited marriage between Asians and whites, it also disallowed marriage between Asians and African Americans.[40]

There was one ethnic group, however, for whom Reuben expressed lifelong dislike and distrust—the Jewish people. In a 1942 letter to Herbert Hoover, he said the Jews "are brilliant, they are able, they are unscrupulous, and they are cruel."[41] Part of the explanation for his anti-Semitism was personal and part political.

He expressed contempt for "the foul sewage of Europe" in his 1898 valedictory, yet Mormons had traditionally gotten along very well with the small population of Jews in Utah.[42] His anti-Jewish attitudes apparently crystallized after he moved to New York City in 1903.

There, in his thirties, Reuben confronted a large Jewish population for the first time in his life. His enrollment at Columbia introduced him to the intense competition of law students, while at the same time he had to interact with the city's Jews. The undergraduate dean starkly and publicly acknowledged a common attitude of that time: "Isn't Columbia overrun with European Jews, who are most unpleasant persons socially?"[43] In Reuben's later law practice in Manhattan, Jewish businessmen numbered among his clients and antagonists in legal cases, and his experiences with them were not always pleasant.[44]

Perhaps most important in the personal side of his anti-Jewish attitudes, he experienced two humiliating defeats for a Senate nomination in the 1920s at the hands of a Jewish opponent, Ernest Bamberger. Reuben was convinced that Jewish money corrupted the political process in these two elections.[45] This followed Simon Bamberger's service as Utah's first

Jewish governor,[46] whose tenure led to an anti-Semitic backlash in Utah, including the appearance of the Ku Klux Klan.[47]

Shortly after Governor Bamberger's term ended, LDS president Grant instructed the general conference in April 1921: "Some of you may be familiar with the agitation that is going on at the present time, in the publications, against the Jewish people. There should be no ill-will, and I am sure there is none, in the heart of any true Latter-day Saint, toward the Jewish people." He added, "I believe in no other part of the world is there as good a feeling in the hearts of mankind towards the Jewish people as among the Latter-day Saints."[48]

Nevertheless, Reuben made notations in his First Presidency office diary about meeting "a typical Jew banker of the worst type" or "a glib Jew army officer."[49] In a letter to his wife, Lute, he referred to an English lord as "a Jew I believe, but a rather nice one 'they say.'"[50] As late as 1957, he wrote that one of his opponents in a ranching dispute was "a jew."[51] As Douglas F. Tobler observed, "Traditional Mormon religious sympathy seemed to have had little influence on his thinking about Jewish matters."[52]

Not surprisingly, Reuben's attitudes influenced his wife and children. In a 1923 letter, Lute wrote, "Mem [Marianne] is on the couch, Luacine at her side, drawing some more Jew faces."[53] While his son and namesake was attending Columbia University, he complained to his father about the advancement of a "Jew boy" into the bishopric of the Manhattan Ward and said that the ward was being taken over by "our incoming Jew Brothers."[54]

Beyond whatever personal reasons Reuben had for his anti-Semitism, there was clearly a political dimension to his attitudes. Some of the most prominent radicals to his knowledge were Jews. Karl Marx was coauthor of *Das Kapital* and the *Communist Manifesto*. Wilhelm Liebknecht founded the German Social Democratic Party. His son Karl cofounded the German Communist Party with Rosa Luxemburg. Morris Hillquit was cofounder of the Socialist Party of America. Leon Trotsky and V. I. Lenin were architects of the Bolshevik Revolution in Russia. Emma Goldman was an American anarchist and pro-Bolshevik. Benjamin Gitlow was cofounder of the American Communist Party and its vice presidential candidate in 1928. Beginning in 1936, Leon Blum was the Socialist premier of France.[55] Reuben owned publications by or about all of these Jews.[56]

In these few, sensational examples of Jewish radicalism, President Clark thought he perceived the basic character of the Jewish people. He told ex-president Hoover in 1942 that the Jews "are essentially revolutionary, but they are not statesmen."[57] Thirty-two percent of surveyed Americans shared his view.[58]

However, there were prominent Jewish opponents of Marxism and Communism,[59] while anti-Semitism flourished in the Soviet Union.[60] A Salt Lake City newspaper headline read, "Anti-Semitism under Soviet Rule Revealed." Reuben owned a book on this subject by the American Jewish League Against Communism.[61]

Yet he never altered his political assessment of the Jewish people. He apparently accepted the argument of another book in his library that the claim for Soviet anti-Semitism was a "big lie."[62] He referred to "communistic tendencies, sponsored mainly by the Jews."[63]

Although not all American anti-Communists were anti-Semitic, the more intense tended to be.[64] Reuben's own fusion of anti-Communism and anti-Semitism was representative of this tendency.

Significantly, the *Protocols of the Elders of Zion* reinforced his attitudes. His enthusiasm for this publication indicated the extent to which he shared his anti-Semitic perceptions with others.

Originating in Russia in 1903, the *Protocols* claimed to be a transcript of a Jewish conspiracy for world dominion as allegedly advocated and planned at the first Zionist Congress.[65] Just as Reuben and millions of others were recoiling in horror at the specter of the Bolshevik Revolution and Russia's adoption of Marx's Communist ideology,[66] the *Protocols* were published in English translation. Beginning in 1920, this anti-Semitic publication was widely publicized in the United States by industrialist Henry Ford in his newspaper, the *Dearborn Independent,* and in his book *The International Jew, the World's Foremost Problem.*[67] The book fueled the previous concern expressed in 1913 by a national magazine's article about "the Jewish invasion of America."[68] Ford's 1920 publication of the *Protocols* is undoubtedly what the LDS president condemned in his April 1921 remarks about "the publications, against the Jewish people."

Furthermore, it was demonstrated as early as 1921, with added verification in later years, that the *Protocols* were fraudulent paraphrases "by officials of the Russian secret police" of far earlier political writings that had nothing to do with Zionism.[69] Reuben was aware of this because he possessed a 1921 refutation published by the American Jewish Committee.[70]

Nevertheless, he ignored pro-Jewish statements written by Jews.[71] After serving more than ten years in the First Presidency, he wrote: "I long ago ceased reading his [Walter Lippmann's] stuff, because he veers like a weather-vane, but I am sure always true when the wind blows from Jewward."[72]

Like an American Fascist publication in his library,[73] Reuben continued to affirm the authenticity of the *Protocols*. He kept several copies in his personal library at all times.[74] As he depleted his own supply by distributing them to others, he obtained six copies at a time from two known sources. He ordered them directly from the Pyramid Book Shop of Houston, Texas, and through his secretary, Rowena Miller, obtained them from Marilyn R. Allen, a Salt Lake City anti-Communist.[75]

Allen's "America Forever" series of Utah publications included the *Protocols*, as well as her *Crucify Him, But Hold the Jews Harmless,* her *Judaic-Communism versus Christian-Americanism ... My Answer to John Roy Carlson,* her *Political Zionism in America Is Subversive,* her *Silencing of Christians by* [sic] *Bnai Brith's Jewish Secret Police: Anti-Defamation League,* and her *Zionist War-Mongering in the U.S.A.: A Primer for the Gullible Goyim.* Reuben owned fifteen of Allen's publications, more than most of Utah's public libraries and universities held. He kept two copies of her *Primer for the Gullible Goyim,* the latter word being the Hebrew term for non-Jews.[76]

In addition, President Clark shared anti-Jewish publications with LDS administrators. In 1949 he recommended the *Protocols* to fellow conservative Ernest L. Wilkinson, commenting that they "will give you the shivers."[77] Reuben owned two other books which linked Jews with American Communism: the 1951 *Iron Curtain over America* and the 1953 *Zion's Fifth Column.*[78] When California stake president Hugh C. Smith, an anti-Communist activist, sent him the latter in 1954, Reuben replied, "I shall put this along with my copy of the 'Protocols of the Learned Elders of Zion,' to which apparently it belongs."[79]

Meanwhile, Utah's Jews were unaware of the Mormon leader's anti-Semitism. In 1953 the author inscribed a copy of his *Pioneer Jews of Utah*: "To President Clark with the kind regards of Leon L. Watters."[80]

Fellow anti-Communist and apostle Ezra Taft Benson sent President Clark a copy of *Towards an Understanding of Communism, the Power Behind It and the Power Using It*. Its second section included the statement, "Communism was established by Jewish and Zionist revolutionaries as an intermediate step to world power." Its third section was titled "Some Milestones in the March of Zionism to World Dominion," which included: "1909—The NAACP [National Association for the Advancement of Colored People] is established by Zionist revolutionaries to spearhead the eventual integration of the white and dark races" and "1933—The New Deal brings Socialism to America under the expert tutelage of Zionists Bernard Baruch, Felix Frankfurter and fellow-traveling intellectuals." In response, Reuben recommended that Apostle Benson, then serving as U.S. Secretary of Agriculture, read the *Protocols*, which "could seem almost prophetic."[81] The book already had been circulating among Mormon anti-Communists since the late 1930s.[82]

However, he was less candid with people he was not well acquainted with. For example, an LDS bishop in California sent him a copy of *The Coming Red Dictatorship: Asiatic Marxist Jews Control Entire World as Last World War Commences* and asked for his opinion of it. Reuben replied, "I do not know how much of the charges made in this printed material is accurate. Apparently some of it at least, is put out by anti-Jewish organizations, and we can only hope that the statements therein made are not true."[83] To those whom he trusted and whom he thought shared his attitudes, he was far more explicit.

The Democratic Party's New Deal provided him with more reasons to distrust "Jewish influence."[84] Just as conservatives were recoiling at the New Deal's innovations, they noticed an unprecedented presence of Jews in the executive branch, creating what one author regarded as a "passing phenomenon" of public opinion against Jews in the federal government.[85] Reuben owned a 1935 anti-Semitic publication titled *Roosevelt's Supreme*

Council: Alien-Asiatic Revolutionaries Control U.S. Politico-Economic Power-Centers, plus a 1936 publication about *Jews in Our Government,* as well as an undated pamphlet on this subject by the same publisher.[86]

As indicated by the publication Elder Benson sent to Clark, President Roosevelt's Jewish appointments provided ultra-conservatives with a rallying cry for decades. One such agitator was Gerald L. K. Smith, a white supremacist and supporter of the Ku Klux Klan.[87] Reuben owned his *Jews in Government and Related Positions of Power*[88] and began acquiring issues of his periodical in 1943. Clark also owned two subsequent publications against Smith's "fascism,"[89] even though he continued to acquire literature from Smith's Christian Nationalist Crusade.[90]

Reuben also warned Mormon Democrat James H. Moyle against the Jews in Roosevelt's administration. Despite being an ardent New Dealer, Moyle replied that he himself "could not understand the President's [FDR's] amenability to Jewish influence."[91] It was certainly no coincidence that Utah's first anti-Semitic pamphlet appeared the year of Roosevelt's first reelection effort.[92]

Of a private meeting with a church member in May 1939, President Clark wrote:

> He then went into some detail explaining to me that Communism came from the Jews: that they were the leaders of it in all parts of the world; that their object was to destroy Christianity and to bring all the world into slavery and bondage under them. ...
>
> Brother Farnsworth charged that all of the policies of the present [FDR] administration in Washington were shaped by the Jews, that they were in all the key positions in the government agencies, and he said they were in a position where they could make a tremendous amount of trouble if they so desired.

To those breathtaking accusations, he replied, "I told Brother Farnsworth that I had heard all of the things that he was telling me before; that some of them I knew to be true; that I felt we were in a serious condition; that I had been preaching about it for four or five years, but that I did not see how we were going to be able to stop the progress of the thing with anything that we might do."[93] Reuben regarded the politically liberal Jews in Franklin D. Roosevelt's administration as cause for concern, if not alarm.

Without explaining this in terms of anti-Roosevelt ideology, Utah political scientist Frank H. Jonas noted in 1940 that "anti-Semitism is beginning to raise its ugly head in the historically congenial and cooperative atmosphere of the Utah metropolis."[94] Unaware of Clark's feelings, President Grant wrote in his diary in 1940: "There is no prejudice in the heart of hearts of the Latter-day Saint people against the Jews. There never has been."[95]

Reuben understood Utah's undercurrent of anti-Semitism better than the political scientist or the LDS president. As he privately acknowledged to "Brother Farnsworth" in 1939, he had preached about Jewish influence in Washington for several years, even though his talks did not specifically identify Jews as the people he condemned.

Instead, like the title of his library's *Alien-Asiatic Revolutionaries,* President Clark used code words in his public references to Jews. For example, he spoke of "German political refugees" and "political emigres" when referring to those who wanted "revenge for ills they had suffered" in Nazi Germany.[96] Likewise, he used the code words "aliens," "alien emigres," and "European political emigres" in nationally publicized talks where he lashed out against the Jews who were "boring termite-like into our whole national structure,—financial, economic, social, and political." He continued that these "alien emigres" (Jews) "with their puppets and tools in or with access to the key positions in administration, they have secured the setting up in our Federal Government of a whole mass of governmental agencies—the alphabetical bureaus."[97] His last comment referred to the Democratic Party's New Deal programs such as the CCC (Civilian Conservation Corps), FDIC (Federal Deposit Insurance Corporation), FHA (Federal Housing Administration), and WPA (Work Projects Administration).[98] In private, Reuben dispensed with such code words as "political emigres" and "alien emigres." He simply referred to "emigre Jews."[99]

His intense feelings against Jews inevitably affected First Presidency decisions. His first administrative impact concerned Nazi Germany, where anti-Semitism was entering a violent phase. More than 12,000 native

German Mormons and hundreds of American missionaries were struggling to coexist with that country's increasingly brutal regime.

Nazi persecution of the Jews was already known to readers of the
LDS newspaper from early 1933 onward.[100] In addition, Reuben had
three publications on this subject.[101] Despite this information, he adopted
a view expressed by Berlin's LDS mission president, Roy A. Welker, in
1937: "Nazi dislike of Jews and hatred of Communism are at the root of
most propaganda against that nation."[102]

In 1938 Reuben alluded to Nazi persecution as his rebuttal to a Jewish critic of his talk in Salt Lake City to the National Congress of Parents
and Teachers:

> One woman's voice, from far back in the hall, arose above the rest:
> "I am a Jewess. May I ask what Mr. Clark intended in his mention of
> 'Christian education'?"
> Mr. Clark stepped to the rostrum to explain that he had employed
> the expression in a broad sense, "as distinguished," he added, "from nazi
> education, for instance."[103]

In mid-1939 he was expressing concern to the rest of the First Presidency that LDS missionaries in Germany might be "thrown into concentration camps, with all the horrors that that entails."[104] He made this
statement knowingly, based on his owning publications of 1933-34 by
survivors of the "murder camp of Dachau" and a Nazi "torture camp."[105]
Like all readers of the *Deseret News,* by 1938 he also knew about mass executions at these concentration camps and about the Nazi goal to exterminate Europe's Jews.[106]

These circumstances caught many Americans in a dilemma of conflicting values, priorities, and realities. They sympathized with the human
suffering of the Nazi oppressed, but how could Depression-racked America absorb millions of Jewish refugees? Those who idealized the Christian
Anglo-Saxon "race" had other reasons to resist Jewish immigration in the
late 1930s. This was particularly true for those who already felt that there
was a "Jewish problem" in the United States.[107]

Reuben had concluded that for the safety of the LDS missionaries
and members in Germany, the church needed to avoid any hint of

criticizing the Nazi regime's Jewish policies.[108] Two months after he was sustained as counselor in 1933, the Nazi Party newspaper in Berlin published an article "Juden und Mormonen" (Jews and Mormons), which criticized the LDS church because it had "always been very friendly with Jews."[109] By his second visit to Germany in 1938, LDS missionaries were assuring German newspapers that Jews were responsible for criticism of the Nazi regime in American newspapers. Missionaries explained that "it is for the lone American almost impossible to preach the truth against the power of Judaism." The First Presidency received a copy of the "Juden und Mormonen" article and its English translation.[110] This statement by the missionaries complied with a warning from Nazi officials to one of Germany's LDS mission presidents that "if we wish to have our church and missionaries remain in Germany," they were to publish statements supportive of the German people and regime and distribute them "to the German Reich"[111] (meaning regime, but also used by the Nazis as "empire").[112]

Reuben was determined that the LDS church would not risk alienating Nazis by helping Jews escape from Germany. Aside from church diplomacy, he did not want to allow more "emigre Jews" into the United States "to bore termite-like into our whole national structure."

This was evident when Jewish families began appealing to the First Presidency in November 1938 for former missionaries to sponsor their exit from Germany and Austria.[113] This was their anguished response to that month's *Kristallnacht* ("Night of Broken Glass") during which mobs burned 171 synagogues and destroyed 7,500 Jewish businesses. Overnight the Nazis arrested 25,000 Jews.[114] The *Deseret News* reported this in front-page articles.[115]

In regard to "your interesting letters," President Clark began his standard reply to these desperate Jews in January 1939, "we have so many requests of this sort from various persons, including members of the Church, that we have found it necessary to ask to be excused from making the required guarantee." His letter recommended that the petitioners, some of whom were LDS, contact Jewish organizations for help.[116] In view of Elder McKay's lifelong interest in promoting the welfare of the Jewish people, it must have been very difficult for him to attach his signature to this letter. But as second counselor, he had no other choice. It may be significant that Reuben did not wait for the return of President Grant before sending this letter which was signed only by the two counselors.

A few months later, State Department operative Allen Dulles asked what Reuben thought of efforts to get Congress to grant immediate asylum to 10,000 children, half of whom were Jewish, whose parents were desperately petitioning to get them out of Nazi Germany. Clark replied on 11 April, "We have had a tremendous meal of aliens in the last two or three years, and I am just a little bit afraid that we may have over-eaten a bit."[117] Mormonism's elder statesman was influencing U.S. policy through a diplomatic acquaintance who apparently had similar attitudes toward Jews.[118]

Three days after writing Dulles, Reuben declined to accept the invitation to serve on a nationwide committee for the placement in American homes of German refugee children, most of whom were Jewish.[119] However, on 24 April 1939 he asked another friend in the State Department to help secure visas for an LDS couple to move from Switzerland to the United States. He assured Greene H. Hackworth that they were "Aryan natives."[120]

While *Aryan* had previously meant any speaker of Indo-European languages, President Clark's letter adopted the well-known Nazi usage of this term. It meant non-Jews of "superior" racial origins: Germanic, Nordic, or Anglo-Saxon. He used "Aryan" in this way despite the fact that his library had two "anti-fascist" publications which condemned such usage. He obviously gave little attention to this criticism which was issued by American Communist publishers.[121]

In January 1940 he persuaded President Grant to reject the plea of Utah's Jewish leaders for the LDS church to donate several hundred thousand dollars in aid for European Jews. Instead, Reuben advised him to donate nothing for that purpose.[122]

However, in September he advised Grant to financially support Marshall Field's privately organized Committee for the Care of European Children because it allowed sponsors to select children according to religious background. Reuben noted that the LDS church "can afford" to make a monetary donation of twenty-one English pounds for each child "as a matter of prestige."[123]

If he could be sure they were not Jewish, President Clark was willing to help Europeans escape the Nazi holocaust. At best, he was indifferent to the plight of Jews in Europe.

In February 1941 the *New York Times* reported that Berlin's Nazi Party newspaper referred to the necessity of "eliminating all Jews."[124] This was an echo of the LDS newspaper's headline in 1938: "Death for 700,000 Jews Threatened: Semites Must Get Out or Die, Nazis Declare."[125] Even this stark Utah report gave less than one-tenth of Adolf Hitler's goal of killing every Jew in Europe. During the balance of 1941 and increasingly thereafter, newspapers in every major American city reported specific examples of the mass execution of Jews throughout Nazi-controlled Europe.[126] In apparent response to such reports, LDS author N. L. Nelson wrote a book against Hitler in the early months of 1941 and referred to the Nazi "butchery" of the Jews.[127]

In his June reply to Nelson's manuscript, Reuben defended Hitler and added: "There is nothing in their history which indicates that the Jewish race loves either free-agency or liberty. 'Law and order' are not facts for the Jews."[128] He was representative of the 60 percent of surveyed Americans who believed that Nazi persecution was the fault of the Jews themselves.[129] Some 35-40 percent of surveyed Americans reported that they would even approve of "an anti-Jewish campaign" within the United States.[130]

For more than one-third of America's adults, Hitler's propaganda minister Josef Goebbels was not exaggerating when he wrote in December 1942, "At bottom, however, I believe both the English and the Americans are happy that we are exterminating the Jewish riff-raff."[131] A month earlier British and American newspapers, including the *Deseret News*, reported that Hitler had already given secret orders to carry out a "Death Decree for All Jews."[132]

In June and July 1942, the *Deseret News* had reported the mass execution of Jews with "poison gas" in the Nazi concentration camp at Oswiechim, Poland (Auschwitz in German).[133] A *News* editorial also stated, "It has been a consistent policy of the Nazis to obliterate the Jews wherever they [the Nazis] have gone."[134]

By March 1943 the front page of the LDS newspaper reported, "All Jews in Five Towns Are Slain," followed a month later by a headline: "Death of All Jews in Europe This Year Expected: Hitler Continues Campaign of Extinction."[135] Clark's library also had a 1943 publication about the mass execution by the Nazis of tens of thousands of Russian Jews living in the city of Kiev, Ukraine.[136] This was his knowledge of European conditions when he wrote in June 1943, "We ought to cease worrying about Europe; they can stew in their own juice without materially affecting us."[137]

Even when the Nazi empire's collapse revealed to the world that this systematic extermination had actually killed millions of Jews,[138] nearly 80 percent of surveyed Americans in 1945 reported that this did not alter their feelings against Jews and Jewish influence in the United States.[139] In this respect, Reuben was typical. He never mentioned the Jewish holocaust in his comments about the tragedies and crimes of World War II.[140]

He also created "some sharp discussions" on the topic at a temple council meeting in 1945 when he opposed the intention of the Quorum of Twelve to endorse the emigration of Jews from Europe to Palestine.[141] The British were in control of Palestine and actively prevented Jewish immigration to their "protectorate," even to the point of seizing shiploads of concentration camp survivors and putting them into barbed-wire camps prior to deportation back to Europe.[142] In this 1945 temple meeting, "Geo. Albert Smith thought we couldn't do too much to aid the cause of the Jews and Pres. Clark remarked that if the Jews had their way they would wreck the country."[143] A year later the published report of one of Reuben's talks likewise used the word "wreck" in condemning America's "alien emigres," his code words for American Jews.[144] His entrenched opinion seemed confirmed when the Communist Party of Britain and the CPUSA supported the creation of a Jewish homeland in Palestine.[145]

Ironically, he was capable of such subtle diplomatic discourse that the executive director of the Jewish National Fund actually thought he was pro-Zionist. After "a precious hour in discussing the Zionist cause" with the LDS counselor, Mendel N. Fisher wrote, "It is good to know that we have your deep and abiding interest and that you expressed yourself so sympathetically with the aspirations of our people to create a Jewish Commonwealth in Palestine."[146] This misperception resulted seven months later in an invitation for Reuben to become a member of the American Palestine Committee. He cited previous commitments as his reason for declining.[147]

From 1945 to 1951 President Clark continued to use his church position and administrative power against what he perceived as "Jewish influence." In a 1946 Constitution Day talk on the LDS radio station,[148] he once again described Jews euphemistically as the "alien emigres" who were undermining the Constitution.[149] During a consultation in his church office in February 1948, he approved of the effort to remove a Jew from the Utah Republican leadership. Reuben told his political visitors that he "did not think we ought to perpetuate the Hebrew dynasty."[150]

He was equally opposed to the establishment of a Jewish nation in Palestine. In April 1948 he drafted a "pretty sharp" refusal to allow participation of any Latter-day Saint in a forum at Columbia University about the creation of the State of Israel.[151]

That same month, his anti-Semitism erupted when he learned that the American Red Cross planned to set up a national blood bank system. This would, in effect, prevent local hospitals from segregating blood donations according to race. Reuben blamed this proposal on "the Jews" and told the president of the American Association of Blood Banks "that it was a Satanic operation by the Jews to break down blood streams while keeping their own fanatically pure."[152] This reflected the view of American ultra-conservatives that Jews supported racial desegregation as part of a plot to undermine white Christian society in the United States.[153]

Because he expressed anti-Jewish attitudes in code words publicly and in specifics privately, Reuben obviously believed that some of his LDS listeners understood and agreed with him. In fact, a resident of Arizona, returned missionary Stewart L. Udall, wrote a private memo in 1947 that "too many members find it easy to be simultaneously devout Mormons and devout anti-Semites."[154]

Although Counselor Clark never altered his personal anti-Semitism, his public allusions and negative influence on LDS policy involving Jewish questions declined markedly after April 1951. The new church president, David O. McKay, was pro-Jewish and pro-Zionist. For example, after the Balfour Declaration established Palestine as a homeland for the Jews, Apostle McKay had publicly declared that this made Christmas of 1917 "one of the most glorious celebrations of our Lord for over 1600 years."[155]

As church president, McKay obtained Reuben's acquiescence in such actions as the 1952-53 purchase of thousands of dollars worth of bonds issued by the State of Israel. McKay explained that this purchase was "merely to show *our sympathy with the effort* being made *to establish the Jews in their homeland.*"[156] One need only remember Reuben's rebuff to George Albert Smith in 1945 to understand the counselor's inner feelings as he listened to these words from his new president.

However, Reuben continued to have influence beyond LDS headquarters. In May 1956, as a member of the board of Western Pacific Railroad, he told this California company's president that he opposed the admission of Jews to that board.[157]

In October 1956 President Clark wrote to one inquirer, "I am sure that the situation of the Jews in Palestine is very, very distressing." But as a hint of his lifelong beliefs, he added: "To what extent they may be responsible for that distress is not the point. As a matter of fact, they are suffering a great many hardships as the situation is represented to me." Concerning his own responsibility for setting the priorities of LDS humanitarian aid, he added:

> We have not sent any Welfare goods as such to the Jews in Palestine, but we do have them in mind and should occasion seem to arise I have no doubt that we will, on proper application, make some kind of a Welfare contribution should the occasion, as I say, arise therefor.[158]

Such an "occasion" never arose while he had oversight of the Welfare Program. In one respect, this reflected what he had previously called "the limitation of our program, which is to take care of our own."[159] In another respect, this 1956 letter was an echo of his response toward the plight of Europe's Jews two decades earlier.

He was capable of great compassion, but there is no evidence that J.

Reuben Clark ever felt compassion for Jews. He never voluntarily supported any humanitarian aid if it included Jewish people.

He also made negative references to Jews in response to LDS situations that did not involve them. In criticizing a chapel as too elaborate and expensive, he told a California stake presidency that "we were getting like Jews in trying to force ourselves into places we were not wanted and showing off with our wealth."[160] When someone expressed "indignation" in 1958 for how government "authorities on Staten Island" had treated an eight-year-old Mormon, President Clark replied: "If the boy had been a Jew, tears would have been flowing across the country from the Pacific to the Atlantic. But we have to take what we have to take."[161] This seemed to be a response to the sympathy many Americans expressed for the suffering of Jews in World War II.

President McKay could not stop Reuben from making hostile remarks about Jews or from distributing copies of the *Protocols*, but he effectively stilled his counselor's administrative voice against Jews. The church president's positive attitudes toward the Jews, Zionism, and the State of Israel were more representative of Mormons generally than were President Clark's anti-Semitic attitudes and administrative actions.[162]

Rivaling his preoccupation with Jews was Clark's personal and administrative interest in people of black African or "Negroid" ancestry, especially African Americans. To understand his response toward blacks, it is necessary to recognize that he was heir to a double-edged legacy: first, traditional American attitudes; and, second, a policy of the LDS church.

Long before Reuben's birth, Americans had already developed definite attitudes toward African Americans. Decades, even centuries, before Joseph Smith founded the LDS church in 1830, the white explorers, philosophers, educators, biologists, politicians, and literary authors had defined black Africans and African Americans as inherently inferior by race in matters of intelligence, civilization, social stability, morality, and physical beauty. Moreover, theologians and clergymen claimed that African Americans were descendants of Adam's son Cain and of Noah's son Ham and that these descendants were cursed by God.[163]

After examining American race relations, a Swedish sociologist observed in 1944:

Without any doubt there is also in the white man's concept of the Negro "race" an irrational element which cannot be grasped in terms of either biological or cultural differences. It is like the concept "unclean" in primitive religion. It is invoked by the metaphor "blood" when describing ancestry. The ordinary man means something particular but beyond secular and rational understanding when he refers to "blood." The one who has got the smallest drop of "Negro blood" is as one who is smitten by a hideous disease. It does not help if he is good and honest, educated and intelligent, a good worker, an excellent citizen and an agreeable fellow. Inside him are hidden some unknown and dangerous potentialities, something which will sooner or later crop up.[164]

Gunnar Myrdal had little or no knowledge of Mormonism and no acquaintance with J. Reuben Clark. Nonetheless, this Swedish sociologist accurately described the attitudes and phrases that cropped up repeatedly in nineteenth-century Mormon teachings about "Negro blood" and in Reuben's writings until his death. As a recent encyclopedia has noted, "By the late nineteenth century, the one-drop rule, which proclaimed that anyone with known African ancestry would be classified as black, prevailed nationally."[165]

These attitudes toward black-skinned people had explicit social and political manifestations. Before the American Civil War, most blacks in the South were legal slaves, whereas nearly all the "free" states and territories of the North enforced laws which disfranchised free blacks and segregated them residentially and socially.[166] Despite the post-Civil War amendments to the Constitution which emancipated Negroes and granted them civil rights, segregation continued in the North.[167] By the time Reuben graduated from the University of Utah in 1898, the U.S. Supreme Court had declared racial segregation Constitutional in such areas as transportation and education. This 1896 court decision gave free reign to practices embodied in the American South's "Jim Crow" laws.[168]

By contrast, more than fifty years earlier, Joseph Smith was an untypical American due to his positive attitude about the potential of American blacks. "Change their situation with the whites, and they would be like them," he said. "Go into Cincinnati or any city, and find an educated negro, who rides in his carriage, and you will see a man who has risen by the powers of his own mind to his exalted state of respectability."[169] Thus, social circumstance alone separated the potential of blacks from that of white Americans. At least, this was the view of the founding Mormon prophet until his death in 1844.

Nevertheless, the Mormons of Utah were consistent with the nearly universal approach of white Americans toward African Americans. Three Negro slaves were among the first company of Mormon pioneers to enter the Salt Lake Valley in 1847. Approximately thirty slaves and an equal number of free blacks lived in Utah from 1850 to the 1860s. Black slaves in Utah were bought, sold, and paid to the LDS church as tithing until the Civil War emancipated them.[170] By contrast, Utah outlawed the slavery of Native Americans in March 1852, a month after Governor Brigham Young signed the bill legalizing black slavery.[171] This reversed Joseph Smith's public proposal in 1844 "to abolish slavery by the year 1850."[172]

Utah Mormon attitudes were consistent with those of other White Anglo-Saxon Protestants (WASPs). While serving as secretary to President Young, George Reynolds instructed Utah's children, "All the other families of men are, as a rule, unequal to the [Caucasian race] in strength, size, beauty, learning and intelligence," whereas "the Negro race [is] the lowest in intelligence and the most barbarous of all the children of men."[173] A decade before he became young Reuben's first mentor, James E. Talmage also wrote:

> Perhaps I am prejudiced—but to look at a Negro face selected almost at random—and then to claim that the Black Man is the equal of the White in ability & mien [i.e., bearing]—appears to me a miserable conclusion—contradicted by all appearances.[174]

Yet that was the claim of racial equality which the church founder had stated decades earlier. Like Talmage, other prominent Utah Mormons made equally negative comments and sometimes used the derogatory term "nigger."[175] This included LDS general authorities, indicating how far the church had departed from the founding prophet's teaching on race.[176]

Instead, Utahns (90 percent of whom were Mormon until the 1950s) shared the nation's belief in scientifically defined racial differences.[177] As elsewhere, Utah imposed legal restrictions on blacks. Prior to the civil rights amendments 13-15 to the Constitution in the 1860s and 1870s, Utah law prohibited free blacks from voting, jury duty, and holding public office. From 1888 to 1963, Utah law prohibited the marriage of a white person to anyone as much as one-eighth Negro, similar to laws in thirty-seven other states.[178] The First Presidency explained in 1947 that "the intermarriage of the Negro and White races, [is] a concept which has heretofore been most repugnant to most normal-minded people from the ancient patriarchs till now."[179] Still, Utah's constitution provided for nonsegregated schooling.[180]

Beyond *de jure* considerations, Utah had a patchwork of *de facto* segregation from the time of Reuben's birth in 1871 until his death. After the Salt Lake City Commission rejected the 1940 petition of a bishop and a thousand fellow petitioners to legally restrict African-American residence to a "Negro District" by the railroad tracks, there was widespread use in all-white neighborhoods of Utah's Uniform Real Estate Contract, Form 30. This prohibited the purchaser of real estate and his or her heirs from reselling property "to any person not of the Caucasian race."[181] While there was no segregation of educational opportunity, the Salt Lake City School District would not hire blacks as teachers.[182] Forty percent of Utah's employers refused to hire Negroes, and those who did discriminated against them in job assignment, promotion, and salary.[183] Blacks were prohibited from eating at the lunch counter of the Salt Lake City-County Building. Utah's bowling alleys excluded African Americans, and theaters required them to sit in the balcony. LDS and Roman Catholic hospitals segregated African-American patients, sometimes requiring them to pay for private rooms. The privately owned resorts of Lagoon and Saltair both prohibited blacks from dancing or swimming.[184] In these respects, Utah and the Mormons were representative of the rest of American society until the 1960s.[185]

But there was one further dimension of Utah Mormon relations with African Americans, and this was an LDS policy in force throughout Reuben's life. All people of black African ancestry were excluded from receiving LDS priesthood ordination. This exclusion included the temple "endowment" and the "sealing" of marriages for "time and eternity."

However, before Mormons relocated to Utah, this was not yet a policy for *all* blacks. Joseph Smith authorized an African American to be ordained to the Melchizedek priesthood, first to the office of elder and then as a Seventy. To Smith's death in 1844, Elijah Abel was the only black man living at LDS headquarters who was both free and Mormon.[186] The prophet's brother also ordained Walker Lewis, a free black living in Lowell, Massachusetts, as an elder.[187] Ordination required a freedom of action that was not possible for slaves, who needed the consent "of their masters" even to be baptized.[188] Therefore, the earliest LDS church policy on African Americans operated within consistent definitions based on slavery or freedom—not race.

It was Brigham Young who defined the issue in terms of race. Aside from some vague references in LDS scripture to ancient priesthood exclusion based on sin,[189] there was no explicit and publicly known mention of racial exclusion until after Smith's death.[190] From 1836 onward, all Mormons living at LDS headquarters in Ohio and Illinois knew that Elder Elijah Abel was a free black who received two ordinations by authorization of the LDS president. Brigham's brother Joseph Young was senior president over the Seventy's quorums of which Abel was an active member.[191]

In support of the 1852 bill to legalize black slavery in Utah, Brigham reminded the legislature of the common belief that African Negroes were the descendants of Cain. He then announced that "any man having one drop of the seed of Cain in him cannot hold the priesthood." In acknowledgment of the fact that this was a departure from Smith's policy, Young added that the exclusion was true even "if there never was a prophet or apostle of Jesus Christ [who] spoke it before."[192]

Thereafter, most LDS leaders rephrased Young's emphasis as "one drop of blood" and inaccurately assumed the doctrine began with Joseph Smith. Leaders also occasionally spoke of a time when Negroes would receive the priesthood. But throughout Reuben's life, the emphasis was on the denial of priesthood for anyone of African descent.[193]

During his secular years as the "Honorable Mr. Clark," Reuben and Lute had an African-American maid who also did the family's cooking.

Evelyn Hall lived at their home in Washington, D.C., from 1915 until 1917, when she traveled with Lute and the children to Utah for the summer. She joined them in their permanent move west in 1920. This "colored woman" was still living with them in 1923 when he returned to Utah. She remained with the family until 1927.[194]

Nevertheless, in his later role as counselor in the First Presidency, Reuben resisted any tendency toward desegregation. He did so based on his own views of race, the racial attitudes of the general white population, the fact that segregation had been the Constitutional law of the land since 1896, and the implications of LDS teachings about Negroes. In 1944 he authorized church leaders in the central part of Salt Lake City to join "a civic organization whose purpose is to restrict and control negro settlement."[195] In 1945 he conferred with church president George Albert Smith and with Nicholas G. Smith, an Assistant to the Twelve, about use of LDS chapels "for meetings to prevent Negroes from becoming neighbors." President Smith's diary did not indicate whether he endorsed or opposed this activity, but his brother Nicholas described it as "race hatred."[196] Nevertheless, in September 1947 Counselor Clark made arrangements for the church to purchase all the residential properties adjoining the Los Angeles temple site "in order to control the colored situation."[197]

At a meeting of the First Presidency and Quorum of Twelve in October 1947, Reuben stated his attitude toward the slow increase of national support for racial integration:

> President Clark called attention to the sentiment among many people in this country to the point that we should break down all racial lines, [and] as a result of which sentiment negro people have acquired an assertiveness that they never before possessed and in some cases have become impudent.[198]

Aside from maintaining the church's social policies of race, he was wary of the fact that, since the 1930s, the Communists were the only political party which had consistently advocated full civil rights and social opportunities for African Americans.[199]

For his own part, he was constantly on the lookout to prevent any tendency in the church that might encourage integration and interracial marriage. In 1947 he complained that an *Improvement Era* photograph portrayed a young man as though he had Negroid features. "Pres. Clark said if he were the boy he would sue them for libel" because this was the son of a local stake president's counselor. His main concern was that the cover photo featured a young white woman with this young man who looked African-American, at least to Clark.[200] On 29 April 1950 the *Deseret News* promoted a multicultural view of "tomorrow's leaders" with a photograph of four young Utahns standing together: an American Indian girl, an Asian-American girl, an Anglo boy, and an African-American boy. In response, Reuben severely lectured the editors for printing this front-page photo: he "did not want anything done to lead his grandchild to marry a negro."[201] During a conversation with an LDS physician four months later, Reuben spoke about "*race tolerance*: the trend is just terrible."[202]

At the same time, various people criticized the church-owned Hotel Utah for refusing to admit Negroes as guests. When an LDS bishop asked about this policy, President Clark, as the hotel's senior vice president, defended this as simply "the practice of the hotel."[203]

For example, internationally renown singer Marian Anderson had to endure such policies. When she gave her first recital at the University of Utah's Kingsbury Hall, this African American was denied entry to any of Salt Lake City's hotels and had to stay with one of the concert's promoters. When she returned in March 1948 to participate in a concert at the Tabernacle, the First Presidency relented, and America's beloved contralto "was allowed to stay at the Hotel Utah on condition that she use the freight elevator." She was not allowed to use the main entrance and lobby.[204]

A year after the First Presidency made this exception, Reuben defended the general policy of refusing to admit African Americans as guests or residents in the Hotel Utah. "Since they are not entitled to the Priesthood, the Church discourages social intercourse with the negro race, because such [social] intercourse leads to marriage, and the offspring possess negro blood and is therefore subject to the inhibition set out in our Scripture." In this September 1949 letter, his secretary, Rowena Miller, relayed his view "that this does not mean that the negro shall not have equal rights before the law, but he does not believe in so-called social equality.

This must be if we are to preserve the purity of the race that is entitled to hold the Priesthood."[205]

He did not explain how African Americans could have equal rights before the law without social equality in the law. Undoubtedly, his attitude was in the context of the Supreme Court's 1896 decision, still in effect, that upheld *de jure* and *de facto* segregation of the races.[206] Nonetheless, he praised the Constitution's nineteenth-century "Amendments which had to do with the destruction of slavery and the enfranchising of the colored man."[207]

He combined his racial attitudes with pleas for compassion toward blacks. After Apostle Harold B. Lee gave a radio talk, "Pres. Clark thought I was just a little severe in my treatment of the negroes and the curse placed upon them."[208] Reuben's office diary also demonstrated this during a conversation with the director of LDS stage plays in October 1950:

> He [JRC] repeated he did not think they should make fun of them. He said that he had a deep sympathy for the negroes, but that did not mean he would want one of his children to marry one, and he did not want them to dance with them, and he did not approve of the breaking down of the color line because anything that breaks down the color line leads to marriage. ...
>
> ... and repeated that he was not against the portraying of the negro but he did not want him [to be] made fun of, which, of course, does not mean that they might not have a character which was humorous or comic, and stated that the Amos and Andy shows [on radio and television] were examples of that.
>
> ... Pres. Clark said there again would have to be the question of just what was intended to be portrayed [of African Americans on stage], that they [LDS plays, should also] have dirty, indolent tramps who are whites, and we make fun of white people [as well]; but what they [drama directors] would have to watch [and prevent] was anything that would degrade them or wound them.[209]

Nevertheless, Reuben sometimes used the race epithets common in the nineteenth century. Nine years before he gave the above instructions, he wrote that Salt Lake temple president Stephen L. Chipman "brought up several matters involving Bro [Joseph] Christensen. The real 'nigger' is they do not trust Bro. Christensen."[210] As previously noted, earlier generations of Utah Mormon leaders used this derogatory word. There is no evidence that Mormonism's founder ever did.

Apparently for the first time since Marian Anderson's concert in the Tabernacle, the visit of a Nobel Prize–winning Negro caused the Hotel Utah in April 1951 again to make an exception to its racial exclusion. A local African-American lawyer wrote that "the Extension Division of the University of Utah invited Dr. Ralph Bunche to Salt Lake City for a lecture. Reservations were made for him at the Utah Hotel, a Mormon owned enterprise. Upon his arrival, the Hotel refused to accept him, but after much pressure, from high places, he [Bunche] was allowed to stay in the hotel on condition that he have his meals in his room and not come to the dining room." The lawyer added that "Congressman Adam Clayton Powell and his wife, Hazel Scott Powell, had a similar experience at the [LDS church-owned] Temple Square Hotel in Salt Lake City." The First Presidency also served as senior officers of that hotel.[211]

However, the pressures against racial segregation were increasing throughout the nation. In May 1954 the U.S. Supreme Court reversed its prior endorsement of racial segregation. In *Brown v. Board of Education of Topeka*, the court ruled that segregation was inherently unequal and therefore illegal under the Constitution. This suddenly thrust the people and institutions of America into a new era of race relations.[212]

Ever the legalist, President Clark now concluded that LDS headquarters should not maintain silence in regard to the new Constitutional decision, and he began preparing a sermon on the status of blacks with regard to the LDS church. Part of his intended talk at the October 1954 general conference dealt specifically with civil rights of Negroes:

> The Latter-day Saints willingly accord to them in civil matters all the rights, privileges, liberties and protection guaranteed them by the Constitution of the United States and laws in this country, and by equivalent instruments in other countries, in all their social, economic and political activities.[213]

This was a stunning reversal of his previous position against "so-called social equality" for African Americans. Despite his own prejudices, he had an unyielding reverence for the supremacy of the law and a rigid respect for the decisions of the Supreme Court in interpreting the Constitution.

Yet, despite his intention to align the LDS church with the Supreme Court's 1954 decision, Reuben never spoke publicly on the topic. This was apparently the decision of President McKay. In February 1949, as a First Presidency counselor, McKay had already expressed his opposition to Arizona's efforts to "guarantee rights of Negroes," commenting that "no matter what the law says, there is going to be discrimination against the colored people." McKay even praised the Jim Crow segregation of Negroes in the South: "I said further that the South knows how to handle them and they do not have any trouble, and the colored people are better off down there—[but] in California they are becoming very progressive and insolent in many cases."[214]

McKay's last phrase in 1949 was an echo of Reuben's previous statement that "negro people ... have become impudent." This was the social attitude of the two counselors toward Negroes, and it was the unstated context of the First Presidency's first official statement about priesthood exclusion in August 1949.[215] There was—and is—a mistaken but generally believed impression that David O. McKay had liberal attitudes toward civil rights for African Americans.[216] Aside from the above contrary evidence, he initiated—without prior consultation with his counselors—a ban in 1952 against LDS Negroes speaking in sacrament meetings or firesides.[217]

Thus it was that the church remained silent about Negro civil rights for nine years after the Supreme Court's 1954 decision. Making specific reference to the desegregation controversy in Little Rock, Arkansas,[218] President Clark in 1957 instructed Relief Society general president Belle Smith Spafford "that she should do what she could to keep the National Council [of Women] from going on record in favor of what in the last analysis would be regarded as negro equality."[219] She had been a vice president of the National Council of Women for nine years.[220] Perhaps Reuben did not need much persuasion from President McKay in 1954 to drop his intended remarks on the "rights, privileges, liberties and protection" of African Americans.

However, by 1963 national fervor for civil rights and resulting criticism of the church's attitude toward African Americans resulted in an endorsement of Negro civil rights at general conference. It was announced by Counselor Hugh B. Brown, a political liberal.[221] By contrast, President Clark had believed that such an endorsement would have received far more credence and a more positive reception if given at the earliest possible date by a counselor who was known to be a conservative.

Still, there were two issues of segregation about which Reuben never altered his position. The first was interracial marriage and the second was blood transfusions.

In one respect, his view of miscegenation was independent of African Americans. He consistently opposed "intermarriage" between any racial and ethnic groups.[222] He wrote to a young man in 1941:

> In the next place, my own observation yields no real exception to the rule that upon an intermarriage, such as is contemplated here, the husband inevitably as time goes on, adopts the standards (above or below his own) of his wife's race. If the situation so worked out with you it would mean that you would become a Brazilian in your habits, your associations, and perhaps in your ideals and concepts.
>
> I know nothing about the young lady in this case, but I do know that Brazilian standards generally are below our standards in matters of morals and frequently in standards of life generally. Their habits are different; their concepts and ideals are different. They are, in fact, a different race.[223]

The ban on blacks receiving the priesthood was a further argument against marriage between Caucasians and Negroes. "For biological and Priesthood reasons, the Church is opposed to intermarriage of the two races," he wrote in his undelivered talk of 1954.[224] In 1960 he told the mission presidents, "Personally, I am unalterably opposed to the amalgamation of the negroes, both on religious and biological grounds."[225] These references to biology indicate that until his death, he retained the belief in eugenics as advocated by his associates at Columbia in the early 1900s.[226]

With regard to blood transfusions, a nationwide hospital practice of segregating the blood of African Americans from Caucasian blood was instituted during World War II. At that time, millions of Americans were donating blood to support the war effort.[227] In Salt Lake City, both the Roman Catholic and LDS hospitals segregated blood by race in accordance with the national practice.[228]

President Clark insisted that the LDS hospitals continue to segregate blood racially "to protect the purity of the blood streams of the people of this Church."[229] Despite medical assurances to the contrary, he feared that if a Caucasian received a transfusion from an African American, this would result in the "one drop" of Negro blood that would disqualify the person from henceforth receiving or exercising the LDS priesthood. This was his understanding of Brigham Young's teaching and of the church's policy after it became headquartered in Utah.[230]

Nevertheless, Reuben declined to advise Mormons to refuse blood transfusions from people of Negroid ancestry. "He has never attempted to direct anybody as to what they should do with reference to blood transfusions," Secretary Miller wrote to one inquirer. She added, "As a matter of fact, however, the L.D.S. Hospital here in Salt Lake City has a blood bank which does not contain any colored blood."[231]

It is important to recognize that Reuben's concerns in this regard also represented the position of President McKay. In 1959 Mark E. Petersen sent the First Presidency a clipping from the *New York Times* quoting a talk at the annual meeting of the American Association of Blood Banks: "Blood transfusions would be safer if a 'race-to-race' policy were followed." Presidents McKay and Clark replied to Apostle Petersen, "The article is a very interesting one and seems to support certain views that we have had for some time on this subject."[232]

The question of blood transfusions led Reuben to another preoccupation—a medical procedure to identify persons with black African ancestry. He called this the "detection of negro blood."[233] For more than a decade, he conversed and corresponded about this quest with Dr. G. Albin Matson, former head of the University of Utah's Blood Grouping Laboratory and subsequent director of the Minneapolis War Memorial Blood Bank.[234] Clark wrote a summary memorandum on 29 November 1960:

It might be well that one step in ruling on this case might be to ask the individual concerned to have an examination made of his blood to see whether or not there are sickle cells therein. If sickle cells are found, it would be proof that he had negro blood. If no sickle cells were found, it would not be absolute proof that there was no negro blood. ...

But those [who are] suspected or charged with having negro blood might be expected to be willing to have the test made if he is a member of the Church, knowing of the attitude of the Church vis-a-vis negroes and the Priesthood. The charge of a taint of negro blood is so serious as involving Priesthood rights that it would seem anyone would be glad to take whatever means are available to clear up the matter of his right to the Priesthood.[235]

As he had written to Matson in 1959, "This question of negro blood is becoming increasingly complicated and for us increasingly difficult."[236] In fact, Clark had been expressing concern for nineteen years about the problems involved in the LDS policy regarding priesthood and blacks.

The joint council of the First Presidency and Quorum of Twelve had not had a significant discussion of the priesthood restriction for thirty years[237] when Reuben initiated a total review of the question in 1940. He had apparently been thinking of this since the First Presidency made a difficult decision in August 1939:

A woman whose father and mother had been through the Temple was applying to go through the Temple herself. She was from the Southern States Mission, and the Church records showed that opposite her name someone had placed the endorsement, "negro blood." Brother McKay talked with me yesterday or the day before about it, and I suggested that he get her patriarchal blessing.

President Clark hoped that this would simplify their decision about this "white" woman with "negro blood." Instead, they discovered that Apostle George F. Richards, who was also an ordained patriarch, "had told her she was of the lineage of Israel through Joseph and Ephraim. We decided that under those circumstances she could not be denied admission to the Temple."[238] This demonstrated to Reuben the nagging inconsistencies of implementing a policy of denial based on "one drop" of black African ancestry.

The minutes of the council meeting of 25 January 1940 indicate that Reuben was not simply asking for a perfunctory reaffirmation of the nearly ninety-year-old policy. He wanted the First Presidency and Quorum of Twelve to give serious consideration to allowing persons of black African ancestry to receive the priesthood:

> President Clark explained that this matter has come up at various times in the past, that it is *the question of what should be done with those people who are faithful in the Church who are supposed to have some Negro blood in their veins.*
>
> President Clark said *at his request* the clerk of the Council had copied from the old records of the Council discussion[s] that have been had in the past on this subject. He said that he was positive that *it was impossible* with reference to the Brazilians *to tell those who have Negro blood and those who have not,* and we are baptizing these people into the Church. The question also arises pertaining to the people in South Africa where we are doing missionary work, and in the Southern States, also in the islands of the Pacific [i.e., black-skinned Fijians and aboriginal Australians].
>
> President Clark suggested that this matter be referred to the Twelve who might appoint *a sub-committee to go into the matter with great care and make some ruling* or re-affirm whatever ruling has been made on this question in the past as to whether or not *one drop of Negro blood* deprives a man of the right to receive the priesthood.[239]

He remained uncertain about the priesthood status of dark-skinned Pacific islanders. Twenty years later his office diary noted: "Mr. Ronald Jones of Morgan, Utah, called Pres. Clark at his home to ask whether or not Polynesians could go to the Temple. ... Pres. Clark said that he could not be positive, but he thought there was no prohibition for Polynesians to go to the Temple, but that he would better call Pres. [ElRay L.] Christiansen on Monday, when he returned."[240]

A month after the January 1940 meeting, the committee of three apostles was split about its recommendation. In their February report, Joseph Fielding Smith and George F. Richards recommended against allowing part-Negroes to receive the priesthood. The other committee member favored an allowance for those with a small portion of black African ancestry. This apostle was Charles A. Callis, a Clark-man who had been president of the Southern States Mission for twenty-five years. He "did not agree [with the majority] but would not file separate report" in dissent. The council accepted the only recommendation the committee made—to continue the policy of one-drop exclusion.[241]

In this regard, Joseph Fielding Smith seemed typical of most twentieth-century LDS leaders who were born a decade after the emancipation of slaves. Living most of his life amid African-American segregation, Apostle Smith later told a newspaper editor, "'Darkies' are wonderful people, and they have their place in our Church."[242] But it was a very limited place.

Despite his own racial attitudes and support of segregation, Reuben continued to be uneasy about a policy based on one drop of blood. With his lifelong emphasis on justice, legalism, and administrative uniformity, he was troubled by the inevitably haphazard manner in which blessings were denied to persons who happened to know of their far-distant Negro ancestry, while priesthood was given to those who were unaware of their African heritage.

A new catalyst for his concerns occurred in August 1947 when the First Presidency and twelve apostles denied a temple recommend to a "sister having one thirty-second of negro blood in her veins."[243] In other words, one of her great-great-great-grandparents was African American. This was a more stringent test than in the segregated South of the 1940s. Virginia's miscegenation law prohibited marrying persons with one-sixteenth African-American ancestry, and Georgia law used the same measure to define a person as Negro. The rest of the South specified one-eighth or one-fourth as the basis for racial restrictions on marriage and against testifying in court.[244]

On 9 October, he asked for another reconsideration of the policy:

> President Clark again repeated what he had previously said on a number of occasions that in South America, and particularly in Brazil, we are entering into a situation in doing missionary work among the people where *it is very difficult if not impossible to tell who has negro blood and who has not*. He said that if we are baptizing Brazilians, we are almost certainly baptizing people of negro blood, and that if the Priesthood is conferred

upon them, which no doubt it is, we are facing a very serious problem. President Clark said that his heart bleeds for the negroes, that he had had them in his home and some of them were very fine people, that he felt we should give them every right and blessing to which they are entitled. *He said he was wondering whether we could not work out a plan, while not conferring the Priesthood as such upon them, we could give them opportunity to participate in the work certainly of the Aaronic Priesthood grades.*[245]

The statement about having "had them in his home" referred to his pre-presidency, live-in "colored" maid, Evelyn Hall.

Only on one known occasion did Reuben ever publicly mention an African American by name. In a meeting with mission presidents, he said: "We have baptized Negroes. Brother [Monroe] Fleming in the Hotel Utah was baptized. He said that he understands our doctrine, but he wanted to join the Church. We have never refused to baptize a Negro but they had better understand it [the priesthood restriction] first."[246]

Although not unprecedented, it was a significant institutional innovation when President Clark proposed in 1947 to allow African Americans to do Aaronic priesthood "work." As an unordained African American, Samuel D. Chambers was called to be an "assistant deacon," or acting deacon, in his Salt Lake City ward from 1873 onward.[247] However, this was not a widespread practice nor an official program of LDS headquarters.

By contrast, after the 1947 temple meeting, Reuben outlined a plan in a document titled "The Afrikan Branches of the Church of Jesus Christ of Latter-day Saints." In it, he recommended that blacks preside over and conduct the auxiliary organizations and be authorized to "preside and conduct" all branch meetings when no ordained priesthood member was present. He further recommended that Negro men be organized into "Preparatory Deacons Groups, Preparatory Teacher Groups, Preparatory Priests Groups."[248] Even those titles implied a not-too-distant ordination for men of black African ancestry.

Nearly eight years later, the apostles accepted Reuben's innovative proposal—at least in part. Without referring specifically to him, their letter mentioned "the survey made some time ago" and concluded:

After much consideration, it is our recommendation that a program be developed which will give to them such blessings as they may properly enjoy—that all of the Negro members in the [Salt Lake] area be organized into a unit which would function somewhat the same as the Deaf Branch or the Spanish-American Branch. Leadership could be brought from elsewhere in the city if felt proper and if needed. Auxiliary organizations could be conducted and the Sacrament could be administered to them in a Sacrament meeting by members of the priesthood from elsewhere in the stake.

In this letter of 30 March 1955, the Quorum of Twelve "respectfully submit the matter for your consideration," assuring the First Presidency that "all of this can be done without danger of intermarriage." It was signed by Joseph Fielding Smith, the Twelve's president.[249]

It does not seem coincidental that the apostles submitted this only a few months after President McKay prevented Elder Clark from giving his talk on this matter at the October 1954 conference. As his biographer, I conclude that Reuben privately urged his allies in the Twelve to promote the proposal he made during the presidency of George Albert Smith. The timing of this letter indicates that the Twelve, with Reuben as their silent partner, hoped that President McKay would agree to such an announcement at the April 1955 conference.

Such would not be the case. An African-American branch was not established during the presidency of David O. McKay. After his death, his successor Joseph Fielding Smith authorized such a congregation, the Genesis Group, involving 200 black Mormons. It began officially in October 1971, ten years after the death of the man who first proposed the idea.[250] In view of the unsuccessful recommendations from Clark since 1947 and the Twelve since 1955, the inescapable conclusion is that President McKay opposed allowing any independence to black Mormons.

Aside from maintaining the priesthood restriction, McKay resisted any liberalization of Mormon culture's social relationships with African Americans during his presidency (1951-70). This was certainly true at the Hotel Utah, over which McKay was president and chairman of the board.[251]

For his part, Reuben continued his practice of not trying to "overpersuade" the LDS president.[252] He repeatedly asked the First Presidency and Twelve to recognize the inequities in then-current procedures of priesthood restriction and to consider altering the policy. However, he loyally supported the church's policy toward blacks and the joint council's decision to continue it. At the same time, he sought medical tests to eliminate the capriciousness in the denials and conferrals of priesthood. Nevertheless, he recommended "preparatory" priesthood quorums and training for blacks because he firmly believed that one day they would receive the priesthood.

In this anticipation, the year 1954 seemed to herald the near approach of that change. Aside from the watershed legal decision of the Supreme Court that year, President McKay had already made a momentous decision regarding blacks outside the United States.

On 17 January 1954 the LDS president began an address to the church's missionaries in South Africa by reaffirming: "Well until the Lord gives us another revelation changing this practice established anciently and adopted in our day we will follow that policy. It is true in the days of the Prophet Joseph one of Negro blood [Elijah Abel] received the Priesthood. Another [still unidentified] in the days of President Brigham Young received it and went through the Temple. These are authenticated facts but exceptions." The president then announced that members in South Africa would no longer have to prove non-Negro ancestry by tracing every ancestral line back to Europe.[253] He recognized that this change would allow the priesthood to some of black African ancestry but: "I should rather, much rather, make a mistake in one case and if it be found out afterwards suspend his activity in the Priesthood than to deprive 10 worthy men of the Priesthood."[254] It is clear that he was seeking to benefit whites, not blacks. Still, he was willing to risk letting some black Africans become the indirect beneficiaries of this change.[255]

When McKay unexpectedly informed his counselors and the Twelve of his announcement, he extended its application to Brazilian Mormons who could not verify a totally white ancestry.[256] This liberalized church policy in Africa and Brazil, but it actually increased the difficulty that Reuben had been describing for nearly fifteen years. White-appearing men who had Negro ancestry but no record of it were being ordained while millions who could not conceal their black African ancestry were denied the priesthood. This is undoubtedly why, on the day President McKay informed his counselors about this revision of the church's race policies, "Pres. Clark was quite perturbed over the change in policy and predicted we would one day return to the old rule."[257]

Not long afterward, McKay made an extraordinary exception for a blond-haired American brother and sister whose "grandmother in South Carolina had Negro blood." Their "brothers and male cousins had been denied ordination" in the South. Now living in Utah, the young man pleaded with apostles Smith and Petersen to allow his sister to be married and sealed in the temple. After this former student told LDS educator Lowell Bennion that the apostles had denied his request, the well-known liberal appealed privately to President McKay, who allowed the temple marriage and authorized the young man to receive the priesthood and serve a full-time mission.[258] In view of McKay's habit of not telling his counselors about decisions he made privately with LDS members, it is unlikely that Reuben learned about these Utah exceptions to the policy. He would have been exasperated that the president extended priesthood privileges to white-appearing Negroes in Utah while their relatives continued to be denied the priesthood in South Carolina.

Nevertheless, the Constitutional and church developments of 1954 seemed to Reuben as steps toward an eventual change when the priesthood would become available to all men, regardless of color or race. He intended to announce that fact to the entire membership in his remarks to the general conference. Although his discourse maintained much of the racial philosophy and terminology of the nineteenth century, his undelivered talk expressed his hopes and anticipations for a new era:

> Furthermore, modern prophets have declared that in the due time of the Lord, the great burden the colored folk now bear will be removed from their shoulders and they will be permitted to enjoy the Priesthood, to the full extent to which they are heirs. But until the Lord again speaks, the situation will remain as it is.
>
> I say again, the Latter-day Saints know that our colored folk will get all the blessings they live for. They know that in the due time of the Lord, the burdens they now carry, and which were placed upon their shoulders

by the Lord, not by the Latter-day Saints, will be lifted and they will come out into the sunshine of the glory of the Priesthood, in such measure as has been decreed and as they have earned. Meanwhile, the Latter-day Saints deeply sympathize with them for the burden they carry, for which the Saints are in no way responsible, and the prayerful hope of the Saints is that the colored folk will carry the burden with fortitude, preparing themselves for the day of release.[259]

As indicated, he was not allowed to give this talk.[260] In 1956 he affirmed that such change would not occur "to meet some political expediency."[261]

On the other hand, he did not endorse statements by those who seemed to exclude the possibility of such change. During a 1960 meeting in the Church Administration Building, a mission president said: "Pope John has recently made the first colored man a cardinal in the Catholic Church. I think that is a good demonstration to us that they do not have the priesthood." Reuben replied, "It looks to me like we will get into deep water here," and changed the subject to interracial marriage, which he opposed.[262]

His private view was that "the early leaders of the Church declared that eventually the disability [of the priesthood restriction] would be removed."[263] He foresaw this "day of release" for all people of black African ancestry, though he did not live to witness the fulfillment of his earnest expectations.

During his lifetime, Utah and the Mormon people were not ready to grant full civil rights to African Americans, let alone confer the LDS priesthood on them. In 1961, the year of Clark's death, a survey of Salt Lake City by the NAACP showed that 12 percent of its cafes, restaurants, and taverns declined to serve blacks and that 80 percent of the city's beauty and barber shops refused to do so. Likewise, 72 percent of the hotels and 49 percent of the motels refused accommodations to African Americans that year.[264] Utah's racial discriminations changed only as a result of the federal Civil Rights Act, enacted less than three years after Reuben's death.[265]

Even then, LDS leaders continued denying priesthood ordination and temple endowment to those who admitted to even "one drop of Negro blood." For example, baptized as a seventeen-year-old convert in Colorado in 1977, blue-eyed, blond Warren Calvin Lathe III was denied priesthood ordination because his great-grandmother had African-American ancestry.[266]

This policy ended in June 1978 when LDS president Kimball announced that God had authorized that henceforth "all worthy male members of the church may be ordained to the priesthood without regard for race or color."[267] Kimball had read Reuben's undelivered talk in 1954.[268]

Although Clark was preeminently a U.S. nationalist, he believed that the LDS church must have a larger destiny. In October 1937 he told the general conference that "too long have we remained somewhat aloof from the organizations of ours on the other side of the water [i.e., the Atlantic Ocean] and in the islands of the sea [Pacific Ocean]."[269] Apparently, it was his idea to recommend as new general authorities some "men from considerable distances from the Church headquarters who could make available to us a knowledge of people and conditions in their areas with which we could not otherwise become acquainted."[270]

Reuben had traveled relatively little among the nations of the world. Still, he knew enough of Americans generally and of Mormon missionaries in particular to recognize their temptation to export American and Utah values throughout the world. He was opposed to cultural imperialism even as a secular idea:

> We must give up this idea too many of us have, that our way of life and living is not only the best, but often the only true way of life and living in the world, that we know what everybody else in the world should do and how they should do it. We must come to realize that every race and every people have their own way of doing things, their own standards of life, their own ideals, their own kinds of food and clothing and drink, their own concepts of civil obligation and honor, and their own views as to the kind of government they should have. It is simply ludicrous for us to try to recast all of these into our mold.[271]

He saw his personal mission as limited to America and the welfare of

Americans, but he had a clear vision of the international implications of the church.

In 1956 he gave even stronger instructions to missionaries about those who had moved to the United States from other countries. "I know what it is to walk down a street and never understand a word that is spoken," he began. "I used to attend the meetings of our Saints down in Mexico, the Mexican Saints. I know how lonely, spiritually, you can get, when you cannot understand what is going on. In addition to that, we have a sort of feeling sometimes that an alien is not quite as good as we are. Oh, he [is] just a 'Wop' or something else. They are just as good as we are. They are just as honest. They are just as sensitive."[272] By using this derogatory word for Italian Americans in his plea for ethnic tolerance,[273] he indicated how much he now rejected America's prejudices of the 1890s against the new immigrants from southern Europe. While his attitudes toward Jews had not changed,[274] he had come a long way from his 1898 speech about immigrant "sewage" from Europe.

Far in advance, Reuben also foresaw that the international mission of the church must be joined with technology. In November 1953 he told the chairman of the Federal Communications Commission that he had hoped for several years that the church could purchase "an international shortwave station." His hopes were not fulfilled until October 1962, a year following his death.[275] In 1954 he told the general priesthood meeting that he could "foresee in no distant future" that the meeting would be broadcast live to an audience of 150,000 men and boys gathered together in their own stakes throughout the United States. That was fulfilled at the April 1969 conference.[276] In 1958 he told the general priesthood that he could "envision within the reasonable future that we shall broadcast throughout the civilized world" sessions of conference translated into the various languages as the conference talks were given. In April 1967 that became the practice.[277]

J. Reuben Clark was clearly a product of the nineteenth century. He alternately accepted and resisted the twentieth century's changing views of race and ethnicity.[278] But supreme to him were the majesty of the law, the principle of justice for all humanity, and the expansiveness of the latter-day gospel. Despite his own acknowledged limitations, he affirmed that the gospel of Christ must be universal: the LDS church must not be confined by its nineteenth-century origins or its Utah headquarters. Despite his American national emphasis, he perceived that the LDS gospel was protected in, but not limited to, the USA. He wanted the church to extend itself in attitude, human resources, and in technology to "all nations, and kindreds, and people, and tongues."

CHAPTER 11.

Precious Things of Every
Kind and Art[1]

J. REUBEN CLARK NEVER CLAIMED TO BE A CULTURAL ESTHETE. HE once characterized his artistic judgment by commenting, "Now I know nothing about art and my opinion about the artistic value of a piece of work is worse than nothing, and, as a matter of fact, is in the red."[2] Yet as a member of the First Presidency, he inevitably became involved in administrative decisions about the church's artistic endeavors. Long before he became a general authority, he already had an untrained interest in both poetry and music that continued throughout his life.

He had little interest in non-poetic literature. Although he collected a massive personal library that he intended to be self-sufficient for his every need, there were only four novels: Jonathan Swift's satirical allegory, *Gulliver's Travels;* James Fennimore Cooper's frontier romance, *The Leatherstocking Saga;* Rudyard Kipling's fantasy, *Puck of Pook's Hill;* and Somerset Maugham's historical novel, *Then and Now.*[3] Novels have often been regarded as a waste of time or as repositories of lewdness. Reuben, who did not have sufficient interest in the genre to take time to sift the wheat from the tares, suspected that there was not much worth the sifting. He wrote to sculptor Avard Fairbanks, "There is more iniquity and devilish filthiness in modern literature than some of us can even dream about, in our naiveness."[4] Even literary essay held little appeal for Reuben. His library had separate imprints of six of Thomas Babington Macaulay's essays and two volumes of Montesquieu's *The Spirit of Laws.*[5] Lute's personal library, however, contained much of the prose literature her husband's lacked.[6]

On the other hand, Reuben had demonstrated an early interest in poetry by composing a six-verse poem when he was thirteen.[7] Shakespeare's *Complete Works* was one of the staples of his early education, and his adult library contained two editions of the Bard's works. There were also two imprints (1897, 1914) of Christopher Pearse Cranch's translation of Virgil's epic, the *Aeneid,* and two editions of John Milton's complete poems. In addition to two anthologies of English poetry, he had copies of Chaucer's *Canterbury Tales* and Edward Fitzgerald's translation of the *Rubaiyat of Omar Khayyám.*[8]

He was not only selective in the number of poetry volumes in his library, but also in the choice of favorite poems. From an extensive anthology of English poetry, he underlined and made marginal notations only on the poems of Burns, Dryden, Goldsmith, Johnson, Milton, and Pope.[9] While in the First Presidency, he manifested particular attachment to the *Rubaiyat.* When he composed a poem to some friends on their departure from Salt Lake City, he introduced it "with abject apologies to Omar."[10] His own copy reminded him on its flyleaf, "See Special verses: vii, xi, xvii, xviii, xix."[11]

The first two of these preferred stanzas from the Muslim poet seem somewhat atypical of Reuben's own disdain for the sensuousness of life: "Come, fill the Cup, and in the Fire of Spring / The Winter Garment of Repentance fling ... Here with a Loaf of Bread beneath the Bough, / A Flask of Wine, a Book of Verse—and Thou."

However, the last three of his favorite stanzas manifested his more somber reflections on the impermanence of power during his last years in the First Presidency: "They say the Lion and the Lizard keep / The Courts where Jamshyd gloried and drank deep; / And Bahram, that great Hunter—the Wild Ass / Stamps o'er his Head, and he lies fast asleep." In keeping with the mood of this and other companion "special verses," he marked only the following lines in his 1945 edition of Bartlett's *Familiar*

Quotations: "Imperious Caesar, dead and turn'd to clay, / Might stop a hole to keep the wind away" (*Hamlet*, V, i, 226).[12] This matched the mood of his 1957 letter to LaRue Sneff, a secretary in the First Presidency's office: "I think there are few duties [in the church] which will count for much in the Hereafter."[13]

President Clark composed poetry infrequently, but during a decade of his service in the First Presidency, church members were occasionally able to see public evidence of his creativity. In June 1941 he published a poem, "When I Would Pass," in the *Relief Society Magazine*. He used the pen name, Jay Rubark. This was a combination of three triads: a three-letter phonetic of his first initial, a three-letter phonetic of the first part of his middle name, and the last three letters of his surname. RUBARK had been the telegraph-cable address for his Washington law firm.[14] In November 1942 he wrote the first draft of a poem titled "A Hymn to the Seed of Ephraim and Manasseh," which he published in January 1946 under his own name in the *Church News*. Four years later he authorized its performance with his daughter Luacine's music score during the June conference of LDS youth organizations.[15] In November 1946 he also wrote a poem, apparently never published, titled "Give Me the Cloudless Day," which associated the symbol of the sun with the Celestial Kingdom and extended this parallel to the earthly effects of the sun.[16] Nevertheless, he did not consider himself a poet and did not project that image to his contemporaries. A common man's feeling for poetry characterized his interest from adolescence to old age.

Although he read little of literature, he had pronounced ideas about the quality of any literary work he happened across. Lute found this out to her chagrin when she asked him to read the manuscript draft of a children's story she hoped to publish. He began his critique by telling her that she had the right idea, but then continued:

> As it now stands however it seems to me it might be improved along the lines suggested below—
> In the beginning of my observations I may say that as I understand it, it is of *vital* importance in a short story that you have no unnecessary words, no unnecessary machinery, no unnecessary description, in other

words—space is almost all important and no word, thought, or incident should be allowed in the story which is not absolutely essential. Every thing in the story should be useful, little or nothing should be purely or-namental.—Again your short story should have a motive, a moral, or a purpose. Of course many stories are told for the sake of the story itself, but I take it yours is not of that class. As I surmise it, you wish to show that ghosts do not exist and that the children's fear of them is groundless. Therefore your whole story should turn around this motive and nothing that does not contribute to it, either directly or indirectly[,] should be admitted within the sacred precincts of your tale.

After his maiden voyage as a literary critic of his wife's first effort at writ-ing, Reuben added a postscript to his letter: "I have also ordered a book on the Art of Short Story telling which I shall send you as soon as it comes." He anticipated that his critique would make Lute "angry enough by this time."[17] He was right. "Thank you very much for the criticism," she replied. "I will simply consign the stuff to the fire, and save any one being persecuted further. It was real sweet of you to take your valuable time for the rot."[18]

Lute was as good as her word, for there is no evidence that the story survived this correspondence. She had apparently already submitted a Christmas story to the *Young Woman's Journal,* which it published four months after this interchange with Reuben. She never published another story in this LDS magazine the remaining sixteen years of its existence.[19] She did, however, publish stories in the LDS magazine for children.[20]

Reuben made few specific comments about painting and sculpture, but his personal papers give some indication of his preferences. He appar-ently enjoyed expressionist caricature that was popular in the early twen-tieth century. While he was ambassador to Mexico, he allowed a Mexican artist to paint at least three watercolor portraits of him in this style. The fact that these caricatures were dated from 1930 to 1931 would indicate that he enjoyed this style enough to return to the same artist several times. Perhaps this was a graphic expression of his famous self-deprecating humor.

During his visits to Europe on government business in 1937-38, he acquired three etchings: one of a forest, another of a snow scene with an isolated country church, and another of a small street in Zurich. He later wrote to his son and daughter-in-law who were visiting Venice, "One of my choicest memories of art work that I saw in Europe (the memory is not too distinct), is of the painting in the Doge's Palace."[21]

In a letter to a friend in New York City, Reuben commented on his visit to the Rock Creek Cemetery. He had liked the "Saint-Gaudens' statue of Nirvana, or as they call it, 'Grief,' and Gutzon Borglum's great statue 'Rabboni.' That was a rare experience for me and for Louise."[22] Sculptor of the Mount Rushmore Monument, Borglum had been raised Mormon.[23]

In the First Presidency, Reuben often had the responsibility of being a critic of church architecture. As usual, he had definite views. His comments about the Celestial Room of the Idaho Falls temple in 1944 indicated his typical firmness:

> I said it looked to me as if we had too much "art"—too much "decorates"; that one of the chief concerns should be properly to give people the proper inspiration; that we must have more and different furniture in this room. I suggested we must have some relief to the bare walls, and spoke of drapes, describing the wall hangings in Mexico, particularly Elizabeth Cabot[']s, though saying that would not do, but were merely illustrative. I thought we might consider some draperies. I also suggested the possibility of introducing some lighting effects in the top of the room—the tower part—a soft radiance that might typify the spirit and its presence ... I also suggested possibility of paneling the walls which would enable us to use a false facing to cover the wall defects.[24]

Since he felt discomfort with too much splendor in temples, which LDS headquarters intended as its best architectural efforts, he was even less pleased with gaudiness in local chapels. When he toured the Oakland Stake Tabernacle in 1945, he gruffly noted that it "looks like an Italian Villa" and complained about Mormons "showing off with our wealth."[25]

Because he was untrained in architecture and the arts, he apparently concluded that contemplation would add nothing to his first impressions. Understandably this approach was disconcerting to the church's architects. LDS architect Georgius Young Cannon described the process by which the First Presidency selected the design of the Los Angeles temple:

President Grant and President Clark and President McKay walked in and almost immediately President Clark stepped in front of President Grant and said, "I don't like this, I don't like this, and I don't like this, I like this, I don't like this," and out they walked. That was all the consideration given to our [architectural] sketches.[26]

Church architecture was one area where Reuben dispensed with his usual pattern of extensive research and reflection prior to announcing a decision.

Music was one of the arts to which he gave more attention. As First Presidency counselor, he told a stake priesthood meeting of his early experiences as a musician:

> As a teenager I tried to take some lessons on a flute in a small country town, not the kind of beautiful flute that you are playing, but just the ordinary, wooden flute. Then later, I do not know how I made the change, but I tried to take some lessons on the piccolo. Finally I degenerated to the tin whistle, (laughter) [from the audience] and out of the tin whistle, partly covering the holes with my fingers to approximate sharps and flats, I finally secured what my wife was kind enough to think was fairly good music. I appreciate your music tonight. I also tried to play a brass horn. The verdict generally was that I did not have the right kind of lip—for *that*. (laughter).[27]

As a workaholic lawyer and civil servant in Washington and New York, he showed little interest in attending concerts or obtaining classical recordings for home listening until he was sixty years old.[28] While his family was isolated in Mexico City, however, the ambassador developed a sudden passion for classical music. The turning point occurred on 25 January 1931. One of the diplomats in Mexico City invited the Clarks to listen to a recording of the entire opera *Aida* one Sunday evening at his home. They stayed until midnight, after which Reuben eagerly obtained a list of musical recommendations for phonograph records.[29]

Three days later he wrote a letter to his daughter Louise in Washington, D.C., asking her to purchase music recordings for him. His list included several light classics of short length, two operas, Stravinsky's *Fire Bird Suite,* plus Dvorak's *New World* and Schubert's *Unfinished* symphonies.

Reuben's letter showed his enthusiasm for the newly discovered world of serious music:

> I would like you to go to the best Victrola store there in Washington and proceed roughly as follows:
>
> Take one forenoon and hear them play "Aida" in the complete record. That will give you a standard by which to judge.
>
> Following this experience, hear, as soon as you can, "La Boheme" (in the album described in the attached list), "Rigoletto" (in the album in the attached list), and "La Tosca", which is not in the catalogue which I have seen, but which, I am told, is as good as "Aida". I have heard some doubt cast upon "La Boheme" and also upon "Rigoletto". You might also hear the two symphonies, the one of Schubert and the other of Dvorak.
>
> Get either or all three of the operas that will compare favorably with "Aida". If the operas are not really good, then of course do not get them.[30]

That was a tall order and an unusual crash course in music criticism, but Louise dutifully followed her father's instructions to the letter.

A week after he first listened to *Aida,* Reuben and Lute devoted an entire Sunday to music. First, they attended a matinee with Leopold Stokowski, then listened to Gilbert and Sullivan's *Mikado* in full on a friend's phonograph, and finally attended another concert in the evening.[31] Soon he was writing from Mexico for recordings of symphonies by Mozart and Beethoven.[32] He was on his way to creating a personal library of recordings that would give him the musical self-sufficiency that his library of books gave him academically.

By the time he entered the First Presidency in 1933, Reuben was a passionate aficionado of classical music and grand opera. However, the Mormon public hardly realized this fact. He disliked the jostling and constraints of audience participation and almost never attended musical productions of any kind. He even declined complimentary tickets to the Utah Symphony after its establishment in Salt Lake City.[33] He preferred listening to music in the comfort of his home.

In fact, for several years he expressed hostility toward the fledgling

Utah Symphony. In 1946 he told Adam S. Bennion, one of its sponsors, "Personally, I am not at all interested in just having a symphony here."[34] In 1949 Reuben opposed the legislature's appropriations for the symphony.[35] This was the continuing fallout of his resentment about professional musicians expecting financial compensation.

In the mid-1940s, he proposed that Leroy Robertson organize an all-volunteer orchestra with church sponsorship. However, "Robertson was absolutely unable to convince President Clark that in order for any orchestra to present such frequent and ongoing programs, the Church would need at least a core of paid professionals." Reuben therefore dropped his idea for a Mormon Tabernacle Symphony.[36] In 1945 the First Presidency pledged $5,000 to the Utah Symphony—only to discover that its organizers were hiring thirty-seven non-Utah musicians. He fumed, "Somebody is taking all of us nitwits for a ride."[37]

He also told local bishops that he disliked the music of J. S. Bach.[38] In published remarks, he notified the women of the church: "Your music—well, I do not know how far above the tom-tom of the jungle it is, but it is not too far. And your drama, plus music—some of it came out of the voodoo huts."[39] The general public had reason to regard Clark as an iconoclast of both classical and modern music.

By contrast, the close associates whom he invited to his home at 80 D Street in Salt Lake City knew him as one who loved serious music. After Harold B. Lee, Henry D. Moyle, and Marion G. Romney went to the Clark home for dinner, they often stayed until midnight listening to full-length musical productions. This included Donizetti's opera *Lucia di Lammermoor* and the Berlioz *Requiem*.[40]

His musical taste often exceeded the experience and appreciation of his guests. Apostle Moyle once innocently recorded that he and other guests stayed at the Clark home until 11 p.m. listening to the Verdi opera "Nutacco."[41] Its actual title is *Nabucco*.[42]

With late-flowering but intense love of music, Reuben could be quite generous in his praise. He never explained why he disliked Bach, but ever the diplomat, he wrote a laudatory letter to Leopold Stokowski for the "beautiful" orchestration of two Bach compositions on an NBC radio broadcast.[43] He commended J. Spencer Cornwall for conducting a "particularly beautiful" performance of the Mormon Tabernacle Choir. He added: "Every once in a while, much to my pleasure, I get the rumble of that basso-profundo. He is as good as the Cossacks."[44] To Florence Jepperson Madsen, he wrote: "As I have many times told you, Sister Madsen, I regard you as the ablest [choir] director in the Church."[45]

But he could also be an unyielding critic. After he listened to a "not so good" radio broadcast of the Tabernacle Choir in 1934, he wrote that the "duet, trio and solo work was poor. [Frank W.] Asper's pieces were poor, and Richard [L.] Evans' announcements were not up to the standard."[46] After hearing a broadcast of BYU's A Capella Choir eighteen years later, he wrote BYU president Ernest L. Wilkinson to inquire whether these students "are yet sufficiently good to sing a capella."[47] He was even critical of Mormon singers with established local reputations. President Wilkinson noted that Reuben "also said we had such a habit in our Church of boasting about the pre-eminence of our singers that he said I ought to get some real vocal experts to come out to listen to what our people are doing to get an appraisal. He commented he did not like the 'adulation society' that is engaged in by most Mormons."[48]

Reuben had contrary responses to devotional music by Roman Catholic composers. On the one hand, he hosted several apostles and their wives at his home in 1954 to listen to the full recording of the Berlioz *Requiem*,[49] even though it was intended for the Mass at Catholic funerals. On the other hand, he criticized a BYU concert in the 1950s because the program included Bruckner's *O Lord Most Holy*. He fumed that it was "a Catholic composition" and observed, "I do not like that kind of music."[50] Shortly thereafter he assessed the program of another BYU concert: "I was happily surprised. I thought there might have been something Catholic, but apparently there is nothing that would be out of harmony with the Gospel."[51]

He had a more intense dislike for contemporary LDS music. He once described Mormon composer Crawford Gates's *Sand in Their Shoes* as "boiler maker music," even though he had not yet heard the music. He declined to listen to the composition because he was "afraid that the music was of a modernistic discordant variety."[52] When LDS musician Robert Cundick composed a modernistic quartet in honor of Reuben's eighty-ninth birthday, President Clark was publicly complimentary at this BYU program. One can imagine his private view since BYU's president wrote that Cundick's "music sounded worse than a funeral dirge."[53]

Reuben's delayed appreciation of serious music, his aloofness from the concert hall, and his tendency to see church administration in light of his government experience all left him ill prepared for one of the ongoing necessities of his position in the First Presidency: dealing with the artistic performer. He began any administrative contact of this type with an assumption that people "of artistic temperament" did not share his rational view of the world. He was also convinced that they "do not have the stability which enables them to meet temptations in the various guises and remain untouched by them."[54] Rightly or wrongly, he assumed that all artists and performers had succumbed to the temptation of pride. Anyone in the arts was therefore at a disadvantage from the outset in any administrative relationship with President Clark.

He chided general authority Richard L. Evans for being "enamored" of the microphone during the "Spoken Word" portion of the Tabernacle Choir broadcasts.[55] Yet he would also say, "I continue to marvel, Richard, at your fertility, unequaled I am sure in the history of the Church, and perhaps in the history of English literature."[56] He likewise praised Cornwall as the conductor of the Tabernacle Choir but criticized him for declining to give assistant conductor Richard P. Condie any opportunity with the baton in performances.[57]

The best example of Reuben's impatience with musicians was his relationship with one of the Tabernacle organists, Alexander Schreiner. He was the only LDS artist about whom Reuben recorded frequent and detailed observations.

Schreiner began playing piano at age five and had been one of several organists at the Salt Lake Tabernacle since 1924. LDS president Heber J. Grant described him as "the greatest organist in the Church."[58] Although he had served at the Tabernacle less than his fellow organists, beginning in 1926 he petitioned the First Presidency for the title of Chief Organist. He argued that his training and experience "qualify me to fill this place," even though the "title, I realize, won't improve my playing but I am sure that it will make it *seem* better to the audiences."[59] The presidency declined to make such an appointment out of deference to the greater seniority of the other organists. In fact, they granted him periodic leaves of absence to perform professionally in Los Angeles and allowed him to serve at the Tabernacle during the summer season.[60] This situation remained unchanged until 1939 when both Schreiner and the First Presidency indicated interest in his becoming engaged full-time at the Salt Lake Tabernacle.

During the process involved in securing Schreiner's employment, President Clark's bias distilled itself on the hapless organist. Reuben began by reassuring his friend Frank W. Asper, an organist with longer tenure, that Schreiner's return would not eclipse the former's work.[61] Concerning Schreiner's request to make Asper "his assistant," President Grant wrote, "Alex is certainly a marvelous organist, but we feel that we can not afford to humiliate Brother Asper."[62]

A month later a meeting with Schreiner to resolve some misunderstandings about his return became unpleasant for both the counselor and the music prodigy. Reuben described the encounter:

> The interview grew a bit stormy, I furnishing the storm when Brother Schreiner tried to "pull some fast ones," so far as I was aware of the facts.
>
> He began to build a story which was designed to make him *The Organist* in fact, even if not in name. I called his attention to the fact that President Grant had told Mrs. Schreiner, her father [Apostle Richard R. Lyman], and her mother [Relief Society leader Amy Brown Lyman], all three separately, that Brother Schreiner could not be *The Organist*. He [Schreiner] was a little bit hazy in many of his statements. He was not quite prepared to say what it was he wanted, but he made it clear that he intended to edge everybody else out, and more or less to take over the Temple Block so far as the music was concerned. He misquoted the letter, which we had written to him, so flagrantly—having in mind the statement which he had made in his letter that he had resigned [from a position with the University of Southern California] "in accordance with your (our) wishes,"—that I felt in doubt about any other statement he made.
>
> I am sure I was unduly rough with him, and I do regret it, but he

seemed to me to be so obviously building up a record, carrying it to a point to such great selfishness, that I allowed myself to get out from under control a bit. He acted very much like a child—a spoiled one at that.[63]

That was a harsh judgment, and the meeting was unexpectedly difficult for both of them. Schreiner's justifiable estimation of his abilities had triggered all of Reuben's suspicions about artistic performers.

He never relaxed his scrutiny of Schreiner. When he and Counselor David O. McKay met with the Presiding Bishopric, who directly supervised the activities of the Tabernacle, Reuben emphasized that the weekly broadcast should not "be made a vehicle for exploiting individuals." He specified that Schreiner "was the senior organist by appointment, but that did not mean *the Church Organist,* and it did not mean *The Organist.*" On learning that Schreiner had given a small group of friends a late-night private recital at the Tabernacle, Reuben told a member of the Presiding Bishopric, "I did not wish to appear to be persecuting Brother Schreiner, but there was just something about such an incident as seemed to me not quite right."[64]

Administratively, he could never forget or forgive what he perceived as vanity in the world-renowned organist. He continued to urge careful monitoring of the musician for any possible manifestation of self-aggrandizement.[65] Although it was an unpleasant circumstance for both men, the situation revealed an important dimension of Reuben's administrative style, attitudes, and influence. His views of this particular matter persisted beyond his own lifetime with respect to the title Schreiner had sought since 1926. Not until April 1965 did he receive the official designation of Chief Organist. This occurred at the retirement of Reuben's close friend Frank Asper to the position of Organist Emeritus.[66] Not surprisingly, Schreiner's published memoirs made no reference to President Clark.[67]

Despite his reactions to Schreiner, Reuben was not dismissive toward those who received national music honors. BYU professor Leroy Robertson had received training from internationally renowned musicians Ernest Bloch (b. 1880) and Arnold Schoenberg (b. 1874). Besting such eminent competitors as Samuel Barber and Aaron Copland, this LDS composer in 1947 won a $25,000 prize plus a concert premier for his new composition. Speaking at a BYU ceremony in Robertson's honor, President Clark said that the Mormon musician's achievement proved that "the loftiest expression can come from the heavenly uplifting influence of a beautiful home where the highest standards of morality and right living are observed."[68]

Nevertheless, because of his own biases toward the priorities and egos of artists, Reuben had little patience with any general authority who took their side in a dispute with him. In 1947 "Pres. Clark became very much agitated toward [Presiding] Bishop [LeGrand] Richards, who persists in pressing the claims of Avard Fairbanks."[69] This was not personal animosity toward the LDS sculptor. Clark had previously advised the church president to pay the storage cost for the sculptor's "unaccepted monument, which he is trying to sell." Despite his famous parsimony with church funds, Reuben did this because Fairbanks was "hard up" financially.[70]

Until he was past eighty, Reuben never cared for motion pictures. But he was involved administratively in the production of the Hollywood film *Brigham Young* in 1939-40. The First Presidency was very concerned about this movie because it was based on the best-selling *Children of God,* and they regarded Vardis Fisher's novel as anti-Mormon. They therefore wanted to influence its production. Luckily, the Hollywood producers were anxious to have the cooperation of LDS leaders.[71]

In October 1939 Reuben accompanied President Grant and Apostle John A. Widtsoe to California where they listened to a reading of the script. They were dissatisfied with the prayer that Brigham Young was to utter at the time the crickets threatened the Mormon people's first harvest in the Salt Lake Valley. Reuben sent a substitute prayer to Jason S. Joy, one of the executives of Twentieth-Century Fox. This proposed text of 193 words began "Our Heavenly Father: Hear the cry of Thine afflicted people" and ended "Help us, in Jesus' name, we ask it, or we starve. Amen."[72] There is no record of the reaction of the movie executives toward Reuben's first attempt as a Hollywood scriptwriter. However, the inclusion of a 193-word prayer was out of the question in a fast-paced movie, and the film instead portrayed Brigham's religious uncertainty in its shorter prayer.[73] President Grant was almost rapturous in his praise of the movie,[74] while Reuben merely "said it was OK."[75]

He maintained this indifference toward motion pictures until he became a sudden enthusiast of Hollywood spectaculars in the 1950s. While he was in New York City in 1952, Lowell Thomas gave him complimentary tickets for a showing of the innovative film process titled Cinerama. He expressed "astonished enjoyment" of the movie to Thomas and to the LDS president. He wrote that President McKay said "he is most anxious to see it as the result of my enthusiasm, because I am notoriously a non-theater goer" and "he wants to see anything that I praise."[76] The next movie that captured Reuben's fancy was the 1955 picture *Martin Luther*. He watched it in a private screening at his home with a few close friends and viewed it a second time afterwards.[77]

His excitement about Hollywood films reached an apex when he viewed Cecil B. DeMille's 1956 production of *The Ten Commandments*. With an effusiveness quite unusual for him, Reuben composed a personal letter to Mr. DeMille:

> The performance was, in the over all, stupendous, magnificent, overwhelming. I am not experienced in these matters, but so far as my knowledge goes, it is the greatest historical pictorial drama ever produced. It dwarfs such predecessors as "Martin Luther," without any disparagement to that picture. ...
>
> I marvel at your powers of imagination, your vision, your ability to see and to develop such a story of one of the most important eras in all human history; your dramatic skill and high artistry, your sense of proportion, indeed your great abilities in all the lines that combined went to make this picture what it is. ...
>
> I tender my homage, Sir, to your true and great genius as a modern dramatic pictoral artist and composer of the highest rank. God bless you.

He had never expressed such unrestrained praise for any other artistic work or artist, or indeed for anyone in any field of endeavor. Ultimately, his own fervor embarrassed him and he decided not to send the letter.[78]

He continued to be awed by subsequent movie spectaculars like the

1957 *Around the World in Eighty Days,*[79] but DeMille's epic found no rival. As Reuben approached ninety, he had no energy for his newfound love of Hollywood's big-budget films. Instead, he limited himself to such home-bound activities as reading, listening to opera on the phonograph, and watching the Lawrence Welk show on television.[80]

J. Reuben Clark was not a common man in the secular world or in the religious world, but he had a common man's appreciation for culture and the arts. He freely acknowledged his limited understanding and appreciation of the artistic value of specific works. Yet as a First Presidency counselor, he was often forced to make administrative decisions about the arts and artists. He did the best he could with the understanding he had. Ultimately, he felt that the Latter-day Saints could absorb very well his own inadequacies as an esthete, as well as the negative comparisons some might make between the culture of Zion and the culture of Babylon:

> You know, I feel, and I have traveled somewhat and lived away from you somewhat—I feel that our cultural standards in this Church will match, if not over-match, the cultural standards of any other people taken as a whole. We do have music, and all the rest, and we get from these ennobling activities in which we engage a spiritual uplift. ...
>
> But in large measure these are but the condiments, valuable as they are. The real food is the spiritual food which must be obtained in addition to the things which shall make it pleasant to eat.[81]

CHAPTER 12.

The Welfare of This People[1]

J. REUBEN CLARK ENTERED THE FIRST PRESIDENCY DURING THE WORST economic crisis in American history. He devoted a major part of his attention to the financial stability of the LDS church. These efforts are often identified with the Welfare Plan, as indicated by Harold B. Lee's eulogy: "Perhaps there was nothing closer to his heart during 28 years of his Presidency than the Welfare Program."[2]

As important as the welfare relief was to him, it was only one of several issues involving what he regarded as his sacred trust in managing church resources. He was also preoccupied with safeguarding the voluntary tithing donations, with the cautious expenditure of those funds, and with the conduct of church business enterprises. As a general authority over an unpaid priesthood, he regarded his tightly circumscribed personal finances as part of that sacred trust. In addition, his thoughts and activities from 1933 onward must be understood in relation to LDS teachings from the previous century regarding the economic ideals of the church.

A few weeks before the organization of the LDS church in April 1830, the newly published Book of Mormon already indicated the ultimate economic goal of the latter-day covenant. After baptism, in order to retain a remission of sins, converts were to "impart of your substance to the poor, every man according to that which he hath, such as feeding the hungry, clothing the naked, visiting the sick and administering to their relief, both spiritually and temporally, according to their wants" (Mosiah 4:26).

Economic equality would be the sign of that covenant. "But it is not given that one man should possess that which is above another, wherefore the world lieth in sin."[3] Also, "every man [should be] equal according to his family, according to his circumstances and his wants and needs" (D&C 49:20). Individual church members were expected to provide for the poor and needy until the church achieved the ultimate goal of real equality.[4]

The means provided to achieve the intended result were the Law of Consecration and Stewardship and the United Order. Basic to the Law of Consecration was the doctrine that the earth and every material thing on it belong to the Lord, that they are his property (D&C 104:14-16). As President Clark later said, "The basic principle of all the revelations on the United Order is that everything we have belongs to the Lord; therefore, the Lord may call upon us for any and all of the property which we have, because it belongs to Him."[5]

By extension, mortals may either aggrandize to themselves alleged property or, in faith, recognize that they are stewards, servants, whom God entrusts with the custody of his property. "Behold, all these properties are mine, or else your faith is vain. ... And if the properties are mine, then ye are stewards" (D&C 104:55-56). Mormon theology did not give spiritual legitimacy to private property despite the revelation's acknowledgment of the social and legal context of private property.

The Saints who accepted this economic perspective indicated their acceptance by consecrating all they possessed to the church by a written deed. In consultation with the bishop, they would receive back by deed whatever was sufficient for their needs. Afterwards they would consecrate each year everything they had earned above their needs (D&C 42:30-37).[6]

At first, the church's leaders sought to define stewardships in the form of lease-and-loan agreements. This "effort to draft the Law of Consecration and Stewardship into the language of civil law" ran into legal and practical difficulties. In 1833 Joseph Smith ordered a restructuring of the deeds to give the steward "his individual property, his private stewardship," even though in the revelatory context a steward did not really own his divine Master's property.[7]

Even with the refinements between 1831 and 1834, the Saints had difficulty living the United Order, which proposed to drastically redistribute wealth "by humbling the rich and proud" (D&C 84:112).[8] In 1838 the founding prophet announced the revelation of a "lesser law" requiring an initial total consecration followed by the tithing of one's annual "increase" or income. Even this proved too difficult for the Mormons to live. In 1841 the initial consecration was reduced to one-tenth of one's property. Within a few decades, Utah leaders dispensed with the initial consecration altogether while retaining the annual tithing requirement.[9]

Joseph Smith established two organizations to care for the poor and needy. In 1831 he announced the office of bishop to administer the consecrated revenues and to supervise the financial operations of the United Order. In 1842 he organized the Relief Society as a women's auxiliary "to provoke the brethren to good works in looking to the wants of the poor —searching after objects of charity, and in administering to their wants to assist."[10] During the 1840s at LDS headquarters in Illinois, "Nauvoo was a new community, its people were all generally poor, and Mormonism definitely stressed both cooperation and generosity. As a result, Nauvoo had no poorhouse or almshouse where paupers were forced to live."[11]

After Brigham Young established the LDS church in Utah, he instituted several practices that provided important points of reference for twentieth-century relief programs:

> My experience has taught me and it has become a principle with me, that it is never any benefit to give, out and out, to man or woman, money, food, clothing, or anything else, if they are able-bodied and can work and earn what they need, when there is anything on the earth for them to do. ... To pursue a contrary course would ruin any community in the world and make them idlers.[12]

To implement this philosophy, President Young adopted several economic policies. First was "cooperatively maintained irrigation systems," followed by "price controls on necessities to prevent those who were well-off from taking advantage of shortages."[13] He also put the unemployed to work building Salt Lake City's Council House, Social Hall, Endowment House, Church Historian's Office, temple foundation, a wall around the city, and numerous other civic projects. The central tithing office soon expanded to a bishop's storehouse in every Mormon settlement where tithing "in kind" (produce, livestock, manufactured items) was stored for the benefit of the poor and for other church purposes. Young also reminded the settlers of the ultimate economic goal of equality by having them consecrate all of their property to the church in the 1850s even though this did not involve a physical transfer of the property. In 1868 he inaugurated in every settlement a cooperative manufacturing and merchandising program. In 1874 he expanded this to a renewal of the United Order.[14]

Of the hundreds of United Orders established in the Great Basin, most failed within a couple of years. The most communal and successful was at Orderville, Utah, where residents subscribed to the principle that "every person is simply a steward and not an owner of property he has in charge, and ... in living as a patriarchal family, and in common, according to their circumstances [all will] fare alike." The residents all dressed alike, ate communal meals at a common dining hall, became nearly self-sufficient, and enjoyed a higher standard of life than most of the settlers had previously experienced. Orderville's United Order lasted until 1885 when LDS headquarters dissolved it amid the U.S. government's economic and political campaign against plural marriage. Some of Orderville's residents moved to Mexico and inaugurated the last church-sponsored United Order, but in 1895 it also disbanded.[15] The official 1930 history of the LDS church referred to the "communistic character" of the United Order in Utah.[16]

Reuben preferred the revelatory ideals of consecration and stewardship rather than the practical attempts to live the United Order from 1831 to 1895. He publicly dismissed Mormon communal experiments as "early deviations ... from the principles set out in the revelations" and insisted that "basic to the United Order was the private ownership of property."[17] Although he disliked the communalism of these church-sponsored efforts, he acknowledged their historical existence in his letter to Frank W. Wylie in Massachusetts:

> I think you may have some misconception about the setup of the Church, since you speak of our "cooperative" system. We do not have a

cooperative system in the Church. In the early days of the Church they set up what was called then the United Order, which was in one sense communal and in another sense wholly individualistic. ...

Then, after a time, Brigham Young again set up a United Order system in some parts of the West, where it was more of a communal order than that set up by the Prophet Joseph Smith in Missouri and Kirtland. Under the plan set up in the West, the community owned the property and they had a common eating hall, and like matters were held in common, though the family relationship was sacredly guarded. This was later abandoned when the Federal Government confiscated all of the Church's property other than churches [i.e., buildings for worship].[18]

He preferred two essential characteristics: first, that the economic program incorporate the early ideals regarding the responsibilities of the church and of the Saints; second, that it enshrine individuality and avoid the kind of cooperation that he identified with socialism and Bolshevik Communism.

A number of changes had occurred in Mormon society since the 1830s that provided a significant background to the situation in the 1930s. Despite efforts at "home industries," Utah was closely linked with the national economy. As a result, the periodic "panics" of small, short-term depressions in the East had an almost immediate effect in Utah, which recovered more slowly than the nation.[19] By 1908 nearly all tithing was in cash rather than in kind, and the First Presidency discontinued the Bishop's General Storehouse in Salt Lake City. Local bishops' storehouses, tithing barns, and granaries were either diverted to other purposes, razed, or left to the elements.[20]

Beginning in 1899, LDS headquarters sent local leaders a handbook that described their responsibilities. The 1901 handbook instructed bishops to give whatever employment possible to persons receiving financial aid. In 1903 the church established an employment bureau in Salt Lake City. Under the direction of the Presiding Bishopric, local bishops provided direct aid to families and individuals as necessary. In the relatively prosperous year of 1915, the church gave financial assistance to 19,547 Latter-day Saints. Under the direction of the Presiding Bishopric, the Relief Society conducted charitable activities in cooperation with both private charities and government agencies. The 1928 *Handbook of Instructions* specified that the responsibility for aiding needy members fell first on their families, second on county relief agencies, and third, as a last resort, on the church. Yet on the eve of the Great Depression, more than 78 percent of needy Mormons turned to the church rather than to county agencies.[21]

For a decade before Wall Street's infamous stock market crash of 1929, Utah's mining, manufacturing, and agricultural economy had been either depressed or stagnant. Because of this statewide depression, "in many ways the 1920s became the graveyard of [LDS] church business ventures."[22] Utah's annual agricultural production declined 20 percent during this period. After 1929 farm income continued to plummet 68 percent. In a nation awash with farm surpluses, Utah farmers would have to triple production to pay pre-1929 debts. By 1933 the result was that nearly half of Utah farm mortgages were delinquent.[23]

The situation in the cities was worse. While the national unemployment rate was 25-30 percent, 63.5 percent of the breadwinners in Salt Lake's Grant Stake were unemployed in 1932. The rest of the city was not much better off. By August 1932 the church's Deseret Employment Bureau was overwhelmed and "would no longer accept applications and place job seekers directly."[24] By 1933 Utah's unemployment rate was the fourth highest in the nation.[25]

As the Great Depression decimated the national and local economy, many wondered if any resource was adequate to meet a crisis that was impoverishing tens of millions. Salt Lake County spent $1,750,000 for direct relief in 1933, and Presiding Bishop Sylvester Q. Cannon noted, "If the Church were to undertake to take care of this amount, it would bankrupt us." The entire church expenditure for relief that year was only one-third of the amount Salt Lake County spent on poor relief.[26]

However, the sources for public assistance seemed to be drying up. State and federal revenues were based on corporate and personal income taxes that vanished as businesses closed their doors and millions went unemployed. County revenues were based on property taxes that were as uncollectible for the newly impoverished majority as were mortgage payments. Church revenues were based on the tithing of personal income that no longer existed for increasing numbers of Mormons.

For the nation at large and for many Latter-day Saints in 1932, the solution to this national crisis seemed to be the election of Franklin D. Roosevelt. He promised a "New Deal" for Americans and implemented it through massive deficit spending by the federal government. This pumped billions of dollars into state and local economies through direct relief, farm price-support programs, and make-work projects through the Public Works Administration (PWA) for unemployed architects, engineers, and construction workers. Its successor was the Work Projects Administration (WPA), which also employed academics, white-collar workers, musicians, artists, and actors on projects chosen by individual states and local jurisdictions. The National Youth Administration (NYA) and Civilian Conservation Corps (CCC) emphasized unemployed youths.[27]

However, many LDS leaders felt that there must be a better way than government charity and deficit spending. For a time, the most innovative responses to the Depression were coming from local LDS leaders rather than from headquarters. Cache Valley's bishops and Relief Society presidents reestablished storehouses for collecting surplus produce and clothing, which they distributed to needy Saints. The greatest innovations occurred during 1932 in the Salt Lake Pioneer Stake under the direction of its youthful president, Harold B. Lee. The stake conducted its own employment agency and obtained permission to keep its tithing revenues. Using its own funds, the Pioneer Stake purchased a farm for the employment of local Mormons in exchange for food, purchased a warehouse to operate as a stake "bishop's storehouse," operated a cannery, marketed excess produce and canned goods to distant points, and built a gymnasium as a make-work project. The stake used its cash profits for purchasing defective products from the Logan Knitting Mills to renovate for sale. All these activities provided jobs for members of the stake where unemployment had reached a high of 70 percent of its adult males.[28]

Nevertheless, all of these local and general church responses depended on Latter-day Saints accepting supplemental government funding, both federal and local.[29] Harold B. Lee himself acknowledged this in May 1933.[30] This was not a departure from LDS policy at the time. It was consistent with the Presiding Bishopric's *Handbook of Instructions* that LDS members seek county relief before turning to the church.[31] Despite this official encouragement, the majority of Mormons had obtained church assistance rather than government aid prior to the Depression.[32] That changed when "over 70 percent of the families receiving public assistance in Salt Lake County were LDS, even though Latter-day Saints were only slightly more than 50 percent of the total population."[33] Mormons were now disproportionately on the government "dole."[34] The reversed proportion of dependency indicated that Mormons generally regarded government as the only resource which could adequately cope with the crisis of the Depression.

However, President Clark was convinced that government resources should not displace the responsibilities of the church and of the individual. During his first talk as a general authority, he affirmed that "no man may rightfully violate [God's] law by living by the sweat from the brow of his brother." But to this April 1933 conference, he admitted that he knew what he opposed better than what to propose as a remedy to the economic tragedy his audience faced:

> The world is moaning in tribulation. I do not know the cure. The questions involved are so nearly infinite in their greatness, that I question whether any human mind can answer them. But it is my faith that if the people shall shun idleness; if they shall cast out from their hearts those twin usurpers, ambition and greed, and then shall re-enthrone brotherly love, and return to the old time virtues—industry, thrift, honesty, self-reliance, independence of spirit, self-discipline, and mutual helpfulness—we shall be far on our way to returned prosperity and worldly happiness.[35]

Typical of his career in government, Reuben was not content merely to criticize one mode of operation but began to devise a new approach.

In mid-May 1933 he started preparing "a possible press announcement in re care of poor" as a proposed statement by the First Presidency. This was the day after he received his first orientation from stake president Lee concerning the Pioneer Stake's program that had been in operation for a year.[36]

As Reuben became more aware of the extent to which Utah's state and local governments, business sector, and citizens were accepting federal funds, he sounded a warning. He told the Salt Lake Community Chest on 19 June: "Interference or help from the central government should be availed or permitted as little as possible. We should not permit our selfishness to interfere with our patriotic duties; nor to blind us to the dangers of centralization in government." He praised the strong social unity of Mexico where the government had not intervened in the economic lives of its people. In Mexico "unemployment was not evident and there had been no appreciable increase of the demands on charitable organizations" despite the Depression and the "repatriation" of nearly 130,000 Mexicans from the United States.[37] Afterwards President Clark wrote, "Made a talk that did not apparently please everybody, though evidently pleasing some."[38]

Concerning the current policy of allowing government funds to supplement LDS church relief activities, he expressed his views in a meeting with the presidents of six Salt Lake City stakes. In discussing their proposal for relief, he said, "My objections to the plan were that it assessed non-Mormons to maintain our churches, and in a reciprocal situation I would object to a scheme which provided money to buy candles for the Roman Catholic altars."[39]

A week after his Community Chest talk, he personally inspected the "relief set up" of the Pioneer Stake. Reuben reported that it was "a very splendid organization doing excellent work."[40]

Two days later, on 30 June, he decided to expand beyond a simple press release. At a luncheon "of representatives of industries and banks" of Utah, he "said we were in the midst of economic revolution [the New Deal]—that we could try to resist the flood—and probably fail—or we can seek to direct it: that theorists know nothing about the human element."[41]

This same day Reuben began the first draft of his "Suggestive Directions for Church Relief Activities." A single sentence from this manuscript indicates the major departure he was hoping to achieve in LDS administration and philosophy: "*Church Aid*. It is to this aid that the Church members must and should primarily look in these times of stress."[42] This would constitute a momentous departure from the thirty-year church policy of cooperation with government relief agencies and away from previous encouragement for Latter-day Saints to accept outside funds.

In 1933 Reuben wanted to cut the umbilical cord of supplemental funds which connected church relief with government relief. This was the primary focus of discussion between the First Presidency and the Presiding Bishopric for the next several years.

He later explained that as early as the 1920s, he opposed the Presiding Bishopric's relief policy. He was visiting Salt Lake City and "heard one of the Presiding Bishopric exhort the brethren and sisters of the audience to make application and send their needy to the County" because Mormons had paid for county services through taxes.[43] I agree with researchers Garth Mangum and Bruce Blumell that this probably referred to Bishop Sylvester Q. Cannon.[44] Reuben said in one of his oft-repeated tellings of this incident: "I never had a greater shock in my life. He just turned around everything I had been more or less bragging about to my acquaintances in the world." He concluded, "So when we began to reconsider this thing in 1933 it seemed to us that we would better get back to the old way."[45]

Reversing three decades of procedure and philosophy was not something that President Clark could achieve in a day. First of all, he was the newly appointed second counselor, while first counselor Anthony W. Ivins was an ardent supporter of President Roosevelt's remedies, such as the National Recovery Administration. In addition, Cannon had promoted the government-linked approach since his appointment as Presiding Bishop in 1925. In July 1933 Cannon also accepted an appointment from Roosevelt to serve as a member of Utah's three-man advisory committee for the Public Works Administration.[46] The Democratic New Deal's NRA and PWA were among the "whole mass of governmental agencies—the alphabetical bureaus" which Reuben later condemned publicly.[47] To him, the Presiding Bishopric of the early 1930s not only maintained an abhorrent tradition of encouraging people to accept government aid, but the Presiding Bishop was also a New Dealer. Therefore, Reuben spent his first few years as counselor in "loyal opposition" about LDS welfare.

When the presidency first discussed Reuben's "Suggestive Directions" draft on 20 July, President Grant recorded, "Brother Clark is to talk with the Presiding Bishopric before a final draft is made or an attempt is made to put the suggestions into operation."[48] Three days previous to this meeting, Reuben had struck from his draft the passage that Latter-day Saints should look primarily to the church for aid. He substituted a revision which softened his proposed reversal of policy:

> *Church Aid.* Reference has already been made to the fact that members of the Church are entitled, because they are tax payers, to receive their fair proportion of all government aid (whether municipal, county, State, or Federal) that may be distributed to needy unemployed. As participants in Community Chest and other relief activities, they are entitled to consideration in the distribution of relief funds by these organizations. *But it is to the Church aid that Church members may rightfully look in these times of stress for a guarantee against hunger and want when other sources fail.*[49]

This was substantially less than the guiding philosophy he really wanted to introduce. Marion G. Romney later observed that the *Suggestive Directions* "wasn't exactly as he [Clark] would have liked it. He left some things out of it and put some things in to get it approved by the other Brethren."[50]

In 1933 Reuben was willing to downplay ideology in order to implement the administrative innovation at the heart of his *Suggestive Directions*: centralizing the relief program at church headquarters rather than in local wards and stakes. Centralized oversight would involve a new committee of which the First Presidency and Presiding Bishop would be part. In addition, there would be regional councils to administer church relief for stakes. This administrative design diminished the previously autonomous role of the Presiding Bishopric in this area. Clark's proposal also reversed the traditional emphasis on decentralization and government cooperation.

Predictably Reuben's suggestions met with a lack of enthusiasm from the Presiding Bishopric. Nonetheless, according to Grant's July instructions, Reuben was trying to accommodate their concerns. By the end of the summer, the second counselor thought a resolution of the viewpoints was imminent. He told Salt Lake City's six stake presidents on 8 August 1933 "that we were working on a plan to be applied to the whole Church and that I thought in a month or six weeks this might be completed."[51] Nearly two months later, he told U.S. president Roosevelt that "the Mormon Church was undertaking to set up an organization for the relief work this winter."[52]

In this regard, it is important to recognize that Reuben did not originate the idea of a churchwide welfare organization. In June 1932 President Grant recorded that a temple meeting of the First Presidency and apostles was "discussing principally the depression and the necessity of some special organization being effected and work [being] done to take care of those who are out of employment and in financial distress needing help."[53] Grant's suggestion for a churchwide "special organization" was eight months before Ambassador Clark left Mexico to begin serving as his counselor. However, the result of this 1932 meeting was a decision a week later to approve and encourage the *local* welfare activities of the Pioneer Stake.[54] Thus, from 1933 onward, Reuben used his administrative skills and broader perspective to give expression to a formative idea previously considered by the church president.

About the time of his August remarks to the local stake presidents, President Clark was drafting a proposed letter about relief. He circulated it to the other members of the First Presidency and Presiding Bishopric for their comments and revisions.[55] The letter's proposed survey of LDS members regarding their relief needs and employment was based on the Pioneer Stake's similar survey earlier in the year, a report of which he filed with his letter draft.[56] In view of the stated goal in his first draft of "Suggestive Directions," it is significant that the final letter of 28 August reaffirmed previous LDS policy: "Our people may properly look, as heretofore, for relief assistance from governmental and perhaps other sources." The letter also reaffirmed that LDS relief programs would originate at the local level and not at headquarters: "The Church will, so far as possible, co-operate in any wise and effective local plan for furthering relief work."[57] Thus, the first statement that Reuben signed actually reaffirmed the policies he wanted to end. When necessary, he compromised.

The crosscurrents at LDS headquarters became apparent in October 1933. During the first week of the month, Bishop Cannon began instructing stake presidents that their stake relief work should be supervised by "qualified and experienced social service workers to be selected by the Stake Presidency and approved by the County Relief Committees, their compensation to be paid by the County Relief Committee."[58] In contrast, at the end of October, the Deseret News Press printed Reuben's *Suggestive Directions*[59] establishing church-only oversight by LDS headquarters.

Despite whatever discussions had occurred since the previous July, Cannon now expressed disagreement with the general and specific intent of Reuben's newly printed pamphlet. In a meeting with the First Presidency on 30 October, Bishop Cannon defended the present administration of relief and said that the pamphlet would demoralize those currently working in long-standing programs for the needy. He asked if the First Presidency was dissatisfied with the LDS relief activities of the Presiding Bishopric.[60]

President Clark was understandably surprised by the bishop's objections to a publication he thought he had sufficiently revised. When Cannon wrote a critique and suggestions for revisions in the pamphlet several days later, Reuben replied at length in a letter of 9 November 1933:

> I observe, however, that you are proposing to eliminate the entire substance of the "Suggestive Directions." ...
>
> Your observations and arguments when you met the Presidency shortly before we left, seem based upon the assumption that our existing Church arrangements are operating satisfactorily and adequately. Your suggestions now made seem based upon the same conclusions.
>
> The reports which have come to me regarding the operation of our Church relief organizations indicate without exception the opposite of such a situation. Federal officers with whom I have talked voiced the same conclusion. I am personally convinced from my own observations and the reports which come to me, that our Church relief system is not now working either satisfactorily or adequately. ... Your proposal seems to contemplate continuing the system as it now exists. ...
>
> I am unalterably opposed to the continuance of the greed, graft, and corruption which has [sic] characterized the use of [government] relief funds among us during the last two years. It is destroying our morale as a people and is seriously undermining our moral and spiritual stamina. If continued, it will make professional paupers of very many of us and our spiritual welfare will be equally threatened. ...

Our course during the last two years has given the lie to our talk about taking care of our own, which was one of our most glorious material achievements and principles.

The plan which was handed you had the approval of all three of us [in the First Presidency], as I suppose you understood. I do not know how President Grant or President Ivins may now feel about it. I shall, of course, be now guided by their wishes, but, subject to their contrary determination, I personally wish that the plan handed to you be put into immediate operation, with such slight modifications as Bishop [John] Wells suggested and such others of a similar character that may be deemed necessary. ...

As already stated, no new Church agencies are set up by the "Suggestive Directions"; all that is contemplated and provided for is a giving of centralized direction to organizations that now operate in a loose, uncoordinated, and largely undirected way. I have not been able to see how any harm could be done by putting such a plan into operation, and on the contrary I think that much good might be accomplished.[61]

Despite its logic, this letter failed to persuade the Presiding Bishop.

Moreover, presidents Grant and Ivins accepted Cannon's viewpoint at their next joint discussion about this matter on 27 November. The minutes of this meeting concluded, "After considerable discussion it was felt that it was not necessary to issue [JRC's pamphlet] ... for the reasons that the relief work throughout the Church is being carried out effectively, and the instructions in the pamphlet might cause some confusion and misunderstanding."[62] This was the exact opposite of Reuben's letter to Cannon: "Our Church relief system is not now working either satisfactorily or adequately."

Instead of distributing Reuben's pamphlet, which had been printed, the Presiding Bishopric published *Care for the Poor* in 1934. It restated the priority of seeking aid first from families and second from the county and that "the Church, therefore, should render financial assistance only in a supplementary way, and chiefly in emergency cases." The Presiding Bishopric also instructed local bishops to be sure that the dependent poor and widows obtained government pensions.[63] Again, this was the exact opposite of Counselor Clark's complaint to Bishop Cannon about "the use of [government] relief funds among us." For a time, Reuben's alternative plan remained on hold.

Although the church had not endorsed the program of welfare independence that Reuben so earnestly hoped for, he continued to state his personal views forthrightly. In the October 1934 general conference, he appealed to the Latter-day Saints to "not soil our hands with the bounteous outpouring of funds which the [federal] government was giving to us." He added, "This people would have been better off materially and spiritually, if we had relied on the Lord's plan and had not used one dollar of government funds."[64] For the general authorities sitting next to him, the last statement was Counselor Clark's not-too-subtle dissent from their recent decision.

Later that month an elderly couple from Grantsville wrote Reuben about their impoverished situation, which they cited in defense of accepting government aid. He gave Brother and Sister Richard M. Robinson, his neighbors, an assessment of government welfare that was the guiding philosophy of the Welfare Program he would promote for the balance of his life:

> But, in all I am saying to you, I am not thinking so much of today and of ourselves; we may be able somehow to squeeze along now and spend these tremendous sums [of federal funding] we are using up and in good part wasting. I am thinking of tomorrow, when your children and grandchildren, and mine, and others, have to shoulder this great burden of [national] debt we are piling up. I am afraid that if the thing goes on, the mere want we have now will become hunger and starvation for them then; I am fearful that our freedom to live and to work and to worship as we wish, those great boons of our free government, may become a cruel tyranny for them with all freedom gone, and with someone telling them where they must live, someone compelling them to work under a whip if necessary—real slavery—and someone forbidding them to worship except as they direct, just as the Governments are doing in Russia and Germany. This possibility, indeed it may be a probability if we continue along our present course, must make all of us stop and think. We must all of us soberly and firmly resolve that we shall personally do nothing to bring this about and on the other hand that we will do everything possible to prevent it.[65]

He restated this in a letter to church member Golden R. Buchanan: "Behind this whole propaganda of 'pensions,' gratuities, [and] doles to which we are now being subjected, is the idea of setting up in America, a socialistic or communistic state, in which the family would disappear, religion would be prescribed and controlled by the state, and we should all become mere creatures of the state, ruled over by ambitious and designing men."[66]

J. Reuben Clark had a somber, conspiratorial view of the consequences of government charity, and many fellow Mormons did not share his fears concerning the ultimate destination of the New Deal's relief programs. But it is necessary to recognize his dark vision in order to appreciate the urgency with which he promoted church relief. This philosophy undergirded every program of LDS welfare he proposed and implemented.

About the time he wrote his Grantsville neighbors, several developments began working in favor of his plans for church welfare. First, Counselor Ivins died in September 1934, thus removing from the First Presidency its only advocate for Roosevelt's New Deal programs. Second, with Reuben's advancement to the position of first counselor, his administrative power increased. Third, the October conference sustained David O. McKay as the new second counselor. He had been a Republican activist in Utah since his appointment as an apostle.[67] Fourth, tensions began surfacing between relief agencies, and "the Church was being pushed toward the position of either abandoning its relief system or striking out separately."[68]

Encouraged by these church-state strains, Reuben urged the First Presidency to announce its own relief program. He drafted a proposed message for the April 1935 conference that would state, "It is the determination of the First Presidency to do the utmost to bring this about and to take people off the Government's back to the fullest possible degree."[69] However, a joint meeting of the First Presidency, Quorum of the Twelve, and Presiding Bishopric decided not to use his proposed statement at this conference.[70]

McKay explained that "President Grant expresses the fear that the people will not sustain it."[71] This referred to the practice of "common consent" by which an assembled conference sometimes voted against a formal motion presented by general authorities, thereby rejecting the proposal.[72] Reuben replied in May that whether or not the Saints accepted it, "I feel now, as I have for the last two years, namely, that this is something we really must attempt to do."[73]

A survey of conditions in September was the occasion for the First Presidency to forge ahead. The survey revealed that 16.3 percent of the LDS population was receiving government relief, whereas only 1.6 percent was receiving church aid.[74]

At the special priesthood meeting of October conference, President Grant severely criticized church members who were receiving government relief: "Instead of being Latter-day Saints [they] have been latter-day sinners." This must have bewildered every local bishop who had read the Presiding Bishopric's *Care for the Poor* pamphlet, which had encouraged church members to accept government assistance. President Clark added that the church had been either thoughtless or guilty of "criminal neglect" because "every comparative table that is issued regarding the distribution of relief in this country shows Utah as one of those States which is receiving the largest per capita amount from the Federal Government for relief." In a reference to Roosevelt's New Deal, he said that the Depression "has made a breeding ground for some of the most destructive political doctrines that have ever found any hold in this country of ours, and I think it may lead us into serious political trouble. I fear we need not be surprised if some blood shall run before we of this nation finally find ourselves."[75]

Two full years after his *Suggestive Directions* was printed but not circulated, the First Presidency's office began preparing correspondence in anticipation of launching a program that was compatible with the ideas expressed in the pamphlet. As was often the case during this period, Reuben was in New York City. His secretary, Valois South, wrote him in November 1935, "At last the Relief project comes forth; I do not know which will overwhelm you more—the fact that it is out at last, or the marvelous changes it has undergone."[76] About this time, the federal government announced plans, ultimately not carried out, to end direct relief assistance. This further prepared the way for the announcement on 7 April 1936 that the LDS church was launching its own relief program.[77] That same year, there were 14,838 Utah farmers receiving direct payments from the New Deal's agricultural programs.[78]

From this time onward, Reuben affirmed that the Welfare Plan was inspired of God. In 1936 he stated, "It is my testimony to you that President Grant was inspired to begin this work and this Plan."[79] While testifying to its inspiration, he also affirmed that it was the product of long administrative deliberations by several general authorities:

> It was not undertaken overnight. It was talked and re-talked, considered and re-considered, and Brother Grant declined to go forward in it until he had the approval of his Counselors and those about him. He always regarded it as a matter of inspiration, revelation if you wish, and I am sure that the effects, direct and indirect, have more than justified the establishment of this plan.[80]

Clark had formulated much of the original philosophy and organization of the plan in collaboration with stake president Harold B. Lee. Still, Reuben saw its churchwide inauguration as the result of a process of revelation that culminated in President Grant's decision to announce "the Church Security Program" in April 1936.[81] Apostle Neal A. Maxwell recently called this deliberative process "tactical revelation."[82]

McKay perceived it differently. Eleven years after the First Presidency's announcement, a reporter for *Time* magazine asked, "I understand that the Welfare Program started in 1936, and that it came as a revelation to President Heber J. Grant." Rather than agree, President McKay responded, "It was not a revelation; it is just a program of the Church."[83]

After the national press headlined the formal announcement of this new program, Reuben wrote presidents Grant and McKay in May: "We are now 'on the spot', and I think we must see to it that the relief program goes over. Personally I am glad that we are 'on the spot', because it is a spur which should increase our speed."[84]

As with Reuben's delayed entry into the First Presidency, his long-delayed program of church relief arrived at full speed. Within six weeks of its announcement, more than 200 welfare projects were established in local stakes. By the end of 1936, more than 17,000 people had already worked on a total of 400 LDS welfare projects.[85] Within one year, fast offerings increased 53 percent and church expenditures for the needy grew by 97 percent.[86]

After its inauguration, Reuben began a campaign to persuade LDS retirees not to accept government pensions. The LDS manager of Arizona's Old Age Revolving Pensions suggested that Reuben did not understand how such a plan operated and sent him a reference guide to read. He replied to George H. Brimhall Jr. in October 1936 that "after years of experience one gathers sufficient experience and knowledge to enable one, for example, to dispense with the necessity of reading a thesis on the superiority of walking on one's hands over walking on one's feet." As an example of his lifelong disinterest in reading anything he thought he would disagree with, his letter concluded, "Life is too short to permit most of us to read such an argument, however ingenious or amusing it may be."[87]

In January 1938 he wrote an editorial that he wanted the LDS newspaper to publish on its front page as "the views" of the First Presidency concerning pensions. Reports had come to their attention "that persons holding responsible positions in the Church are urging and inducing aged Church members to 'qualify' for and seek these 'pensions,' and that misled by such Church officials, even bishops and presidents of Stakes have joined in such persuasions."[88] This was an assault on Presiding Bishop Cannon's long-standing advice to church members.

Grant and his second counselor declined to publish this statement because they did not share the intensity of Reuben's views. McKay explained: "We agree with you that the condition here in Utah regarding old age 'pensions' is serious, and needs remedying, but whether it should go on the operating table and be put under the knife at once, as you suggest, or be given a milder treatment first is the problem President Grant is now considering. An operation without previous preparation will produce a lot of pain in many quarters."[89] The first counselor replied that he was "quite content to abide by whatever you and President Grant decide, but I do think the situation is critical as affecting our people and that something should be done before it is too late." Concerning Elder McKay's comment that ending pensions would cause "pain in many quarters," Reuben replied, "If in the hind quarters, I think it would be all right."[90]

Lacking First Presidency backing, Reuben nevertheless denounced pensions in his April 1938 general conference address.[91] He wrote about this, "I tried to indicate that I did not have a granite heart and yet I hoped to display something of a hard head."[92]

He continued pressing the issue. In a 1942 meeting at the Welfare Office with Apostle Albert E. Bowen, Presiding Bishopric counselor Joseph L. Wirthlin, the Welfare Committee's vice-chairman Robert L. Judd, and Elder Romney, then serving as an Assistant to the Twelve, "President Clark made it clear and definite that Old Age Pensions were unsound and were direct relief; that the Church's attitude was to become self-sustaining and advise our people to not rely upon Old Age Pensions or any other kind of public relief; that the Church would take care of its own; stressing, however, the necessity of families taking care of their own as far as they can."[93] This opposition to pensions was in the 1944 handbook for the Welfare Program.[94]

However, his objections did not extend to unemployment compensation, old-age insurance, or Social Security. The 1944 handbook stated: "Workers who are entitled to unemployment compensation and individuals covered by old-age insurance, as distinguished from old-age assistance described in Section 79 ["sometimes called pensions"], should be counseled to accept these benefits."[95] In encouraging an LDS inquirer to accept such assistance, Reuben's secretary, Rowena Miller, relayed his view: "The Government pays no part of the Social Security, although it takes the money which has been contributed and deposited with it, uses it for its own purposes, and holds its own bonds as security for what it takes."[96] In this respect, his views about accepting Social Security were less negative and strident than those of his protégé Harold B. Lee.[97]

While Reuben affirmed the right of wage earners to accept the benefits of the taxes they and their employers paid into Social Security, he frequently condemned what he saw as the system's fundamental flaw:

> The great bulk of the people still do not understand that their money has gone, been spent, just as much, just as fully, and just as irretrievably as have the sales taxes they have paid; they do not understand that the only way the government can make good its promises to pay old age security, those unemployment stipends, and other payments is by levying more taxes, thus making the people pay themselves twice."[98]

In conjunction with its relief activities, the church began a Beautification Program in 1937. Reuben said this should begin with "the places to be seen by tourists" but should include private residences and ultimately the entire community.[99] He advised a general conference three years later: "Paint your meeting houses, your town hall, repair your sidewalks, keep your park or public grounds looking neat, keep up your fences."[100]

He also encouraged the legal entity of the relief program, the Cooperative Security Corporation, to provide two-year college tuition aid to returned missionaries. LDS leadership backed away from this proposal as too expensive. Meeting alone with the Welfare Committee a week later, "President McKay stated that if we begin this assistance we will have too large a field of it and will expend our funds just for this purpose."[101]

In 1938 the church incorporated Deseret Industries after Reuben received briefings from two Mormons about the California-based Goodwill Industries which refurbished donated goods for resale and provided employment for the unskilled and disabled.[102] Orson H. Hewlett was the originator of the LDS version.[103]

The same year, construction began on a massive Bishop's Central Storehouse complex, Welfare Square, in Salt Lake City. Labor came primarily from unemployed Mormons.[104] In many respects, the new Church Security Program, renamed the Welfare Plan in 1938, moved at great speed.

Nevertheless, typical of his entire administrative style, President Clark resisted proposals for the program to promise too much, either in social change or economic recovery. A month before the official announcement, he expressed hope "that Brother [Harold B.] Lee will not try to insist upon a new social set-up in the situation. It seems to me that our problem is very small in its scope, namely, to relieve the present situation. The plans for social reform can wait until we get back on our feet and see things a little more clearly and with a little more perspective."[105]

Reuben was particularly careful about insisting that the church not promise to do more than it could achieve, lest the faith of the Saints be injured. As he told a general conference in 1940: "It would have been a simple matter to begin visionary undertakings that would not only have bankrupted the Church but that would have broken the heart and courage of all of us by the greatness of our disaster. We have therefore gone slowly and watched each step taken. The Lord has been with us in this plan."[106] To another general conference, he said: "One of the most difficult things that we have had to do [in welfare] is to stick to our knitting, to see that we did not get off into lines of activity which we could not successfully carry on, because the Church—do not forget this, brethren—the Church must not fail!"[107]

Reuben was also especially anxious to avoid any suggestion that the Welfare Plan was a step toward the United Order. A month after the announcement of the program, he suggested that the First Presidency not allow "certain of our people to expect and to hope that we are going to undertake some sort of new economic order. I feel very strongly that we should confine this statement merely to the work which we now have in hand[,] reduced to its lowest proportions. We can always enlarge our plans. It will be all but impossible to contract it. ... Let us try to change the emphasis by promising relatively little and doing much."[108]

For that reason, he criticized a talk that Harold B. Lee gave to the October 1941 conference about the need for "absolute economic equality" among Mormons. Reuben "doubted the Lord provided for that" and "doubted if that were the United Order." Such phrasing about economic equality was absent from the published report of Apostle Lee's conference talk, which was apparently edited to remove passages to which his mentor objected.[109]

Perhaps because of his protégé's emphasis on total economic equality, Reuben adopted a middle position in his general conference sermon a year later: "We have all said that the Welfare Plan is not the United Order and was not intended to be. However, I should like to suggest to you that perhaps, after all, when the Welfare Plan gets thoroughly into operation—it is not so yet—we shall not be so very far from carrying out the great fundamentals of the United Order."[110] In fact, because of the Welfare Program, he thought "the Church was [now] living the United Order as it was revealed by the Lord to Joseph Smith as nearly now as it is possible to live it in an industrial age."[111]

In only one respect did he allow his economic and political philosophy to proclaim a goal for the Welfare Program that was beyond the resources of the church. Although he consistently denied that it was intended to reestablish the United Order, he proclaimed his intention for LDS welfare to supplant the New Deal in the economic lives of Latter-day Saints. In May 1936 the *New York Times* and Associated Press reported his talk in New York City that the church's relief program intended to remove 88,000 needy Latter-day Saints from government relief rolls and make them self-supporting.[112] At the October 1936 general conference, Reuben proclaimed: "If we should fail in this, and the Lord will not let us fail, great would be our condemnation."[113] Less than a year later, the General Church Welfare Committee agreed "to take one county at a time in the State of Utah and to clear this county entirely of the L.D.S. cases now on county relief."[114]

Officially, the First Presidency did not oppose the government's make-work programs such as the WPA.[115] Nonetheless, Reuben maintained that any form of economic relief was the responsibility of churches and charitable organizations "and not a problem of government."[116] He publicly described himself as "anti-Welfare State."[117] He was convinced that "many of those on W.P.A. were not very active members of the Church ... [and] were members in name only."[118]

The LDS Welfare Program succeeded in many ways, but it failed to fulfill President Clark's hope that it would supplant New Deal aid among Latter-day Saints. In 1937 the Welfare Committee verified that Utah ranked fifth nationally in direct relief from the federal government and "that in every county in the state[,] L.D.S. cases were increasing instead of decreasing." The committee learned the following year that even more LDS members were turning to the government for financial relief.[119]

Likewise, by 1938 the percentage of Utah's working population in federal projects was above the national average. Utah was above the national average by 19.6 percent for the WPA, 100 percent for the CCC, 33.3 percent for NYA, and 33.3 percent for participation in other New Deal agencies. As committee member William E. Ryberg told the General Welfare Committee in 1938, "more success could be attained by the Church Security Program if there was not the excellent competition offered by the Government."[120]

The national press emphasized these statistics in proclaiming the "failure" of the LDS program in its goal of replacing federal relief.[121] This negative publicity was compounded by the furor over the LDS newspaper's mistake in reporting that a successful WPA project in the Uintah Basin was the church's project. As a result of this media flap, Reuben said that it was important to keep stories about the Welfare Program "out of the papers and to do this was never more important than at the present."[122]

However, this was easier said than done. Ever since the announcement in 1936, the national media were interested in what LDS leaders said about their Welfare Plan and what they did with it. This was especially true whenever the former ambassador spoke publicly about welfare.[123]

President Clark's intention to substitute the Welfare Plan for New Deal relief inevitably undercut his repeated affirmations that the LDS program was not politically motivated. The result was that anti–New Dealers supported the program and New Dealers opposed it. Politically conservative magazines throughout the nation regarded it as "an anti–New Dealer's dream come true" and the liberal press labeled the Welfare Program as "an ultra-conservative gesture of withdrawal."[124]

In this respect, nearly all of the general authorities shared Reuben's attitudes toward government assistance. They wholeheartedly supported the philosophy and conduct of the Welfare Plan as he envisioned it. On the other hand, there were a few who continued to be sympathetic to the New Deal's approach. These LDS leaders wanted to soften the church program's effort to supplant government aid to the needy. As Elder Lee's biographer wrote, "From the beginning, and without cessation for years, opposition was everywhere, even in high places."[125]

President Clark commented on this in a memo to President Grant in October 1937 after the church's general conference. He noted first that Democratic apostle Stephen L Richards wanted "to leave the money side of relief to the Government (State and Federal) while the Church confined itself to spiritual and character rehabilitation." As a reflection of Reuben's four years of direct conflict with the Presiding Bishop, he made this assessment of Cannon: "For four years he has either fought the Plan the Presidency then proposed or has willfully failed to support it." He said that Cannon should decide "to get in line or to get out of the way."

Reuben added that Presiding Bishopric counselor David A. Smith was also "against the Church Security Plan." He was convinced that Smith would continue to follow Cannon in this regard.[126] Grant agreed and warned the Welfare Committee that the First Presidency would not allow "one of the Presiding Bishopric ... to hinder what we are doing and what apparently is a success."[127]

At the next general conference in April 1938, the First Presidency released Cannon as Presiding Bishop. They ordained him an apostle and appointed him to the newly created position of Associate to the Quorum of Twelve, which had no vacancies at the time.[128] In a similar manner, presidents Grant and Clark had previously replaced his brother Joseph J. Cannon as editor of the *Deseret News.* For the Cannon family, supporting Roosevelt's New Deal had resulted in one brother becoming a mission president and the other an assistant apostle.[129]

Bishop Cannon's successor was LeGrand Richards, one of Reuben's former students. Each regarded the other as a "long-time friend."[130] Grant and Clark selected him despite opposition from Counselor McKay.[131] Cannon was surprised to learn that his successor retained neither Smith nor John Wells as counselors, choosing instead Marvin O. Ashton and Joseph L. Wirthlin. Both had been members of the General Welfare Committee for nearly a year.[132] Reuben felt that he now had like-minded associates in place to direct the work of local bishops in the Welfare Program.

Nevertheless, the installation of this new bishopric did not solve the divergence in opinion about the relationship of church welfare and government assistance. "We had quite a discussion this morning as to the relationship of the Welfare Program to the relief agencies of the federal[,] state and county governments," Romney wrote in 1942. "As usual, the Welfare Committee and President Clark [were] on one side, and the Relief Society and Presiding Bishopric [were] on the other."[133] Bishop Richards and his counselors were following the traditional role of the bishopric as an ally and "an advocate for Relief Society" in its charity work.[134] A year earlier the Presiding Bishopric had also given an official "slight and an affront to the Welfare Committee," as Apostle Lee described it.[135]

Despite these tensions, Bishop Richards and his counselors sought to carry out decisions of the First Presidency. Richards later wrote about "what I said to President Clark a few years ago after we had disagreed on a matter, 'President Clark, you can't be angry at me because I love you too much.'"[136]

Opposition to the Welfare Program was even more dramatic among local LDS leaders and members, 70 percent of whom were New Dealers. Apostle Romney said that "some stake presidents would even tear up the written instructions they received and throw them in the waste paper basket right in front of some of the brethren" of the Welfare Committee.[137] Reuben told welfare workers that "all the critics of the Welfare Program were members of the Church"[138] and that from the beginning these critics thought it was "a scheme of Republican Clark to turn out the Democratic Party."[139] In January 1939 he confided to a stake president that "all of us were having difficulty in getting the people to follow along, particularly on the welfare work at the present moment, and that there were times when those in authority had to go on, even against great odds, if they felt they were right."[140] In September, President Clark admitted to the Welfare Committee: "I am rather convinced in my own mind that 90% of our difficulty comes from the fact that our Bishops and Stake Presidents are not converted to the Plan, the distribution, etc. I do not know what we can do. The loyalty, support, that used to come to the Church when it undertook something of this kind before is just not here."[141]

As late as 1944-45, Reuben complained at general conferences that bishops and stake presidents were refusing to support the Welfare Program.[142] These opponents proclaimed that it was a failure, "professing to see in it some deep-laid political scheme."[143] After the death of Franklin D. Roosevelt in 1945, the New Deal ceased to be such a divisive issue among the Latter-day Saints. Yet nine years later President Clark informed welfare workers: "The other day we had a letter that was very distressing to me; it came from an official of a stake who was criticizing the very foundations of this Welfare Plan."[144] Eventually, most Mormons could see the real achievements of the program in a nonpartisan light.

Reuben himself was able to make a positive assessment less than three years after its announcement, although not without making reference to the New Deal. In view of criticism by the national press and opposition by LDS members at this time, his remarks to the General Welfare Committee deserve close attention:

> I don't believe that you have a thorough appreciation of what you have really done. I think the achievements of this Welfare Plan are not only outstanding, but they are so great that we had no right really to expect that they could be what they have been.
>
> I think your achievements can be divided into two headings, and the first and most important item I would call the intangibles. In the first place you have thoroughly mapped the terrain, the whole area, over which you are operating, and that is no small job. ... In the second place you have discovered your weak spots. ... Then, the third thing you have done is to bring to the people a consciousness of the program and what it is trying to do. That is no small achievement. ...
>
> Your tangibles you fail to appreciate and what you have done in this way. Your central storehouses, your stake storehouses, your industries— you have your projects you have taken on, your coal mine, saw-mills and all of the others. They are all really great achievements not only of themselves but in the fact that you have shown the way.
>
> Then, of course, you have done a marvelous job in the production of foodstuffs, clothing, fuel, shelter. That was in a way, your initial problem, and you have particularly brought the consciousness of the people to this problem. If you have to intensify it at a later time there will be no real difficulty in increasing it. The problem of distribution you have been working on. ... Labor is still your greatest problem. How are you going to put these people to work and at what, and to get to them the idea that they should work for what they get. You will not be able to do this fully until a change comes in our national policy. With the [federal] government spending billions, compared with our thousands, it isn't possible not to have a reaction against the plan. This will all work out in time.[145]

He spoke these words at a meeting of the General Welfare Committee in January 1939. This was the year the church reached its Depression apex of providing assistance to 155,460 Latter-day Saints.[146]

Nevertheless, Garth Mangum and Bruce Blumell have stressed that the New Deal "dwarfed the church's sharing and self-help activities until war-related economic recovery allowed its phasing out in 1941." Before that time, up to three-fourths of Utah's rural population received federal relief. The WPA employed an average of 11,000 Utahns annually and "the NYA enrolled an average of 2,200 young Utahns per year." Moreover, a higher proportion of LDS Utahns obtained federal relief than did non-LDS Utahns.[147]

As the wartime economy and mobilization ended the Depression that the New Deal was unsuccessful in ending,[148] Mormons participated in the general economic recovery. From 1939 to 1940, the numbers receiving Welfare Program assistance declined 13 percent.[149] At the welfare meeting of the April 1940 general conference, Reuben was euphoric:

> Now, my brothers and sisters, we are over the hump. There have been times when I have been anxious about this work. I wondered, my faith must have been weak, I wondered whether we could compete with all of the free stuff that was being handed out. But I am over that and this enterprise is undertaking. It is over the hump.[150]

This same year the church completed its towering grain elevator at Welfare Square.[151] From 1941 to 1942, the numbers receiving church assistance plummeted 75 percent.[152] A wartime economy allowed Roosevelt to claim that the New Deal ended the Depression for the nation—and Reuben to perceive that the Welfare Program finally supplanted the New Deal in Utah.

Correspondingly, the church and its various businesses were now in solid financial shape—a dramatic change from their precarious situation during the 1920s and 1930s. In March 1942 the First Presidency's financial secretary, Frank Evans, wrote that "all Church institutions—Church owned or controlled"—held a total of "nearly twenty million dollars" in U.S. bonds.[153] This did not include the deposits of the LDS Corporation of the President in church-owned banks, which was Reuben's preferred location for the church's "reserve fund." Nonetheless, he had sufficient confidence in the financial situation that in July and August of 1942 he authorized the transfer of $150,000 from the Utah State National Bank to purchase additional U.S. War Bonds, series G.[154]

At this time he was also launching a reorganization of the church's general finances. Elder Romney described it as the second most important contribution that Clark made to the church.[155]

This began with the establishment of a general budget for each year's expenditures. In Reuben's words:

> Living within your income requires the making of a budget, then of course afterwards living within your budget. I may say that I think until 1938 or 1939 the Church had never had really a budget prepared beforehand; there was always a complete accounting for funds expended, but apparently before that time it was never projected what would be needed for this item, that item, and the other item. Since 1939 we have had a budget and we have guided our course by it.[156]

He proposed a comprehensive budget to control in advance the kinds of expenditures that had exceeded church revenues during the previous two years. He had announced to general conferences that the church experienced spending deficits of $100,000 in 1937 and nearly $500,000 part way through 1938.[157] In his view, voluntary disclosure of such deficits encouraged greater austerity at headquarters and elsewhere. The following year he confided to BYU president Franklin S. Harris that the church had spent "between $800,000 and $900,000 more than our revenues."[158] Welfare activities severely drained church resources, but Reuben was determined that the church would not attempt to relieve economic distress through deficit spending.

In his effort to have the church live well within its income, he gained a reputation for parsimony. "Some of our own members seem to be thinking that the Church too has a pile of gold," he told the April 1938 general conference. "It has not. All the Church has is the moderate income it receives from investments it has made out of the savings from your past contributions, and the tithing and donations which you faithful members—usually not the critics and fault-finders—make for the support of the work." He later observed that "the tithing is paid by the moderately circumstanced and poor of the Church."[159] Publicly and privately, he insisted that the general authorities protect the sacred trust of donated monies by the most careful expenditure of funds.

From 1943 to 1945, he pared down expenditures to 27 percent of annual revenues. The balance went into a reserve fund for the postwar depression he expected.[160] But he was not satisfied with saving 73 percent of LDS income annually. In 1945 he privately "expressed some anxieties about Church finances."[161]

Nevertheless, he had to balance budget cutting with necessary expenses. The latter included substantial allotments for relief of the poor. In 1944 he preached: "I repeat, all should be cared for, no one should suffer, no one should be hungry, no one unclothed, no one without shelter, no one without coal, but I also say again, bishops cannot clothe their needy in silks and satins or house them in modern palaces."[162] He acknowledged this same year the "tradition that has come up through the Church that we ought to be self-sustaining and there has come to attach to Church relief some kind of stigma which people are loath to bring upon themselves." Therefore, he instructed local bishops that "one of the tasks which you have is to make those who need help—worthy members of the Church—feel that they may properly take it."[163]

The end of World War II brought continued prosperity and a long postponed opportunity to build needed chapels, which meant that expenditures increased. Reuben was able to hold only 36 percent of church income in reserve in 1947.[164] In January 1948 he spoke with Apostle Lee "about the increasing financial burden of the Church."[165] Reuben expressed this anxiety to the general conference the following April: "The expenditures of the Church are increasing at what seems to me to be a disquieting rate. ... I should like to urge the people to cease building cathedrals for ward meetinghouses, and to stop furnishing them as if they were palaces."[166] For example, when Chicago's stake president John K. Edmunds wanted to build a stake center with expensive lannon stone for its exterior surface, President Clark "told them they could have any kind of chapel they desired as long as it was constructed with red brick. The church, he told them, was not in the business of building monuments."[167]

In 1949 he asked the church's bishops to try to reduce their expenditures by 20 percent. This was not easy, as he commented in 1950: "Sometimes when some of you bishops, as it comes to me, find yourselves in a tight spot, you put the blame on the welfare program rather than assuming the responsibility yourselves."[168]

Still, Reuben was open to persuasion about the need for new expenditures. He had opposed funding a temple microfilming project in 1939 but changed his view after World War II. First, there had been indiscriminate destruction of Christian cathedrals and their centuries-old archives during saturation bombing raids on European cities.[169] This was a clear argument for microfilming the records that had survived. Given Clark's natural pessimism and views on war, he was convinced that this should be done before another war destroyed them all. Second, an LDS genealogical executive "took a microfilm reader to the office of President J. Reuben Clark Jr., chairman of the Church finance committee, and spent hours showing him the possibilities." This hands-on demonstration settled any remaining doubts, and he "soon began using his influence to get money budgeted for the program" of microfilming European and American records of vital statistics.[170]

Aside from his philosophy about budgets and lower expenditures, he introduced an administrative reorganization of LDS finances. At a First Presidency meeting early in 1941, President Grant referred to the periodic efforts during the previous sixty years to satisfactorily balance the roles of the presidency and the Presiding Bishopric in the administration of church funds.[171] Reuben later noted, "I took it therefore upon myself to make a study of the financial operations of the Church from the beginning down through and until after the death of the Prophet." His sources for that understanding were the revelations to Joseph Smith in the Doctrine and Covenants and the seven-volume *History of the Church.*[172] He also spent five months in 1941 consulting with the financial secretaries of the First Presidency in order to ask them questions about church finances. The first result was a "Compendium of Information on Financial and Property Interests of the Church," compiled by the financial secretaries at Clark's request.[173]

Having amassed the necessary sources, he began to study them carefully. Because he did this at his own initiative, his administrative sense of propriety dictated that it had "to be done of course always at nights." It took Reuben two years of evenings in his home library to research these sources, to contemplate the doctrinal, historical, and current financial situation, and to draft a proposal for reorganizing the administration of funds.[174] On 8 April 1943 he presented his proposal to the combined First Presidency and Quorum of Twelve.

In a comprehensive presentation, he reviewed the revelations concerning the collection and administration of funds. He noted:

> I am impressed with this fact, that while the Prophet in his thinking was frequently ahead of the revelations which he received due to inspiration of course, nevertheless, he did not see the thing from the beginning, and the Lord gave these general instructions, and the brethren more or less floundered about within broad limits as to the details of the situation which they set up.[175]

He then proposed first that the Presiding Bishopric be responsible for receipt of tithing and fast offerings, the Welfare Committee for the proceeds of welfare production, and the First Presidency for all other revenues from all other sources. Second, he proposed the organization of a Committee on Budget to approve in advance a binding budget of expenses. Its members were to be the First Presidency, two or three members of the Council of Twelve, and the Presiding Bishopric. Third, he proposed the organization of a Committee on Expenditures which would have the same membership and have responsibility for the actual expenditure of budgeted funds. Fourth, his proposal recommended that there be subcommittees on expenditures for such areas as building construction and maintenance, purchases, missions, and ranches. Fifth, he recommended that members of the First Presidency, Presiding Bishopric, and Welfare Committee administer the use of fast offerings and the production of welfare projects.[176]

Apostle Lee described this as "a most historic meeting."[177] Soon to become president of the Twelve, Apostle George Albert Smith noted: "I think the proposition now involves this body of men individually as nothing else has in a long time. We will be assuming a responsibility that we have been relieved of for a long time—I speak of the Twelve. The Presidency have carried the burden and [also] the Presiding Bishopric."[178]

Reuben was gratified by the enthusiastic response but he was stunned by a document he saw after the meeting. The Church Historian showed him a copy of an unpublished revelation that President Joseph F. Smith received on 1 November 1918. It provided for the kind of reorganization of church finances that Reuben had just presented. "I had never seen or heard of this 'revelation' till Brother Joseph Fielding Smith mentioned it in Council Meeting on April 8/43. He brought it to me to read at 3:30 p.m. April 8/43, my first view." For Reuben, this was an inspiring and humbling evidence that the work he had taken on himself had divine approval.[179]

The outline of responsibilities for the receipt and disbursement of church funds was only the first part of the financial reorganization. At the heart of his two years of work was his detailed "General Principles Underlying Church Finances."[180] On 28 April he presented it to President Grant, who approved it.[181] The following day he presented this document to the Quorum of Twelve, which unanimously approved it, after Stephen L Richards modified the motion to allow more flexibility in budgeting and expenditures.[182] Reuben's opening remarks provided a sufficient summary of the philosophy governing this lengthy document:

> We start out with the basic purpose and mission of the Church which may be briefly stated thus: To work out the purposes of God among and for His children upon this earth by saving the living and by saving the dead. Therefore the test of every Church financial operation, both incoming and outgoing, is, Does this help to carry out the purpose and mission of the Church? This principle we have behind us at all times.[183]

Similar to his comment about the temple meeting's first discussion of the financial reorganization on 8 April, Apostle Lee wrote on 29 April: "This was a historic meeting and the decisions made were received by a unanimous expression that indicated divine approval."[184] Following the hierarchy's approval and implementation of the plan, Reuben announced its basic outlines to the October 1943 general conference.[185] At the Committee on Expenditures meeting a week later, Apostle Lee noted that "Pres. Clark definitely put an end to 'rubber stamp' expenditures of the P.B.O. [Presiding Bishop's Office]"[186]

In addition, he regarded a detailed and published report of church finances as a right of LDS members. When he read the financial report at April 1944 conference, Elder Romney described it as "more comprehensive and complete than any financial report which has been given to the

Church in my day."[187] But as spending increased during the administration of David O. McKay, the church president wanted to reduce the report, and he and first counselor Richards approved a less detailed disclosure in April 1953. The second counselor objected. "They ought to tell the people all they can tell them," Reuben said. "He hated to see what they tell them cut down, [because] it might raise some comment."[188] The church stopped issuing annual reports with dollar amounts in 1960. By that time, Reuben was in physical decline, President McKay was excluding him from decision making, and Counselor Henry D. Moyle was promoting an expansive program of deficit spending.[189]

In pursuing his philosophy toward the financial mission of the church, Reuben regarded church-owned or -controlled businesses as a special challenge. He explained his attitude toward these enterprises in a letter to Elder John A. Widtsoe:

> Furthermore, I think there was none of them organized for the mere purpose of making money. They were all organized to help develop this great Intermountain community and to help stabilize the financial and industrial conditions to the direct benefit of all our people in the areas affected.[190]

Because of that view, President Clark actually wanted to discourage church businesses from "making so much money; there is no difficulty in making money, the question is making too much," as he told the temple meeting of apostles.[191] When the president of one church company said that it was "making too much money, I told him that was the situation of all of our enterprises."[192]

Reuben was an officer or director of many church businesses, but he displayed a consistent disdain for commercialism. To him, these businesses were part of the sacred trust of the church rather than free-wheeling enterprises of capitalism.

That trust sometimes involved compromises. For example, in 1941 President Clark ended a business practice that had enmeshed LDS headquarters in ethical compromise for fifty years.[193] Beginning in 1891, the church's real estate holding company leased properties to individuals who converted them into houses of prostitution on Commercial Street, now Regent Street, in Salt Lake City.[194]

This came up for discussion in 1897 during the temple meeting of the First Presidency and Quorum of Twelve. Apostle Anthon H. Lund wrote that "the matter of the Brigham Young Trust Co. having fitted up a first class whore-house and President [George Q.] Cannon being President of the company was brought up."[195] At a meeting in 1900, Apostle Brigham Young Jr. wrote that there was "much talk about B.Y. Trust Co running a whore house on Commercial Street." Instead of requiring the church holding company to terminate these leases, counselors George Q. Cannon and Joseph F. Smith and Apostle Young simply resigned as officers and trustees of the company by 1901.[196]

In 1908 the *Salt Lake Tribune* proclaimed that the Brigham Young Trust Company still "filled these houses on Commercial Street." The *Tribune* listed the church's annual income as $2,400 from just one of the brothel leases.[197] At that time, $2,300 was the purchase price for a "12-room modern house, 3 blocks from the Temple."[198] Although the LDS church was technically and legally only the lessor of the buildings, some general authorities regarded the church's leadership as morally implicated in brothel management.[199]

As an apostle, Heber J. Grant had also complained that "Brigham Young Trust Co. kept a Whorehouse."[200] But as church president after 1918, he did not require the church holding company, by then Clayton Investment Company, to terminate the leases. Apparently, the income was too important to the financial struggle of LDS headquarters at the time.

The LDS holding company failed to divest its houses of prostitution until 1941 when its president confided to Reuben that the church still "has 'whorehouses' on Clayton Investment." Because the holding company was merging with the higher-profile Zion's Securities Corporation, Reuben gave instructions to "clean or close all Clayton Investment houses of shoddy character." He added that the First Presidency "cared nothing about the money involved."[201] To the presidency's financial secretary, Frank Evans, Clark explained why he insisted on ending the LDS church's relationship with brothels: "Money is not the primary objective but morality and cleanliness."[202]

Ten years later, he decided to compromise when confronting a lesser ethical conflict in LDS business operations. At a meeting of the KSL board of directors on 25 October 1951, "President Clark then raised for discussion the question as to whether or not KSL and KSL-TV should accept programs sponsored by beer accounts." He explained that "under the circumstances it appeared clear that neither KSL nor KSL-TV could be dominant and influential if the Corporation continued to refuse to accept beer programs." In response to his presentation, the board of directors "voted unanimously to authorize the Management to negotiate such contracts as are necessary to protect and best serve the combined interests of KSL-AM and KSL-TV, including beer business as may be required to this end."[203] This was a clear departure from the church's decades of requiring abstinence from alcoholic beverages.[204] His papers contain a draft of the announcement to the "Ladies and Gentlemen of the KSL Television audience" which explained this acceptance of beer commercials: "We have so far as we have been able, kept faith with you. The unescapable necessities incident to television operation have forced us to yield something from our ideals, because a television station must have programs and must have revenues in order to live." He wrote this as president of KSL.[205]

In his administration of church finances as a sacred trust, Reuben went to great lengths to avoid both the appearance and substance of profiting from his church position. In April 1935 he told the general priesthood meeting: "There is a general impression, I am told, that I am a man of wealth. My Brethren, I am not."[206] Nine months later he confided to his wife that he was asking only a small fee for his non-church responsibilities as a means of enhancing the status of Mormons among influential non-Mormons. "I did not wish too much money and I want to leave them, if I can, with a good impression about the stability, morals, etc of our people," he told Lute. These were "some of the biggest financial men in England" and each one "not only knows I am a Mormon but one of the First Presidency."[207]

In February 1941 he was amused to receive an invitation from a New York law firm for him to purchase the Yankees baseball team. Reuben answered: "Your letter of the thirtieth ultimo constitutes one of the high spots in my life. It is one of the few real compliments I have ever had paid me. ... I could not buy the boy that carries the water to the team, much less the team itself."[208]

Two months later he tried to persuade his daughter Louise against buying a new car. "I have now bought a secondhand Ford pick-up which has all of the usual and unusual Ford noises," he wrote. "This I intend to use for running in and out to Grantsville, *provided* your Mother's sense of dignity and fitness is not too much violated by my riding in a Ford of the kind I have described. That leaves the Zephyr for you and Mother."[209]

He also refused to accept payment or royalties for his speeches and publications after he entered the First Presidency. This was especially true of his many LDS publications, some of which he actually paid to publish.[210] He also declined honoraria for speaking at non-church functions.[211] If organizers still sent him a check in payment for such activities, he usually returned it. Other checks he simply endorsed over to the Primary Children's Hospital or to the Relief Society.[212] If he received an honorarium for speaking at a college or university, he "turned it back and let them use it for some needy students."[213]

In 1945 President Clark wanted to establish a policy to prevent LDS general authorities from "producing books for which they receive sizeable income."[214] In this, he was unsuccessful with most of the general authorities.[215] However, he could be very persuasive with his protégés. The family biography of Apostle Petersen noted:

> His first book was *Your Faith and You*, a collection of Church editorials, which was published in October 1953. Shortly after, he was called into President Clark's office, congratulated on breaking into print, and reminded that he had already been paid for the editorials. The royalties should go to the *Deseret News*. The great love and respect Mark felt for President Clark compelled him to accept this suggestion, and he willingly donated his royalties to the paper. Six additional volumes of editorials were subsequently published over the years, with over 52,000 copies sold.[216]

Likewise, Reuben's former student and "long-time friend" LeGrand Richards accepted no royalties for either *Marvelous Work and a Wonder* or *Israel, Do You Know?* Before his death, the first sold 2 million English-language copies and 50,000 translated copies, while the second sold 40,000 copies.[217]

In terms of church compensation, President Clark often declined to accept the salary he was authorized as an officer of church-affiliated corporations. In other cases, he accepted only part of it.[218] In 1949 he wrote that "the General Authorities of the Church get precious little from the tithing of the Church. They are not paid as much as a first-class, stenographic secretary of some of the men who run industry."[219]

This "precious little" was evident to two of his Welfare associates after they entered the Mormon hierarchy in April 1941. Appointed an Assistant to the Twelve, Romney learned that his church "allowance amounted to less than half of what he was earning from his law practice when he was called as a General Authority."[220] Ordained an apostle that same month, Elder Lee discovered that his financial allowance was less than the salary of some staff members at LDS headquarters.[221]

After President George Albert Smith approved an increase in these allowances in 1950, his first counselor refused to accept it. Reuben usually called the allowance to general authorities a "salary."[222] Nevertheless, two weeks later "Pres. Clark thought the allowance should be doubled" for surviving dependents of deceased general authorities.[223] This reflected a view he expressed before his appointment to the hierarchy: "Personally I think it is most regrettable that a man may devote his entire life to the Church and then have his family left penniless when he dies. I am sure that sooner or later this situation will be changed."[224] He opposed the LDS president's approval of "an insurance plan for all Church employees" in 1950 because it was "discriminating in favor of a few."[225]

Regarding the compensation he did accept, "I pay my tithing on my gross income without any deductions."[226] In addition to his personal tithing and other regular LDS donations, he gave the use of his flour mill in Grantsville to the Welfare Program.[227] Reuben sought in every dimension of his life to safeguard the awesome responsibility of managing the funds of the church and of responding to the general welfare of its membership.

Despite his personal generosity, he took a dim view of those who advertised their charitable donations. When he dedicated a chapel in Westchester, New York, he publicly humiliated Isaac M. Stewart who "had made a large contribution which apparently had been rather widely known." In his remarks, Reuben referred to pharisees who boast of their donations. Everyone in the audience knew who he meant, and Stewart's "non-Mormon neighbors who were present hadn't helped matters when they now refer to him as their 'Pharisee' friend."[228] This may also reflect a grudge Reuben had held for nearly thirty years, ever since Stewart served as secretary to Reed Smoot. The senator had ignored Reuben's own 1903 application as secretary and then treated him with condescension thereafter.[229]

Reuben's personal investments were primarily in real estate. "I might say that I have not acquired them with a thought that I could thereby make myself wealthy," he explained. "I have gradually taken them on with the thought that I was adding security to my children."[230] His only other financial investment was in the stock of church-owned Zion's First National Bank.[231]

However, it was his small cattle ranch that put him into conflict with Apostle Ezra Taft Benson, whom Reuben had first befriended as a newly appointed stake president.[232] In 1945 they were of one mind "on the subject of [farm] Cooperatives," and Reuben had suggested that the junior member of the Twelve write "a statement of the policy of the Church on this subject."[233] The first strain in their relationship surfaced in 1948 when Clark expressed "disgust" that Benson "had purchased a six-story building on 5th Avenue in New York as the headquarters of the Eastern States Mission at a cost of $105,000."[234]

When Apostle Benson began his duties as U.S. Secretary of Agriculture in March 1953, Reuben confided that "he is apprehensive of Bro Benson in Washington."[235] A month later Clark bluntly told him "that I thought he was talking too much." In May he told a rank-and-file Mormon that "Secy Benson has no jurisdiction over the Church, in his capacity of Secy of Agriculture, and [Clark] said to tell the people to get in touch with the Brethren up here."[236]

Dissatisfaction with Secretary Benson was Reuben's subtext when he commented on federal policies toward small ranchers at general conference meetings devoted to the Welfare Program. In April 1955 he said: "But I assure you there is a problem that you brethren at the A.C. [Utah

State Agricultural College] and you men who are handling the Agricultural Department in Washington must not overlook. What can the farmer afford to do, and live?"[237] Elder Benson was the only person at general conference who was "handling the Agriculture Department." In October of that same year, President Clark said, "But as I see the tendency and the trend of our governmental policy, for which Secretary Benson is not responsible—it is something that he inherited—it means (unless some remedial steps are taken) the practical elimination of the small man, the little man."[238] This was also a public message to Apostle Benson that he *should* make such remedial changes in the federal policies that he had inherited.

From Reuben's point of view, their relationship steadily deteriorated over conflicts regarding the rights and obligations of Utah ranchers, like himself, whose cattle grazed on federal lands. In a private meeting with the Secretary of Agriculture in July 1957, Reuben complained "that he [Benson] was talking of a reduction of grazing privileges by 20% this year, and increasing it [the reduction] this year and next until it was 50%." He told Benson "that stockmen could not conduct their business" that way.[239] On 11 October, President Clark had a two-hour private meeting with Secretary Benson in Washington, D.C. "I urged him to understand," he wrote. "He readily saw that carrying out of their announced plans for Grantsville meant ruin for us out there."[240]

Six days later Benson compounded their conflict over grazing policies. Reuben was offended to learn that the apostle ignored his advice "not to take his family with him on his round-the-world trip" as Secretary of Agriculture. Apostle Lee referred to this in two separate diary entries a week apart.[241]

After four years of increasing dissatisfaction with Secretary Benson's policies, President Clark began retaliating. On 29 October he instructed Apostle Mark E. Petersen to "print the adverse comment[s] on Sec'y Benson" in the *Deseret News*. Significantly, Reuben recorded this in his "Ranch Diary" rather than in his office diary at LDS headquarters.[242]

In the last days of November and first days of December, Apostle Benson increased the tension when he advised the counselor not to include "a statement pointed at preferential treatment of the livestock industry" in his upcoming talk to the Utah Cattlemen's Association. In an obvious effort to put pressure on Reuben, whom President McKay had demoted to the position of second counselor, the still-junior apostle sent a copy of this letter to McKay.[243] On 4 December, Clark icily wrote an LDS member, Karl D. Butler, that by Benson's statement to the newspapers, "the Secretary seems to have already made up his mind to stay in the Cabinet. I would have thought that he ought to have let the [U.S.] President be the one to decide this; maybe he was."[244] Within days he gave the kind of talk that Benson had tried to enlist President McKay to prevent.[245]

Aside from Utah's cattlemen, Mormon reaction to this December talk was negative. An LDS woman complained that "our 1st Presidency through Pres. J. Reuben Clark has demanded the United States Forest Service to permit the livestock men to continue with their past practices when it appears such practices are detrimental to our mountain watersheds." With experience on his family's small farm and ranching operation, a Mormon had worked twenty-four years for the U.S. Forest Service and expressed dismay at Clark's characterization of Forest Service employees as "tyrants." Sending a copy of this letter to President McKay, he told Reuben, "Many of us [Forest Service employees] are members of the Church and holding, or have held, responsible positions in wards and stakes." Due to the counselor's speech, he wrote, he and others were receiving "increasing ridicule from non-members." Another LDS man warned that non-Mormons "may label the Church as a selfish group which is opposed to conservation of our natural resources" and then suggested to McKay, "Inasmuch as President Clark cannot speak unless he is thought to be representing the L.D.S. Church it might be better for the Church if President Clark were represented only by [legal] counsel." Another described Reuben's televised talk as "impassioned" and "inflammatory," and made his own impassioned plea: "I am appealing to you, President McKay, to use your authority and influence and publish any facts misrepresented by President Clark. He has harmed the cause of conservation in Utah." Like the other LDS members, this correspondent signed his name to his letter of complaint about Reuben's speech.[246]

Two bishops and another Mormon from Wellsville, Utah, met with President McKay to protest. They expressed their concern that his counselor's talk could undermine efforts to "replant the devastated area caused by overgrazing" and the consequent flooding. The church president wrote, "I assured these brethren that the Church was in favor of conservation of our mountain areas." When they "asked if some such statement could be made in the public press to that effect," McKay hesitated to repudiate his counselor publicly. He did encourage local leaders to quote his own views "publicly and privately."[247] This would have the effect of undercutting Reuben.

Aside from the counselor's criticism of Secretary Benson's policies, these were the reactions that the apostle had feared. In a letter to Reuben in January 1958, he said that "I am disturbed by your remarks." Again Benson sent a copy to President McKay.[248]

Nevertheless, in various statements to rank-and-file Mormons, President Clark increased his direct and implied criticisms of Apostle Benson. In February 1958 he recorded in his "Home Diary" a conversation with one Mormon: "I said State had nothing to do with it. It was grazing and Fed. Govt. I said it looked as if Sec'y [Benson] wanted to get it into the hands of game people [hunters] where the votes were."[249] At the April 1958 general conference, Reuben told Welfare workers that the U.S. Departments of Agriculture and Interior held 73 percent of Utah's land. He concluded, "We are something of a plaything of some professionals."[250] Two weeks later he spoke with the chairman of the Utah Cattlemen's Association and chairman of the National Woolgrowers Association: "I told them I did not think the Secretary of Agriculture would yield to argument."[251] In December 1959 he told a rank-and-file Mormon that Ezra Taft Benson "was doing more to destroy the small farmer than anyone else had done."[252]

Reuben made his most public criticism of Apostle Benson at a Welfare meeting in April 1960: "Is the Secretary of Agriculture here? (After a pause) Apparently not. I am very sorry. I may make an uncomplimentary remark about government policy. I would not like him to feel that I was saying it behind his back."[253] In his farm diary for June, he wrote: "Sec'y Benson's policies have about extinguished the small farmer and small cattleman."[254]

Thomas G. Alexander has noted that "as a [federal] permittee on the [Grantsville] allotment, Clark opposed the [grazing] reductions, even though range allotment analysis showed the range [was] seriously over-stretched." This BYU historian interpreted the strident opposition by Reuben and his protégé Henry D. Moyle, who was also a rancher, "as the last gasp of a dying way of life rather than as the effort of a group of power-ful community leaders to promote their interests."[255] Actually, it was both.

During the last decade of Reuben's life, the expansion of the church brought tremendous increases both in revenues and in expenditures. In April 1950 "Pres. Clark stressed the need for economy to keep within our income and to lighten the financial burdens upon our people." He named a committee "to go over the budget requests in an attempt to pare them down to our estimated income."[256] By contrast, a new financial secretary to the First Presidency wrote, "A new year in the financial history of the church began in 1950-51!" William F. Edwards reported that tithing reve-nues had paralleled the state and national rise in personal income for eleven years. But starting with 1951, church income began to rise inde-pendently.[257]

Beginning with McKay's presidency in 1951, church membership grew at a dizzying pace. Corresponding increases in tithing revenues re-quired either increased investment of the church's reserve income or greatly increased church expenditures. President McKay chose to do both and ushered in a new financial era.

The church's investment portfolio expanded and diversified as the church simultaneously spent tens of millions of dollars. These expendi-tures funded the expansion of BYU and other educational facilities, con-struction of new temples and chapels throughout the world, microfilming of genealogical records, increased welfare needs of a membership that was doubling every fifteen years, development of exhibits for public relations, expansion of media broadcast and ownership, and related projects. The momentum had been growing for years but seemed to explode during the McKay presidency. His optimistic, expansive personality was equal to the new financial circumstances that confronted the church as it acceler-ated toward becoming a world religion.

This was a new circumstance that President Clark could not adapt to. He had supervised LDS finances and welfare projects through the har-rowing Great Depression and the uncertainties of a wartime economy. It was difficult, if not impossible, for him to accept expansively administered church finance.

In April 1955 he reluctantly agreed to allow presidents McKay and Richards to invest tithing funds in municipal bonds, but he expressed his dissent to Apostle Lee: "Nothing that smacks of speculation should ever be done with the funds of the Church."[258] This was an example of Reuben's larger conflict of personality and philosophy with presidents McKay and Richards.

In a conversation with the first counselor during September 1956, Reuben was not subtle about his opposition. The church's investment in municipal bonds had suffered a $1 million loss in just a few months. He reminded Richards that "he knew I never had approved of the investment of Church funds in Governments or in other securities; but that I had gone along with him and Brother McKay on this matter." Reuben then said simply that he would nevertheless not oppose the rest of the presidency in approving a contract to set aside two-thirds of tithing income for continued investment, despite the recent losses.[259] That same month he complained to Apostle Lee "about the fact that the expenditures for this year would reach a record high."[260]

Reuben's reactions in these 1956 discussions were aggravated by a report circulated at LDS headquarters that year. "There is too much of a feeling among the general authorities that only President Clark and elders Moyle, Lee, and Romney are the Welfare Program leaders." As Moyle's biographer has written, this "upset" all four of them.[261]

In January 1959 Romney wrote that Clark "seemed full of concern about the course of Church affairs, including its banking policy."[262] After nearly three decades, Reuben was still haunted by his discovery that the church-owned Utah State National Bank had lost $1,374,900 in the first years of the Great Depression.[263] A week after Romney's comment, President McKay released Clark as president of the KSL radio station and released his son-in-law Ivor Sharp as head of the broadcasting company.[264] This may have had no connection to Reuben's growing dissent over the direction McKay was taking church finances, but it was easy to regard these changes at KSL as a form of punishment.

By April 1959, the last full month in which Richards served as first counselor, the second counselor's festering dissatisfaction led him to make an extraordinary statement to general conference. He stated that "wherever you begin to make great expenditures of money there is always some lack of wisdom, sometimes a lack of foresight, occasionally, oh so occasionally in this Church, a lack of integrity."[265] Long before then, Clark, Lee, and Romney had aligned themselves against Richards in disputes about the Welfare Program.[266]

Reuben also expanded on his remarks about "lack of integrity" in church finances. "I think it is terrible for any man in the Church to begin to use his Church position, particularly in finances, to his own advantage," he told the Quorum of Twelve. "So far as I know there are none of you who are trying to use the Church to your own self-advantage. That cannot be said for all our Church members."[267] He gave an example: "Even mission presidents have not been above padding payrolls."[268]

As church-affiliated businesses became more profitable, he told financial secretary Edwards that this "was not, as I had always understood, the prime purpose. I then said it looked as if we were going to take the funds of the Church and try to make money out of them."[269] Clark regarded this as profiteering at the expense of those whom Mormon enterprises seek to benefit, the Latter-day Saints.[270] Nonetheless, in January 1960 Edwards reported commercial investments of $3,675,000 in thirteen national corporations including International Harvester, Pacific Finance Corporation, Westinghouse, General Electric, International Shoe Corporation, and Archer-Daniels-Midland.[271]

By February 1960 Reuben opposed new construction for the church's existing schools in the United States because "it all might be blown up." Likewise, he did not want to build chapels in Europe because "if war comes we cannot know where bombs might light."[272] "How much money do you want today?" he asked BYU's president Ernest L. Wilkinson in October. Wilkinson answered, "As far as you are concerned, I will settle for 10 cents," and he privately complained about Reuben's "parsimony."[273]

This was vintage J. Reuben Clark, who had carefully husbanded church finances for nearly two decades in his responsibility for the "welfare of this people." But his cousin and devoted admirer, LDS president

Spencer W. Kimball, observed that Reuben's opposition to the church's expanded investments and expenditures after 1950 was "short-sighted."[274]

Not surprisingly, this put President Clark into direct conflict with the First Presidency's financial secretary. Before coming to BYU to serve as dean of its business college and as vice president, William F. Edwards had been the senior portfolio manager and vice president of New York City's "second largest group of Mutual Funds." Like Reuben, Edwards regarded LDS employment as a self-sacrificing calling and he went to BYU for "approximately fifteen percent [of] what I was earning" in Manhattan. When President McKay asked him to leave BYU to be chief financial advisor to the First Presidency, Edwards said: "The first problem I turned to was the banks ... there was a substantial build-up in the reserves that were controlled by the Church. I'm talking of tens of millions." What Reuben regarded as his greatest achievement in LDS finances—the reserve fund—this financial expert regarded as a "problem" to be remedied through investments in the stock market. There were two obstacles. Bank president Orval Adams "was the closest financial advisor to the Church and very, very close to President Clark." The result was constant conflict, which Edwards ruefully described: "Working in the Church office building as I did the next few years, I never felt a spirit comparable to the spirit I felt working with the faculty at the BYU. There [at LDS headquarters] I found more backbiting, more resistance, more problems, than I experienced at the Y. Maybe I shouldn't record it because I have such tremendous faith in the Brethren."[275]

In May 1960 Edwards submitted his resignation. Decades later he blamed second counselor Moyle for persuading President McKay to "release" him.[276] While it is certain that Moyle had greater influence with McKay at this time than Reuben, Wilkinson's 1960 diary showed that Clark had a significant role in this: "He said the things Edwards had done had gotten them in a lot of trouble." Wilkinson wrote: "I do not personally believe this. Edwards was operating on instructions of President McKay. Obviously he and President Clark did not agree on certain matters, and I think in this respect President Clark was entirely wrong."[277]

In the last years of his life, Reuben's apprehensions about church growth and the permanence of the Welfare Program brought him unnecessary distress.[278] His views mirrored the somber assessment of a 1957 entry in the diary of his protégé Elder Lee:

> Marion Romney expressed anxiety that we had lost almost every one of our cherished principles in the welfare program, even including the question of accepting government aid. ... Our ablest welfare men are called to preside over missions and no new committee members are approved. The Canadians are informed by telegram that they are to counsel the people to accept government dole. We are told to put money in the bank rather than in commodities for a year in home storage. City stakes are now proposing to build old folks homes in lieu of production projections; [and] government social security benefits are gradually replacing the Church employees welfare aid.[279]

By this time, the Welfare Program was again under the main jurisdiction of the Presiding Bishopric despite the opposition of Apostle Lee and President Clark to this change.[280]

Nevertheless, from 1939 on, President Clark had stated that the growth of the church would one day bring such large revenues that it would be problematical to either spend or maintain them. He also foresaw that the Welfare Program might need to contract as well as expand.[281] When President McKay began such changes in the 1950s, Reuben felt himself in decline administratively and physically. Therefore, he regarded these developments with suspicion. But it was his decade-long policy of keeping more than 70 percent of church revenues in reserve that provided the solid financial basis for the enormous expansion of expenditures during the last decade of his life.

In 1946 the Welfare Program became international as the church prepared to send aid to Mormons living in war-devastated countries. The first shipment was 85 railroad freight cars of food, clothing, and bedding to Germany. Eventually this totaled 140 freight cars to Europe, plus "nearly a thousand packages to needy people in Japan at war's end."[282] Even so, President Clark "thought we might wish to be a bit careful about our statements as to the great work we were doing for the Saints in Europe." With typical bluntness, he explained to President George Albert Smith that "the Quakers had made perhaps 100 times more shipments to

Europe than we had, with half the Church membership."[283]

He regarded this post-war aid as a dramatic exception to general policy. In a 1953 discussion of requests for the church to send humanitarian aid to non-Mormons in Europe, Asia, and Arab countries, Reuben said "that while we have sympathy for the suffering of people in foreign countries, we cannot undertake from our resources to relieve it everywhere. We must keep in mind the limitation of our program, which is to take care of our own, so far as we are able, and then to alleviate what other suffering we can."[284]

The continued vitality of the Welfare Plan and its importance to the LDS membership are evident in its expansion prior to President Clark's death in 1961. The value of commodities in bishops' storehouses increased from $385,836 in 1946 to $2,420,770 in 1960, while total assets of the Welfare Program increased from $4 million to $44 million. The number of assisted families increased from 8,000 to 27,000.[285] Midway through that period of growth, he joined with apostles Lee, Moyle, and Romney at his "Grantsville home rewriting and reducing the text of the *Welfare Handbook* until there was nothing left but sheer pearls and power."[286]

It was three decades before the church had sufficient resources to depart from the limitation on international aid that Reuben had emphasized in 1953. From 1982 onward, LDS headquarters gave both supplies and financial aid for emergency relief to non-LDS populations in sub-Saharan Africa, Latin America, the Soviet Union, Eastern Europe, the People's Republic of China, Iran, the Philippines, and elsewhere.[287]

Throughout his service in the First Presidency, J. Reuben Clark's devotion to the cause of his people, the Latter-day Saints, was unfailing. His contributions to their welfare and to the financial stability of the church remain lasting legacies.

AFTERWORD

In Honorable Remembrance[1]

J. Reuben Clark's life was one-third in the nineteenth century and two-thirds in the twentieth, and he reflected both eras. The educated, middle-class, white, Anglo-Saxon Americans of the late nineteenth century tended to be intensely nationalistic, pessimistic regarding human nature but optimistic toward America's destiny, fearful of foreigners, confident of natural laws and of one's own world view, apprehensive of social change, opposed to government domestic intervention except to preserve civil order, intensely partisan in politics, legalistic, and fervent in the belief that the U.S. Constitution and capitalism were divinely sanctioned.[2] In all these respects, Reuben was a typical nineteenth-century American throughout his life as a civil servant, ambassador, elder statesman, and counselor.

But even while relatively young, he also was more typically a twentieth-century Mormon. He did not feel the nineteenth-century Mormon zeal for the security of life in the tightly knit Zion of the West, nor did he regard the metropolitan East as simply an unpleasant stopover. Like most mid-twentieth-century Mormons, Reuben appreciated the headquarters culture of Zion but was willing to live in a religious minority or in isolation in order to develop his talents and profession.

The intersection of his civic life and his service to the church demonstrated the Mormon rejection of the traditional division between secular and sacred. "All things unto me are spiritual" were the words of an early revelation to Joseph Smith (D&C 29:34). Theologically, Mormonism rejected the idea that the spiritual and material are distinct or that the religious and secular are incompatible. Prior to his call to the First Presidency, Reuben unflinchingly demonstrated his Mormonism while at the same time he was undeniably very much in the world. He was a secular Saint and maintained his integrity in both the secular and religious spheres of his life. As an elder statesman in the First Presidency, he continued to be a secular Saint and contributed to both spheres of endeavor. His life stands as a refutation of the idea that one cannot be both religious and secular.

However, the unusual circumstances of his call to the First Presidency will probably always distinguish Clark in LDS administrative history. At an obvious level, it is unlikely that anyone else will enter the Mormon hierarchy after serving as a U.S. ambassador and second-ranking member of the State Department.

The lesser known qualities of his religious background are also without parallel for anyone raised as a Mormon prior to becoming a member of the First Presidency. Aside from no full-time proselytizing mission, he had no administrative experience in branch, ward, district, stake, or mission leadership. He was absent most of his adult life, including the years immediately prior to his call, from an organized church stake. His previous LDS leadership experience was limited to Sunday School teacher and auxiliary board member. In addition, for decades he had chosen not to attend LDS meetings regularly, nor pay tithing, nor participate in Mormon temple ordinances. Finding himself sliding toward atheism, he maintained faith as an act of will.

Yet he was called to be a counselor to the LDS president and went on to serve in that capacity longer than anyone else in Mormon history. Among Latter-day Saints, J. Reuben Clark is one of the most recognized names of former LDS leaders aside from church presidents.

Of the many tributes expressed concerning his church service, Spencer W. Kimball's brief statement may be the best: "What leadership you have given to this Church! What power! What vigor! You have been an example to all the people and will be long remembered and quoted."[3]

In fact, quotes from President Clark's talks have found their way into dozens of LDS lesson manuals, hundreds of general conference talks, and several anthologies in the years since his death. Quite simply, Reuben was eminently quotable. He was a profound exponent of the topics he treated and was a master of the English language. In a nearly unprecedented way, he introduced the Latter-day Saints to sermons that were both scholarly and eloquent. But he could have had the halting speech of Moses and still left a profound legacy through his administrative influence on the church.

The LDS church was more than a century old when he entered the office of the First Presidency, but he permanently altered the conduct of administrative matters there. Nearly twenty years after his death, First Presidency secretary D. Arthur Haycock said, "In the Presidency's office today, most of the procedures and language phrasing we use were developed by J. Reuben Clark."[4] With the perspectives gained as a second-ranking official in the burgeoning federal bureaucracy, he anticipated the necessary administrative adjustments that the First Presidency's office would need as it coped with the massive growth in membership that was increasingly international.

For current readers, Reuben entered the highest leadership of a very small church in 1933. That year the LDS membership was barely 700,000. In 1961, the year of his death, Mormons numbered 1.8 million. Today—forty years later—the church has 12 million members.

Although the LDS presidents whom Clark served made final decisions regarding any recommendations, the elder statesman advocated an impressive list of innovations. Heber J. Grant and George Albert Smith authorized him to implement some of these innovations, while others were refined and introduced years later by other general authorities. Among the long-lasting contributions that Reuben originally proposed were the centrally directed church Welfare Plan, reorganization of church finances, establishment of Assistants to the Quorum of Twelve Apostles, "simplification" of the relationship between the church's auxiliaries and its priesthood leadership, establishment of regional priesthood leadership, closed-circuit media broadcasts of general conferences to outlying wards and stakes, simultaneous translation of general conferences into the languages of non-English speakers, construction of multi-ward buildings, and the administrative anticipation of the conferral of priesthood on men of black African descent by establishment of "preparatory" priesthood groups and branches. Although resistant to social change, President Clark was in the vanguard of LDS administrative innovation.

Equally important was the seeming contradiction that such an innovative man was also a bulwark of stability within an often-buffeted First Presidency. He distinguished himself during the 1930s and 1940s as an articulate, calm, and unyielding exponent of views approved by LDS president Heber J. Grant but opposed by a large sector of the membership. When the church for the first time faced the challenge of the prolonged sickness of its prophet, Reuben provided complete stability and avoided self-aggrandizement. His life will remain as an extraordinary example of integrity and loyalty.

Although his strongly stated views were not always the universal expression of other general authorities, including LDS president David O. McKay, President Clark became an advocate for several positions to which LDS leaders and members continue to refer. These include the dangers of rationalized religion, the evils of government support as a social system, the difficulties of exporting Americanism to non-U.S. Mormons, the necessity for LDS church members to be loyal citizens within repressive regimes, the imperatives of peace compared with the horrors of even a "just war," the unparalleled threat of philosophical and institutional Communism, the stability of the U.S. Constitution, and the importance of refraining from dogmatism about unessential theologies.

An obvious manifestation of President Clark's administrative heritage lies in the men whom he trained and influenced, who continued to lead the church. In the years since his death, his protégés and close associates have included LDS presidents Joseph Fielding Smith, Harold B. Lee, Spencer W. Kimball, Ezra Taft Benson, and Gordon B. Hinckley, and First Presidency counselors Henry D. Moyle and Marion G. Romney. Literally thousands of other church leaders—from general authorities to ward bishops—look to J. Reuben Clark as their spiritual, philosophical, and administrative mentor as Mormonism has entered the twenty-first century. The measure of his continuing legacy is that many of these Latter-day Saints were not adults nor even born during this elder statesman's service as church leader.

NOTES

Works frequently cited in the notes are identified by the following abbreviations:

B   Leonard J. Arrington, Feramorz Y. Fox, and Dean L. May. *Building the City of God: Community and Cooperation among the Mormons.* 2d ed. Urbana: University of Illinois Press, 1992.

C   Frank W. Fox, *J. Reuben Clark: The Public Years* (Provo, UT: Brigham Young University Press; Salt Lake City: Deseret Book, 1980).

Clarkana   J. Reuben Clark's personal library, the Clarkana collection of books, Special Collections, Lee Library, Brigham Young University

CN   Church News (previously Church Section) in the *Deseret News*

Conf   *Conference Reports.* Salt Lake City: Church of Jesus Christ of Latter-day Saints, semi-annual. The years 1897–1970 are also available in *New Mormon Studies CD-ROM: A Comprehensive Resource Library* (San Francisco: Smith Research Associates, 1998), which has phrase-search capability.

D   Gene A. Sessions, ed. *Mormon Democrat: The Religious and Political Memoirs of James Henry Moyle.* Salt Lake City: Signature Books/Smith Research Associates, 1998.

D&C   *The Doctrine and Covenants of The Church of Jesus Christ of Latter-day Saints.* Published at Salt Lake City in various editions.

DA   Louis Filler. *Dictionary of American Conservatism.* New York: Philosophical Library, 1987.

Dial   *Dialogue: A Journal of Mormon Thought*

DM   Francis M. Gibbons. *David O. McKay: Apostle to the World, Prophet of God.* Salt Lake City: Deseret Book, 1986.

DN   *Deseret News* (weekly), *Deseret Evening News,* and *Deseret News* (daily).

E   D. Michael Quinn. *The Mormon Hierarchy: Extensions of Power.* Salt Lake City: Signature Books/Smith Research Associates, 1997.

EA	*Encyclopedia Americana: International Edition.* 30 vols. Danbury, CT: Grolier, 2000.
EM	Daniel H. Ludlow, ed. *Encyclopedia of Mormonism: The History, Scripture, Doctrine, and Procedure of the Church of Jesus Christ of Latter-day Saints,* 5 vols. New York: Macmillan, 1992. Please consult for such LDS terms as branch, stake, ward, high priest, Seventy, and so on.
ER	Christian Zentner and Friedemann Beduerftig, eds. *The Encyclopedia of the Third Reich.* Amy Hackett, trans. 2 vols. New York: Macmillan, 1991.
F	J. Reuben Clark Jr. *Stand Fast by Our Constitution.* Salt Lake City: Deseret Book, 1962.
FHL	Family History Library, The Church of Jesus Christ of Latter-day Saints, Salt Lake City, Utah
G	Francis M. Gibbons. *George Albert Smith: Kind and Caring Christian, Prophet of God.* Salt Lake City: Deseret Book, 1990.
H	L. Brent Goates. *Harold B. Lee: Prophet and Seer.* Salt Lake City: Bookcraft, 1985.
HBLL	Department of Archives and Special Collections, Harold B. Lee Library, Brigham Young University.
I	Harvard S. Heath, ed. *In the World: The Diaries of Reed Smoot.* Salt Lake City: Signature Books/Smith Research Associates, 1997.
J	*Journal of Discourses ...,* 26 vols. London and Liverpool, England: Latter Day Saints' Book Depot, 1854–86. All sermons published in the *Journal of Discourses* are also available on the *New Mormon Studies CD-ROM,* which has phrase-search capability.
JMH	*Journal of Mormon History*
JRC	J. Reuben Clark Jr.
JRCP	J. Reuben Clark Jr. Papers, Department of Archives and Special Collections, Harold B. Lee Library, Brigham Young University, Provo, Utah
JWML	Manuscripts Division, J. Willard Marriott Library, University of Utah, Salt Lake City
K	Merlo J. Pusey. *Builders of the Kingdom: George A. Smith, John Henry Smith, George Albert Smith.* Provo, UT: Brigham Young University Press, 1981.
L	Francis M. Gibbons. *Harold B. Lee: Man of Vision, Prophet of God.* Salt Lake City: Deseret Book, 1993.
LDSA	Archives, Historical Department, The Church of Jesus Christ of Latter-day Saints, Salt Lake City, Utah. For manuscripts.

LDSL   Library, Historical Department, The Church of Jesus Christ of Latter-day Saints, Salt Lake City, Utah. For published works.

M   James R. Clark, ed. *Messages of the First Presidency of The Church of Jesus Christ of Latter-day Saints*. 6 vols. Salt Lake City: Bookcraft, 1965-75.

NYT   *The New York Times*

O   D. Michael Quinn. *The Mormon Hierarchy: Origins of Power.* Salt Lake City: Signature Books/Smith Research Associates, 1994.

OC   I. C. B. Dear and M. R. D. Foot, eds. *The Oxford Companion to World War II.* Oxford, Eng.: Oxford University Press, 1995.

P   Garth Mangum and Bruce Blumell. *The Mormons' War on Poverty: A History of LDS Welfare, 1830-1990.* Salt Lake City: University of Utah Press, 1993.

R   Jerry C. Roundy. *Ricks College: A Struggle for Survival.* Rexburg, ID: Ricks College Press, 1976.

SA   David H. Yarn Jr., ed. *J. Reuben Clark: Selected Papers on Americanism and National Affairs.* Provo, UT: Brigham Young University Press, 1987.

SI   David H. Yarn Jr., ed. *J. Reuben Clark: Selected Papers on International Affairs.* Provo, UT: Brigham Young University Press, 1987.

SLT   *The Salt Lake Tribune*

SR   David H. Yarn Jr. *J. Reuben Clark: Selected Papers on Religion, Education, and Youth.* Provo, UT: Brigham Young University Press, 1984.

T   Thomas G. Alexander. *Mormonism in Transition: A History of the Latter-day Saints, 1890-1930.* Urbana: University of Illinois Press, 1986.

U   Allan Kent Powell, ed. *Utah History Encyclopedia.* Salt Lake City: University of Utah Press, 1994.

UHQ   *Utah Historical Quarterly*

W   Richard D. Poll. *Working the Divine Miracle: The Life of Apostle Henry D. Moyle.* Stan Larson, ed. Salt Lake City: Signature Books, 1999.

Note: The author regrets that some readers may find the abbreviations confusing. The publisher employed them as a space-saving measure.

NOTES TO PREFACE

[1] Francis M. Gibbons, "Perspectives in Writing Biography," *New Perspectives* 16 (Spring 1999): 1-2. *New Perspectives* is a publication of Ricks College in Rexburg, Idaho. I believe readers will find little of "innuendo" in the restored portions of my biography since Clark stated his views so clearly and emphatically. I did my best to portray these within the context in which Reuben expressed himself. However, Gibbons is accustomed to writing biographies that tell readers how to regard people's actions and statements, frequently indicating how he himself judges them. What he dismissed as innuendo was apparently my decision to allow readers to make their own value judgments about what people said or did.

[2] Lawrence Coates, "A Response to Francis M. Gibbons's Perspectives in Writing Biography," *New Perspectives* 16 (Spring 1999): 5. I admire the church-owned college for publishing such a response by a faculty member to remarks by an emeritus church authority.

[3] See my discussion and source notes in the editor's introduction to *The New Mormon History: Revisionist Essays on the Past* (Salt Lake City: Signature Books, 1992) and in the preface to D. Michael Quinn, *Early Mormonism and the Magic World View,* rev. and enl. ed. (Salt Lake City: Signature Books, 1998).

[4] This letter of February 1993 listed two of my recent publications: "One Hundred Fifty Years of Truth and Consequences about Mormon History," *Sunstone* 16 (Feb. 1992): 12-14, and "Mormon Women Have Had the Priesthood Since 1843" in Maxine Hanks, ed., *Women and Authority: Re-emerging Mormon Feminism* (Salt Lake City: Signature Books, 1992), 365-409. This letter also identified as "apostasy" my statements to the *SLT* and *NYT* that current leadership of the LDS church wants "cookie-cutter Mormons" and does not accept the existence of a "loyal opposition," contrary to the more pluralistic view of LDS prophets in the nineteenth century.

For more details, see "Apostasy Investigation Launched against Historian," *SLT,* 13 Feb. 1993, A-6, A-7 (local story only); "Mormons Investigating Him, Critic Says," *The Los Angeles Times,* 13 Feb. 1993, B-4, B-5 (Associated Press wire-service story); "Michael Quinn Investigated for Apostasy," *Sunstone* 16 (Mar. 1993): 69; "Historian Assails LDS Research Barriers: Quinn Contends 'Golden Age' of Access to Data by Scholars Has Come and Gone," *Standard-Examiner* [Ogden, UT], 15 May 1993, C-2; "Six Facing Censure Accuse Mormon Church of Purge," *The Los Angeles Times,* 18 Sept. 1993, B-5; "Mormons Penalize Dissident Members: Six Who Criticized Leaders or Debated Doctrine Await Sanctions by Church," *NYT,* 19 Sept. 1993, 31; "As Mormon Church Grows, So Does Dissent from Feminists and Scholars," *NYT,* 2 Oct. 1993, 7; "Elders Banishing Dissidents in Struggle over Mormon Practices," *Washington Post,* 26 Nov. 1993, A-3; "Ex-Mormon Warns LDS Historians to Be Wary," *University of Utah Daily Utah Chronicle,* 9 Dec. 1993, 1; "Mormon Church Ousts Dissidents," *The Los Angeles Times,* 30 Dec. 1993, E-2; "SUU Cancels Excommunicated LDS Historian's Talk," *Daily Spectrum* [Cedar City, UT], 6 Jan. 1994, A-3; "Historian to Speak on LDS Issues after All: Private, Faculty Funds Will Bring Quinn to SUU and Snow

College," *SLT,* 1 Mar. 1994, D-5; "Mormon Church Excommunicates Five Scholars over Their Books," *Publishers Weekly* 241 (25 Apr. 1994): 12.

NOTES TO CHAPTER 1

[1] Psalms 137:1; *D&C* 101: 18.

[2] In my 1981 draft, I intended a similar phrase to be ironic. For example, Reuben reminded LDS members in the Salt Lake Tabernacle that they "gained the most of the land which we possess, including that on which we stand, by conquest ... I loathe conquest, I loathe oppression ..." See *Conf,* Oct. 1938, 138.

The displacement of the Native Americans from their ancestral lands had the same result as elsewhere in North America but was somewhat different in its process and very different in its ideology. A three-page bibliography on this topic is in *E,* 521-23.

[3] Donna Hill, *Joseph Smith: The First Mormon* (1977; Salt Lake City: Signature Books, 1999); Richard L. Bushman, *Joseph Smith and the Beginnings of Mormonism* (Urbana: University of Illinois Press, 1984); Monte S. Nyman and Lisa Bolin Hawkins, "Book of Mormon: Overview," Bushman and Larry C. Porter, "History of the Church: ca. 1820-31, Background, Founding, New York Period," and Bushman and Dean L. Jessee, "Smith, Joseph: The Prophet," in *EM* 1:140, 2:603, 3:1331-39. For general histories, see Leonard J. Arrington and Davis Bitton, *The Mormon Experience* (New York: Alfred A. Knopf, 1979); D. Michael Quinn, *Early Mormonism and the Magic World View,* rev. and enl. ed. (Salt Lake City: Signature Books, 1998); and James B. Allen and Glen M. Leonard, *The Story of the Latter-day Saints,* 2d ed., rev., enl. (Salt Lake City: Deseret Book, 1992).

[4] There are several scholarly studies of the causes and manifestations of this anti-Mormonism during the lifetime of founder Joseph Smith. See, for instance, Lawrence Foster, *Religion and Sexuality: Three American Communal Experiments of the Nineteenth Century* (New York: Oxford University Press, 1981); Annette P. Hampshire, *Mormonism in Conflict: The Nauvoo Years* (New York: Edwin Mellen Press, 1985); Stephen C. LeSueur, *The 1838 Mormon War in Missouri* (Columbia: University of Missouri Press, 1987); Kenneth H. Winn, *Exiles in a Land of Liberty: Mormons in America, 1830-1846* (Chapel Hill: University of North Carolina Press, 1989); Marvin S. Hill, *Quest for Refuge: The Mormon Flight from American Pluralism* (Salt Lake City: Signature Books, 1989); various essays in Arnold K. Garr and Clark V. Johnson, eds., *Regional Studies in Latter-day Saint Church History: Missouri* (Provo, UT: Department of Church History and Doctrine, Brigham Young University, 1994); John E. Hallwas and Roger D. Launius, eds., *Cultures in Conflict: A Documentary History of the Mormon War in Illinois* (Logan: Utah State University Press, 1995).

[5] Joseph I. Bentley, "The Martyrdom of Joseph and Hyrum Smith," in *EM* 2:860-62; Kenneth W. Godfrey, "Remembering the Deaths of Joseph and Hyrum Smith," and Danel W. Bachman, "Joseph Smith, a True Martyr," in Susan Easton Black and Charles D. Tate Jr., eds., *Joseph Smith: The Prophet, the Man* (Provo, UT: Religious Studies Center, Brigham Young University, 1993), 301-15, 317-22; *O,*

137-41; Davis Bitton, *The Martyrdom Remembered: A One Hundred Fifty Year Perspective on the Assassination of Joseph Smith* (Salt Lake City: Aspen Books, 1994); Reed H. Blake and Spencer H. Blake, *The Carthage Tragedy: The Martyrdom of Joseph Smith* (Provo, UT: LDS Book Publications, 1994).

⁶ Ronald K. Esplin, "'A Place Prepared': Joseph, Brigham and the Quest for Promised Refuge in the West," *JMH* 9 (1982): 85-111; Leonard J. Arrington, *Brigham Young: An American Moses* (New York: Alfred A. Knopf, 1985), 127-51; also "The Ascension of Brigham Young" in *O*, 173-82.

⁷ Joseph Smith Jr., et al., 7 vols., *History of the Church of Jesus Christ of Latter-day Saints*, 2d rev., B. H. Roberts, ed. (Salt Lake City: Deseret Book, 1960), 7:516, 520-22; Leonard J. Arrington, *Great Basin Kingdom: An Economic History of the Latter-day Saints, 1830-1900* (Cambridge, MA: Harvard University Press, 1958), 24.

⁸ *J* 6:87 (G. A. Smith/1857).

⁹ "Zion" in Davis Bitton, *Historical Dictionary of Mormonism* (Metuchen, NJ: Scarecrow Press, 1994), 273.

¹⁰ Joshua R. Clark diary, autobiographical summary, JRCP; also "A History of the Early Life of Joshua Reuben Clark, Sr. Covering a Period of About 30 Years, Written at the Home of His Son Joshua Reuben in Washington, D.C. an[d] in My Home at Grantsville, Utah, 1910 and 1911 also 1912, 1914 and 1915, 1922 and 1925," typed document, 2 (father "a minister of the Dunker Church," Joshua's enlistment in Indiana Volunteers in December 1861), 3 (medical discharge early in 1863), 6 (arrival at Farmington on 9 March 1867, hearing his first Mormon sermon, and Joshua's baptism on 14 April 1867), 7 ("On April 22, 1867 I quit drinking tea and coffee and also smoking tobacco. I intended to try to keep the 'Word of Wisdom' and as far as smoking is concerned I have kept that part of the Word of Wisdom pretty well, for a few years after I may have smoked a few cigars"), 10 (his arrival at Grantsville in November 1868 to teach school and his marriage of Mary L. Woolley on 11 July 1870), microfilm of Clark diary and miscellaneous papers, Henry E. Huntington Library, San Marino, California; David H. Yarn Jr., *Young Reuben: The Early Life of J. Reuben Clark, Jr.* (Provo, UT: Brigham Young University Press, 1973); *C*, 4-5; federal census of Utah, 1870, National Archives, Washington, D.C., also microfilm copy in FHL.

¹¹ "Hot Shot from Cannon. An Interview with the Utah Delegate," *Washington Post*, 6 Feb. 1878, reprinted in *DN*, 12 Feb. 1878, [2].

¹² Joshua R. Clark diary, 24 Oct. 1880, 2 Sept. 1891.

¹³ Alma A. Gardiner, "The Founding and Development of Grantsville, Utah, 1850-1950," M.A. thesis, Brigham Young University, 1959; federal censuses of Utah, 1930 and 1960. One of my pioneer Utah ancestors, Mary Elizabeth Hardy, was born in Grantsville in 1861.

¹⁴ For his secular career, see *C*.

¹⁵ *C*, 439, made a similar observation: "The careers of a Reed Smoot or a James H. Moyle remained essentially western careers built upon local [Utah] bases of support." For these federal officials, see Mark W. Cannon, "The Mormon Issue in Congress, 1872-1882, Drawing on the Experience of Territorial Delegate

George Q. Cannon," Ph.D. diss., Harvard University, 1960; Milton R. Merrill, *Reed Smoot: Apostle in Politics* (Logan: Utah State University Press, 1990); Harvard S. Heath, "Reed Smoot: The First Modern Mormon," Ph.D. diss., Brigham Young University, 1990; *E*, 262-65, 280-81, 283, 294, 301, 314, 322, 324, 343, 356. See also *D* and Davis Bitton, *George Q. Cannon: A Biography* (Salt Lake City: Deseret Book, 1999).

Never a general authority, James H. Moyle served as Assistant Secretary of the U.S. Treasury Department (1917-21). I did not include him in the comparison because Reuben's 1930 appointment as U.S. ambassador to Mexico exceeded the status of Moyle's federal appointment and rivaled the congressional status of Cannon and Smoot.

[16] *C*, 389.

[17] Born less than a generation after Reuben's birth, Lowry Nelson provided the first scholarly analysis of this culture in his *The Mormon Village: A Study in Social Origins* (Provo, UT: Research Division, Brigham Young University, 1930).

[18] Yarn, *Young Reuben*; *C*, 7-12.

[19] Andrew Jenson, *Encyclopedic History of the Church of Jesus Christ of Latter-day Saints* (Salt Lake City: Deseret News, 1941), 299.

[20] Gardiner, "Founding and Development of Grantsville, Utah"; Leonard J. Arrington, *From Quaker to Latter-day Saint: Bishop Edwin D. Woolley* (Salt Lake City: Deseret Book, 1976), 73, 74, 375, 404, 455; William E. Hunter, *Edward Hunter, Faithful Steward* (Salt Lake City: Mrs. William E. Hunter, 1970), 234-50; also Douglas D. Alder, "The Mormon Ward: Congregation or Community?," *JMH* 5 (1978): 61-78.

[21] James B. Allen, "Ecclesiastical Influence on Local Government in the Territory of Utah," *Arizona and the West: A Quarterly Journal of History* 8 (Spring 1966): 35-48; Allen, "The Unusual Jurisdiction of County Probate Courts in the Territory of Utah," *UHQ* 36 (Spring 1968): 132-42; Alvin Charles Koritz, "The Development of Municipal Government in the Territory of Utah," M.A. thesis, Brigham Young University, 1972, 74; Raymond T. Swenson, "Resolution of Civil Disputes by Mormon Ecclesiastical Courts," *Utah Law Review* (1978): 573-95; Donald Gene Pace, "Community Leadership on the Mormon Frontier: Mormon Bishops and the Political, Economic, and Social Development of Utah Before Statehood," Ph.D. diss., Ohio State University, 1983.

[22] Stan L. Albrecht, "Stake," in *EM* 3:1411-14.

[23] JRC membership certificate in Deceased LDS Members File (1941-74), microfilm, FHL.

[24] Francis M. Lyman diary, entries for 1877-80, original holographs in vault of the First Presidency, Salt Lake City, Utah, with typed transcription at one time in the office of the Church Historian, LDSL, where I researched Lyman's early diaries and took extensive notes; also Albert R. Lyman, *Biography: Francis Marion Lyman, 1840-1916, Apostle 1880-1916* (Delta, UT: Melvin A. Lyman, 1958), 84-94.

[25] Heber J. Grant journal, 30 Oct. 1880 (details of stake conference and first quote), 11 Nov. 1880 (final quote), LDSA; also Francis M. Gibbons, *Heber J. Grant:*

Man of Steel, Prophet of God (Salt Lake City: Deseret Book, 1979), 39-40 (stake conference and second quote). While "diary" is the standardized term I use to identify personal documents with daily entries, Grant kept several different kinds of such records which must be identified separately in order to locate the quotations.

26 Heber J. Grant letterbook journal, 19 July 1889. As indicated by the year of this entry, Grant's unpopularity continued and grew after he became a member of the Quorum of Twelve Apostles in 1882. Otherwise-devout Mormons expressed personal dislike and criticism of him even after he became prophet and church president in 1918; also chapter 3, note 159.

27 Arrington, *From Quaker to Latter-day Saint,* 482-83; Gibbons, *Heber J. Grant,* 19-20; Ronald W. Walker, "Young Heber J. Grant's Years of Passage," *BYU Studies* 24 (Spring 1984): 149; Walker, "Heber J. Grant," in Leonard J. Arrington, ed., *The Presidents of the Church: Biographical Essays* (Salt Lake City: Deseret Book, 1986), 230; Walker, "'Going to Meeting' in Salt Lake City's Thirteenth Ward, 1849-1881: A Microanalysis," in Davis Bitton and Maureen Ursenbach Beecher, eds., *New Views of Mormon History: A Collection of Essays in Honor of Leonard J. Arrington* (Salt Lake City: University of Utah Press, 1987), 138-61.

28 "Journal of Rachel Emma Woolley Simmons," *Heart Throbs of the West* 11 (1950): 197.

29 Heber J. Grant journal, 7 Oct. 1881; also Ronald W. Walker, "Young Heber J. Grant and His Call to the Apostleship," *BYU Studies* 18 (Fall 1977): 121.

30 *Revelation Given through President John Taylor, at Salt Lake City, Utah Territory, October 13th, 1882* (Salt Lake City: Church of Jesus Christ of Latter-day Saints, 1882). Though officially published, this "Thus saith the Lord" revelation was never added to the *D&C* in English. Its full text was included in foreign editions: in Swedish in 1888; German in 1893, 1903, and 1920; and Danish in 1900.

31 *C,* 12.

32 Joshua R. Clark diary, 22 Dec. 1880.

33 Yarn, *Young Reuben,* 24-25.

34 Joshua R. Clark diary, 9 Dec. 1885, 19 Dec. 1887.

35 Joshua R. Clark diary, 30 Mar. 1890; entry for JRC in genealogy of members, 31st Quorum of the Seventy records, vol. 2, LDSA and FHL.

Reuben reported in 1941 that the man who ordained him a Seventy was Apostle Francis M. Lyman. Not since 1880 had Lyman been Tooele's stake president, and at this time stake presidents did not have authority to ordain men to the office. See JRC membership certificate in Deceased LDS Members File (1941-74).

36 *D&C* 107:97; James Norman Baumgarten, "The Role and Function of Seventies in L.D.S. Church History," M.A. thesis, Brigham Young University, 1960.

37 JRC, "What I Read as a Boy," *Children's Friend* 43 (Mar. 1943): 99.

38 Yarn, *Young Reuben,* 45-54; also *C,* 10-12. "Common school" was the nineteenth-century term for "elementary school."

[39] JRC remarks to general priesthood meeting, 8 Oct. 1933, transcript, box 151, JRCP; JRC to Roscoe Grover, 18 Apr. 1934, fd 3, box 351, JRCP.

[40] JRC office diary, 23 Oct. 1959, JRCP.

[41] Joshua R. Clark diary, 13 Feb. 1884; quoted with slight difference in *C*, 11.

[42] Yarn, *Young Reuben,* 45-54; also *C*, 10-12; also various entries in Joshua R. Clark diary through August 1890.

[43] Yarn, *Young Reuben,* 59; also *C*, 12, used the "barefoot boy" image of JRC on the brink of moving to Salt Lake City to attend LDS College.

[44] *C*, 15.

[45] "Editor's Introduction" in James Harris, ed., *The Essential James E. Talmage* (Salt Lake City: Signature Books, 1997). See also John R. Talmage, *The Talmage Story: Life of James E. Talmage—Educator, Scientist, Apostle* (Salt Lake City: Book-craft, 1972).

[46] "Pres. Clark's Address at MIA Conference," *CN* 23 June 1956, 4, referring to the Mutual Improvement Associations for LDS youth from the 1870s to the 1970s. For most people "MIA" refers to military personnel who are missing-in-action. That may be the reason why, during the last years of the Vietnam War, the First Presidency changed the name of the youth organizations and dropped the term "MIA" from Mormon usage.

[47] Concerning the intertwined histories of the three institutions, see D. Michael Quinn, "The Brief Career of Young University at Salt Lake City," *UHQ* 41 (Winter 1973): 69-89.

[48] JRC scrapbook, 6 Oct. 1897, JRCP; Joshua R. Clark diary, 15 June 1898; "The State University: The Twenty-Ninth Annual Commencement Exercises," *The Salt Lake Herald,* 16 June 1898, 5; "Commencement Oration," in *SA*, 11-16.

[49] James E. Talmage diary, 14 Sept. 1898, HBLL.

[50] Joshua R. Clark diary, 1 Jan. 1891.

[51] Joshua R. Clark diary, 16 Jan. 1891.

[52] Spencer J. Condie, "Missionary, Mission Life," in *EM* 2:911-12.

[53] *C*, 13, 15.

[54] David J. Whittaker, "Articles of Faith," in *EM* 1:67-69.

[55] Talmage, *The Talmage Story,* 154-59. For examples of doctrines that were standardized or rejected altogether, see James E. Talmage diary, 29 Nov. 1893, 5 Jan. 1894, 13 Jan. 1899; also Thomas G. Alexander, "The Reconstruction of Mormon Doctrine: From Joseph Smith to Progressive Theology," *Sunstone* 5 (July-Aug. 1980): 27-31; *T,* 281.

[56] "Pres. Clark's Address at MIA Conference," *CN* 23 June 1956, 4.

[57] *C*, 18; also Bradley W. Richards, *The Savage View: Charles Savage, Pioneer Mormon Photographer* (Nevada City, CA: Carl Mautz, 1995).

[58] JRC, "Two Years in the Service Can Be Profitable," *Improvement Era* 55 (Aug. 1952): 611.

[59] *C*, 18 (for Savage's role in securing this teaching position); William James Mortimer, ed., *How Beautiful Upon the Mountains: A Centennial History of Wasatch County* (n.p.: Wasatch County Chapter of the Daughters of Utah Pioneers, 1963), 85 (quote).

[60] *C*, 18 (honeymoon departure), 609n59 (Fox's observation and quote from Luacine's autobiography).

[61] Lute to Ida, 25 Jan. 1899, box 328, JRCP.

[62] *C*, 19; cf. woman's alleged accusation in note 160 below.

[63] Yarn, *Young Reuben*, 98.

[64] Yarn, *Young Reuben*, 102-16; *C*, 19-20.

Apostle M. Russell Ballard recently told a general conference, "However, in the Lord's Church there is no such thing as a 'loyal opposition.'" See M. Russell Ballard, "Beware of False Prophets and False Teachers," *Ensign* 29 (Nov. 1999): 64.

[65] JRC to George W. Decker, 23 Nov. 1901 (quotes) and 14 Feb. 1902 (outcome), both in box 1, JRCP. *C*, 21, wrote simply: "While in Cedar City he had dabbled in coal-bearing properties and had gained a sense of the importance of minerals to the state."

[66] *C*, 21-22.

[67] JRC remarks to missionary meeting, 4 Apr. 1958, transcript, in April 1958 conference binder, box 167, JRCP.

[68] JRC to R. W. Madsen, Orval W. Adams, and Herbert A. Snow, 5 Sept. 1951, fd 2, box 364, JRCP.

[69] JRC to William Cullen Dennis, 30 June 1910, fd 10, box 343, JRCP; quoted in *C*, 435.

[70] JRC remarks to bishops' meeting, 3 Apr. 1953, transcript, box 151, JRCP.

[71] *C*, 27-41.

[72] *C*, 30-33 (influence of professors on JRC), 31 (quote), and 238-39 (Bassett's future in the State Department).

[73] *C*, 42-86.

[74] *C*, 86-233 (discussion of the *Right* memorandum, 196-97); *SI*, 321-24; references to JRC in Samuel Flagg Bemis, *The Latin American Policy of the United States: An Historical Interpretation* (New York: Harcourt, Brace, 1943), 165; Peter Calvert, *The Mexican Revolution, 1910-1914: The Diplomacy of Anglo-American Conflict* (Cambridge, Eng.: Cambridge University Press, 1968), 44, 112.

[75] John A. Widtsoe, "President J. Reuben Clark, Jr.: A Defender of the Gospel," *Improvement Era* 54 (Aug. 1951): 563; *C*, 234-365; *SI*, 39-59, 163-91, 209-31.

[76] *C*, 362-63, also 596.

[77] Term first used in Wilbur Zelinsky, "An Approach to the Religious Geography of the United States: Patterns of Church Membership in 1952," *Annals of the Association of American Geographers* 51 (June 1961): 163-64, 193; D. W. Meinig, "The Mormon Culture Region: Strategies and Patterns in the Geography of the American West, 1847-1964," *Annals of the Association of American Geographers* 55 (1965): 191-220; Samuel S. Hill, "Religion and Region in America," *Annals of the American Academy of Political and Social Science* 480 (July 1985): 137; D. Michael Quinn, "Religion in the American West," in William Cronon, George Miles, and Jay Gitlin, eds., *Under an Open Sky: Rethinking America's Western Past* (New York: W. W. Norton, 1992), 146, 160; Lowell C. "Ben" Bennion, "The Geographic Dynamics of Mormondom, 1965-95," *Sunstone* 18 (Dec. 1995): 21, 27-32.

[78] JRC talk in young men's portion of Mutual Improvement Associations

conference, 9 June 1934, transcript, box 151, JRCP; paraphrased in *DN*, 9 June 1934, 1.

[79] Luacine to JRC, 30 Apr. 1909, box 329, JRCP; *C*, 366-74, 374 (quote from above letter), 435.

[80] Marianne Clark Sharp oral history, 1977, typescript, 2, 9, LDSA.

[81] Lute to JRC, 5 Sept. 1920, fd 3, box 332, JRCP; Lute to JRC, 24 Apr. 1923 (quote), fd 1, box 333, JRCP; Luacine S. Clark autobiography, JRCP; *C*, 414, also 386 (photo caption: "Luacine and the children, circa 1920: No mere happenstance that daddy was missing from the picture").

[82] *C*, 414.

[83] *C*, 379; Luacine S. Clark letters to JRC, boxes 332 and 333, JRCP.

[84] JRC, "The Prophet's Sailing Orders to Relief Society," *Relief Society Magazine* 36 (Dec. 1949): 797.

[85] Marianne Clark Sharp 1977 oral history, 7.

[86] Marianne Clark Sharp 1977 oral history, 18; *C*, 380-81 (quote).

[87] Marianne Clark Sharp 1977 oral history, 5-7; *C*, 377; Joshua R. Clark diary, 7 Jan. 1886 (family prayers), 14 Aug. 1910 (Marianne's baptism), 1 Aug. 1917 (Reuben III's baptism); Lute to JRC, 6 Jan. 1923 (young Luacine's baptism), fd 3, box 333, JRCP.

[88] Marianne Clark Sharp 1977 oral history, 14.

[89] Anthon H. Lund diary, 11 July 1900, microfilm, LDSA. By stipulation of its donor, the Lund diary is available to all researchers at LDSA.

[90] *Proceedings Before the Committee on Privileges and Elections of the United States Senate in the Matter of the Protests Against the Right of Hon. Reed Smoot, a Senator from the State of Utah, to Hold His Seat*, 4 vols. (Washington, D.C.: Government Printing Office, 1904-07), 3:183, 184, 189, 207, often called the Smoot Hearings.

[91] Marianne Clark Sharp 1977 oral history, 6; Reed Smoot diary, 14 Feb., 7 Mar. 1909, HBLL, with photocopy at JWML; Smoot diary, 4 July 1909, in *I*, 19; Carlos A. Badger diary, 6 Apr., 24 Apr. 1904, LDSA. Badger was Smoot's secretary.

[92] Marianne Clark Sharp 1977 oral history, 6; Reed Smoot diary, 16 Jan., 6 Mar., 17 Apr. 1910, in *I*, 43, 45, 47; *D*, 208-09.

[93] Carlos A. Badger diary, 29 Mar. 1903, 16 Apr. 1905, 27-28 May 1905, 15 Oct. 1905, partly published in Rodney J. Badger, ed., *Liahona and Iron Rod: The Biography of Carl A. and Rose J. Badger* (n.p.: Family History, 1985), 203, 269, 273.

[94] *C*, 433.

[95] Reed Smoot diary, 4 July 1909, 27 Mar., 10, 17 Apr., 12 June 1910, 22 Jan., 5 Feb., 5 Mar., 13 Aug., 12, 19 Nov. 1911, 21 Jan., 4 Feb., 25 Feb., 3 Mar., 24 Mar., 7 Apr., 14 Apr., 21 Apr., 28 Apr., 2 June, 30 June 1912, 2 Mar. 1913, in *I*, 19, 45, 46, 47, 49, 89, 90, 93, 109, 128, 129, 133, 134, 136, 137, 139, 142, 144, 145, 146, 152, 179.

[96] Reed Smoot diary, 18 Apr., 4 July 1909, 10 Apr. 1910, 15 Jan. 1911, 18 Feb., 3 Mar. 1912, in *I*, 14, 19, 46, 88-89, 135, 137.

[97] Reed Smoot diary, 23 Jan., 10 Apr., 1 May 1910, 22 Jan., 19 Nov. 1911, 21 Jan., 3 Mar., 31 Mar., 28 Apr. 1912, 6 Apr., 20 Apr., 15 June, 24 Aug. 1913, in *I*, 44, 46, 47, 89, 129, 133, 138, 140, 145, 185, 186, 188, 191.

[98] Reed Smoot diary, 1 May 1910, 29 Jan. 1911, in *I*, 47, 90.

[99] Reed Smoot diary, 12 Jan. 1930, in *I*, 720; also Heath's comment (720n2): "In an interview with Milton R. Merrill in 1940, Elbert D. Thomas, [a Mormon] who defeated Smoot in 1932, claimed that Smoot purposefully kept missionaries out of the Washington, D.C., area so that he alone could represent the church there."

[100] Lute to JRC, 3 Oct. 1906; also 21 Sept. 1906, box 328, JRCP; *C*, 432.

[101] *D*, 210; also *C*, 432.

[102] *C*, 432.

[103] "J. Reuben Clark Speaker," *DN*, 4 Dec. 1911, 12; "Now Before U.S. Senate: Address Delivered in Salt Lake Tabernacle, Sunday, November 26, 1911, by Elder J. Reuben Clark, Jr.," *DN*, 9 Dec. 1911, 30.

[104] JRC manuscript outlines of talks and sermons in box 90, JRCP.

[105] JRC diary, 19 July, 8 Nov. 1914, 3 Jan., 22 Aug. 1915, 23 Apr. 1922, JRCP; also New York District Conference history (1910-19), LDSA; New York Branch Sunday School record (1913-18), LDSA; Brooklyn Branch priesthood minutes (1922-23), LDSA; Brooklyn Branch historical and priesthood record (1924-28), LDSA; Washington, D.C. Branch sacrament meeting minutes (1923-30), LDSA. One of the few references to attending Sunday School from 1913 to 1922 is in his diary, 21 May 1922.

[106] JRC 1907 memorandum book, box 2, JRCP; quoted more fully in *C*, 437.

[107] JRC, "Letter to Pa on my position," in 1907 notebook, fd E9, box 16, JRCP; partly quoted in *C*, 437.

[108] JRC conversation with Mathonihah Thomas in JRC memorandum #6, fd J9, box 90, JRCP, dated 4 Feb. 1914, but from context written on 4 March.

[109] JRC 1917 memorandum, "Knowledge and Belief," #31, fd J9, box 90, JRCP.

[110] *SA*, 370.

[111] Brad E. Hainsworth, "Utah State Elections, 1916-1924," Ph.D. diss., University of Utah, 1968, 230-32.

[112] Donald Bruce Gilchrist, "An Examination of the Problem of L.D.S. Church Influence in Utah Politics, 1890-1916," M.S. thesis, University of Utah, 1965; Hainsworth, "Utah State Elections, 1916-1924"; Jan Shipps, "Utah Comes of Age Politically: A Study of the State's Politics in the Early Years of the Twentieth Century," *UHQ* 35 (Spring 1967): 91-111; *E*, 347-49, 353, 356.

[113] Lute to JRC, 30 Oct. 1906, box 328, JRCP ("it has been so long since you have been able to pay tithing"); also *C*, 433.

[114] JRC financial records, box 512, JRCP. The apparent reason for paying a full tithing in 1925 was that he was called to the general board of the Young Men's Mutual Improvement Association. See "Thousands Attend M.I.A. Jubilee Sessions," *DN*, 8 June 1925, 2; *C*, 444. In accepting such a prominent position, his strict sense of propriety required him to fully live the same standards of conduct expected of teenage boys. Otherwise he might have continued to pay part-tithing until called to the First Presidency in 1931.

[115] JRC to James E. Talmage, 24 Nov. 1912, box 346, JRCP; *C*, 432.

[116] Lute to JRC, second letter of 12 Feb. 1923 ("only been once" to the temple in his life, after many letters referring to her own regular participation), all in fd 1, box 333, JRCP; Emma Fugal, "Salvation of the Dead," in *EM* 3:1258, for quote.

[117] *C*, 433 (complaints and advice); Evelyn T. Marshall, "Garments," in *EM* 1:534-35.

[118] Lute to Reube, 26 May 1923, fd 1, box 333, JRCP: "I must tell you another of your predictions has come true[—]our garments are modified[—]no collars, buttons[,] elbow sleeve, new length"; Reed Smoot diary, 17 May 1923, in *I*, 534, concerning First Presidency and apostles who "agreed that certain changes in the Latter day Saints garments will be allowed. They were as follows: Buttons instead of strings, no collar; sleeves above the elbow and few inches below the knee and a change in the crotch so as to cover the same. George A[lbert] Smith and Jos F Smith Jr. [Joseph Fielding Smith] were opposed to the change. This action will be approved especially by the women."

[119] Lute to JRC, 5 Sept. 1920; *C*, 436.

[120] *Proceedings before the Committee ...*, passim, in Clarkana; also Jay R. Lowe, "Fred T. Dubois, Foe of the Mormons: A Study of the Role of Fred T. Dubois in the Senate Investigation of the Hon. Reed Smoot and the Mormon Church, 1903-1907," M.A. thesis, Brigham Young University, 1960; Alan Elmo Haynes, "Brigham Henry Roberts and Reed Smoot: Significant Events in the Development of American Pluralism," M.A. thesis, Catholic University of America, 1966, iii-vi, 40-74; Shipps, "Utah Comes of Age Politically," 92-99; M. Paul Holsinger, "Philander C. Knox and the Crusade Against Mormonism, 1904-1907," *Western Pennsylvania Magazine* 51 (Jan. 1969): 47-56; Holsinger, "For God and the American Home: The Attempt to Unseat Senator Reed Smoot, 1903-1907," *Pacific Northwest Quarterly* 60 (July 1969): 154-60; David Brudnoy, "Of Sinners and Saints: Theodore Schroeder, Brigham Roberts, and Reed Smoot," *Journal of Church and State* 14 (Spring 1972): 261-78; Gary James Bergera, "Secretary to the Senator: Carl A. Badger and the Smoot Hearings," *Sunstone* 8 (Jan.-Apr. 1983): 36-41; Richard O. Cowan, *The Church in the Twentieth Century* (Salt Lake City: Bookcraft, 1985), 29-31; *T*, 16-27; Church Educational System, *Church History in the Fulness of Times* (Salt Lake City: Church of Jesus Christ of Latter-day Saints, 1989), 467-70; Allen and Leonard, *The Story of the Latter-day Saints*, 444-47.

[121] *C*, 435.

[122] JRC to Preston D. Richards, 21 Mar. 1915, box 345, JRCP, with my addition of question marks.

[123] Preston D. Richards to JRC, 26 Mar. 1915, and JRC to Richards, 26 Mar. 1915, both in box 345, JRCP. *C*, 438, dismissed this proposal as "a fantastic scheme" without noting the church president's serious interest in it.

[124] *C*, 438.

[125] *C*, 434-35; Joseph Lynn Lyon, "Word of Wisdom," in *EM* 4:1584-85.

[126] JRC conversation with Mathonihah Thomas, 1914.

[127] JRC memorandum, "Knowledge and Belief"; partly quoted in *C*, 431.

[128] JRC memorandum, "Are We Not Only Entitled but Expected to Think for Ourselves?" box 90, JRCP; partly quoted in *C,* 433; "Man's Free Agency," in James E. Talmage, *The Articles of Faith: A Series of Lectures on the Principal Doctrines of the Church of Jesus Christ of Latter-day Saints … Written by Appointment; and Published by the Church* (Salt Lake City: Deseret News, 1899), 54-57; "Agency," in Bruce R. McConkie, *Mormon Doctrine,* 2d ed. (Salt Lake City: Bookcraft, 1966), 26-28; David Bohn, "Freedom," in *EM* 2:525.

[129] JRC memorandum #3, fd J9, box 90, JRCP.

[130] *D&C* 76:57-58, 132:20; Smith, et al., *History of the Church,* 6:306; Joseph Fielding Smith, ed., *Teachings of the Prophet Joseph Smith …* (Salt Lake City: Deseret News Press, 1938), 346; McConkie, *Mormon Doctrine,* 577; Richard C. Galbraith, ed., *Scriptural Teachings of the Prophet Joseph Smith …* (Salt Lake City: Deseret Book, 1993), 391; Quinn, *Early Mormonism and the Magic World View,* 233, 299.

[131] JRC memorandum #20, fd J9, box 90, JRCP.

[132] JRC to Leroy W. Morris, 17 June 1952, fd 5, box 386, JRCP. This made no specific reference to his own crisis of faith, nor did JRC claim the quoted statement was original to him: "Someone used the simile of which I am very fond."

[133] JRC to Cloyd H. Marvin, 1 Dec. 1956, binder of JRC-Marvin correspondence, box 189, JRCP; originals of JRC letters in Marvin papers, Archives, George Washington University, Washington, D.C.

[134] JRC to Cloyd H. Marvin, 9 Dec. 1959, emphasis in original.

[135] JRC talk in young men's portion of Mutual Improvement Associations conference, 9 June 1934, transcript, box 151, JRCP; remarks paraphrased in *DN,* 9 June 1934, 1.

[136] JRC to Mrs. Harold M. Stephens, 4 Nov. 1960, fd 13, box 409, JRCP; JRC to Cloyd H. Marvin, 1 Dec. 1956; *C,* 445. Contrast Reuben's concept of personal faith with "Testimony" in *EM* 4:1741: "It reaches beyond secondhand assent, notional conviction, or strong belief."

[137] *Conf,* Apr. 1950, 182; JRC to Jesse R. S. Budge, 15 Oct. 1953, fd 3, box 390, JRCP.

[138] JRC to meeting of general authorities, 4 Oct. 1956, transcript, 3, box 151, JRCP.

[139] *C,* 414-18; *U,* 160. In anticipation of serving in the U.S. Senate, Reuben specified his political views in several publications in 1922, in *SA,* 333-64.

[140] Lute to JRC, 6 Jan. 1923.

[141] Lute to JRC, 14 Jan. 1923, fd 3, box 333, JRCP.

[142] Lute to JRC, 24 Apr. 1923 (first quote), 3 Apr. 1923 (second quote), 25 Apr. 1923 (widow), 5 Mar. 1923 (re-marriage), 14 Mar. 1923 ("refinement"), 17 Mar. 1923 (last quote), 29 Apr. 1923 (anniversary), all in fd 1, box 333, JRCP.

[143] Lute to JRC, 9 Apr. 1923, first letter of that date; *C,* 442.

[144] JRC diary, 27 May 1923, JRCP.

[145] *C,* 360.

[146] Carl S. Hawkins, "Professional Service as a Christian Ministry," *Clark*

Memorandum (Fall 1999): 11. The *Memorandum* is a publication of the BYU law school.

[147] Lute to JRC, 17 July 1923 (first quote), 21 July 1923 (second quote), fd 1, box 333, JRCP.

[148] JRC sermon manuscript, box 114, JRCP.

[149] JRC sermons and talks, boxes 114 and 115, JRCP; Washington, D.C., Branch sacrament meeting minutes (1923-30).

[150] JRC talk to Deseret Sunday School Union, 6 Oct. 1947, transcript, box 151, JRCP: "The bulk of the work which I did in the Church ... was as a teacher in the Sunday Schools," with reference to classes he taught, including the adult class in 1923-25. See course outlines in box 115, JRCP; also *C*, 444.

[151] "Thousands Attend M.I.A. Jubilee Sessions," *DN*, 8 June 1925, 2; *C*, 444.

[152] JRC talks and sermons, box 115, JRCP.

[153] JRC to Fred Morris Dearing, 23 Apr. 1925, box 343, JRCP; quoted in *C*, 387.

[154] William W. Johnson, *Heroic Mexico: The Violent Emergence of a Modern Nation* (Garden City, NY: Doubleday, 1968); Ronald Atkin, *Revolution! Mexico, 1910-20* (New York: John Day, 1970); Robert F. Smith, *The United States and Revolutionary Nationalism in Mexico, 1916-32* (Chicago: University of Chicago Press, 1972); John W. F. Dulles, *Yesterday in Mexico: A Chronicle of the Revolution, 1919-36* (Austin: University of Texas Press, 1961).

[155] *C*, 451-75.

[156] *C*, 476-502; *SI*, 287-308; also Dulles, *Yesterday in Mexico*, 329; George Philip, *Oil and Politics in Latin America: Nationalist Movements and State Companies* (Cambridge, Eng.: Cambridge University Press, 1982), 39, for reference to JRC in 1928.

[157] *C*, 420-23; also *J. Reuben Clark for Senator of the United States from Utah* (Salt Lake City: Campaign Committee, 1928) and *Republican Leadership for Utah* (Salt Lake City: [JRC Campaign Committee], 1928). The latter pamphlet began its bio of JRC with the words: "Candidate for United States Senator from Utah, Subject to Republican State Convention, August 16th," and ended with italicized words: *Nominate and Elect Him*. These pre-convention pamphlets are in LDSL.

[158] JRC "Daily Summaries of Conversations," vol. 2 (1928-29), 29 Oct. 1928, JRCP, regarding previous day (Sunday, 28 October).

[159] Reed Smoot diary, 29 Oct. 1928, in *I*, 694, as follow-up to "Rueben [*sic*] Clark" on 27 October, p. 693. Smoot usually misspelled Reuben's name, which Heath's edition sometimes corrected.

[160] Concerning Reuben's appointment, Smoot mentioned something about which I have no other information: "The Secy to the President telephoned to me telling me the action of Sen [William] Borah [of Idaho] in Executive Session asking that the President return to the Senate the nomination of Rueben [sic] Clark as Under Secy of State as some woman had made serious charges against Clark. I was told by Sanders the Secy that it was too late as Clark had taken the oath of office and was sworn in. I talked with Borah and he said he knew nothing about it but [was] requested by Sen [George] Norris [a Republican] to do it. I asked him

[what] the charges were and he handed me a letter from the woman addressed to Senator Norris [of Nebraska]. I phoned Clark and told him to prepare an answer to same that I could use in executive session when the question came up. He stated he would do so." See Reed Smoot diary, 31 Jan. 1929, in *I*, 534. Heath noted (534n3): "This incident was not mentioned in Fox's biography. He may have felt it unimportant or perhaps no documents were found to shed additional light on the incident."

[161] Lee H. Burke, "J. Reuben Clark, Jr.: Under Secretary of State," *BYU Studies* 13 (Spring 1973): 396-409; Michael Elvin Christensen, "The Renunciation of Domination: A Study into the Origins of the Clark Memorandum," M.S. thesis, Utah State University, 1973; *C*, 503-30; also *SI*, 371-80; Bemis, *The Latin American Policy of the United States,* 220-21, 222, 260, 272-73; Federico G. Gil, *Latin American-United States Relations* (New York: Harcourt Brace Jovanovich, 1971), 80-81.

[162] *C*, 520-21, 687; also Bemis, *The Latin American Policy of the United States* (New York: Harcourt, Brace, 1943), 222; Robert H. Ferrell, "Repudiation of a Repudiation," *Journal of American History* 51 (Mar. 1965): 669-73; Gene A. Sessions, "The Clark Memorandum Myth," *The Americas* 34 (July 1977): 40-58.

[163] *C*, 531-35. Aside from BYU's collection, carbon copies of Dwight Morrow's letters and JRC originals are available in the Morrow papers, College Archives, Robert Frost Library, Amherst College, Amherst, Massachusetts.

[164] JRC to John J. Esch, 21 July 1930, box 30, JRCP.

[165] JRC memorandum, 5 Sept. 1931, box 131; *C*, 409.

[166] *C*, 536-38.

[167] Susa Young Gates to JRC, 31 July 1930 and JRC to SYG, 6 Sept. 1930, both in fd R3, box 35, JRCP. Her report seems strange in light of Smoot's diary entry that the president would "appoint Rueben [sic] Clark as Ambassador to Mexico if possible." See Smoot diary, 18-21 Feb. 1930, in *I*, 721. It is possible that Smoot did not want to promote rumors, but in view of their mutual antagonism, it is likely that he tried to undermine Reuben's appointment.

[168] *C*, 540-84; also "Principal Diplomatic Agents, March 4, 1789-January 1, 1931," in *Register of the Department of State, January 1, 1931* (Washington, D.C.: Government Printing Office, 1931), 321-37, for list of ambassadors. One had been serving for three decades.

[169] *C*, 521, 541, 549, 551-52, 583 (quote from Mexico City's *Excelsior*, 9 Nov. 1932).

[170] JRC to Ira C. Bennett, undated, box 35, JRCP, quoted in *C*, 537.

[171] *C*, 541, 579-80.

[172] JRC office diary, 8 Jan. 1943; also versions in *Improvement Era* 36 (Sept. 1933): 674; David O. McKay office diary, 11 May 1960, LDSA; JRC remarks to temple meeting of First Presidency and Quorum of Twelve, 27 Apr. 1961, transcript, box 264, JRCP; *C*, 409.

[173] *C*, 550. In the midst of the Great Depression, $800,000 was a staggering amount equal to more than $10 million today. I rely on Fox but am skeptical that even a collection of the finest wines had this value in 1930.

[174] *C*, 580 (quote concerning cigarettes). Clark's annual budget included cigars. See his account book for the embassy (1932-33), fd R46, box 45a, JRCP.

[175] JRC to S. Wayne Clark, 23 Aug. 1943, fd 1, box 367, JRCP; also based on an interview with JRC's daughter Luacine. *C*, 436, summarized this.

[176] Clarkana includes William F. Montavon, *The Facts Concerning the Mexican Problem* (Washington, D.C.: National Catholic Welfare Conference, 1926); Montavon, *Religious Crisis in Mexico* (Washington, D.C.: National Catholic Welfare Conference, 1926); Montavon, *Religious Persecution in Mexico: The Verdict of the Mexican Press* (Washington, D.C.: National Catholic Welfare Conference, 1927); Ernesto Galarza, *The Roman Catholic Church as a Factor in the Political and Social History of Mexico* (Sacramento, CA: Capital Press, 1928); Emilio Portes Gil (Attorney General of Mexico), *The Conflict Between the Civil Power and the Clergy: Historical and Legal Essay* (Mexico City: Press of the Ministry of Foreign Affairs, 1935); see also G. Baez Camargo and Kenneth G. Grubb, *Religion in the Republic of Mexico* (London: World Dominion Press, 1935); Charles S. Macfarland, *Chaos in Mexico: The Conflict of Church and State* (New York: Harper and Brothers, 1935), esp. 246; Robert E. Quirk, *The Mexican Revolution and the Catholic Church, 1910-1929* (Westport, CT: Greenwood Press, 1986).

[177] Luacine S. Clark diary, 16 Nov. 1930-Feb. 1933, JRCP.

[178] JRC to J. R. Bost, 22 July 1932, fd R17, box 40, JRCP.

[179] Luacine S. Clark diary, 4 Jan., 1 Mar., 16 Aug. 1931.

[180] Luacine S. Clark diary, 4 Apr., 16 Aug. 1931, 12 Feb. 1933.

[181] JRC ("Hubpop") to Lute, undated, 1930 fd, box 335, JRCP.

[182] *C*, 569.

[183] Heber J. Grant letters to JRC, fd 3, box 334, JRCP; JRC to Anthony W. Ivins, 9 Feb. 1931, Ivins papers, Utah State Historical Society, Salt Lake City; Luacine S. Clark diary, 18 Aug. 1932, 12 Feb. 1933.

[184] Examples in Luacine S. Clark diary, 23 Nov., 14, 28 Dec. 1930, 18 Jan., 25 Jan., 8 Feb. (leather riding suit), 15 Feb., 15, 22 Mar., 17, 24 May, 7, 21 June, 5, 19, 26 July, 9, 23 Aug., 25 Oct., 15 Nov., 13 Dec. 1931, 2 Jan., 31 July 1932.

[185] Luacine S. Clark diary, 1, 15 Feb., 8 Mar., 12 July, 30 Aug., 6 Sept., 1 Nov., 8 Nov., 22 Nov., 29 Nov., 27 Dec. 1931, with references to "Ace Duce."

[186] Luacine S. Clark diary, 15 Nov. 1931.

[187] Luacine S. Clark, "Old Mexico," *Relief Society Magazine* 18 (Oct. 1931): 549-53; Luacine S. Clark, "Christmas in Old Mexico," *Relief Society Magazine* 18 (Dec. 1931): 681-82, with reference to Christmas 1930; cf. "Index to Relief Society Magazine, Volumes 1-19 (1914-1932)," bound typescript, LDSL.

[188] JRC to J. Reuben Clark III, 23 May 1929, box 335, JRCP.

[189] JRC to Ivor Sharp, undated, in box 335, JRCP; also *C*, 445.

[190] Clyde J. Williams, "Standard Works," in *EM* 3:1415-16.

[191] JRC to John A. Widtsoe, 8 Dec. 1929, box 27, JRCP.

[192] George D. Parkinson, "How a Utah Boy Won His Way," *Improvement Era* 17 (Apr. 1914): 557.

[193] Lute to JRC, 15 Aug. 1918, fd 1, box 332, JRCP; *C*, 438.

[194] "Ten Thousand Hear Clark's Analysis of League," and "Here's Text of

Maj. Clark's Speech on League of Nations," *The Salt Lake Herald*, 3 Sept. 1919, 1; "The Clark Lecture," editorial, *The Salt Lake Herald*, 4 Sept. 1919, 6; James B. Allen, "J. Reuben Clark, Jr. on American Sovereignty and International Organization," *BYU Studies* 13 (Spring 1973): 347-72; Allen, "Personal Faith and Public Policy: Some Timely Observations on the League of Nations Controversy in Utah," *BYU Studies* 14 (Autumn 1973): 83-98; *C*, 279-98 (work against Versailles Treaty and speech writer for Senator Knox of Pennsylvania), 293-95 (role in Utah's League controversy); also *SI*, 167-91, 209-12.

[195] JRC diary, 18, 28 June 1920.

[196] Brigham H. Roberts, *A Comprehensive History of the Church ...* 6 vols. (Salt Lake City: The Church of Jesus Christ of Latter-day Saints, 1930), 6:636-68; Truman G. Madsen, *Defender of the Faith: The B. H. Roberts Story* (Salt Lake City: Bookcraft, 1980), 241-68; *T*, 11; Gary James Bergera, ed., *The Autobiography of B. H. Roberts* (Salt Lake City: Signature Books, 1990), 212-19; Bitton, "The Exclusion of B. H. Roberts from Congress," in Bitton, *The Ritualization of Mormon History and Other Essays* (Urbana: University of Illinois Press, 1994), 150-70.

[197] JRC to Heber J. Grant, 24 May 1922, box 344, JRCP, and in box 24, CR 1/44, LDSA.

[198] Ronald W. Walker, "Crisis in Zion: Heber J. Grant and the Panic of 1893," *Arizona and the West* 21 (Autumn 1979): 257-78; Walker, "Heber J. Grant and the Utah Loan and Trust Company," *JMH* 8 (1981): 21-36; Walker, "Heber J. Grant: Entrepreneur Extraordinary," in Thomas G. Alexander and John F. Bluth, eds., *The Twentieth Century American West* (Provo, UT: Charles Redd Center for Western Studies, Brigham Young University, 1983), 104; Walker, "Heber J. Grant," in Arrington, *The Presidents of the Church*, 243-44, 245.

[199] Heber J. Grant to JRC, 8 June 1922, box 24, CR 1/44.

[200] JRC church document #9, box 114, JRCP.

[201] See previous notes 106-110, 112.

[202] "Utah Will Be for Coolidge," *SLT*, 10 May 1924, 7; also in the next election, "Reuben Clark Urges Utah to Retain Smoot," *SLT*, 2 Nov. 1932, 18.

[203] Folder N5, box 29, JRCP; JRC to Heber J. Grant and David O. McKay, 18 May 1936, fd 1, box 355, JRCP, also in JRC fd, CR 1/48, LDSA; Heber J. Grant journal, 2 Feb. 1926.

[204] *Conf*, Apr. 1926, 11.

[205] *Conf*, Oct. 1930, 97.

[206] S. J. Quinney to JRC, 19 May 1931, fd 13, box 39, JRCP.

[207] JRC to S. J. Quinney, 27 May 1931, fd 13, box 39.

[208] Heber J. Grant journal sheets, 21 May 1931; also N. Eldon Tanner, "The Administration of the Church," *Ensign* 9 (Nov. 1979): 44, on voting for a new apostle.

[209] Heber J. Grant journal sheets, 29 May, 1 Oct. 1931; *E*, 672-73.

[210] Reed Smoot diary, 28 May 1925, in *I*, 599. For clarity I changed Smoot's first-person references to third-person.

[211] *E*, 711, 721, for biographical details on Wells and Young; *EM* 4:1678 (for dates of service).

212 Related by Heber J. Grant to his granddaughter's husband, Waldo M. Anderson. Anderson to Rowena J. Miller, 31 Jan. 1961, with comment by JRC to his secretary, typescript, fd 1, box 410, JRCP; also *C,* 446.

213 Louise Clark Bennion and Marianne Clark Sharp interview by D. Michael Quinn, 7 Nov. 1977; also *C,* 580.

214 Heber J. Grant and Anthony W. Ivins to JRC, 19 Dec. 1931, JRC fd, CR 1/48. JRC referred to his foreknowledge of the letter's contents in Spencer W. Kimball diary, 4 July 1960, private possession.

215 Marianne C. Sharp, "Born to Greatness: The Story of President J. Reuben Clark, Jr.," *Children's Friend* 53 (Sept. 1954): 362.

216 Composite quotes from JRC to Mrs. Levi Edgar Young, 23 Feb. 1938, attached to JRC letter to Heber J. Grant and David O. McKay, 23 Feb. 1938, JRC fd, CR 1/48; JRC to Oscar R. Houston, 4 Mar. 1957, fd 1, box 399, JRCP.

217 JRC to Heber J. Grant and Anthony W. Ivins, 19 [*sic*] Dec. 1931, JRC fd, CR 1/48. Clark was dealing with the Rio Grande River boundary where it passed through El Paso's Chamizal District. He achieved a tentative agreement, but not finality, in August 1932. See Dulles, *Yesterday in Mexico,* 594-96; *C,* 133, 552-54, 563-64, 576-79.

218 Louise Clark Bennion, Marianne Clark Sharp, and J. Reuben Clark III interview by D. Michael Quinn, 7 Nov. 1977; Joseph Anderson, *Prophets I Have Known* (Salt Lake City: Deseret Book, 1973), 90; Marianne Clark Sharp 1977 oral history, 42.

In 1977 Reuben III called his father "The Great Sphinx." He told another interviewer: "We knew better than to try and pump him. I don't think any of his kids were smart enough to wheedle anything out of him. If he wanted to tell you, he would volunteer it; if he didn't want to tell you, no amount of questioning would ever have elicited any information." See J. Reuben Clark III oral history, 1982, typescript, 13, HBLL.

219 JRC to Heber J. Grant and Anthony W. Ivins, 28 Dec. 1931, folded like accompanying letter and memorandum, JRC fd, CR 1/48. By contrast, *SR,* 8, claimed that Clark received the letter "by mail just before Christmas in 1931" and "accepted the call immediately."

220 Anthony W. Ivins diary, 2 Jan. 1932, Utah State Historical Society; A. W. Ivins to Heber J. Grant, 2 Jan. 1932, JRC fd, CR 1/48.

221 JRC to Heber J. Grant, 9 Jan. 1932, JRC fd, CR 1/48; also Philip, *Oil and Politics in Latin America,* 211, for reference to JRC in 1932.

222 Heber J. Grant to JRC, 4 Mar. 1932, JRC fd, CR 1/48; JRC to Heber J. Grant, 11 Mar. 1932, JRC fd, CR 1/48; JRC to Anthony W. Ivins, 11 Mar. 1932, Ivins papers.

223 Related by JRC in Spencer W. Kimball diary, 4 July 1960; also Heber J. Grant journal sheets, 9 Mar. 1932. It is the perspective of the LDS hierarchy's gerontocracy that a sixty-year-old is "a young man." See discussion in D. Michael Quinn, "From Sacred Grove to Sacral Power Structure," *Dial* 17 (Summer 1984): 31-34.

224 JRC to Heber J. Grant and A. W. Ivins, 11 Mar., 20 June 1932, JRC fd, CR 1/48.

225 JRC to A.W. Ivins, 28 Aug. 1932, Ivins papers.

226 JRC to "Dear Brethren," 16 Dec. 1932, Ivins papers; also *C*, 581-82; text of his farewell speech in *SI*, 309-11.

227 JRC to Louis S. Cates, 4 May 1932, fd R17, box 40, JRCP.

228 "Church Officials Make Statement Regarding Election," *DN*, 29 Oct. 1932, 1.

229 "Grant Declares Election Stand," *Salt Lake Telegram,* 3 Nov. 1932, 1, which reprinted an interview Grant gave to the Ogden newspaper.

230 E. C. Davies to JRC, 12 Jan. 1933, box 336, JRCP; Marianne C. Sharp ("Mem") to JRC, 12 Mar. 1933, box 336, JRCP.

231 *Austin Statesman,* 16 Feb. 1933, in JRC scrapbook.

232 "Reuben Clark Back in S.L. after Years: Former Ambassador to Mexico Returns to Civil Life," *SLT,* 19 Mar. 1933, B-10.

233 Heber J. Grant journal sheets, 20 Mar. 1933; also "J. Reuben Clark Welcomed Home with Reception," *DN*, 21 Mar. 1933, 8.

234 *Deseret News 1999-2000 Church Almanac* (Salt Lake City: Deseret News, 1998), 436-37 (organized stakes as of 1933), 552 (LDS membership).

235 Louise Clark Bennion, Marianne Clark Sharp, and J. Reuben Clark III interview by D. Michael Quinn, 7 Nov. 1977, for what their father told them. They humorously noted that this was the inscription above the gates of Hell in Dante's *Inferno*.

NOTES TO CHAPTER 2

1 *D&C* 47:15.

2 JRC to Deseret Sunday School Union, 6 Oct. 1947, typescript, box 151, JRCP.

3 Marion G. Romney oral history, 1976, typescript, 14, LDSA; Spencer W. Kimball interview by D. Michael Quinn, 2 Feb. 1979.

4 Frank W. Asper to JRC, 5 Aug. 1939, fd 1, box 361, JRCP.

5 "I feel you won't consider this at all, feeling your way is best. I only tell you this hoping you may get some one's viewpoint besides your own" (Lute to JRC, 15 May 1923, fd 1, box 333, JRCP).

6 JRC to Frank and Gertrude Clark, 17 Nov. 1953, fd 5, box 388, JRCP.

7 JRC to W. Paul Chipman, 8 Mar. 1956, fd 1, box 396, JRCP.

8 Examples in JRC office diary, 13 Feb. 1935, 5; 24 Apr. 1936, 2; 8 July 1940; 17 July 1940; JRCP.

9 JRC office diary, 23 Nov. 1949.

10 JRC to Mrs. B. H. Stradling, 27 Dec. 1949 (quote), fd 4, box 379, JRCP; Marion G. Romney interview by D. Michael Quinn, 26 Oct. 1977 (JRC's gruff tone).

11 JRC office diary, 10 July 1939.

[12] JRC to "Brother and Sister" Reynold Irwin, 2 Mar. 1956, fd 2, box 397, JRCP.

[13] JRC office diary, 2 July 1948. David O. McKay also stated this in "Teaching is Best by Example," *CN*, 11 June 1952, 3.

[14] "Elder Lee Pays Tribute to a Great Leader," *CN*, 14 Oct. 1961, 14.

[15] JRC to Frank R. Clark, 1 June 1945, fd 3, box 371, JRCP.

[16] Ernest L. Wilkinson diary, 17 Apr. 1960, photocopy, JWML. Henry D. Moyle made this statement while he and JRC were in the First Presidency. The apostle was Mark E. Petersen.

[17] JRC office diary, 7 Mar. 1947.

[18] JRC office diary, 24 May 1933.

[19] JRC office diary, 19 Apr. 1950.

[20] *Conf*, Apr. 1940, 14.

[21] JRC to Frank H. Jonas, 17 Aug. 1943, fd 2, box 411, JRCP; also Jonas papers, JWML.

[22] This statement was in the 1983 book published by BYU Press.

[23] Marion G. Romney diary, 18 Nov. 1952, private possession.

[24] Ernest L. Wilkinson diary, 30 Mar. 1956.

[25] Rowena J. Miller to Mrs. Robert F. Bird, 20 Mar. 1950, fd 2, box 381, JRCP.

[26] Related by several general authorities to John K. Edmunds, former president of the Chicago Stake and of the Salt Lake temple (Edmunds oral history, 1979-80, typescript, vol. 2:102, LDSA).

[27] JRC to Richard R. Lyman, 31 Oct. 1933, box 349, JRCP.

[28] JRC to Franklin S. Harris, 5 Nov. 1931, box 38, JRCP.

[29] JRC to bishops' meeting, 5 Apr. 1949, typescript, box 151, JRCP.

[30] Heber J. Grant journal sheets, 8 Apr. 1933, LDSA.

NOTES TO CHAPTER 3

[1] *D&C* 107:22

[2] Heber J. Grant journal sheets, 20 Mar. 1933, LDSA; "Utah Republicans Welcome Hoover," *DN*, 20 Mar. 1933, sec. II, 1.

[3] *Conf*, Apr. 1933, 102.

[4] Heber J. Grant to John A. Widtsoe, 20 Mar. 1936, box 97, CR 1/44, LDSA.

[5] Lester V. Chandler, *America's Greatest Depression, 1929-1941* (New York: Harper and Row, 1970), 34.

[6] *B*, 338-39.

[7] See William E. Leuchtenburg, *Franklin D. Roosevelt and the New Deal, 1932-1940* (New York: Harper and Row, 1963).

[8] Heber J. Grant journal sheets, 7 Aug. 1940.

[9] Heber J. Grant journal sheets, 2 Nov. 1920: "It is amusing for me to pose as a Democrat, and when I come to vote at our State and National elections divide my vote for a larger number of Republicans than Democrats"; also *E*, 336.

[10] Heber J. Grant to Morton J. Theiband, 21 Nov. 1936, box 96, CR 1/44; Heber J. Grant journal sheets, 8 Nov. 1938; also *D*, 283.

[11] *E*, 332, 338, 343, 347, also 663 (summary and chronology of Anthony W. Ivins's activities in the Democratic Party); *D*, 261, 282.

[12] Ronald W. Walker, "Crisis in Zion: Heber J. Grant and the Panic of 1893," *Arizona and the West* 21 (Autumn 1979): 257-78; Walker, "Heber J. Grant and the Utah Loan and Trust Company," *JMH* 8 (1981): 21-36; Walker, "Heber J. Grant: Entrepreneur Extraordinary," in Thomas G. Alexander and John F. Bluth, eds., *The Twentieth Century American West* (Provo, UT: Charles Redd Center for Western Studies, Brigham Young University, 1983), 104; Walker, "Heber J. Grant," in Leonard J. Arrington, ed., *The Presidents of the Church: Biographical Essays* (Salt Lake City: Deseret Book, 1986), 243-44, 245.

[13] JRC to J. C. Grey (editor of the *New York Sun*), 20 Oct. 1941, fd 1, box 363, JRCP. Reuben's comment about praying "hermits" was a reference to the monastic life of Roman Catholicism.

[14] JRC to Bryant S. Hinckley, 20 Sept. 1956, fd 6, box 395, JRCP; "Pres. Clark Notes 88th Anniversary," *DN*, 1 Sept. 1959, A-1.

[15] "Holders Here Get Brazilian Bond Aid: J. R. Clark Says New Plan, in Effect in April, Will Add Millions to Annual Interest ... Tells State Department of the Recent Negotiations in Rio," *NYT*, 25 Feb. 1934, sec. II, 7; "World Court Foes See War Peril in It," *NYT*, 17 May 1934, 1 (JRC testimony to U.S. Senate); "Reich Debt Parley Comes to an End," *NYT*, 30 May 1934, 9; "Dominican Bonds Are Re-amortized," *NYT*, 17 Aug. 1934, 1; "Governor and J. R. Clark Say Policy Holders Oppose Any Centralized Regulation," *NYT*, 16 Dec. 1939, 10; *C*, 598, 600.

[16] JRC fd of correspondence, Post-Presidential Individual File, Hoover Presidential Library, West Branch, Iowa; JRC memorandum, 14 Sept. 1944, fd 5, box 370, JRCP; also the *New York Sun*, 4 June 1934, in JRC scrapbook, JRCP; James W. Gerard (former ambassador to Germany) telegrams to JRC, 11 Apr., 14, 29 Oct. 1947, fds 1 and 5, box 376, JRCP; "Gerard Calls Pact Bar to Early War," *NYT*, 7 May 1949, 4; Cloyd H. Marvin correspondence, box 189, JRCP; also JRC originals in Marvin papers, Archives, George Washington University, Washington, D.C.

[17] JRC scrapbook.

[18] William H. Ryan (editor of *Sunday New York Journal American*) to JRC, 6 Oct. 1937, fd 1, box 357, JRCP.

[19] JRC office diary, 17 Apr. 1933, JRCP.

[20] Francis M. Gibbons, *Heber J. Grant: Man of Steel, Prophet of God* (Salt Lake City: Deseret Book, 1979), 26-27; Walker, "Heber J. Grant: Entrepreneur Extraordinary," 88, 92, 94-95.

[21] JRC office diary, 17 Apr. 1933.

[22] JRC office diary, 18 Feb. 1958; "Pres. Clark Retires as Insurance Director," *DN*, 18 July 1958, B-1; boxes 433-39, JRCP; *H*, 326-27, 381; *L*, 139: "In turn, President Clark had begun to regard Harold B. Lee as a protégé and almost as a son."

[23] JRC scrapbook; JRC office diary; JRC 1933 memorandum book, JRCP.

[24] JRC office diary, Apr.–June 1933.

[25] JRC office diary, 3 May 1933.

[26] JRC office diary, 22, 24 May 1933; *M* 5:315-30.

[27] JRC office diary, 23 June 1933.

[28] Heber J. Grant journal sheets, 20 July 1933.

[29] JRC office diary, 28 Aug., 31 Aug. 1933.

[30] JRC office diary, 1 Sept. 1933.

[31] JRC office diary, 12 Sept. 1933. For the National Recovery Administration (NRA), see *EA* 19:777-78; Leuchtenburg, *Franklin D. Roosevelt and the New Deal.*

[32] JRC office diary, 13 Sept. 1933.

[33] JRC office diary, 22-25 Sept. 1933.

[34] *C*, 36.

[35] JRC office diary, 25 Sept. 1933.

[36] *C*, 586; JRC office diary, 25 Sept. 1933 onward.

[37] *Conf,* Oct. 1933, 64-65, 89; cf. chapters 8, 12.

Reuben acknowledged two enormous problems with industrial capitalism and the modern system of free enterprise. First was the exploitation of workers. Second was the enormous disparity between society's rich and financially comfortable versus its financially struggling and impoverished. In response to the first problem, he suggested the need for Constitutional amendments to protect workers and support labor unions. In response to the second problem, he advocated charitable service by churches and other voluntary associations while he steadfastly opposed any actions by government, local or national, to aid the poor.

[38] Gibbons, *Heber J. Grant,* 198.

[39] JRC office diary, 13 Oct. 1933 onward.

[40] JRC to Samuel O. Bennion, 8 Nov. 1937, fd 1, box 356, JRCP; *C*, 586.

[41] "Plan to Aid Bondholders Outlined," *NYT,* 21 Oct. 1933, 25; "Clark to Leave on Saturday to Take New Post," *SLT,* 27 Oct. 1933, 22.

[42] "To Head Bond Group: J. R. Clark to Be Acting President of Foreign Holders' Council," *NYT,* 24 Feb. 1934, 22; "Heads Bond Protectors: J. Reuben Clark, Ex-ambassador Is Elected by Council," *NYT,* 3 May 1934, 32; *C*, 594-96; Gene A. Sessions, *Prophesying Upon the Bones: J. Reuben Clark and the Foreign Debt Crisis, 1933-39* (Urbana: University of Illinois Press, 1992); boxes 412-20, JRCP.

[43] Dana G. Munro, "Sweetening Sour Bond Issues," *World Affairs* 122 (Fall 1959): 81; also *SI*, 381-89.

[44] JRC to Orval W. Adams, 30 Oct. 1937, fd 1, box 356, JRCP; also Leonard J. Arrington, "Banking and Finance in Utah," in *U,* 31.

[45] Lute apparently had the same feelings toward Alice Taylor Sheets Smoot, a widow whom the senator-apostle had married in 1930 as a widower. Concerning "a very nice luncheon" of the general authority wives, she wrote about Sister Smoot's conduct during Lute's talk to the group: "Mrs. Smoot was so bored. She left before I finished. The only interest she showed was to say she sat by the President at the dinner we attended at the White House before leaving [for Mexico]."

See Lute to JRC, 8 Mar. 1935, box 336, JRCP; also Reed Smoot diary, 30 June 1930 (proposal to "Mrs. Sheets"), 2 July 1930 (marriage), 16 Nov. 1930 (dinner with Hoover and wife and "Ambassador and Mrs. J. Reuben Clark"), in *I*, 726, 740.

[46] *E*, 685-86 (summary and chronology of Stephen L Richards's activities in the Democratic Party).

[47] "Pres. Grant Calls upon Pres. Roosevelt at White House," *DN*, 4 Nov. 1933, 1; "L.D.S. Chapel Dedicated in U.S. Capital," *SLT*, 6 Nov. 1933, 16; Heber J. Grant journal sheets, 4-6 Nov. 1933; "Clark Chosen Pan-American Meet Delegate," *DN*, 10 Nov. 1933, 1; "Leaders in Church Speak at Opening of Capital Chapel," *CN*, 11 Nov. 1933, 1.

[48] JRC office diary, 9 Jan. 1934.

[49] JRC office diary, 14 Jan., 6, 7, 11, 12 Feb. 1934. For JRC activities at the Seventh Pan-American Conference, see Samuel Flagg Bemis, *The Latin American Policy of the United States: An Historical Interpretation* (New York: Harcourt, Brace), 274, 339 (JRC as "a plenipotentiary at the Montevideo Conference"), 433n26; *C*, 590-94; boxes 143-47, JRCP.

[50] JRC office diary, 6 Feb. 1934.

[51] JRC office diary, 15-17 Feb. 1934; also Bemis, *The Latin American Policy of the United States*, 339: "The president of the Council was J. Reuben Clark, Jr., former solicitor of the Department of State, whom we have met so often in this study."

[52] Lute to JRC, 23 Oct. 1934, box 336, JRCP.

[53] Folder labeled "Speeches, etc. (lists)" in box 302, JRCP.

[54] JRC to Samuel O. Bennion, 8 Nov. 1937.

[55] JRC office diary, 29 July 1933, 21 Feb., 4 Mar. 1934.

[56] Eugene E. Campbell and Richard D. Poll, *Hugh B. Brown: His Life and Thought* (Salt Lake City: Bookcraft, 1975), 107.

[57] JRC to J. H. Gipson, president of Caxton Printers, 11 Mar. 1954, fd 1, box 391, JRCP.

[58] JRC office diary, 5 Mar. 1934.

[59] Heber J. Grant journal sheets, 3 Apr. 1934.

[60] Heber J. Grant to JRC, 20 June 1934, JRC fd, CR 1/48, LDSA.

[61] Heber J. Grant journal sheets, 5 May 1934; also Noble Warrum to JRC, 7 May 1934, fd 1, box 351, JRCP. For his biographical sketch, see Warrum, *Utah Since Statehood*, 4 vols. (Chicago: S.J. Clarke Publishing, 1919), 3:1118 (not specifically identifying Warrum as non-LDS, but listing his membership in Utah's Masonic Lodge and Order of Elks, both of which Mormons declined to join). In the early 1890s, Warrum had been associated as a fellow Democrat with Grant in the operation of the *Salt Lake Herald*.

[62] "Presidents Grant and Clark Return," *DN*, 7 Mar. 1934, 2; JRC scrapbook.

[63] JRC to Noble Warrum, 21 May 1934, fd 1, box 351, JRCP.

[64] Harry Chandler to Heber J. Grant, 4 June 1934, and Albert A. Tilney to

Heber J. Grant, 5 June 1934, in JRC fd, CR 1/48; also *Who Was Who in America, Vol. 3* (Chicago: A.N. Marquis, 1960), 1,241.

[65] "Clark Silent about Senate Race Rumors," *The Salt Lake Telegram*, 2 June 1934, 1.

[66] "Clark Silence Is Interpreted as Acceptance," *The Salt Lake Telegram*, 12 June 1934, [13].

[67] JRC to Heber J. Grant, 17 June 1934, 1:52 a.m., JRC fd, CR 1/48; "Clark Gives Position on Nomination," *SLT,* 18 June 1934, 16; "Pres. Clark Refuses to Be Candidate," *DN,* 18 June 1934, [9]. By the time the telegram was received, the morning newspapers were already in print. At this time the *DN,* an evening newspaper, did not have a Sunday edition.

[68] "Pres. Clark Refuses to Be Candidate," *DN,* 18 June 1934, [9]; "Clark Refuses to Run in Utah, *NYT,* 19 June 1934, 21; Heber J. Grant to Preston D. Richards, 18 June 1934, JRC fd, CR 1/48.

[69] JRC memorandum, "The Problem," 18 July 1934, box 347, JRCP.

[70] Albert E. Bowen to JRC, 13 July 1934, box 347, JRCP.

[71] JRC memorandum, "The Problem," 18 July 1934.

[72] "Clark Gives Position on Nomination," *SLT,* 18 June 1934, 16 (quote); also Harry S. Joseph to JRC, 18 June 1934, box 347, JRCP, and in JRC fd, CR 1/48.

[73] JRC to J. Parley White, 2 July 1934, JRC fd, CR 1/48; also White's letter to JRC of 26 June and JRC to Harry S. Joseph, both in box 347 of Clark and in JRC fd of CR 1/48.

[74] JRC to Heber J. Grant, 4 July 1934, in three repositories: box 347, JRCP; JRC fd, CR 1/48; Manuscript A550, Utah State Historical Society, Salt Lake City. *C,* 597, overstated these as "letters of resignation from the First Presidency," whereas JRC asked for only a "furlough." The church president's letter was "to relieve you from your active duties" and not from the position itself.

[75] Heber J. Grant journal sheets, 9 July 1934; Grant to JRC, 9 July 1934 (quote), JRC fd, CR 1/48.

[76] Heber J. Grant journal sheets, 10 July 1934.

[77] *C,* 414–18, 420–23.

[78] JRC to Heber J. Grant, 13 July 1934, box 347, JRCP; JRC fd, CR 1/48.

[79] Robert Murray Stewart to JRC, 25 July 1934, fd 1, box 351, JRCP. Stewart was a son-in-law of Apostle George Albert Smith and one of JRC's staunch advocates for the 1934 nomination.

[80] JRC memorandum, "The Problem," 18 July 1934, with parentheses in original.

[81] John Gunther, *Inside U.S.A.* (New York: Harper and Brothers, 1947), 202. Gunther cited the counselor's son H. Grant Ivins on page 927 as a source. When asked about this telephone conversation with Anthony W. Ivins, Reuben replied in 1946 that "he did not remember any conversation with the authorities on his nomination to the Senate, he wrote some letters, but did not have any conversation" (JRC office diary, 19 Nov. 1946). This must have been a lapse of memory because Reuben definitely discussed his possible nomination with members of

the First Presidency in conversations on 5 March, 3 April, and 16 July 1934. If the Ivins-Clark telephone conversation occurred, it was a dramatic catalyst for the self-doubts JRC expressed in the memorandum.

[82] JRC memorandum, "The Problem," 18 July 1934.

[83] Transcript of telephone conversation between JRC and Heber J. Grant, 16 July 1934, JRC fd, CR 1/48; Heber J. Grant journal sheets, 16 July 1934; also JRC to Heber J. Grant, 13 July 1934, with "Received" stamp of 16 July 1934, JRC fd, CR 1/48.

[84] JRC to Byron D. Anderson, 17 July 1934, quoted in full in concurrent telegram of JRC to Heber J. Grant, 17 July 1934, 12:10 a.m., JRC fd, CR 1/48; "G.O.P. Names Slate at S.L. Convention," *SLT*, 19 July 1934, 6.

[85] "G.O.P. Names Slate at S.L. Convention," and "Friends Lose in Effort to Draft Clark," *SLT*, 19 July 1934, 6, 9; Doris F. Salmon, "Don Byron Colton," and John Sillito, "William Henry King," in *U*, 110, 303-04.

[86] Heber J. Grant journal sheets, 18 July 1934.

[87] "The Ticket and the Platform," editorial, *SLT*, 20 July 1934, 4.

[88] O. N. Malmquist, *The First 100 Years: A History of the Salt Lake Tribune, 1871-1971* (Salt Lake City: Utah State Historical Society, 1971), 227, 234-35, 237, 282-83, 291.

[89] JRC letter to S. Norman Lee, president of the Box Elder Stake, copy enclosed in JRC to John F. Fitzpatrick, 13 Oct. 1933, box 72, CR 1/44. Italics added.

[90] Heber J. Grant journal sheets, 9 July 1938, also 9 Nov. 1932; Malmquist, *The First 100 Years*, 295, 297, 384-85; John S. McCormick, "Salt Lake City," in *U*, 482; David Lawrence McKay, *My Father, David O. McKay*, ed. Lavina Fielding Anderson (Salt Lake City: Deseret Book, 1989), 214.

[91] John A. Widtsoe to JRC, 26 July 1934, fd 1, box 351, JRCP; also *E*, 715 (summary and chronology of Widtsoe's activities in the Republican Party).

[92] Heber J. Grant journal sheets, 2 June 1934.

[93] Heber J. Grant to JRC, 18 Oct. 1940, fd 7, box 362, JRCP.

[94] Heber J. Grant journal sheets, 9 June 1936, 17 June 1940; also *D*, 288.

[95] Franklin J. Murdock oral history, 1973, typescript, 52, LDSA.

[96] Heber J. Grant journal sheets, 12 Dec. 1941.

[97] Heber J. Grant journal sheets, 21 Sept. 1933, 4 Oct., 11 Oct. 1934.

[98] *O*, 167-68, 246-47, 250-54, 258, 260-61.

[99] *L*, 145 (first part of quote); *G*, 270-71 (second part of quote).

[100] *D*, 282.

[101] Heber J. Grant journal sheets, 31 Oct. 1934 (reference to Clark), 30 Oct. 1934 (reference to Ivins); and 18 October 1934, where Grant wrote that Democratic apostle "Stephen L. Richards said it was our fault that we have been talking about Joseph [J. Cannon]'s editorials not being satisfactory, and he [Richards] said he was ready to make a promotion to release him [as editor of the *DN*]. And finally, after some discussion, it was decided to do so and to appoint him President of the British Mission. I was very glad for this suggestion; it will be a very nice way to promote him."

[102] JRC office diary, 5 Mar. 1934.

[103] Heber J. Grant journal sheets, 28 July 1932.

[104] LeGrand Woolley to JRC, 17 Apr. 1935, attached to April 1935 conference binder, box 152, JRCP; *Conf,* Oct. 1934, 98; *Conf,* Apr. 1935, 95, for quotes.

[105] Clarkana has Alex Bittelman, *How Can We Share the Wealth? The Communist Way Versus Huey Long* (New York: Workers' Library Publishers, 1935); and Sender Garlin, *The Real Huey P. Long* (New York: Workers' Library Publishers, 1935). The Communist publishing houses often had *worker* in their names.

It seems significant that Clarkana does not include Long's famous *Share Our Wealth: Every Man a King,* but he had anti-Long publications by the American Communist Party. This indicates that Clark was interested only in the fact that Communists attacked him. See also Harnett T. Kane, *Louisiana Hayride: The American Rehearsal for Dictatorship, 1928-1940* (New York: W. Morrow, 1941); Reinhard H. Luthin, *American Demagogues: Twentieth Century* (Boston: Beacon Press, 1954); Allan P. Sindler, *Huey Long's Louisiana: State Politics, 1920-1952* (Baltimore: Johns Hopkins University Press, 1956); Edwin W. Green, *The Man Bilbo* (Baton Rouge: Louisiana State University Press, 1963); T. Harry Williams, *Huey Long* (New York: Alfred Knopf, 1970); and Alan Brinkley, *Voices of Protest: Huey Long, Father Coughlin, and the Great Depression* (New York: Alfred A. Knopf, 1982).

[106] *ER,* 2:622-23, for "Nazi" as the designation for the German acronym NSDAP which referred to the National Socialist German Workers Party; also "20,000 Nazi Allies Denounce Boycott," *NYT,* 18 May 1934, 3, with photo caption: "A General View of the Demonstration Held Last Night to Protest Against 'the Unconstitutional Jewish Boycott of Germany.' The Figures in the Aisles Are Ushers Who Wore the Uniform of the Nazi Storm Troopers Except for the Shirt, Which Was White Instead of Brown"; also Sander A. Diamond, *The Nazi Movement in the United States, 1924-1941* (Ithaca, NY: Cornell University Press, 1974).

[107] Gaetana Salvemini, *Italian Fascist Activities in the United States* (New York: Center for Migration Studies, 1977); Philip V. Cannistraro, *Black Shirts in Little Italy: Italian Americans and Fascism, 1921-1939* (West Lafayette, IN: Bordighera, 1999); also R. N. L. Absalom, *Mussolini and the Rise of Italian Fascism* (London: Methuen, 1969).

[108] Clarkana has A. B. Magil, *The Truth about Father Coughlin* (New York: Workers' Library Publishers, 1935); Magil, *The Real Father Coughlin* (New York: Workers' Library Publishers, 1939); General Jewish Council, *Father Coughlin, His "Facts" and Arguments* (New York City: American Jewish Committee, et al., 1939). Since Clark did not have any of Coughlin's publications, he seems to have been interested only in the fact that Jews and a Communist publisher attacked him. See also Charles J. Tull, *Father Coughlin and the New Deal* (Syracuse, NY: Syracuse University Press, 1965); Sheldon Marcus, *Father Coughlin: The Tumultuous Life of the Priest of the Little Flower* (Boston: Little, Brown, 1973); and Brinkley, *Voices of Protest.*

[109] Peter H. Buckingham, *America Sees Red: Anti-Communism in America,* 1870s to 1980s (Claremont, CA: Regina Books, 1988), 42-43.

[110] Jules Archer, *The Plot to Seize the White House* (New York: Hawthorne Books, 1973).

[111] Raymond Gram Swing, *Forerunners of American Fascism* (New York: J. Messner, 1935); Lawrence Dennis, *The Coming American Fascism* (New York: Harper and Brothers, 1936); Leuchtenburg, *Franklin D. Roosevelt and the New Deal,* 277-78; David H. Bennett, *Demagogues in the Depression: American Radicals and the Union Party* (New Brunswick, NJ: Rutgers University Press, 1969).

[112] "J. Reuben Clark Voices Defense of Constitution," *SLT,* 8 June 1935, 32.

[113] JRC to Heber J. Grant and David O. McKay, 18 May 1935, HJG and DOM to JRC, 21 May 1935, both in JRC fd, CR 1/48; also in fd U1, box 149 and fd 1, box 365, JRCP.

[114] JRC scrapbook; *C,* 586, 597; also George Philip, *Oil and Politics in Latin America: Nationalist Movements and State Companies* (Cambridge, Eng.: Cambridge University Press, 1982), 206-07, 208 (JRC activity with oil company).

[115] Lute to JRC, 28 May 1935, box 336, JRCP.

[116] Lute to JRC, 5 Nov. 1935, box 336, JRCP; also Douglas D. Alder, "The Mormon Ward: Congregation or Community?" *JMH* 5 (1978): 61-78.

[117] JRC scrapbook and office diary, September 1934, 15 June-11 July 1935.

[118] JRC to Monte L. Bean, 4 Mar. 1952, fd 2, box 385, JRCP. This may have referred to a Maori, rather than Samoan, war dance.

[119] Louise and Reuben [III] to "Hon. and Mrs. J. Reuben Clark," 11 July 1935, box 336, JRCP, spelling and punctuation standardized.

[120] JRC to J. Reuben Clark III, 12 July 1935, box 336, JRCP, spelling and punctuation standardized.

[121] Walker, "Heber J. Grant" (1986), 231.

[122] Gibbons, *Heber J. Grant,* 164; also Heber J. Grant journal sheets, 18 Apr. 1936: "I brought four [dictaphone] cylinders of letters to the office this morning."

[123] Heber J. Grant to Melvin D. Wells, 22 Apr. 1936, quoted in Grant journal sheets of same date; also entry of 18 April.

[124] Heber J. Grant to John Connelly, 15 Dec. 1937, box 98, CR 1/44; Heber J. Grant journal sheets, 15 June 1936.

[125] Example from Heber J. Grant journal, 23 July 1924.

[126] *D,* 283.

[127] *Deseret News 1999-2000 Church Almanac* (Salt Lake City: Deseret News, 1998), 552.

[128] Heber J. Grant journal sheets, 20 Jan. 1936 (first quote), 29 Jan. 1936 (second quote).

[129] JRC to David O. McKay, 6 Mar. 1936, fd 1, box 355, JRCP.

[130] *E,* 671 (summary and chronology of McKay's Republican activities); also *DM,* 316.

[131] JRC to David O. McKay, 6 Mar. 1936, fd 1, box 355, JRCP.

[132] JRC office diary, 24 May 1958; Donald R. McCoy, *Landon of Kansas* (Lincoln: University of Nebraska Press, 1966), 349n19.

[133] "Buck Says Landon Will Be Nominated ... E. G. Calladay and J. Reuben Clark Also Predict Republican Victory," *NYT,* 31 Mar. 1936, 27.

[134] JRC 1936 personal diary, 7-12 June 1936, JRCP; Heber J. Grant journal sheets, 15 June, 5 July 1936; JRC scrapbook.

[135] Lute to JRC, 19, 20 Aug. 1936, box 337, JRCP. For George Wilson's Republican "political machine" in Utah and alleged involvement in "kick-back and protection rackets," see *C*, 415-16.

[136] Ted Clark to JRC, 1 Oct. 1936, box 337, JRCP.

[137] JRC to Fred S. Purnell, director of the National Speakers Bureau of the Republican National Committee, 7 Oct. 1936, box 347, JRCP.

[138] JRC 1936 personal diary, 25-26 Sept., 18-22 Oct.; *The New York Sun*, 22 Oct. 1936, in JRC scrapbook.

[139] Heber J. Grant journal sheets, 31 Oct. 1936. In the quoted phrase, Grant referred to himself.

[140] "An Editorial: The Constitution," *DN*, 31 Oct. 1936, 1, repeated in full on page 2: "A Message to *Deseret News* Readers." The editorial reflected the perspectives of the following publications from Clarkana: Frank S. Bell, *The New Deal: The Masque Torn off; The Issue: Americanism vs. Communism Masquerading under the Term Liberalism* (Twin Falls, ID: By the author, 1934); Ethan Colton, *Four Patterns of Revolution: Communist U.S.S.R., Fascist Italy, Nazi Germany, New Deal America* (New York: Association Press, 1935); *International "New" Dealism, The Fact That a "New" Deal Has Been Proposed in Great Britain, Canada, and Switzerland Is Sufficient Evidence of Its International Character: Is This Part of a World Conspiracy?* (New York: League for Constitutional Government, 1935); *Dictator or President? Which Do You Want in the United States?* (New York: Campaign Committee, Women's National Republican Club, [1936?]); *Herbert Hoover, American Ideals Versus the New Deal* ... (New York: Scribner Press, 1936); Erik McKinley Eriksson and Trent Hewitt Steele, *Constitutional Basis for Judging the New Deal* (Rosemead, CA: Rosemead Review Press, 1936); *The System of "Stealing" Party Nominations* (New York: League for Constitutional Government, 1936).

[141] *B*, 348-50; *Conf*, Apr. 1945, 25. Technically *Welfare Plan* emphasized the philosophy while *Welfare Program* emphasized the organization and conduct, but the terms were used interchangeably.

[142] *D*, 283.

[143] A. L. H—— to Heber J. Grant, 1 Nov. 1936; [returned missionary] to Heber J. Grant, 1 Nov. 1936; O.H. M——, J— N. B——, and H. D. J—— to First Presidency, 1 Nov. 1936; O. H. M—— to First Presidency, 1 Nov. 1936; P—— J. C—— to Heber J. Grant, 2 Nov. 1936; G—— H. C—— to Samuel O. Bennion (copy to Heber J. Grant), 2 Nov. 1936; R—— T. S—— to Heber J. Grant, 2 Nov. 1936; J— R. N—— Jr. to Heber J. Grant, 3 Nov. 1936; W—— W——, A. W. C——, J— J. R——, and R. O. L—— to *DN*, 2 Nov. 1936, all in fd 6, box 8, CR 1/33, LDSA.

[144] Frank Herman Jonas, "Utah: Sagebrush Democracy," in Thomas C. Donnelly, ed., *Rocky Mountain Politics* (Albuquerque: University of New Mexico Press, 1940), 34; Frank H. Jonas and Garth N. Jones, "Utah Presidential Elections, 1896-1952," *UHQ* 24 (Oct. 1956): 305.

[145] Heber J. Grant journal sheets, 17 Apr. 1938.

146 F. Burton Howard, *Marion G. Romney: His Life and Faith* (Salt Lake City: Bookcraft, 1988), 109.

147 Esther to "Reube, Lute and All," 12 Nov. 1936, box 337, JRCP.

148 JRC to general priesthood meeting, 5 Apr. 1937, typescript, box 151, JRCP.

149 JRC to general priesthood meeting, 2 Oct. 1937, typescript, box 151, JRCP.

150 See fd 6, box 8, CR 1/33; LeGrand Woolley to JRC, 17 Apr. 1935; Heber J. Grant to David O. McKay, 16 Aug. 1936, JRC fd, CR 1/48; *Conf,* Apr. 1944, 113-14; Marion G. Romney oral history, 1972-73, typescript, 15-16, LDSA; *D,* 285.

151 JRC to Daniel J. McRae, 1 Sept. 1938, fd 2, box 359, JRCP; JRC to Herbert Hoover, 14 May 1942, 2, Hoover Presidential Library; "Pres. Clark Testifies of Divinity of Church Welfare Program," *CN,* 8 Aug. 1951, 13. Carbon copies of Clark's letters to Hoover are also in JRCP.

152 *Conf,* Oct. 1942, 58; *SR,* 40-41.

153 Anonymous/Crank folders in boxes 358, 361, 371, 373, 390, 392, 398, 401, 404, 407, 410, JRCP.

154 JRC to N—— J——, 15 Apr. 1943, attached to April 1943 conference binder, box 175, JRCP.

155 Unsigned, undated letter to Heber J. Grant, in JRC fd (1939-49), CR 1/48. For President Clark's acceptance of his own unpopularity with LDS members, see JRC to Milton R. Merrill, 2 June 1941, fd 2, box 363, JRCP; JRC office diary, 26 Mar. 1945.

156 JRC to general priesthood meeting, 4 Oct. 1947, typescript, box 151, JRCP.

157 JRC office diary, 11 Jan. 1943.

158 JRC to Fred Morris Dearing, 7 Nov. 1958, fd 6, box 402.

159 JRC to General Welfare Committee, 10 Apr. 1938, typescript, CR 255/5, LDSA; also Grant's statement: "Some of our wisest and most faithful and diligent Latter-day Saints ... felt that it was almost a calamity when I came to the Presidency," in Walker, "Heber J. Grant" (1986), 242-43; and *E,* 358: "Heber J. Grant was the most unpopular church president in Mormon history," with corroborating quotes on 358-59.

160 JRC to Lee B. Valentine, 15 Aug. 1954, fd 19, box 391, JRCP.

161 Until 1940 David O. McKay had primary responsibility for governing the Welfare Program. In 1937, for example, JRC met only nine times with the General Welfare Committee in company with McKay or Grant, whereas McKay met alone with the committee in exactly two-thirds of the meetings that year (CR 255/18, LDSA).

162 JRC to Heber J. Grant and David O. McKay, 1 Dec. 1936, fd 1, box 355, JRCP.

163 Luacine to JRC, 9 Feb. 1937, box 337, JRCP. LDSL has a copy of this one-reel "March of Time." See also photo stills and excerpts in "'Time Marches On' with the Church Security Plan," *Improvement Era* 40 (Apr. 1937): 214-15.

¹⁶⁴ Heber J. Grant journal sheets, 2 Mar. 1937.

¹⁶⁵ Heber J. Grant journal sheets, 7 Apr. 1937. For background, see Leuchtenburg, 231-38.

¹⁶⁶ Heber J. Grant to David O. McKay, 20 Apr. 1937, and DOM to HJG, 21 Apr. 1937, fd 13, box 101, CR 1/44.

¹⁶⁷ "President Clark Takes Party Post," *DN,* 28 Dec. 1937, 1.

¹⁶⁸ JRC memorandum, 21 Mar. 1939, fd 6, box 112, CR 1/44.

¹⁶⁹ Heber J. Grant letterbook-journal, 1886-87, 276 (25 July 1887); Grant journal sheets, 23 Sept. 1934.

¹⁷⁰ Heber J. Grant to JRC, 2 June 1937, JRC fd, CR 1/48.

¹⁷¹ Heber G. Wolsey, "The History of Radio Station KSL from 1922 to Television," Ph.D. diss., Michigan State University, 1967, 222.

¹⁷² CR 255/18.

¹⁷³ Lute to JRC, 9 May 1940, box 338, JRCP.

¹⁷⁴ CR 255/18.

¹⁷⁵ Heber J. Grant journal sheets, 9 Dec. 1938.

¹⁷⁶ JRC to special priesthood meeting, 8 Apr. 1939, typescript, box 151, JRCP. After Reuben's death, five years became the standard period of service for bishops.

¹⁷⁷ JRC to bishops' meeting, 4 Oct. 1940, typescript, box 151, JRCP; also Emma Fugal, "Salvation of the Dead," in *EM* 3:1258.

¹⁷⁸ *EA* 29:372-80; various entries in *ER* and *OC.*

¹⁷⁹ Gilbert W. Scharffs, *Mormonism in Germany: A History of the Church of Jesus Christ of Latter-day Saints in Germany Between 1840 and 1970* (Salt Lake City: Deseret Book, 1970), 91.

¹⁸⁰ JRC office diary, 21 July 1939.

¹⁸¹ Heber J. Grant journal sheets, 25 [*sic*] Aug. 1939; Scharffs, *Mormonism in Germany,* 92; James B. Allen and Glen M. Leonard, *The Story of the Latter-day Saints,* 2d ed., rev., enl. (Salt Lake City: Deseret Book, 1992), 536-37.

¹⁸² Heber J. Grant journal sheets, 27 Aug. 1939 (quote); JRC to David O. McKay, 25 Aug. 1939, for "what has happened since you left yesterday."

¹⁸³ Heber J. Grant journal sheets, 27 Aug. 1939 (quote), 31 Aug. 1939 (Grant, JRC, and Anderson starting to work on "a telegram to Europe" at 11 p.m.).

¹⁸⁴ Joseph Fielding Smith Jr. and John J. Stewart, *The Life of Joseph Fielding Smith, Tenth President of The Church of Jesus Christ of Latter-day Saints* (Salt Lake City: Deseret Book, 1972), 275; also Francis M. Gibbons, *Joseph Fielding Smith: Gospel Scholar, Prophet of God* (Salt Lake City: Deseret Book, 1992), 304.

¹⁸⁵ Scharffs, *Mormonism in Germany,* 92: "The East German Mission President Alfred C. Rees had just been released on August 16, 1939, and President Thomas E. McKay, who had replaced him, presided only a few days before he too had to leave Germany." This is the only reference by Scharffs to the evacuation from Berlin and areas of East Prussia and the Polish border. The Frankfurt area is typically emphasized by LDS writers because an LDS apostle and his wife were there at the time.

¹⁸⁶ Smith and Stewart, *The Life of Joseph Fielding Smith,* 276-81; Scharffs

Mormonism in Germany, 92–99; Gibbons, *Joseph Fielding Smith,* 305, 307; David F. Boone, "The Worldwide Evacuation of Latter-day Saint Missionaries at the Beginning of World War II," M.A. thesis, Brigham Young University, 1981; Terry Bohle Montague, *"Mine Angels Round About": Mormon Missionary Evacuation from Western Germany, 1939* (Murray, UT: Ken Earl/Roylance, 1989), 84 (departure of Norman Seibold).

[187] Heber J. Grant journal sheets, 26 Dec. 1939.

[188] Examples from the *New York Sun*: 18 Oct., 15 Dec. 1939, 11 Sept. 1940, in JRC scrapbook; from *NYT,* 2 Aug. 1937, 21; 19 Sept. 1937, sec. II, 1; 20 Sept. 1937, 44; 17 Nov. 1938, 37; 21 June 1939, 2; 16 Dec. 1939, 10; 21 Nov. 1945, 31.

[189] JRC memorandum, 6 May 1938, fd 10, box 360, JRCP.

[190] JRC office diary, 4 Feb. 1940; also refusal on 27 February to accept the suggestion by Apostle Charles A. Callis.

[191] JRC to J. H. Gipson, president of Caxton Printers, 22 Sept. 1943, fd 2, box 367, JRCP.

[192] JRC to Clarence Cowan, 18 June 1945, fd 3, box 371, JRCP.

[193] Heber J. Grant journal sheets, 20 Oct. 1933, 7 Nov. 1939, 19 Oct. 1942.

[194] JRC to LDS welfare committees, Apr. 1938, typescript, box 151, JRCP.

[195] David O. McKay office diary, 30 Nov. 1939, LDSA; Gibbons, *Heber J. Grant,* 214–18; *Conf,* Oct. 1941, 6.

[196] Reported retrospectively in Spencer W. Kimball diary, 30 Dec. 1943, microfilm at LDSA, original in private possession.

[197] *E,* 652, 659, 700; *Deseret News 1999-2000 Church Almanac,* 53, 59.

[198] Frank Evans diary, 15 Sept. 1942, LDSA; Gibbons, *Heber J. Grant,* 218–30; Preston Nibley, *The Presidents of the Church,* rev. ed. (Salt Lake City: Deseret Book, 1971), 258–60; Heber J. Grant journal sheets, 1–20 Jan. 1941, 1 July–31 Dec. 1943; Joseph Fielding Smith typed diary, 3 June 1943, 15 Feb. 1945, LDSA.

[199] JRC office diary, 2, 4 Mar. 1940; David O. McKay office diary, 14 Mar. 1940, 3 Dec. 1943.

[200] David O. McKay office diary, passim; Nibley, *Presidents of the Church,* 338.

[201] JRC to Louise Bennion, 13 Dec. 1940, box 338, JRCP.

[202] Marion G. Romney diary, 28 Aug. 1942, private possession. Romney was an Assistant to the Quorum of Twelve at this time; also, *D,* 284.

[203] JRC to Heber J. Grant and David O. McKay, 15 Feb. 1940, JRC fd in CR 1/48, and fd 3, box 4, McKay papers, LDSA.

[204] JRC office diary, 15 Mar. 1940.

[205] JRC office diary, 22 May 1940, 28 Apr. 1943, 24 Oct. 1944, 16, 25 Feb., 11 Mar. 1945; Heber J. Grant journal sheets, 24 Aug. 1941.

[206] JRC office diary, 26 Jan. 1943.

[207] JRC office diary, 4 Mar., 1 Apr. 1940.

[208] JRC office diary, 3 June 1940.

[209] JRC office diary, 12 Jan. 1943; Heber J. Grant journal sheets, 27 Jan. 1943.

[210] JRC office diary, 22 May 1940, 5, 16 Feb. 1945.

[211] JRC office diary, 15 Oct. 1943.

[212] *C,* 603.

[213] Heber J. Grant journal sheets, 29 July 1940.

[214] Heber J. Grant journal sheets, 7 Aug., 30 Sept., 1, 18 Oct. 1940.

[215] JRC office diary, 13 Oct. 1940.

[216] Heber J. Grant journal sheets, 30 Oct. 1940.

[217] JRC to "Brother and Sister" Reynold Irwin, 2 Mar. 1956, fd 2, box 397, JRCP.

[218] "Church and State," *DN*, 31 Oct. 1940, 4; "The Third Term Principle," *DN*, 1 Nov. 1940, 4; drafts of JRC editorials, box 208, JRCP. Clarkana has Sterling E. Edmunds, *The Roosevelt Coup d'Etat of 1933-40* ... (Charlottesville, VA: Michie, 1940); Thomas E. Dewey, *The Case Against the New Deal* (New York: Harper and Brothers, 1940); and Edwin C. Riegel, *The Aggressor in the White House* (New York: League for Constitutional Government, 1940).

[219] Jonas and Jones, "Utah Presidential Elections," 304. By contrast, Armand L. Mauss, *The Angel and the Beehive: The Mormon Struggle with Assimilation* (Urbana: University of Illinois Press, 1994), 49, was wrong in asserting, "With the arrival of the New Deal era, however, Mormons began to see the Democratic party increasingly as representing big government and big labor, rather than the common people per se, and so began to move toward the Republicans." The election data and statements of LDS leaders from 1932 to 1950 show that the opposite was true of Mormons generally. Mauss later accurately stated (114): "Mormons at the grass roots voted consistently for Roosevelt and the New Deal throughout the thirties and forties, just as the rest of the nation did, and many of them found careers in federal government during this period. This was despite the hostility of President Grant and much of the Mormon hierarchy to the New Deal and to its exponents, such as Utah senator Elbert Thomas."

[220] Heber J. Grant journal sheets, 5 Nov. 1940.

[221] John Sillito, "Democratic Party," and Miriam B. Murphy, "Herbert Brown Maw," in *U*, 134 (quote), 351; *W*, 118-20.

[222] "Cornerstone Laid for Temple in Idaho: Eleven Church Authorities Attend Rites," *DN*, 19 Oct. 1940, 1; also Delbert V. Groberg, *The Idaho Falls Temple: The First LDS Temple in Idaho* ([Salt Lake City]: Publishers Press, 1985), 79-81 (JRC at ceremony), 102-07 (full text of JRC talk).

[223] JRC office diary, 19 Feb. 1941; Gibbons, *Heber J. Grant,* 226.

[224] Minutes of temple meeting, 13 Mar. 1941, in "Assistants to the 12" fd, CR 1/48; also Heber J. Grant journal sheets, 13 Mar. 1941; Gibbons, *Joseph Fielding Smith,* 325; *E,* 148. For men who lived as ordained apostles while not serving in the quorum, see *O,* 534, 549, 554, 562; *E,* 40, 54, 136, 149, 650, 653, 659, 696, 706, 709, 711, 719-22.

[225] "Assistants to the 12" fd, CR 1/48; JRC office diary, 14 Mar. 1941.

[226] "Assistants to the 12" fd, CR 1/48.

[227] *Conf,* Apr. 1941, 1; Heber J. Grant journal sheets, 6 Apr. 1941. With the exception of Alvin R. Dyer, the Assistants to the Twelve were high priests rather than apostles from 1941 until their position was merged with the First Quorum of Seventy on 1 October 1976 when they were ordained to the office of Seventy. See Byron R. Merrill, "Assistants to the Twelve," in *EM* 1:81-82.

[228] Marion G. Romney oral history, 1976, typescript, 8, LDSA; *H*, 177, 311, 312.

[229] JRC office diary, 9 Mar. 1941; Heber J. Grant journal sheets, 9 Mar., 6 Apr. 1941.

[230] Heber J. Grant journal sheets, 7 June 1941, referring to the Mutual Improvement Associations from the 1870s to the 1970s.

[231] *H*, 365.

[232] Jill Mulvay Derr, Janath Russell Cannon, and Maureen Ursenbach Beecher, *Women of Covenant: The Story of Relief Society* (Salt Lake City: Deseret Book, 1992), 297-98.

[233] *H*, 365.

[234] *L*, 223; also *H*, 363-77; Richard O. Cowan, *The Church in the Twentieth Century* (Salt Lake City: Bookcraft, 1985), 305-17; Allen and Leonard, *The Story of the Latter-day Saints*, 593-623; Frank O. May Jr., "Correlation of the Church," and James B. Allen and Cowan, "History of the Church: 1945-1950," in *EM* 1:324, 2:642-43; Mauss, *The Angel and the Beehive*, 163-67; Jan Shipps, "Making Saints in the Early Days and the Latter Days," in Marie Cornwall, Tim B. Heaton, and Lawrence A. Young, eds., *Contemporary Mormonism: Social Science Perspectives* (Urbana: University of Illinois Press, 1994), 77, 80.

[235] JRC office diary, 22 Dec. 1938; *DN,* first Sunday edition 16 May 1948 continuing through 31 August 1952. The *DN* did not resume a Sunday edition until 16 January 1983.

[236] Gordon W. Prange, *December 7, 1941: The Day the Japanese Attacked Pearl Harbor* (New York: McGraw-Hill, 1988); Stanley Weintraub, *Long Day's Journey into War: December 7, 1941* (New York: Dutton, 1991).

[237] JRC to Gordon W. Clark, 30 Oct. 1940, box 338, JRCP.

[238] JRC office diary, 7 Dec., 10 Dec. 1941.

[239] Harold B. Lee diary, 13 Dec. 1941 (quote), 18 Sept. 1942 (expectation of apostleship for Mervyn Bennion), private possession; also JRC to Severo Mallet-Prevost, 2 Feb. 1942, fd 2, box 365, JRCP.

[240] Heber J. Grant journal sheets, 6 Apr. 1942.

[241] Heber J. Grant journal sheets, 3 Oct. 1942 ("Brother Clark practically wrote it all").

By declining President Grant's offers to identify him as the author of First Presidency statements, Clark was able to say, when challenged: "While at our conference I read the Message of the First Presidency, it was not my message but the message of all the members of the Presidency, who all approved and signed it." (JRC to Jonathan W. Snow, 9 Dec. 1942, attached to October 1942 conference binder, box 156, JRCP).

[242] George F. Richards diary, 10, 24 Dec. 1942, LDSA. For discussion of the second anointing, see *M* 3:228, 5:112; David John Buerger, "The Fulness of the Priesthood: The Second Anointing in Latter-day Saint Theology and Practice," *Dial* 16 (Spring 1983): 10-46; *O,* 36, 55, 56, 115, 168-72, 184-85, 205, 206, 207-08, 245, 495-500, 503, 505, 647-48, 655; *E,* 120, 127, 130, 149; also James E. Talmage,

The House of the Lord (1912; Salt Lake City: Signature Books, 1998), 138-41, for discussion and photo of "Holy of Holies."

243 Heber J. Grant journal sheets, 6 Feb. 1943; also "Regional Conferences," *CN*, 3 Apr. 1943, 1; Richard E. Turley Jr., "Solemn Assemblies," in *EM* 3:1390.

244 JRC, "Budget Beginnings," bound volume, box 188, JRCP; Heber J. Grant journal sheets, 28 Apr. 1943.

245 Heber J. Grant journal sheets, 19 Feb. 1943; also Moyle's account of their meeting in *D*, 2-5.

246 Joseph Fielding Smith typed diary, 3 June 1943.

247 Heber J. Grant journal sheets, 1 July 1943, and entry for the inclusive period 1 July–31 Dec. 1943.

248 A. Hamer Reiser interview by D. Michael Quinn, 1 Mar. 1980. Reiser was former manager of Deseret Book Company, counselor in the general Sunday School presidency, and former assistant secretary to the First Presidency. He served as Clark's chauffeur from 1957 to 1961, the period when Reuben had difficulty in driving and walking.

Based on interviews with twenty-one influential Utahns, John Gunther, in his *Inside U.S.A.* (New York: Harper and Brothers, 1947), stated on page 202: "Clark's great days came in the period of Grant's senescence. Ivins died, and from 1934 to 1945, he [Clark] practically ran the church singlehanded. Not since the days of Brigham Young have the Latter Day [*sic*] Saints known such vigorous rule, I heard it said, and as a consequence Clark became highly unpopular in some circles." Reuben dismissed Gunther's assessment with the comment "that the stuff about his taking over the Church is the purest kind of bunk" (JRC office diary, 6 May 1947).

249 "Churchmen Plan Tour," *DN*, 13 July 1943, [9]; "Pres. Clark Finishes Trip: Fourteen Stakes Visited by Church Leader," *DN*, 11 Aug. 1943, [9]; "U.S. Freedom Threat Seen: Pres. Clark Warns of Communism," *DN*, 7 Oct. 1943, 1.

250 JRC office diary, 10, 12 Jan., 24 Feb., 26 Mar., 1, 3 Apr., 2 May 1944.

251 Harold B. Lee diary, 5, 11-12, 18, 31 July 1944.

252 *H*, 177.

253 JRC to Irving S. Olds of New York City, 31 July 1957, fd 5, box 400, JRCP; also *Who Was Who in America, Volume IV: 1961-1968* (Chicago: A. N. Marquis, 1968), 718.

254 JRC office diary, 10 Aug., 8 Nov. 1944, 26 June 1950.

255 JRC memorandum, 14 Sept. 1944, fd 5, box 370, JRCP.

256 JRC office diary, 24 Oct., 3 Nov. 1944; also *E*, 149, for jurisdictional tensions involving the Seventy.

257 JRC office diary, 20-23 Jan., 2-5 Mar., 27 Sept.-1 Oct., 20 Nov. 1944.

258 Harold B. Lee diary, 1 Feb. 1945.

259 JRC office diary, 4, 16, 25 Feb., 11 Mar. 1945 (visits with Grant), 26 Mar. 1945 (quotes); also discussion of gerontocracy in D. Michael Quinn, "From Sacred Grove to Sacral Power Structure," *Dial* 17 (Summer 1984): 31-34.

Even after becoming a general authority, Hugh B. Brown continued to express concern about this problem. At nearly ninety himself, he recommended an age for retirement from the Quorum of Twelve that would have made him the first emeritus apostle. The hierarchy did not accept his proposal but provided mandatory retirement for everyone except apostles and members of the First Presidency. See Edwin B. Firmage, ed., *An Abundant Life: The Memoirs of Hugh B. Brown* (Salt Lake City: Signature Books, 1988), 143; *O*, 259, 459n75.

[260] Marianne Clark Sharp oral history, 1977, typescript, 47, 52, LDSA; Belle S. Spafford oral history, 1975-76, typescript, 79-80, LDSA. For general authorities who expressed concerns about nepotism before Clark, see *E*, 51, 172-73; also Sheri L. Dew, *Go Forward with Faith: The Biography of Gordon B. Hinckley* (Salt Lake City: Deseret Book, 1996), 467 (president's concern about "charges of nepotism" because his daughter was a counselor in the young women's organization).

[261] JRC office diary, 4-5 Apr. 1945; *Conf,* Apr. 1945, 14.

[262] Marianne C. Sharp to JRC, 10 Oct. 1946, JRC to Marianne C. Sharp, 11 Dec. 1946, Oct. 1946 fd, box 158, JRCP.

[263] *Conf,* Apr. 1945, 4.

[264] Harold B. Lee diary, 6 Apr. 1945.

[265] Joseph Fielding Smith typed diary, 12 Apr. 1945.

[266] Gibbons, *Joseph Fielding Smith,* 316; also *E*, 697 (summary and chronology of Joseph Fielding Smith's Republican Party activities).

[267] JRC to Preston D. Richards, 7 May 1945, fd 11, box 372, JRCP.

[268] George F. Richards diary, 14 May 1945.

[269] *H*, 189.

[270] Spencer W. Kimball diary, 18 May 1945, emphasis in original.

[271] Two books on American manifestations of "loyal opposition" provide the context for Clark's joining with former U.S. president Herbert Hoover in publicly opposing U.S. participation in World War II. See Harold Wolfe, *Herbert Hoover: Public Servant and Leader of the Loyal Opposition* (New York: Exposition Press, 1956); Richard E. Darilek, *A Loyal Opposition in Time of War: The Republican Party and the Politics of Foreign Policy from Pearl Harbor to Yalta* (Westport, CT: Greenwood Press, 1976).

[272] See *T.*

NOTES TO CHAPTER 4

[1] D&C 107:22

[2] George Albert Smith patriarchal blessing by Zebedee Coltrin, 16 Jan. 1884, fd 13, box 96, George A. Smith Family papers, JWML; *K*, 114, 196, 208; *G*, 2.

[3] "First Presidency Chosen," *DN*, 21 May 1945, 1; *G*, 272-73; Edward L. Kimball and Andrew E. Kimball Jr., *Spencer W. Kimball, Twelfth President of The Church of Jesus Christ of Latter-day Saints* (Salt Lake City: Bookcraft, 1977), 220-21; *H*, 190. For 1889 as the first occasion when a new president retained the same counselors, see *EM* 4:1678; *E*, 631-32.

[4] C. N. Lund to George Albert Smith, ca. May 1945, fd 8, box 63, Smith Family papers, JWML. Cf. the negative perspective about Clark's influence in *D*, 282, 284, 285.

[5] David O. McKay office diary, 2 June 1945, LDSA.

[6] "Presidency's Offices Changed," *CN*, 9 June 1945, 5.

[7] Eldred G. Smith interview by D. Michael Quinn, 21 Oct. 1977. Smith was Patriarch to the Church from 1947 to 1979.

[8] Harold B. Lee diary, 26 May 1945, private possession.

[9] JRC to James Grafton Rogers of FBPC, 15 June 1945, fd 11, box 372, JRCP.

[10] *K*, 316.

[11] Heidi S. Swinton, *In the Company of Prophets: Personal Experiences of D. Arthur Haycock with Heber J. Grant, George Albert Smith, David O. McKay, Joseph Fielding Smith, Harold B. Lee, Spencer W. Kimball, and Ezra Taft Benson* (Salt Lake City: Deseret Book, 1993), 32; with different version in *K*, 316.

[12] *K*, 316.

[13] George Albert Smith diary, 27 June 1945, Smith Family papers, JWML.

[14] Preston Nibley, *The Presidents of the Church*, rev. ed. (Salt Lake City: Deseret Book, 1971), 276.

[15] George Albert Smith diary, 25 Feb. 1909; Dr. Heber J. Sears to George Albert Smith, 12 Apr. 1909, fd 11, box 27, Smith Family papers, JWML; Glen R. Stubbs, "A Biography of George Albert Smith, 1870 to 1951," Ph.D. diss., Brigham Young University, 1974, 101; Reed Smoot diary, 15 Sept. 1909, in *I*, 28; Heber J. Grant journal sheets, 16 Aug. 1930, LDSA.

[16] George Albert Smith diary, 8 Jan., 24 Jan., 25 Feb., 19-23 Mar., 31 Mar.-21 Apr., 24, 28 Aug., 3 Oct. 1909, 3 Nov. 1909-8 May 1910, 25 June, 10 July, 1 Aug., 12 Sept., 24 Oct., 28 Nov. 1910, 20 Jan. 1911, 14 May 1912-18 May 1913; Stubbs, "Biography of George Albert Smith," 101-21; *K*, 245, 250-52; Merlo J. Pusey, "George Albert Smith," in Leonard J. Arrington, ed., *The Presidents of the Church: Biographical Essays* (Salt Lake City: Deseret Book, 1986), 258-59; *G*, 60-63, 65-68, 70-72 (Gray's Sanitarium). Stubbs and Pusey called the facility a "Sanitorium," but the *Salt Lake City Directory, 1913* (Salt Lake City: R.L. Polk, 1913), 408, listed "Gray's Sanitarium" which was "for the cure of Liquor and Tobacco Habits and Nervous Diseases."

[17] Heber J. Grant journal sheets, 16 Aug. 1930.

[18] George Albert Smith diary, 14, 19 Jan., 3, 7 Mar. 1932, 2, 6 Jan. 1933; also earlier entries for 12 Aug.-26 Oct. 1930, 23-24 Sept., 9, 27 Oct. 1931; *K*, 287, 303; Pusey, "George Albert Smith," in Arrington, *Presidents of the Church*, 263.

[19] JRC to Robert Murray Stewart, 8 Jan. 1947, fd 4, box 373, JRCP.

[20] JRC office diary, 15 Sept. 1950, JRCP.

[21] JRC office diary, 22 Jan. 1949.

[22] *D*, 283.

[23] JRC office diary, 11 July 1950; also *K*, 316.

[24] JRC office diary, 15 Sept. 1950.

[25] David O. McKay office diary, 11-12 Jan. 1932; George Albert Smith diary, 13, 19 Jan., 3 Mar., 30-31 Dec. 1932, 2 Feb. 1933; Heber J. Grant journal sheets, 15 Jan. 1932, 2-3 Feb., 21, 23 Mar., 1, 25 Apr. 1933; May Anderson, Isabelle S. Ross, and Edna H. Thomas to Emily S. Stewart, 21 Jan. 1932, fd 8, box 149, Smith

Family papers, JWML; Emily S. Stewart to Earl Pardoe, 12 May 1948, 7-8, fd 1, box 96, Smith Family papers; *K*, 286-88; Pusey, "George Albert Smith," 263-64; *G*, 152-54; *E*, 63-64.

[26] Heber J. Grant journal sheets, 23 Mar. 1933.

[27] *K*, 294, 342; *G*, 169-70.

[28] Spencer W. Kimball interview by D. Michael Quinn, 2 Feb. 1979.

[29] A. Hamer Reiser interview by D. Michael Quinn, 1 Mar. 1980.

[30] *G*, 34-35. Gibbons made no comment about the administrative influence of Emily Smith Stewart.

[31] JRC office diary, 26 Apr. 1949.

[32] JRC office diary, 22 Jan. 1949 (quote). For Winslow Farr Smith's assessment of Emily during the Primary controversy, see Heber J. Grant journal sheets, 23 Mar. 1933.

[33] JRC office diary, 3 Aug. 1945; ch. 3.

[34] Summary of activities, April 1933 to April 1945, in folder labeled "Speeches, etc. (lists)," box 302, JRCP; JRC office diary, 3 Aug. 1945.

[35] JRC attendance (1945-51) at respective directors' meetings, boxes 412-19, 423-39, JRCP.

[36] "Pres. Clark Warns U.S. on Foreign Loans," *DN*, 21 Nov. 1945, 1; "U.S. Heads for War, Pres. Clark Warns: Leader Urges America [to] Mind Own Business," *DN*, 14 Nov. 1947, 1; JRC office diary, 3 Apr. 1948; boxes 299, 440-42, and JRC scrapbook, JRCP.

[37] JRC office diary, 21 Mar. 1946.

[38] JRC scrapbook, 4 Apr. 1949.

[39] "First Session: Importance of Temple Ordinances Is Stressed," *CN*, 29 Sept. 1945, 2.

[40] "Detailed Program," *CN*, 29 Sept. 1945, 2-7; Albert Zobell Jr., "Dedication Proceedings," *Improvement Era* 48 (Oct. 1945): 565; Delbert V. Groberg, *The Idaho Falls Temple: The First LDS Temple in Idaho* ([Salt Lake City]: Publishers Press, 1985), 205, 207, 208, 209, 210; Lael J. Woodbury, "Hosannah Shout," EM 2:659.

[41] JRC to bishops' meeting, 5 Apr. 1946, transcript, box 151, JRCP.

[42] JRC outline notes for sermons, attached to transcriptions of his talks, including conference talks for 1960, box 169, JRCP.

[43] Harold B. Lee diary, 2-3 Oct. 1943; *L*, 224-25.

[44] Joseph Fielding Smith typed diary, 6 Apr. 1945, LDSA.

[45] JRC to bishops' meeting, 5 Apr. 1946. JRCP has only Reuben's comments at this meeting and does not fully identify Hinckley. It may have been Bryant S. Hinckley, an author and orator who sometimes spoke at general conference, or it could have been his son, Gordon B., chief administrator of the Radio, Publicity, and Mission Literature Committee. Neither was a general authority at this time, and Gordon would not be in a ward bishopric until several weeks later. Gordon's uncle, Alonzo A. (b. Arza Alonzo Hinckley), a church apostle, died in 1936. See Sheri L. Dew, *Go Forward with Faith: The Biography of Gordon B. Hinckley* (Salt Lake City: Deseret Book, 1996); *E*, 634, 737.

[46] Marion G. Romney diary, 8 Apr. 1958, private possession.

[47] JRC office diary, 2 May 1944. Decades before Clark, other Mormons objected to recreation in LDS youth programs. See Charles L. Olsen letter in "Editor's Table: Hints to the Editors," *Improvement Era* 14 (Sept. 1911): 1,038; Edward P. Kimball, "Character of Music Programs for Joint M.I.A. Meetings," *Improvement Era* 25 (Jan. 1922): 274-75.

The quotes by Olsen and Kimball appear in Richard Ian Kimball, *"To Make True Latter-day Saints": Mormon Recreation in the Progressive Era* (forthcoming from University of Illinois Press). His chapter "Athletics, Socialization, and the 'Selling' of the Word of Wisdom" observes, "Calls for reining in the church's recreational activities remained in the minority for most of the early twentieth century, however."

[48] For the extent and history of these church-sponsored activities, see *M.I.A. Year-Round Program of Recreation, 1925-26* (Salt Lake City: Mutual Improvement Association, 1925); *Recreational Program for M.I.A. Summer Camps, Especially Planned for Girls* (Salt Lake City: Mutual Improvement Association, 1926); Rex A. Skidmore, "Mormon Recreation in Theory and Practice: A Study of Social Change," Ph.D. diss., University of Pennsylvania, 1941; *Materials for Dance Festivals: Ward, Stake, and All-Church, also Ballroom and Floor Show Numbers* (Salt Lake City: General Boards of MIA, 1947); *Athletic Handbook, 1952-53: Outline and Rules for All-Church M-Men Basketball, Golf, M.I.A. Relay, Softball (Junior and Senior), Tennis, Volleyball* (Salt Lake City: Young Men's Mutual Improvement Association, [1952]); A. Walter Stevenson, Marvin J. Ashton, and Elbert R. Curtis (M.I.A. general board members), "Why An All-Church Basketball Tournament?" in *BYU Speeches of the Year, 1953-54* (Provo, UT: Brigham Young University Press, 1954); Gordon N. Osborn, "An Historical Study of the All-Church Softball Tournament of the Church of Jesus Christ of Latter-day Saints," M.S. thesis, Brigham Young University, 1961; Ruth Andrus, "A History of the Recreation Program of the Church of Jesus Christ of Latter-day Saints," Ph.D. diss., State University of Iowa, 1962.

[49] Harold B. Lee diary, 12 Nov. 1946. For President Smith's enthusiasm for activities, see *K*, 289; *G*, 329-30.

[50] James B. Allen and Glen M. Leonard, *The Story of the Latter-day Saints,* 2d ed., rev., enl. (Salt Lake City: Deseret Book, 1992), 600.

[51] JRC office diary, 7 May 1947.

[52] See *E*, 24.

[53] JRC office diary, 7 May 1947.

[54] JRC office diary, 8 May 1947.

[55] JRC office diary, 15 Sept. 1949.

[56] Edward Leo Lyman, *Political Deliverance: The Mormon Quest for Utah Statehood* (Urbana: University of Illinois Press, 1986), 12.

[57] JRC office diary, 8 Feb. 1947.

[58] Harold B. Lee diary, 6 June 1947.

[59] *L*, 251-52; also *H*, 365-66.

[60] JRC to bishops' meeting, 3 Oct. 1947, transcript, box 151, JRCP.

[61] *Conf*, Oct. 1947, 155, 160; also JRC, *To Them of the Last Wagon* (Salt Lake City: Deseret News Press, 1947); *SR*, 67-74.

[62] *L*, 250, emphasis in original.

[63] *Conf*, Oct. 1947, 158.

[64] Marion G. Romney interview by D. Michael Quinn, 26 Oct. 1977; also John J. Shumway to JRC, 8 Apr. 1943, in April 1943 conference fd, box 157, JRCP; cf. Herbert L. Stewart, *Winged Words: Sir Winston Churchill as Writer and Speaker* (New York: Bouregy and Curl, 1954); James C. Humes, *Churchill: Speaker of the Century* (New York: Stein and Day, 1980).

[65] Henry D. Moyle diary, 10 June 1951, LDSA.

[66] George Albert Smith diary, 9 Apr. 1950.

[67] *Conf*, Oct. 1947, 156-57.

[68] JRC, *On the Way to Immortality and Eternal Life* (Salt Lake City: Deseret Book, 1949), 20-21.

[69] JRC, "Note" on xiii.

[70] JRC office diary, 25 Feb. 1948.

[71] Monsignor D. G. Hunt, *The People, the Clergy and the Church: An Answer to Accusations against the Catholic Church Made by a Mormon Writer of Utah* (New York: Paulist Press, 1936). Bernice M. Mooney, "The Catholic Church in Utah," in *U*, 78, stated: "The writings and radio addresses of Bishop Duane G. Hunt (1884-1960), fifth bishop of the diocese, kept Utah Catholics in the national spotlight."

[72] JRC office diary, 25 Feb. 1948. For Fitzpatrick, see *G*, 318-19; John S. McCormick, "Salt Lake City," in *U*, 482.

[73] JRC office diary, 2 Mar. 1948.

[74] Clarkana has many anti-Catholic works published from the early 1800s onward, including: Thomas James, *A Treatise of the Corruptions of Scripture ... for the Maintenance of Popery* (London: J.W. Parker, 1843); John Purvey, *Remonstrance Against Romish Corruptions in the Church ...* (London: Longman, Brown, Green and Longmans, 1851); John W. Burgon, *England and Rome: Three Letters to a Pervert* (New York: E.P. Dutton, 1869); Joseph McCabe, *Vice in German Monasteries ...* (Girard, KS: Haldeman-Julius, 1937); Lester F. Sumrall, *Roman Catholicism Slays ...* (Grand Rapids, MI: Zondervan Publishing House, [1940]); D. Tomitch, *Those Responsible for the Second World War*, trans. L. H. Lehmann (New York: Fulfillment Press, 1947); Lucien Vinet, *I Was a Priest* (Englewood, CO: Protestant Information Bureau, 1949); Paul Blanshard, *American Freedom and Catholic Power* (Boston: Beacon Press, 1949).

[75] Peggy Petersen Barton, *Mark E. Petersen: A Biography* (Salt Lake City: Deseret Book, 1985), 75-76: "President Clark kept his eye on the young man. He chose Mark Petersen as a protégé, and Mark cherished this great man as teacher and example."

[76] JRC office diary, 1 Nov. 1945.

[77] Clark, *On the Way to Immortality and Eternal Life*, 225-44; cf. the following entries in *New Catholic Encyclopedia*, 15 vols. (New York: McGraw-Hill, 1967): "Hagiography" (6:894), "Images, Veneration of" (7:370-72), "Indulgences"

(7:482-86), "Mariology" (9:223-27), "Relics" (12:234-40), and "Simony" (13:227-28).

[78] JRC office diary, 8 Mar. 1948.

[79] Harold B. Lee diary, 6 Apr. 1949; cf. *Conf,* Apr. 1949, 162.

[80] George Albert Smith diary, 24 Sept. 1949; David O. McKay office diary, 28 Aug., 12 Oct. 1949, 3 June 1954, 10 Oct. 1957.

[81] *The Christian Register* 129 (Apr. 1950): 2; reprinted in "Pres. Clark's Newest Book Ably Reviewed," *CN,* 17 June 1950, 3, 10.

[82] "Bishop Answers Criticisms: Infallibility of Church Offers Certainty" [KSL broadcast of 24 April 1949], *The Register: Intermountain Catholic Edition,* 1 May 1949, 5-6.

[83] Heber G. Wolsey, "The History of Radio Station KSL from 1922 to Television," Ph.D. diss., Michigan State University, 1967, 222.

[84] JRC office diary, 12 June 1948.

[85] See *E,* 155-61.

[86] *K,* 335-36; *G,* 339-40; Swinton, *In the Company of Prophets,* 16.

[87] *H,* 214-15.

[88] Harold B. Lee diary, 1 July 1948.

[89] George Albert Smith diary, 6 Oct. 1948, 14 Jan., 8 Feb.-Mar. 1949; *Conf,* Apr. 1949, 1; *K,* 344-46; *G,* 346-49.

[90] JRC office diary, 13 Apr. 1949. *K,* 334, for Arthur W. Moulton and the 1947 dedication of the "This Is the Place" monument. See Moulton's biographical sketch in J. Cecil Alter, *Utah: The Storied Domain,* 3 vols. (Chicago: American Historical Society, 1932), 2:179-80; in *Who Was Who in America, Volume IV, 1961-1968* (Chicago: A.N. Marquis, 1968), 685; also references in Smith Family papers, JWML; James W. Beless Jr., "The Episcopal Church in Utah," *UHQ* 36 (Winter 1968): 92-94.

[91] See sources in ch. 8, note 204.

[92] JRC office diary, 13 Apr. 1949.

[93] JRC office diary, 19 Mar. 1947. Clarkana has Gerhart Eisler, *My Side of the Story: The Statement the Newspapers Refused to Print, Prepared to Be Read before the House Committee on Un-American Activities* (New York: Civil Rights Congress, 1947). In that regard, see Robert K. Carr, *The House Committee on Un-American Activities* (Ithaca, NY: Cornell University Press, 1952); Walter Goodman, *The Committee: The Extraordinary Career of the House Committee on Un-American Activities* (New York: Farrar, Straus and Giroux, 1968); *DA,* 155-56.

[94] JRC office diary, 13 Apr. 1949.

[95] JRC office diary, 22 Jan. 1949.

[96] JRC to John C. Traphagen and Hendon Chubb, 11 Apr. 1949, fd 11, box 380, JRCP.

[97] JRC to A. Helen Morgan, 3 May 1949, fd 4, box 380, JRCP.

[98] George Albert Smith diary, 5 May 1949.

[99] David O. McKay office diary, 15 July 1949, emphasis in original.

[100] JRC to VaLois [South] Chipman, 14 Sept. 1949, fd 3, box 379, JRCP. She married Walter Chipman.

[101] George Albert Smith diary, 9 Oct. 1949.

[102] JRC office diary, 19 Oct. 1949.

[103] For example, George Albert Smith diary, 3 Aug. 1949.

[104] George Albert Smith diary, 27 Dec. 1949.

[105] George Albert Smith diary, 12 Jan.-27 Feb., 17-27 Mar., 30 July-29 Aug. 1950; *K*, 352-55; *G*, 360-62.

[106] JRC to A. Helen Morgan and Archer Morgan, 23 Jan. 1950, fd 6, box 382, Clark.

[107] For example, George Albert Smith diary, 12 Jan.-27 Feb. 1950, during recuperation at Laguna Beach.

[108] JRC office diary, 19-22 Sept. 1950; George Albert Smith diary, 18-19 Sept. 1950; Harold B. Lee diary, 22 Sept. 1950.

[109] JRC to Monte L. Bean, 26 Sept. 1950, fd 2, box 381, JRCP, emphasis in original.

[110] Harold B. Lee diary, 5 Oct. 1950.

[111] *G*, 365-66.

[112] George Albert Smith diary, 24 Oct., 18 Nov. 1950, 29 Jan. 1951; JRC office diary for the same period; Stubbs, "Biography of George Albert Smith," 428; *G*, 366.

[113] George Albert Smith diary, 14 Feb. 1951; also *G*, 366.

[114] Nurses' notes, 25 Feb.-4 Apr. 1951, fd 6, box 96, Smith Family papers, JWML; George Albert Smith diary, 25 Feb.-4 Apr. 1951; JRC office diary, 13 Mar., 30 Mar. 1951. In contrast with the nurses' notations, *G*, 367 claimed: "He was lucid and responded understandingly to his nurses, members of the family, and visitors." President Smith's diary maintains a first person narrative, but others, including Haycock, made entries on his behalf for the last several months of his life; also *K*, 357-58.

[115] James B. Allen, "David O. McKay," in Leonard J. Arrington, ed., *The Presidents of the Church: Biographical Essays* (Salt Lake City: Deseret Book, 1986), 301; Sheri L. Dew, *Ezra Taft Benson: A Biography* (Salt Lake City: Deseret Book, 1987), 247, used "recognize them."

[116] David O. McKay office diary, 2 Apr. 1951; also quoted in *DM*, 273.

[117] David O. McKay office diary, 4 Apr. 1951; JRC office diary, 4 Apr. 1951; *K*, 359; *G*, 365-66.

[118] *DM*, 273; also *G*, 270-71.

[119] Spencer W. Kimball diary, 6 Apr. 1951, private possession; also *Conf*, Apr. 1951, 3, 38.

NOTES TO CHAPTER 5

[1] *D&C* 107:22.

[2] Lute ("Wiflets") to JRC, 19 July 1908, box 328, JRCP.

[3] Heber J. Grant journal sheets, 27 Sept. 1934, LDSA. For Clark's 1933 ordination as a high priest, see JRC membership certificate in Deceased LDS Mem-

bers File (1941-74), microfilm, FHL; JRC to Seventy's conference, 6 Oct. 1934, transcript, box 151, JRCP; also *EM* 4:1679 for list of apostles in seniority.

⁴ *Conf,* Oct. 1934, 90.

⁵ Leonard J. Arrington and Davis Bitton, *The Mormon Experience* (New York: Alfred A. Knopf, 1979), 339-40; *EM* 4:1678; *E,* 631-33.

⁶ Arrington and Bitton, *The Mormon Experience,* 339-40; *EM* 4:1678. Since 1951 this has also occurred with counselors N. Eldon Tanner and Harold B. Lee (president in 1972) and with counselors Thomas S. Monson and Gordon B. Hinckley (president in 1995). See *E,* 635-39.

⁷ Jeanette McKay Morrell, *Highlights in the Life of President David O. McKay* (Salt Lake City: Deseret Book, 1966), 13-62; David Lawrence McKay, *My Father, David O. McKay,* ed. Lavina Fielding Anderson (Salt Lake City: Deseret Book, 1989), 39, 57; Newell G. Bringhurst, "The Private Versus the Public David O. McKay: Profile of a Complex Personality," *Dial* 31 (Fall 1998): 25-27; membership certificates of JRC and David O. McKay in Deceased LDS Members File (1941-74).

⁸ McKay was not related by kinship or marriage to any other general authority, living or dead, at the time of his appointment to the Twelve in 1906. JRC had only distant in-law relationships with other general authorities, all but two of whom were dead when the general conference sustained him to the First Presidency in 1933. At least a fifth of the new general authorities during this same period were closely related to other general authorities. See *E,* 169, 170, 189, 192.

Reuben's connections included a brother who was married to a granddaughter of Presiding Bishopric counselor Robert T. Burton. Reuben's deceased uncle had been a stepfather of Seventy's president Brigham H. Roberts. His uncle had married an aunt of former apostle Matthias F. Cowley. His first cousin had married former apostle John W. Taylor. A cousin and an uncle married children of former apostle Erastus Snow. An uncle married a daughter of former apostle Charles C. Rich. Other cousins married descendants of former apostles Orson Hyde and Marriner W. Merrill and of former Bishopric counselor Orrin P. Miller. See Preston W. Parkinson, *The Utah Woolley Family* (Salt Lake City: By the author, 1967), 198-200, 219, 232-33, 321, 334, 357, 459, 549, 612; *O,* 212, 552; *E,* 643, 652, 673, 681, 686, 700, 705. First cousin S. W. Kimball was appointed later.

⁹ *E,* 363-64 (McKay's public endorsement of Richard M. Nixon), 671 (summary of McKay's lifelong Republican activities); also "Pres. McKay Hails Ike as Good Omen," *DN,* 22 Jan. 1953, A-1; Dean E. Mann, "Mormon Attitudes toward the Political Roles of Church Leaders," *Dial* 2 (Summer 1967): 33-35; Frank H. Jonas, "Utah: The Different State," in Jonas, ed., *Politics in the American West* (Salt Lake City: University of Utah Press, 1969), 335; *DM,* 316, 375.

¹⁰ Marion G. Romney diary, 28 Aug. 1942, private possession.

¹¹ Marion G. Romney interview by D. Michael Quinn, 26 Oct. 1977.

¹² CR; box 151, JRCP; David O. McKay, *Gospel Ideals* (Salt Lake City: The *Improvement Era,* 1953), index; David O. McKay, Clare Middlemiss, comp. *Treasures of Life* (Salt Lake City: Deseret Book, 1962), index. A comprehensive list would

also include Byron, Carlyle, Dickens, Emerson, Goethe, Longfellow, Milton, Tennyson, Tolstoy, and Wordsworth.

[13] Ernest L. Wilkinson diary, 31 July 1960, photocopy, JWML.

[14] *DM*, 401.

[15] Jeremiah Stokes, *Modern Miracles: Authenticated Testimonies of Living Witnesses* (Salt Lake City: Deseret News Press, 1935), 97-106, 186-87; Clare Middlemiss, comp., *Cherished Experiences from the Writings of David O. McKay* (Salt Lake City: Deseret Book, 1955), 14, 16, 18, 67, 73-78, 101-02, 145, 155, 161-63; *Conf,* Apr. 1949, 182.

[16] JRC talk "Testimony," 23 Sept. 1928, transcript, #45, box 114, JRCP.

[17] Heber J. Grant journal sheets, 4 Oct. 1942; also his similar statement in entry of 15 March 1921 dismissing Apostle John W. Taylor's experience of "seeing the Savior" and having "the gift of tongues" because Taylor "followed his own course, which took him out of the Church."

[18] JRC to W. D. LeCheminant, 19 Feb. 1946, fd 1, box 374, JRCP, for the quote; also *Conf,* Apr. 1949, 187.

[19] JRC to Ira C. Fletcher, 15 Apr. 1949, fd 8, box 379, JRCP.

[20] JRC, "Testimony: A Sacred Gift," *Improvement Era* 52 (Aug. 1949): 495.

[21] "Pres. Clark's Address at Conference," *CN,* 20 June 1953, 4.

[22] JRC to Mrs. Francis Huntington-Wilson, 29 Mar. 1947, fd 13, box 378, JRCP.

[23] JRC to Cloyd H. Marvin, 2 Aug. 1957, binder of JRC-Marvin correspondence, box 189, JRCP; also originals of JRC letters in Marvin papers, Archives, George Washington University, Washington, D.C.

[24] JRC office diary, 22 Aug. 1939, JRCP

[25] Marion G. Romney oral history, 1976, typescript, 14 (quote), LDSA; also Spencer W. Kimball interview by D. Michael Quinn, 2 Feb. 1979.

[26] A. Hamer Reiser interview by D. Michael Quinn, 1 Mar. 1980.

[27] Harold B. Lee diary, 11 Aug. 1944, private possession.

[28] JRC office diary, 6 Mar. 1947.

[29] Ernest L. Wilkinson diary, 20 Aug. 1957.

[30] JRC to Milton R. Merrill, 2 June 1941, fd 2, box 363, JRCP.

[31] Frank W. Asper to JRC, 5 Aug. 1939, fd 1, box 361, JRCP.

[32] *DM*, 263.

[33] Ernest L. Wilkinson diary, 12 Aug. 1959; also *E*, 28, 30.

[34] Ernest L. Wilkinson diary, 11 June 1960. For other comments on this susceptibility, see Wilkinson's entries for 22 July 1954, 25 Feb. 1955, 24 May 1957. This is implicit throughout McKay's office diary.

[35] Rowena J. Miller to Mrs. Robert F. Bird, 20 Mar. 1950, fd 2, box 381, JRCP.

[36] *C,* 231; also *SA,* 52-53: "The law notwithstanding, men are still selfish, still love power, still will lie, steal, and oppress, still are prepared to adopt the means necessary to gratify their wants."

[37] David O. McKay, *True to the Faith,* comp. Llewelyn R. McKay (Salt Lake City: Bookcraft, 1966), 192-93; McKay, *Treasures of Life,* 536; *Conf,* Oct. 1928, 37.

[38] Preston Nibley, *The Presidents of the Church*, rev. ed. (Salt Lake City: Deseret Book, 1971), 313-33; *DM*, 18, 37-53, 102-28.

[39] *Conf,* Apr. 1927, 82.

[40] John Gunther, *Inside U.S.A.* (New York: Harper and Brothers, 1947), 202-03. Gunther later wrote, "Incidentally, of all the cities that were affronted by *Inside U.S.A.* when it came out, Salt Lake City was affronted most" (Gunther, *A Fragment of Autobiography: The Fun of Writing the INSIDE Books* [New York: Harper and Row, 1961], 52).

[41] Spencer W. Kimball interview by D. Michael Quinn, 2 Feb. 1979.

In *DM*, 405-406, Gibbons disputed this discussion as it appeared in my 1983 edition, writing about "some observers, unacquainted with the inner workings of the Church hierarchy" who use "generic terms 'McKay men' and 'Clark men.'" These terms were volunteered by LDS president Spencer W. Kimball, second counselor Marion G. Romney, and others who had administrative positions at LDS headquarters prior to Clark's death in 1961. Gibbons himself identified several church leaders as "protégés" or "disciples" of Clark, and his 1990 biography of George Albert Smith gave a remarkable summary of how these leaders felt toward their mentor.

[42] *G*, 276. Romney and Affleck both told me that President Clark called them "kid" while talking with them individually.

[43] Interviews of Gordon Burt Affleck and A. Hamer Reiser by D. Michael Quinn, summarized in a chart I prepared in 1979-80 along with the identifications Reuben's children made. This chart is with my papers at the Beinecke Library, Yale University, New Haven, Connecticut. My interviews with various LDS administrators have supported these groupings. In identifying church positions in the text, I listed the highest quorum in which they served during a significant portion of the time period under consideration.

[44] Sheri L. Dew, *Ezra Taft Benson: A Biography* (Salt Lake City: Deseret Book, 1987), 251, 296-97, 385; Francis M. Gibbons, *Ezra Taft Benson: Statesman, Patriot, Prophet of God* (Salt Lake City: Deseret Book, 1996), 125, 239-41, 264; *W,* 185-88, 195-96, 199-200.

[45] Armand L. Mauss, *The Angel and the Beehive: The Mormon Struggle with Assimilation* (Urbana: University of Illinois Press, 1994), 80, demonstrates a too inflexible view of McKay men and Clark men by asserting that Apostle Matthew Cowley was closer to McKay and "clearly not [one of the] Clark men." By contrast, Louise Clark Bennion and Affleck both regarded Cowley as a "strong" Clark man. Mauss gave no reason for his statement, nor cited any evidence. I suspect that his conclusion was based solely on the impressionistic evidence of Cowley's sermons which emphasized spirituality, miracle-working, and love. See Henry A. Smith, *Matthew Cowley: Man of Faith* (Salt Lake City: Bookcraft, 1954), 180-302.

[46] Eugene E. Campbell and Richard D. Poll, *Hugh B. Brown: His Life and Thought* (Salt Lake City: Bookcraft, 1975), 89 (law partnership), 101 (study group), 106 (quote and end of partnership), 144-48 (militarism), 205 (liberal arts), 205-06 (optimism), 262-63 (positive view of mankind); Hugh B. Brown, "An Eternal Quest: Freedom of the Mind," *Dial* 17 (Spring 1984): [78] ("We are not so much

concerned with whether your thoughts are orthodox or heterodox as we are that you shall have thoughts"); also Brown viewed by Sterling M. McMurrin and L. Jackson Newell, *Matters of Conscience: Conversations with Sterling M. McMurrin on Philosophy, Education, and Religion* (Salt Lake City: Signature Books, 1996), 209.

[47] *E*, 35, adds that as counselors in the First Presidency from 1985 to 1995, Gordon B. Hinckley and Thomas S. Monson "combined 'McKay man' N. Eldon Tanner's moderation and calmness with 'Clark man' Harold B. Lee's administrative tutelage."

[48] Sheri L. Dew, *Go Forward with Faith: The Biography of Gordon B. Hinckley* (Salt Lake City: Deseret Book, 1996), 266.

[49] JRC office diary, 29 Oct. 1948.

[50] Dew, *Go Forward with Faith*, 237 (quote about JRC), 86 (Hinckley's first association with Richards), 102 (Richards as "the young writer's mentor"), 194-95 (Hinckley's 1958 appointment), 207 (1959 death of mentor), 308 (quote about McKay), 563 (time line for 1935 appointment with Mission Literature Committee).

[51] Harold B. Lee diary, 10 July 1941, 24-25 Dec. 1944, 6 Aug. 1951, 26 June 1952, 13 Apr., 30 Aug., 19 Nov. 1955, 10 Feb. 1960; Marion G. Romney diary, 18 July, 29 Aug. 1951, 30 July 1954, 10, May 1955, 2 Nov. 1959; Henry D. Moyle diary, 30 Nov. 1949, 6 Aug. 1951, LDSA; JRC office diary, 12 July 1952.

[52] See references to Benson, Bowen, Brown (only at study group), Carl W. Buehner, ElRay L. Christiansen, Cowley, Hinckley, Isaacson (only on 22 Mar. 1951), Kimball, John Longden, Petersen, Joseph Fielding Smith, Nicholas G. Smith, Stapley, LeGrand Richards, Richard L. Evans, and George Q. Morris attending private socials with JRC, Lee, Moyle, and/or Romney, in Nicholas G. Smith diary, 23 Apr., 7 May, 29 July, 30 Dec. 1942, 8 Apr., 22 Apr., 7 May, 16 Dec. 1943, 27 Jan., 10, 24 Feb., 27 Apr., 8 May, 9 June, 29 July, 16 Sept. 1944, 22 Feb., 12-13 Apr., 1, 7, 13, 30 Aug. 1945, LDSA; Harold B. Lee diary, 29 July 1942, 13 July 1951, 27 Feb. 1952, 31 Aug. 1953, 13 May 1955, 19 July 1956, 8 Aug., 24 Oct. 1957, 6 Dec. 1958, 20 Sept. 1960; Henry D. Moyle diary, 4 Jan. 1950, 22 Mar. 1951, 21 June 1951, 31 Aug. 1953, 23 Oct. 1957; Marion G. Romney diary, 3 Aug. 1941, 13 July, 12 Sept. 1952, 24 June, 23 Sept. 1953, 12 May 1954, 29 Aug., 23 Oct. 1957; JRC ranch diary, 31 Aug. 1954, 16 Nov. 1955, JRCP; Joseph Fielding Smith typed diary, 27 Feb., 26 Aug. 1952, 23 Nov. 1954, LDSA; Spencer W. Kimball diary, 4 Oct. 1943, 22 Mar. 1951, 23 Oct. 1957, 6 Dec. 1958, private possession.

Also in attendance at several of these socials were Joseph Anderson and his wife. As a staff employee, Anderson could not express philosophical alignment with one counselor over another, nor personal preferences for individual members of the presidency. When I interviewed Reiser in 1980, I asked if he thought Anderson would be willing to comment on the Clark-man and McKay-man issue from his perspective as secretary for nearly fifty years. Released in 1970 to become a general authority, Anderson became emeritus in 1978 but had a reputation for his extraordinary memory. Reiser told me that an interview would probably not be worthwhile because Anderson defined himself as "the First Presidency's *secret*-ary." Several administrators quoted Anderson's humorous self-description to me, and I found that he was universally loved and respected at church headquarters.

53 Marion G. Romney diary, 29 Aug. 1951; Joseph Fielding Smith typed diary, 14 Feb. 1952, 22 Dec. 1953.

54 Lute to JRC, 11 Aug. 1936, box 337, JRCP; JRC office diary, 10 Sept. 1946; Louise Clark Bennion interview by D. Michael Quinn, 7 Nov. 1977.

55 JRC to David O. McKay, 6 June 1938, fd 7, box 26, McKay papers, LDSA.

56 David O. McKay office diary, 11 Apr., 13 May 1938, 20 July 1945, LDSA; JRC office diary, 2 Mar. 1940, 13 Nov. 1946, 28 Apr. 1950.

57 Lute to JRC, 14 Jan. and 10 Nov. 1935, box 336, JRCP.

58 Anthony W. Ivins diary, 4 Jan. 1910, Ivins papers, Utah State Historical Society, Salt Lake City; *E*, 212.

59 *C*, 595 (annual salary), 597 (fee).

60 JRC income tax return for 1936, Form 710 (Gift Tax), including his description of this gift (required by the form), box 514, JRCP; also D. Michael Quinn's research notecard in 1981 about a Reuben III statement to Frank Fox that JRC felt guilty about leaving McKay alone to run the office when JRC's outside income from these trips was so great and "McKay was in debt and had only his church allowance." This notecard is with my research papers at the Beinecke Library, Yale University.

61 Joseph A. Geddes, "I Remember the Utah Self-Help Cooperative Board," 4, Utah State Historical Society.

62 Lute to JRC, 26 Apr. 1938, box 337, JRCP, referring to Robert ("Bert") Judd, husband of Grant's daughter Mary.

63 JRC office diary, 20 May 1940 (first quote), 14 June 1940 ("division"). For the context of McKay's views, see Mark L. Chadwin, *The Warhawks: American Interventionists before Pearl Harbor* (New York: W.W. Norton, 1970).

64 "Mormon Mixup," *Time* 40 (19 Oct. 1942): 42. In view of his disagreements with Clark about Hitler and World War II, it seems significant that McKay retained a copy of C. N. Lund, *Reply to Clark's Speech* (Salt Lake City: Progressive Opinion, [1943]), broadside (fd 4, box 50, McKay papers). Although once located in Clarkana, Lund's publication does not currently appear in BYU's computerized catalog.

65 *ER*, 2:622-23.

66 *Conf*, Oct. 1942, 15-16 (references to this message); *M* 6:170-85; Heber J. Grant journal sheets, 3 Oct. 1942 ("Brother Clark practically wrote it all").

67 *Conf*, Oct. 1942, 68. For "Axis" allies of Nazi Germany, see *EA*, 2:882.

68 For example, JRC to Jonathan W. Snow, 9 Dec. 1942, attached to October 1942 conference binder, box 156, JRCP.

69 Spencer W. Kimball diary, 4 July 1960.

70 Harold B. Lee diary, 3 May 1943.

71 A. Hamer Reiser interview by D. Michael Quinn, 1 Mar. 1980.

72 John W. Young became first counselor in 1877 on the same day he first entered the ranks of general authorities even though Daniel H. Wells had been

second counselor since 1857. In 1901 John R. Winder was sustained first counselor and Anthon H. Lund second counselor although Lund had been an apostle since 1889, whereas Winder had been a counselor in the subordinate Presiding Bishopric. Lund was sustained first counselor in 1910 on the same day that John Henry Smith was sustained second despite Smith's nine years' longer service in the quorum than Lund's. See Arrington and Bitton, *The Mormon Experience,* 339-40; *EM* 4:1678; *E*, 631, 632, 633, 667, 694, 711, 717, 721.

[73] *Conf,* Apr. 1951, 151.

[74] JRC office diary, 2 June 1944.

[75] *K*, 316.

[76] Gibbons, in *DM*, 273, wrote, "George Albert Smith passed away quietly at 7:27 P.M. At that moment the burden of Church leadership shifted to the capable shoulders of David Oman McKay."

[77] Spencer W. Kimball diary, 8 Apr. 1951.

[78] Ernest L. Wilkinson diary, 28 Apr. 1960.

[79] *DM*, 278.

[80] JRC office diary, 8 Apr. 1951; Louise Clark Bennion interview by D. Michael Quinn, 7 Nov. 1977.

[81] *Conf,* Apr. 1951, 80.

[82] JRC to Lute, 4 June 1929, box 335, JRCP.

[83] Edward L. Kimball and Andrew E. Kimball Jr., *Spencer W. Kimball, Twelfth President of The Church of Jesus Christ of Latter-day Saints* (Salt Lake City: Bookcraft, 1977), 268; Harold B. Lee diary, 8 Apr. 1951.

[84] Gibbons, *Ezra Taft Benson,* 171.

[85] Spencer W. Kimball diary, 8 Apr. 1951, quoted in part in Kimball and Kimball, *Spencer W. Kimball,* 268.

[86] Dew, *Ezra Taft Benson,* 247.

[87] Harold B. Lee diary, 9 Apr. 1951 (previous evening), partly quoted in *H*, 239; Henry D. Moyle diary, 8 Apr. 1951. By contrast, James B. Allen, "David O. McKay," in Leonard J. Arrington, ed., *The Presidents of the Church: Biographical Essays* (Salt Lake City: Deseret Book, 1986), 302, claimed: "President Clark expressed no dismay at all." Allen's statement contradicted previously published quotes of Reuben's dismay about this change.

[88] Interview of Louise Clark Bennion, Marianne Clark Sharp, Luacine Clark Fox, and J. Reuben Clark III by D. Michael Quinn, 7 Nov. 1977. Reuben III called his father "the Great Sphinx." He later told another interviewer, "Anything that he ever told us about, you could almost be sure would be in the paper the next day, or was common knowledge." See J. Reuben Clark III oral history, 1982, typescript, 13, HBLL.

[89] Marianne C. Sharp to "Dearest Daddy," 19 Apr. 1951, fd 7, box 383, JRCP.

[90] *Conf,* Apr. 1951, 151. Gibbons, in *DM*, 278, repeated the official explanation that there was no rift in the First Presidency and that Clark's changed status was not a demotion. He then undercut that explanation by saying that McKay was wise to make "the selection of Elder Richards as first counselor so that in the event the chemistry was wrong after the change, the administration of the Church

would not suffer because of any differences between the Prophet and the one second in authority."

91 *Conf,* Apr. 1951, 154; JRC, "Not Where You Serve, but How," *Improvement Era* 54 (June 1951): 412; *SR,* 76.

92 Spencer W. Kimball diary, 9 Apr. 1951. I altered the order of the quotes.

93 Joseph Anderson, *Prophets I Have Known* (Salt Lake City: Deseret Book, 1973), 82. This was an echo of Harold B. Lee's diary, 9 Apr. 1951, "seldom equaled and perhaps never excelled," quoted in *H,* 240.

94 Cf. discussion in ch. 7, note 130.

95 Marion G. Romney diary, 9 Apr. 1951.

96 Spencer W. Kimball diary, 9 Apr. 1951.

97 Tyler Abell, ed., *Drew Pearson Diaries, 1949-1959* (New York: Holt, Rinehart, and Winston, 1974), 201 (talking with J. Bracken Lee about "my old friend Reuben Clark ... a reactionary of the worst sort"); Drew Pearson, "Washington Merry-Go-Round," *St. Louis Post-Dispatch,* 25 Feb. 1952, B-1 (main quotes), with copy in JRC scrapbook, JRCP. Although several Utah newspapers regularly published Pearson's nationally syndicated column, they refused to print this particular article.

98 JRC office diary, 28 May 1951.

99 A. Hamer Reiser oral history, 1974, typescript, vol. 3:17, LDSA (quote); Reiser interview, 1 Mar. 1980 (self-description as "a McKay man").

100 John K. Edmunds oral history, 1979-80, typescript, vol. 2:103, LDSA.

101 Conway B. Sonne, *A Man Named Alma: The World of Alma Sonne* (Bountiful, UT: Horizon, 1988), 179.

102 Marianne C. Sharp to JRC, 19 Apr. 1951.

103 JRC office diary, 11 Apr. 1951.

104 JRC to A. Helen Morgan, 12 May 1951, fd 1, box 384, JRCP.

105 Marion G. Romney diary, 13 Apr. 1951.

106 David O. McKay office diary, 20 Apr. 1951; *Report of "This Is the Place Monument" Commission* (Salt Lake City: n.p., 1947), 5.

107 JRC to Stephen L and Irene Richards, 27 Dec. 1957 and 14 Sept. 1949, boxes 399 and 380, JRCP.

108 Harold B. Lee diary, 3 May 1951.

109 *CN,* 20 June 1951, 4.

110 E. LeRoy Hatch oral history, 1974, typescript, 43-44, LDSA.

111 Harold B. Lee diary, 7 June 1951.

112 Stephen L Richards office diary, 30 Aug. 1951, LDSA.

113 Harold B. Lee diary, 22 Oct. 1946, 3 Apr. 1947.

114 A. Hamer Reiser interview by D. Michael Quinn, 1 Mar. 1980; also mentioned in Reiser 1974 oral history, 3:78.

115 Marion G. Romney diary, 11 Jan. 1952.

116 David O. McKay office diary, 8 Oct. 1953.

117 JRC statement in Harold B. Lee diary, 22 Apr. 1955. Cf. statement by Apostle Ballard, speaking in general conference, "However, in the Lord's Church

there is no such thing as a 'loyal opposition'" (M. Russell Ballard, "Beware of False Prophets and False Teachers," *Ensign* 29 (Nov. 1999): 64).

[118] Pearson article, 25 Feb. 1952, B-1; copy in JRC scrapbook.

[119] JRC office diary, 25 Feb. 1952.

[120] Marion G. Romney 1976 oral history, 8; also indicated in JRC office diary, 12 July 1952; *H*, 311, 312, 381; *W*, 147.

[121] *H*, 310; *L*, 290; *W*, 91-92.

[122] *H*, 312. The conference was held in January 1952.

[123] Marion G. Romney diary, 11 Jan. 1952 (quote), 26 Feb. 1952.

[124] Harold B. Lee diary, 6 Oct. 1955.

[125] JRC office diary, 18 June 1951; also Ernest L. Wilkinson diary, 24 Feb. 1960.

[126] Harold B. Lee diary, 6 Apr. 1954 (quote). For JRC telling Lee of his becoming church president, see Lee diary, 15 Nov. 1941, 19 May 1949, 15 Dec. 1950, 10 Nov. 1951, 20 Nov. 1953, 4 Aug. 1954, 21-22 Nov. 1956; *H*, 178, 222.

[127] Ernest L. Wilkinson diary, 24 Feb. 1960.

[128] *L*, 264-65.

[129] Keith Terry, *David O. McKay: Prophet of Love* (Santa Barbara, CA: Butterfly, 1980), 100; also Dorothy O. Rea, "Secretary to a Prophet," *CN*, 21 May 1966, 13. It was in this well-known context that JRC wrote Middlemiss about "your great devotion to your Chief" (JRC to Middlemiss, 1 Sept. 1958, fd 7, box 401, JRCP).

[130] Ernest L. Wilkinson diary, 7 Mar. 1967.

[131] *DM*, 419.

[132] Henry D. Moyle diary, 3 Jan. 1953; also Heidi S. Swinton, *In the Company of Prophets: Personal Experiences of D. Arthur Haycock with Heber J. Grant, George Albert Smith, David O. McKay, Joseph Fielding Smith, Harold B. Lee, Spencer W. Kimball, and Ezra Taft Benson* (Salt Lake City: Deseret Book, 1993), 45: "For Arthur it was a difficult transition" to be displaced by Middlemiss. After McKay's death in 1970, Middlemiss left the office and the new presidency invited Haycock to return to his former position. In this capacity, he served Presidents Smith, Lee, Kimball, and, briefly, Benson. See Swinton, *In the Company of Prophets,* 53ff.

[133] U.S. Senator Frank E. Moss to U.S. Representative Ken W. Dyal [also LDS], 2 Mar. 1966, fd 5, box 184, Moss papers, JWML. Moss's observation was based on interviews with "the Brethren" a week earlier.

[134] Terry, *David O. McKay,* 183.

[135] Ernest L. Wilkinson diary, 14 Sept. 1960.

[136] A. Hamer Reiser interview by D. Michael Quinn, 1 Mar. 1980.

[137] For specific references to the "end run" phenomenon of the McKay administration, see Neal A. Maxwell oral history, 1976-77, typescript, 24-25, LDSA; Ernest L. Wilkinson diary, passim; JRC office diary, 22 May 1961.

[138] *DM*, 419.

[139] This statement was in the draft I submitted for review by LDS administrators in 1981.

[140] JRC office diary, 10-11 May, 18 June 1951.

[141] JRC office diary, 17 Mar. 1953 (quote), also 14 July 1953.

[142] David O. McKay office diary, 6 Dec. 1956.

[143] JRC office diary, 2 Jan. 1957.

[144] "Crowd," *DN,* 27 July 1952, 4.

[145] Ernest L. Wilkinson diary, 19 Feb. 1959. For references to the illnesses and hospitalizations of McKay and Richards, see Wilkinson diary, 27 Mar., 2 June, 3 Sept. 1958; Harold B. Lee diary, 3 May, 29 Aug. 1951, 14 May 1958; JRC office diary, 3 May 1951, 5 Jan., 30 Jan. 1953; JRC farm diary, 25 Aug. 1951, JRCP; Spencer W. Kimball diary, 22 Feb. 1953; Marion G. Romney diary, 29 Jan., 5 Feb. 1953, 2 Sept. 1958; David O. McKay office diary, 26 June, 7 July 1958; JRC to Dr. J. LeRoy Kimball, 17 Aug. 1958, fd 14, box 402, JRCP.

[146] JRC to Leonard E. Read, 21 Dec. 1954, attached to copy of Read, *Government: An Ideal Concept* (Irvington-on-Hudson, NY: Foundation for Economic Education, 1954) in Clarkana.

[147] JRC memorandum, 8 May 1959, removed from JRCP in 1977 by David H. Yarn because he regarded it as too controversial for other researchers to see but given to me by J. Reuben Clark III for my own information and note-taking. I do not know what happened to this document after I returned it.

[148] Ernest L. Wilkinson diary, 6 Feb. 1959.

[149] Harold B. Lee diary, 28 June 1958.

[150] *"Brother Stephen L's Attitude,"* in JRC memorandum, "Church Security Plan," 19 Oct. 1937 (emphasis in original), fd 1, box 358, JRCP; also *W,* 84; *E,* 685-86 (Stephen L Richards activities in Democratic Party).

[151] Harold B. Lee diary, 29 Feb. 1952.

[152] David O. McKay office diary, 2 Mar. 1953.

[153] Harold B. Lee diary, 4 Mar. 1952.

[154] Harold B. Lee diary, 14 May 1952; also *H,* 327-28.

[155] David O. McKay office diary, 7 Nov. 1952.

[156] Henry D. Moyle diary, 20 Nov. 1952; Marion G. Romney diary, 9 Jan. 1953.

[157] Harold B. Lee diary, 31 July 1953; also *H,* 328; *L,* 296.

[158] Harold B. Lee diary, 7 Jan. 1955.

[159] Marion G. Romney diary, 26 Mar. 1957.

[160] Harold B. Lee diary, 30 Mar. 1957.

[161] *H,* 328; also Harold B. Lee diary, 3 Sept. 1957.

[162] JRC ranch diary, 6 Oct. 1957.

[163] Harold B. Lee diary, 31 Dec. 1957, with paraphrase in *H,* 330.

[164] Marion G. Romney 1976 oral history, 6.

[165] Stephen L Richards office diary, 7 Dec. 1953.

[166] Harold B. Lee diary, 4 May 1956 ("socialistic"); Ernest L. Wilkinson diary, 4 May 1956 (last quote), echoed in Lee's comment: "While Pres. McKay announced that personally he had returned all such government gratuities from his own farm, he was inclined to go along with Stephen L. Richards' idea."

[167] Harold B. Lee diary, 10 Feb 1955; related entry in Henry D. Moyle diary, 10 Feb. 1955.

[168] Harold B. Lee diary, 18 Mar. 1955.

[169] JRC, *Our Lord of the Gospels: Course of Study for the Melchizedek Priesthood Quorums of the Church of Jesus Christ of Latter-day Saints, 1958* (Salt Lake City: Deseret Book, 1957); *A Teacher's Manual: A Study Guide for Our Lord of the Gospels* (Salt Lake City: Deseret Book, 1957).

[170] Gordon Burt Affleck interviews with D. Michael Quinn. His quote was in the first draft I submitted for review by LDS administrators in 1981, but they recommended that I change it to a softened paraphrase for the 1983 book.

[171] Marion G. Romney diary, 12 Apr. 1955.

[172] JRC scrapbook, 1 Oct. 1954; cf. published photo in *SLT,* 1 Oct. 1954, A-1.

[173] For JRC's concern during David O. McKay's illnesses, see Harold B. Lee diary, 29 Aug. 1951; JRC office diary, 3 May 1951, 30 Jan. 1953; transcript of their telephone conversation, 29 Jan. 1957, transcript, fd 13, box 174, McKay papers; Ernest L. Wilkinson diary, 27 Mar. 1958; McKay office diary, 7 July 1958. For JRC during illnesses of Stephen L Richards, see Harold B. Lee diary, 7 Apr. 1949; JRC farm diary, 25 Aug. 1951; JRC to J. LeRoy Kimball, 17 Aug. 1958.

[174] David O. McKay statement in Ernest L. Wilkinson diary, 11 June 1960. Clare Middlemiss stated in 1975 that "no decision he made in all his years as president of the Church caused him so much worry and anxiety." See *R*, 210, 240. This school is now known as BYU-Idaho.

[175] *R*, 187-247; Ernest L. Wilkinson and Leonard J. Arrington, eds., *Brigham Young University: The First One Hundred Years,* 4 vols. (Provo, UT: Brigham Young University Press, 1975-76), 3:156-62.

[176] *R*, 190.

[177] Ernest L. Wilkinson diary, 11 July 1957.

[178] *R*, 192.

[179] Ernest L. Wilkinson diary, 25 Mar., 21 Apr., 21 May 1954.

[180] *R*, 187, 196-207, 233-39; Ernest L. Wilkinson diary, 23 Apr., 1 June 1957.

[181] Ernest L. Wilkinson diary, 1 July 1957; David O. McKay office diary, 1 July 1957.

[182] *R*, 210-11; later referred to in Ernest L. Wilkinson diary, 17 July 1957.

[183] Ernest L. Wilkinson diary, 17 July 1957 (learning from newspaper), 21 July 1957 (statements by Richards).

[184] *R*, 210-11.

[185] Ernest L. Wilkinson diary, 22 July 1957 (JRC quote), 27 Sept. 1957 (lawsuit).

[186] Ernest L. Wilkinson diary, 10 Apr. 1958.

[187] David O. McKay office diary, 31 Oct. 1958; Ernest L. Wilkinson diary, 30 June, 14-15 Oct., 3 Nov. 1958.

[188] *R*, 220-22.

[189] Ernest L. Wilkinson diary, 3 Nov. 1958.

[190] David O. McKay office diary, 6 Feb. 1959.

[191] *R*, 224-25, 228 ("hammered"), 230 ("hurt President McKay"), 239.

[192] JRC report to the First Presidency and Quorum of the Twelve, 20 Nov.

1958 (quote), in David O. McKay office diary, 15 Nov. 1958; also related comments in Marion G. Romney diary, 15 Nov. 1958.

[193] Ernest L. Wilkinson diary, 17 Dec. 1958; *R*, 226-27.

[194] *R*, 227-37.

[195] David O. McKay office diary, 10 Feb. 1959, for the meeting's transcript, 1, 25, 28.

[196] "First Presidency Issues Notice on Ricks College Situation," *CN*, 14 Feb. 1959, 2; *R*, 236-37.

[197] *R*, 224-25, 233, 239.

[198] "Reaction Varied in Rexburg on College Issue," *DN*, 14 Feb. 1959, A-2.

[199] Ernest L. Wilkinson diary, 3 June 1959; also entries for 11 June and 29 June regarding outside pressures on McKay and his vacillation.

[200] JRC report to the First Presidency and Quorum of Twelve, 20 Nov. 1958, in David O. McKay office diary, 15 Nov. 1958.

[201] Ernest L. Wilkinson diary, 11 Feb. 1959.

[202] Ernest L. Wilkinson diary, 23 Nov. 1960.

[203] David O. McKay office diary, 30 June 1960; also *R*, 244-45, for a different view of McKay's final decision.

[204] JRC to "Brother and Sister" Reynold Irwin, 2 Mar. 1956, fd 2, box 397, JRCP.

[205] For a general survey of his activities from 1951 onward, see JRC scrapbook.

[206] Thomas S. Monson, "Miracles—Then and Now," *Ensign* 22 (Nov. 1992): 68, reprinted in Monson, *Inspiring Experiences That Build Faith* (Salt Lake City: Deseret Book, 1994), 233-34; also Monson, "The Call of Duty," *Ensign* 16 (May 1986): 37: "It was my privilege to know President Clark rather well. I was his printer."

[207] JRC scrapbook; Chad M. Orton, *More Faith Than Fear: The Los Angeles Stake History* (Salt Lake City: Bookcraft, 1987), 181, 190-91; Richard O. Cowan and William E. Homer, *California Saints: A 150-Year Legacy in the Golden State* (Provo, UT: Religious Studies Center, Brigham Young University, 1996), 331, 348.

[208] Harold B. Lee diary, 12 June 1953, quoted in parts in *L*, 307-08; *Conf*, Sept.-Oct. 1967, 25-26.

[209] JRC to Fred Morris Dearing, 7 Nov. 1958, fd 6, box 402, JRCP.

[210] JRC to Mrs. A. Helen Morgan, 25 Feb., 11 Sept. 1952, fd 5, box 386, JRCP. The friend was Preston Richards.

[211] Harold B. Lee diary, 12, 30 Aug., 1 Sept. 1955; "Family, Friends, Admirers Honor Pres. Clark on His 84th Birthday," *CN*, 3 Sept. 1955, 2 (quote).

[212] JRC to Mrs. A. Helen Morgan, 16 June 1953, fd 2, box 389, JRCP.

[213] For example, JRC to Ernest L. Wilkinson, 9 Sept. 1957, fd 8, box 398, JRCP.

[214] Eleanor Knowles, *Howard W. Hunter* (Salt Lake City: Deseret Book, 1994), 133-34; also Harold B. Lee diary, 7 July 1956.

[215] JRC to LaRue Sneff, 28 Dec. 1957, fd 5, box 399, JRCP.

[216] David O. McKay office diary, 19 May 1959; Spencer W. Kimball diary, 21 May 1959; Gordon B. Hinckley, "An Appreciation of Stephen L Richards," *Improvement Era* 54 (July 1951): 499 (for quote); also *DM*, 134, regarding "Stephen L Richards of the Twelve, who was like a Jonathan to this David."

[217] David O. McKay office diary, 20 May 1959, emphasis in original.

[218] Ernest L. Wilkinson diary, 19 May 1959.

[219] Francis M. Gibbons, *Spencer W. Kimball: Resolute Disciple, Prophet of God* (Salt Lake City: Deseret Book, 1995), 224.

[220] Harold B. Lee diary, 12 June 1959, quoted in *H*, 335; *L*, 357; *W*, 187.

[221] David O. McKay office diary, 12 June 1959.

[222] Ernest L. Wilkinson diary, 20 July 1954; Gordon B. Affleck interviews by D. Michael Quinn; *W*, 90, 91, 150, 184.

[223] For example, JRC to Carl W. Buehner, 11 June 1959, fd 3, box 404, and JRC to President and Mrs. Arwell L. Pierce, 26 June 1959, fd 13, box 406, JRCP.

[224] "Pres. Clark Instructs MIA Leaders," *CN*, 20 June 1959, 3.

[225] Marion G. Romney diary, 15, 25 Jan., 4 Apr. 1959; JRC home diary, 17 Feb., 3 Mar. 1959, JRCP.

[226] JRC to Dr. Lawrence Foss Woolley, 16 Sept. 1959 (quote), fd 22, box 406, JRCP; also stated as "a nervous break-down and fatigue" in JRC to Walter and Ebba Mathesius, 15 Apr. 1960, fd 6, box 409, JRCP.

[227] Ernest L. Wilkinson diary, 5 Aug. 1959.

[228] Marion G. Romney diary, 18 Nov. 1959; Harold B. Lee diary, 21 Nov. 1959; JRC office diary, 8, 9 Mar. 1960; JRC to Walter and Ebba Mathesius, 15 Apr. 1960.

[229] JRC to Fortunato Anselmo, 30 Mar. 1943, fd 1, box 367; JRC to William P. Knecht, 20 Aug. 1946, fd 14, box 373; JRC to President and Mrs. Henry A. Smith, 9 Sept. 1957, fd 8, box 398; all in JRCP.

[230] JRC to John J. Massey, 4 Dec. 1957, fd 1, box 400, JRCP; also JRC to J. Willard Marriott, 19 June 1945, fd 6, box 372, and JRC to Lloyd Howard, 13 Oct. 1950, fd 11, box 381, both in JRCP.

[231] JRC to Mrs. A. Helen Morgan, 5 June 1957, fd 1, box 400, JRCP.

[232] Ernest L. Wilkinson diary, 3 June 1959.

[233] Marion G. Romney diary, 18 Nov. 1959.

[234] JRC to Frank R. Clark, 9 July 1960, fd 6, box 408, JRCP.

[235] JRC office diary, 15 Feb. 1960.

[236] Ernest L. Wilkinson diary, 3 June 1959.

[237] Marion G. Romney diary, 6 Nov. 1959, 15 Apr. 1960.

[238] JRC office diary, 4 Dec. 1959. Like most of this chapter, the reference to Apostle Benson was in the first draft I submitted for review in 1981 to LDS administrators. At that time he was the Twelve's president; he became church president in 1985.

[239] Ezra Taft Benson, *The Red Carpet* (Salt Lake City: Bookcraft, 1962), 144 (quote); also references to JRC in Dew, *Ezra Taft Benson,* 251; Benson, *Cross Fire: The Eight Years with Eisenhower* (Garden City, NY: Doubleday, 1962), 585; Benson, *Title of Liberty*, comp. Mark A. Benson (Salt Lake City: Deseret Book, 1964), 9, 74,

78-79, 82, 97, 108-10, 191, 222-25; Benson, *God, Family, Country: Our Three Great Loyalties* (Salt Lake City: Deseret Book, 1974), 38-39, 224-25, 229, 238, 255, 259, 261-62, 267, 271, 320, 323, 340-41, 342, 372, 375-76, 385, 395-97; Benson, *This Nation Shall Endure* (Salt Lake City: Deseret Book, 1977), 11, 19, 32, 33, 35, 43, 46, 97.

[240] JRC office diary, 13 Apr. 1961.

[241] Spencer W. Kimball interview with D. Michael Quinn, 2 Feb. 1979; also Derek A. Cuthbert, *The Second Century: Latter-day Saints in Great Britain, 1837-1987* (Salt Lake City: By the author, 1987), 52-53; D. Michael Quinn, "I-Thou vs. I-It Conversions: The Mormon Baseball Baptism Era," *Sunstone* 16 (Dec. 1993): 30-44; Richard Williams, "Crying on Cue," *Sunstone* 17 (June 1994): 6-7; Michael Rayback, "Gospel as Commodity," *Sunstone* 17 (Sept. 1994): 7-8; statements by a female missionary and by Apostle Joseph Fielding Smith in Mary Lythgoe Bradford, *Lowell L. Bennion: Teacher, Counselor, Humanitarian* (Salt Lake City: Dial Foundation, 1994), 142; *E*, 27-30; *W*, 208, 211-12.

[242] JRC office diary, 10 Nov. 1959.

[243] Marion G. Romney diary, 27 July 1960.

[244] JRC to meeting of mission presidents, 30 Mar. 1960, transcript, 1, box 151, JRCP.

[245] Ernest L. Wilkinson diary, 6 Sept. 1960, also 25 May 1961; *W*, 214, 216.

[246] Harold B. Lee diary, 23 June 1960.

[247] David O. McKay office diary, 7 Oct. 1960.

[248] Spencer W. Kimball diary, 9 Oct. 1960.

[249] *Conf*, Oct. 1960, 88.

[250] Marion G. Romney diary, 27 Oct. 1960.

[251] Harold B. Lee diary, 28 Oct. 1960, quoted in *L*, 387.

[252] Harold B. Lee diary, 10 Nov., 7 Dec., 18 Dec. 1960.

[253] Marion G. Romney diary, 9 Nov. 1960; Harold B. Lee diary, 7, 18 Dec. 1960; Harold B. Lee to Spencer W. Kimball, 1 Nov. 1960, in Kimball diary of that date; *L*, 388; also Ernest L. Wilkinson diary, 6 Sept. 1960.

[254] Ernest L. Wilkinson diary, 28 Apr., 7 Sept. 1960; also Gary James Bergera, "Building Wilkinson's University," *Dial* 30 (Fall 1997): 125-26, 128, 128n98.

[255] Marion G. Romney diary, 16 Jan. 1959; Harold B. Lee diary, 30 Mar. 1959 (first quote), 7 Jan. 1960 (second quote); Ernest L. Wilkinson diary, 4 Feb. 1960; also *W*, 212.

[256] Ernest L. Wilkinson diary, 9 Jan. 1960 (first pair of quotes), 10 Oct. 1961 (for last pair of quotes).

[257] Ernest L. Wilkinson diary, 24 Jan. 1958; also JRC to J. H. Gipson (president of Caxton Printers), 22 Sept. 1943, fd 2, box 367, JRCP.

[258] Dennis L. Lythgoe, *Let 'Em Holler: A Political Biography of J. Bracken Lee* (Salt Lake City: Utah State Historical Society, 1982), 101.

[259] Hugh B. Brown interview, 30 Nov. 1969, side 2, transcription, 23-24, now located in Edwin B. Firmage papers, JWML; also a revised version in Edwin B. Firmage, ed., *An Abundant Life: The Memoirs of Hugh B. Brown* (Salt Lake City: Signature Books, 1988), 131.

[260] Ernest L. Wilkinson diary, 7 Sept. 1960 (first set of quotes), 13 Oct. 1960 (last quote); also *DA*, 58, for "calamity howlers."

[261] Harold B. Lee to Spencer W. Kimball, 1 Nov. 1960, in Kimball diary of that date.

[262] David O. McKay office diary, 14 Nov. 1960.

[263] JRC to U.S. Senator Wallace F. Bennett, 2 Jan. 1961, JRCP; also David C. Gessel, "Wallace F. Bennett," in *U*, 39. President Clark's friends honored his wishes until he died, when a collection of his religious talks in *Behold the Lamb of God* (Salt Lake City: Deseret Book, 1962) and of his political talks in *F* were published.

[264] JRC to Milton R. Hunter, 2 Mar. 1953, fd 10, box 388; Rowena J. Miller to Nels B. Lundwall, 2 Apr. 1953, fd 1, box 389; JRC memorandum, 9 July 1958, unnumbered box; all JRCP.

[265] JRC office diary, 27 Feb. 1961.

[266] David O. McKay office diary, 14 Oct. 1960.

[267] Spencer W. Kimball diary, 13 Apr. 1961.

[268] JRC remarks to temple meeting of First Presidency and Quorum of the Twelve Apostles, 27 Apr. 1961, transcript, box 264, JRCP.

[269] Gordon B. Affleck interviews by D. Michael Quinn; A. Hamer Reiser interview by D. Michael Quinn, 1 Mar. 1980. After publication of the 1983 biography, I happened to meet a member of my LDS stake who had done repairs in the Church Administration Building. In this first encounter with a member of the First Presidency, Reuben, who was being wheeled down the hallway, apologized for not being able to stand and said: "Young man, old age is a sonofabitch!"

[270] JRC office diary, 15 May 1961.

[271] Ernest L. Wilkinson diary, 22 May 1961.

[272] David O. McKay office diary, 14 June 1961.

[273] JRC office diary, 15 June 1961.

[274] David O. McKay office diary, 22 June 1961.

[275] *Conf,* Oct. 1960, 88.

[276] David O. McKay office diary, 22 June 1961; Harold B. Lee diary, 22 June 1961; Campbell and Poll, *Hugh B. Brown,* 239-40. "Wept like the dickens" is in Hugh B. Brown interview, 30 Nov. 1969, side 2, transcription, 23, and in Firmage, ed., *An Abundant Life*, 131.

[277] Marion G. Romney diary, 5 July, 19 July 1961.

[278] Marion G. Romney diary, 19 July, 7 Aug. 1961; Harold B. Lee diary, 15 Aug. 1961.

[279] Marion G. Romney diary, 1 Sept. 1961; David O. McKay office diary, 1 Sept. 1961.

[280] David O. McKay office diary, 23 Sept. 1961.

[281] JRC office diary, 26 Sept. 1961; Harold B. Lee diary, 29 Sept. 1961.

[282] JRC office diary, 3 Oct. 1961.

[283] Jay Rubark, pseud. [JRC], "When I Would Pass," *Relief Society Magazine* 28 (June 1941): 375; box 224, JRCP.

[284] *Deseret News 1999-2000 Church Almanac* (Salt Lake City: Deseret News, 1998), for LDS membership in 1961.

[285] Marion G. Romney diary, 6 Oct. 1961; also *C*, 603, "For a man of hope, there was something undeniably tragic about his life."

NOTES TO CHAPTER 6

[1] 2 Cor 8:4.

[2] JRC office diary, 11 July 1950, JRCP; JRC to welfare meeting, 5 Apr. 1958, transcript, box 151, JRCP.

[3] This book uses the standard English forms of *proselytize* rather than the LDS variant *proselyte* (verb). See EM 4:1771.

[4] "Stokowski Tells of Mexico Visit with Pres. Clark," *DN*, 6 May 1936, 6; cf. Luacine S. Clark diary, 1 Feb. 1931, JRCP.

[5] JRC 1936 diary, 5 Sept., JRCP; JRC office diary, 9 Oct. 1951.

[6] JRC to Reeve Schley, 6 May 1941, fd 3, box 363, JRCP; *Who's Who in America*, 1940-41 ed. (Chicago: A.N. Marquis, 1940), 2283-84.

[7] JRC to Mrs. Francis M. Huntington-Wilson, 29 Mar. 1947, fd 13, box 378, JRCP; binder of JRC correspondence with Cloyd H. Marvin, box 189, JRCP; also originals of JRC letters in Marvin papers, Archives, George Washington University, Washington, D.C.

[8] Marion G. Romney diary, 29 Oct. 1943, private possession.

[9] JRC to A— H———, 15 Sept. 1948, fd 10, box 377, JRCP.

[10] JRC to D. Arthur Haycock, president of the Hawaiian Mission, 4 Mar. 1957, fd 11, box 399, JRCP.

[11] Derek A. Cuthbert, *The Second Century: Latter-day Saints in Great Britain, 1837-1987* (Salt Lake City: By the author, 1987), 52-53; D. Michael Quinn, "I-Thou vs. I-It Conversions: The Mormon Baseball Baptism Era," *Sunstone* 16 (Dec. 1993): 30-44; Richard Williams, "Crying on Cue," *Sunstone* 17 (June 1994): 6-7; Michael Rayback, "Gospel as Commodity," *Sunstone* 17 (Sept. 1994): 7-8; statements by a female missionary and by Apostle Joseph Fielding Smith in Mary Lythgoe Bradford, *Lowell L. Bennion: Teacher, Counselor, Humanitarian* (Salt Lake City: Dialogue Foundation, 1994), 142; *E*, 27-30; *W*, 208, 211-12.

[12] JRC office diary, 4 Oct. 1947.

[13] JRC to missionary meeting, 6 Apr. 1956, transcript, 2, box 151, JRCP.

[14] Related by Mr. and Mrs. Clifford Hunter in JRC office diary, 9 Apr. 1956.

[15] JRC to Mrs. Nephi Probst, 7 Nov. 1958, fd 7, box 403, JRCP.

[16] Spencer W. Kimball diary, 20 Apr., 23 Apr. 1950, private possession; Edward L. Kimball and Andrew E. Kimball Jr., *Spencer W. Kimball, Twelfth President of The Church of Jesus Christ of Latter-day Saints* (Salt Lake City: Bookcraft, 1977), 264.

[17] JRC office diary, 25 July 1939; Heber J. Grant journal sheets, 25 July 1939, LDSA.

[18] Melvin R. Ballard, *Melvin J. Ballard: Crusader for Righteousness* (Salt Lake City: Bookcraft, 1966), 95.

[19] *Conf,* Apr. 1960, 21.

[20] Harold B. Lee diary, 7 May 1947 (administration), private possession; *H*, 211.

[21] Marion G. Romney diary, 11 Feb. 1945.

[22] JRC office diary, 23 Nov. 1960.

[23] JRC office diary, 24 Mar. 1959.

[24] *Conf,* Oct. 1952, 84; JRC office diary, 3 Nov. 1952; also Roger L. Miller, "Mormon Tabernacle Choir," in *U,* 380.

[25] JRC to Mrs. M——— G. L——, 6 May 1949, fd 1, box 380, JRCP.

[26] JRC to Mrs. Romania Woolley, 16 Sept. 1957, fd 16, box 400, JRCP.

[27] JRC to Mr. and Mrs. Arthur Bliss Lane, 25 Apr. 1947, fd 11, box 376, JRCP.

[28] Harold B. Lee diary, 25 Apr. 1946.

[29] JRC office diary, 23 June 1949.

[30] JRC to Mrs. Marie Ryberg, 11 Feb. 1950, fd 12, box 382, JRCP; also JRC to Irving S. Olds of New York City, 31 July 1957, fd 5, box 400, JRCP.

[31] JRC office diary, 2 Aug. 1951.

[32] Harold B. Lee diary, 30 June 1952.

[33] W——— C— to JRC, 9 July, 3 Sept. 1933, in "Cranks 1937" fd, box 358, JRCP; also "disfellowshipment" in the glossary of *EM* 4:1767.

[34] T— G—— to JRC, undated, and JRC to T— G——, 18 Apr. 1938, both in box 153, JRCP.

[35] Folder 2, box 398, JRCP.

[36] JRC office diary, 11 Sept. 1945 (first quote), 14 Dec. 1945 (last quote), 27 June 1947, 17 Mar. 1948.

[37] Folder 6, box 403, JRCP.

[38] JRC office diary, 8 July 1949.

[39] JRC to W——— D——, 9 Oct. 1933, fd 7 ("Cranks"), box 358, JRCP.

[40] JRC to Spencer W. and Camilla Kimball, 6 Sept. 1958, fd 7, box 401, JRCP.

[41] JRC office diary, 20 Mar. 1951.

[42] G——— W. A—— to JRC, 30 Dec. 1946, fd 4, box 373, JRCP.

[43] *C,* 556.

[44] Transcript of JRC ordination of Samuel W. Clark to office of bishop, 15 Feb. 1941, fd 1, box 363, JRCP.

[45] Thomas S. Monson, "A Provident Plan—A Precious Promise," *Ensign* 16 (May 1986): 62.

[46] JRC to meeting of stake presidencies, ward bishoprics and other officers, 5 Apr. 1937, transcript, box 151, JRCP.

[47] JRC to Milton H. Ross, 28 Mar. 1951, fd 6, box 384, JRCP.

[48] JRC to bishops' meeting, 1 Oct. 1948, transcript, box 151, JRCP.

[49] JRC to bishops' meeting, 5 Apr. 1949, transcript, box 151, JRCP.

[50] Bruce C. Hafen, "J. Reuben Clark: The Man and the Message," *BYU Today* 42 (Sept. 1988): 2.

[51] Marion G. Romney, "Political Thought and Life of J. Reuben Clark, Jr.,"

in *Speeches of the Year: BYU Devotional Addresses, 1972-1973* (Provo, UT: Brigham Young University Press/Young House, 1973), 55.

[52] JRC office diary, 28 May 1939.

[53] For example, JRC to R— M. R———, 18 Mar. 1953, fd 8, box 389, JRCP.

[54] JRC office diary, 2 June 1943.

[55] For the transition from a less stringent approach, see Leonard J. Arrington, "An Economic Interpretation of the Word of Wisdom," *BYU Studies* 1 (Winter 1959): 37-49; Lester E. Bush Jr., "The Word of Wisdom in Early Nineteenth-Century Perspective," and Thomas G. Alexander, "The Word of Wisdom: From Principle to Requirement," *Dial* 14 (Autumn 1981): 47-65, 78-88; *T,* 258-71; Joseph Lynn Lyon, "Word of Wisdom," in *EM* 4:1584-85; Clyde Ford, "The Origin of the Word of Wisdom," *JMH* 24 (Fall 1998): 129-54; also *E* (consult index).

[56] JRC to bishops' meeting, 1 Oct. 1948. He said this during the presidency of George Albert Smith but not during that of Heber J. Grant, who stridently emphasized the Word of Wisdom. In April 1932 Apostle Stephen L Richards made a similar statement in general conference and President Grant refused to publish his talk. Grant asked Richards to recant during the temple meeting of the presidency and Twelve on 5 May 1932. Richards refused and offered to resign from the Twelve. His status as an apostle was in jeopardy until he apologized three weeks later. See Heber J. Grant journal sheets, 8, 11, 21 Apr., 5, 26-27 May 1932; David O. McKay office diary, 26 Apr., 5 May 1932, LDSA; David O. McKay personal diary, 5 May 1932, in David Lawrence McKay papers, JWML; Reed Smoot diary, 8 May 1932, in *I,* 686.

[57] *D&C* 89.

[58] JRC pencil notes, described as "draft not used," October 1947 conference fd, box 159, JRCP. His statement in 1948 was a toned down version of this.

[59] JRC office diary, 30 Jan. 1950; also John A. Widtsoe and Leah D. Widtsoe, *The Word of Wisdom: A Modern Interpretation* (Salt Lake City: Deseret Book, 1937); Ralph B. Simmons, ed., *Utah's Distinguished Personalities: A Biographical Directory of Eminent Contemporaneous Men and Women Who Are the Faithful Builders and Defenders of the State* (Salt Lake City: Personality Publishing, 1933), 216, for her sketch.

[60] To place Clark's counsel on sexual conduct in perspective, see Marvin Rytting and Ann Rytting, "Exhortations for Chastity: A Content Analysis of Church Literature," *Sunstone* 7 (Mar.-Apr. 1982): 15-21. Clarkana includes Auguste Forel, *La Question Sexuell: Exposé aux Adultes Cultives* (Paris: G. Steinheil, 1906); Walter S. Keating, *pseud.* [Henrietta Rosenberg], *Sex Studies from Freud to Kinsey* (New York: Plaza Book, 1954).

[61] "Chastity Held Vital to Welfare of Youth," *DN,* 9 June 1941, [1].

[62] JRC, "Plain Talk to Girls," *Improvement Era* 49 (Aug. 1946): 492; *SR,* 209-10.

[63] *Conf,* Oct. 1949, 195.

[64] JRC to bishops' meeting, 7 Apr. 1950, transcript, box 151, JRCP.

[65] *Conf,* Oct. 1951, 171.

[66] Gordon Burt Affleck statement to me after a high council meeting in 1979; *E*, 307, for the context of this surveillance.

[67] JRC, "Home, and the Building of Home Life," *Relief Society Magazine* 39 (Dec. 1952): 793-94, also 791 (second quote). These quotes from the LDS magazine, which I deleted under protest from the 1983 book, were in my 1981 draft.

[68] JRC, "Home, and the Building of Home Life," 793-94, order of quotes reversed; also in D. Michael Quinn, *Same-Sex Dynamics among Nineteenth-Century Americans: A Mormon Example* (Urbana: University of Illinois Press, 1996), 373; *E*, 839 (entry for 2 Oct. 1952).

[69] *Conf,* Oct. 1954, 79. This quote was in the first draft I submitted for official review in 1981. BYU administrator Robert K. Thomas asked me to delete it as one of the revisions recommended by apostles Hunter and Monson. I protested that officially published statements should not be censored from the authorized biography.

In 1981 my own beliefs were in stark contrast to Reuben's views of homosexuality, which I nonetheless wanted to portray as he expressed them. As I wrote in *Same-Sex Dynamics among Nineteenth-Century Americans*, 4: "I conclude that heterosexuality is no more moral than right-handedness and that homosexuality is no less moral than left-handedness. Homosexuality is simply left-handed sexuality, and bisexuality is simply ambidextrous sexuality. ... The exceptional in nature is still 'natural,' whether the exception is left-handedness or the homosexual orientation of erotic desire."

[70] JRC home diary, 2 Oct. 1960, JRCP.

[71] Wilford E. Smith, "Mormon Sex Standards on College Campuses, or Deal Us Out of the Sexual Revolution," *Dial* 10 (Autumn 1976): 77. This was the finding of Professor Smith from questionnaires distributed over a twenty-year period to BYU sociology students identified on page 77 as "Mormons in a large church university." While I was enrolled in a BYU sociology course during the 1962-63 school year, I took this survey, which was identified to us as Wilford E. Smith's questionnaire. I was one of those homosexually inclined persons who had remained celibate, yet I declined to answer "yes" when this survey asked if I had homosexual feelings. I have talked with other males who declined to report the fact that they had had homoerotic experiences. For this reason I believe that Smith's article under-reported the percentage of those who privately regarded themselves as homosexual and under-reported those with homoerotic experience.

A comparison with surveys conducted at other universities with high percentages of Mormon students is instructive. For example, a survey of 200 single men (median age: 19) enrolled in marriage-preparation courses at the University of Utah during 1949 showed that 16.5 percent of them reported "active participation in some kind of homosexual practice." Since these men were preparing to marry women, there was probably a smaller percentage of self-identified homosexuals in this study than in the general population. Sixty-nine percent of this total group were LDS, 80 percent reporting active attendance at church. See John Albert Pennock, "A Study of the Sexual Attitudes and Behavior of Two Hundred Single College Men," M.A. thesis, University of Utah, 1949, 22, 24, 50.

[72] *Conf,* Oct. 1949, 194; *SR,* 161.

[73] *Conf,* Oct. 1951, 58; also JRC, "Home, and the Building of Home Life," 793-94; Quinn, *Same-Sex Dynamics among Nineteenth-Century Americans,* 392n45 (first line); Eric G. Swedin, "'One Flesh': A Historical Overview of Latter-day Saint Sexuality and Psychology," *Dial* 31 (Winter 1998): 1-29.

[74] JRC office diary, 28 Nov. 1941, 24 Aug. 1948.

[75] Marginal notation in Edward Gibbon, *The Decline and Fall of the Roman Empire,* 5 vols. (New York: International Book, 1845), 1:406, in Clarkana.

[76] JRC, "Home, and the Building of Home Life," 795.

[77] JRC office diary, 11 Sept. 1950. For the context and significance of JRC's instructions to this stake president, see Quinn, *Same-Sex Dynamics among Nineteenth-Century Americans,* 372-73.

[78] JRC memorandum, 12 July 1937, box 385, JRCP.

[79] JRC to Richard R. Lyman, 18 Apr. 1956, fd 15, box 396, JRCP.

[80] Elder Lyman's situation is described in Kimball and Kimball, *Spencer W. Kimball,* 208-09, 346; *E,* 669, 670; Quinn, *Same-Sex Dynamics among Nineteenth-Century Americans,* 372, 388n25.

[81] JRC office diary, 1 Oct. 1950.

[82] JRC to Thaddeus A. Davis (chief of Probation Department, U.S. District, Los Angeles, California), 21 June 1938, fd 1, box 359, JRCP.

[83] JRC office diary, 29 Nov. 1945; more fully quoted in *E,* 832.

[84] JRC remarks to bishops' meeting, 3 Oct. 1947, transcript, box 151, JRCP.

[85] Jill Mulvay Derr, Janath Russell Cannon, and Maureen Ursenbach Beecher, *Women of Covenant: The Story of Relief Society* (Salt Lake City: Deseret Book, 1992), 340-41.

[86] Harold B. Lee diary, 14 June 1946 (quote), also: "I spoke my mind frankly and perhaps with considerable impatience"), as well as entry for 15 June 1946: "Pres. Clark talked with me later and told me his daughter [in the Relief Society presidency] had informed him I had walked out on a previous meeting where this same question was under discussion."

[87] JRC to R— T—— W———, 7 Feb. 1941, fd 3, box 363, JRCP.

[88] JRC to H.H. W—, 24 Apr. 1953, fd 14, box 389, JRCP.

[89] Ancestral File, FHL (also available in every stake of North America), for Brigham Young (b. 1801) and cousin-wife Rhoda Richards (beyond child-bearing age), Lorenzo Snow (b. 1814) and cousin-wife Mary A. Goddard (3 children), Joseph F. Smith (b. 1838) and cousin-wife Levira A. C. Smith (first wife, divorced after eight years, no children); Willard Richards (b. 1804) and cousin-wife Jennetta Richards (3 children), Abraham H. Cannon (b. 1859) and cousin-wife Wilhelmina M. Cannon (6 children), Franklin D. Richards (b. 1821) and cousin-wife Susan S. Peirson (3 children); William W. Taylor (b. 1853) and cousin-wife Sarah T. Hoagland (6 children). The cousin relationships can be ascertained by selecting the *pedigree* function key for each of their names. Apostle Willard Richards (b. 1804) also married his niece Amelia E. Peirson (1 child).

[90] JRC to Mrs. D—— T——, 3 June 1941, copy in JRCP, original in possession of her granddaughter from whom I received a photocopy. For clarity I added

the parentheses in the last sentence around the phrase that was in the original letter.

⁹¹ Letter from their daughter C—— T—— Z———— to D. Michael Quinn, 8 Aug. 2000.

⁹² Jessie L. Embry, "Ultimate Taboos: Incest and Mormon Polygamy," *JMH* 18 (Spring 1992): 103 (Utah's 1907 law), 104–05 (Watt's marriage); also *E*, 752, for Brigham Young's public sermon, "I beleive [sic] in Sisters marrying brothers and brothers haveing [sic] their sisters for Wives." See Scott G. Kenney, ed., *Wilford Woodruff's Journal, 1833-1898 Typescript,* 9 vols. (Midvale, UT: Signature Books, 1983-85), 4: 290, for Watt as stenographer and Woodruff's statement that this was "the greatest sermon that ever was delivered to the Latter day Saints since they have been a people." Cf. *The Essential Brigham Young* (Salt Lake City: Signature Books, 1992), 98.

Lorenzo Snow told a fellow apostle that "brothers and sisters would marry each other in this church. All our horror at such a union was due entirely to prejudice, and the offspring of such unions would be as healthy and pure as any other. These were the decided views of Pres. Young, when alive, for Bro. S[now] talked to him freely on this matter." See Abraham H. Cannon diary, 15 July 1886, HBLL, with photocopies at the JWML and Utah State Historical Society, Salt Lake City.

⁹³ JRC to general priesthood meeting, 4 Oct. 1947, transcript, box 151, JRCP. His reference to "seventy-five years" shows that this conversation probably occurred after his seventy-fifth birthday on 1 September 1946.

⁹⁴ JRC to Mutual Improvement Associations, 15 June 1958, transcript, box 151, JRCP.

⁹⁵ JRC to B— C——, 19 Aug. 1947, fd 6, box 399, JRCP.

⁹⁶ JRC to bishops' meeting, 3 Oct. 1947, transcript, box 151, JRCP.

⁹⁷ JRC office diary, 17 Aug. 1953.

⁹⁸ JRC to L— C——, 28 Nov. 1959, box 405, JRCP.

⁹⁹ Rowena J. Miller to Mrs. T—— R. M——, 14 Mar. 1952, fd 5, box 386, JRCP.

¹⁰⁰ Kirk H. Porter and Donald Bruce Johnson, comps., *National Party Platforms, 1840-1956* (Urbana: University of Illinois Press, 1956), 393, 412, 453.

¹⁰¹ *Conf,* Apr. 1944, 115–16.

¹⁰² *Congressional Record* 96:861; Joan Hoff-Wilson, ed., *Rights of Passage: The Past and Future of the ERA* (Bloomington: Indiana University Press, 1986), 122. The phrase "hysteric opposition" was in the first draft I submitted for review by LDS administrators in 1981.

¹⁰³ JRC office diary, 25 Jan. 1950; also *E*, 373–401, for the different response of subsequent LDS leaders to the proposed Equal Rights Amendment.

¹⁰⁴ JRC, "Home, and the Building of Home Life," 791.

¹⁰⁵ JRC office diary, 10 Aug. 1933. LDS church headquarters has recently returned to JRC's policy about individually decided birth control. See "LDS Handbook Says Family Size Up to Couple, God," *SLT,* 5 Dec. 1998, A-1, A-6; also for the rank-and-file realities which led to this 1998 change, see Tim B. Heaton,

"Contraceptive Use among Mormons, 1965-75," *Dial* 16 (Autumn 1983): 106-09.

From McKay's presidency in 1951 to the incapacitation of President Benson in 1992, two years before his death, various LDS presidents, apostles, and handbooks condemned the individual initiative of married couples in delaying childbearing and/or limiting the number of children. See Lester E. Bush Jr., "Birth Control among the Mormons: Introduction to an Insistent Question," *Dial* 10 (Autumn 1976): 27-29, 41n100, 42nn101-02, who also quoted (25-26) JRC's 1949 statement to general conference: "Remember the prime purpose of sex desire [is] to beget children. Sex gratification must be had at that hazard." That is what his 1933 statement referred to as "the principles of the Church that govern such matters," yet he regarded all such matters to be "left for determination to each individual man and wife." On the issue of individual choice, see "Man's Free Agency" in James E. Talmage, *The Articles of Faith: A Series of Lectures on the Principal Doctrines of the Church of Jesus Christ of Latter-day Saints ... Written by Appointment; and Published by the Church* (Salt Lake City: Deseret News, 1899), 54-57; and "Agency" in Bruce R. McConkie, *Mormon Doctrine,* 2d ed. (Salt Lake City: Bookcraft, 1966), 26-28.

106 JRC memorandum, 8 Feb. 1936, box 87, CR 1/44, LDSA.

107 JRC office diary, 12 May 1933.

108 JRC office diary, 28 Apr. 1958.

109 *Conf,* Oct. 1951, 58.

110 JRC to David A. Broadbent, 12 May 1948, fd 2, box 377, JRCP; also his entry in Ancestral File, FHL. He was no relation to the Mormon fundamentalist leader Joseph Leslie Broadbent.

111 JRC to bishops' meeting, 3 Oct. 1947. For one of Kimball's statements about LDS leaders neglecting their own children, see Thomas E. Cheney, *The Golden Legacy: A Folk History of J. Golden Kimball* (Santa Barbara, CA: Peregrine Smith, 1974), 134-35.

NOTES TO CHAPTER 7

1 *D&C* 88: 118.

2 Lute to JRC, 23 Aug. 1906, box 328, JRCP.

3 Reported in Lute to JRC, 14 Apr. 1940, box 338, JRCP.

4 JRC dictation, 1 Sept. 1956, transcript, box 225, JRCP.

5 Ernest L. Wilkinson diary, 28 Mar. 1956, photocopy, JWML.

6 Clarkana.

7 JRC, *Why the King James Version?* (Salt Lake City: Deseret Book, 1956), vii-viii.

8 JRC office diary, 7 July 1955, JRCP. This conversation occurred while Deseret Book was preparing to publish his study.

9 JRC office diary, 5 June 1956.

10 JRC to Ernest L. Wilkinson, 8 Feb. 1950 (first set of quotes) and 28 Feb. 1950 (second set), both in fd 18, box 382, JRCP.

[11] See discussion and quotes for notes 12 and 15.

[12] JRC to Frank R. Clark, 4 Mar. 1946, with manuscript draft (12 Jan. 1946) of Clark's general observations about Brodie's biography, plus a proposed review (18 Feb. 1946) of her book, all in box 234, JRCP. Cf. Fawn M. Brodie, *No Man Knows My History: The Life of Joseph Smith, the Mormon Prophet* (New York: Alfred A. Knopf, 1945); Marvin S. Hill, "Brodie Revisited: A Reappraisal," *Dial* 7 (Winter 1972): 72-85; Newell G. Bringhurst, "Fawn M. Brodie, 'Mormonism's Lost Generation,' and *No Man Knows My History*," *JMH* 16 (1990): 11-24; William O. Nelson, "Anti-Mormon Publications," in *EM* 1:50; Bringhurst, "Fawn McKay Brodie," in *U*, 58.

[13] JRC office diary, 9 May 1946; also Peggy Petersen Barton, *Mark E. Petersen: A Biography* (Salt Lake City: Deseret Book, 1985), 75-76: "President Clark kept his eye on the young man. He chose Mark Petersen as a protégé, and Mark cherished this great man as teacher and example."

[14] "Appraisal of the So-Called Brodie Book," *CN*, 11 May 1946, 1, 6, 8.

[15] A. Hamer Reiser memorandum to JRC, 15 May 1959, and JRC to A. Ray Olpin (president, University of Utah), 30 May 1959, attached to Olpin's presentation copy of McMurrin's *The Philosophical Foundations of Mormon Theology*, along with Olpin to JRC, 11 May 1959, in Clarkana.

[16] JRC to Sidney B. Sperry, 11 Jan. 1956, fd 7, box 397, JRCP.

[17] JRC to Nephi Jensen, 13 Dec. 1940, fd 2, box 362, JRCP. Clarkana has Septimus J. Hanna, *Christian Science History* ... (Boston: Christian Science Publication Society, 1899); also Ellen G. White, *The Great Controversy between Christ and Satan: The Conflict of the Ages in the Christian Dispensation* (Mountain View, CA: Pacific Press Publishing, 1911); also *The New Encyclopaedia Britannica,* 15th ed., 30 vols. (Chicago: Encyclopaedia Britannica, 1998), 4:364 (for Mary Baker Eddy, founder of Christian Science). Neither the *Britannica* nor *EA* has an article about Ellen G. White, the "prophetess and cofounder" of Seventh-day Adventism. See Ronald L. Numbers, "White, Ellen Gould," in Mircea Eliade, ed., *The Encyclopedia of Religion,* 15 vols. (New York: Macmillan Publishing, 1987), 15:337-79.

[18] Rowena J. Miller to Mrs. Walter H. Durrant, 27 Oct. 1959, fd 7, box 405, JRCP; Clarkana has Edwin Arnold, *The Light of Asia; Or the Great Renunciation ... Being the Life and Teachings of Gautama, Prince of India and Founder of Buddhism* ... (New York: A. L. Burt, 1879); *Religions in Japan* (Tokyo: General Headquarters, Supreme Commander for the Allied Powers, Civil Information and Education Section, Religions and Cultural Resources Division, 1948).

[19] JRC to Thomas I. Parkinson, 11 July 1947, fd 16, box 376, JRCP.

[20] For example, Marion G. Romney diary, 16 Jan. 1959, private possession; also President Clark's negative comment about "intellectuals" in *Conf,* Oct. 1956, 96. The only publications titled *intellectual, intellectuals, intellectualism, liberals,* or *liberalism* in Reuben's personal library focused on socialism or Communism, both of which he despised and feared. Clarkana has the following: Paul Lafargue, *Socialism and the Intellectuals,* trans. Charles H. Kerr (Chicago: C. H. Kerr, 1900); Santeri Nuorteva, *An Open Letter to American Liberals ...* (New York: Socialist Publication Society, 1918); George H. Soule, *The Intellectual and the Labor Movement* (New

York: League for Industrial Democracy, 1923); Frank S. Bell, *The New Deal: The Masque Torn off: The Issue, Americanism vs. Communism Masquerading under the Term Liberalism* (Twin Falls, ID: By the author, 1934); Joseph Stalin, *Marxism vs. Liberalism* (New York: International Publishers, 1935); V. J. Jerome, *Intellectuals and the War* (New York: Workers' Library Publishers, 1940); Carey McWilliams, *The Liberals and the War Crisis* (Los Angeles: Southern California Branch of the American Civil Liberties Union, [1940]); Howard Fast, *Intellectuals in the Fight for Peace* (New York: Masses and Mainstream, 1949). The Communist Party's publishing houses often had "international" or "worker" in their names.

²¹ JRC to Cloyd H. Marvin, 1 Dec. 1956, 9 Dec. 1959, binder of JRC-Marvin correspondence, box 189, JRCP; originals of JRC letters in Marvin papers, Archives, George Washington University, Washington, D.C.

²² *Conf,* Oct. 1954, 38; JRC, "Our Priceless Special Blessings," *Improvement Era* 57 (Dec. 1954): 879.

²³ *Conf,* Apr. 1952, 95; JRC, "Our Destiny Was Planned," *Improvement Era* 55 (June 1952): 412.

²⁴ Richard Hofstadter, *Anti-Intellectualism in American Life* (New York: Alfred A. Knopf, 1963), 27.

²⁵ Leonard J. Arrington, "The Intellectual Tradition of the Latter-day Saints," *Dial* 4 (Spring 1969): 22n22; cf. Richard F. Haglund Jr. and David J. Whittaker, "Intellectual History," in *EM* 2:689 (for "J. Reuben Clark, Jr. in international affairs").

²⁶ JRC to Ormand Coulam, 3 Sept. 1938, fd 1, box 359, JRCP.

²⁷ The Book of Mormon. For recent works on the historicity of the Book of Mormon, see D. Michael Quinn, *Early Mormonism and the Magic World View,* rev. and enl. ed. (Salt Lake City: Signature Books, 1998), 352n101.

²⁸ JRC memorandum #3, fd J9, box 90, JRCP.

²⁹ JRC to J. Willard Marriott, 6 Mar. 1946, fd 2, box 347, JRCP.

³⁰ JRC office diary, 22 Aug. 1959.

³¹ JRC to Thomas Stuart Ferguson, 16 May 1957, box 340, JRCP; his letter to Ferguson on 29 March 1957 referred to "this Catholic veneer" (box 340); see also Stan Larson, *Quest for the Gold Plates: Thomas Stuart Ferguson's Archaeological Search for The Book of Mormon* (Salt Lake City: Freethinker Press, 1996), with specific references to JRC on 18, 37, 47, 72-73.

³² Ernest L. Wilkinson and Leonard J. Arrington, eds., *Brigham Young University: The First One Hundred Years,* 4 vols. (Provo, UT: Brigham Young University Press, 1975-76), 2:224.

³³ JRC, "The Chartered Course of the Church in Education," in *CN,* 13 Aug. 1938, 6; in *Improvement Era* 41 (Sept. 1938): 572; in Wilkinson and Arrington, eds., *Brigham Young University,* 2:246; with full reprint in *SR,* 243-59.

³⁴ Lucile C. Tate, *Boyd K. Packer: A Watchman on the Tower* (Salt Lake City: Bookcraft, 1995), 199; also David E. Buchanan, "An Analysis of the Immediate and Long-Range Implications of Three Speeches Delivered by J. Reuben Clark, Jr.," M.A. thesis, Brigham Young University, 1976, 22-39 (for "The Chartered Course of the Church in Education"); Bruce C. Hafen, "J. Reuben Clark: The

Man and the Message," *BYU Today* 42 (Sept. 1988): 3; Bryan Waterman and Brian Kagel, *The Lord's University: Freedom and Authority at BYU* (Salt Lake City: Signature Books, 1998), 443-45.

[35] Boyd K. Packer, *Teach Ye Diligently* (Salt Lake City: Deseret Book, 1975), 307-21.

[36] Sterling M. McMurrin and L. Jackson Newell, *Matters of Conscience: Conversations with Sterling M. McMurrin on Philosophy, Education, and Religion* (Salt Lake City: Signature Books, 1996), 115.

[37] JRC office diary, 21 Apr., 27 Apr. 1944, 4 Mar. 1946, 21 Apr. 1950.

[38] Heber J. Grant, JRC, and David O. McKay to Committee on Publications (Joseph Fielding Smith, John A. Widtsoe, Harold B. Lee, and Marion G. Romney), 9 Aug. 1944, LDSA, quoted in *M* 6:208-11.

[39] Wilkinson and Arrington, eds., *Brigham Young University,* 2:261, 3:139-40. JRC office diary, 21 Apr. 1950, expressed his first objection to "a postgraduate school at the BYU."

[40] JRC to Ernest L. Wilkinson, 17 Nov. 1956, fd 5, box 15, Wilkinson papers, HBLL; quoted in part in Wilkinson and Arrington, eds., *Brigham Young University: The First One Hundred Years,* 2:651.

The previous quotes highlight the decades-old conflict between Mormons like Clark who want BYU to be an LDS "divinity school" for all its students versus those who want it to become a "real" university of both committed faith and rigorous academic freedom like Notre Dame, the country's pre-eminent Catholic university. BYU came closest to the latter synthesis while Dallin H. Oaks was its president from the early 1970s to early 1980s, but in recent years administrators and trustees have enforced the kind of emphasis that Clark advocated. See Gary James Bergera and Ronald Priddis, *Brigham Young University: A House of Faith* (Salt Lake City: Signature Books, 1985), 32-40, 342, 357, 367, 385n69; Waterman and Kagel, *The Lord's University*; Martha C. Nussbaum, *Cultivating Humanity: A Classical Defense of Reform in Education* (Cambridge, MA: Harvard University Press, 1997), 257-99 (for specific comparison of BYU and Notre Dame), reviewed by BYU and Notre Dame graduate R. Dennis Potter, "Religious Education in a Liberal World," *Sunstone* 22 (June 1999): 64-69.

[41] Ernest L. Wilkinson diary, 6 Jan., 24 Feb., 28 Apr., 7 Sept., 19 Oct. 1960; JRC office diary, 13 Feb. 1960; Gary James Bergera, "Building Wilkinson's University," *Dial* 30 (Fall 1997): 125-26, 128, 128n98.

[42] JRC pencil notes, marked "draft not used," attached to October 1947 conference fd, box 159, JRCP.

[43] JRC to Frank L. Perris, 29 Jan. 1936, fd 1, box 354, JRCP.

[44] Ernest L. Wilkinson diary, 18 July 1956.

[45] JRC to N. L. Nelson, 24 June 1941, fd 2, box 363, JRCP. JRC was outraged when Nelson used quotes from this letter to advertise his book. See JRC to Nelson, 5 Feb. 1942, fd 2, box 365, JRCP; also Davis Bitton, "N. L. Nelson and the Mormon Point of View," *BYU Studies* 13 (Winter 1973): 157-71.

[46] JRC office diary, 16 Apr. 1948. Petersen was specifically mentioned in the first draft I submitted in 1981 for review by LDS administrators. The 1983

printing changed the reference to "someone." Elder Petersen was then a senior member of the Twelve and died in 1984.

[47] JRC pencil notes, "draft not used," attached to October 1947 conference folder; also Susan Easton Black, "Celestial Kingdom," in *EM* 1:259-60; Shamma Friedman and Leib Moscovitz, "Talmud," in R. J. Zwi Werblowsky and Geoffrey Wigoder, eds., *The Oxford Dictionary of the Jewish Religion* (New York: Oxford University Press, 1997), 669-72. Clarkana has the following: Michael L. Rodkinson, *New Edition of the Babylonian Talmud,* 2d ed., rev. and enl. (Boston: Talmud Society, 1918), including JRC underlinings and marginal notations; *Hebraic Literature: Translations from the Talmud, Midrashim and Kabbala* (New York: Tudor Publishing, 1936); Eugene N. Sanctuary, *The Talmud Unmasked: The Secret Rabbinical Teachings Concerning Christians* (New York: N.p., 1939); Charles L. Russell, *The Babylonian Talmud: In Selection* (New York: Philosophical Library, 1944).

[48] *J* 8:9 (B. Young/1860).

[49] JRC to J. Reuben Clark III, 23 May 1929, box 355, JRCP.

[50] *Conf,* Apr. 1949, 187.

[51] JRC statement to temple meeting of the First Presidency and Quorum of Twelve, 8 Apr. 1943 (quote), transcript in "Budget Beginnings," bound volume, 15, box 188, JRCP; also "A Conversation with Elder Neal Maxwell," in Hugh Hewett, *Searching for God in America* (Dallas, TX: Word, 1996), 128; "Tactical Revelation," *Sunstone* 19 (Dec. 1996): 80.

[52] JRC to M——— R. R—, 24 Sept. 1953, fd 8, box 389, JRCP. For statements by LDS apostles and prophets about God as a progressing personage, see Gary James Bergera, "Does God Progress in Knowledge?," *Dial* 15 (Spring 1982): 179-81; *E*, 757, 763, 764, 803, 846, 874. Cf. Bruce R. McConkie, "The Seven Deadly Heresies," in *1980 Devotional Speeches of the Year: BYU Devotional and Fireside Addresses* (Provo, UT: Brigham Young University Press, 1981), 75: "Heresy One: There are those who say that God is progressing in knowledge and is learning new truths. This is false—utterly, totally, and completely."

[53] *M* 4:266-67. For studies of the complexity of this matter, see Rodney Turner, "The Position of Adam in Latter-day Saint Scripture and Theology," M.A. thesis, Brigham Young University, 1953; David John Buerger, "The Adam-God Doctrine," *Dial* 15 (Spring 1982): 14-58; Quinn, *Early Mormonism and the Magic World View,* 234, 304.

In 1992 *EM* adopted a curious approach to this matter. The index (4:1776) stated: "Adam-God. *See* God," but there was no reference to Adam under God, God the Father, Godhead, nor Godhood (4:1799-1800). Volume one had: "ADAM-GOD. See: Young, Brigham: Teachings of Brigham Young." In that entry (4:1611) Hugh Nibley did not cite the First Presidency's official statement but instead referred to this well-documented doctrine/theory in an oblique manner: "Brigham Young recognized that many people were not prepared to understand the mysteries of God and godhood. 'I could tell you much more about this,' he said, speaking of the role of ADAM, but checked himself, recognizing that the world would probably misinterpret his teaching (*J* 1:51)." Aside from the fact that Brigham Young did talk about Adam as God in this 1852 sermon and in increasing detail for twenty-five years afterward, Nibley's approach allowed his readers to conclude that Adam was actually God the Father.

[54] JRC to D—— C. L——, 2 July 1946, fd 1, box 374, JRCP.

[55] JRC to G—— E. W———, 28 Oct. 1936, fd 2, box 354, JRCP. The controversy among general authorities in the nineteenth century concerning the Adam-God doctrine is discussed in Gary James Bergera, "The Orson Pratt-Brigham Young Controversies: Conflict within the Quorums, 1853-1868," *Dial* 13 (Summer 1980): 7-49.

[56] John A. Widtsoe, ed., *Discourses of Brigham Young, Second President of the Church of Jesus Christ of Latter-day Saints* (Salt Lake City: Deseret Book/copyrighted "by Heber J. Grant for the Church of Jesus Christ of Latter-day Saints," 1925), 99, in Clarkana. Widtsoe was quoting from *J* 2:123. Cf. M. Russell Ballard, "Beware of False Prophets and False Teachers," *Ensign* 29 (Nov. 1999): 64: "However, in the Lord's Church there is no such thing as a 'loyal opposition.'"

[57] Clark, *On the Way to Immortality and Eternal Life,* 314-35.

[58] *New Catholic Encyclopedia,* 15 vols. (New York: McGraw-Hill, 1967), 6:821-22 ("Guadalupe, Our Lady of" and sub-heading "Cult and Its Extension").

[59] JRC to Joseph T. Bentley, 26 Sept. 1956, fd 2, box 395, JRCP.

[60] JRC to missionary meeting, 5 Apr. 1957, transcript in April 1957 conference fd, box 166, JRCP; also *SR*, 182-83, as "I don't know."

[61] JRC office diary, 28 Apr. 1952; also Jeanne B. Inouye, "Stillborn Children," in *EM* 3:1419, "the Church has made no official statement on the matter."

[62] Rowena J. Miller to L—— R——, 25 Aug. 1953, fd 3, box 389, JRCP; also Rodney Turner, "Sons of Perdition," in *EM* 3:1391-92.

[63] JRC office diary, 24 Jan. 1950. Cf. Joseph Fielding Smith, *Answers to Gospel Questions, Volume II,* comp. and ed. by Joseph Fielding Smith Jr. (Salt Lake City: Deseret Book, 1958), 159, for "Was the Holy Ghost on the Earth before the Time of Our Savior?" Elder Smith gave this condescending answer: "A little ordinary thinking would reveal to us the fact that the ancient prophets could not have spoken by prophecy and revelation unless they were in possession of this great gift."

[64] JRC to LeRoie Woolley, 5 Nov. 1959, fd 22, box 406, JRCP.

[65] Joseph Fielding Smith, "The Perfect Resurrection," *Improvement Era* 57 (Feb. 1954): 78. To a member's question, "If we lose a part of the body, like a hand, arm, or leg, will we be made whole?" Apostle Smith appealed to common sense and scripture to conclude: "All deformities and imperfections will be removed." Reprinted in Bruce R. McConkie, comp., *Doctrines of Salvation: Sermons and Writings of Joseph Fielding Smith,* 3 vols. (Salt Lake City: Bookcraft, 1955), 2:289.

[66] JRC to Ivan E. Lawrence, 20 May 1957, fd 16, box 399, JRCP.

[67] JRC to Harvey L. Taylor, 2 Jan. 1957, "Copyrights" fd, box 277, JRCP.

[68] JRC office diary, 1 June 1948. For discussion of the historical nature of doctrinal differences among members of the First Presidency and Quorum of Twelve, see *M* 2:214-23, 229-40; Brigham H. Roberts, *A Comprehensive History of the Church* ... 6 vols. (Salt Lake City: The Church of Jesus Christ of Latter-day Saints, 1930), 4:61n16, 5:269-271; Bergera, "Orson Pratt-Brigham Young Controversies"; Donald Q. Cannon, "The King Follett Discourse: Joseph Smith's

Greatest Sermon in Historical Perspective," *BYU Studies* 18 (Winter 1978): 191-92; Thomas G. Alexander, "The Reconstruction of Mormon Doctrine: From Joseph Smith to Progressive Theology," *Sunstone* 5 (July–Aug. 1980): 27-31; *T,* 259-306.

[69] JRC office diary, 21 June 1948.

[70] JRC, "Jesus Christ—Our Head," *CN,* 23 May 1953, 3; Bruce R. Mc-Conkie, "Who Is the Author of the Plan of Salvation?" *Improvement Era* 56 (May 1953): 322.

[71] Rowena J. Miller to Ernest C. Cook, 26 Jan. 1954, fd 1, box 388, JRCP. By contrast, LDS headquarters, through pre-publication approval and editing of its official encyclopedia, followed McConkie's rejection of the term "plan" when referring to Lucifer's alternative. See Gerald N. Lund, "Plan of Salvation, Plan of Redemption," and Brent L. Top, "War in Heaven," in *EM* 3:1088 ("the Father's plan" and Lucifer's "proposal"), 4:1546 ("God the Father instituted the eternal *plan of salvation*" and "Lucifer's proposal"). President Clark regarded this as a semantic distinction without a difference.

[72] Duane E. Jeffery, "Seers, Savants and Evolution: The Uncomfortable Interface," *Dial* 8 (Nos. 3/4, 1973): 63-65; Richard Sherlock, "A Turbulent Spectrum: Mormon Reactions to the Darwinist Legacy," *JMH* 5 (1978): 33-46; Sherlock, "'We Can See No Advantage to a Continuation of the Discussion': The Roberts/Smith/Talmage Affair," *Dial* 13 (Fall 1980): 63-78; Truman D. Madsen, *Defender of the Faith: The B. H. Roberts Story* (Salt Lake City: Bookcraft, 1980), 344-45; First Council of Seventy minutes, 20 Sept. 1928, 12 Feb., 9 Apr. 1931, LDSA; George F. Richards diary, 21 Jan., 7 Apr. 1931, LDSA; James E. Talmage diary, 2, 7, 14, 21 Jan., 7 Apr., 5, 17, 21 Nov. 1931, HBLL; Heber J. Grant journal sheets, 25 Jan., 23 Feb., 30 Mar. 1931, LDSA.

[73] JRC notes for talk, "Evolution," 29 Nov. 1915, box 90, JRCP; JRC notes for talk, "Science Truths—Theory vs. Fact," 7 Sept. 1924, box 114, JRCP.

[74] JRC to Joseph Fielding Smith, 2 Oct. 1946, marked "Not sent," in fd for Relief Society conference of Oct. 1946, box 158, JRCP. Five years before his exchange of letters with Apostle Smith, Reuben wrote that "there are absolutely no time periods or limitations for the material creation, the creation of the material world and its living beings" (JRC to Frank R. Clark, 3 Mar. 1941, fd 1, box 363).

[75] Second draft of JRC talk, "Our Wives and Our Mothers in the Eternal Plan," fd for Relief Society conference of Oct. 1946.

[76] Previous note 72; also quoted in William E. Evenson, "Evolution," in *EM* 2:478.

[77] Author's presentation copy of *Man: His Origin and Destiny* in Clarkana. For reference to part of the controversy the book caused, see Joseph Fielding Smith Jr. and John J. Stewart, *The Life of Joseph Fielding Smith, Tenth President of The Church of Jesus Christ of Latter-day Saints* (Salt Lake City: Deseret Book, 1972), 319; detailed references in Joseph Fielding Smith typed diary, 2 Apr., 28 Aug., 7 Sept., 29 Dec. 1954, LDSA.

[78] "Pres. Clark Talks on 'Man—God's Greatest Miracle,'" *CN,* 10 July 1954, 9; also full text in *SR,* 113-29.

79 "Our Relationship to God—Theme of BYU Lecture," *CN,* 17 July 1954, 2, 10-11; "Pres. Smith Lectures at BYU: Discusses Organic Evolution, Opposed to Divine Revelation," *CN,* 24 July 1954, 4, 13-15; Joseph Fielding Smith typed diary, 28 June 1954; Francis M. Gibbons, *Joseph Fielding Smith: Gospel Scholar, Prophet of God* (Salt Lake City: Deseret Book, 1992), 241.

As an example of Apostle Smith's rejection of science, he instructed a stake conference in 1961: "We will never get a man into space. This earth is man's sphere and it was never intended that he should get away from it. The moon is a superior planet to the earth and it was never intended that man should go there. You can write it down in your books that this will never happen." See *E,* 848 (entry for 14 May 1961), with commentary a few days later in George S. Tanner diary, JWML. Smith wanted this view to be taught to "the boys and girls in the Seminary System." However, U.S. astronauts walked on the moon six months before he became president of the church in January 1970.

80 See previous note 72.

81 "President Clark's Lecture: When Are Church Leader's Words Entitled to Claim of Scripture?" *CN,* 31 July 1954, 10-11.

82 David O. McKay office diary, 18 Aug. 1954, LDSA.

83 Ernest L. Wilkinson diary, 10 Mar. 1960.

84 David O. McKay office diary, 29 Dec. 1954. President McKay expressed the basic ideas of his December 1954 comments in a letter to William Lee Stokes on 15 Feb. 1957, widely circulated and published in Stokes, "An Official Position," *Dial* 12 (Winter 1979): 90-92; also David O. McKay to Dr. A. Kent Christensen, 3 Feb. 1959, quoted in *E,* 844.

85 Quotes and discussion for previous notes 74-75, 77-78, 81-82.

86 JRC, *When Are* ... (Provo, UT: Department of Seminaries and Institutes, 1966); *Melchizedek Priesthood Course of Study, 1969-1970: Immortality and Eternal Life* (Salt Lake City: First Presidency of The Church of Jesus Christ of Latter-day Saints, 1969), 215-25; *Dial* 12 (Summer 1979): 68-81; *SR,* 95-112. The title of this talk has varied in these publications.

87 JRC office diary, 29 Mar. 1940.

88 Heber J. Grant, JRC, and David O. McKay to Committee on Publications (Joseph Fielding Smith, John A. Widtsoe, Harold B. Lee, and Marion G. Romney), 9 Aug. 1944, quoted in *M* 6:208-11; also JRC office diary, 10 Jan., 12 Jan., 28-29 June 1944.

89 *H,* 363-77, 519; Richard O. Cowan, *The Church In the Twentieth Century* (Salt Lake City: Bookcraft, 1985), 305-17; James B. Allen and Glen M. Leonard, *The Story of the Latter-day Saints,* 2d ed., rev., enl. (Salt Lake City: Deseret Book, 1992), 593-623; Frank O. May Jr., "Correlation of the Church: Administration," and James B. Allen and Richard O. Cowan, "History of the Church: 1945-1990," in *EM* 1:324, 2:642-43; Jan Shipps, "Making Saints in the Early Days and the Latter Days," in Marie Cornwall, Tim B. Heaton, and Lawrence A. Young, eds., *Contemporary Mormonism: Social Science Perspectives* (Urbana: University of Illinois Press, 1994), 77, 80.

[90] JRC to Heber J. Grant and David O. McKay, 1 Dec. 1936, fd 1, box 355, JRCP.

[91] JRC office diary, 26 Jan. 1942.

[92] JRC to Louis F. Thomann, 18 Oct. 1943, fd 3, box 367, JRCP.

[93] JRC office diary, 1, 14-15 Nov. 1949; with quote from JRC to D. D. Moffatt, 21 Nov. 1949, one of several related documents in fd 5 (labeled "Dale Morgan"), box 8, CR 1/19, LDSA; also John Philip Walker, ed., *Dale Morgan on Early Mormonism: Correspondence and a New History* (Salt Lake City: Signature Books, 1986).

[94] Thomas G. Alexander, *Utah, the Right Place: The Official Centennial History*, rev. ed. (Salt Lake City: Gibbs-Smith Publisher/Utah Division of State History, 1996), 228, 409; also Leonard J. Arrington, *"The Richest Hole on Earth": A History of Bingham Copper Mine* (Logan: Utah State University Monograph Series, 1963).

[95] Heber J. Grant journal sheets, 13 Jan. 1945; cf. Maurine Whipple, *This Is the Place: Utah* (New York: Alfred A. Knopf, 1945); also Jessie L. Embry, "Maurine Whipple: The Delicate Dissenter," in Roger D. Launius and Linda Thatcher, eds., *Differing Visions: Biographical Essays on Mormon Dissenters* (Urbana: University of Illinois Press, 1994), 310-18. Contrast JRC's censorship with his response to the proposed biography of Apostle John W. Taylor. Taylor was dropped from the Quorum of Twelve in 1906 for marrying polygamously after the 1890 Manifesto, then excommunicated in 1911 for marrying yet another plural wife. See chapter 8.

[96] JRC office diary, 8, 13 Nov. 1951.

[97] Juanita Brooks, *The Mountain Meadows Massacre* (Stanford, CA: Stanford University Press, 1950), 165n9 (last para.); also Levi S. Peterson, "Juanita Brooks: The Mormon Historian as Tragedian," *JMH* 3 (1976): 47-54; Peterson, *Juanita Brooks: Mormon Woman Historian* (Salt Lake City: University of Utah Press, 1988); Peterson, "Juanita Brooks," in *U*, 58-59.

[98] JRC to John M. Riggs, 12 Mar. 1951, fd 6, box 384, JRCP. Unwillingness to discuss Higher Criticism was consistent with Clark's "fundamental rules" against reading anything he thought he would disagree with.

[99] Unused draft of JRC to Hud Stoddard, undated, regarding *Life* magazine's issue of 16 September 1954, fd 6, box 391, JRCP.

[100] JRC memorandum, 19 Oct. 1957, unnumbered box, JRCP.

[101] James R. Clark, "The Kingdom of God, the Council of Fifty and the State of Deseret," *UHQ* 26 (Apr. 1958): 131-48; cf. D. Michael Quinn, "The Council of Fifty and Its Members, 1844-1945," *BYU Studies* 20 (Winter 1980): 163-97; Andrew F. Ehat, "'It Seems Like Heaven Began on Earth': Joseph Smith and the Constitution of the Kingdom of God," *BYU Studies* 20 (Spring 1980): 253-79; also *O* and *E* (consult index). Although deeply flawed in interpretation and with gaps of significant evidence, Klaus J. Hansen's *Quest for Empire: The Political Kingdom of God and the Council of Fifty in Mormon History* (Lansing: Michigan State University Press, 1967) continues to be the only book on this subject.

[102] *M* 1:viii.

[103] In case current readers assume this statement is a reflection of my 1993

excommunication from the LDS church, it was in the 1981 draft I submitted to LDS administrators and in the 1983 book as published by BYU Press.

[104] Harold B. Lee diary, 28-29 Jan. 1944 (concerning Leah), 10 Oct. 1947 (concerning John, with commas added for clarification), private possession; also *E*, 714-16 (summary of John's activities in education, business, politics, government, and LDS administration); see John A. Widtsoe and Leah D. Widtsoe, *The Word of Wisdom: A Modern Interpretation* (Salt Lake City: Deseret Book, 1937); Ralph B. Simmons, ed., *Utah's Distinguished Personalities: A Biographical Directory of Eminent Contemporaneous Men and Women Who Are the Faithful Builders and Defenders of the State* (Salt Lake City: Personality Publishing, 1933), 216, for her sketch.

[105] JRC office diary, 18 Oct. 1948. For the introduction of tea and coffee into the "Word of Wisdom" and transition to a commandment, see Leonard J. Arrington, "An Economic Interpretation of the Word of Wisdom," *BYU Studies* 1 (Winter 1959): 37-49; Lester E. Bush Jr., "The Word of Wisdom in Early Nineteenth-Century Perspective," and Thomas G. Alexander, "The Word of Wisdom: From Principle to Requirement," *Dial* 14 (Autumn 1981): 47-65, 78-88; *T,* 258-71; Joseph Lynn Lyon, "Word of Wisdom," in *EM* 4:1584-85.

[106] Harold Lee Snow, "Refined Sugar: Its Use and Misuse: A Summary of Scientific Evidence," *Improvement Era* 51 (Mar. 1948): 140 (I quote the article's first sentence. The second reads: "One hundred years ago less than one-tenth as much sugar per capita was consumed as food in this country, as compared with today." Widtsoe and Widtsoe, *The Word of Wisdom,* is the only source given [176n1] for these statements); Leonard J. Arrington, *Beet Sugar in the West: A History of the Utah-Idaho Sugar Company, 1891-1966* (Seattle: University of Washington Press, 1966), 179, for JRC position.

[107] *Improvement Era* 51 (Mar. 1948): 130 (Widtsoe as coeditor); JRC office diary, 12 Apr. 1948 (quote); also Reed Millard, "Sugar Goes to Work for Science," *Improvement Era* 53 (June 1950): 492, 520, which the editors introduced, contrary to President Clark's intent, as a response to the March 1948 article.

[108] George Albert Smith diary, 1 July 1949, in George A. Smith Family papers, JWML.

To understand why Clark thought the information "would be better not circulated," I examined the *Year Book of Facts and Statistics: Church of Jesus Christ of Latter-day Saints* (Salt Lake City: "Council of the Twelve," 1949), copies located in LDSL and Clarkana. Besides discrepancies in the figures reported for temple "ordinations" and "endowments," page 25 showed that Latter-day Saints were not always healthier than non-Mormons: they had a higher mortality rate than Utahns generally for "diseases of the circulatory system" and a higher rate than either Utahns or Americans generally for "diseases of the respiratory system." Moreover Clark may have been perturbed that page 30 gave the illegitimate birth rate for Utah and Idaho, even though it was 1/4 the national rate and the unidentified author, John A. Widtsoe, specifically used these statistics to praise the LDS membership's higher morality. Widtsoe's authorship is known only through the above entry in Smith's diary.

[109] JRC office diary, 26 Sept. 1955. This referred to John A. Widtsoe, "Tem-

ple Worship," in *The Utah Genealogical and Historical Magazine* 12 (Apr. 1921): 49-74, which has recently been reprinted as an appendix in James E. Talmage, *The House of the Lord* (1912; Salt Lake City: Signature Books, 1998), 185-97.

[110] The first advertisement appeared in the *Improvement Era* 58 (Dec. 1955): 882. The book was not included in the publisher's Christmas advertisement in *DN,* 13 Dec. 1955, B-4. When I submitted this narrative for review by LDS administrators in 1981, Elder McConkie was a member of the Quorum of Twelve. He died in 1985.

[111] JRC office diary, 16 Mar. 1956. Slightly less than twenty years after the First Presidency stopped this series, McConkie, now an apostle, had his oldest son, Joseph F. McConkie, publish the 1955 book under the title *Journal of Discourses Digest, Volume 1.* This had little better success than the earlier effort, and no subsequent volume was published.

[112] Bruce R. McConkie, *Mormon Doctrine* (Salt Lake City: Bookcraft, 1958), 3-5.

[113] David O. McKay office diary, 7 Jan. 1960.

[114] See also *E,* 846 (entry for 7-8 Jan. 1960).

[115] JRC, *Why the King James Version?,* preface.

[116] JRC memorandum, 9 July 1958, unnumbered box, JRCP.

[117] Marion G. Romney diary, 16 Jan. 1959; David O. McKay office diary, 5 Mar. 1959.

[118] David O. McKay office diary, 7 Jan. 1960.

[119] David O. McKay office diary, 27 Jan. 1960, with parenthetical statement in the original.

[120] David O. McKay office diary, 7 Jan. 1960 (first quote), 28 Jan. 1960 (second quote); both quoted in *E,* 846 (entry for 7-8 Jan. 1960).

[121] David O. McKay to Dr. A. Kent Christensen, 3 Feb. 1959, quoted in *E,* 844; also 844-45 for McConkie's effort on 17 February 1959 to prevent the suppression of *Mormon Doctrine* by making public disclaimers, to which the First Presidency replied the next day that "you cannot be disassociated from your official position in the publication of such a manuscript" and that "pending the final disposition of this problem[,] no further edition of the book be printed."

[122] Bruce R. McConkie, *Mormon Doctrine,* 2d ed. (Salt Lake City: Bookcraft, 1966); Gibbons, *Joseph Fielding Smith,* 391 (McConkie as son-in-law and compiler), 437-38 (Smith as additional counselor). David O. McKay's office diary (7 Jan. 1960) did not list all 1,067 "errors and misstatements" but did give thirty-six objections. With reference to those, the second edition deleted McConkie's ecclesiastical position from the title page and eliminated his description of the work as a "compendium of the whole gospel," stating instead that it was an expression of scriptures and prophetic interpretation.

The second edition dropped such cross references as (1958 ed., 108) "*Catholicism.* See Church of the Devil." It dropped articles on Eternal City, Indulgences, Penance, and Supererogation. It deleted the Catholic church from articles on Abominations, Agency, Babylon, Church of the Devil, Exorcism, Harlots, and Magic. It toned down references to Catholicism in entries for Extreme Unction and Inquisition. It eliminated the word *apostate* from entries on Church, Cross, Deaconess, Epiphany, Kingdoms of Glory, Priests, Protestants, and Sacred Grove. It toned down the article on Palm Sunday and references to other churches in Ministerial Titles and Prayer. It tempered its RLDS church reference in Article on Marriage and Josephites. It dropped organic evolution and evolutionists from the entries on Animals, Civilization, Devil, and Evil Spirits. It deleted the earth's age in the Creation section. It qualified references to the status of animals and plants in the Garden of Eden in the Animals entry. It dropped the statement that reading a prepared sermon was "a mockery of sacred things" under Sermons. It mitigated instructions on the conduct of family prayers in Prayer, and it dropped that article's reference to resumption of the School of the Prophets.

Due to oversight, negotiation, or some other reason, the second edition failed to delete or modify references to the following items specified as either objectionable or doctrinally false by President McKay in 1960: the RLDS church (Common Consent), Christian churches (Clergy), the Catholic church (Immaculate Conception), organic evolution (Believers), the entire article on evolution (Evolution), pre-Adamites (Adam; First Flesh), the status of animals and plants in the Garden of Eden (Animals), the time of creation (Day), Moses as a translated being (Elijah; Moses), the origin of individuality (Life), marriage out of the temple as a defilement of one's priesthood (Melchizedek Priesthood), literal intercourse part of Christ's conception (Only Begotten Son), stillborn children being resurrected (Stillborn Children), Old Testament baptism (Brazen Sea), one's calling and election confirmed (Calling and Election Sure), Paul's marriage (Celibacy), unspecified errors (Church of Enoch; Consecration of Oil), councils and schools among gods (Council in Heaven), Sunday observance (Family Reunions), the earth's geological changes (Flood of Noah), the Holy Ghost as a spirit man (Holy Ghost), specific conduct (Hosannah Shout), women as gods (Queens), the interpretation of *D&C* 93:1 (Revelation), interpretation of D&C 93:38 and the status of children in the Celestial Kingdom (Salvation of Children), climatological changes after Noah's flood (Seasons), interpretation of 3 Nephi 21:20 (Second Chance Theory), and the "discourteous" use of the word *apostate* (Christendom; Ethics).

[123] Citing the First Presidency's objections to the book in 1958-60, Armand L. Mauss, *The Angel and the Beehive: The Mormon Struggle with Assimilation* (Urbana: University of Illinois Press, 1994), 162-63, noted the irony of its current status within LDS culture: "At the Mormon grass roots, it is considered authoritative, if not definitive, and easily ranks alongside the older *Articles of Faith* by Talmage in its importance as a quasi-canonical source for popular reference. There is a tremendous irony in this fact, one that shows clearly how the persistence of one strong-willed leader with fundamentalist leanings can prevail against the preferences of other leaders, even some of the most powerful, in a lay ministry with ambiguous limits to legitimate authority."

[124] *Conf,* Apr. 1949, 162 (first quote), 187 (second quote).

[125] *Conf,* Apr. 1945, 55; JRC, "Postwar Planning," *Improvement Era* 48 (May 1945): 237; *SR,* 196.

[126] JRC to missionary meeting, 4 Apr. 1960, transcript, 1, box 151, JRCP.

[127] *Conf,* Apr. 1952, 95.

[128] *Conf,* Apr. 1949, 187.

[129] JRC to general priesthood meeting, Oct. 1946, transcript, box 151, JRCP.

[130] I was unable to say in the biography I submitted for official review that JRC's 1946 statement contradicted his own private views and the revelations of the first LDS prophet. Clark sometimes regarded the decisions of three living prophets as simply wrong or contrary to his own understanding of God's will. He thought that several of President McKay's financial decisions were clearly leading the church "astray." He advised one general authority what to do if the LDS president "asks you to do anything which is wrong" (Marion G. Romney diary, 9 Apr. 1951). See also chap. 5.

The 1951 revision of *Doctrine and Covenants Commentary* by Joseph Fielding Smith, Harold B. Lee, and Marion G. Romney referred, in its discussion of *D&C* 43:3-4, to the possibility that the LDS president could be in a "fallen condition" due to "apostasy." All three apostles were closely aligned with President Clark. See Hyrum M. Smith and Janne M. Sjodahl, *Doctrine and Covenants Commentary* [cover title], rev. ed. (Salt Lake City: Deseret Book, 1951), 241.

Another revelation (*D&C* 107:82-84) provided for the trial and excommunication of the president in such a circumstance. The church's official centennial history stated, "Therefore if the time should ever come that the church should be so unfortunate as to be presided over by a man who transgressed the laws of God and became unrighteous, a means in the church system of government is provided for deposing him without destroying the church, without revolution, or even disorder" (Roberts, *A Comprehensive History of the Church,* 2:376). In other words, Joseph Smith's revelations maintain that there are no limits to the ability of the LDS president and prophet to be in error and to commit sin.

This leaves two options. Either what Reuben publicly stated in 1946 was a claim that he knew to be false or he did not specify the context for his claim that God would not allow the LDS prophet to lead the church "astray." I believe that his seemingly unconditional statement in 1946 must be understood within the emphasis of his 1949 conference address about a prophet being a prophet "only when he was acting as such." By a legalistic interpretation of that statement, President Clark apparently concluded that (when functioning as God intended) "the Prophet" could never mislead the Latter-day Saints, but that the same man could mislead them in his capacity as "President of the Church." By that convoluted logic, when the church president was not speaking or acting as God intended, the man ceased to be "the Prophet" and thus could lead the LDS church astray.

In an 1890 sermon Wilford Woodruff was the first LDS president to claim infallibility. His exact words were: "The Lord will never permit me or any other man who stands as President of this Church to lead you astray. It is not in the programme. It is not in the mind of God. If I were to attempt that, the Lord would remove me out of my place, and so He will any other man who attempts to lead the children of men astray from the oracles of God and from their duty." (*DN,* 11

Oct. 1890, 2) This was his defense against widespread criticism of his Manifesto which officially ended LDS plural marriage. Unlike Clark, President Woodruff did not refer to Joseph Smith's statement that "a prophet was a prophet only when he was acting as such" because that would have invited members to question whether he issued the Manifesto as a prophet or not. Nevertheless, the LDS church has virtually canonized Woodruff's statement by including it in the *D&C* (for example, 1981 edition, page 292).

As indicated above, Woodruff's claim contradicted the founding prophet's revelations, including the doctrine of free agency. For example, "Men and women may not evade or escape their freedom, for reality always appears as a set of choices informed by some kind of understanding of good, the outcome of which defines in some measure the course of human events," in David Bohn, "Freedom," in *EM* 2:525; also "Man's Free Agency," in James E. Talmage, *The Articles of Faith: A Series of Lectures on the Principal Doctrines of the Church of Jesus Christ of Latter-day Saints … Written by Appointment; and Published by the Church* (Salt Lake City: Deseret News, 1899), 54-57; "Agency," in McConkie, *Mormon Doctrine* (1966), 26-28.

[131] Widtsoe, ed., *Discourses of Brigham Young*, 214, in Clarkana. Widtsoe quoted *J* 7:281.

[132] *Conf*, Apr. 1940, 14.

[133] *Conf*, Apr. 1949, 186; previous note 130; cf. Joseph Smith Jr., et al., 7 vols., *History of the Church of Jesus Christ of Latter-day Saints,* 2d rev., B. H. Roberts, ed. (Salt Lake City: Deseret Book, 1960), 5:265, that the founding prophet "visited with a brother and sister from Michigan, who thought that 'a prophet is always a prophet'; but I told them that a prophet was a prophet only when he was acting as such."

[134] "President Clark's Lecture: When Are Church Leader's Words Entitled to Claim of Scripture?" *CN*, 31 July 1954, 11.

[135] Widtsoe, ed., *Discourses of Brigham Young*, 209, in Clarkana. Widtsoe quoted *J* 9:150.

[136] *J* 1:312 (B. Young/1853).

NOTES TO CHAPTER 8

[1] This restores the chapter's original title (Romans 16:17) as well as its full discussion of post–1890 polygamy. Both were in the first draft I submitted in 1981 for review by LDS administrators. I also expand a section from the 1983 book about Reuben's views on the U.S. Constitution.

[2] See quote and discussion for note 75.

[3] *Conf*, Apr. 1949, 162; also "heresy" and "inquisition," in *New Catholic Encyclopedia,* 15 vols. (New York: McGraw-Hill, 1967), 6:1062-69, 7:535-41.

[4] *Conf*, Oct. 1944, 117.

[5] *Conf*, Oct. 1945, 166.

[6] JRC office diary, 29 Oct. 1948, JRCP, referring to the upcoming publica-

tion of his book, *On the Way to Immortality and Eternal Life* (Salt Lake City: Deseret Book, 1949).

[7] JRC to bishops' meeting, 29 Sept. 1950, transcript, box 151, JRCP.

[8] *Conf,* Apr. 1952, 81.

[9] JRC, "The Place of the M.I.A. in the Church Program," *Improvement Era* 39 (Mar. 1936): 133; JRC, "Truth and Simplicity in Church Ordinances," *Improvement Era* 48 (Nov. 1945): 636; Clark, *On the Way to Immortality and Eternal Life,* 54. Clarkana has Benjamin F. Cocker, *Christianity and Greek Philosophy ...* (New York: Carlton and Lanahan, 1870); also see *New Catholic Encyclopedia,* 6:736 ("Nevertheless, the influence especially of Stoic and Neoplatonic philosophy soon made itself felt in the vocabulary and external structure of Christian thinking."); Everett Ferguson, ed., *Encyclopedia of Early Christianity,* 2d ed., 2 vols. (New York: Garland Publishing, 1997), 2:914 ("A more explicit and substantial encounter between early Christianity and Hellenistic philosophy took place in the second century apologists, particularly Justin Martyr.").

[10] For background on the history and approaches of Higher Criticism, see Robert M. Grant, *A Short History of the Interpretation of the Bible,* rev. ed. (New York: Macmillan, 1963); *Interpreter's Dictionary of the Bible,* 4 vols. (New York: Abingdon Press, 1962) 1:407-18; also the following publications by Fortress Press of Philadelphia, most of which are pamphlet-sized: William A. Beardslee, *Literary Criticism of the New Testament* (1970), Norman C. Habel, *Literary Criticism of the Old Testament* (1971), Ralph W. Klein, *Textual Criticism of the Old Testament ...* (1974), Edgar Krentz, *The Historical-Critical Method* (1975), Edgar V. McKnight, *What Is Form Criticism?* (1969), McKnight, *Meaning in Texts ...* (1978), J. Maxwell Miller, *The Old Testament and the Historian* (1976), Daniel Patte, *What Is Structural Exegesis?* (1976), Norman Perrin, *What Is Redaction Criticism?* (1969), Walter E. Rast, *Tradition History and the Old Testament* (1972).

[11] For the reaction against Higher Criticism, see William Henry Green, *The Hebrew Feasts in Their Relation to Recent Critical Hypotheses* (New York: R. Carter and Brothers, 1885); L. W. Munhall, *Anti-Higher Criticism, or Testimony to the Infallibility of the Bible* (New York: Hunt and Eaton, 1894); Green, *Higher Criticism of the Pentateuch* (New York: Charles Scribner's Sons, 1895); William Edward Biederwolf, *The New Paganism and Other Sermons* (Grand Rapids, MI: William B. Eerdmans, 1934); Willis B. Glover, *Evangelical Nonconformists and Higher Criticism in the Nineteenth Century* (London: Independent Press, 1955); Ernest R. Sandeen, *The Roots of Fundamentalism: British and American Millenarianism, 1800-1930* (Chicago: University of Chicago Press, 1970); Paul A. Carter, *The Spiritual Crisis of the Gilded Age* (DeKalb: Northern Illinois University Press, 1971); James Barr, *Fundamentalism* (London: SCM Press, 1977); Richard A. Grusin, *Transcendentalist Hermeneutics: Institutional Authority and the Higher Criticism of the Bible* (Durham, NC: Duke University Press, 1991).

[12] Philip L. Barlow, *Mormons and the Bible: The Place of the Latter-day Saints in American Religion* (New York: Oxford University Press, 1991), 149.

[13] John A. Widtsoe, *In Search of Truth* (Salt Lake City: Deseret Book, 1930), 90

(first quote), 81 (second quote); also his biographical sketches in *U,* 635-36; *E,* 714-16.

[14] JRC to John A. Widtsoe, 29 June 1930, JRCP.

[15] Charles W. Penrose to Joseph W. McMurrin, 31 Oct. 1921, in *American History: A Syllabus for Social Science 100* (Provo, UT: Brigham Young University Press, 1977), 428-29; *T,* 283; also *E,* 662-63, 678-79 (summary of religious and secular activities of Anthony W. Ivins and Charles W. Penrose).

[16] Articles by Sidney B. Sperry and H. Grant Vest in *CN,* all on page 3: "Brief History of Criticism of Isaiah," 9 Sept. 1933; "The Problem of Isaiah in the Book of Mormon," 16 Sept. 1933; "The Synoptic Problem in Its Relation to Modern Revelation," 30 Sept. 1933; and "The Johannine Problem in Its Relation to Modern Revelation," 7 Oct. 1933; also "Sidney B. Sperry," *Journal of Book of Mormon Studies: Foundation for Ancient Research and Mormon Studies* 4 (Spring 1995): x–xiv.

[17] JRC office diary, 7 Feb. 1934.

[18] Carl E. Hatch, *The Charles A. Briggs Heresy Trial: Prologue to Twentieth Century Liberal Protestantism* (New York: Exposition Press, 1969).

[19] John A. Widtsoe, "Is the Bible Translated Correctly?" *Improvement Era* 43 (Mar. 1940): 161.

[20] John A. Widtsoe, *Evidences and Reconciliations: Aids to Faith in a Modern Day* (Salt Lake City: Bookcraft, 1943), 99. Many general authorities published with the independently managed Bookcraft. Clark's religious works were published exclusively by LDS-owned Deseret Book Company where the church exercised more direct control over editorial decisions. Bookcraft later became an imprint of Deseret Book.

[21] JRC to Milton Bennion, 19 Apr. 1943, fd 1, box 367, JRCP.

[22] Heber J. Grant, JRC, and David O. McKay to Committee on Publications (Joseph Fielding Smith, John A. Widtsoe, Harold B. Lee, and Marion G. Romney), 9 Aug. 1944, in *M* 6:211; also JRC office diary, 10, 12 Jan., 28-29 June 1944.

[23] Richard Sherlock, "Faith and History: The Snell Controversy," *Dial* 12 (Spring 1979): 31-32; also *E,* 672-73, 723-24 (summary of religious and secular activities of Joseph F. Merrill and Levi Edgar Young).

[24] JRC, "The World Crisis Today," *CN,* 16 June 1945, 4, 9, 11-12; also *SA,* 121, 126, 128, 129-32. For political terms, see Adam B. Ulam, *The Bolsheviks: The Intellectual and Political History of the Triumph of Communism in Russia* (New York: Macmillan, 1965); Gaetana Salvemini, *Italian Fascist Activities in the United States* (New York: Center for Migration Studies, 1977); *ER,* 2:622-23.

[25] *Conf,* Apr. 1949, 163.

[26] JRC to John M. Riggs, 12 Mar. 1951, fd 6, box 384, JRCP.

[27] For beginnings of his biblical studies, see JRC to John A. Widtsoe, 8 Dec. 1929, box 27, JRCP.

[28] JRC office diary, 31 Oct. 1946.

[29] The preferred transliteration among scholars has been YHWH or Yaweh, or JHVH for Jehovah. See John Allen, *Modern Judaism: Or a Brief Account of the Opinions, Traditions, Rites, and Ceremonies of the Jews in Modern Times,* 2d ed., rev.

(1816; London: R. B. Seeley and W. Burnside, 1830), 87; J. Newton Brown, ed., *Fessenden and Co.'s Encyclopedia of Religious Knowledge* ... (Brattleboro, VT: Fessenden; Boston: Shattuck, 1835), 674; Samuel Macauley Jackson, ed., *The New Schaff-Herzog Encyclopedia of Religious Knowledge,* 12 vols. (New York: Funk and Wagnalls, 1908-12), 6:116-17; George Arthur Buttrick, ed., *The Interpreter's Bible,* 12 vols. (New York: Abingdon Press, 1951-57), 2:817; Louis F. Hartman, "God, Names of," in Cecil Roth, ed., *Encyclopaedia Judaica,* 16 vols. (Jerusalem: Macmillan/Keter, 1971-72), 7:680; Jacob Neusner and William Scott Green, eds., *Dictionary of Judaism in the Biblical Period, 450 B.C.E. to 600 C.E.,* 2 vols. (New York: Macmillan Library Reference USA/Simon and Schuster Macmillan, 1996), 2:629.

[30] "Pres. Clark's Address at Conference," *CN,* 20 June 1953, 4. Based on the English language of the 1500s, the KJV translators in 1611 rendered the Greek word *agape* (love) as *charity,* which means something different in modern English. Twenty-six years after this sermon, LDS headquarters specified that *charity* in I Corinthians 13 does indeed refer to the Greek word for *love.* See *The Holy Bible ... Authorized King James Version with Explanatory Notes and Cross References to the Standard Works* (Salt Lake City: The Church of Jesus Christ of Latter-day Saints, 1979), 1454n. Thus the hierarchy officially rejected Clark's emphatic statement about this matter.

[31] *Conf,* Apr. 1954, 38-47; *SR,* 77-94.

[32] See JRC, *Why the King James Version?* (Salt Lake City: Deseret Book, 1956); cf. JRC to John A. Widtsoe, 8 Dec. 1929 (Reuben's proposed study); JRC to Ivor Sharp, undated (ca. 1929-31), box 335, JRCP (request for books); *C,* 445; JRC office diary, 27 Sept. 1954, "he had prepared this outline in 1935-1936"; also Harold B. Lee diary, 22, 25 Jan. 1954, private possession.

[33] Barlow, *Mormons and the Bible,* 149; also the insightful analysis in Armand L. Mauss, *The Angel and the Beehive: The Mormon Struggle with Assimilation* (Urbana: University of Illinois Press, 1994), 102-08, who interprets this as an example of "retrenchment reaction of the Mormon leadership to half a century of assimilation with American society."

[34] JRC office diary, 26 Jan. 1956. McKay seems to me to be exasperated and irritated.

[35] JRC office diary, 27 Sept. 1954, spelling in original. Even though he had taught Latin at LDS College and had training in Latin legal terms, the accurate phrase is *magnum opus.* Clark mistakenly assumed that the word endings had to be the same in this Latin phrase.

[36] JRC to Cloyd H. Marvin, 10 Mar. 1958, binder of JRC-Marvin correspondence, box 189, JRCP; also originals of JRC letters in Marvin papers, Archives, George Washington University, Washington, D.C.

From 1956 to JRC's death, no Mormon with training in biblical languages and literature wanted to go on record with a candid assessment of his book. Beyond not knowing the original languages, Clark misunderstood their history and translation. He asserted the necessity of the KJV's formal style despite the fact that the original authors rejected formal Greek in favor of the most basic, colloquial form of the language. Moreover, JRC sometimes misunderstood the scholarly sources he used and sometimes ignored their discussions of the meaning of words and phrases. See Philip L. Barlow, "Why the King James Version? From the Common to the Official Bible of Mormonism," *Dial* 22 (Summer 1989): 29-30, 33-34; Barlow, *Mormons and the Bible,* 162-63, 166-67, 170, 180-81; Douglas F. Salmon, "As Translated Correctly: The Inspiration and Innovation of the Eighth Article of Faith," *Dial* 31 (Summer 1998): 144-47.

[37] Eldin Ricks to Ernest L. Wilkinson, 30 June 1958, Wilkinson to JRC, 8 Aug. 1958, and JRC to Wilkinson, 30 Aug. 1958, all in fd 2, box 108, Wilkinson papers, HBLL.

[38] JRC office diary, 5 Feb. 1955; also Brian Capener, *The Faith of an Observer: Conversations with Hugh Nibley* (Provo, UT: Brigham Young University/Foundation for Ancient Research and Mormon Studies, 1985).

[39] JRC to P. H. Gates, 5 June 1957, fd 10, box 399, JRCP.

[40] JRC office diary, 31 Aug. 1933; also discussion of pre-1940 LDS manuals in Mauss, *The Angel and the Beehive,* 27-28.

[41] JRC to Heber J. Grant and Anthony W. Ivins, 13 Mar. 1934, JRC fd, CR 1/48, LDSA.

[42] JRC, "The Chartered Course of the Church in Education," *CN,* 13 Aug. 1938, 6; also in the *Improvement Era* 41 (Sept. 1938): 572; quoted in Ernest L. Wilkinson and Leonard J. Arrington, eds., *Brigham Young University,* 2:246; and in David E. Buchanan, "An Analysis of the Immediate and Long-Range Implications of Three Speeches Delivered by J. Reuben Clark, Jr.," M.A. thesis, Brigham Young University, 1976, 22-39.

[43] JRC office diary, 3 Nov. 1940.

[44] JRC office diary, 4 Mar. 1946.

[45] JRC to Irvin Hull, 9 Mar. 1946, fd 12, box 373, JRCP.

[46] JRC office diary, 31 Aug. 1933, 3 Nov. 1940, 18 Apr. 1941, 25 Apr. 1950; Merrill Y. Van Wagoner to JRC, 22 Aug. 1938, fd 3, box 111, CR 1/44, LDSA.

[47] Marion G. Romney diary, 16 Jan. 1959, private possession.

[48] Ernest L. Wilkinson diary, 24 Feb. 1960, photocopy, JWML. For the situation from the mid-1950s to JRC's death in 1961, see Gary James Bergera and Ronald Priddis, *Brigham Young University: A House of Faith* (Salt Lake City: Signature Books, 1985), 65-70, 152-61. For the continued influence of Clark's various recommendations "to get rid of" the "so-called liberals at Brigham Young University," see Bryan Waterman and Brian Kagel, *The Lord's University: Freedom and Authority at BYU* (Salt Lake City: Signature Books, 1998).

[49] For the situation of LDS academics during the period beginning with JRC's entry into the First Presidency, see Thomas F. O'Dea, *The Mormons* (Chicago: University of Chicago Press, 1957), 224-40; Claude J. Burtenshaw, "The Student: His University and His Church," *Dial* 1 (Spring 1966): 89-101; Davis Bitton, "Anti-Intellectualism in Mormon History," *Dial* 1 (Autumn 1966): 124-28; "Birchers Spied on [BYU] Professors, Hialeah Student Says," *Miami Herald,* 3 Mar. 1967, A-32; "Wilkinson Admits 'Spy Ring' Existence at 'Y,'" *Daily Herald* [Provo, UT], 14 Mar. 1967, 1, 4; "Y. Ouster Not Linked to Spying," *DN,* 13 Apr.

1967, B-14; "Letters to the Editor," *Dial* 1 (Summer 1966): 9-10, 2 (Spring 1967): 7-8, 2 (Summer 1967): 15-16, 3 (Spring 1968): 8, 4 (Autumn 1969): 7-8; William Mulder, "Problems of the Mormon Intellectual," *Dial* 5 (Autumn 1970): 121-23; T. Edgar Lyon oral history, 1977, typescript, LDSA; Sterling M. McMurrin papers, JWML; Scott Kenney, "E. E. Ericksen: Loyal Heretic," *Sunstone* 3 (July-Aug. 1978): 22-27; Hugh W. Nibley, "Zeal without Knowledge," in *Nibley on the Timeless and the Timely* (Provo, UT: Religious Studies Center, Brigham Young University, 1978), reprinted in *Dial* 11 (Summer 1978): 101-12; Sherlock, "Faith and History," 27-41; George T. Boyd, *Views on Man and Religion,* ed. James B. Allen, Dale C. LeCheminant, and David J. Whittaker (Provo, UT: Friends of George T. Boyd, 1979), 160-68; Bergera and Priddis, *Brigham Young University,* 49-70, 148-61; Mary Lythgoe Bradford, *Lowell L. Bennion: Teacher, Counselor, Humanitarian* (Salt Lake City: Dialogue Foundation, 1995); Sterling M. McMurrin and L. Jackson Newell, *Matters of Conscience: Conversations with Sterling M. McMurrin on Philosophy, Education, and Religion* (Salt Lake City: Signature Books, 1996); *E,* 93-94.

[50] A brief but useful historical survey is Stanley S. Ivins, "Notes on Mormon Polygamy," *Western Humanities Review* 10 (Summer 1956): 229-39, reprinted in *UHQ* 35 (Fall 1967): 309-21, reprinted in D. Michael Quinn, ed., *The New Mormon History: Revisionist Essays on the Past* (Salt Lake City: Signature Books, 1992), 169-80. The best book-length survey remains Richard S. Van Wagoner, *Mormon Polygamy: A History* (Salt Lake City: Signature Books, 1986). In addition, B. Carmon Hardy, *Solemn Covenant: The Mormon Polygamous Passage* (Urbana: University of Illinois Press, 1992), 39-126, is especially good in examining the American Victorian hysteria over the alternative marriage practices of a tiny minority, as if they could have threatened the institution of marriage generally.

For statistics on how many Mormon men were polygamists, see Dean L. May, "People on the Mormon Frontier: Kanab's Families of 1874," *JMH* 1 (Winter 1976): 172; Lowell "Ben" Bennion, "The Incidence of Mormon Polygamy in 1880: Dixie versus Davis Stake," *JMH* 11 (1984): 29-38; Larry M. Logue, *A Sermon in the Desert: Belief and Behavior in Early St. George, Utah* (Urbana: University of Illinois Press, 1988), 50-51; Kathryn M. Daynes, "Plural Wives and the Nineteenth-Century Mormon Marriage System: Manti, Utah, 1849-1910," Ph.D. diss., Indiana University, 1991, 157, 159; Jessie L. Embry, "Polygamy," in *U,* 428-29; Dean L. May, *Three Frontiers: Family, Land, and Society in the American West, 1850-1900* (Cambridge, Eng.: Cambridge University Press, 1994), 121. For statistics on Mormon women, including the fact that polygamous wives sometimes outnumbered monogamous wives in Utah's population, see Marie Cornwall, Camela Courtright, and Laga Van Beek, "How Common the Principle? Women as Plural Wives in 1860," *Dial* 26 (Summer 1993): 148-49.

On legal issues, see "The Raid," in Leonard J. Arrington, *Great Basin Kingdom: An Economic History of the Latter-day Saints, 1830-1900* (Cambridge, MA: Harvard University Press, 1958), 353-79; Orma Linford, "The Mormons and the Law: The Polygamy Cases," *Utah Law Review* 9 (Winter 1964/Summer 1965): 308-70, 543-91; Joseph H. Groberg, "The Mormon Disfranchisements of 1882 to

1892," *BYU Studies* 16 (Spring 1976): 399-408; Robert G. Dyer, "The Evolution of Social and Judicial Attitudes toward Polygamy," *Utah State Bar Journal* 5 (Spring 1977): 35-45; James L. Clayton, "The Supreme Court, Polygamy, and the Enforcement of Morals in Nineteenth Century America: An Analysis of Reynolds v. United States," *Dial* 12 (Winter 1979): 46-61; Rosa Mae McClellan Evans, "Judicial Prosecution of Prisoners for LDS Plural Marriage: Prison Sentences, 1884-1895," M.A. thesis, Brigham Young University, 1986; Edwin B. Firmage, "The Judicial Campaign against Polygamy and the Enduring Legal Questions," *BYU Studies* 27 (Summer 1987): 91-117; Ken Driggs, "The Prosecutions Begin: Defining Cohabitation in 1885," *Dial* 21 (Spring 1988): 109-21; Firmage and R. Collin Mangrum, *Zion in the Courts: A Legal History of the Church of Jesus Christ of Latter-day Saints* (Urbana: University of Illinois Press, 1988), 160-260; Tracey E. Panek, "Search and Seizure in Utah: Recounting the Antipolygamy Raids," *UHQ* 62 (Fall 1994): 316-34; Sarah Barringer Gordon, "'The Twin Relic of Barbarism': A Legal History of Anti-Polygamy in Nineteenth-Century America," Ph.D. diss., Princeton University, 1994; also "excommunication" in the glossary of *EM* 4:1767.

[51] D. Michael Quinn, "LDS Church Authority and New Plural Marriages, 1890-1904," *Dial* 18 (Spring 1985): 15 (quote), 9-105; also see Henry J. Wolfinger, "A Reexamination of the Woodruff Manifesto in the Light of Utah Constitutional History," *UHQ* 39 (Fall 1971): 328-49; Victor W. Jorgensen and B. Carmon Hardy, "The Taylor-Cowley Affair and the Watershed of Mormon History," *UHQ* 48 (Winter 1980): 4-36; Kenneth L. Cannon II, "After the Manifesto: Mormon Polygamy, 1890-1906," *Sunstone* 8 (Jan.-Apr. 1983): 27-35; Jan Shipps, "The Principle Revoked: A Closer Look at the Demise of Plural Marriage," *JMH* 11 (1984): 65-77; *T,* 3-15, 60-73; Edward Leo Lyman, *Political Deliverance: The Mormon Quest for Utah Statehood* (Urbana: University of Illinois Press, 1986), 139-42; Martha Sonntag Bradley, "Changed Faces: The Official LDS Position on Polygamy, 1890-1990," *Sunstone* 14 (Feb. 1990): 26-33; Hardy, *Solemn Covenant,* 84-335; Dan Erickson, "Star Valley, Wyoming: Polygamous Haven," *JMH* 26 (Spring 2000): esp. 152-64.

[52] *M* 3:193; and for background of this 1890 document, see Kenneth W. Godfrey, "The Coming of the Manifesto," *Dial* 5 (Autumn 1970): 11-25; Quinn, "LDS Church Authority," 32-50 (including 44-45 for the committee that edited the 510-word first draft to 356 words); Lyman, *Political Deliverance,* 124-39; *T,* 60-73; Francis M. Gibbons, *Wilford Woodruff: Wondrous Worker, Prophet of God* (Salt Lake City: Deseret Book, 1988), 358-59; Thomas G. Alexander, "The Manifesto: Mormonism's Watershed," *This People* 11 (Fall 1990): 21-27; Lyman, "The Political Background of the Woodruff Manifesto," *Dial* 24 (Fall 1991): 26-29; Alexander, "The Odyssey of a Latter-day Prophet: Wilford Woodruff and the Manifesto of 1890," *JMH* 17 (1991): 169-206; Alexander, *Things in Heaven and Earth: The Life and Times of Wilford Woodruff, a Mormon Prophet* (Salt Lake City: Signature Books, 1991), 265-68; *E,* 328-29.

[53] Richard D. Poll, "The Twin Relic: A Study of Mormon Polygamy and the Campaign by the Government of the United States for Its Abolition, 1852-1890,"

M.A. thesis, Texas Christian University, 1939; Poll, "The Political Reconstruction of Utah Territory, 1866-1890," *Pacific Historical Review* 27 (May 1958): 111-26; Gustive O. Larson, *The "Americanization" of Utah for Statehood* (San Marino, CA: The Huntington Library, 1971); Lyman, *Political Deliverance,* 150-295.

[54] Kenneth L. Cannon II, "Beyond the Manifesto: Polygamous Cohabitation among LDS General Authorities," *UHQ* 46 (Winter 1978): 24-36; also Quinn, "LDS Church Authority," 49-52, 67, 69, 75, 81, 83, 85-86, 90; *E*, 647, 658, 687, 696, 702, for attempted and successful criminal indictments against first counselor George Q. Cannon (prevented in 1893 by bribing Utah's attorney general), Apostle Heber J. Grant (1899, 1903, 1906), Seventy's president Brigham H. Roberts (1899), second counselor Joseph F. Smith (prevented in 1893 through bribe; indicted in 1906), Apostle Lorenzo Snow (1899).

[55] Quinn, "LDS Church Authority and New Plural Marriages, 1890-1904," 57-104; Hardy, *Solemn Covenant,* 167-283.

[56] These are my unpublished calculations based on the highest annual number of plural marriages performed before and after September 1890. The same trend is apparent in comparing annual polygamous versus monogamous marriages for twenty years before and after the watershed 1890.

[57] *M* 4:151-52.

[58] Francis M. Gibbons, *Joseph F. Smith: Patriarch and Preacher, Prophet of God* (Salt Lake City: Deseret Book, 1984), 221.

[59] *Proceedings Before the Committee on Privileges and Elections of the United States Senate in the Matter of the Protests Against the Right of Hon. Reed Smoot, a Senator from the State of Utah, to Hold His Seat,* 4 vols. (Washington, D.C.: Government Printing Office, 1904-07), 1:114, 2:397-400, with JRC underlinings and marginal notations in Clarkana; Preston Woolley Parkinson, *The Utah Woolley Family* (Salt Lake City: By the author), 251, 340; *Tooele Utah Stake History, 1847 to 1900* (n.p., 1977), 190; "Appendix II: Post-Manifesto Polygamous Marriages: A Tentative List with Remarks," in Hardy, *Solemn Covenant,* 46, 148, 191, 217; Spencer W. Kimball oral history, 1972, typescript, 17-18, LDSA ("It was about 1902. I don't know just when the Manifesto was made operative in all the world, including Canada and Mexico, but Aunt Fannie [Woolley Parkinson] was married before the late President Joseph F. Smith 'locked the gate'").

[60] J. P. Taylor, trans., *The Civil Code of the Mexican Federal District* (1884; San Francisco: American Book and Printing, 1904), 8, 9, 23, 33-35, 42, 470, 472, 482; Jorgensen and Hardy, "Taylor-Cowley Affair," 18n26; Quinn, "LDS Church Authority and New Plural Marriages, 1890-1904," 17; B. Carmon Hardy, "Mormon Polygamy in Mexico and Canada: A Legal and Historiographical Review," in Brigham Y. Card, et al., eds., *The Mormon Presence in Canada* (Edmonton: University of Alberta Press, 1987; reissued, Logan: Utah State University Press, 1990), 188-89.

[61] Jorgensen and Hardy, "Taylor-Cowley Affair"; Quinn, "LDS Church Authority and New Plural Marriages, 1890-1904," 98-103; Hardy, *Solemn Covenant,* 262-67.

[62] JRC 1907 memorandum book, box 2, JRCP; quoted fully in *C*, 432, with the "vehemently" description.

[63] See discussion and sources for note 59.

[64] D. Michael Quinn's unpublished research files, Western Americana, Beinecke Rare Book and Manuscript Library, Yale University, New Haven, Connecticut; Hardy; also Spencer J. Condie, "Missionary, Mission Life," *EM* 2:911.

[65] Reed Smoot diary, 8, 27 Sept. 1910, in *I*, 63-64, 69. Smoot's numbered diary books before 1909 are missing but might possibly be among the historical documents in the First Presidency's vault, Salt Lake City.

[66] Reed Smoot diary, 15-16 Nov. 1910, 14 Mar., 2 Apr. 1911, in *I*, 78-79, 94-95, 99.

[67] JRC to Lute, 1906. In note taking I accidentally omitted the specific date of this letter in box 328, JRCP. For Wrathall's 1906 release as bishop, see Alma A. Gardiner, "The Founding and Development of Grantsville, Utah, 1850-1950," M.A. thesis, Brigham Young University, 1959, 430.

[68] Family Group Sheets for James L. Wrathall and Grantsville Ward records, microfilms, FHL; computerized Ancestral File, FHL, and in every stake of North America; entries for James L. Wrathall in Tooele Stake Form E reports (1906-25), microfilms, FHL, also LDSA.

[69] *M* 4:218; Quinn, "LDS Church Authority," 105; my research files on Judson Tolman.

[70] "Excommunication," *DN*, 31 Mar. 1914, 1; Joshua R. Clark to JRC, 30 Apr. 1914, box 330, JRCP; *C*, 440-41; my research files on John W. Woolley.

[71] After his excommunication in 1914, Patriarch John W. Woolley was the verified officiator (or probable officiator) for the following polygamous marriages in Centerville, Farmington, and Salt Lake City or the vicinity: Reuel J. Alder and Rita Vickers, 14 October 1918; George F. Hickman and Zina A. Woolf, 24 January 1915; Alpha J. Higgs and Amy F. E. Gill, 9 September 1921; Adolphus D. Rogers and Bernice L. Warren, 17 July 1915; Milford B. Shipp Jr. and Nellie V. Wood, 6 October 1917; Edward R. South and Nancy A. Porter, 16 June 1915; Thomas J. Steed and Josephine Sandberg, 14 June 1918; Walter W. Steed and Lillie E. Sandberg, 25 January 1918; Alvin F. Sundberg and Catharina Debry, October 1915; Otto N. Toomey and Rosa A. Cornwall, 24 March 1915; Lorin C. Woolley and Alice Simmons, about 1914. Most of these dates can be verified through the Ancestral File, FHL. My unpublished research provides the connections of these marriages to John W. Woolley.

[72] Ancestral File, FHL, for VaLois South as daughter of Edward R. South and the legal wife he married prior to his 1915 polygamous marriage.

[73] "Visitation of Jesus Christ and Joseph Smith to John Taylor as Related By Lorin C. Woolley," in Lynn L. Bishop and Steven L. Bishop, *The Keys of the Priesthood Illustrated* (Draper, UT: Review and Preview, 1971), 119-23; *M* 5:242; Van Wagoner, *Mormon Polygamy*, 183-84.

[74] *M* 4:84-85, 151-52, 217-18, 301; 5:193-97, 242, 249, 292-95.

[75] JRC church document #9, box 114, JRCP.

76 J. Max Anderson, *The Polygamy Story: Fiction and Fact* (Salt Lake City: Publishers Press, 1979), 146.

77 For frequent statements by Mormon fundamentalists about the LDS church, individual families, or rival groups being "out of order" or "in order," see various quotes throughout my "Plural Marriage and Mormon Fundamentalism," *Dial* 31 (Summer 1998): 1-68.

78 Heber J. Grant journal sheets, 15 Apr. 1933.

79 JRC office diary, 26 Apr. 1957; also Mark J. and Rhea A. Baird, *Reminiscences of John W. Woolley and Lorin C. Woolley,* 4 vols. (Draper, UT: Np, nd). For *Lamanite,* see Book of Mormon title page, also Bruce A. Chadwick and Thomas Garrow, "Native Americans," in *EM* 3:981-82.

80 JRC office diary, 21 June 1948; also Lynn L. Bishop and Steven L. Bishop, *The Truth about John W. Woolley, Lorin C. Woolley and the Council of Friends* (Draper, UT: By the authors, 1972); Anderson, *The Polygamy Story;* Fred C. Collier, *Re-Examining the Lorin Woolley Story* (Salt Lake City: Collier's, 1981).

81 Quinn, "LDS Church Authority," 18.

82 *Conf,* Apr. 1921, 202; *M* 5:195, quoted word part of Grant's denunciation. By contrast, in *Conf,* Apr. 1931, 8, and *M* 5:295, Grant said that the claims by polygamy advocates were "provoking and annoying ... but I do not speak in anger."

83 JRC office diary, 25 Apr. 1933, concerning apostles Taylor, Merrill, Cowley, and Woodruff (with an unrelated reference to Moses Thatcher resisting the political activities of the First Presidency). Although he knew that Apostle Abraham H. Cannon married a plural wife shortly before his death in 1896, Grant always emphasized the following four violators of the Manifesto whose marriage dates are shown here: John W. Taylor (1890 in Salt Lake City and two in 1901 at Farmington, Utah), Marriner W. Merrill (1901 in Salt Lake City), Matthias F. Cowley (1899 in the Logan temple, 1905 in Canada), and Abraham Owen Woodruff (1901 in Preston, Idaho). See Appendix II in Hardy, *Solemn Covenant,* 36, 56, 132, 191, 214; *E,* 644, 653, 673, 705, 717 (details of their marriages); also my unpublished research. Cf. Heber J. Grant to A. W. Ivins, 1 Sept. 1906, Grant papers, LDSA; Heber J. Grant journal, 23 July 1924, LDSA; Grant to Linnie Keeler Naegle, 29 Oct. 1934, CR 1/44, LDSA; Grant to Mrs. Katherine H. Allred, 15 Nov. 1935, First Presidency 1935-36 letterbook, 163-64, LDSA.

Grant did not seem to know about two other apostles who married post-Manifesto polygamous wives: Brigham Young Jr. (1901 in Salt Lake City) and Rudger Clawson (1904 in Grand Junction, Colorado). See Hardy, *Solemn Covenant,* 51, 219 (without wife's name); David S. Hoopes and Roy Hoopes, *The Making of a Mormon Apostle: The Story of Rudger Clawson* (Lanham, MD: Madison Books, 1990), 215-17, 227; *E,* 651, 718 (for details of their marriages). My unpublished research verifies that apostles Young and Clawson performed post-Manifesto plural marriages for other Mormons as well.

84 JRC office diary, 22-24 May 1933.

85 *M* 5:316-30 (quotations from 1933 statement); Hel 1:9-12; 2:3-11, in Book of Mormon; Paul R. Cheesman, "Book of Mormon: Book of Helaman," in *EM* 1:153.

[86] JRC to William Cullen Dennis, 1 Aug. 1933, box 349, JRCP.

[87] "First Presidency Statement on Marriage to Be Read in All Wards," *CN*, 1 July 1933, 1.

[88] *C*, 165-66, quote on 166; also "It did a great deal of harm," wrote Peter Calvert. "The rebels were installed on the border, their cause was strengthened." See Calvert, *The Mexican Revolution, 1910-1914: The Diplomacy of Anglo-American Conflict* (Cambridge, Eng.: Cambridge University Press, 1968), 112 (JRC authorship of message), 113 (quotes).

[89] Harold B. Lee diary, 21 Mar. 1945.

[90] *Scriptures of The Church of Jesus Christ of Latter-day Saints, for the Sunday Schools* (Salt Lake City: Deseret Sunday School Union, 1968): 159: "A few were married after 1890 in Mexico, Canada and on the high seas—outside the jurisdiction of the United States. It was not until 1904, under the leadership of Joseph F. Smith, that plural marriage was banned finally and completely, everywhere in the world, by the Church"; Paul H. Peterson, "Manifesto of 1890," in *EM* 2:853: "While nearly all Church leaders in 1890 regarded the Manifesto as inspired, there were differences among them about its scope and permanence. Some leaders were understandably reluctant to terminate a long-standing practice that was regarded as divinely mandated. As a result, a limited number of plural marriages were performed over the next several years."

[91] The role of Anthony W. Ivins in performing post-1890 polygamous marriages in Mexico became public knowledge beginning with the Smoot Investigation of 1904-07. See H. Grant Ivins, *Polygamy in Mexico as Practiced by the Mormon Church, 1895-1905* (Salt Lake City: Collier's, 1981), 4, 6, 10; Quinn, "LDS Church Authority," 78-79, 86, 93; Hardy, "Mormon Polygamy in Mexico and Canada," 191-92; Hardy, *Solemn Covenant*, 171-72, 176, 187, 259, 316-17, 321-22. Grant Ivins claimed that his father performed these marriages only after receiving a coded letter of authorization for each couple. This was the procedure for nonresident visitors to the Juarez Stake over which Anthony W. Ivins was president. Eventually the First Presidency authorized him to perform polygamous marriages for worthy members of the stake without the necessity of receiving specific authorization from the First Presidency. See Quinn, "LDS Church Authority," 68, 70, 80, 88, 93. Ivins performed the polygamous marriage in 1903 for his own daughter Anna Ivins and another local resident, Guy C. Wilson. However, his on-and-off willingness to do this put him at odds with members of his stake and with general authorities who sometimes performed the polygamous ceremonies for local Mormons whom Ivins had turned down in Mexico.

[92] Edward L. Kimball and Andrew E. Kimball Jr., *Spencer W. Kimball, Twelfth President of The Church of Jesus Christ of Latter-day Saints* (Salt Lake City: Bookcraft, 1977), 91.

[93] Several of the apostles in attendance, including Grant, recorded in their diaries detailed accounts of these meetings, but the most available is in Abraham H. Cannon diary, 30 Sept. 1890 and 1 Apr. 1892, HBLL, with photocopies at the JWML and Utah State Historical Society, Salt Lake City; "Revelation Given to President John Taylor, September 27, 1886, copied from the original manuscript

by Joseph F. Smith Jr., August 3, 1909," Joseph Fielding Smith papers, LDSA; Minutes of the Quorum of Twelve Apostles, 22 Feb., 1 Mar. 1911, fd 5, box 18, John Taylor Family papers, JWML.

[94] In 1985 I stated in "LDS Church Authority," 104n382, that "these men fathered more than 3,300 children, many of whom are still alive, as well as the fact that some of these post-Manifesto polygamists have sixth-generation descendants at present."

[95] These statements were in the draft I submitted for review by LDS administrators in 1981.

[96] This statement was in the draft I submitted for review by LDS administrators in 1981.

[97] Joseph W. Musser diary, 4 Apr. 1931, 25 June 1933, 25 Feb. 1934, LDSA; also Martha S. Bradley, "Joseph W. Musser: Dissenter or Fearless Crusader of Truth?" in Roger D. Launius and Linda Thatcher, eds., *Differing Visions: Biographical Essays on Mormon Dissenters* (Urbana: University of Illinois Press, 1994), 262-78.

[98] Joseph W. Musser diary, 1921-44. There was a significant exception to the pattern of polygamy advocates not holding schismatic meetings until after the 1933 statement. In May 1929 Lorin C. Woolley began ordaining a few men, including Musser, as "high priest apostles" to be members of his own priesthood council, and this "Council of Friends" met frequently.

Most published works on Mormon fundamentalist history have tended to be sensationalistic or partisan, but the following are useful: Kimball Young, *Isn't One Wife Enough?* (New York: Henry Holt, 1954); Samuel W. Taylor, *I Have Six Wives* [a pseudonym biography of Fundamentalist leader Rulon C. Allred] (New York: Greenburg, 1956); Jerry R. Andersen, "Polygamy in Utah," *Utah Law Review* 5 (Spring 1957): 381-89; Dean C. Jessee, "A Comparative Study and Evaluation of the Latter-day Saint and 'Fundamentalist' Views Pertaining to the Practice of Plural Marriage," M.A. thesis, Brigham Young University, 1959; Jerold A. Hilton, "Polygamy in Utah and Surrounding Area Since the Manifesto of 1890," M.A. thesis, Brigham Young University, 1965; Bishop and Bishop, *The Keys of the Priesthood Illustrated;* Van Wagoner, *Mormon Polygamy,* 177-217; Dorothy Allred Solomon, *In My Father's House* (New York: Franklin Watts, 1984); Ogden Kraut, *The Fundamentalist Mormon: Presented at the Sunstone Symposium, August 1989* (n.p., 1989); Ken Driggs, "After the Manifesto: Modern Polygamy and Fundamentalist Mormons," *Journal of Church and State* 32 (Spring 1990): 367-89; Martha S. Bradley, "The Women of Fundamentalism: Short Creek, 1953," and Driggs, "Fundamentalist Attitudes toward the Church: The Sermons of Leroy S. Johnson," *Dial* 23 (Summer 1990): 15-37, 39-60; Driggs, "Twentieth-Century Polygamy and Fundamentalist Mormons in Southern Utah," *Dial* 24 (Winter 1991): 44-58; Martha Sonntag Bradley, *Kidnapped from That Land: The Government Raids on the Polygamists of Short Creek* (Salt Lake City: University of Utah Press, 1993); Irwin Altman and Joseph Ginat, *Polygamous Families in Contemporary Society* (Cambridge, Eng.: Cambridge University Press, 1996); Quinn, "Plural Marriage and Mormon Fundamentalism," 1-68.

[99] In 1905 Reuben, possibly while visiting Utah during a break from Columbia University, received one of the first of these post-Manifesto, pro-polygamy publications. Clarkana has John T. Clark, *The Last Record to Come Forth: The Lord's Strangest Act: The Manifesto, a Covenant with Death and an Agreement with Hell* (Salt Lake City: By the author, 1905), inscribed: "Compliments of John T. Clark."

[100] Joseph W. Musser diary, 23, 25 June, 8 Aug., 11 Sept., 22 Oct. 1933, 23 Jan., 3 Aug. 1934; B. Harvey Allred, *A Leaf in Review* (Caldwell, ID: Caxton Printers, 1933); Joseph W. Musser, *The New and Everlasting Covenant of Marriage* (Salt Lake City: Truth Publishing, 1933); Musser and Joseph Leslie Broadbent, *Supplement to the New and Everlasting Covenant of Marriage: An Interpretation of Celestial Marriage, Plural Marriage, Priesthood* (Salt Lake City: Truth Publishing, 1934); Arnold Boss, *A Voice from the Dead, Being an Answer to the Official Statement of the Church of Jesus Christ of Latter-day Saints of June 17, 1933 ...* (n.p., n.d.); Kirk Arnold, *Civil or Divine Sovereignty* (Salt Lake City: By the author, 1934); *Truth*, 21 vols. (Salt Lake City, 1935-56); *Star of Truth*, 4 vols. (Salt Lake City, 1953-56); Gilbert A. Fulton Jr., *The Most Holy Principle*, 4 vols. (Murray, UT: Gems Publishing, 1970-75).

[101] Joseph W. Musser diary, 2 Dec. 1934, also various entries (1933-44) for references to conversions and names of affiliated Fundamentalists. For Joseph Leslie Broadbent as the priesthood successor of Lorin C. Woolley, see Bishop and Bishop, *The Keys of the Priesthood Illustrated*, 289.

[102] The statements of this paragraph were in the draft I submitted for review by LDS administrators in 1981.

[103] See quotes and discussion for previous notes 89, 93, 95, 101.

[104] JRC office diary, 15 Jan. 1948, for conversation with Samuel and Raymond W. Taylor. Samuel published his father's biography as *Family Kingdom* (New York: McGraw-Hill; London: Hodder and Stoughton, 1951).

[105] JRC met with Mrs. Mary Bennion Powell, daughter of Heber Bennion (1858-1932) who married plural wives Emma Jane Webster in 1901 and Mary Bringhurst in 1902. See John Bennion, "Mary Bennion Powell: Polygamy and Silence," *JMH* 24 (Fall 1998): 85-128; also my unpublished research. Heber Bennion's pro-polygamy pamphlets in the 1920s were *An Open Letter, Gospel Problems,* and *Supplement to Gospel Problems.*

[106] Conversation with Mrs. Mary Bennion Powell in JRC office diary, 11 Apr. 1949.

[107] George F. Richards diary, 15 Apr. 1921, LDSA, partially quoted in *E*, 304; also James Kirkham diary, 12 Jan. 1928, microfilm, FHL.

[108] *C*, 263; also for its Utah manifestation, see Joerg A. Nagler, "Enemy Aliens and Internment in World War I: Alvo von Alvensleben in Fort Douglas, Utah, a Case Study," *UHQ* 58 (Fall 1990): 388-405.

[109] Blank forms in First Presidency files, LDSA; example in *Truth* 1 (1 Mar. 1936): 128; also Bradley, *Kidnapped from That Land,* 57.

[110] *Handbook of Instructions for Stake Presidencies, Bishops and Counselors, Stake and Ward Clerks, Number Fifteen* (Salt Lake City: Church of Jesus Christ of Latter-day Saints, 1934), 10 (temple recommend requirement that the person

"should not join nor be a member of any secret oath-bound organization and should sustain without reservation the general and local authorities of the Church"); also Robert A. Tucker, "Temple Recommend," in *EM* 4:1446; Edward L. Kimball, "The History of LDS Temple Admission Standards," *JMH* 24 (Spring 1998): 145-46 (polygamy emphasis in interviews), 147 (1934 requirement for loyalty to current leadership).

[111] Still living in the mid-1930s were the following couples who were married between 1890 and 1904, listed as husband, followed by post-Manifesto wife or wives: Isaac Alldredge and Maria Delila Van Leuven; Heber S. Allen and Elizabeth S. Hardy; Orin E. Barney and Sarah E. Fenn; John C. Beecroft and Lettie A. Farnsworth; Joseph C. Bentley and Maud M. Taylor; David P. Black and Alzada Kartchner; Morley L. Black and Rachel A. Lunt; Benjamin B. Brown and Mary V. Hansen; Orson P. Brown and Jane B. Galbraith, Eliza Skousen; George H. Budd and Mary J. Duke; John F. Burton and Florence A. Porter; Anson B. Call and Julia S. Abegg; Willard Call and Leah Pratt; Angus J. Cannon and Annie R. Bockholt; George M. Cannon and Ellen C. Steffensen; Louis P. Cardon and Edith J. Done, Mary I. Pratt; James F. Carroll and Annie E. Burrell; Hyrum D. C. Clark and Mary A. Robinson; Amos Cox and Grace E. Chestnut; Joseph H. Dean and Amanda W. Peterson; Abraham Done and Louisa M. W. Haag, Ellen P. Moffett; Edward C. Eyring and Emma Romney; Heber E. Farr and Rosemilda R. Bluth; Arthur W. Hart and Evadyna Henderson; George M. Haws and Martha H. Wall; Victor C. Hegsted and Hannah Grover; James Hood and Jamima J. Russell; John J. Huber Jr. and Percis L. Maxham; Benjamin J. Johnson and Harriet J. Hakes; Franklin D. Leavitt and Jane S. Glenn; Walter B. Lewis and Esther D. Wilson; Robert L. McCall and Christina Southeimer; George A. McClellan and Nellie Allan; Olonzo D. Merrill and Mary L. Hansen; Edward W. Payne and Lucy A. Farr, Rosalia Tenney; Brigham H. Pierce and Sarah E. Harris; Joseph E. Robinson and Willmia Brown, Harriet Spencer; Miles A. Romney and Elizabeth Burrell; Robert Sherwood and Alice T. Shoenfeld; Luman E. Shurtliff and Mary J. Roundy; Daniel Skousen and Sarah A. Spilsbury; James N. Skousen Jr. and Emma F. Mortensen; Jesse M. Smith and Priscilla Smith; Walter W. Steed and Alice B. Clark; David A. Stevens and Mary A. Boice; Brigham Stowell and Ellen M. Skousen; Frank Y. Taylor and Alice M. Neff, Annie S. Campbell; Joseph H. Turley and Joanna McLaws; David K. Udall and Mary A. Linton; John J. Walser Jr. and Elizabeth Braithwaite; Guy C. Wilson and Agnes M. Stevens, Anna L. Ivins; Edward J. Wood and Adalaide Solomon; Newton Woodruff and Elizabeth S. Weekes; Newel K. Young and Geneva Cooley. Much of this can be verified through the Ancestral File, FHL; the rest is in my unpublished research.

[112] On the basis of a limited sample of thousands of Mormon polygamists in 1890, I found the following ten examples of what must have been dozens of couples still living in the mid-1930s, listed here as husband, followed by pre-Manifesto wife (Ancestral File, FHL): Israel Bennion and Matilda Pehrson, Anson V. Call Jr. and Rosa E. Stayner, Benjamin Cluff Jr. and Harriet Cullimore, Matthias F. Cowley and Luella S. Parkinson, Joseph H. Dean and Florence Ridges, George M. Haws and Susan A. Cluff, Josiah E. Hickman and Martha A. Lawisch, Don M.

LeBaron and Vilate E. Johnson, David Spilsbury and Mary E. Haight, John J. Walser Jr. and Marie L. Frischknecht.

[113] Bishop Fred E. H. Curtis and counselors John L. Riley and Ernest Blackmore to JRC, 1 Oct. 1938, Curtis to First Presidency, 10 Nov. 1938, Curtis to First Presidency (with copy to Presiding Bishop LeGrand Richards), 9 June 1939, JRC and David O. McKay to Curtis, 24 June 1939, Curtis to First Presidency, 4 Oct. 1939, Curtis to JRC, 30 Sept. 1940, all in fd marked "First Presidency—Plural Marriage—Investigation of Meetings of 'Fundamentalist' Musser-Darter Groups," in CR 1/48, with cover sheet: "They later checked the license numbers with the State license department in order to ascertain car owners. Next, they checked car owners with the City Directory, and in some cases with the Bishops of the wards where these people reside"; also Rowena J. Miller memorandum to JRC, 12 Nov. 1940: "Bishop Curtis has not completed this work, [because] some people come by street car and it is taking more time to identify them. Will keep you advised," also in CR 1/48; JRC office diary, 2 May 1939; Bradley, *Kidnapped from That Land*, 65, 226n5, 226n10; *E*, 305–06. My first draft and 1983 biography did not identify Curtis by name because I did not realize that he publicly testified in 1944 as the leader of this surveillance team.

[114] JRC office diary, 15 Oct. 1940 (quote), 21 Aug. 1944.

[115] Joseph W. Musser diary, 17 July 1938, 8 May 1939.

[116] "An Open Letter to J. Reuben Clark, Jr.," *Truth* 5 (Aug. 1939): 50.

[117] JRC to Fred E. H. Curtis, 16 Oct. 1940, Curtis to First Presidency, Attn: JRC, 25 Feb., 25 Aug. 1941, all in "First Presidency—Plural Marriage—Investigation of Meetings" file, CR 1/48; also *E*, 306.

[118] Fred E. H. Curtis to First Presidency, Attn: JRC, 4 Oct. 1939 (for quotes), CR 1/48; JRC office diary, 25 Jan. 1940, 26-27 Feb., 9 Apr. 1941, 29 Jan. 1943.

[119] JRC office diary, 30 Dec. 1940.

[120] JRC office diary, 2 May 1939, 28 Feb. 1940.

[121] JRC office diary, 27 Mar. 1940, also 4 May 1944; Frank Evans diary, 4 May 1944, LDSA.

[122] Richard R. Lyman diary, 10-11 Feb., 17 Feb. 1922, HBLL (first references to Anna S. Jacobsen who married Victor C. Hegsted as a polygamous wife in 1907). Hegsted had another polygamous wife from May 1904, a month after the Second Manifesto, as described in Julie Hemming Savage, "Hannah Grover Hegsted and Post-Manifesto Plural Marriage," *Dial* 26 (Fall 1993): 102-17, with no reference to Jacobsen.

For the Lyman-Jacobsen case, see Harold B. Lee diary, 13 Oct. 1943; JRC office diary, 2 Nov., 31 Dec. 1943; Joseph Fielding Smith typed diary, 2, 4, 11 Nov. 1943, LDSA; George Albert Smith diary, 9 Nov. 1943, George A. Smith Family papers, JWML; Richard R. Lyman to Stephen L Richards, 12 Nov. 1949, Richards papers, LDSA; *K*, 309; John R. Sillito, "Enigmatic Apostle: The Excommunication of Richard R. Lyman," paper given at Sunstone Symposium, Aug. 1991; Francis M. Gibbons, *Joseph Fielding Smith: Gospel Scholar, Prophet of God* (Salt Lake City: Deseret Book, 1992), 355 ("Elder Smith and Elder Harold B. Lee, who had the unpleasant task of corroborating the facts that led to the excommunication");

L, 205 ("Elder Lee was assigned by the First Presidency to work with President Joseph Fielding Smith to investigate charges that had been made against Elder Lyman"); *E*, 669-70.

[123] Hilton, "Polygamy in Utah," 19; George Albert Smith diary, quoted in *K*, 310; George F. Richards diary, 12 Nov. 1943; Spencer W. Kimball diary, 12 Nov. 1943, quoted in Kimball and Kimball, *Spencer W. Kimball,* 209.

[124] Richard R. Lyman to Stephen L Richards, 12 Nov. 1949; Sillito, "Enigmatic Apostle"; *E*, 669.

[125] "The Lyman Case," *Truth* 9 (Feb. 1944): 223-24.

[126] JRC office diary, 4 Dec. 1951.

[127] "Polygamy," *DN*, 29 Sept. 1944, 17; "State Rests Cult Case: Recess Follows 4 Days of Testimony," *DN*, 30 Sept. 1944, 12; Bradley, *Kidnapped from That Land*, 64, 84-87; *E*, 306-07.

[128] JRC office diary, 20 May 1944, emphasis in the original; also Frank Evans diary, 4 May 1944.

[129] JRC office diary, 1 Oct. 1951; "Statement to be given to Mr. Gordon of the Burns Detective Agency, who is investigating the Short Creek situation," 2 Oct. 1951, fd 3, box 383, JRCP.

[130] JRC office diary, 12 Jan. 1948, 4 Dec. 1951, 26 Oct. 1953, 20 Oct. 1954.

[131] Bradley, *Kidnapped from That Land,* 124-25.

[132] JRC office diary, 5 Aug. 1953 (statement of ten-day notice); Howard Pyle telegram to Delbert L. Stapley, 25 July 1953 and memorandum by LaRue Sneff (First Presidency Office) and Theron Liddle (*DN*), 25 July 1953, both in fd marked "Ultra Confidential JRC," CR 1/45, LDSA.

[133] *Truth* 19 (Sept.-Oct. 1953): 97-160; "Arizona: The Great Love-Nest Raid," *Time* 63 (3 Aug. 1953): 16.

[134] Bradley, *Kidnapped from That Land,* 127-81; fd marked "First Presidency —Statement on Short Creek Situation (Polygamy) July 27, 1953" in CR 1/45.

[135] JRC office diary, 7 Nov. 1955.

[136] *C*, 261-62; "Pres. Clark Warns of Plot to Wreck U.S.," *DN*, 18 Sept. 1946, 1. Clarkana has Vladimir Stepankowsky, *The Russian Plot to Seize Galicia (Austrian Ruthenia),* 2d ed. (Jersey City, NJ: Ukrainian National Council, 1915); Edgar C. Sisson and George Creel, *The German-Bolshevik Conspiracy* (Washington, D.C.: Committee on Public Information, 1918); *International "New" Dealism, ... Is This Part of a World Conspiracy?* (New York: League for Constitutional Government, 1935); Jules Bolivar, *Shall We, as a Nation, Survive or Perish? ... Communism and Its Conspiracy to Overthrow the United States Government* (Los Angeles: Americans' National Security League, 1936); Jeremiah Stokes, *A Nation-Wide Red Plot to Repeal All State Crime-Prevention Syndicalism Laws Revealed ...* (Salt Lake City: Continental Fact-Finding Committee, 1939); Stokes, *The Communist Plot to Purge American Patriots from Congress* (Salt Lake City: Federated Libraries, 1942); George A. Dondero, *Communist Conspiracy in Art Threatens American Museums* (Washington, D.C.: Government Printing Office, 1952); Eustace C. Mullins, *The Federal Reserve Conspiracy,* 2d ed. (Union, NJ: Common Sense, 1954); Usher L. Burdick, *The Great Conspiracy to Destroy the United States* (Washington, D.C.: Government Printing

Office, 1954). For the historical context, see David Brion Davis, *The Fear of Conspiracy: Images of Un-American Subversion from the Revolution to the Present* (Ithaca, NY: Cornell University Press, 1971).

[137] JRC to Roy Matthews, 11 Mar. 1954, fd 7, box 391, JRCP.

[138] "Ten Thousand Hear Clark's Analysis of League," and "Here's Text of Maj. Clark's Speech on League of Nations," *The Salt Lake Herald*, 3 Sept. 1919, 1; "The Clark Lecture," editorial, *The Salt Lake Herald*, 4 Sept. 1919, 6; also *C*, 294.

[139] *Conf*, Oct. 1942, 58; also *Conf*, Oct. 1950, 172, Apr. 1957, 50-51; Floyd Melvin Hammond, "Some Political Concepts of J. Reuben Clark, Jr.," M.A. thesis, Brigham Young University, 1962, 76-86 ("Constitutional Conservatism"); Martin B. Hickman, "J. Reuben Clark, Jr.: The Constitution and the Great Fundamentals," *BYU Studies* 13 (Spring 1973): 255-72; J. David Gowdy, "The Constitutional Thought of J. Reuben Clark, Jr.," *Clark Memorandum* (Spring 1999): 10-15.

[140] *D&C*. Drafted in 1787, the Constitution was ratified in 1789.

[141] JRC to ElRay L. Christiansen, 30 May 1957, fd 1, box 399, JRCP.

[142] *Conf*, Apr. 1944, 115.

[143] He used various phrases for the corporate rape of workers. It appeared as "the greed and rapacity of capital" in JRC office diary, 27 May 1944 and in JRC to Charles Edmundson (associate editor of *Fortune* magazine), 16 Dec. 1944, fd 2, box 369, JRCP.

[144] "President Clark Proposes Labor-Capital Partnership," *DN*, 7 Dec. 1946, 6; also *SA*, 567-68.

[145] JRC to special Welfare meeting, 7 Apr. 1956, box 151, JRCP. Clarkana has hundreds of publications about labor unions; also *DA*, 343-44 (unions).

[146] *SA*, 543.

[147] JRC memorandum, 30 Nov. 1951, box 244, JRCP.

[148] JRC office diary, 6 Dec. 1950.

[149] Marion G. Romney, "Political Thought and Life of J. Reuben Clark, Jr.," in *Speeches of the Year: BYU Devotional Addresses, 1972-1973* (Provo, UT: Brigham Young University Press/Young House, 1973), 60, also with reference to Clark's public advocacy of a six-year limit for the U.S. president.

[150] *Conf*, Apr. 1957, 44; also *Conf*, Oct. 1942, 59.

[151] *Conf*, Oct. 1942, 58; also JRC office diary, 8 Jan. 1943.

[152] JRC to Robert LeFevre, president of the Freedom School, 22 Jan. 1957, fd 8, box 396, JRCP.

[153] Rowena J. Miller to Leroy A. Wilson, 17 Nov. 1949, fd 14, box 380, JRCP.

[154] *Conf*, Apr. 1957, 51.

[155] JRC to Ernest L. Wilkinson, 5 Feb. 1949, fd 16, box 380, JRCP; also JRC to Herbert Hoover, 1 Sept. 1951: "Dr. Wilkinson is a thorough American; while titularly a Democrat, he is anti-New Deal, anti-Communist, and anti-all of the new fads and fancies and fallacies" (fd 13, box 383, JRCP, also in JRC fd of correspondence, Post-Presidential Individual File, Hoover Presidential Library, West Branch, Iowa).

¹⁵⁶ Computerized title-search of publications in Clarkana. Aside from 700 books with *Bolshevik, Communism, Lenin, Marx,* or *Trotsky* in the title, there are others about Russia and the Soviet Union.

¹⁵⁷ Clark specified that his valedictory talk at the University of Utah (in 1898) was the beginning of his campaign against "Socialism, which is a form of Marxism." See JRC to J. Howard Nelson, 5 Jan. 1960, attached to *The Iron Curtain over America* in Clarkana; cf. "Commencement Oration," in *SA*, 11-16.

This chapter emphasizes Marxism and Communism for two reasons. First, socialists have not always identified their views with Marx. Second, socialists usually emphasized the democratic process and rejected the Communist emphasis on "the dictatorship of the proletariat." Reuben regarded these as distinctions without a difference. For the philosophy, conduct, and history of socialism versus Communism, see Lewis A. Coser and Irving Howe, *The American Communist Party* (Boston: Beacon Press, 1957); "Communism Versus Socialism," in *EA* 7:439, also 25:146-47 (pre-Marx socialism), 25:147-48 (Christian socialism), 25:148-49 (democratic socialism); also John R. Sillito, "Socialist Saints: Mormons and the Socialist Party in Utah, 1900-20," *Dial* 18 (Spring 1985): 121-31.

¹⁵⁸ By his July 1915 letter, Clark had added at least some of these to Clarkana: Karl Marx, *Der Bürgerkrieg in Frankreich* ... (Leipzig: Genossenschaftsbuchdruckerei, 1876); Paul Lafargue, *Der Wirtschaftliche Materialismus nach den Auschauunger von Karl Marx* (Zurich: Volksbuchhandlung, 1886); *Karl Marx vor den Kölner Geschwornen* ... (Berlin: Expedition, 1895); Paul Fischer-Berlin, *Die Marxische Werttheorie* ... (Berlin: Expedition, 1896); Errico Malatesta, *A Talk about Anarchist Communism between Two Workers* (San Francisco: Free Society, 1898); Gabriel Deville, *The People's Marx* ..., trans. Robert Rives La Monte (New York: International Library Publishing, 1900); V. I. Lenin, *The Reorganization of the Party,* reprinted from New Life (issues of 10, 15-16 Nov. 1905); Daniel DeLeon, *Marx on Mallock, or Fact vs. Fiction* ... (New York: National Executive Committee, Socialist Labor Party, [1908?]); Anton Pannekoek, *Marxism and Darwinism* (Chicago: C.H. Kerr/Cooperative, 1912); *Karl Marx, Value, Price, and Profit: Addressed to Working Men,* ed. Eleanor Marx Aveling (Chicago: C.H. Kerr, [1913]); Emma Goldman, *Syndicalism: The Modern Menace to Capitalism* (New York: Mother Earth Publishing Association, 1913); I. M. Rubinow, *Was Marx Wrong?* ... (New York: Cooperative Press/Marx Institute of America, 1914); Heinz Neumann, *Marx and Engels on Revolution in America* (Chicago: Daily Worker, nd).

¹⁵⁹ JRC to Lucy Wilson, 12 July 1915, box 346, JRCP; also *C*, 256, which used her maiden name James in the narrative but in his source note (636n27) correctly identified her married name.

¹⁶⁰ Aside from other sources cited in this chapter, Clarkana has Osip A. Piatnitskii, *The Bolshevisation of the Communist Parties by Eradication of the Social-Democratic Traditions,* 2nd Reprint (London: Modern Books, 1932).

¹⁶¹ Clarkana has the following from Communist publishing houses: Charles E. Ruthenberg, *The Workers (Communist) Party* (Chicago: Workers Communist Party, [1920]); Max Bedacht, *The Menace of Opportunism* (Chicago: Daily Worker Publishing, 1926); *The Platform of the Class Struggle* (New York: Workers' Library

Publishers, 1928); *Why Every Worker Should Join the Communist Party* (New York: Communist Party of the United States of America, [1929?]); *What's the Answer? Twelve Questions That Country Workers and Farmers Are Asking* (London: Communist Party of Great Britain, 1944); and *Russia with Our Own Eyes: Report of the British Workers' Delegation to the Soviet Union, 1950* (New York: SRT Publisher, 1951).

See Edward L. Shapsmeier and Frederick H. Schapsmeier, *Political Parties and Civic Action Groups* (Westport, CT: Greenwood Press, 1981), 110-12, for "Workers (Communist) Party," original name of the Communist Party of the United States of America (CPUSA). See also Coser and Howe, *The American Communist Party*; Neal Wood, *Communism and the British Intellectuals* (New York: Columbia University Press, 1959); David Caute, *Communism and the French Intellectuals* (New York: Macmillan, 1964); Martin Dubovsky, *We Shall Be All: A History of the Industrial Workers of the World* (Chicago: Quadrangle Books, 1969); Helen Z. Papanikolas, "Unionism, Communism, and the Great Depression: The Carbon County Coal Strike of 1933," *UHQ* 41 (Summer 1973): 254-300; Glenn V. Bird, "The Industrial Workers of the World in Utah: Origins, Activities, and Reactions of the Church of Jesus Christ of Latter-day Saints," M.A. thesis, Brigham Young University, 1976; John S. McCormick, "Hornets in the Hive: Socialists in Early Twentieth-Century Utah," *UHQ* 50 (Summer 1982): 224-40.

[162] *F,* 84; *Conf,* Oct. 1941, 16; also Hammond, "Some Political Concepts of J. Reuben Clark, Jr.," 32-39.

[163] *C,* 664.

[164] JRC, "Memorandum for American Preparatory Committee for Third Hague Conference," Sept. 1913, box 76, JRCP; *C,* 666.

[165] John A. Widtsoe, ed., *Discourses of Brigham Young, Second President of the Church of Jesus Christ of Latter-day Saints* (Salt Lake City: Deseret Book/copyrighted "by Heber J. Grant for the Church of Jesus Christ of Latter-day Saints," 1925), 99, in Clarkana. Widtsoe was quoting from *J* 10:191.

[166] *SI,* 347.

[167] Although "white Russian" can apply to a resident of Byelorussia, during the 1917-20 civil war a white Russian was an anti-Bolshevik whose goals included democratic socialism. For early accounts by American soldiers in the civil war against Bolshevik "reds," see Joel R. Moore, Harry H. Mead, and Lewis E. Jahns, comps., *The History of the American Expedition Fighting the Bolsheviki* (Detroit, MI: Polar Bear Publishing, 1920); Ralph Albertson, *Fighting without a War: An Account of Military Intervention in North Russia* (New York: Harcourt, Brace, and Howe, 1920). Reuben's former mentor, James Brown Scott, wrote the introduction for a 1937 book about this matter by Leonid I. Strakhovsky. For scholarly analysis, see John Lewis Gaddis, *Russia, the Soviet Union, and the United States: An Interpretive History* (New York: John Wiley and Sons, 1978), 72-82; David S. Foglesong, *America's Secret War against Bolshevism: U.S. Intervention in the Russian Civil War, 1917-1920* (Chapel Hill: University of North Carolina Press, 1995). *EA* 29:339-40 discusses only the beginning of the U.S. intervention.

[168] JRC work diary, 18 Jan. 1929, box 530, JRCP; quoted fully in *C,* 666. Clarkana has the following books concerning Josif Stalin's rule in Russia after

Lenin's death in 1924: Maria Reese, *I Accuse Stalinism!* (New York: Pioneer Publishers, [1933]); Leon Trotsky, *Stalinism and Bolshevism* (New York: Pioneer Publishers, 1937); J. C. Hunter, *The Murder of Trotsky and the Fight against Stalinism* (New York: Leninist League, [1940]); James P. Cannon, *American Stalinism and Anti-Stalinism* (New York: Pioneer Publishers, 1947); Fred E. Beal, *The Red Fraud: An Exposé of Stalinism* (New York: Tempo Publishers, 1949); see also Alan Bullock *Hitler and Stalin: Parallel Lives* (New York: Alfred A. Knopf, 1992).

[169] Gaddis, *Russia, the Soviet Union, and the United States,* 87-117.

[170] *Conf,* Oct. 1941, 16.

[171] Marion G. Romney diary, 8 May 1942.

[172] JRC to David O. McKay, 1 Nov. 1934, fd 3, box 351, JRCP.

[173] "Church Members Warned to Eschew Communism: Leaders Cite Threat to Home, Nation and Church," and "Warning to Church Members," *DN,* 3 July 1936, 1; "Editorial Warning to Church Members," Improvement Era 39 (Aug. 1936): 488; *M* 6:17-18.

[174] Fraser M. Ottanelli, *The Communist Party of the United States from the Depression to World War II* (New Brunswick, NJ: Rutgers University Press, 1991), 12, 43; Frank H. Jonas and Garth N. Jones, "Utah Presidential Elections, 1896-1952," *UHQ* 24 (Oct. 1956): 305; John Sillito, "Third Parties in Utah," in *U,* 554. In *E,* 304, I stated that 772 Communist votes were reported in the post-election tallies of the *SLT.* I forgot that those immediate tallies did not include absentee votes or some precincts which were included in the totals given by Jonas and Jones.

[175] Clarkana has the CPUSA election platforms for 1928, 1929, 1932, 1936, 1937, 1938, and 1940, as well as local state publications *Defend Yourself! Save Free Speech!* (Salt Lake City: Utah Communist Party, 1940?) and *United Mass Struggle against Hunger: The Communist Party Call to Workers and Farmers of Utah* (Salt Lake City: State Campaign Committee, Utah Communist Party, nd).

[176] JRC to David O. McKay, 22 July 1936, fd 1, box 355, JRCP; also in CR 1/48.

[177] Samuel O. Bennion to First Presidency, 27 July 1936, fd 5, box 34, David O. McKay papers, LDSA; Wendell J. Ashton, *Voice in the West: Biography of a Pioneer Newspaper* (New York: Duell, Sloan and Pearce; Salt Lake City: Deseret News Press, 1950), 301-02.

[178] Lester Wire to First Presidency, 20, 23, 30 July, 12 Aug. 1936, fd 5, box 34, McKay papers; *Municipal Record* 25 (Salt Lake City, July 1936): 1, for Finch as chief of police; Andrew Jenson, *Latter-day Saint Biographical Encyclopedia,* 4 vols. (Salt Lake City: Deseret News/Andrew Jenson History, 1901-36), 4:726; "Retired Police Officer, Inventor Dies In S.L.," *DN,* 15 Apr. 1958, A-16, for Wire.

[179] Jonas and Jones, "Utah Presidential Elections," 305; *Presidential Elections Since 1789* (Washington, D.C.: Congressional Quarterly, 1987), 137, but the vote tallies in this source omitted the Communist Party's votes in the 1932 election; Ottanelli, *The Communist Party of the United States,* 103.

[180] JRC office diary, 1 May 1939; also Stanford J. Layton, "Charles Rendell Mabey," in *U,* [341].

[181] Jeremiah Stokes to David O. McKay, 16 Apr. 1940, with "copy of a secret

report of Officer Lester Wire of the City Police force"; also McKay to Stokes, 19 Apr. 1940, acknowledging receipt of "a copy of a report made to Officer Lester Wire of the City Police Force of two Communist meetings held recently in Salt Lake City," both in fd 5, box 34, McKay papers.

[182] David O. McKay to Jeremiah Stokes, 19 Apr. 1940.

[183] "Nazis Infest Utah," *Sugar House Post Sentinel, Extra* 5, no. 42 (25 May 1940), Clarkana 320.53, A1, #534.

[184] *E*, 308-12.

[185] *M* 6:18.

[186] *Conf,* Oct. 1942, 54; JRC, "Private Ownership under the United Order and the Guarantees of the Constitution," *Improvement Era* 45 (Nov. 1942): 688.

[187] JRC to bishops' meeting, 1 Oct. 1943, transcript, box 151, JRCP.

[188] JRC to Edgar B. Brossard, 2 May 1944, fd 1, box 369, JRCP; Jenson, *Latter-day Saint Biographical Encyclopedia,* 4:335, for Brossard as former president of the French Mission; for Communism as "the real threat," rather than Nazism, see JRC to Jonathan W. Snow, 9 Dec. 1942, binder for October 1942 conference, box 156, JRCP.

[189] JRC, *Let Us Have Peace* (Salt Lake City: Deseret News Press, 1947), 15; *F,* 70.

[190] *C*, 66, which added: "As long as Hitler and Stalin behaved themselves internationally, Reuben had no quarrel with either of them. In point of fact, neither one behaved; on those grounds Reuben wound up opposing them both." The latter statement is only half correct. JRC did not like to read criticisms of Hitler even after Nazi armies invaded neutral countries, conquered most of Europe, and were killing American soldiers. See chapter 9.

[191] Marion G. Romney diary, 8 May 1942.

[192] JRC to Frank H. Jonas, 15 Feb. 1943, fd 2, box 411, JRCP; also in Jonas papers, JWML.

[193] George Albert Smith, JRC, and David O. McKay to U.S. Senator Elbert D. Thomas, 27 Aug. 1946, and Thomas to "The First Presidency," 10 Sept. 1946, both in unnumbered fd "General File—1946—Misc. (Lat-1)," box 99, Thomas papers, Utah State Historical Society.

[194] Rowena J. Miller to U.S. Senator Wallace F. Bennett, 27 Aug. 1954, fd 4, box 390, JRCP. Nevertheless, Reuben exerted this influence on the content of the First Presidency's letters without feeling that he was over-persuading the president. See chap. 2.

[195] JRC office diary, 1 Feb. 1947 (first set of quotes), 6 Mar. 1947 (quotes about the first list); also entry for Paul Robeson in Jack Salzman, David Lionel Smith, and Cornel West, eds., *Encyclopedia of African-American Culture and History,* 5 vols. (New York: Macmillan Library Reference USA/Simon & Schuster, 1996), 4:2346-48. Clarkana has Paul Robeson, "Forward," in Amanke Okafor, *Nigeria: Why We Fight for Freedom* (Watford, Eng.: Farleigh Press, 1949).

[196] JRC office diary, 17 Oct. 1949.

[197] JRC to G. Homer Durham, 6 May 1948, fd 4, box 377, JRCP.

[198] Ernest L. Wilkinson diary, 2 Mar. 1960.

[199] *SI*, 274.

[200] "Pres. Clark Holds Service Insurance Aim," *DN*, 15 Dec. 1939, 3; "U.S. Freedom Threat Seen: Pres. Clark Warns of Communism," *DN*, 7 Oct. 1943, 1; "Pres. Clark Warns of Plot to Wreck U.S.," *DN*, 18 Sept. 1946, 1; "Common Law Government in U.S. Endangered," *CN*, 21 Sept. 1946, 2; JRC to Thorpe B. Isaacson, 13 Feb. 1947, fd 7, box 376, JRCP; *SA*, 121-22, 186-87, 463, 524, 548-49; also JRC, *Inroads upon the Constitution by the Roman Law: A Constitution Day Address by President J. Reuben Clark, Jr. (September 17, 1946)* (Salt Lake City: Deseret News Press, 1946).

[201] JRC to G. Homer Durham, 6 May 1948.

[202] JRC office diary, 19 Aug. 1949 (meeting on 16 August).

[203] JRC to C. W. Barton, 9 Apr. 1947, fd 2, box 375, JRCP.

[204] JRC to Hugh C. Smith, 6 Dec. 1954, fd 15, box 391, JRCP. As of 1981, William F. Buckley's syndicated newspaper editorials were still favorable toward Joseph R. McCarthy's anti-Communism.

Interpretations of McCarthy and the anti-Communist crusade of the 1950s continue to be divided along ideological lines, but useful studies are: Victor Navasky, *Naming Names* (New York: Viking Press, 1980); Thomas C. Reeves, *The Life and Times of Joe McCarthy* (Briar Cliff Manor, NY: Stein and Day, 1981); Stanley I. Butler, *The American Inquisition* (New York: Hill and Wang, 1982); Peter L. Steinberg, *The Great "Red Menace"* (Westport, CT: Greenwood Press, 1985); Jeff Broadwater, *Eisenhower and the Anti-Communist Crusade* (Chapel Hill: University of North Carolina Press, 1992); Joel Kovel, *Red Hunting in the Promised Land* (New York: Basic Books, 1994); Ellen Schrecker, *Many Are the Crimes: McCarthyism in America* (Boston: Little, Brown, 1998).

Because of the political grandstanding and tactics of McCarthy's Senate committee and the House Un-American Activities Committee (HUAC), there were impassioned pleas of innocence by many of those accused in 1945-55. This was especially true for Alger Hiss and for Julius and Ethel Rosenberg. Their children, friends, and many liberal scholars continued to maintain their innocence for decades. Hiss died in 1996 still claiming that he was falsely accused and unjustly imprisoned. In addition to the above sources, see *DA*, 150-51, 155-56, 198-200, 287-88.

Their guilt was demonstrated in the late 1990s when the KGB made available for scholarly research the files on Americans who served as spies for the Soviet Union to the 1950s. See Allen Weinstein and Alexander Vassiliev, *The Haunted Wood: Soviet Espionage in America—the Stalin Era* (New York: Random House, 1999) for Alger Hiss (code names Lawyer and Ales) and Julius Rosenberg (code names Antenna, Liberal, and King). This remarkable book demonstrates that in addition to wrongly accusing hundreds of U.S. citizens, McCarthy and HUAC often overlooked those who had been operating as Soviet spies in the U.S. Army Signals Security Agency, the War Production Board, Aviation Department, Civil Service Commission, Commerce Department, Treasury Department, State Department, U.S. embassy in Germany, and the Office of Strategic Operations (precursor of the CIA). Soviet agents included a U.S. congressman, a member of the New York State Supreme Court, and one of Franklin D. Roosevelt's assistants in the White House.

²⁰⁵ Clarkana has three volumes by Joseph R. McCarthy and three books about him.

²⁰⁶ In response to a Mormon's complaint about *DN* editorials against Senator McCarthy as "a pathological character assassin" whose activity "reeks of totalitarianism," JRC's secretary wrote: "Mr. Clark wishes me to acknowledge your letters of February 16th and February 22nd, and to say that the editorials in the Deseret News, to which you refer, are no more pleasing to him than they apparently are to you. Mr. Clark does not believe that you will find similar articles appearing hereafter in the News" (Richard S. Morrison to JRC, 16 Feb. 1952 and Rowena J. Miller to Morrison, 1 Apr. 1952, both in fd 5, box 386, JRCP). This correspondence referred to "McCarthy's Busy Rut," *DN,* 10 Feb. 1952, B-2, and "Hitting below the Belt," *DN,* 16 Feb. 1952, B-2; see also F. Ross Peterson, "McCarthyism in the Mountains, 1950-1954," in Thomas G. Alexander, ed., *Essays on the American West, 1974-1975* (Provo, UT: Brigham Young University, 1976), 47-77; Richard Swanson, "McCarthyism in Utah," M.A. thesis, Brigham Young University, 1977.

²⁰⁷ David O. McKay office diary, 3 June 1954, LDSA. Contrast with the perspective of Utah's senator Arthur V. Watkins in his *Enough Rope: The Inside Story of the Censure of Senator Joe McCarthy by His Colleagues* (Englewood Cliffs, NJ: Prentice-Hall, 1970); Michael Whitney Straight, *Trial by Television: The Army-McCarthy Hearings* (Boston: Beacon Press, 1954); Emile DeAntonio and Daniel Talbot, *Point of Order! A Documentary of the Army-McCarthy Hearings* (New York: Norton, 1964).

²⁰⁸ "Gerard Calls Pact Bar to Early War," *NYT,* 7 May 1949, 4.

²⁰⁹ JRC to U.S. Senator Henry C. Dworshak, 16 Apr. 1948, fd 5, box 377, JRCP.

²¹⁰ *C,* 263.

²¹¹ Clarkana has seven Stokes volumes, including (all published in Salt Lake City by Federated Libraries) *Americans' Castle of Freedom under Bolshevik Fire on Our Home Front,* 1944; *For Freedom's Sake Stop America's Leftist Course toward Self-Annihilation,* 1946; and *Communists Have Solemnly Decreed That They Will Destroy Your Right to Life, Liberty, Property, Free Agency, Sovereignty, Free Speech, Free Press, Free Public Assembly, and Freedom of the Exercise of Religious Faith and Worship,* n.d.; also David O. McKay to Stokes, 15 Apr. 1940: "You are doing an excellent work in furnishing to the people information regarding the menace of Communism" (fd 5, box 34, McKay papers); JRC to Joseph E. Olsen, 25 May 1940: "I am sorry to say I know nothing about the matter which Jeremiah Stokes and his associates are putting out regarding Communism" (fd 2, box 362, JRCP).

²¹² JRC to Jeremiah Stokes, 13 Feb. 1945, fd 13, box 372, JRCP. For Stokes's correspondence with other members of the First Presidency, see Stokes papers, HBLL.

²¹³ JRC office diary, 30 Apr. 1948; also entry of 28 May 1948 for President Clark's similar view about another kind of extremism: "Mr. Harvey Dixon came

in to see me about masonry. He evidently is very extreme in anti-masonry. ... I did not approve of his arguments and statements because they were very extreme."

214 JRC office diary, 23 Sept. 1946 (quote), also 3 Sept. 1946 (first refusal to meet).

215 JRC to Hugh C. Smith, 6 Dec. 1954.

216 JRC correspondence with Ezra Taft Benson and memorandums of their conversations, JRCP.

217 JRC to Sumner Gerard, treasurer of the Committee for Constitutional Government, 15 Sept. 1947, fd 16, box 376, JRCP. Clarkana has Robert Hunter, *Revolution: Why, How, When?* 4th ed. (New York: Committee For Constitutional Government, 1943); Wilford I. King, *The Keys to Prosperity* (New York: Constitution and Free Enterprise Foundation/Committee for Constitutional Government, 1948); John T. Flynn, *The Road Ahead: America's Creeping Revolution* (New York: Committee for Constitutional Government/Devin-Adair, 1949); Frank E. Holman, *Story of the "Bricker" Amendment: The First Phase* (New York: Committee for Constitutional Government, 1954); Thomas James Norton, *The Constitution of the United States: Its Sources and Its Applications* (New York: Committee for Constitutional Government, 1956); also chapter 3, note 140.

218 JRC office diary, 3 Apr. 1948.

219 Samuel Barrett Pettengill, *Where Karl Marx Went Wrong* (Irvington-on-Hudson, NY: Foundation for Economic Education, 1953); also *DA*, 126, for this organization.

220 Among this organization's publications in Clarkana are Ludwig Von Mises, *Planned Chaos*, 1947; Paul L. Poirot, *The Pension Idea*, 1950; F. A. Harper, *Morals and the Welfare State*, 1951; and Russell J. Clinchy, *Human Rights and the United Nations*, 1952; also the author's presentation copy of Leonard E. Read, *Why Not Freedom?*, 1958; see Hammond, "Some Political Concepts of J. Reuben Clark, Jr.," 40–51, for "welfare state."

221 "UN Versus US," *Freeman* 5 (Mar. 1955): 365–67; "The Collectivist Menace," *Freeman* 6 (Aug. 1956): 53–56; "Blindspots in the New Socialism," *Freeman* 7 (May 1957): 51–55; "Not Victories for Communism," *Freeman* 8 (Apr. 1958): 32–38; "The Nature of Socialistic Disaster," *Freeman* 8 (Nov. 1958): 14–20; "Khrushchev's Bogus Challenge," *Freeman* 9 (Jan. 1959): 3–10. This 1950s publication should not be confused with the ultra-conservative magazine of the same name published decades later by W. Cleon Skousen, a Mormon. See *E*, 468n336, 471n372.

222 Previous note 158; Clarkana also has *The American Economic System Compared with Collectivism and Dictatorship* (Washington, D.C.: Chamber of Commerce of the United States, [1936]); see *DA*, 77, for *collectivism*.

223 JRC office diary, 19 Aug. 1949, described this meeting of August 16.

224 JRC to Leonard E. Read, 19 Aug. 1949, also JRC office diary, 19 Aug. 1949.

225 JRC office diary, 8 Sept. 1950, emphasis in original; *World Affairs*, Fall 1947, inside front cover (Hiss first listed as an American Peace Society director), and Spring 1949, inside back cover (Hiss no longer listed as a director); note 204.

[226] JRC office diary, 21 Sept. 1951.

[227] Mark E. Petersen to "The First Presidency," 11 Apr. 1952; David O. Mc-Kay, Stephen L Richards, and JRC to Petersen, 14 Apr. 1952, both in Petersen fd, CR 1/48.

[228] Statement of Merwin K. Hart, president of the National Economic Council, in "Organizations: The Ultras," *Time* 78 (8 Dec. 1961): 24; Robert M. Buck, *The Grim Truth about Fluoridation*, bound with Frank S. Meyer, *The Moulding of Communists* (New Rochelle, NY: Conservative Book Club, 1961); also Benjamin R. Epstein and Arnold Forster, *The Radical Right: Report on the John Birch Society and Its Allies* (New York: Vintage Books/Random House, 1967), 28; *DA*, 124.

[229] JRC office diary, 8 Nov. 1955, with account of his later conversation with Spencer F. Hatch on 22 November. Still, JRC had "a general prejudice, he thinks it is, against fluoridation" (Rowena J. Miller to Mrs. H. Pistorius, 31 May 1957, fd 8, box 400, JRCP).

[230] JRC to W. Cleon Skousen, 28 Mar. 1958, fd 12, box 403; also JRC to Skousen, 20 July 1953, fd 10, box 389, JRCP. Cf. the assessment by LDS historian Richard D. Poll, *This Trumpet Gives an Uncertain Sound: A Review of W. Cleon Skousen's The Naked Communist* (Provo, UT: By the author, 1962), partly quoted in *E*, 82, 450n145.

[231] Joseph Anderson to David A. Law, 13 Nov. 1959, fd 6, box 406, JRCP.

[232] David O. McKay office diary, 17 Aug. 1961.

[233] JRC talk outline, box 210, JRCP.

[234] JRC office diary, 9 July 1940.

[235] JRC office diary, 4 May, 19 July, 2 Aug. 1939, 26, 29-30 Apr., 24, 29 May, 28 June, 5, 8-9, 11-12, 17, 20, 23, 29 July, 3, 13 Aug., 9 Dec. 1940, 8 Sept. 1941, 1 June 1943, 27 Jan., 21 Apr., 2, 22, 26-27 May 1944, 22 May 1946, 11 Mar. 1947, 28 Feb., 22 Mar., 2, 29 July, 6, 9 Aug., 24 Sept., 14 Oct. 1948, 1 Nov. 1949, 31 Jan., 14 Apr., 26 May, 8 June 1950, 6, 20 June, 25 July 1951, 18 Apr., 31 Dec. 1952, 2, 4 Mar. 1953, 10 Sept., 19 Oct., 12 Nov. 1954, 19 Jan., 18 Mar. 1955, 25 Nov. 1957; *H*, 185.

[236] JRC office diary, 12 May 1944.

[237] JRC office diary, 4 Feb. 1939.

[238] JRC office diary, 9 Mar., 24 Oct. 1944, 10 Sept. 1954.

[239] JRC office diary, 20 July 1940, 11 Mar. 1947, 1 Nov. 1949, 16 May 1952, 2 Mar. 1953; Henry D. Moyle diary, 26 July, 3, 10 Oct. 1940, 10 Oct. 1950, 10, 19 Jan., 18, 22-24, 26 Feb., 7, 23 Mar., 25 July, 27 Dec. 1951, 12 Aug., 1 Oct. 1952, 5, 14 Jan., 6, 10, 12 Mar., 30 Oct. 1953, LDSA; Harold B. Lee diary, 26 June 1942, 3 May 1943; Leonard J. Arrington, "Banking and Finance in Utah," in *U*, 31; *W*, 85 (General Welfare Committee), 121 (1947 apostleship and "the mechanism by which Henry Moyle and his good friend Harold B. Lee became liaisons between the church leadership and the political process in Utah").

[240] JRC office diary, 18 Apr. 1952.

[241] JRC office diary, 11 Feb. 1943.

[242] JRC office diary, 9 Aug. 1948.

[243] JRC to J. H. Gipson, president of Caxton Printers, 8 Sept. 1949, fd 9, box 379, JRCP.

[244] JRC office diary, 1 Nov. 1949.

[245] JRC to Drew Pearson, 27 Nov. 1950, fd 11, box 382, JRCP.

[246] Paul Jennens, "Elbert D. Thomas," in *U*, 557-58.

[247] JRC, *Some Factors of a Now-Planned Post-War Governmental and Economic Pattern* (Salt Lake City: Deseret News Press, 1943), 5, published in *Commercial and Financial Chronicle*, 25 Nov. 1943; also JRC talk for Constitution Day, 17 Sept. 1946, given over LDS radio station KSL, summarized in "Pres. Clark Warns of Plot to Wreck U.S.," *DN*, 18 Sept. 1946, 1 (quoted phrase), published as "Common Law Government in U.S. Endangered," *CN*, 21 Sept. 1946, 2, in *Commercial and Financial Chronicle*, 3 Oct. 1946, and Clark, *Inroads upon the Constitution by the Roman Law*, 5; see also *SA*, 143-44, 191, 195, 232-33, 235, 245, 246, 253-54, 488, 491, 522, 543-44.

In 1946 JRC named only one "alphabetical bureau" of the federal government—the OPA (Office of Price Administration) which Franklin D. Roosevelt established in 1941. See *EA* 20:649 (OPA); *DA*, 30, 225 ("alphabet agencies"); also "OPA Official Praises Foresight of Church," *CN*, 20 Feb. 1943, 4.

[248] Beth Smith Jarman, "Isolationism in Utah, 1935-1941," M.S. thesis, University of Utah, 1970, 22, 103 (Thomas an opponent of U.S. neutrality), 27-28, 76-78, 134 (JRC the opposite).

[249] David S. Wyman, *The Abandonment of the Jews: America and the Holocaust, 1941-1945* (New York: Pantheon Books, 1984), 146 (Thomas a founding member of the 1943 Emergency Conference to Save the Jewish People of Europe), 153 (drafting legislation for that purpose), 193-94 (cosponsor of a Senate resolution which unsuccessfully tried to give military priority to rescuing Jews from Nazi concentration camps); also Douglas F. Tobler, "The Jews, the Mormons, and the Holocaust," *JMH* 18 (Spring 1992): 72-75.

[250] JRC office diary, 5 May 1950.

[251] For plausible denial as the First Presidency's twentieth-century policy, see *E*, 355.

[252] JRC office diary, 14 July, 18 July 1950, emphasis in original.

[253] George Albert Smith diary, 18 July 1950.

[254] JRC office diary, 6 June 1951.

[255] Henry D. Moyle diary, 19 Jan., 23-24 Feb., 1 Mar. 1951; for more details, see *E*, 360, 591n265; *W*, 123-24, 126.

[256] Henry D. Moyle statement quoted in interview, 4 Apr. 1956, in Kenneth Holmes Mitchell, "The Struggle for Reapportionment in Utah," M.A. thesis, University of Utah, 1960, 96-97.

[257] Mitchell, "Struggle for Reapportionment in Utah," 97-102; JRC office diary, 2 Mar. 1953, 2 Dec. 1954; Henry D. Moyle diary, 29 Jan., 6, 10, 12 Mar. 1953; David O. McKay office diary, 12 Mar. 1953.

[258] JRC office diary, 2 Mar. 1953, also 2 Dec. 1954. For the outcome, see Mitchell, "Struggle for Reapportionment in Utah," 113-19; Frank H. Jonas, "Reapportionment in Utah and the Mormon Church," *Proceedings of the Utah Acad-*

emy of Sciences, Arts, and Letters 46, pt. 1 (1969): 19-25; Q. Michael Croft, "Influence of the L.D.S. Church on Utah Politics, 1945-1985," Ph.D. diss., University of Utah, 1985, 222-23; *E*, 361-62.

259 Mitchell, "Struggle for Reapportionment in Utah," 118-19; Jonas, "Reapportionment in Utah," 21-25; Croft, "Influence of the L.D.S. Church," 222-23; *E*, 360-61; *W*, 124-25.

260 Harold B. Lee diary, 18 Dec. 1954. For a description of this "distribution of literature," see Mitchell, "Struggle for Reapportionment in Utah," 113-14, 118-19; *E*, 361.

261 Composite quote from his statements in Harold B. Lee diary, 9 Nov. 1956 and in JRC to Howard W. Hunter, 14 Nov. 1956, fd 11, box 396, JRCP.

262 JRC to A. Helen Morgan, 30 July 1956, fd 18, box 396, JRCP.

263 Harold B. Lee diary, 13 Sept. 1956.

264 *SA*, 242-43, 291; also *EA* 6:353.

265 JRC to Roland Rich Woolley, 19 July 1960 (marked "not sent"), fd 18, box 409, JRCP.

266 Dean E. Mann, "Mormon Attitudes Toward the Political Roles of Church Leaders," *Dial* 2 (Summer 1967): 33-35; Frank H. Jonas, "Utah: The Different State," in Jonas, ed., *Politics in the American West* (Salt Lake City: University of Utah Press, 1969), 335; *DM*, 375; *E*, 363-64.

267 Dennis L. Lythgoe, "A Special Relationship: J. Bracken Lee and the Mormon Church," *Dial* 11 (Winter 1978): 76, 79, 80, 84; Dennis L. Lythgoe, *Let 'Em Holler: A Political Biography of J. Bracken Lee* (Salt Lake City: Utah State Historical Society, 1982), 33-34, 91-92, 101-02, 104.

268 JRC office diary, 10 Apr. 1956.

269 JRC office diary, 9 Aug., 14 Oct. 1948, 6 Jan. 1949, 25 July 1951, 23 Jan., 3, 8 May, 25 July, 31 Dec. 1952.

270 JRC office diary, 31 Jan. 1950.

271 JRC office diary, 12 June 1951, 2 Mar. 1955 (quote).

272 Henry D. Moyle diary, 2 Mar. 1951, 31 Jan. 1953.

273 Lythgoe, *Let 'Em Holler*, 98.

274 JRC office diary, 30 Jan. 1953.

275 Lythgoe, "Special Relationship," 82-83; Lythgoe, *Let 'Em Holler*, 98-99.

276 JRC office diary, 14 July 1953.

277 JRC to general priesthood meeting, 6 Apr. 1935, transcript, box 151, JRCP.

278 JRC, *Our Dwindling Sovereignty* (Salt Lake City: Deseret News Press, 1952), 4-5; *F*, 96-97; *SA*, 200.

Clark's emphasis on "the free country we had grown to be in the first 130 years of our national existence" referred to the period from the drafting of the U.S. Constitution in 1787 until troops were sent to Europe in 1917. He believed that such foreign interventions had corrupted the United States. Regarding the labels in this quote, Clarkana has *Karl Marx and Friedrich Engels: Reactionary Prussianism* (New York: International Publishers, 1944); *The Struggle for Communism: The Position of the Internationalist-Communists of the United States* (New York:

Communist League of Struggle, 1935); and Harper, *Morals and the Welfare State.* Also *DA*, 165 (*interventionism*), 273 (*reactionary*). As an indication of Reuben's divergence from most conservatives, Filler's article begins: "Intervention, crucial to United States relations in the world."

NOTES TO CHAPTER 9

[1] The New Testament, Matt. 26:52. For pacifism and the LDS church, and more generally in the United States, see D. Michael Quinn, "The Mormon Church and the Spanish-American War: An End to Selective Pacifism," *Pacific Historical Review* 43 (Aug. 1974): 342-66, reprinted in *Dial* 17 (Winter 1984); *T,* 13-14; *O,* 82-84; Davis Bitton, "The Ordeal of Brigham Young, Jr.," in Bitton, *The Ritualization of Mormon History and Other Essays* (Urbana: University of Illinois Press, 1994), 141; also Peter Brock, *Pacifism in the United States from the Colonial Era to the First World War* (Princeton, NJ: Princeton University Press, 1968); John A. Rohr, *Prophets without Honor: Public Policy and the Selective Conscientious Objector* (Nashville, TN: Abingdon Press, 1971).

[2] Joshua R. Clark autobiography, 1-29, and 1865-67 diary, 1-36, in JRCP; "A History of the Early Life of Joshua Reuben Clark, Sr. Covering a Period of about Thirty Years, Written at the Home of His Son Joshua Reuben in Washington, D.C. an[d] in My Home at Grantsville, Utah," typed document, 2 (father a "Dunker" minister; Joshua with Indiana Volunteers), 3 (medical discharge), end of microfilm of Clark diary and miscellaneous papers, Henry E. Huntington Library, San Marino, California; Leonard J. Arrington, *From Quaker to Latter-day Saint: Bishop Edwin D. Woolley* (Salt Lake City: Deseret Book, 1976), 358; also Norman F. Furniss, *The Mormon Conflict, 1857-1859* (New Haven: Yale University Press, 1960), 95-103; Howard Roberts Lamar, *The Far Southwest, 1846-1912: A Territorial History* (New Haven: Yale University Press, 1966), 338-45; Eugene E. Campbell, *Establishing Zion: The Mormon Church in the American West, 1847-1869* (Salt Lake City: Signature Books, 1988), 233-38; Donald R. Moorman and Gene A. Sessions, *Camp Floyd and the Mormons: The Utah War* (Salt Lake City: University of Utah Press, 1992); Richard D. Poll, "Utah Expedition," in *EM* 4:1500-02; Poll, "The Utah War," in *U,* 607-08.

[3] JRC to Joshua and Mary Clark, 21 May 1898, box 328, JRCP; also A. Prentiss, *The History of the Utah Volunteers in the Spanish-American War and in the Philippine Islands* (Salt Lake City: W.F. Ford, 1900); Quinn, "The Mormon Church and the Spanish-American War"; Brian M. Linn, *The U.S. Army and Counterinsurgency in the Philippine War, 1899-1902* (Chapel Hill: University of North Carolina Press, 1989); *The World Almanac and Book of Facts: 2000* (Mahwah, NJ: World Almanac Books, 1999), 217 (casualties).

[4] JRC to Theodore Marburg, 24 Oct. 1912, in American Peace Society fd, box 343, JRCP; also text of JRC memorandum, written at Marburg's request, on the judicial settlement of international disputes, in *SI,* 61-79.

[5] *C,* 260 (hordes), 255 (barbarians); *EA* 6:187, 29:231 (Central Power alliance); also Bernadotte E. Schmitt, *The Origins of the First World War* (London: The

Historical Association, 1958); Barbara W. Tuchman, *The Guns of August* (New York: Macmillan, 1962).

⁶ JRC to John W. Clark, 25 Jan. 1915, fd 11a, box 90, JRCP; *C*, 254-58, also 635n20 (America's "obsolete," "impossible," and "lopsided" demands) and 622n36 (JRC's similar "double-talk" about U.S. neutrality in Mexican Revolution).

⁷ *EA* 29:335, Wilson's 1917 speech.

⁸ *C*, 252, 271.

⁹ Schmitt, *Origins of the First World War;* Tuchman, *Guns of August; EA* 29:216-31, 332-35.

¹⁰ JRC to Theodore Marburg, 4 May 1914 (resignation request), JRC to Arthur Deering Call, 9 Dec. 1914 (resignation request), JRC to Theodore Marburg, 18 Dec. 1914 (quote), JRC to Theodore Marburg, 15 Apr. 1916 (resignation), all in American Peace Society fd; also *C*, 253.

¹¹ JRC to Theodore Marburg, 3 Mar. 1917, in American Peace Society fd. Reuben's definition of pacifism was similar to the category of "radical pacifist" in Robert S. Wood, "War and Peace," in *EM* 4:1547.

¹² Ernest R. May, *The World War and American Isolation, 1914-1917* (Cambridge, MA: Harvard University Press, 1959), 142-56; Louis W. Koenig, *Bryan: A Political Biography of William Jennings Bryan* (New York: G.P. Putnam's Sons, 1971), 502-69. Clarkana has William Jennings Bryan and William J. Stone, *Neutrality* (Washington: Government Printing Office, 1915); *The Proposal for a League to Enforce Peace* (New York: American Association for International Conciliation, [1916]); and Bryan, *The Prince of Peace* (Independence, MO: Zion's Printing and Publishing, 1925).

¹³ *EA* 29:335; *The World Almanac and Book of Facts,* 217 (casualties).

¹⁴ *C*, 263; also for its Utah manifestation, see Joerg A. Nagler, "Enemy Aliens and Internment in World War I: Alvo von Alvensleben in Fort Douglas, Utah, A Case Study," *UHQ* 58 (Fall 1990): 388-405.

¹⁵ "Address of Major J. Reuben Clark on Peace," *DN*, 6 Sept. 1919, sec. 4, vii; also James B. Allen, "J. Reuben Clark, Jr., on American Sovereignty and International Organization," *BYU Studies* 13 (Spring 1973): 347-59; *C*, 273-98.

¹⁶ "Brand Clark as Unfair and Illogical," *DN,* 6 Sept. 1919, 5, in which George W. Middleton, E. A. Smith, George E. Fellows, and Joshua H. Paul criticized his talk as "pro-German, illogical and one-sided," and as "not false merely, but traitorous."

¹⁷ John Albert White, *The Siberian Intervention* (Princeton, NJ: Princeton University Press, 1950); Betty Miller Unterberger, *American Intervention in the Russian Civil War* (Lexington, MA: D.C. Heath, 1968); John Lewis Gaddis, *Russia, the Soviet Union, and the United States: An Interpretive History* (New York: John Wiley and Sons, 1978), 72-82; David S. Foglesong, *America's Secret War against Bolshevism: U.S. Intervention in the Russian Civil War, 1917-1920* (Chapel Hill: University of North Carolina Press, 1995).

¹⁸ *C*, 299-321; Edwin Brown Firmage and Christopher L. Blakesley, "J. Reuben Clark, Jr., Law and International Order," *BYU Studies* 13 (Spring 1973): 336-42.

[19] Salmon O. Levinson to JRC, 9 May 1923, in American Committee for the Outlawry of War fd, box 345, JRCP.

[20] JRC, "Criticism of Plan to Outlaw War," 17 Jan. 1922, box 47, JRCP, summarized and quoted in *C*, 643n35; full text in *SI*, 193-96.

[21] JRC to J. C. Maxwell Garnett, 11 Mar. 1924, in American Committee for the Outlawry of War fd.

[22] *C*, 513.

[23] JRC to E. Worth Higgins, 12 Oct. 1938, fd 3, box 359, JRCP.

[24] John J. Esch to JRC, 9 May, 21 July 1930, both in box 30, JRCP.

[25] "The Distinction of Just and Unjust Wars," in James Hastings, ed., *Encyclopaedia of Religion and Ethics,* 13 vols. in 7 vols. (New York: Scribners, 1928), 12:681-83, in Clarkana; also Floyd Melvin Hammond, "Some Political Concepts of J. Reuben Clark, Jr.," M.A. thesis, Brigham Young University, 1962, 52-62 (chapter on war).

[26] For example, David Rees, *The Age of Containment: The Cold War, 1945-1965* (New York: St. Martin's Press, 1968).

[27] *ER* 2:622-23 for *Nazi* as English designation for the NSDAP, the German acronym for the National Socialist German Workers Party.

[28] *ER* 2:622-23.

[29] JRC to Salmon O. Levinson, 9 July 1934, fd 1, box 351, JRCP. Clarkana has one publication on this topic, by a Communist: Georgi Dimitrov, *The Legal System of German Fascism* (New York: Workers' Library Publishers, 1936); also see Kurt G. W. Ludecke, *I Knew Hitler: The Story of a Nazi Who Escaped the Blood Purge* (London: Jarrolds, 1938); Donald M. McKale, *The Nazi Party Courts: Hitler's Management of Conflict in His Movement, 1921-1945* (Lawrence: University of Kansas Press, 1974). The Communist publishing houses often had "worker" in their names.

[30] JRC to David O. McKay, 14 June 1937, fd 1, box 358, JRCP. *Kaiserism* referred to the leader of Imperial Germany during World War I, Kaiser [Emperor] Wilhelm II. Clarkana has R. Floyd Clarke, *In the Matter of Position of William Hohenzollern, Kaiser of Germany, under International Law* (New York: n.p., 1918).

[31] JRC to general priesthood meeting, 8 Oct. 1938, transcript, box 151, JRCP.

[32] Wayne S. Cole, *Charles A. Lindbergh and the Battle against American Intervention in World War II* (New York: Harcourt Brace Jovanovich, 1974), 31. *C*, 666, was the first to compare JRC with Lindbergh.

[33] Dorothy Herrmann, *Anne Morrow Lindbergh: A Gift for Life* (New York: Ticknor and Fields, 1992), 33-36, 51-53 (father Dwight Morrow), also 207 ("I felt that England, France and U.S.A. had *forced* the use of force on Germany," emphasis in original).

[34] Douglas F. Tobler, "The Jews, the Mormons, and the Holocaust," *JMH* 18 (Spring 1992): 75.

[35] *C*, 288, 290-92; Firmage and Blakesley, "J. Reuben Clark, Jr., Law and International Order," 55.

[36] JRC to Hiram W. Johnson, 18 Mar. 1935, fd 4, box 352, JRCP; also *C*, 598.

Clarkana has *Germany Rearms in the Air* (Paris: Centre d'Informations Documentaires, 1935).

[37] Clarkana has *Understanding Germany: Reichskanzler Adolf Hitler Addressing the German Reichstag on May 17, 1933* (Berlin: Liebheit and Thiessen, 1933); *One Year of National Socialism in Germany: Speech Delivered by Chancellor Adolf Hitler in the Reichstag on January 30, 1934* (Berlin: Liebheit and Thiessen, 1934).

[38] Dale Clark, "Mormonism in the New Germany," *CN,* 9 Dec. 1933, 3, 7; also Mary Jolley, "Fast and Testimony Meeting," "Genealogy," and Joseph Lynn Lyon, "Word of Wisdom," in *EM* 2:502, 538, 4:1584-85. Dale Clark was not related to JRC, whose brother Elmer Dale was already dead.

[39] Photographs in *CN,* 25 Jan. 1936, 1, 6; 18 July 1936, 2; 7 Aug. 1937, 2; *Webster's New World Dictionary of the American Language,* 2d college ed. (New York: Simon and Schuster, 1986), 1323, for *Sieg Heil* as "hail to victory; a Nazi salute"; also *ER* 2:938 for meaning of swastika, examples of this salute on 2:623, 625, 801, 875. William W. Slaughter, *Life in Zion: An Intimate Look at the Latter-day Saints, 1820-1995* (Salt Lake City: Deseret Book, 1995), 145, reprinted the photo of President Grant in front of the swastika banner and gave this explanation: "In Germany at this time, all public assemblies were required to display the Nazi (National Socialist Party) flag." What the Nazi government required was a different matter from what LDS headquarters chose to emphasize in *CN* photographs.

[40] Luacine S. Clark diary, 4-9 Aug. 1937; JRC 1937 diary, 4-9 August; JRC 1938 diary, 24-27 June; all in JRCP.

[41] *ER* 2:831.

[42] "Governor and J. R. Clark Say Policy Holders Oppose Any Centralized Regulation," *NYT,* 16 Dec. 1939, 10; *SA,* 458, 488, 491, 493.

[43] "Hitler Champions Business Freedom," *NYT,* 17 May 1934, 13; "Hitler Derides Russia for Asking Assistance of Capitalist Nations," *SLT,* 17 May 1934, 8; Clarkana has *Economic Development of Germany under National Socialism* (New York: National Industrial Conference Board, 1937), with JRC underlinings and marginal notations.

[44] JRC, *Let Us Have Peace* (Salt Lake City: Deseret News Press, 1947), 15; *F,* 70.

[45] "Europe War Scares Discounted," *SLT,* 8 Sept. 1937, 17.

[46] Interviews with Roy Anson Welker, 2-3 Feb. 1972, also listed as 1973 in the source notes, in Maja B. Wensel, "How Was the Mormon Church in Germany Affected during Hitler's Reich," 4 (quote), typed term paper, 18 Nov. 1982, for history class, Brigham Young University, copy in LDSL. More information about the Nazi women's leader, Gertrude Scholtz-Klink, is in David C. Nelson, "The Huebener Syndrome: How Mormons Remember Church History in Nazi Germany," copy in my possession.

[47] Ruth Welker Pugmire, comp., *Roy Anson Welker and Elizabeth Hoge: Their History* (Logan, UT: By the author, [1987]), 24, LDSL. This family history reported Hitler's words to Sister Welker, "I would like every woman in Germany to have a symbol just as you have." Fifty years later, the Welker family still did not

recognize the irony of the narcissistic Führer's remark about the narcissus flower as a symbol for German women.

Wensel, "How Was the Mormon Church in Germany Affected," 4, stated that the Nazis provided a limousine and uniformed chauffeur for these meetings. Pugmire's history, 25, described Sister Welker's visit to a Nazi youth camp after British Mormons reported rumors of immorality in the camps, which she dispelled.

Written four decades after the Nazi holocaust, these pleasant defenses of Hitler by the Welkers are jarring to read. Nevertheless, it is commendable that their daughter chose to accurately portray her parents' late-1930s enthusiasm for the German dictatorship.

[48] JRC memorandum, 18 July 1938, fd 4, box 215, JRCP, with my correction in his spelling of *Fuehrer.*

[49] JRC to "Brother and Sister Richard M. Robinson," 28 Oct. 1934, fd 1, box 351, JRCP.

[50] "Nazi Terrorizing of Jews Reported," *DN,* 22 Mar. 1933, 1; "Jews Flee from German Boycott," *DN,* 1 Apr. 1933, 1; "Hitler Deprives Jews of Citizenship," *DN,* 16 Sept. 1935, 1.

[51] Clarkana has *The Jews in Nazi Germany; the Factual Record of Their Persecution by the National Socialists* (New York: American Jewish Committee, 1933), Max J. Kohler, *The United States and German Jewish Persecutions—Precedents for Popular and Governmental Action* (Cincinnati: B'nai B'rith Executive Committee, 1934); Theodore Deak and Rae Einhorn, *Women and Children under the Swastika: A Collection of News Items and Factual Reports of the Unbridled Terror and Oppression in the Third Reich* (New York: Universum, 1936).

[52] *Conf,* Oct. 1937, 59; also John S. Conway, *The Nazi Persecution of the Churches, 1933-45* (New York: Basic Books, 1968); Ernst Christian Helmreich, *The German Churches under Hitler: Background, Struggle, and Epilogue* (Detroit, MI: Wayne State University Press, 1979). Tobler, "The Jews, the Mormons, and the Holocaust," 78, wrongly dated Welker's statement 1938 in the text, but accurately as 1937 in source note.

[53] Clarkana has H. S. Leiper, "The Plight of Religion," in M. B. Schnapper, ed., *Five Years of Hitler* (New York: American Council on Public Affairs, 1938).

[54] *Conf,* Oct. 1937, 59.

[55] JRC memorandum, 18 July 1938. For support of Nazis among German Latter-day Saints, see Joseph M. Dixon, "Mormons in the Third Reich: 1933-1945," *Dial* 7 (1972), no. 1:71-72, 77; Alan F. Keele and Douglas F. Tobler, "The Fuehrer's New Clothes: Helmuth Huebener and the Mormons in the Third Reich," *Sunstone* 5 (Nov.-Dec. 1980): 27; Christine Elizabeth King, *The Nazi State and the New Religions: Five Case Studies in Non-Conformity* (New York: Edwin Mellen Press, 1982), 67-71, 74-77, 79, 81, 84-87.

By contrast, seventeen-year-old Helmuth Huebener was tortured and beheaded for leading fellow LDS youths in anti-Nazi activities at Hamburg. Two of his LDS friends were sent to concentration camps and later immigrated to Utah. See Gilbert W. Scharffs, *Mormonism in Germany: A History of the Church of Jesus*

Christ of Latter-day Saints in Germany between 1840 and 1970 (Salt Lake City: Deseret Book, 1970), 102–04; Keele and Tobler, "The Fuehrer's New Clothes"; Karl-Heinz Schnibbe, Alan F. Keele, and Douglas F. Tobler, *The Price: The True Story of a Mormon Who Defied Hitler* (Salt Lake City: Bookcraft, 1984); Rudi Wobbe and Jerry Borrowman, *Before the Blood Tribunal* (American Fork, UT: Covenant Communications, 1992); Schnibbe, *When Truth Was Treason: German Youth against Hitler*, trans. Blair R. Holmes and Alan F. Keele, eds. (Urbana: University of Illinois Press, 1995).

[56] *Conf,* Oct. 1938, 136; also a secular version of this in JRC, "Religion in a Democracy," talk to the National Conference of Jews and Christians at Estes Park, Colorado, 26 July 1938, marked "ESTES PARK Not Delivered," transcript, page G, box 210, JRCP.

[57] Joseph Smith Jr., et al., 7 vols., *History of the Church of Jesus Christ of Latter-day Saints,* 2d rev., B. H. Roberts, ed. (Salt Lake City: Deseret Book, 1960), 4:541; James E. Talmage, *The Articles of Faith: A Series of Lectures on the Principal Doctrines of the Church of Jesus Christ of Latter-day Saints ... Written by Appointment; and Published by the Church* (Salt Lake City: Deseret News, 1899), later titled *A Study of the Articles of Faith: Being a Consideration of the Principal Doctrines ...* 13th ed. Salt Lake City: Church of Jesus Christ of Latter-day Saints, 1924), 413–28; translated as *Die Glaubensartikel ...* (Basel: Schweizerisch-Deutschen Mission, 1919), 510–30.

[58] Statement of LDS mission president Oliver H. Budge, 8 Sept. 1933, quoted at length in Tobler, "The Jews, the Mormons, and the Holocaust," 79; also *ER* 2:864 for Secret State Police, *Geheime Staatspolizei* and acronym *Gestapo.*

[59] Similar views appear in the works of interpreters and scholars whose writings have been the subject of varying degrees of controversy. For World War I, see Harry Elmer Barnes, *The Genesis of the World War: An Introduction of the Problem of War Guilt* (New York: Alfred A. Knopf, 1926), esp. 654–62; Arthur Ponsonby, *Falsehood in War-Time, Containing an Assortment of Lies Circulated Throughout the Nations During the Great War* (New York: E.P. Dutton, 1928); C. Hartley Grattan, *Why We Fought* (New York: Vanguard Press, 1929); Walter Millis, *Road to War: America 1914-1917* (Boston: Houghton Mifflin, 1935); James D. Squires, *British Propaganda at Home and in the United States from 1914 to 1917* (Cambridge, MA: Harvard University Press, 1935): Edwin Borchard and William Potter Lage, *Neutrality for the United States* (New Haven: Yale University Press, 1937); Charles Callan Tansill, *America Goes to War* (Boston: Little, Brown, 1938); H.C. Peterson, *Propaganda for War: The Campaign against American Neutrality, 1914-1917* (Norman: University of Oklahoma Press, 1939); Warren I. Cohen, *The American Revisionists: The Lessons of Intervention in World War I* (Chicago: University of Chicago Press, 1967).

For World War II, see Harold Nicolson, *Peacemaking, 1919* (Boston: Houghton Mifflin, 1933); Harold Lavine and James Wechsler, *War Propaganda and the United States* (New Haven: Yale University Press, 1940); Thomas A. Bailey, *Woodrow Wilson and the Great Betrayal* (New York: Macmillan, 1945); A. J. P. Taylor, *The Origins of the Second World War* (London: Hamilton, 1961); Robert A.

Divine, *The Illusion of Neutrality* (Chicago: University of Chicago Press, 1962); David L. Hoggan, *Der erzwungene Krieg: Die Ursachen and Urheber des 2. Weltkriegs* [The Forced War: The Causes and Originators of the Second World War] (Tübingen: Verlag der Deutschen Hochschullehrer-Zeitung, 1963); Richard M. Watt, *The Kings Depart, The Tragedy of Germany* (New York: Simon and Schuster, 1968); Mark L. Chadwin, *The Warhawks: American Interventionists before Pearl Harbor* (New York: W.W. Norton, 1970); Charles Roetter, *The Art of Psychological Warfare, 1914-1945* (New York: Stein and Day, 1974); Anthony Rhodes, *Propaganda, the Art of Persuasion: World War II* (New York: Chelsea House, 1976); Joseph P. Lash, *Roosevelt and Churchill, 1939-1941: The Partnership that Saved the West* (New York: W.W. Norton, 1976); D. J. Goodspeed, *The German Wars, 1914-1945* (Boston: Houghton Mifflin, 1977).

[60] Joseph M. Kenworthy [Strabolgi] (previously of British naval intelligence) and George Young, *Freedom of the Seas* (London: Hutchinson; New York: Liveright, 1928), 211 ("The *Lusitania* was sent [by the British Admiralty] at considerably reduced speed into an area where a U-boat was known to be waiting and with her escorts withdrawn," Kenworthy having been present when this decision was made). Colin Simpson, *The Lusitania* (Boston: Little, Brown, 1973), 131n observed that Kenworthy's "original manuscript stated 'was *deliberately* sent.' The word *deliberately* was deleted after representations [formal requests] from the Admiralty to Mssrs. Hutchinson, the publishers," also 35-36, 78-80, 130-31, for Simpson's discussion of young Winston Churchill's role in allowing German submarines to sink ships with American passengers.

In *The Lusitania Disaster: An Episode in Modern Warfare* (New York: Free Press/Macmillan, 1975), 186-91, Thomas A. Bailey and Paul B. Ryan attacked Simpson's interpretations in sections titled "The Alleged Plot to Embroil America" and "Churchill's Dubious Guilt." They did not mention the British intelligence officer Joseph Kenworthy or his book *Freedom of the Seas*. While I agree with Bailey and Ryan that many conspiracy theories are based on ill-founded suspicion, a refutation requires engaging the significant evidence that such theorists do cite.

[61] Simpson, *Lusitania*, 108-09 (photocopies of the manifests listing contraband munitions), 104 (diagram); Bailey and Ryan, *Lusitania Disaster,* 355n12 (State Department received the manifests in 1915), 101-02 (argument that the four million cartridges of rifle ammunition would not have exploded), also 107 (volatile "high explosives" under other names unlikely).

In a strange line of reasoning, Bailey and Ryan also argued (101) that this 1915 shipment to Britain was legal because the Department of Commerce had ruled in 1911 that "small arms ammunition" could be legally transported on passenger ships. However, this ruling was three years before the outbreak of war and before the U.S. declaration of neutrality. The burden of proof for Bailey and Ryan was to demonstrate that the U.S. government restated this exception after August 1914 when U.S. neutrality made ammunition "wartime contraband."

[62] JRC to general priesthood meeting, 4 Apr. 1938, transcript, box 151, JRCP.

[63] JRC to general priesthood meeting, 8 Oct. 1938, transcript, box 151, JRCP.

[64] Although Reuben rejected pro-British publications, Clarkana has Special Committee on Un-American Activities, *Investigation of Nazi Propaganda Activities* (Washington, D.C.: Government Printing Office, 1934).

[65] JRC to James T. Williams, 21 Nov. 1938, fd 3, box 359, JRCP; also Donald F. Drummond, *The Passing of American Neutrality, 1937-1941* (Ann Arbor: University of Michigan Press, 1955).

[66] Before his 1938 letter, Reuben had apparently acquired the following publications about the Spanish Civil War that are now in Clarkana: *Spain's War of Independence* (Washington, D.C.: Spanish Embassy, 1937); *Madrid, the "Military" Atrocities of the [Franco] Rebels* (London: Victoria House Printing, 1937); Andre Marty, *Heroic Spain* (New York: Workers' Library, 1937); *The Story of the Abraham Lincoln Brigade* (New York: Friends of the Abraham Lincoln Brigade, 1937); Isabel de Palencia, "What the Civil War May Mean to Spanish Trade Unions," in Francis J. Gorman, ed., *The Fate of Trade Unions under Fascism* (New York: Anti-Fascist Literature Committee, 1937); Ignacio G. Menendez-Reigada, *La Guerra Nacional Española ante la Moral y el Derecho* (Bilbao: Editora Nacional, 1937); *Attentats et Terreur: Instruments de Conquete Politique* (Paris: Comite Franco-Espagnol, [1937?]); [Salaria Kee], *A Negro Nurse in Republican Spain* (New York: Negro Committee to Aid Spain, with the Medical Bureau and North American Committee to Aid Spanish Democracy, 1938).

[67] James W. Cortada, *Historical Dictionary of the Spanish Civil War, 1936-1939* (Westport, CT: Greenwood, 1982), 5-6, 11, 144-46, 236-38, 251; also *EA* 25:421-22.

[68] "Pres. Clark Joins Attack on Spanish Rebels' Cruelty," *DN*, 29 May 1937, 5. Beth Smith Jarman, "Isolationism in Utah, 1935-1941," M.S. thesis, University of Utah, 1970, 38, mistakenly cited the *DN* article as an editorial on a different page.

[69] Paul H. Lambert ("Secretary East German Mission"), "German Paper Prints Mormon Article," *CN*, 20 May 1939, 2.

[70] *M* 6:89-92.

[71] *Conf*, Oct. 1939, 11-12.

[72] *Conf*, Apr. 1941, 20.

[73] JRC to Orval Adams, 25 Apr. 1941, fd 1, box 363, JRCP; also Firmage and Blakesley, "J. Reuben Clark, Jr., Law and International Order," 305.

[74] See JRC statement quoted for note 83.

[75] *Conf*, Oct. 1939, 11-12; also *SI*, 272, 393.

[76] *Conf*, Oct. 1939, 13.

[77] *M* 6:89; letters in box 153, JRCP, including JRC to Greene H. Hackworth (legal adviser, Department of State), 23 Oct. 1939, and JRC to William E. Borah (Senate Committee on Foreign Relations), 23 Oct. 1939.

[78] "Welfare," *DN*, 7 Oct. 1939, 9.

[79] "U.S. Attache Killed in Nazi Airplane Raid," *DN*, 22 Apr. 1940, [1].

[80] *SLT*, 22 May 1940, 8; 29 June 1940, 8.

[81] See JRC statement quoted for note 208.

[82] JRC office diary, 9 July 1940, JRCP. Clarkana has Edwin C. Riegel, *The Aggressor in the White House* (New York: League for Constitutional Government, 1940), which had the alternate title *Quarantine the Aggressor in the White House.*

[83] JRC to Amy Brown Lyman, 15 July 1940, fd 2, box 362, JRCP; also this German view in Hoggan, *Der erzwungene Krieg* [The Forced War].

[84] "Hitler Takes Nine Days in Drive on Paris," *DN*, 14 June 1940, 2; for Amy Brown Lyman as general president in 1940, see Jill Mulvay Derr, Janath Russell Cannon, and Maureen Ursenbach Beecher, *Women of Covenant: The Story of Relief Society* (Salt Lake City: Deseret Book, 1992), 436.

[85] *Conf,* Oct. 1940, 14.

[86] William L. Langer and S. Everett Gleason, *The Undeclared War, 1940-41* (New York: Harper, 1953); Thomas A. Bailey and Paul B. Ryan, *Hitler vs. Roosevelt: The Undeclared Naval War* (New York: Free Press, 1979); William J. Casey (director, CIA), *The Secret War Against Hitler* (Washington, D.C.: Regnery Gateway, 1988); and the "Provoking War" chapter in Irwin F. Gellman, *Secret Affairs: Franklin Roosevelt, Cordell Hull, and Sumner Welles* (Baltimore: Johns Hopkins University Press, 1995), 247-60.

[87] JRC to Gordon W. Clark, 30 Oct. 1940, box 338, JRCP.

[88] Relevant entries in *ER; OC.*

[89] JRC draft of talk, box 223, JRCP; also "Church Leaders Pay High Tribute to Life and Teachings of Lincoln: Pres. Clark Asks Freedom Be Preserved," *DN*, 13 Feb. 1941, [13], 18; full text in *SA*, 503-19, with my last quote on 517.

[90] Afton Lowder (executive secretary, Utah chapter, America First Committee) to JRC, 29 May 1941, and JRC to Lowder, 2 June 1941, both in fd 1, box 364, JRCP. Clarkana has eight of the organization's publications, all published in Chicago, 1940-41: *Aims and Activities*; *Our Foreign Policy*; *Can Hitler Cripple America's Economy?*; John T. Flynn, ed., *Can Hitler Invade America?*; D. Worth Clark, *Peace or War?*; *Address by Charles A. Lindbergh*; *Convoy: A Funeral Train*; and *"I Hate War."*

In 1941 Reuben "was greatly agitated over the criticism that had come to the First Presidency because of them allowing the Tabernacle to be used for an America First Rally where young Senator [Rush] Holt of [West] Virginia is to speak. He intimated that approval had been given without their consent" (Harold B. Lee diary, 13 Nov. 1941, private possession). For background, see Wayne S. Cole, *America First: The Battle against Intervention, 1940-1941* (Madison: University of Wisconsin Press, 1953); *DA*, 31; Justus D. Doenecke, ed., *In Danger Undaunted: The Anti-Interventionist Movement of 1940-1941 as Revealed in the Papers of the America First Committee* (Stanford, CA: Hoover Institute Press, 1990.)

[91] In her zeal to criticize Clark, the woman made this mistaken reference to the infamous destruction of Rotterdam during Germany's 1940 invasion of neutral Holland. See *EA* 29:389.

[92] J— R. S—— to JRC, 13 Feb. 1941; Mrs. J. S. B— to JRC, 13 Feb. 1941; Z— B. S——— to JRC, 14 Feb. 1941; all in box 223, JRCP.

[93] JRC to John Bassett Moore, 18 Feb. 1941, fd 15, box 223, JRCP.

[94] Jarman, "Isolationism in Utah, 1935-1941," 11.

[95] For *Blitzkrieg,* see *ER* 1:90; *OC,* 140.

[96] JRC to Alfred M. Landon, 28 Apr. 1941, fd 11, box 364, JRCP; also Thomas Pakenham, *The Boer War* (New York: Random House, 1979).

[97] N. L. Nelson, *The Second War in Heaven, As Now Being Waged by Lucifer through Hitler as a Dummy* (Independence, MO: Zion's Printing and Publishing, 1941). For decades this was the LDS church's Midwestern publishing house, directed primarily by the president of the Central States Mission, who was sometimes also an LDS general authority.

[98] JRC to N. L. Nelson, 24 June 1941, 2, 6, in fd 2, box 363, JRCP, partly quoted in *E,* 828. See "N. L. Nelson and the Mormon Point of View," *BYU Studies* 13 (Winter 1973): 157-71.

[99] For Europe's status in June 1941, see relevant entries in *ER; OC.* Many readers may not realize that the following countries were military allies of Nazi Germany: Bulgaria, Croatia, Finland, the Vichy Regime of southern France, Hungary, Italy, Romania, and Slovakia, and that the Baltic states of Estonia, Latvia, and Lithuania provided military units for Nazi forces. In most of these cooperating countries, the local police, judges, and ordinary people aided the SS and *Gestapo* in arresting and executing fellow citizens. This cooperation also occurred in conquered countries. The extraordinary exceptions were conquered Denmark and Axis ally Bulgaria, both of which rescued their Jews from being sent to concentration camps. See Leo Goldberger, ed., *The Rescue of the Danish Jews: Moral Courage under Stress* (New York: New York University Press, 1987); Michael Bar-Zohar, *Beyond Hitler's Grasp: The Heroic Rescue of Bulgaria's Jews* (Holbrook, MA: Adams Media, 1998).

In addition, there has been enormous distortion in the emphasis on Germany's 1938 annexation of Austria. Prior to its 1938 absorption into Germany, Austria had a higher percentage of Nazi Party membership than did Germany. In the April 1938 plebiscite, 99.7 percent of its voters wanted their country to merge with Germany. Even taking into consideration voting fraud, the anti-Nazi Austrians were a very small minority. See *ER* 1:26; Bruce F. Pauley, *Hitler and the Forgotten Nazis: A History of Austrian National Socialism* (Chapel Hill: University of North Carolina Press, 1981); Pauley, "The Austrian Nazi Party before 1938: Some Recent Revelations," in F. Parkinson, ed., *Conquering the Past: Austrian Nazism, Yesterday and Today* (Detroit, MI: Wayne State University Press, 1989), 34-56.

[100] Clarkana has Hans Beimler, *Four Weeks in the Hands of Hitler's Hell-Hounds: The Nazi Murder Camp of Dachau* (New York: Workers' Library Publishers, 1933); and *The Sonnenburg Torture Camp, By an Escaped Prisoner* (New York: Workers' International Relief and International Labor Defense, 1934). Even though these narratives were printed by Communist publishers, his 1939 statement to Presidents Grant and McKay (see following note) showed that Reuben accepted the basic truth of these publications in his private library.

[101] JRC office diary, 21 July 1939.

[102] "Concentration Camp Prisoners Shot Down, *DN,* 19 Nov. 1938, 2, regarding a mass execution of Jews at Buchenwald, with reference to the camps at Sachsenhausen and Dachau.

[103] "Fifteen GOP Leaders Demand U.S. Steps toward War End," *DN,* 5 Aug. 1941, 1; "Fifteen Republicans Score War 'Steps,'" *NYT,* 6 Aug. 1941, 6; also "Hoover Visits S.L. on Way to Vacation: Former President Declines to Elaborate on Anti-War Statement," *DN,* 6 Aug. 1941, 1; Harold Wolfe, *Herbert Hoover: Public Servant and Leader of the Loyal Opposition* (New York: Exposition Press, 1956), 379-401, with mention of Clark on page 171.

[104] Manfred Jonas, *Isolationism in America, 1935-1941* (Ithaca, NY: Cornell University Press, 1966); Wayne S. Cole, *Roosevelt and the Isolationists, 1932-45* (Lincoln: University of Nebraska Press, 1983), with mention of Clark on page 205; also Martin B. Hickman and Ray C. Hillam, "J. Reuben Clark, Jr.: Political Isolationism Revisited," *Dial* 7 (Spring 1972): 37-46; reprinted in *BYU Studies* 13 (Spring 1973): 426-40.

[105] Jarman, "Isolationism in Utah, 1935-1941," 134. She prefaced this assessment with these tentative words: "It may not be stating the case too strongly to suggest that ..." She failed to mention Clark's Lincoln Day talk or his participation in the August 1941 denunciation of U.S. aid to Britain.

[106] "Former Admirer" to JRC, Aug. 1941, fd 6, box 371, JRCP; also *ER* 1:34-35 (appeasement); *OC,* 354 (Fifth Columnists); Harold Lavine, *Fifth Column in America* (New York: Doubleday, Doran, 1940).

[107] *Scoop Magazine* (Aug. 1941): 22, in JRC scrapbook, JRCP, emphasis in original.

[108] See discussion, quotes, and sources for notes 39, 89-92, 104-105.

[109] "F.D.R. Gives 'Fire First' Order: Axis Denounces Roosevelt; Makes Threat on U.S. Ships," *DN,* 12 Sept. 1941, 1; also Langer and Gleason, *Undeclared War,* 742-50; Bailey and Ryan, *Hitler vs. Roosevelt,* 179-83.

[110] *Conf,* Oct. 1941, 15-16.

[111] In 1939 Canadian Mormons lived mainly in the southern part of Alberta province; cf. Kenneth W. Tingley, *For King and Country: Alberta in the Second World War* (Edmonton, Can.: Reidmore Books/Provincial Museum of Alberta, 1995); *Raymond Remembered: Settlers, Sugar and Stampedes* (Raymond, Can.: The History Book Committee, 1993), 13-165; also Eugene E. Campbell and Richard D. Poll, *Hugh B. Brown: His Life and Thought* (Salt Lake City: Bookcraft, 1975), 150-53, concerning Hugh B. Brown's Canadian-born son who volunteered for service with the Eagle Squadron of the Royal Air Force. President Clark would have known about this because he and Brown were friends. Cf. Michael D. Melinchuk, "Eagles for the Allies: Recruiting American Volunteers for the Royal Air Force and Royal Canadian Air Force, 1939-1945," Ph.D. diss., Kent State University, 1997.

[112] *Conf,* Oct. 1941, 15-16. Clarkana has the anti-British publication of Frederick F. Schrader, *The Enemy Within: Americans Looking in the Wrong Direction for the Dangers That Menace Our Institutions* (New York: N.p., 1940).

[113] Heber J. Grant, JRC, and David O. McKay to William C. FitzGibbon (Defense Savings staff, U.S. Treasury Department), 11 Oct. 1941, copy in Marriner S. Eccles papers, JWML; Heber J. Grant journal sheets, 5 Aug. 1942, LDSA.

[114] JRC to J. C. Grey, 20 Oct. 1941, fd 1, box 363, JRCP.

[115] *EA* 29:422-25; *OC*, 434-36; *ER* 2:820-21; "Russ Lose Four Million Men, Nazis Say," *DN*, 6 Aug. 1941, 1; "Nazis Take Leningrad Defenses," *DN*, 18 Sept. 1941, 1; "Nazis Capture 574,000 Reds: Trapped Armies at Kiev Reported Near Collapse," *DN*, 26 Sept. 1941, 1: "Reds Crushed Forever, Says German Chief," *DN*, 3 Oct. 1941, 1; "Nazis Launch New Drive on Front: Moscow Held to Be Newest German Goal," *DN*, 6 oct. 1941, 1; "Nazi Drive Pushes within 125 Miles of Red Capital," *DN*, 8 oct. 1941, 1; "Russ Lines Pierced: 350,000 Reds Taken," *DN*, 13 Oct. 1941, 1.

[116] Warren F. Kimball, *The Most Unsordid Act: Lend-Lease, 1939-1941* (Baltimore: Johns Hopkins University Press, 1969), 40ff; V. R. Cardozier, *The Mobilization of the United States in World War II* (Jefferson, NC: McFarland, 1995), 132-48.

[117] JRC statement in Marion G. Romney diary, 14 Nov. 1941, private possession; JRC office diary, 22 Nov. 1941; also Mary Peach, "Clearfield," Thomas G. Alexander and Rick J. Fish, "The Defense Industry of Utah," Charles G. Hibbard, "Fort Douglas," Hibbard, "Hill Air Force Base," in *U*, 99-100, 130-31, 199-200, 253-54; Leonard J. Arrington and Thomas G. Alexander, "World's Largest Military Reserve: Wendover Air Force Base, 1941-63," *UHQ* 31 (Fall 1963): 324-35; Arrington and Alexander, "Sentinels on the Desert: The Dugway Proving Ground (1942-63) and Deseret Chemical Depot (1942-1955), *UHQ* 32 (Winter 1964): 32-43; Arrington and Alexander, "Utah's Small Arms Ammunition Plant during World War II," *Pacific Historical Review* 34 (May 1965): 185-96.

[118] JRC office diary, 22 Nov. 1941; also note 155.

[119] JRC office diary, 1 July 1940, JRCP, with parenthetical expression in original; also see "Nazis Infest Utah," *Sugar House Post Sentinel, Extra,* 25 May 1940, HBLL.

[120] For Gaeth, see Andrew Jenson, *Latter-day Saint Biographical Encyclopedia,* 4 vols. (Salt Lake City: Deseret News/Andrew Jenson History, 1901-36), 4:326-27; Kahlile Mehr, "Czech Saints: A Brighter Day," *Ensign* 24 (Aug. 1994): 47-48. As an example of Gaeth's anti-Nazi views that were published before JRC could suppress them, see "If Christ Came to Germany," *CN*, 25 Jan. 1941, 5-6, 8, which included a photograph of "prisoners in a German concentration camp." This was part of a scheduled series of articles which ended on 1 March 1941, after which Reuben made sure that the LDS newspaper did not publish any more of Gaeth, and JRC office diary stated on 17 November 1941: "*President Clark:* Of course we can suppress him [Gaeth], I do not know how long it will last." Three weeks later, the U.S. declaration of war against Nazi Germany made such a ban unnecessary, and the *CN* began publishing anti-Nazi articles far more strident than Gaeth's 1941 article.

[121] Gordon W. Prange, *December 7, 1941: The Day the Japanese Attacked Pearl Harbor* (New York: McGraw-Hill, 1988); Stanley Weintraub, *Long Day's Journey into War: December 7, 1941* (New York: Dutton, 1991).

[122] *EA* 2:882 (Japan and Axis).

[123] Cole, *Charles A. Lindbergh*, 212-28.

[124] JRC office diary, 9 July 1940; *Conf,* Oct. 1940, 16; JRC to Gordon W. Clark, 29 Oct. 1940, box 338; JRC to Philip Marshall Brown, 1 Feb. 1941, fd 1,

box 363, JRCP; *Conf,* Oct. 1941, 16-17. Clarkana has John T. Flynn, *The Truth about Pearl Harbor* (New York: by the author, 1944). This interpretation has been voiced by liberals, conservatives, and apolitical naval officers and military historians. Aside from books in the late 1940s and 1950s by Harry Elmer Barnes, Charles A. Beard, William Henry Chamberlain, John T. Flynn, Admiral Husband E. Kimmel, Frederic R. Sanborn, Charles Callan Tansill, and Admiral Robert A. Theobald, see John Toland, *Infamy: Pearl Harbor and Its Aftermath* (Garden City, NY: Doubleday, 1982); James Rusbridger and Eric Nave, *Betrayal at Pearl Harbor: How Churchill Lured Roosevelt into World War II* (New York: Summit Books, 1991); Edward Beach, *Scapegoats: A Defense of Kimmel and Short at Pearl Harbor* (Annapolis, MD: Naval Institute Press, 1995); Robert B. Stinnett, *Day of Deceit: The Truth about FDR and Pearl Harbor* (New York: Free Press/Simon and Schuster, 2000); and the televised documentary, "Sacrifice at Pearl Harbor," BBC/History Channel, 1997.

[125] Cole, *Charles A. Lindbergh,* 207-08.

[126] Heber J. Grant journal sheets, 12 Dec. 1941.

[127] After the Henry L. Stimson diary became available at the Library of Congress, where I researched it, most studies have quoted this last sentence of this entry for 25 November 1941 but have only paraphrased Roosevelt's first observation. A fuller set of quotes appeared in Robert Smith Thompson, *A Time for War: Franklin Delano Roosevelt and the Path to Pearl Harbor* (New York: Prentice Hall Press, 1991), 381. The crucial sentence of this quote seems to be a continuation of Roosevelt's statements, but it could also have been Stimson's own assessments as Secretary of War.

For two examples of pro-Roosevelt views, see Gordon W. Prange, *At Dawn We Slept: The Untold Story of Pearl Harbor* (New York: McGraw-Hill, 1981), 371-72 ("No one who has examined the great mass of historical evidence on Pearl Harbor can doubt that the United States wanted to maintain peace with Japan for as long as possible. ... Certainly the Japanese needed no encouragement from Washington to open hostilities."); Henry C. Clausen (author of volume 35 of the federal hearings) and Bruce Lee, *Pearl Harbor: Final Judgement* (New York: Crown Publishers, 1992), 2 ("One merely has to employ common sense and remember that Roosevelt was a Navy man through and through. He loved his ships; he loved the men who sailed them. Never, never would he allow his battleships to be sunk and his sailors drowned.").

Prange and other FDR defenders have ignored the very specific meaning of "*maneuver* them into the position of firing the first shot" (emphasis added). Stimson was not simply describing a wait-and-see approach but was describing Roosevelt's open-the-way approach for a Japanese attack. They probably thought the U.S. installations in the Philippines, Guam, and Wake Island would be the first-strike targets, which would not allow "too much danger to ourselves." If so, they miscalculated.

[128] Harold B. Lee diary, 27 Oct. 1942.

[129] JRC unused editorial (intended as a First Presidency message), box 208, JRCP.

[130] JRC office diary, 20 May, 14 June 1940.

[131] Prange, *At Dawn We Slept,* 539 (for 2,403 dead or missing at Pearl Harbor); also Ronald H. Spector, *Eagle against the Sun: The American War with Japan* (New York: Free Press/Macmillan, 1985), 93-109, for bombing and strafing raids against U.S. forces in Guam, Wake Island, and the Philippines in early December 1941.

[132] *M* 6:139-41.

[133] *M* 6:158-60.

[134] Heber J. Grant, JRC, and David O. McKay to U.S. senators Elbert D. Thomas and Abe Murdock and to U.S. Congressmen J. W. Robinson and Walter K. Granger, 17 Dec. 1941, in unnumbered fd, "Personal File—1941: Corr, LDS," box 30, Thomas papers, Utah State Historical Society, Salt Lake City.

[135] Heber J. Grant journal sheets, 6 Apr. 1942; cf. ch. 3, note 241.

[136] JRC to U.S. Representative Henry C. Dworshak, 6 Oct. 1941, fd 6, box 364, JRCP.

[137] JRC to William Cullen Dennis, 8 July 1942, fd 1, box 365, both in JRCP; see also *Who Was Who in America, Volume IV: 1961-1968* (Chicago: A.N. Marquis, 1968), 244.

[138] *M* 6:183; *Conf,* Oct. 1942, 16; see also *EA* 29:396 for "Allies," *EA* 29:398 for "Allied land forces."

[139] *The New Encyclopaedia Britannica,* 15th ed., 30 vols. (Chicago: Encyclopaedia Britannica, 1998), 4:404-05. Not until 24 December 1943 was Eisenhower appointed "Supreme Commander" of all Allied Forces in Europe.

[140] Heber J. Grant journal sheets, 3 Oct. 1942; cf. ch. 3, note 241.

[141] *Conf,* Oct. 1942, 68; also *ER* 2:821-22; *OC,* 439-45.

[142] Jonathan W. Snow to JRC, undated, in October 1942 conference binder, box 156, JRCP.; *ER* 2:821-22; *OC,* 439-45.

[143] "Mormon Mixup," *Time* 40 (19 Oct. 1942): 42.

[144] See *ER* 2: 11; *OC,* 814-18.

[145] JRC to Herbert Hoover, 15 Jan. and 22 Apr. 1943, box 344, JRCP; also JRC fd of correspondence, Post-Presidential Individual File, Hoover Presidential Library, West Branch, Iowa. When I did the original research for this biography, carbon copies of Clark's letters to Hoover were in JRCP but not available to the general public. I referenced controversial quotes to the originals in the Hoover Presidential Library, a public archives, after verifying their existence there.

[146] JRC to Stephen Abbot, 30 June 1943, fd 1, box 367, JRCP.

[147] *Conf,* Oct. 1943, 28.

[148] See quote for note 107; Clarkana has *May Day Manifesto: Open the Second Front Now! Smash Hitler and Crush the Axis!* (New York: Communist Party of the United States of America, 1943); also *An Appeal of the German Communists: Destroy Hitler! Free Germany!* (New York: Workers' Library Publishers, 1942).

[149] *SI,* 432.

[150] See quote for note 142.

[151] *The New York Sun,* 1 Apr. 1944, in JRC scrapbook.

[152] "Concentration Camp Prisoners Shot Down," *DN,* 19 Nov. 1938, 2, re-

garding mass execution of Jews at Buchenwald, reference to Sachsenhausen and Dachau; "Death for 700,000 Jews Threatened: Semites Must Get Out or Die, Nazis Declare," *DN*, 23 Nov. 1938, [2]; "700,000 Polish Jews Allowed to Die of Disease, Hunger: Nazis Accused of Hastening End for Race; Poison Gas Used," *DN*, 26 June 1942, 2; "Threat to Palestine," editorial, *DN*, 3 July 1942, 4 ("It has been a consistent policy of the Nazis to obliterate the Jews wherever they have gone"); "Poles Charge Schmeling Headed Worst German Camp," *DN*, 9 July 1942, 1, referring to Oswiechim (*Auschwitz* in German); "Death Decree for All Jews Charged to Hitler: Dr. Wise Claims to Have Proof of Order," *DN*, 25 Nov. 1942, 3; "All Jews in Five Towns Are Slain," *DN*, 20 Mar. 1943, 1; "Death of All Jews in Europe This Year Expected: Hitler Continues Campaign of Extinction, Says London Investigator," *DN*, 19 Apr. 1943, 2; "Jews Driven to Gulch, Stripped, Killed by Nazis," *DN*, 17 Nov. 1943, 1. Concerning the November 1942 report in the *DN* that "approximately half of the estimated 4,000,000 Jews in Nazi-occupied Europe already had been killed," Tobler, "The Jews, the Mormons, and the Holocaust," 89n91, observed: "Post-war research has confirmed the accuracy of these figures."

[153] Richard E. Darilek, *A Loyal Opposition in Time of War: The Republican Party and the Politics of Foreign Policy from Pearl Harbor to Yalta* (Westport, CT: Greenwood Press, 1976); Wolfe, *Herbert Hoover*, 402-17.

[154] JRC to Philip Marshall Brown, president of the American Peace Society, 1 Nov. 1944, fd 1, box 369, JRCP; also "American Forces Capture Aachen: Nazis Battle to Last Man," *DN*, 20 Oct. 1944, [1]; *OC*, 1334.

[155] Welfare Committee minutes, 28 Nov. 1941, CR 255/18, LDSA.

[156] JRC to Henry L. Stimson, 11 Feb. 1942, fd 5, box 366, JRCP.

[157] JRC office diary, 17 Feb. 1943, fully quoted in *E*, 830; also JRC to O. S. McBride, 27 May 1941, fd 2, box 363, JRCP; JRC office diary, 10 Mar. 1943.

[158] Diary of Frank Evans, financial secretary to First Presidency, 12 Mar., 30 July, 4 Aug. 1942, LDSA.

[159] JRC office diary, 7 Jan. 1944.

[160] Frank Evans diary, 21 Mar. 1942 (quote), 30 July, 4 Aug. 1942.

[161] "MIA Bond Sale Drive Totals $3,123,000," *CN*, 7 Aug. 1943, [1].

[162] JRC office diary, 11 Apr. 1944.

[163] JRC office diary, 10 Aug. 1944, follow-up on 11 Aug., 8 Sept.

[164] JRC office diary, 18 Sept. 1944, similar decision 29 Nov.

[165] JRC to Arthur Deering Call, 26 June 1939, fd 1, box 361, JRCP; also *World Affairs*, 1939-61, inside front/back cover for establishment of American Peace Society in 1828.

[166] *L*, 180.

[167] See previous note 1.

[168] JRC to William Cullen Dennis, 19 June 1942, fd 1, box 365, JRCP.

[169] JRC to Edward W. Evans, 14 June 1943, and JRC to Joshua L. Baily Jr., 14 June 1943, both in fd for October 1942 conference.

[170] JRC to Philip Marshall Brown, president of American Peace Society, 1

Nov. 1944, fd 1, box 369, JRCP; *World Affairs*, 1945-61, inside front/back cover for JRC as a national director of American Peace Society.

[171] JRC, *Some Factors of a Now-Planned Post-War Governmental and Economic Pattern* (Salt Lake City: Deseret News Press, 1943); published in full in *Commercial and Financial Chronicle*, 25 Nov. 1943; *SA*, 521-39.

[172] C. N. Lund, *Reply to Clark's Speech* (Salt Lake City: Progressive Opinion, [1943]), broadside, fd 4, box 50, David O. McKay papers, LDSA, also in JWML and LDSL. Once located in Clarkana, Lund's publication does not currently appear in BYU's computerized catalog.

[173] The executive vice president of the Hawaiian Sugar Planters' Association said, "It is the best, clearest, most direct and most impressive analysis of what the managers of the New Deal have done to our country that I have seen" (Briant H. Wells to JRC, 22 May 1944). Ten years later, the chairman of the board of Metropolitan Life repeated the main points of JRC's 1943 talk in his own address to a convention and recommended JRC's original talk (Leroy A. Lincoln to JRC, 8 Oct. 1953). The president of Occidental Life wrote, "I remember vividly your stirring address of ten years ago ... You were indeed a prophet" (Laurence F. Lee to JRC, 3 Nov. 1953); all in box 227, JRCP.

[174] JRC office diary, 1 July 1940.

[175] John Roy Carlson, *pseud*. [Arthur Derounian], *Under Cover: My Four Years in the Nazi Underworld of America* (New York: E. P. Dutton, 1943), 367, 373-85; cf. listed names with Ancestral File, Patriarchal Blessing Index, Family Group Sheets, and LDS church census reports, FHL. This book had seventeen printings in its first four months. Clarkana has the Carlson book, plus Jeremiah Stokes, *Guilty: Condemned Derounian Alias John Roy Carlson!: "Under Cover" Author Found Guilty of Defamatory Libel and Fined Ten Thousand Dollars by a Federal Court Jury* (Salt Lake City: Federated Libraries, 1946); also the JWML's copy of Marilyn R. Allen's *Judaic-Communism versus Christian-Americanism ... My Answer to John Roy Carlson* (Salt Lake City: By the Author, 1946).

[176] "Counter Intelligence Weekly Report, for Week Ending 27 November 1942," 6, District Intelligence Office, Ninth Naval District, Naval Investigative Service, Suitland, Maryland; report of Salt Lake City's FBI office on Internal Security and Custodial Detention Case 100-1487, dated 2 Jan. 1943, in Records Management Division, Federal Bureau of Investigation, Washington, D.C., obtained through a Freedom of Information Act request; also follow-up telephone conversation of D. Michael Quinn with FBI headquarters, 4 Dec. 1980.

[177] Peach, "Clearfield," 99-100, for its Naval Supply Depot. Similar to the FBI's central storage of reports by its field offices, U.S. Army Intelligence stored its surveillance reports in a central location. As part of my own training as a Military Intelligence agent, in the fall of 1968 I toured a large warehouse which stored the army's investigative files on tens of thousands of American civilians. My group of agents-in-training was told that these files predated World War II. Before 1980 I read a newspaper report that the army had allegedly destroyed these massive investigative files on private citizens.

[178] *C*, 263.

[179] JRC office diary, 19 Dec. 1941.

[180] JRC to Frank R. Clark, 23 Mar. 1942 (for first quote), and JRC to S. Wayne Clark, 13 Nov. 1942 (second set of quotes), both in fd 1, box 365, JRCP.

[181] Heber J. Grant journal sheets, 30 Jan. 1943. Clarkana has *The Facts about Conscientious Objectors in the United States (under the Selective Service Act of May 18, 1917)* (New York: National Civil Liberties Bureau, 1918).

[182] *M* 6:157-59. During my pre-1983 research in JRCP, I did not think to examine the preliminary drafts for references to conscientious objection. In view of Clark's position with the American Peace Society since 1939 and his continued hostility toward American involvement in World War II even after Pearl Harbor, my guess is that Reuben's early draft of the 1942 statement would have included some mention of conscientious objection as an alternative to entering the armed forces.

[183] JRC office diary, 6 Apr. 1943.

[184] JRC to J— L— B——, 9 Nov. 1943, fd 1, box 367, JRCP.

[185] JRC office diary, 1 Apr., 3 Apr., 2 May 1944, and reference to March 1942 decision.

[186] JRC office diary, 8 May 1944; also Mulford Q. Sibley and Philip E. Jacob, *Conscription of Conscience: The American State and the Conscientious Objector, 1940-1947* (Ithaca, NY: Cornell University Press, 1952); Gordon C. Zahn, *Another Part of the War: The Camp Simon Story* (Amherst: University of Massachusetts Press, 1979).

[187] JRC office diary, 2 Oct. 1945.

[188] George Albert Smith and JRC letter, 25 June 1946, in Conscientious Objector file, fd 2, box 3, CR 1/33, LDSA.

[189] Clarkana has *Report of Treatment of Conscientious Objectors at the Camp Funston Guard House* (Brooklyn, NY: Relatives and Friends of Conscientious Objectors, 1918).

[190] JRC "Postwar Planning in the Home," *Improvement Era* 47 (Nov. 1944): 656; also *Conf.* Apr. 1945, 54; JRC, "Postwar Planning," *Improvement Era* 48 (May 1945): 236-37, a restatement of his remarks to the Utah Wool Growers convention, reprinted in *SA*, 556-57.

[191] JRC to Philip Marshall Brown, 1 Nov. 1944.

[192] "Utah Loses More Than Her Share in War Deaths, U.S. Report Shows," *DN*, 27 June 1946, 1; *New Encyclopaedia Britannica*, 29:1022 (sixty million war-related deaths); *The World Almanac and Book of Facts: 2000* (Mahwah, NJ: World Almanac Books, 1999), 217 (total for U.S. armed forces).

[193] Richard O. Cowan, *The Church in the Twentieth Century* (Salt Lake City: Bookcraft, 1985), 192.

[194] Scharffs, *Mormonism in Germany*, 116, provided war deaths for LDS Germans, but I have not found similar reports for the significant pre-1945 Mormon populations in Canada, Britain, Denmark, Holland, Australia, or New Zealand.

[195] *F,* 72; cf. Whitney R. Harris, *Tyranny on Trial: The Evidence of Nuremberg* (Dallas, TX: Southern Methodist University Press, 1954); William J. Bosh, *Judgment on Nuremburg: American Attitudes toward the Major War-Crimes Trials* (Chapel

Hill: University of North Carolina Press, 1970); Bradley F. Smith, *Reaching Judgment at Nuremburg* (New York: Basic Books, 1977).

[196] JRC to Ezra Taft Benson, 20 Aug. 1946, fd 2, box 373, JRCP.

[197] Clarkana has a set of the Chief Counsel for the Prosecution of Axis Criminality, *Nazi Conspiracy and Aggression,* 11 vols. (Washington, D.C.: Government Printing Office, 1946-48), inscribed: "To Pres. J. Reuben Clark with affectionate regards, Ernest L. Wilkinson, 4/14/47"); also the author's presentation copy to JRC of Shinsh Hanayama, *The Way of Deliverance: Three Years with the Condemned Japanese War Criminals,* trans. Hideo Suzuki, et al. (London: Gollancz, 1955).

[198] JRC to Greene H. Hackworth (legal adviser to the U.S. State Department), 24 Apr. 1939, marked "Personal," box 113, CR 1/44, quoted more fully in *E*, 827.

[199] *ER* 1:45 (*Aryan*); also *Webster's New World Dictionary of the American Language,* 79: "*Aryan* has no validity as an ethnological term, although it has been so used, notoriously and variously by the Nazis, to mean 'a Caucasian of non-Jewish descent,' 'a Nordic,' etc."

Clarkana has Margaret Schlauch, *Who Are the Aryans?* (New York: Anti-Fascist Literature Committee, [1935 or 1940]); Gino Bardi, *Are We Aryans?* (New York: Workers' Library Publishers, 1939). HBLL catalogers put the publication date for Schlauch as "194?". WorldCat shows 1935 and 1940 editions of the same page length, but HBLL lists dimensions midway between the two in WorldCat.

[200] JRC draft of editorial, 8 Aug. 1945, box 232, JRCP; published in *SI*, 262-63.

[201] "Pres. Clark Represents Church at Salt Lake Mass Peace Meet," *CN*, 8 Sept. 1945, 12, emphasis added.

[202] "Welfare Meet Considers Farm Matters," *DN*, 4 Oct. 1952, A-1.

[203] JRC office diary, 27 Aug. 1958 ("I had been urging this for over twelve years, next as a result of a rather recent meeting of the First Presidency it had been agreed that we should try to go forward ... and had secured options on the cliff situation down by the mouth of Little Cottonwood.").

[204] "Church Dedicates Canyon Record Vault," *DN*, 23 June 1966, A-1, A-6, crediting JRC with the idea; *In a Granite Mountain* (Salt Lake City: Genealogical Society of The Church of Jesus Christ of Latter-day Saints, [1968]); "What Is the Granite Mountain Records Vault?" *Improvement Era* 69 (Aug. 1966): 699-701 also gave JRC credit and mentioned the vault's resistance to atomic and hydrogen bombs while denying this was its specific purpose.

[205] JRC, "Conference Address," *Instructor* 81 (June 1946): 277.

[206] JRC to Ben L. Rich, 6 Aug. 1946, fd 6, box 374, JRCP.

[207] JRC office diary, 2 Apr. 1947. Because of McKay's intensely pro-war sentiment since 1939, my guess is that Reuben's entry referred to him.

[208] *Conf,* Oct. 1946, 88-89; *C*, 589; also Richard F. Haglund Jr. and David J. Whittaker, "Intellectual History," in *EM* 2:689 ("President J. Reuben Clark, Jr. warned that the alliance forged in wartime between science and government had created a military-industrial complex."). The latter phrase was coined by U.S.

president Dwight D. Eisenhower. See *The Penguin Dictionary of Twentieth-Century Quotations* (London: Viking, 1993), 116.

For the specific incidents referred to, see David Irving, *The Destruction of Dresden* (London: William Kimber, 1963); "The Bombing of Dresden," in Garold N. Davis and Norma S. Davis, comps. and trans., *Behind the Iron Curtain: Recollections of Latter-day Saints in East Germany, 1945-1989* (Provo, UT: BYU Studies, 1996), 1-45; for lower British estimates of deaths, see *OC*, 311 (50,000 deaths at Dresden); *New Encyclopaedia Britannica,* 4:221 ("killing between 35,000 and 135,000 people, but achieved little militarily"); also Robert C. Batchelder, *The Irreversible Decision, 1939-1950* (Boston: Houghton Mifflin, 1962); Barton J. Bernstein, ed., *The Atomic Bomb: The Critical Issues* (Boston: Little Brown, 1976); Gordon Thomas and Max Morgan-Wills, *Ruin from the Air: The Atomic Mission to Hiroshima* (London: Hamilton, 1977).

[209] JRC office diary, 3 Aug. 1950. This is the emphasis of Gar Alperovitz, *The Decision to Use the Atomic Bomb and the Architecture of an American Myth* (New York: Alfred A. Knopf, 1995), quoting such authorities as General Dwight D. Eisenhower about the military non-necessity of dropping an atomic bomb on the already defeated Japanese. For a contrary view, see Richard B. Frank, *Downfall: The End of the Imperial Japanese Empire* (New York: Random House, 1999).

[210] JRC draft of unused editorial, 22 Sept. 1950, box 208, JRCP. Clarkana has Henry DeWolf Smyth, *Atomic Energy for Military Purposes: The Official Report on the Development of the Atomic Bomb under the Auspices of the United States Government* (Princeton, NJ: Princeton University Press, 1947); Henry J. Taylor, *Oak Ridge: The Amazing Firsthand, On-the-Scene Story of How Free Enterprise Met the Challenge of the Atom Bomb* (Detroit, MI: General Motors, 1948).

[211] JRC to agricultural meeting of Welfare Program, 5 Apr. 1954, transcript, 5, box 151, JRCP.

[212] Mark E. Petersen to JRC, 2 Feb. 1945, fd 7, box 371, JRCP.

[213] JRC manuscript draft, 5 Feb. 1945, of proposed statement against peacetime conscription, fd 7, box 371, JRCP.

[214] Computer word-search on *imperialism* and *imperialistic* in *Conf,* 1897-1970; also Clark's statement that World War II was "unrighteous" because it was "a war for empire." See quotes for notes 72-73.

[215] JRC office diary, 4 Feb. 1945; Mark E. Petersen to JRC, 6 Feb. 1945, fd 7, box 371, JRCP.

[216] JRC to Arthur Deering Call, 9 Dec. 1914; JRC to Theodore Marburg, 18 Dec. 1914.

[217] Harold B. Lee diary, 7 June 1945.

[218] JRC to Tucker P. Smith, American Friends Service Committee, 15 June 1945, fd 7, box 371, JRCP.

[219] George Albert Smith, JRC, and David O. McKay to U.S. Senator Elbert D. Thomas, 14 Dec. 1945, Thomas papers; "Church Opposes Military Bill: Letter Sent Utah Salons December 14," *DN,* 3 Jan. 1946, 1, 5.

[220] *M* 6:239-42; cf. JRC manuscript draft, 5 Feb. 1945, of proposed statement against peacetime conscription; also J. D. Williams, "The Separation of Church

and State in Mormon Theory and Practice," *Dial* 1 (Summer 1966): 47, reprinted in *Journal of Church and State* 9 (Spring 1976); Q. Michael Croft, "Influence of the L.D.S. Church on Utah Politics, 1945-1985," Ph.D. diss., University of Utah, 1985, 88. Clarkana has *Resolutions against Universal Military Training, 1945-1947* (Washington, D.C.: Friends Committee on National Legislation, [1947]).

221 JRC office diary, 16 Jan. 1947.

222 JRC office diary, 22 Sept. 1947; also *C*, 589; ch. 3, note 241.

223 Clark, *Let Us Have Peace*, 15-16; *F,* 71; also "U.S. Heads for War, Pres. Clark Warns: Leader Urges America [to] Mind Own Business," *DN,* 14 Nov. 1947, 1, 3; *C,* 589; *SI,* 275.

224 Harold B. Lee diary, 2 Jan. 1951; also JRC office diary, 6 May 1950, for his similar statement "to the group at Adam Bennion's." Adam S. Bennion, a McKay man, became a member of the Quorum of Twelve in 1953.

225 JRC to U.S. Senator Arthur H. Vandenberg, 31 Dec. 1947, fd 22, box 376, JRCP.

226 JRC office diary, 2 Mar. 1948.

227 *Conf,* Apr. 1948, 174-75.

228 Rowena J. Miller to David I. Folkman, 16 Nov. 1959, fd 11, box 405, JRCP.

229 Clarkana has six publications that oppose atomic weapons, all published by leftist presses, including William Wainwright, *H Bomb Tests, End Them Now* (London: Communist Party of Great Britain, 1957); *To Live or to Die: The H-Bomb versus Mankind: Public Statements by Albert Schweitzer ... with a Foreword by W. E. B. Dubois* (New York: New Century Publishers, 1957); and John Gollan, *Labour and the Bomb* (London: Communist Party of Great Britain, 1960).

230 Peggy Petersen Barton, *Mark E. Petersen: A Biography* (Salt Lake City: Deseret Book, 1985), 94; *W,* 149.

231 Francis M. Gibbons, *Joseph Fielding Smith: Gospel Scholar, Prophet of God* (Salt Lake City: Deseret Book, 1992), 401.

232 Without mentioning JRC, Justus D. Doenecke provided the national setting in *Not to the Swift: The Old Isolationists in the Cold War Era* (Lewisburg, PA: Bucknell University Press, 1979).

233 James W. Gerard telegram to JRC, 11 Apr. 1947, JRC telegram to Gerard, 15 Apr. 1947, and JRC to U.S. Senator Henry C. Dworshak, 30 Apr. 1947, all in fd 1, box 376, JRCP. Clarkana has *"Ikaria Will Be the Largest Cemetery of Those Who Have Died for Their Political Ideals"* (Philadelphia: American Council for a Democratic Greece, Philadelphia Chapter, 1947); *American Intervention in Greece, 1947-1948* (New York: American Council for a Democratic Greece, 1948); *The Youth of Greece Is Fighting for Freedom, Independence, and Democracy: The Heroic Struggle of EON* (New York: American Youth for the Youth of Greece, 1948); Olive Sutton, *Murder Inc. in Greece* (New York: New Century Publishers, 1948).

234 James W. Gerard telegrams to JRC, 14, 29 Oct. 1947, JRC telegrams to Gerard, 14, 29 Oct. 1947, all in fd 5, box 376, JRCP. Clarkana has twenty-two books on Communism in China, including eight by Mao Tse-tung (e.g., *China's New Democracy* [New York: Workers' Library Publishers, 1944]), several others

from Communist presses (e.g., Arthur Clegg, *No War with China* [London: Communist Party of Great Britain, 1951]), and some with an anti-Communist slant (e.g., Committee on Un-American Activities, *Communist Persecution of Churches in Red China and Northern Korea* ... [Washington, D.C.: Government Printing Office, 1959]).

235 *SI,* 473.

236 JRC to James W. Gerard, 14 Apr. 1949, fd 9, box 379, JRCP; "Gerard Calls Pact Bar to Early War, *NYT,* 7 May 1949, 4; also Robert Endicott Osgood, *NATO: The Entangling Alliance* (Chicago: University of Chicago Press, 1962). As a result of Gerard's testimony, JRC wrote to him, 30 Sept. 1949: "Having in mind the unauthorized use you made of my opinion about the Atlantic Treaty ... I shall refrain from expressing my views at this time on the questions asked in your telegram" (fd 9, box 379). Gerard was formerly a U.S. ambassador to Germany. See *Who Was Who in America, Vol. 3* (Chicago: A.N. Marquis, 1960), 319.

237 "Atlantic Treaty Wrong, S.L. Trust Meet Told," *The Salt Lake Telegram,* 17 Aug. 1949, 1; *F,* 84-94; *SA,* 177-84. Clarkana has Abraham Chapman, *The North Atlantic Pact: For Peace or War?* (New York: New Century Publishers, [1949]); Jessica Smith, *Jungle Law or Human Reason? The North Atlantic Pact and What It Means to You* (New York: SRT Publications, 1949).

238 Carl Berger, *The Korean Knot: A Military Political History,* rev. ed. (Philadelphia: University of Pennsylvania Press, 1964); Glenn D. Paige, *The Korean Decision (June 24-30, 1950)* (New York: Free Press, 1969); J. Lawton Collins, *War in Peacetime: The History and Lessons of Korea* (Boston: Houghton Mifflin, 1969).

239 *The World Almanac and Book of Facts,* 217 (total deaths in U.S. armed forces).

240 JRC office diary, 27 June 1950.

241 JRC office diary, 13 Dec. 1950.

242 JRC office diary, 8 Sept. 1950.

243 Clarkana has Bernard Freed, *Is This the Last War? A Timely Discussion and Exposé of the Danger That Threatens to Start World War III* (San Francisco: For Enduring Peace, [1944?]); Tabitha Petran, *Open Secret: Reports on the Betrayal of Roosevelt's Peace Policy and American Preparations for World War III* (Washington, D.C.: National Committee to Win the Peace, 1946); *Shadow of the Swastika: German Rearmament and Renazification, the Road to World War III* (Los Angeles: West Side Committee against Renazification of Germany, 1950).

244 JRC, *Our Dwindling Sovereignty* (Salt Lake City: Deseret News Press, 1952), 32-33, reprinted in *F,* 128-29. Clarkana has *Statements by Two American Air Force Officers, Kenneth Lloyd Enoch and John Quinn, Admitting Their Participation in Germ Warfare in Korea, and Other Documents* (Peking: n.p., 1952); Robert Mann, *From Korean Truce to World Peace* (New York: New York State Communist Party, [1953?]).

245 *C,* 273-308, 412-13, 588; *SI,* 167-91, 209-12.

246 JRC office diary, 4 Oct. 1948, 8 Sept. 1950, 17 Oct. 1955; also James B. Allen, "J. Reuben Clark, Jr., on American Sovereignty and International Organi-

zation," and Stan A. Taylor, "J. Reuben Clark, Jr., and the United Nations," *BYU Studies* 13 (Spring 1973): 347-72, 415-25.

[247] JRC memorandum on the United Nations San Francisco Charter, ca. June-July 1945, box 231, JRCP. For studies of the United Nations, see William A. Scott and Stephen B. Withey, *United States and United Nations: The Public View, 1945-1955* (New York: Manhattan, 1958); Julius Stone, *Aggression and World Order: A Critique of United Nations Theories of Aggression* (Berkeley: University of California Press, 1958); Ernest A. Gross, *The United Nations: Structure for Peace* (New York: Harper, 1962); James J. Wadsworth, *The Glass House: The United Nations in Action* (New York: Praeger, 1966); *DA*, 344.

[248] For example, JRC to Staff Sergeant James S. Arringona, 3 Dec. 1945, fd 1, box 371, JRCP.

[249] JRC, *Our Dwindling Sovereignty*, 23-24, 26-32, reprinted in *F,* 118-19, 122-28.

[250] JRC office diary, 15 Oct. 1955.

[251] *SI*, 437-70.

[252] Folders 1-3, 7, box 167, George A. Smith Family papers, JWML.

[253] David O. McKay office diary, 23 Oct. 1955, LDSA.

[254] JRC office diary, 17 Oct. 1955.

[255] See ch. 5 for Clark men and McKay men.

[256] Stephen L Richards office diary, 29 Oct. 1951, LDSA; cf. Albert R. Bowen, "The Constitution and the United Nations Charter," *Relief Society Magazine* 38 (Aug.-Nov. 1951): 507-11, 580-85, 654-57, 727-29.

[257] See ch. 5 for Marianne Clark Sharp's refusal in April 1951 "to ascribe the secondary action to the Lord" when President McKay demoted her father to second counselor.

[258] JRC to Mrs. A. Helen Morgan, 16 June 1953, fd 2, box 389, JRCP.

[259] See published studies in note 247.

[260] JRC office diary, 22 Oct. 1951, for this criticism that was specifically directed at LDS political scientist G. Homer Durham.

[261] Clarkana has Myron C. Fagan, *U.N. Is U.S. Cancer* (Hollywood, CA: Cinema Educational Guild, 1952); also Marilyn R. Allen, *Admiral Nimitz and the United Nations* (Salt Lake City: By the author, 1950); Russell J. Clinchy, *Human Rights and the United Nations* (Irvington-on-Hudson, NY: Foundation for Economic Education, 1952); Usher L. Burdick, *The Great Conspiracy to Destroy the United States* (Washington, D.C.: Government Printing Office, 1954).

[262] See previous discussion here and in ch. 5.

[263] David O. McKay office diary, 19 Sept. 1961.

[264] JRC, "Two Years in the Service Can Be Profitable," *Improvement Era* 55 (Aug. 1952): 568.

[265] Harold B. Lee diary, 11 July 1952.

[266] Stephen L Richards office diary, 24 Apr. 1953.

[267] Ray C. Hillam and David M. Andrews, "Mormons and Foreign Policy," *BYU Studies* 25 (Winter 1985): 63; also notes 26 and 276.

[268] Clark, *Let Us Have Peace,* 15; also *F,* 70; Hillam and Andrews, "Mormons and Foreign Policy," 68.

[269] JRC to Alfred M. Landon, 26 July 1955, fd 15, box 393, JRCP.

[270] JRC to William Hard, 3 Dec. 1951, fd 12, box 383, JRCP, for quote.

[271] Verbatim transcription of JRC conversation with Ezra Taft Benson, 21 Mar. 1955, fd 5, box 392, JRCP.

[272] JRC to Alfred M. Landon, 26 July 1955; JRC to Landon, 15 Aug. 1956, fd 16, box 396, JRCP.

[273] *Conf,* Oct. 1959, 46.

[274] Clarkana has *Tactical and Organizational Questions of the Communist Parties of India and Indo-China* ([Sydney, Australia:] Pan-Pacific Worker, 1933); also Sanzo Nosaka, *The War in the Far East and the Tasks of the Communists ...* (New York: Workers' Library Publishers, 1932); Wang Ming, pseud. [Ch'en Shao-yu], *The Revolutionary Movement in the Colonial Countries* (New York: Workers' Library Publishers, 1935); *Bolshevik Leninist Trotskyist Programme Stands for Violent Expulsion of British Imperialism* ([Bombay]: Fourth International, Indian Section, [1941]).

[275] JRC to U.S. Senator Henry C. Dworshak, 17 May 1954, fd 15, box 390, JRCP; also *C,* 589; and *E,* 840.

[276] Rees, *Age of Containment;* William J. Duiker, *U.S. Containment Policy and the Conflict in Indochina* (Stanford, CA: Stanford University Press, 1994).

[277] Dwight D. Eisenhower, *Mandate for Change, 1953-1956* (Garden City, NY: Doubleday, 1963), 372; *The Pentagon Papers* (New York: Quadrangle Books, 1971), 23, 47.

When the United States in 1967 allowed South Vietnam's anti-Communist dictatorship to hold elections, there were no Marxist, Communist, or Viet Cong candidates. Neither this nor any other election allowed a plebiscite on whether to reunite peacefully with North Vietnam. The Viet Cong denounced the elections as a fraudulent effort to legitimize America's "puppet regime" in Saigon. Moreover, South Vietnam's elected leaders routinely jailed their political opponents. See "National Legitimacy," in Timothy J. Lomperis, *The War Everyone Lost—and Won: America's Intervention in Viet Nam's Twin Struggles* (Baton Rouge: Louisiana State University Press, 1984), 48-87; also Frances FitzGerald, *Fire in the Lake: The Vietnamese and the Americans in Vietnam* (New York: Vintage Books, 1973), 317: "Created, financed, and defended by Americans, the Saigon regime was less a government than an act of the American will."

[278] JRC to Fred Morris Dearing, 18 Aug. 1958, fd 6, box 402, JRCP. This apparent humor masks the seriousness of Clark's convictions. Concerning the possibility of war "between the free world and the communistic world," he wrote less than two years earlier to the president of George Washington University: "Next, as to the international situation,—the news we get out here about matters of that sort, first, is fragmentary; second, we do not get the whole truth as to the matters touched upon; third, we do not know as to the matters touched upon, which is truth and which is fiction; finally, we do not know the importance of the things that are not given to us" (JRC to Cloyd H. Marvin, 1 Dec. 1956, binder of

JRC-Marvin correspondence, box 189, JRCP; original in Marvin papers, Archives, George Washington University, Washington, D.C.)

[279] "Army Lists Victims of Red Attack: Terrorists Raid Viet Nam Base," *SLT,* 10 July 1959, A-1; "Yanks Given Extra Guards in Viet Nam: Protection Increased after Five Die in Red Terrorist Attack," *DN,* 10 July 1959, 1 (including number of "advisors"); also *DA,* 26, for advisors in Vietnam.

[280] JRC to U.S. Senator Henry C. Dworshak, 17 May 1954.

[281] Guenter Lewy, *America in Vietnam* (New York: Oxford University Press, 1978); George C. Herring, *America's Longest War: The United States and Vietnam, 1950-1975* (New York: Wiley, 1979).

[282] Anthony O. Edmonds, *The War in Vietnam* (Westport, CT: Greenwood Press, 1998), 83 ("Between 1.5 and 2 million Vietnamese died ... [and] some three hundred thousand missing Vietnamese have never been found"), 88 (58,209 American deaths and 2,000 MIAs); *The World Almanac and Book of Facts,* 217 (total deaths in U.S. armed forces).

[283] Lewy, *America in Vietnam*; Herring, *America's Longest War*; Edmonds, *War in Vietnam*; Jay R. Jensen, *Six Years in Hell: A Returned POW Views Captivity, Country, and the Nations [sic] Future* (Bountiful, UT: Horizon Publishers, 1974); Douglas Valentine, *The Phoenix Program* (New York: Morrow, 1990); Charles DeBenedetti, *An American Ordeal: The Antiwar Movement of the Vietnam Era* (Syracuse, NY: Syracuse University Press, 1990); Michael Bilton and Kevin Sim, *Four Hours in My Lai* (New York: Viking/Penguin, 1992), 48, 111, 124, 216, 218, 223 (Mormon participants); *E,* 308, 855-62, 864, 868, 881.

[284] Allan Kent Powell, "The Vietnam Conflict and Utah," in *U,* 613; also for Marriner S. Eccles, see Leonard J. Arrington, "Banking and Finance in Utah," in *U,* 31.

[285] Hugh W. Nibley, "Denounce War," *Brigham Young University Daily Universe,* 26 Mar. 1971.

[286] Questionnaires indicated that 9-13 percent of BYU's students expressed opposition to the Vietnam War. See Knud S. Larsen and Gary Schwendiman, "The Vietnam War through the Eyes of a Mormon Subculture," *Dial* 3 (Autumn 1968): 152-62. On a personal note, I volunteered for military service during the Vietnam War, along with a former missionary companion and several other missionary associates. I served nearly three years. One of my friends, Roy Lee Richardson, died during the invasion of Cambodia in 1970. Another former missionary associate, Richard W. Glade, protested against the war and became a permanent exile in Canada. Most of my LDS friends avoided military service through various kinds of deferments. At the time I wrote this source note in the biography's first draft, I felt admiration for both deceased veteran Richardson and for war protestor Glade. I still do.

[287] At the general conference of April 1968, Boyd K. Packer condemned those who were conscientious objectors. In "The Member and the Military," *Improvement Era* 71 (June 1968): 58, he began: "There have emerged in our society groups composed mostly of restless, unchallenged young people. In the name of peace and love and brotherhood, they criticize those who, obedient to the laws of

the land, have answered the call to military duty. ... They declare on moral grounds, as an act of virtue, that they will not serve." While not acknowledging that conscientious objection was also a legal option in the United States, he continued (60): "First, the scriptures are not silent on the subject," followed by quotes from the Book of Mormon in praise of military service.

Significantly, and clearly as an intentional omission, he did not acknowledge the Book of Mormon passages about righteous people who refused to participate in war or refused to serve in a specific war due to scruples about its conduct (Al 24:6, Morm 3:11, 16). The latter position fits those who opposed the Vietnam War as an "immoral" intervention in a civil conflict but who would support a war they considered "moral" or "just." These are the "selective conscientious objectors" described in Rohr, *Prophets without Honor.* For the context of Elder Packer's statement within LDS history and doctrine, see D. Michael Quinn, "Conscientious Objectors or Christian Soldiers? The Latter-day Saint Position on Militarism," *Sunstone* 10 (Mar. 1985): 22.

[288] An example of Mormon anti-Vietnam writings that used JRC quotes is Gordon C. Thomasson, ed., *War, Conscription, Conscience and Mormonism* (Santa Barbara, CA: Mormon Heritage, 1971), esp. 9-12, 29-36, 44-72, 76, 84-85. For other examples, see Knud S. Larsen, "A Voice against the War," *Dial* 2 (Autumn 1967): 163-66; Eugene England, "The Tragedy of Vietnam and the Responsibility of Mormons," *Dial* 2 (Winter 1967): 71-91; "Letters to the Editor," *Dial* 3 (Spring 1968): 7-8; "A Conversation with Arthur V. Watkins," (former U.S. senator from Utah), *Dial* 3 (Winter 1968): 118-20; Hugh W. Nibley, "Denounce War," *Daily Universe*, 26 Mar. 1971; and Jay Christensen, et al., *An Important Message to the Men of BYU* (Provo, UT: n.p., [1971]). The latter included conscientious objector Andrew E. Kimball Jr., grandson of then-apostle Spencer W. Kimball. As a military veteran of the Vietnam era, I wrote this source note in the biography's first draft and felt admiration for the views of President Clark, Eugene England, Andrew Kimball, Knud Larsen, Hugh Nibley, and Gordon Thomasson against participation in the Vietnam War. My feelings have not changed.

[289] JRC to Everett De La Mare, 6 Mar. 1956, fd 1, box 395, JRCP.

NOTES TO CHAPTER 10

[1] The Bible, Rev 7:9. I acknowledge that questions have been raised in the biological and social sciences about the concept of race. During the time periods under consideration, this concept had not yet been challenged. In fact, it formed the basis for political life, for domestic social policies, for international diplomacy, and for the termination of human lives.

For general information on the topic, see John S. Halber, *Outcasts from Evolution: Scientific Attitudes of Racial Inferiority, 1859-1900* (Urbana: University of Illinois Press, 1971); Christine Bolt, *Victorian Attitudes to Race* (London: Routledge and Kegan Paul, 1971). On the related issue of imperialism, see Richard W. Van Alstyne, *The Rising American Empire* (New York: Oxford University Press, 1960); Walter LaFeber, *The New Empire: An Interpretation of American Expansion, 1860-*

1898 (Ithaca, NY: Cornell University Press, 1963); Richard Faber, *The Vision and the Need: Late Victorian Imperialist Aims* (London: Faber, 1966); Agnes Murphy, *The Ideology of French Imperialism, 1871-1881* (New York: H. Fertig, 1968); Rubin F. Weston, *Racism in U.S. Imperialism: The Influence of Racial Assumptions on American Foreign Policy, 1893-1946* (Columbia: University of South Carolina Press, 1972); C. C. Eldridge, *England's Mission: The Imperial Idea in the Age of Gladstone and Disraeli* (Chapel Hill: University of North Carolina Press, 1973).

[2] Halber, *Outcasts from Evolution;* Bolt, *Victorian Attitudes to Race;* Peter Roberts, *The New Immigration: A Study of the Industrial and Social Life of Southeastern Europeans in America* (New York: Macmillan, 1912); John Higham, *Strangers in the Land: Patterns of American Nativism, 1860-1925* (New Brunswick, NJ: Rutgers University Press, 1955); Thomas J. Curran, *Xenophobia and Immigration, 1820-1930* (Boston: Twayne, 1975).

[3] JRC to Herbert Hoover, 14 May 1942, 7, Post-Presidential Individual File, Hoover Presidential Library, West Branch, Iowa; carbon copies in JRCP.

[4] See note 2; *Webster's New World Dictionary of the American Language,* 2d college ed. (New York: Simon and Schuster, 1986) for *nativism* and *xenophobia.*

[5] "The State University: The Twenty-ninth Annual Commencement Exercises," *The Salt Lake Herald,* 16 June 1898, 5 (complete text of JRC's valedictory); also "Commencement Oration," in *SA,* 14 (which noted that JRC's quote was from an unidentified source), also 361-62 (same opinion in 1922, JRC's own words). The quoted statement and audience reaction are in the Joshua R. Clark diary, 15 June 1898, JRCP.

[6] *C,* 631n2; also *Webster's New World Dictionary of the American Language* for *egalitarianism* and *Saxon.*

For the specifically racist expression of American eugenics in the early 1900s, see Charles B. Davenport, *Eugenics: The Science of Human Improvement by Better Breeding* (New York: Henry Holt & Co., 1910); Prince A. Morrow, *Eugenics and Racial Poisons* (New York: The Society of Sanitary and Moral Prophylaxis, 1912); also scholarly analysis in Donald K. Pickens, *Eugenics and the Progressives* (Nashville, TN: Vanderbilt University Press, 1968); Steven Selden, *Inheriting Shame: The Story of Eugenics and Racism in America* (New York: Teachers College Press, 1999).

[7] JRC to Herbert Hoover, 14 May 1942, 7.

[8] *C,* 86-233, 451-583; Samuel Flagg Bemis, *The Latin American Policy of the United States: An Historical Interpretation* (New York: Harcourt, Brace, 1943), with specific reference to JRC on 165; also John W. F. Dulles, *Yesterday in Mexico: A Chronicle of the Revolution, 1919-36* (Austin: University of Texas Press, 1961); William W. Johnson, *Heroic Mexico: The Violent Emergence of a Modern Nation* (Garden City, NY: Doubleday, 1968); Peter Calvert, *The Mexican Revolution, 1910-1914: The Diplomacy of Anglo-American Conflict* (Cambridge, Eng.: Cambridge University Press, 1968); Ronald Atkin, *Revolution! Mexico, 1910-20* (New York: John Day, 1970); Robert F. Smith, *The United States and Revolutionary Nationalism in Mexico, 1916-32* (Chicago: University of Chicago Press, 1972).

[9] JRC to bishops' meeting, 5 Apr. 1956, transcript, box 151, JRCP; *C,* 632.

[10] F. Lamond Tullis, *Mormons in Mexico: The Dynamics of Faith and Culture* (Logan: Utah State University Press, 1987), 137-58.

[11] First Presidency letter of 2 Nov. 1936, quoted in JRC memorandum, 26 June 1944, 7, box 228, JRCP; summarized in Tullis, *Mormons in Mexico,* 142; also title page and 2 Ne 4:3-11 in the Book of Mormon.

This letter demonstrates Clark's unwillingness to talk down to rank-and-file Mormons by simplifying the language he typically used with leaders of the U.S. government and LDS church. I am sure that his phrasing was translated as literally as possible by the Spanish-speaking mission president, who undoubtedly felt obligated to maintain the wording of the First Presidency's letter. However, as a Chicano and sometime resident in a Mexican town, I am sure that Reuben's convoluted phrasing would have been nearly incomprehensible to the common Mexicans who comprised the Third Convention.

[12] JRC memorandum, 26 June 1944.

[13] "1,200 Mexican Members Return to Church During Pres. Smith's Visit," *CN,* 15 June 1946, [1]; *K,* 326-27; Tullis, *Mormons in Mexico,* 157-58.

[14] JRC to F. W. Smith, 29 Nov. 1941, fd 3, box 363, JRCP.

[15] JRC to Isaias Juarez (Tlalpan, D.F., Mexico), 27 May 1953, fd 12, box 388, JRCP, with addition of italics. *Mole* is a spicy sauce, usually for chicken. *Mole negro,* made with chocolate, is the most common, but non-chocolate *mole* can be a red, yellow, or green sauce.

[16] JRC office diary, 13 July 1950, JRCP; Jessie L. Embry, *"In His Own Language": Mormon Spanish-Speaking Congregations in the United States* (Provo, UT: Charles Redd Center for Western Studies, Brigham Young University, 1997); Jorge Iber, *Hispanics in the Mormon Zion, 1912-1999* (College Station: Texas A&M University Press, 2000).

[17] JRC to Spencer W. and Camilla Kimball, 30 Sept. 1956, fd 7, box 395, JRCP, copied in Spencer W. Kimball diary, 30 Sept. 1956, private possession; also Edward L. Kimball and Andrew E. Kimball Jr., *Spencer W. Kimball, Twelfth President of The Church of Jesus Christ of Latter-day Saints* (Salt Lake City: Bookcraft, 1977), 236-45, 247, 249-50, 257-59, 274-75, 296-98, 320-23, 340-42, 361-63, 366-67, 404, for his decades of emphasis on Native Americans; also Bruce A. Chadwick and Thomas Garrow, "Native Americans," in *EM* 3:981-82; Clarence R. Bishop, "Indian Placement: A History of the Indian Placement Program of the Church of Jesus Christ of Latter-day Saints," M.S.W., University of Utah, 1967.

[18] Kimball and Kimball, *Spencer W. Kimball,* 296 (which quoted from the above letter), also 366 (opposition by some apostles).

[19] Spencer W. Kimball interview by D. Michael Quinn, 2 Feb. 1979.

[20] *Conf,* Oct. 1938, 138; "Zion" in Davis Bitton, *Historical Dictionary of Mormonism* (Metuchen, NJ: Scarecrow Press, 1994), 273.

The primary emphasis of Clark's above talk was Germany's 1938 annexation of Austria and part of Czechoslovakia. He reminded his audience of their own historical expropriation of native lands in order to dismiss their criticism of Nazi expansionism. See ch. 9, discussion for notes 62-64.

[21] JRC to Alfred M. Landon, 21 Nov. 1938, fd 8, box 360, JRCP.

[22] JRC to Hamilton Fish Armstrong, 23 Oct. 1939, fd 1, box 361, JRCP.

[23] *C*, 631n2 (first quote), also 316 ("Nipponophobia" in the context of the 1921 Washington Arms Conference and Japan's naval power); also "The Yellow Peril" in Roger Daniels, *The Politics of Prejudice: The Anti-Japanese Movement in California and the Struggle for Japanese Exclusion* (Berkeley: University of California Press, 1962), 65-78; Richard A. Thompson, *The Yellow Peril, 1890-1924* (New York: Arno Press, 1978); Jenny Clegg, *Fu Manchu and the Yellow Peril: The Making of a Racist Myth* (Stoke-on-Trent, Eng.: Trentham Books, 1994). For the U.S. as a colonial power in the western Pacific after 1898, see Alstyne, *Rising American Empire;* Julius W. Pratt, *Expansionists of 1898: The Acquisition of Hawaii and the Spanish Islands* (Chicago: Quadrangle Books, 1964); Stanley Karnow, *In Our Image: America's Empire in the Philippines* (New York: Random House, 1989).

[24] *C*, 346; also Daniels, *Politics of Prejudice,* 31-64. Clarkana has William Draper Lewis, *Can the United States by Treaty Confer on Japanese Residents in California the Right to Attend the Public Schools?* (Princeton, NJ: Princeton University Press, 1907).

[25] JRC office diary, 6 June 1951.

[26] *C*, 632n2, with my addition of a comma.

[27] Gordon W. Prange, *December 7, 1941: The Day the Japanese Attacked Pearl Harbor* (New York: McGraw-Hill, 1988); Stanley Weintraub, *Long Day's Journey into War: December 7, 1941* (New York: Dutton, 1991).

[28] For example, "New Jap Army Head," *DN,* 13 Sept. 1941, [2]; "Japs Threaten to Invade China, India from Burma," *DN,* 4 May 1942, [1]; "What the Japs Covet," editorial, *DN,* 2 Oct. 1942, [4]; "S.L. Jap Asks 'Chinaman's Chance,'" *DN,* 3 July 1943, [1]; "Boise Serviceman Writes from Jap Prison Camp," *CN,* 18 Mar. 1944; "Japs Warned to Oust War Lords," *DN,* 10 Feb. 1944, 5; *CN,* 29 Jan. 1945; "Japs Prepare for Invasion," *DN,* 9 May 1945, [1].

[29] JRC to Paul Shoup, president, Merchants and Manufacturers Association of Los Angeles, 3 Mar. 1942 (using "Japanese" repeatedly in contrast to the "Japs" of Shoup's letter), both in fd 3, box 365, JRCP.

[30] JRC office diary, 13 Mar. 1942.

[31] JRC office diary, 2 Nov. 1942; also Dillon S. Myer, *Uprooted Americans: The Japanese Americans and the War Relocation Authority, during World War II* (Tucson: University of Arizona Press, 1971); Roger Daniels, *Concentration Camps USA: Japanese Americans and World War II* (New York: Holt, Rinehart, Winston, 1971); John Tateishi, comp., *And Justice for All: An Oral History of the Japanese American Detention Camps* (New York: Random House, 1984); Mary Tsukamoto and Elizabeth Pinkerton, *We the People: A Story of Internment in America* (Elk Grove, CA: Laguna Publishers, 1987); Deborah Gesenway and Mindy Roseman, *Beyond Words: Images from America's Concentration Camps* (Ithaca, NY: Cornell University Press, 1987).

There are two indications that the federal relocation program catered to California's prejudices against Asian Americans. See Eldon R. Penrose, *California Nativism: Organized Opposition to the Japanese, 1890-1913* (San Francisco: R.&E. Research Associates, 1973); Roger Daniels, *The Politics of Prejudice: The Anti-Japa-*

nese Movement in California and the Struggle for Japanese Exclusion, 2d ed. (Berkeley: University of California Press, 1977).

First, despite the attack on Pearl Harbor, there was no general internment of Hawaii's Japanese immigrants, nor its Japanese-American population. See R. Lanier Britsch, *Moramona: The Mormons in Hawaii* (Laie, HI: Institute for Polynesian Studies, Brigham Young University-Hawaii, 1989), 159: "In Hawaii it would have been impossible to place all AJAs [Americans of Japanese ancestry] under arrest because they were the largest racial group in the islands. ... and no cases of sabotage were ever detected among them."

Second, there was no equivalent internment of the German Americans on the East Coast, despite the arrest of Nazi spies there and the torpedoing of a 10,000-ton tanker by a German submarine just outside New York Harbor. See William Wise, *When Saboteurs Came: The Nazi Sabotage Plot against America in World War II* (New York: Dutton, 1967); W. A. Swanberg, "The Spies Who Came in from the Sea," *American Heritage* 21 (Apr. 1970): 66-69, 87-91; William B. Breuer, *Hitler's Undercover War: The Nazi Espionage Invasion of the U.S.A.* (New York: St. Martin's Press, 1989); Jean-Philippe Dallies-Labourdette, *U-Boote, 1935-1945: The History of the Kriegsmarine U-Boat* (Paris: Historie & Collections, 1996), 47.

[32] Leonard J. Arrington, *The Price of Prejudice: The Japanese-American Relocation Center in Utah during World War II* (Logan: Utah State University Press, 1962); Sandra C. Taylor, *Jewel of the Desert: Japanese American Internment at Topaz* (Berkeley: University of California Press, 1993); Jane Beckwith, "Topaz Relocation Center," in *U,* 560-61; Michael O. Tunnell and George W. Chilcoat, *The Children of Topaz: The Story of a Japanese-American Internment Camp, Based on a Classroom Diary* (New York: Holiday House, 1996); "The Camp: Americans Jailed for Their Country," *SLT,* 1 May 1998, E-1, E-4.

[33] JRC office diary, 2 Nov. 1942.

[34] Sources cited in previous notes 31-32.

[35] Spencer W. Kimball interview by D. Michael Quinn, 2 Feb. 1979.

[36] *Conf,* Oct. 1946, 88-89; *C,* 589.

[37] JRC to G—— C. B———, 3 Aug. 1945, fd 2, box 371, JRCP. This young woman was able to serve an LDS mission during World War II because the government did not imprison Hawaii's Japanese-American population. See Britsch, *Moramona,* 160 (Japanese Hawaiians as missionaries during the war); also Jessie L. Embry, *Asian American Mormons: Bridging Cultures* (Provo, UT: Charles Redd Center for Western Studies, Brigham Young University, 1999).

[38] JRC to H—— R. C————, 30 Oct. 1952, fd 5, box 385, JRCP, for quote, marriage outcome, and sending copies of the letter to others.

[39] Chieko N. Okazaki, *Cat's Cradle* (Salt Lake City: Bookcraft, 1993), 59.

[40] "Woman of Mixed Blood Desirous of Marrying a Chinaman—License Refused," *DN,* 16 Sept. 1898, 2; Irving G. Tragen, "Statutory Prohibitions against Interracial Marriage," *California Law Review* 32 (1944): 271n9.

[41] JRC to Herbert Hoover, 14 May 1942, 8. Most of this section on anti-Semitism was in the first draft I submitted in 1981 for review by Reuben's

children and by LDS administrators. Although my draft and 1983 book presented Clark's view without refutation, I had previously responded to anti-Semitic statements by a Utah woman, Charlotte M. Howe, who frequently expressed support for ultra-conservative political views in letters to the editor. See D. Michael Quinn to the editor, *SLT,* 21 Sept. 1978.

[42] Rudolf Glanz, *Jew and Mormon: Historic Group Relations and Religious Outlook* (New York: Waldron Press, 1963); Juanita Brooks, *History of the Jews in Utah and Idaho* (Salt Lake City: Western Epics, 1973), 69-70; *O,* 107, 632, 639; *E,* 235, 763, 796, 806, 815, 819; Douglas F. Tobler, "The Jews, the Mormons, and the Holocaust," *JMH* 18 (Spring 1992), 60-68.

[43] Frederick Paul Keppel, *Columbia* (New York: Oxford University Press, 1914), 179 ("The question is so often asked ..."), also Keppel's own statement on 180 ("but it is evident that the proportion of Jewish students is decreasing rather than increasing"). Columbia's undergraduate dean published this eleven years after JRC entered the university.

[44] Tobler, "The Jews, the Mormons, and the Holocaust," 70, stated that JRC "had some unhappy experiences [with Jews] while living in the Eastern United States, according to his son." For example, while working for the Foreign Bondholders' Protective Council, Clark wrote in his office diary, 1 Mar. 1934: "Last night worked more or less in the line I might take in talking with Jimmy Speyer today. I see no advantage in being tender with him. I can imagine no better advertisement—favorable—than his complaint that we refused to ask Brazil to revamp this plan in the interest of one Jew issue house [brokerage], to the detriment of the great bulk of American bondholders," and "I returned to get ready to take on the Jew." For the biographical sketch of James Speyer, see *Who Was Who in America, Vol. 1, 1897-1942* (Chicago: A.N. Marquis, 1942), 1163.

[45] Candidacies of Ernest Bamberger in Allan Kent Powell, "Elections in the State of Utah," *U,* 160; discussion and allegations of corruption in *C,* 415-19, 422-27.

[46] Frank Thomas Morn, "Simon Bamberger: A Jew in a Mormon Commonwealth," M.A. thesis, Brigham Young University, 1966; Miriam B. Murphy, "Simon Bamberger," in *U,* 26; S. George Ellsworth, "Simon Bamberger: Governor of Utah," *Western States Jewish Historical Quarterly* 5 (July 1973): 231-42.

[47] Larry R. Gerlach, *Blazing Crosses in Zion: The Ku Klux Klan in Utah* (Logan: Utah State University Press, 1982); Gerlach, "Ku Klux Klan," in *U,* 307-08.

[48] *Conf,* Apr. 1921, 124.

[49] JRC office diary, 17 Feb. 1934, 25 Feb. 1944.

[50] JRC to Lute, 7 Jan. 1935, box 337, JRCP.

[51] JRC ranch diary, 26 May 1957, JRCP, with added capitalization, which stated in full: "Cozio seems to be *Kozial* a jew," emphasis in original. This referred to Felix C. Koziol, Wasatch National Forest Supervisor. See Thomas G. Alexander, *The Forest Service and the LDS Church in the Mid-Twentieth Century: Utah National Forests as a Test Case* (Ogden, UT: Weber State College Press, 1988), 10.

[52] Tobler, "The Jews, the Mormons, and the Holocaust," 70.

[53] Lute to JRC, 1923, fd 1, box 333.

[54] J. Reuben Clark III (as a graduate student) to JRC, 9 Oct. 1950, referring to Jerome Horowitz in first quote; also Reuben III to JRC, 9 Apr. 1950 (second quote), in full: "Best we give the Ward back to the Mission and the Island back to our Red Brothers before our incoming Jew Brothers (Poles, Germans, Russians, Greeks, etc.) take it for nothing," both in fd 6, box 361, JRCP.

[55] Branko Lazitch [Lazic] and Milorad M. Drachkovitch, *Biographical Dictionary of the Comintern* (Stanford, CA: The Hoover Institution Press/Stanford University, 1973), 121; Joan Comay, *Who's Who in Jewish History after the Period of the Old Testament* (New York: David McKay, 1974), 99, 169, 255-56, 265-66, 278-79, 406-09; Robert S. Wistrich, *Revolutionary Jews from Marx to Trotsky* (London: George C. Harrap, 1976), 3, 4, 19, 26-45, 57, 61, 64, 67, 76-92, 153-70, 189-207; Gerald Sorin, *The Prophetic Minority: American Jewish Immigrant Radicals, 1880-1920* (Bloomington: Indiana University Press, 1985), 79; also *The New Encyclopaedia Britannica*, 15th ed., 30 vols. (Chicago: Encyclopaedia Britannica, 1998), 7:341-42, for Karl Liebknecht, who was executed in 1919 on the same day as Rosa Luxemburg. Benjamin Gitlow fell out of favor and eventually became an anti-Communist.

[56] Clarkana has five books by Wilhelm Liebknecht, including *Wissen Ist Macht—Macht Ist Wissen* (Leipzig: Genossenschaftsbuchdruckerei, 1873) and *No Compromise, No Political Trading*, rev. ed., trans. A. M. Simons and Marcus Hitch (Chicago: C.H. Kerr, 1919); one by William Liebknecht and Paul Lafargue, *Karl Marx: His Life and Work* ... (New York: International Publishers, 1943); five by V. I. Lenin, including *The State and Revolution: Marxist Teaching on the State and the Task of the Proletariat in the Revolution* (London: British Socialist Party, 1919) and an additional, serialized article by Lenin: "The Reorganization of the Party," *New Life*, 10, 15, 16 Nov. 1905; three volumes by Rosa Luxemburg, including *The Crisis in the German Social-Democracy* (New York: Socialist Publication Society, 1919); three by Morris Hillquit, including *The Civic Federation and Labor: A Reply to P. M. Easley* (Chicago: National Office of the Socialist Party, 1911); two by Leon Trotsky, including *Terrorismus und Kommunismus, Anti-Kautsky* (Petrograd [St. Petersburg]: Verlag der "Kommunistischen Internationale," 1920); and Karl Marx and Friedrich Engels, *Manifesto of the Communist Party*, trans. Samuel Moore (New York: International Publishers, 1937); W. Tcherkesoff, *Let Us Be Just: An Open Letter to [Karl] Liebknecht* (London: James Tochatti/Liberty Press, 1896); Gabriel Deville, *The People's Marx: A Popular Epitome of Karl Marx's Capital*, trans. Robert Rives La Monte (New York: International Library Publishing, 1900); Emma Goldman, *Syndicalism: The Modern Menace to Capitalism* (New York: Mother Earth Publishing Association, 1913); and Max Shachtman, *Lenin, [Karl] Liebknecht, Luxemburg* (Chicago: Young Workers' League, 1920?); see also Gitlow as vice presidential candidate in *The Platform of the Class Struggle: National Platform of the Workers' (Communist) Party, 1928* (New York: National Election Campaign Committee/Workers' Library Publishers, 1928).

[57] JRC to Herbert Hoover, 14 May 1942, 8.

[58] Charles Herbert Stember, et al., *Jews in the Mind of America* (New York: Basic Books, 1966), 157.

59 Comay, *Who's Who in Jewish History,* 63, 81, 132. During the 1950s the Jewish anti-Communists included Rabbi Benjamin Schultz, Roy M. Cohn (Senator Joseph McCarthy's principal assistant), and other members of the American Jewish League Against Communism. For this organization, see M. J. Heale, *American Anti-Communism: Combating the Enemy Within, 1830-1970* (Baltimore: Johns Hopkins University Press, 1990), 173.

60 Ronald I. Rubin, ed., *The Unredeemed: Anti-Semitism in the Soviet Union* (Chicago: Quadrangle Books, 1968); William Korey, *The Soviet Cage: Anti-Semitism in Russia* (New York: Viking Press, 1973); Hedrick Smith, *The Russians* (New York: Quadrangle/New York Times Book, 1976), 473-80.

61 "Anti-Semitism under Soviet Rule Revealed," *The Salt Lake Telegram,* 6 Dec. 1949, 8; also Gregor Aronson, *Soviet Russia and the Jews,* trans. Benjamin Schultz (New York: American Jewish League Against Communism, 1949), in Clarkana.

62 Moses Miller, *Soviet "Anti-Semitism": The Big Lie* (New York: Jewish Life, 1949), in Clarkana.

63 JRC office diary, 8 Jan. 1943; also Denis Fahey, *The Rulers of Russia,* 3d ed., rev. and enl. (Dublin: Holy Ghost Missionary College, 1939), in Clarkana.

64 Stember, et al., *Jews in the Mind of America,* 168; Charles Y. Glock and Rodney Stark, *Christian Beliefs and Anti-Semitism* (New York: Harper & Row, 1966), 118.

65 *New Encyclopaedia Britannica,* 9:742; *ER* 2:738-39.

66 See ch. 8 for JRC's affirmation that the Russian people had the right to engage in revolution and to accept a Leninist-Stalinist government; also ch. 9 for his affirmation that Indo-China had this right to throw off "corrupt colonial government" and adopt "an enlightened Communism."

67 [Henry Ford], *The International Jew, the World's Foremost Problem* (Dearborn, MI: Dearborn Independent, 1920); Michael N. Dobkowski, *The Tarnished Dream: The Basis of American Anti-Semitism* (Westport, CT: Greenwood Press, 1979), 199-200; Norman Cohn, *Warrant for Genocide: The Myth of the Jewish World-Conspiracy and the Protocols of the Elders of Zion* (New York: Harper & Row, 1966), 58-59; Albert Lee, *Henry Ford and the Jews* (New York: Stein and Day, 1980). Clarkana does not have Ford's publications, but it does have a similar book, *The Cause of World Unrest* ... (New York: G.P. Putnam, 1920).

68 Burton J. Hendrick, "The Jewish Invasion of America," *McClure's Magazine* (Mar. 1913): 125-65.

69 *New Encyclopaedia Britannica,* 9:742 (quote); *ER* 2:738-39; also Herman Bernstein, *The History of a Lie, "The Protocols of the Wise Men of Zion"* (New York: J. S. Ogilivie, 1921); Bernstein, *The Truth about "The Protocols of Zion"* (New York: Covici, Friede, 1935); John S. Curtiss, *An Appraisal of the Protocols of Zion* (New York: Columbia University Press, 1942). Henry Ford's role in popularizing the *Protocols* in the United States is absent from *EA* 22:694.

70 *The "Protocols," Bolshevism, and the Jews* (New York: American Jewish Committee, 1921), in Clarkana.

71 Aside from such publications by the American Jewish Committee and

another by the B'nai B'rith, Clarkana has J. Soltin, *The Struggle against Anti-Semitism: A Program of Action for American Jewry* (New York: Jewish Bureau of the National Committee, Communist Party, 1938); James W. Ford, *Anti-Semitism, the Struggle for Democracy, and the Negro People* (New York: Workers' Library, 1939): "based on the report of a special meeting of the Harlem division of the Communist Party by Theodore R. Bassett (December 22, 1938), and the speech of James W. Ford at the national conference of the Jewish Communists, December 24, 25, 26, 1938"; William Gallacher, *Anti-Semitism: What It Means to You* (London: Communist Party of Great Britain, 1943); Gallacher and Earl Browder, *Anti-Semitism, What It Means and How to Combat It* (New York: Workers' Library, 1943); ch. 8 for Browder.

[72] JRC to Herbert Hoover, 28 Oct. 1943, Hoover Presidential Library; also Ronald Steel, *Walter Lippmann and the American Century* (Boston: Little, Brown, 1980).

[73] Clarkana has *Out of Their Own Mouths: The Jewish Will for Power and the Authenticity of the "Protocols"* (New York: American Nationalist Press, [1937]). Pro-Nazi and pro-Fascist publishing houses often had "Nationalist" in their names. This publication was translated from articles in *La Vita Italiana,* Rome's Fascist newspaper.

[74] Clarkana has three copies of *The Protocols of the Wise Men of Zion,* all inscribed "J. Reuben Clark."

[75] Marilyn R. Allen to JRC, 18 July 1946 (JRC notation, "ask for 6 to my home"), and Rowena J. Miller to Marilyn R. Allen, 7 Dec. 1949, both in fd 1, box 379, JRCP; JRC to Pyramid Book Shop, 22 Sept. 1958 ("supply me with one-half dozen copies"), fd 7, box 403, JRCP.

[76] Cf. Allen's publications in Clarkana with BYU's non-Clarkana holdings and the catalogs for the Salt Lake City Public Library (main branch), the University of Utah, Weber State University, Utah State University, and Southern Utah University. My tally of Reuben's collection of fifteen titles did not include his second copy of Allen's *Zionist War-Mongering* .... Some of her publications had the series title "I Love America." See ch. 9, note 175, for discussion of Carlson.

[77] JRC to Ernest L. Wilkinson, 5 Feb. 1949, fd 16, box 380, JRCP.

[78] Clarkana has John O. Beaty, *The Iron Curtain over America* (Dallas, TX: Wilkinson Publishing, 1951); Jack B. Tenney, *Zion's Fifth Column* (Tujunga, CA: Standard Publications, 1953); also a 1958 edition of Beaty's book.

[79] JRC to Hugh C. Smith, 10 Aug. 1954, fd 15, box 391, JRCP.

[80] Inscription in presentation copy of Leon L. Watters, *The Pioneer Jews of Utah* (New York: American Jewish Historical Society, 1952), in Clarkana.

[81] Ezra Taft Benson to JRC, 9 Dec. 1957, and JRC undated reply to Ezra Taft Benson, both in fd 4, box 398, JRCP; cf. Harry I. Shumway, *Bernard M. Baruch: Financial Genius, Statesman, and Adviser to Presidents* (Boston: L.C. Page, 1946); Clyde E. Jacobs, *Justice Frankfurter and Civil Liberties* (Berkeley: University of California Press, 1961). As noted in *E,* 835, this apostle's correspondence with Clark about Communist subversion by Jews "may be the reason Benson organizes secret surveillance of employees (especially Jews) in U.S. Department of Agriculture."

[82] On 30 August 1939, E. Hollings of Salt Lake City sent a copy of the *Protocols* to Apostle Joseph F. Merrill with the comment, "International Jewry finances and sponsors Communism." See carbon copy of letter in fd 5, box 34, David O. McKay papers, LDSA.

[83] JRC to E—— M. W——, 26 Feb. 1954, fd 20, box 391, JRCP.

[84] JRC office diary, 8 Jan. 1943.

[85] Stember, et al., *Jews in the Mind of America,* 126-27.

[86] Clarkana has Robert E. Edmondson, *Roosevelt's Supreme Council: Alien-Asiatic Revolutionaries Control U.S. Politico-Economic Power-Centers, Washington and New York* (New York: Edmondson Economic Service, 1935); William D. Pelley, *What Every Congressman Should Know: Jews in Our Government* (Asheville, NC: Pelley Publishers, 1936); *Hidden Empire* (Asheville, NC: Pelley Publishers, nd); also William D. Pelley, *The Blot on North Carolina: Have Effective Critics of the New Deal Forfeited Their Rights to the Protection of the Statutes in State or Federal Courts?* (Indianapolis: Fellowship Press, 1941).

[87] David H. Bennett, *Demagogues in the Depression: American Radicals and the Union Party* (New Brunswick, NJ: Rutgers University Press, 1969), 113-44, 251-53, 282-86.

[88] Gerald L. K. Smith, *Jews in Government and Related Positions of Power* (St. Louis, MO: Christian Nationalist Crusade, 1951), in Clarkana. This demonstrates that Clark's concern about Jews in the federal government had not diminished since his 1943 discussion with James H. Moyle, cited in note 91; also note 73.

[89] Clarkana has two issues from 1943 of *The Cross and the Flag,* the periodical of Gerald L. K. Smith's Christian Nationalist Crusade, plus *Los Angeles against Gerald L. K. Smith: How a City Organized to Combat Native Fascism!* (Los Angeles: Mobilization for Democracy, 1945); Jonathan E. Perkins, *The Biggest Hypocrite in America: Gerald L. K. Smith Unmasked* (Los Angeles: American Foundation, 1949).

[90] Clarkana has Gerald L. K. Smith, *Too Much and Too Many Roosevelts* (St. Louis: Christian Nationalist Crusade, 1950); Smith, *Jews in Government and Related Positions of Power* (1951).

[91] JRC office diary, 8 Jan. 1943.

[92] When "Rubbie Gordon and a companion Jew" brought this to the attention of McKay, the second counselor expressed "regret that the hitherto expressed pleasant relations between Jews and Mormons should be disturbed by agitators." See McKay office diary, 16 Apr. 1936, LDSA.

[93] JRC office diary, 1 May 1939.

[94] Frank Herman Jonas, "Utah: Sagebrush Democracy," in Thomas C. Donnelly, ed., *Rocky Mountain Politics* (Albuquerque: University of New Mexico Press, 1940), 19. Jesse B. Stone wrote a pamphlet about 1940 titled "Jewish Influence on the Mormon Church," stating: "It behooves the Mormon People to hold a few mass meetings, to determine what ails them and their church, and spend less time troubling about Hitler's work in Germany." See typed copy in fd 5, box 34, McKay papers.

[95] Heber J. Grant journal sheets, 2 Jan. 1940, LDSA.

[96] *SI*, 272. Clark consistently used "emigres" rather than "immigrants" ap-

parently because the former is often used for people who have been forced from their country of origin; *DA*, 75 (*"Code words,* distinguished from euphemisms (q.v.), an effort to disguise coldness or antagonism toward members of ethnic or racial groups. They are often found in public discourse.")

[97] JRC, *Some Factors of a Now-Planned Post-War Governmental and Economic Pattern* (Salt Lake City: Deseret News Press, 1943), 5, published in full in *Commercial & Financial Chronicle*, 25 Nov. 1943; also JRC talk for Constitution Day, 17 Sept. 1946, given over LDS radio station KSL, quoted and summarized in "Pres. Clark Warns of Plot to Wreck U.S.," *DN*, 18 Sept. 1946, 1, and published in full in "Common Law Government in U.S. Endangered," *CN*, 21 Sept. 1946, 2, in *Commercial & Financial Chronicle*, 3 Oct. 1946, and JRC, *Inroads upon the Constitution by the Roman Law: A Constitution Day Address by President J. Reuben Clark, Jr. (September 17, 1946)* (Salt Lake City: Deseret News Press, 1946), 5; also *SA*, 143-44, 191, 195, 232-33, 235, 245, 246, 253-54, 488, 491, 522, 543-44.

In 1946 JRC named only one "alphabetical bureau" of the federal government—the OPA (Office of Price Administration), which President Roosevelt established in 1941. See *EA* 20:649 (OPA); *DA*, 30, 225 ("alphabet agencies"), 51 ("boring from within"); also "OPA Official Praises Foresight of Church," *CN*, 20 Feb. 1943, 4.

[98] William E. Leuchtenburg, *Franklin D. Roosevelt and the New Deal, 1932-1940* (New York: Harper and Row, 1963), 60, 125-28, 135, 174; Lester V. Chandler, *America's Greatest Depression, 1929-1941* (New York: Harper & Row, 1970), 148, 154, 197-98, 202-03.

[99] JRC to Herbert Hoover, 14 May 1942, 2.

[100] "Nazi Terrorizing of Jews Reported," *DN*, 22 Mar. 1933, [1]; "Jews Flee from German Boycott," *DN*, 1 Apr. 1933, [1]; "Hitler Deprives Jews of Citizenship," *DN*, 16 Sept. 1935, [1]; "Nazi Minister Asks Halt to Anti-Jew Riots: Mobs Smash Stores, Burn Synagogues to Avenge Agent Slaying," *DN*, 10 Nov. 1938, [1]; "Jews Hide in Fear of Renewed Attacks," *DN*, 16 Nov. 1938, [1]; "Nazis Place Ban On Name of Jehovah: Mention of Jewish Prophets also Forbidden," *DN*, 19 Nov. 1938, [1].

[101] Clarkana has *The Jews in Nazi Germany: The Factual Record of Their Persecution by the National Socialists* (New York: American Jewish Committee, 1933); Max J. Kohler, *The United States and German Jewish Persecutions—Precedents for Popular and Governmental Action* (Cincinnati: B'nai B'rith Executive Committee, 1934); Theodore Deak and Rae Einhorn, *Women and Children under the Swastika: A Collection of News Items and Factual Reports of the Unbridled Terror and Oppression in the Third Reich* (New York: Universum, 1936).

[102] "Europe War Scares Discounted," *SLT*, 8 Sept. 1937, 17. Concerning Welker's conversation with "a Jewish woman, a Frau Kammerling, who had often rented rooms to missionaries in the past," Tobler quoted from Welker's 1934 diary: "She told us many stories of the [Nazi] government's persecution of the Jews, which revealed another side of things to us. We were surprised and shocked at her stories." See Tobler, "The Jews, the Mormons, and the Holocaust," 82.

[103] "Warm Debates Enliven P.T.A.," *The Salt Lake Telegram*, 18 May 1938, 7;

also Carl W. Binder, *Education under the Hitler Regime* (New York: Commission Investigating Fascist Activities, 1934), in Clarkana.

[104] JRC office diary, 21 July 1939.

[105] Clarkana has Hans Beimler, *Four Weeks in the Hands of Hitler's Hell-Hounds: The Nazi Murder Camp of Dachau* (New York: Workers' Library Publishers, 1933); *The Sonnenburg Torture Camp, by an Escaped Prisoner* (New York: Workers' International Relief and International Labor Defense, 1934). Even though these were printed by Communist publishers, his 1939 statement to Presidents Grant and McKay showed that Clark accepted the basic truth of these publications.

[106] For example, "Concentration Camp Prisoners Shot Down," *DN*, 19 Nov. 1938, 2, regarding a mass execution of Jews at Buchenwald, with added reference to the camps at Sachsenhausen and Dachau; "Death for 700,000 Jews Threatened: Semites Must Get Out or Die, Nazis Declare," *DN*, 23 Nov. 1938, [2]; also Eugen Kogon, *The Theory and Practice of Hell: The German Concentration Camps and the System behind Them* (New York: Berkley Press, 1950); Nora Levin, *The Holocaust: The Destruction of European Jewry, 1933-1945* (New York: Thomas R. Crowell, 1968).

[107] This is the emphasis of David S. Wyman, *Paper Walls: America and the Refugee Crisis, 1938-1941* (Amherst: University of Massachusetts Press, 1968).

[108] Minutes of meeting of Presiding Bishopric with First Presidency, 29 July 1935, 4, LDSA.

[109] Tobler, "The Jews, the Mormons, and the Holocaust," 83–84; *E*, 823.

[110] Statements of missionaries Burke M. Snow and Edwin Q. Cannon to the *Stettiner General-Anzeiger*, 24 Oct. 1938 (original and translation), CR 1/44, LDSA.

[111] Minutes of meeting of Presiding Bishopric with First Presidency, 28 July 1936, 3.

[112] *ER* 2:763.

[113] Egon E. Weiss (LDS Jew) to First Presidency, 23 Nov. 1938 (stamped "received" 16 Jan. 1939), fd 6, box 111, CR 1/44, partly quoted in *E*, 826; Richard Siebenschein to LDS church president, 25 and 28 Dec. 1938 ("received" 16 Jan. 1939), in fd 5, box 110, CR 1/44. Siebenschein's second letter enclosed two photographs of him with Heber J. Grant and LDS missionaries in 1901. There were no notations on this correspondence to explain why letters mailed a month apart by different Jews from different residences were stamped "received" on the same day in the First Presidency's office.

[114] *ER* 1:515-16.

[115] "Nazi Minister Asks Halt to Anti-Jew Riots: Mobs Smash Stores, Burn Synagogues to Avenge Agent Slaying," *DN*, 10 Nov. 1938, [1]; "London, Berlin Pact Menaced by Jew Attack," and "Goebbels Warns Foreign Jews Treatment at Home Will Depend Partly upon Conduct Abroad: Propaganda Chief Claims Violence Not Organized," *DN*, 11 Nov. 1938, [1]; "Nazis Fine Jews $400,000,000 for Slaying," *DN*, 12 Nov. 1938, [1]; "Jews Hide in Fear of Renewed Attacks," *DN*,

16 Nov. 1938, [1]; "Nazis Place Ban on Name of Jehovah: Mention of Jewish Prophets also Forbidden," *DN*, 19 Nov. 1938, [1].

[116] For example, JRC and David O. McKay to Richard Siebenschein, 27 Jan. 1939, in fd 5, box 110, CR 1/44; also quoted in *E*, 827.

[117] JRC to Allen Dulles, 11 Apr. 1939 (regarding Dulles to JRC, 31 Mar. 1939), both in fd 1, box 361, JRCP. Wyman, *Paper Walls: America and the Refugee Crisis, 1938-1941* did not cite this correspondence, but Wyman described the State Department's resistance to Jewish immigration.

[118] In 1944-45 Dulles was the station chief of the Office of Strategic Services (OSS, precursor of the CIA) in Bern, Switzerland. He continued to show "minimal interest in the extermination of the Jews" and "indifference" about proposals to liberate the extermination camps or at least bomb the train tracks leading to them. See David S. Wyman, *The Abandonment of the Jews: America and the Holocaust, 1941-1945* (New York: Pantheon Books, 1984), 314, 411n11, also 206, 288-307 (discussion of failed proposals for Allied air force raids).

As a fellow Republican, Dulles had joined the Foreign Service in 1913, the last year Clark served as Solicitor in the State Department. This younger man served for ten years as one of the "new cadre of diplomatic-intelligence officers" in Europe. Like Clark, as an attorney in private practice, Dulles continued to receive State Department assignments with international conferences for arms control and negotiation of national disputes. They both served as advisers at the Washington Arms Conference of 1921-22. Like Clark, Dulles had conferred with the Nazi finance minister, Hjalmar Schacht. Unlike Reuben, he had also met Adolf Hitler in 1933, after which he warned the State Department about Nazi intentions for conquest. At the time of this correspondence about Jewish immigration in 1939, Dulles was expanding his role as U.S. spy master in Europe, having previously had oversight of intelligence-gathering operations in the Middle East, including Palestine. Like Clark (see note 146), Dulles diplomatically expressed pro-Zionist views to members of Zionist organizations. He needed Zionists for intelligence gathering on Nazi-occupied Europe. He eventually became director of the Central Intelligence Agency. See James Srodes, *Allen Dulles: Master of Spies* (Washington, D.C.: Regnery Publishing, 1999), 50 (above quote), 133-37, 141, 144-53, 171-72, 185-89, 194.

[119] JRC to Clarence E. Pickett, 14 Apr. 1939, fd 2, box 361, JRCP.

[120] JRC to Greene H. Hackworth (legal adviser to the U.S. Department of State), 24 Apr. 1939, marked "Personal," box 113, CR 1/44, quoted more fully in *E*, 827. Wyman, *Paper Walls*, did not cite this correspondence.

[121] *ER* 1:45 (Aryan); also *Webster's New World Dictionary of the American Language*, 79: "Aryan has no validity as an ethnological term, although it has been so used, notoriously and variously by the Nazis, to mean 'a Caucasian of non-Jewish descent,' 'a Nordic,' etc."

Clarkana has Margaret Schlauch, *Who Are the Aryans?* (New York: Anti-Fascist Literature Committee, [1935 or 1940]); Gino Bardi, *Are We Aryans?* (New York: Workers' Library Publishers, 1939).

[122] Heber J. Grant journal sheets, 2 Jan. 1940. Tobler, "The Jews, the Mor-

mons, and the Holocaust," 81, theorized that Clark's opposition to aiding European Jews was influenced by continued contacts with his State Department friend Wilbur J. Carr: "Carr's unwillingness to believe that the Holocaust was taking place and his subsequent foot-dragging were significant impediments to publicizing it in America or developing any significant rescue efforts." However, Reuben did not need Carr's persuasion to oppose helping Jews escape Hitler.

[123] JRC memorandum, 23 Sept. 1940, "British Refugee Children" fd, box 361, JRCP. The Field Committee ended this program when German submarines sank a ship carrying English refugee children, killing seventy-nine. See "Children's Exodus Halted by Britain," *NYT,* 3 Oct. 1940, 3.

[124] "Nazis Stress Ousting of Jews from Europe," *NYT,* 4 Feb. 1941, 6.

[125] "Death for 700,000 Jews Threatened: Semites Must Get Out or Die, Nazis Declare," *DN,* 23 Nov. 1938, [2].

[126] Wyman, *Abandonment of the Jews,* 20-26, 36n12, for newspaper articles during 1941-42 in major newspapers; also Robert Ross, *So It Was True: The American Protestant Press and the Nazi Persecution of the Jews* (Minneapolis: University of Minnesota Press, 1980).

[127] N. L. Nelson, *The Second War in Heaven, as Now Being Waged by Lucifer through Hitler as a Dummy* (Independence, MO: Zion's Printing and Publishing, 1941), 126.

[128] JRC to N. L. Nelson, 24 June 1941, 4, fd 2, box 363, JRCP; see Davis Bitton, "N. L. Nelson and the Mormon Point of View," *BYU Studies* 13 (Winter 1973): 157-71. Clark's defense of Hitler after Nelson's condemnation of Nazi "butchery" (see quote for ch. 9, note 98) is the background for Tobler, "The Jews, the Mormons, and the Holocaust," 91: "Perhaps it would not have saved lives, but it would have meant a great deal in terms of ethical awareness if the [LDS] Church had taken a moral stand in behalf of the Jews, whom they professed to consider as siblings."

[129] Stember, et al., *Jews in the Mind of America,* 138.

[130] Wyman. *The Abandonment of the Jews,* 15.

[131] Louis P. Lochner, trans. and ed., *The Goebbels Diaries, 1942-1943* (Garden City, NY: Doubleday, 1948), 241.

[132] "Death Decree for All Jews Charged to Hitler: Dr. Wise Claims to Have Proof of Order," *DN,* 25 Nov. 1942, 3. Concerning this report that "approximately half of the estimated 4,000,000 Jews in Nazi-occupied Europe already had been killed," Tobler, "The Jews, the Mormons, and the Holocaust," 89n91, observed: "Post-war research has confirmed the accuracy of these figures."

[133] "700,000 Polish Jews Allowed to Die of Disease, Hunger: Nazis Accused of Hastening End for Race; Poison Gas Used," *DN,* 26 June 1942, 2; "Poles Charge Schmeling Headed Worst German Camp," *DN,* 9 July 1942, 1, referring to the Nazi extermination camp in Oswiechim, Poland (Auschwitz in German); also see the *New Encyclopaedia Britannica,* 1:707-08; Wieslaw Kielar, *Anus Mundi: 1,500 Days in Auschwitz/Birkenau,* trans. Susanne Flatauer (New York: New York Times Book, 1980), by a young Polish Catholic political prisoner.

[134] "Threat to Palestine," editorial, *DN,* 3 July 1942, 4.

[135] "All Jews in Five Towns Are Slain," *DN*, 20 Mar. 1943, [1]; "Death of All Jews in Europe This Year Expected: Hitler Continues Campaign of Extinction, Says London Investigator," *DN*, 19 Apr. 1943, 2; also "Jews Driven to Gulch, Stripped, Killed by Nazis," *DN*, 17 Nov. 1943, 1.

[136] John Gibbons, *The Most Terrible Place in the World* (London: Communist Party of Great Britain, 1943), in Clarkana; also note 105.

At the National Archives in the 1980s I read a captured Nazi document which matter-of-factly described the machine-gun shootings and mass-burials of Kiev's Jews in September 1941. In this initial report, the German officer estimated the dead at 20,000. Other reports from German military commanders showed that they killed a total of 33,771 Jews during a thirty-six-hour period in the woods of Babi Yar outside Kiev. See Erhard Roy Wiehn, ed., *Die Schoaeh von Babij Jar: Das Massaker deutscher Sonderkommandos an der jüdischen Bevölkerung von Kiew 1941* (Konstanz, Ger.: Verlag Hartung-Gorre, 1991); *New Encyclopaedia Britannica,* 1:769; Internet website, "The History Place: Holocaust Timeline" for "Massacre at Babi Yar," including photographs taken by the Germans in 1941.

[137] JRC to Stephen Abbot, 30 June 1943, fd 1, box 367, JRCP. Quoting a title from a book about Americans generally, Tobler, "The Jews, the Mormons, and the Holocaust," 89, stated: "Mormons and their leaders, like most Americans, found the reports [of the mass executions of Jews] 'beyond belief.'" Because Clark regarded the Jews as "essentially revolutionary" (note 57), he felt that they brought this persecution and death upon themselves. See note 158.

[138] "Nazis Massacre 5 Million Jews," *DN*, 11 Apr. 1945, [1]; "This Camp Shows Yanks Nazi Horror," *DN*, 1 May 1945, 2; "Nazis Slaughtered 6,000,000 Jews," *DN*, 14 Dec. 1945, 6; Kogon, *Theory and Practice of Hell*; Levin, *Holocaust*; Michael R. Marrus, ed., *The Nazi Holocaust: Historical Articles on the Destruction of European Jews*, 15 vols. (Westport, CT: Mecker, 1989); Israel Gutman, ed., *Encyclopedia of the Holocaust*, 4 vols. (New York: Macmillan; London: Collier Macmillan, 1990).

[139] Stember, et al., *Jews in the Mind of America,* 143. This applied to the surveyed Americans who reported in 1945 that they previously had anti-Semitic feelings. The survey showed that 80 percent of this anti-Semitic group still retained those attitudes after learning about the annihilation of Jews in Nazi concentration camps. See notes 58, 129-30.

[140] In reading through more than 600 boxes of Clark's personal papers, I found criticisms of British and American atrocities but no similar complaints about Japanese or German conduct during World War II. Yet from the 1940s onward, Clark acquired several publications about Nazi concentration camps. Clarkana has Bruno Bettelheim, "My Life in Nazi Concentration Camps," in L. M. Birkhead, ed., *Pattern for Revolution* (Girard, KS: Haldeman-Julius Publications, 1943); Fernand Grenier, *Ceux de Chateaubriant* (London: Communist Party of Great Britain, 1943), about a concentration camp in France; *Fascist Murderers: Pictures of the Concentration Camps You Must Never Forget* (London: Communist Party of Great Britain, 1945); *Letter from Ernst Thaelmann in Reply to a Letter from a Fellow-Prisoner at Bautzen Concentration Camp: Written in January 1944* (Bombay: People's Publishing House, 1951).

Because I found no evidence that Clark ever mentioned the Nazi slaughter of Jews, there is likewise no known evidence that he ever denied it. Cf. Deborah E. Lipstadt, *Denying the Holocaust: The Growing Assault on Truth and Memory* (New York: Free Press, 1993).

[141] Harold B. Lee diary, 22 Mar. 1945, private possession.

[142] Martin Jones, *Failure in Palestine: British and United States Policy after the Second World War* (London: Mansell, 1986), 80, 83-84, 115, 116, 153, 156, 197.

[143] Harold B. Lee diary, 22 Mar. 1945. For George Albert Smith's pro-Israel activities in 1948-49, see Tobler, "The Jews, the Mormons, and the Holocaust," 62, 62n9, citing Jack Goodman, "Jews in Zion," in Helen Z. Papanikolas, ed., *The Peoples of Utah* (Salt Lake City: Utah State Historical Society, 1976), 217; Louis Zucker, "A Jew in Zion," *Sunstone* 6 (Sept.-Oct. 1981): 44.

[144] "Pres. Clark Warns of Plot to Wreck U.S.," *DN*, 18 Sept. 1946, [1]. His speech's text did not use the word "wreck," but he may have suggested this title to the editors. The full text soon appeared in two *DN* publications: *CN*, 21 Sept. 1946, and the pamphlet, *Inroads upon the Constitution by the Roman Law.*

[145] Clarkana has *European Jewry and the Palestine Problem* ... (London: Communist Party of Great Britain, 1946); Alexander Bittelman, *To Secure Jewish Rights: The Communist Position* (New York: New Century Publishers, 1948). The publisher's imprint, New Century, referred to the centennial of the *Communist Manifesto.* The publisher was the Communist Party of the United States of America.

[146] Mendel N. Fisher to JRC, 23 Nov. 1943, fd 2, box 367, JRCP.

[147] JRC to Robert F. Wagner (chairman of the American Palestine Committee at Washington, D.C.), 28 June 1944, fd 1, box 369, JRCP.

[148] Heber G. Wolsey, "The History of Radio Station KSL from 1922 to Television," Ph.D. diss., Michigan State University, 1967, 222; JRC office diary, 3 Aug. 1945.

[149] "Pres. Clark Warns of Plot to Wreck U.S.," *DN*, 18 Sept. 1946, [1].

[150] JRC office diary, 28 Feb. 1948.

[151] JRC office diary, 16 Apr. 1948; also *Zionists Misleading World with Untruths for Palestine Conquest* ... (New York: Herald Tribune, 1947), in Clarkana.

[152] JRC office diary, 10 Apr. 1948.

[153] See note 81; Robert H. Williams, *Know Your Enemy* (Santa Ana, CA: By the author, 1950), 43; "Zionists Control NAACP," *Common Sense: America's Newspaper against Communism*, 1 Nov. 1960, 1.

[154] Stewart L. Udall's 1947 memorandum, "I feel to state some of the reasons why I cannot be a practicing Mormon in full fellowship," typescript, fd 3, box 209, Udall papers, Archives, University of Arizona, Tucson, quoted in F. Ross Peterson, "'Do Not Lecture the Brethren': Stewart L. Udall's Pro-Civil Rights Stance, 1967," *JMH* 25 (Spring 1999): 273; also Armand L. Mauss, "Mormon Semitism and Anti-Semitism," *Sociological Analysis* (Spring 1968): 11-27.

[155] David O. McKay's 1921 sermon in New Zealand concerning Christmas of 1917, quoted in Tobler, "The Jews, the Mormons, and the Holocaust," 65; also *EA* 3:88, for the December 1917 Balfour Declaration; *Conf,* Oct. 1918, 47 (McKay's early commentary about this declaration).

156 David O. McKay office diary, 14 Oct. 1952, emphasis in original; also David O. McKay and JRC to Tracy-Collins Trust Co., 11 Feb. 1953, CR 1/46, LDSA; *E*, 839, 845, 869, 872, 882, 884, 893.

157 JRC office diary, 14 May 1952.

158 JRC to Robert C. Joyce, 10 Oct. "1955" (1956), fd 13, box 396, JRCP.

159 Minutes of Welfare Committee meeting with First Presidency, 19 June 1953, CR 255/18.

160 JRC office diary, 27 Jan. 1945.

161 JRC to James T. Williams Jr., 30 Sept. 1958, fd 8, box 401, JRCP, in response to letter of "indignation," same location.

162 See notes 155, 156 (McKay quotes); cf. Mauss, "Mormon Semitism and Anti-Semitism"; Glanz, *Jew and Mormon*.

163 Winthrop D. Jordan, *White over Black: American Attitudes toward the Negro, 1550-1812* (Chapel Hill: University of North Carolina Press, 1968); George M. Fredrickson, *Black Image in the White Mind: The Debate on Afro-American Character and Destiny, 1817-1914* (New York: Harper & Row, 1971). For a useful summary of the diversity, complexity, and achievements of blacks in Africa, see John Hope Franklin and Alfred A. Moss Jr., *From Slavery to Freedom: A History of Negro Americans*, 6th ed. (New York: Alfred A. Knopf, 1988), 1-26.

164 Gunnar Myrdal, *An American Dilemma: The Negro Problem and Modern Democracy* (New York: Harper & Brothers, 1944), 100.

165 "Miscegenation and Intermarriage," in Jack Salzman, David Lionel Smith, and Cornel West, eds., *Encyclopedia of African-American Culture and History*, 5 vols. (New York: Macmillan Library Reference USA/Simon & Schuster, 1996), 4:1814.

166 Leon F. Litwack, *North of Slavery: The Negro in the Free States, 1790-1860* (Chicago: University of Chicago Press, 1961); Eugene H. Berwanger, *The Frontier against Slavery: Western Anti-Negro Prejudice and the Slavery Extension Controversy* (Urbana: University of Illinois Press, 1967).

167 James M. McPherson, *The Struggle for Equality: Abolitionists and the Negro in the Civil War and Reconstruction* (Princeton, NJ: Princeton University Press, 1964), 223-37; C. Vann Woodward, *The Strange Career of Jim Crow*, 3d rev. ed. (New York: Oxford University Press, 1974); Joel Williamson, *The Crucible of Race: Black-White Relations in the American South Since Emancipation* (New York: Oxford University Press, 1984).

168 Text of 1896 *Plessy v. Ferguson* in Anthony J. Cooper, ed., *The Black Experience, 1865-1978: A Documentary Reader* (Dartford, Eng.: Greenwich University Press, 1995), 73-76; *EA* 22:247; also Woodward, *Strange Career of Jim Crow*; I. A. Newby, *Jim Crow's Defense: Anti-Negro Thought in America, 1900-1930* (Baton Rouge: Louisiana State University Press, 1965).

169 Joseph Fielding Smith, ed., *Teachings of the Prophet Joseph Smith* (Salt Lake City: Deseret News Press, 1938), 269; Richard C. Galbraith, ed., *Scriptural Teachings of the Prophet Joseph Smith* (Salt Lake City: Deseret Book, 1993), 303-04.

170 Jack Beller, "Negro Slaves in Utah," *UHQ* 3 (Oct. 1929): 122-26; Roldo V. Dutson, "A Study of the Attitude of the Latter-day Saint Church in the Terri-

tory of Utah toward Slavery as It Pertained to the Indian as Well as to the Negro from 1847 to 1865," M.A. thesis, Brigham Young University, 1964; Kate B. Carter, *The Negro Pioneer* (Salt Lake City: Daughters of Utah Pioneers, 1965); Dennis L. Lythgoe, "Negro Slavery in Utah," *UHQ* 39 (Winter 1971): 40-54; Ronald Gerald Coleman, "A History of Blacks in Utah, 1825-1910," Ph.D. diss., University of Utah, 1980, 32-41, 46-55; Coleman, "Blacks in Utah History: An Unknown Legacy," in Papanikolas, *Peoples of Utah*, 116-20; Newell G. Bringhurst, *Saints, Slaves, and Blacks: The Changing Place of Black People within Mormonism* (Westport, CT: Greenwood Press, 1981), [218]-21, 224-27; entry for "Utah" in Salzman, et al., *Encyclopedia of African-American Culture and History,* 5:2728.

[171] *Acts, Resolutions and Memorials, Passed at the Several Sessions of the Legislative Assembly of the Territory of Utah* (Salt Lake City: Joseph Cain, Public Printer, 1855), 161, 173-74; Bringhurst, *Saints, Slaves, and Blacks,* 67-70, 226; *E,* 267, 272, 286, 749-50.

[172] Joseph Smith Jr., et al., 7 vols., *History of the Church of Jesus Christ of Latter-day Saints,* 2d rev., B. H. Roberts, ed. (Salt Lake City: Deseret Book, 1960), 6:205.

[173] G[eorge] R[eynolds], "Man and His Varieties," *Juvenile Instructor* 3 (15 Sept. 1868): 141; compare with Jordan, *White over Black*; Fredrickson, *Black Image in the White Mind*; also *DA,* 361, for WASP.

[174] James E. Talmage diary, 22 Feb. 1884, HBLL.

[175] Franklin and Moss, *From Slavery to Freedom,* 296, on the "insulting" designations of "nigger," "coon," and "darkies." Cf. uses of "nigger" in Brigham Young statement, 29 May 1847, quoted in Bringhurst, *Saints, Slaves, and Blacks,* 98; in *J* 4:39 (B. Young/1856), 5:121 (B. Young/1857), 5:119 (J. Taylor/1857), 5:127 (J. Taylor/1857); in "How to Impress Niggers," DN, 22 Feb. 1860, 403; in Salt Lake Stake high council minutes, 9 Oct. 1889 ("The man was about 1/6 [sic] Nigger from his appearance"), LDSA; in Abraham Owen Woodruff diary, 6 Mar. 1902, LDSA (with photocopy of this apostle's diary in HBLL); in "Social Hall Theatre," *DN,* 22 Mar. 1919, sec. 3, IV, for laudatory review of the play, "The Nigger"; also examples in *E,* 256, 755, 759, 764, 782, 790, 804, 816.

[176] In April 1835 the official *Latter Day Saint Messenger and Advocate* published an anti-Negro editorial, apparently by Associate President Oliver Cowdery: "Must we open our houses, unfold our arms, and bid these degraded and degrading sons of Canaan, a hearty welcome and a free admittance to all we possess! ... and low indeed must be the mind, that would consent for a moment, to see his fair daughter, his sister, or perhaps, his bosom companion in the embrace of a NEGRO!" See *O,* 625 (quote), also 44-45 (position of Associate President), and other statements about African Americans on 81, 122, 478, 619-20, 624, 628, 636, 642, 659-60.

[177] See previous notes 1, 166.

[178] Coleman, "History of Blacks in Utah," 197-98; *Utah Code Annotated* (1953), Replacement Volume 3, Title 30-1-2.2; cf. Tragen, "Statutory Prohibitions against Interracial Marriage," 269-80; Robert J. Sickels, *Race, Marriage, and*

the Law (Albuquerque: University of New Mexico Press, 1972), 64 (states with miscegenation laws), also 64–74.

[179] First Presidency letter to Lowry Nelson, 17 July 1947, quoted in John J. Stewart, *Mormonism and the Negro: An Explanation and Defense of the Doctrine of the Church of Jesus Christ of Latter-day Saints in Regard to Negroes and Others of Negroid Blood* (Orem, UT: Bookmark/Community Press Publishing, 1964), 47, citation on 55n20.

[180] Wallace R. Bennett, "The Negro in Utah," *Utah Law Review* 3 (Spring 1953): 340–41, 347.

[181] David H. Oliver, *A Negro on Mormonism* (Salt Lake City: By the author, 1963), 25–26 (discussion of 1940 petition); Elmer R. Smith, *The Status of the Negro in Utah* (Salt Lake City: National Association for the Advancement of Colored People, 1956), 12 (racially restrictive real estate covenant).

[182] Bennett, "Negro in Utah," 341.

[183] Utah Legislature, "Report of Senate Committee to Investigate Discrimination against Minorities in Utah," 27th Sess. (1947), *Senate Journal*, 66.

[184] James Boyd Christensen, "A Social Survey of the Negro Population of Salt Lake City, Utah," M.S. thesis, University of Utah, 1948, 51, 53–55; Bennett, "Negro in Utah," 341–43; Smith, *Status of the Negro in Utah*, 6–7; Douglas Monty Trank, "A Rhetorical Analysis of the Rhetoric Emerging from the Mormon-Black Controversy," Ph.D. diss., University of Utah, 1973; Bringhurst, *Saints, Slaves, and Blacks*, 167–69; "Interviews with Blacks in Utah, 1982-88," JWML; Ronald G. Coleman, "African Americans in Utah," in *U*, 2; "Stepping Back? The Racial Situation in Utah's Homogenous Culture Today Is Threatening to Minorities," *DN*, 23 Feb. 1997, B-1; "Utah," in Salzman, et al., *Encyclopedia of African-American Culture and History*, 5:2729.

[185] Woodward, *Strange Career of Jim Crow*; Franklin and Moss, *From Slavery to Freedom*, 147–48, 238, 280, 296–97, 314–15, 379, 420–21; Lester A. Sobel, ed., *Civil Rights, 1960-66*, 2 vols. (New York: Facts on File, 1967); photographs of "Jim Crow Signs," in Langston Hughes, Milton Meltzer, and C. Eric Lincoln, *A Pictorial History of African Americans*, 4th rev. ed. (New York: Crown, 1973), 298–99; also comparison of LDS and non-LDS attitudes in Armand L. Mauss, "Mormonism and Secular Attitudes toward Negroes," *Pacific Sociological Review* 9 (Fall 1966): 91–99; Charles Harold Ainsworth, "Religious and Regional Sources of Attitudes toward Blacks among Southern Mormons," Ph.D. diss., Washington State University, 1982; Armand L. Mauss, *The Angel and the Beehive: The Mormon Struggle with Assimilation* (Urbana: University of Illinois Press, 1994), 52–53.

[186] Andrew Jenson, *Latter-day Saint Biographical Encyclopedia*, 4 vols. (Salt Lake City: Deseret News/Andrew Jenson History, 1901-36), 3: 577; "Journal History of the Church of Jesus Christ of Latter-day Saints (1830-1972)," 31 May 1879, 246 reels, microfilm, JWML; William E. Berrett ("Vice President of Brigham Young University"), *The Church and the Negroid People*, 7–11 (separately paged), in Stewart, *Mormonism and the Negro*; Lester E. Bush Jr., "Mormonism's Negro Doctrine: An Historical Overview," *Dial* 8 (Spring 1973): 16–21; Newell G. Bringhurst, "Elijah Abel and the Changing Status of Blacks within Mormonism,"

Dial 12 (Summer 1979): 23-36; Bringhurst, *Saints, Slaves, and Blacks,* 37-38; "Mormons," in Salzman, et al., *Encyclopedia of African-American Culture and History,* 4:1854-55.

[187] William I. Appleby diary, 170-71 (19 May 1847), LDSA; Berrett, *The Church and the Negroid People,* 7; Bringhurst, *Saints, Slaves, and Blacks,* 90. Demonstrating the emphasis after Joseph Smith's death, Appleby commented that this ordination was "contrary, though[,] to the order of the Church of the Law of the Priesthood, as the Descendants of Ham, are not entitled to that privilege."

[188] *D&C* 134:12; also Bush, "Mormonism's Negro Doctrine," 13.

[189] Al 13:3-4 in the Book of Mormon; "The Book of Abraham," *Times and Seasons* 3 (1 Mar. 1842): 705; Abr 1:21-27 in the Pearl of Great Price. Concerning the latter, Lester Bush has reported his conversation in 1976 with BYU scholar Hugh Nibley: "He does not find any clear support for the priesthood denial/ Book of Abraham relationship in early texts—or 'I would be shrieking it from the house tops.' He does not think the blacks are related to Cain, or the early Canaan[ites], and probably not to Ham, Egypt, Canaan or Pharoah." Notes of 25 Oct. 1976, summarizing their meeting on 24 October, quoted in full in Lester Bush, "Writing 'Mormonism's Negro Doctrine: An Historical Overview' (1973): Context and Reflections, 1998," *JMH* 25 (Spring 1999): 268.

[190] The first transitional reference was John Taylor's editorial, "A Short Chapter on a Long Subject," *Times and Seasons* 6 (1 Apr. 1845): 857, which referred to "descendants of Cain" as black-skinned "apostates of the Holy Priesthood." The ambiguity here is that Mormon usage by this time used "apostates" as religious rebels, which clearly did not apply to Abel and Lewis. Taylor, a former Methodist minister, did not share the founding prophet's positive view of African Americans, whom Taylor publicly referred to as "niggers" at least twice in Utah sermons. See *J* 5:119 (J. Taylor/1857), 5:157 (J. Taylor/1857). Bush, "Mormonism's Negro Doctrine," 25, quoted Brigham Young's similar view.

[191] Previous note 186; *O,* 67-69 (office of Seventy), 611-12 (Joseph Young).

[192] Manuscript versions of Brigham Young discourse, 5 Feb. 1852, in Young papers, LDSA, and in Scott G. Kenney, ed., *Wilford Woodruff's Journal, 1833-1898 Typescript,* 9 vols. (Midvale, UT: Signature Books, 1983-85), 4:97; published and quoted in Matthias F. Cowley, *Wilford Woodruff ...* (Salt Lake City: Deseret News Press, 1909), 351; Joseph Fielding Smith, *The Way to Perfection* (Salt Lake City: Genealogical Society of Utah, 1931), 106; Daniel H. Ludlow, *Latter-day Prophets Speak* (Salt Lake City: Bookcraft 1942), 204; Bush, "Mormonism's Negro Doctrine," 26; Ronald K. Esplin, "Brigham Young and Priesthood Denial to the Blacks: An Alternative View," *BYU Studies* 19 (Spring 1979): 400-01; Bringhurst, *Saints, Slaves, and Blacks,* 124-25.

Lester Bush has further reported his conversation in 1976 with Hugh Nibley: "He's unsure but would guess now that Brigham Young was 'wrong' relating blacks to Cain. He said—'we all have Negro blood'—there was intermixture everywhere. I asked about the accounts of the early [biblical] patriarchs marrying apparent blacks. He exclaimed yes[.] I mentioned Moses—Yes. But the real 'irony' was Joseph marrying a daughter of the priest of On—who he says by definition had to have been a Hamite—and their sons were Ephraim and Manasseh, who[m] we are all so proud to claim. He said it was as though the Lord was trying to tell us something." Notes of 25 Oct. 1976, summarizing their meeting on 24 October, quoted in full in Bush, "Writing 'Mormonism's Negro Doctrine,'" *JMH* 25 (Spring 1999): 268.

Salzman et al., *Encyclopedia of African-American Culture and History,* 4:1854, follows Bringhurst's analysis (*Dial*) that Brigham Young first conceived of the priesthood restriction in 1846-47 as a way of repudiating the claims of an upstart African-American prophet in Iowa. My quote from John Taylor in 1845 (note 190) indicates that within months of the founder's death, this apostle was already preaching the conventional view of white Southern Protestants.

[193] *J* 7:290-91 (B. Young/1859), 11:272 (B. Young/1866); First Presidency statement, 17 Aug. 1949, in Berrett, *Church and the Negroid People,* 16; and historical discussion in Bush, "Mormonism's Negro Doctrine," 43-44; Bringhurst, *Saints, Slaves, and Blacks,* 165-67.

[194] Joshua R. Clark diary, 27 June, 17 July 1917, 3 July 1919 ("colored woman"), 3 June 1920 (same quote); *Salt Lake City Directory, 1922* (Salt Lake City: R. L. Polk, 1922), 210, 389; Lute to JRC, 15 Feb. 1923, box 333, JRCP; *Salt Lake City Directory, 1927* (Salt Lake City: R. L. Polk, 1927), 351, 537, but no entry for Evelyn Hall thereafter.

[195] JRC office diary, 30 Aug. 1944.

[196] George Albert Smith diary, 16 June 1945 (long quote), George A. Smith Family papers, JWML; Nicholas G. Smith diary, 16 June 1945 (last quote), microfilm, LDSA.

[197] JRC to Preston D. Richards, 16 Sept. 1947, fd 17, box 376, JRCP.

[198] Minutes of council meeting, Salt Lake temple, 9 Oct. 1947, fd 7, box 78, Smith Family papers; in fd 15, box 5, H. Michael Marquardt papers, JWML. A similar document, with entries to the 1950s, was in the Adam S. Bennion papers, donated by his family to HBLL shortly after his death in 1958. Later the library withdrew the document from public access (Bush, "Writing 'Mormonism's Negro Doctrine,'" 260). However, a transcription remains available in Bush's "Compilation on the Negro in Mormonism," photocopied typescript of 386 pages (catalog number: Americana BX 8643.622/C738/1970z), HBLL.

[199] Clarkana has 13 books on Negro rights, issued by Communist publishing houses, including *Negro Rights Must Be Granted Now! Communists Declare* (New York: Communist Party of the United States of America, nd); James W. Ford and James S. Allen, *The Negroes in a Soviet America* (New York: Workers' Library Publishers, 1935); *Draft Resolution on the Negro Question* ([New York]: National Committee, Communist Party of the United States of America, 1946); [Solomon Freeman], *Why a Negro Pastor Joined the Communist Party* (New York: Communist Party of the United States of America, nd); and John Moss, *Together, Say No to Discrimination* (London: Communist Party of Great Britain, 1961).

[200] JRC office diary, 4 Mar. 1947. To my eye, the boy in the cover photo did not have Negroid features.

[201] JRC office diary, 1 May 1950; cf. photo of "Tomorrow's Leaders," *DN,* 29

Apr. 1950, A-1. The day before Reuben's instructions, the LDS newspaper published a photo of a possibly Negro girl with white children, plus a photo of a white boy with a Hispanic boy. See *DN,* 30 Apr. 1950, A-11, B-4.

[202] JRC office diary, 8 Sept. 1950, emphasis in original.

[203] Harold B. Lee diary, 29 Nov. 1949; also JRC position in Leonard J. Arrington and Heidi S. Swinton, *The Hotel: Salt Lake's Classy Lady; The Hotel Utah, 1911-1986* (Salt Lake City: Publishers Press/Westin Hotel, 1986), 97.

[204] For Anderson's exclusion from Salt Lake hotels, see "Famous Contralto Had to Use Freight Lift in Hotel Utah," *SLT,* 9 Apr. 1993, A-3, as related by Elva Plummer, widow of Gail Plummer, manager of Kingsbury Hall. Plummer remembered that this visit was in 1937, but the first concert was apparently "Contralto Singer Impresses with Voice, Sincerity," *Daily Utah Chronicle,* 4 Mar. 1943, [1]. Plummer accurately remembered that the second event was in 1948, as in "'Ave Maria' Will Be an Encore," *SLT,* 19 Mar. 1948, 18. See also Salzman, et al., *Encyclopedia of African-American Culture and History,* 1:133-34, for Anderson.

As reported in "Mormon's Mission Led Him to Fight for Civil Rights," *SLT,* 19 Apr. 1993, B-1, when Mick Duncan, founder of Utah's chapter of the ACLU, learned that "the black diva was forced to take the freight elevator to her room in the Hotel Utah," he unsuccessfully lobbied the legislature to outlaw racial discrimination at hotels. This was in 1955, seven years after the event.

[205] Rowena J. Miller to Mrs. Guy B. Rose, 20 Sept. 1949, fd 8, box 380, JRCP; also JRC office diary, 29 Nov. 1949: "Pres. Clark read to him [Harold B. Lee] the letter he wrote to Mrs. Rose in New York about the negro question."

[206] *EA* 22:247.

[207] JRC to ElRay L. Christiansen, 30 May 1957, fd 1, box 399, JRCP.

[208] Harold B. Lee diary, 6 May 1945.

[209] JRC office diary, 24 Oct. 1950. For his reference to the Amos and Andy shows, see Bart Andrews and Ahrgus Juilliard, *Holy Mackerel! The Amos 'n' Andy Story* (New York: E.P. Dutton, 1986); Melvin P. Ely, *The Adventures of Amos 'n' Andy: A Social History of an American Phenomenon* (New York: Maxwell Macmillan International, 1991); Salzman, et al., *Encyclopedia of African-American Culture and History,* 1:128.

[210] JRC office diary, 5 Nov. 1941; also *The Salt Lake Temple: A Centennial Book of Remembrance, 1893-1993* (Salt Lake City: The Church of Jesus Christ of Latter-day Saints, 1993), for Chipman and Christensen.

[211] Oliver, *A Negro on Mormonism,* 23 (which inaccurately dated this talk at the University of Utah as occurring "during World War II"); cf. "UN Mediator, Nobel Winner to View 'Peace Prospects,'" *Daily Utah Chronicle,* 25 Apr. 1951, [1]; also Salzman, et al., *Encyclopedia of African-American Culture and History,* for Ralph J. Bunche and Adam Clayton Powell.

Again, at the time I researched the office diaries of JRC and David O. McKay, I did not realize the significance of the visits by Anderson, Bunche, and Powell. Therefore, I overlooked the references in these First Presidency office diaries at the time. However, as the senior executive officers for both the Hotel Utah and the Temple Square Hotel, McKay and Clark had to approve these exceptions to the policy against allowing African Americans to stay there in the 1940s-1950s.

212 "Highest Court Bans School Segregation: Jurists Make Decision Unanimously," *DN*, 17 May 1954, [1]; Benjamin Muse, *Ten Years of Prelude: The Story of Integration Since the Supreme Court's 1954 Decision* (New York: Viking Press, 1964); *EA* 4:634; text of *Brown v. Board of Education* in Cooper, *Black Experience*, 236-38.

213 Draft #3 of JRC talk for general conference (undelivered), 13 Sept. 1954, typescript, 17, fd 5, box 210, JRCP.

214 David O. McKay's instructions to an Arizona stake president (McKay office diary, 25 Feb. 1949). As late as 1967, Fawn McKay Brodie wrote that "bigotry is endemic in the Church" and made the following comment about her uncle: "I know ... something of his private prejudices and would be astonished to see him abandon them at this late date." See Brodie to Stewart L. Udall, 4 Apr. 1967, fd 3, box 209, Udall papers, University of Arizona, quoted in Peterson, "'Do Not Lecture the Brethren,'" 279.

But McKay said whatever he thought his faithful Mormon listener wanted to hear (note 216). In contrast with his 1949 statement, he wrote the following in a 1947 letter to a Mormon who was disturbed about the LDS church's policy: "This is a perplexing question, particularly in the light of the present trend of civilization to grant equality to all men irrespective of race, creed, or color. ... George Washington Carver was one of the noblest souls that ever came to earth. He held a close kinship with his Heavenly Father, and rendered a service to his fellowmen such as few have ever excelled. For every righteous endeavor, for every noble impulse, for every good deed performed in his useful life George Washington Carver will be rewarded, and so will every man [—] be he red, white, black or yellow, for God is no respector of persons." See full text of letter in Llewelyn R. McKay, *Home Memories of President David O. McKay* (Salt Lake City: Deseret Book, 1956), 226-31.

215 Bush, "Mormonism's Negro Doctrine," 39, 43-44. Despite Bush's 1973 publication of the August 1949 statement, this crucial document did not appear in *M* undoubtedly due to sensitivity at LDS headquarters about giving publicity to the church's policy.

216 Bush, "Mormonism's Negro Doctrine," 45-46; Armand L. Mauss, "The Fading of the Pharaoh's Curse: The Decline and Fall of the Priesthood Ban against Blacks in the Mormon Church," *Dial* 24 (Autumn 1981): 11; Sterling M. McMurrin and L. Jackson Newell, *Matters of Conscience: Conversations with Sterling M. McMurrin on Philosophy, Education, and Religion* (Salt Lake City: Signature Books, 1996), 199-201.

I do not doubt the accuracy of McMurrin's accounts of McKay's private statements to him in favor of civil rights for African Americans and against the LDS "policy" of denying priesthood to persons of black African ancestry. President McKay likewise privately gave support to opponents of moving Ricks College from Rexburg, Idaho, at the same time he voted with church councils to move the college. For years he privately encouraged ultra-conservative Apostle Ezra Taft Benson's support of the John Birch Society while at the same time privately endorsing the efforts of his politically liberal counselor Hugh B. Brown to undercut Apostle Benson and attack the Birch Society. See *E*, 66-108. It didn't matter if he was praising Jim Crow laws to an LDS stake president who was a segregationist or speaking in favor of civil rights with a Mormon liberal he liked, President MCKay said whatever he thought his LDS listener would love him for saying, which was the consistency undergirding his contradictory statements. I say this as one who met President McKay and felt love for him, but who discovered this characteristic of his personality by reading historical documents and interviewing LDS administrators.

[217] David O. McKay office diary, 6 Aug. 1952. This paragraph was in a source note of the draft I submitted for review by LDS administrators in 1981.

[218] Tom Cowan and Jack Maguire, *Timelines of African-American History: Five Hundred Years of Black Achievement* (New York: Roundtable/Perigee, 1994), 230; Charles M. Gristian and Sari J. Bennett, *Black Saga: The African American Experience* (Boston: Houghton Mifflin, 1995), 395; Roy Reed, *Faubus: The Life and Times of an American Prodigal* (Fayette: University of Arkansas Press, 1997), 205-32.

[219] JRC office diary, 2 Dec. 1957; also Maureen Ursenbach Beecher, "Relief Society," in *U*, 459.

[220] *E*, 834.

[221] "Give Full Civil Equality to All, LDS Counselor Brown Asks," *SLT*, 7 Oct. 1963, [1]; Hugh B. Brown, "The Fight between Good and Evil," *Improvement Era* 66 (Dec. 1963): 1,058; "Bush, "Mormonism's Negro Doctrine," 44-45; Eugene E. Campbell and Richard D. Poll, *Hugh B. Brown: His Life and Thought* (Salt Lake City: Bookcraft, 1975), 256; Sterling M. McMurrin, "A Note on the 1963 Civil Rights Statement," *Dial* 12 (Summer 1979): 60-63.

[222] Discussion and quotes for notes 37-38, 200-201, 205, 209, 223-224, 262.

[223] JRC to T—— J. P———, 8 Dec. 1941, fd 2, box 365, JRCP.

[224] Draft #3 of JRC talk for general conference (undelivered), 13 Sept. 1954, transcript, 18.

[225] JRC to mission presidents' meeting, 30 Mar. 1960, transcript, April 1960 conference fd, box 169, JRCP.

[226] See discussion and sources for previous notes 6, 37, 224, 225.

[227] James G. Martin and Clyde W. Franklin, *Minority Group Relations* (Columbus, OH: Charles E. Merrill, 1973), 75; Michael W. Williams, ed., *The African American Encyclopedia*, 6 vols. (New York: Marshall Cavendish, 1993), 2:479.

[228] Bennett, "Negro in Utah," 347n52.

[229] JRC to Dr. G. Albin Matson, 12 Apr. 1948, fd 1, box 378, JRCP; also JRC office diary, 9 July 1951.

[230] JRC office diary, 9 June 1949, 9 July 1951.

[231] Rowena J. Miller to O. Boyd Mathias, 3 Mar. 1953, fd 2, box 389, JRCP, in response to Mathias to JRC, 18 Feb. 1953 (same location): "It has been said that you advised members of the Church of Jesus Christ of Latter-day Saints to refuse blood transfusions from people with Negro ancestry. Is that correct?"; also quoted in *E*, 839.

[232] Mark E. Petersen to "The First Presidency," 16 Nov. 1959, with attached

clipping: "Blood Expert Says Transfusion between Races May Be Perilous"; also David O. McKay and JRC to Petersen, 11 Dec. 1959, both in Petersen fd, CR 1/45, LDSA.

233 JRC to Dr. G. Albin Matson, 22 July 1954, fd 7, box 391, JRCP.

234 Correspondence between JRC and Matson in boxes 295, 378, 391, and 406, JRCP; G. Albin Matson, *The Distribution of the Four Blood Groups among the Ute Indians of Utah* (Salt Lake City: Utah Academy, 1947) was the publication that brought the author to Clark's attention.

235 JRC memorandum, 29 Nov. 1960, "Negro" fd, box 295, JRCP, which folder also contains G. Albin Matson to JRC, 20 Oct. 1958, with JRC's reply on 7 Nov.

236 JRC to Dr. G. Albin Matson, 19 Jan. 1959, "Negro" fd, box 295, JRCP.

237 The previous discussion had been on 26 August 1908. See excerpts from minutes of First Presidency and Quorum of Twelve meetings in fd 7, box 78, Smith Family papers; in fd 15, box 5, Marquardt papers; and (restricted access) the Adam S. Bennion papers, HBLL. See note 198.

238 JRC office diary, 18 Aug. 1939. For Apostle George F. Richards as Acting Patriarch to the Church from 1937 to 1942, see *E*, 51-52, 129, 684-85.

239 Minutes of council meeting, Salt Lake temple, 25 Jan. 1940, fd 7, box 78, Smith Family papers, emphasis added; also in fd 15, box 5, Marquardt papers.

240 JRC office diary, 19 Mar. 1960.

241 JRC office diary, 27 Feb. 1940; Jenson, *Latter-day Saint Biographical Encyclopedia,* 4:380.

242 Quoted in "Editor's Note," *Look*, 22 Oct. 1963, [unnumbered page 78 or 80], reporting Apostle Smith's statements to managing editor William B. Arthur during the previous summer "at his office in the Mormon Church's office building in Salt Lake City." Bush, "Writing 'Mormonism's Negro Doctrine,'" 268, paraphrased this and called it "a notorious Joseph Fielding Smith quotation." Like other white Americans raised in the nineteenth century, Apostle Smith still regarded "darkies" an affectionate reference to Negroes. However, see Franklin and Moss, *From Slavery to Freedom,* 296, for the fact that African Americans considered this insulting.

243 Temple meeting of 28 Aug. 1947, typescript minutes in fd 7, box 78, Smith Family papers; in fd 15, box 5, Marquardt papers; cited in Bush, "Mormonism's Negro doctrine," 66n184; and (restricted access) Adam S. Bennion papers, HBLL. See note 198.

244 Tragen, "Statutory Prohibitions against Interracial Marriage" (1944), 274n26, for one-fourth Negro ancestry in Alabama, Maryland, North Carolina, Tennessee, and West Virginia (also Oregon), one-eighth in Florida and Mississippi (also Indiana, Nebraska, and North Dakota), and one-sixteenth in Virginia; Sickels, *Race, Marriage, and the Law,* 71, for Georgia's definition of a great-great-grandparent (one-sixteenth) as the legal test.

245 Temple council meeting, 9 Oct. 1947, quoted in part in Bush, "Mormonism's Negro Doctrine," 41, emphasis added.

246 JRC to mission presidents' meeting, 30 Mar. 1960.

Monroe H. Fleming was one of the Hotel Utah's waiters who served meals to LDS missionaries during their week-long orientation in Salt Lake City. As a missionary in September 1963, I listened to Fleming give a spontaneous testimony of the LDS gospel in the hotel's dining room where he told us not to worry about the priesthood restriction that was upon his race. See "LDS Leader Eulogizes Former Black Busboy," *Standard-Examiner* [Ogden, UT], 6 Aug. 1982, included in "Journal History of the Church," 5 Aug. 1982, 1, with the article's statement: "Fleming and men like him, were often criticized as 'Uncle Toms' by blacks who felt betrayed by the Mormon policy." For views similar to Fleming's, see Carey C. Bowles, *A Mormon Negro Views the Church* (Newark, NJ: By the author, 1968). In 1967 I arranged for Fleming to speak to my BYU ward.

[247] "Saint without Priesthood: The Collected Testimonies of Ex-Slave Samuel D. Chambers," *Dial* 12 (Summer 1979): 13-21; William G. Hartley, "Samuel D. and Amanda Chambers," *New Era* 4 (June 1974): 46, reprinted in *Celebrating the LDS Past: Essays Commemorating the 20th Anniversary of the 1972 Founding of the LDS Church Historical Department's "History Division"* (Provo, UT: Joseph Fielding Smith Institute for Church History, Brigham Young University, 1992), 79.

[248] JRC memorandum, "The Afrikan Branches of the Church of Jesus Christ of Latter-day Saints," undated, box 207, JRCP.

[249] Joseph Fielding Smith (on behalf of the Quorum of Twelve) to "President David O. McKay and Counselors," 30 Mar. 1955, Joseph Fielding Smith fd, CR 1/46.

[250] Jessie L. Embry, *Black Saints in a White Church: Contemporary African American Mormons* (Salt Lake City: Signature Books, 1994), 182; Sheri L. Dew, *Go Forward With Faith: The Biography of Gordon B. Hinckley* (Salt Lake City: Deseret Book, 1996), 296.

[251] Arrington and Swinton, *The Hotel: Salt Lake's Classy Lady,* 97.

[252] JRC to "Brother and Sister" Reynold Irwin, 2 Mar. 1956, fd 2, box 397, JRCP.

[253] David O. McKay office diary, 17 Jan. 1954; also Farrell Ray Monson, "History of the South African Mission of the Church of Jesus Christ of Latter-day Saints, 1853-1970," M.A. thesis, Brigham Young University, 1971, 45-46; A. Hamer Reiser oral history, 1974, typescript, vol. 2:165-69, LDSA; James B. Allen, "David O. McKay," in Leonard J. Arrington, ed., *The Presidents of the Church: Biographical Essays* (Salt Lake City: Deseret Book, 1986), 305.

[254] David O. McKay office diary, 17 Jan. 1954.

[255] JRC memorandum, 29 Nov. 1960 (quote).

[256] David O. McKay office diary, 25 Feb. 1954.

[257] Harold B. Lee diary, 25 Feb. 1954.

[258] Mary Lythgoe Bradford, *Lowell L. Bennion: Teacher, Counselor, Humanitarian* (Salt Lake City: Dialogue Foundation, 1995), 165 (quotes), 166 (outcome); Paul V. Hyer, "Temple Sealings," in *EM* 3:1289.

[259] Draft #3 of JRC talk for general conference (undelivered), 13 Sept. 1954, typescript, 16-17.

[260] See discussion in previous notes 214-217 and for notes 250-251.

[261] JRC memorandum, 18 May 1956, fd 4, box 395, JRCP.

[262] Remarks of F— A. T—— and JRC to mission presidents' meeting, 30 Mar. 1960, transcript (statement about interracial marriage).

[263] JRC memorandum, "The Afrikan Branches," numbered para. 8 (quote); also JRC to Hugh C. Smith, 6 May 1960, fd 13, box 409, JRCP.

[264] Margaret Judy Maag, "Discrimination against the Negro in Utah and Institutional Efforts to Eliminate It," M.S. thesis, University of Utah, 1971, 34.

[265] Text and provisions of the Civil Rights Act of 1964 in Cooper, *Black Experience*, 254-55; *EA* 6:778-79. It would be an overstatement to say Utah's racial discrimination ended at a certain date. See "Stepping Back? The Racial Situation in Utah's Homogenous Culture Today Is Threatening to Minorities," *DN*, 23 Feb. 1997, B-1; "Utah Is Unwelcoming to Blacks, NAACP Says," *DN*, 10 Dec. 2000, B-4.

[266] Warren Calvin ("Trey") Lathe III to D. Michael Quinn, 30 Nov. 1999. Trey is a convert and returned missionary with a Ph.D. in molecular biology.

[267] "LDS Church Extends Priesthood to All Worthy Male Members," *DN*, 9 June 1978, [1]; "Priesthood of LDS Opened to Blacks," *SLT*, 10 June 1978, A-1; also photograph of "Joseph Freeman, Jr., the first black to receive the priesthood following President Kimball's 1978 revelation," in Richard O. Cowan, *The Church in the Twentieth Century* (Salt Lake City: Bookcraft, 1985), 392.

For the administrative processes which preceded this, see Mark L. Grover, "The Mormon Priesthood Revelation and the Sao Paulo, Brazil Temple," *Dial* 23 (Spring 1990): 39-53; Francis M. Gibbons, *Spencer W. Kimball: Resolute Disciple, Prophet of God* (Salt Lake City: Deseret Book, 1995), 238-39, 292-96; *E*, 14-17; also Mary Lou McNamara, "Secularization or Sacralization: The Change in LDS Church Policy on Blacks," in Marie Cornwall, Tim B. Heaton, and Lawrence A. Young, eds., *Contemporary Mormonism: Social Science Perspectives* (Urbana: University of Illinois Press, 1994), 310-25.

[268] Spencer W. Kimball's notation on front of draft #3 of JRC talk for general conference (undelivered), 13 Sept. 1954.

[269] *Conf,* 1937, 105.

[270] JRC to Spencer W. Kimball, undated response to Kimball's letter of 4 Aug. 1943, fd 2, box 367, JRCP.

[271] JRC, *Public Loans to Foreign Countries* (Salt Lake City: Deseret News Press, 1945), 20; quoted in Edwin Brown Firmage and Christopher L. Blakesley, "J. Reuben Clark, Jr., Law and International Order," *BYU Studies* 13 (Spring 1973): 301-02; partly quoted in *C*, 588. While said in the context of U.S. government issues, it also expressed Clark's view about LDS policies and missionary work. See also Sterling M. McMurrin, "Problems in Universalizing Mormonism," *Sunstone* 4 (Dec. 1979): 14-17; Lamond Tullis, "The Church Moves outside the United States," and Jiro Numano, "How International Is the Church in Japan?" *Dial* 13 (Spring 1980): 67-70, 87; Murray Boren, "Worship through Music: Nigerian Style," *Sunstone* 10 (May 1985): 64-65; Michael Hicks, *Mormonism and Music: A History* (Urbana: University of Illinois Press, 1989), 221-22; David Martin, *Tongues of Fire: The Explosion of Protestantism in Latin America* (Oxford, Eng.: Basil Black-

wood, 1990), 208-09; Marjorie Newton, "'Almost Like Us': The American So-
cialization of Australian Converts," *Dial* 24 (Fall 1991): 9-20; David Knowlton,
"Thoughts on Mormonism in Latin America," *Dial* 25 (Summer 1992): 42-43;
Knowlton, "'Gringo Jeringo': Anglo-Mormon Missionary Culture in Bolivia," in
Cornwall, Heaton, and Young, *Contemporary Mormonism*, 227-28, 231; James B.
Allen, "On Becoming a Universal Church: Some Historical Perspectives," *Dial*
25 (Spring/Mar. 1992): 14 ("a kind of cultural imperialism").

[272] JRC to missionary meeting, 6 Apr. 1956, transcript, 3, box 151, JRCP.

[273] See *Webster's New World Dictionary of the American Language* for *wop* as
slang for "an Italian or a person of Italian descent; an offensive term of hostility
and contempt."

[274] See quotes and discussion for previous notes 51, 75-76, 78-79, 81, 157,
158, 161.

[275] JRC office diary, 30 Nov. 1953; *Deseret News 1999-2000 Church Almanac*
(Salt Lake City: Deseret News, 1998), 507.

[276] *Conf,* Oct. 1954, 78; Apr. 1969, 92; cf. Oct. 1968, 83.

[277] *Conf,* Apr. 1958, 88; *Deseret News 1999-2000 Church Almanac,* 508.

[278] While not commenting specifically about racial views, *C,* 604, noted:
"Some of these contradictions were not personal—they were aspects of the clash
between the nineteenth and twentieth centuries."

NOTES TO CHAPTER 11

[1] The Book of Mormon, Hel 12:2.

[2] JRC to Alvin S. Nelson, 19 June 1942, fd 2, box 365, JRCP.

[3] Clarkana's presentation copy of a Paul Bailey novel is excluded from consideration here.

[4] JRC to Avard Fairbanks, 18 June 1952, fd 13, box 385, JRCP.

[5] Clarkana.

[6] Information supplied by JRC children.

[7] Joshua R. Clark diary, 26 Dec. 1884, JRCP.

[8] Clarkana.

[9] *Hale's Longer English Poems* (1892), in Clarkana.

[10] The details of this letter are now missing from my research notes.

[11] Edward Fitzgerald's translation of the *Rubaiyat of Omar Khayyam* (1952), in
Clarkana.

[12] Bartlett's *Familiar Quotations* (1945), in Clarkana.

[13] JRC to LaRue Sneff, 28 Dec. 1957, fd 5, box 399, JRCP.

[14] Jay Rubark, *pseud.* [JRC], "When I Would Pass," *Relief Society Magazine* 28
(June 1941): 375; also cablegrams with sender's and receiver's addresses of
RUBARK (1913-23) in JRCP.

[15] "A Hymn to the Seed of Ephraim and Manasseh," *CN,* 5 Jan. 1946, 4; "Inspiring Music by MIA Chorus Thrills Throng," *CN,* 25 June 1950, 12, referring
to the Mutual Improvement Associations for LDS youth.

[16] JRC, "Give Me the Cloudless Day," box 235, JRCP.

¹⁷ JRC to Lute, 28 Aug. 1913, box 330, JRCP, emphasis in original.

¹⁸ Lute to JRC, 4 Sept. 1913, box 330, JRCP.

¹⁹ Luacine S. Clark, "Our Christmas," *Young Woman's Journal* 24 (Dec. 1913); with no other entries in this magazine's index at LDSL.

²⁰ Information supplied by her children. There are no author indices for stories in the *Children's Friend,* and the table of contents for each issue lists only titles, not authors. I therefore simply accepted her children's statement that Lute published stories in this periodical.

²¹ JRC to J. Reuben Clark III and his wife Emily, 6 Aug. 1953, fd 5, box 388, JRCP; also etchings in JRCP.

²² JRC to G. Stanley McAllister, 21 Oct. 1957, fd 3, box 400, JRCP.

²³ Richard L. Jensen, *The Mormon Years of the Borglum Family* (Salt Lake City: History Division, Historical Department, The Church of Jesus Christ of Latter-day Saints, 1979); Howard Shaff and Audrey Karl Shaff, *Six Wars at a Time: The Life and Times of Gutzon Borglum, Sculptor of Mount Rushmore* (Sioux Falls, SD: Center for Western Studies, Augustana College, 1985).

²⁴ JRC office diary, 18 Feb. 1944, JRCP; also *C,* 555, for Elizabeth Lewis Cabot as the wife of Ambassador Clark's protocol officer John M. Cabot in the Mexican embassy. Clark did not indicate whether his "illustrative" example of the Boston Brahmin's "wall hangings" referred simply to "drapes" or to tapestries.

²⁵ JRC office diary, 27 Jan. 1945.

²⁶ Georgius Young Cannon oral history, 1973, typescript, 16, LDSA.

²⁷ JRC remarks to Wilford Stake priesthood meeting, Monday, 16 Jan. 1956, at Grandview Ward meeting house, transcript, JRCP, emphasis in original.

²⁸ The only concert reference I found before 1931 was in JRC's personal diary, 30 Apr. 1922, JRCP, which recorded his attendance at the Brooklyn Academy of Music for a performance by singer Emma Lucy Gates Bowen. This demonstrated support for a Mormon and friend rather than interest in music itself. She was married to his Utah law partner, Albert E. Bowen; also Carol Cornwall Madsen, "Emma Lucy Gates Bowen," in *U,* 49-50.

²⁹ Luacine S. Clark diary, 25 Jan. 1931, JRCP.

³⁰ JRC to Louise Clark Bennion, 28 Jan. 1931, box 336, JRCP.

³¹ Luacine S. Clark diary, 1 Feb. 1931.

³² JRC to Lute, 30 Sept. 1931, JRCP.

³³ For example, JRC to Thorpe B. Isaacson, 8 Nov. 1950, JRCP.

³⁴ JRC to Adam S. Bennion, 5 Nov. 1946, fd 2, box 373, JRCP. Conrad B. Harrison, *Five Thousand Concerts: A Commemorative History of the Utah Symphony* (Salt Lake City: Utah Symphony Society, 1986), 123-24, credited Clark with providing the Salt Lake Tabernacle essentially free-of-charge for symphony rehearsals and performances "late in September of 1946." This continued until Salt Lake City constructed a concert hall in the 1980s. In view of the counselor's negative attitude about the symphony, it was probably President George Albert Smith's idea, communicated to the symphony by Reuben.

³⁵ Harold B. Lee diary, 7 Feb. 1949, private possession.

[36] Marian Robertson Wilson, *Leroy Robertson: Music Giant from the Rockies* (Salt Lake City: Blue Ribbon Publications, 1996), 270.

[37] Michael Hicks, *Mormonism and Music: A History* (Urbana: University of Illinois Press, 1989), 178.

[38] JRC to bishops' meeting, 7 Apr. 1950, transcript in April 1950 conference fd, box 160, JRCP.

[39] JRC, "Home, and the Building of Home Life," *Relief Society Magazine* 39 (Dec. 1952): 792. These references to "jungle" and "voodoo huts" reflect his view of black Africans and African Americans. See chapter 10.

[40] For example, Henry D. Moyle diary, 6 Aug. 1951, LDSA; Harold B. Lee diary, 6 Aug. 1951; Marion G. Romney diary, 19 Dec. 1954, 2 Nov. 1959, private possession.

[41] Henry D. Moyle diary, 31 Aug. 1953.

[42] *EA* 28:17.

[43] JRC to Leopold Stokowski, 28 Apr. 1933, box 349, JRCP.

[44] JRC to Richard L. Evans, 18 May 1936, fd 1, box 355, JRCP; also Roger L. Miller, "Mormon Tabernacle Choir," in *U*, 379. Historically "Cossacks" refers to ethnic and military groups of Russia, but Reuben was referring to a Russian singing group of the mid-1930s.

[45] JRC to Florence Jepperson Madsen and Alberta Huish Christensen, 1 Nov. 1956, fd 18, box 396, JRCP. For Madsen, see Ralph B. Simmons, ed., *Utah's Distinguished Personalities: A Biographical Directory of Eminent Contemporaneous Men and Women Who Are the Faithful Builders and Defenders of the State* (Salt Lake City: Personality Publishing, 1933), 141; "Dr. Florence Jepperson Madsen: Her Fascinating Life Story," *Millennial Star* 123 (Mar. 1961): 104–09; Jill Mulvay Derr, Janath Russell Cannon, and Maureen Ursenbach Beecher, *Women of Covenant: The Story of Relief Society* (Salt Lake City: Deseret Book, 1992), 41.

[46] JRC office diary, 18 Feb. 1934; also Miller, "Mormon Tabernacle Choir," 379-80.

[47] JRC to Ernest L. Wilkinson, 12 May 1952, fd 1, box 16, Wilkinson papers, HBLL.

[48] Ernest L. Wilkinson diary, 3 June 1959, photocopy, JWML.

[49] Marion G. Romney diary, 19 Dec. 1954.

[50] JRC to Ernest L. Wilkinson, 12 May 1952 (with follow-up letter of Gerrit de Jong Jr. to Wilkinson on 23 May, with the exact title of the Bruckner composition), both in fd 1, box 16, Wilkinson papers.

[51] JRC to Ernest L. Wilkinson, 8 Aug. 1952, fd 1, box 16, Wilkinson papers.

[52] Ernest L. Wilkinson diary, 3 June 1959; also Gerald S. Argetsinger, "Cumorah Pageant," and Michael D. Hicks, "Music," in *EM* 1:347, 2:974.

[53] Ernest L. Wilkinson diary, 7 Sept. 1960; also Miller, "Mormon Tabernacle Choir," 380.

[54] JRC to Joseph J. Cannon, 28 Jan. 1936, fd 1, box 355, JRCP.

[55] JRC office diary, 3 Mar. 1943. From 1938 to 1953, Richard L. Evans was one of the Seventy's presidents, but he much preferred his other role as speaker for the Sunday morning broadcast of the Tabernacle Choir. Heber J. Grant wrote: "I

then called Richard L. Evans to come to my office, and told him of his selection to be one of the Seven Presidents of the Seventies. I could see that he was very much disappointed." The president added, "He said he told his brother [that] the one and only place of authority in all the Church that he hoped he would never be called to fill is one of the Seven Presidents of the Seventies" (Grant journal sheets, 6 Oct. 1938, LDSA). In addition, Richard L. Evans Jr., *Richard L. Evans: The Man and the Message* (Salt Lake City: Bookcraft, 1973), 47, noted, "His wife says she never saw him so depressed and forlorn as during the several days after this call came from President Grant."

⁵⁶ JRC to Richard L. and Alice Evans, 26 Dec. 1955, fd 6, box 393, JRCP.

⁵⁷ JRC office diary, 29 Nov. 1944; also Miller, "Mormon Tabernacle Choir," 379.

⁵⁸ Heber J. Grant journal sheets, 23 Feb. 1936.

⁵⁹ Alexander Schreiner to Heber J. Grant and counselors, 14 July 1926, box 43, CR 1/44, LDSA; Schreiner to the First Presidency, 14 May 1930, in Schreiner fd, CR 1/45, LDSA, emphasis in original.

⁶⁰ Alexander Schreiner fd, CR 1/45; Heber J. Grant journal sheets, 11, 17-18 July 1933, 23 Feb. 1936, 28 June, 26 Aug. 1938.

⁶¹ JRC office diary, 3 Feb., 3 May 1939.

⁶² Heber J. Grant journal sheets, 15 May 1939.

⁶³ JRC office diary, 22 June 1939, emphasis in original. Grant had a similar experience with Schreiner nine years earlier: "I have a fairly good memory, but if I ever made you a promise in July 1926, such as you refer to, it has entirely failed me in this instance. It is only fair to say to you that the exact opposite is my understanding of what happened in July 1926. I usually record promises that I make, and my journal shows no such promise to you. ... I do not know how in the world I could make language any plainer, my dear Brother Schreiner, than that Brother Kimball was entitled to and would have his position back [as Tabernacle organist] when he returned from his mission" (Grant to Schreiner, 16 Sept. 1930, in CR 1/45).

⁶⁴ JRC office diary, 23 June, 18 July 1939, emphasis in original.

⁶⁵ JRC office diary, 7 Feb. 1949.

⁶⁶ *Conf,* Apr. 1965, 102.

⁶⁷ *Alexander Schreiner Reminisces* (Salt Lake City: Publishers Press, 1984), index, which did list Heber J. Grant and Charles W. Nibley (JRC's predecessor as counselor).

⁶⁸ Hicks, *Mormonism and Music,* 178-79; also "Message in 'Trilogy': Robertson Believes Spiritual Theme Responsible for Recognition Given His Now Famous Work," *DN,* 8 Nov. 1947, "Magazine" section, 2.

⁶⁹ Harold B. Lee diary, 10 June 1947.

⁷⁰ JRC office diary, 3 Feb. 1940; also Eugene F. Fairbanks, *A Sculptor's Testimony in Bronze and Stone: The Sacred Sculpture of Avard T. Fairbanks,* rev. ed. (Salt Lake City: Publishers Press, 1994).

⁷¹ James V. D'Arc, "The Saints on Celluloid: The Making of the Movie *Brigham Young," Sunstone* 1 (Fall 1976):11-28; Heber J. Grant journal sheets, 11

Sept. 1939; also Joseph M. Flora, "Vardis Fisher and the Mormons," *Dial* 4 (Autumn 1969): 48-55; William O. Nelson, "Anti-Mormon Publications," in *EM* 1:50.

[72] Heber J. Grant journal sheets, 27 Oct. 1939; JRC to Jason S. Joy, 31 Oct. 1939, fd 5, box 361, JRCP.

[73] James Vincent D'Arc, "Two Articles: 'Darryl F. Zanuck's *Brigham Young:* A Film in Context,' and 'So Let It Be Written ...': The Creation of Cecil B. DeMille's Autobiography," Ph.D. diss., Brigham Young University, 1986, 44.

[74] Heber J. Grant journal sheets, 13 Aug. 1940; "Church Officials See 'Brigham Young': President Grant Endorses Film Heartily after Private Screening," *DN*, 13 Aug. 1940, [13]; James V. D'Arc, "Darryl F. Zanuck's *Brigham Young:* A Film in Context," *BYU Studies* 29 (Winter 1989): 17.

[75] JRC office diary, 14 Aug. 1940.

[76] JRC to Lowell Thomas, 3, 13 Jan. 1953, fd 12, box 389, JRCP.

[77] JRC ranch diary, 16 Nov. 1955, JRCP; JRC to Robert R. Mullen, 5 Dec. 1955, fd 16, box 393, JRCP.

[78] JRC to Cecil B. DeMille, 16 Aug. 1956, marked "Not sent," box 255, JRCP; also JRC to John Krier, 29 Aug. 1956, fd 21, box 396, JRCP.

[79] JRC to John O. Denman, 24 Aug. 1957, fd 15, box 400, JRCP.

[80] JRC home diary, 26 Apr. 1958, JRCP.

[81] "Pres. Clark's Address at Conference," *CN*, 20 June 1953, 4; *SR*, 156.

NOTES TO CHAPTER 12

[1] The Book of Mormon, Al 60:9

[2] "Elder Lee Pays Tribute to a Great Leader," *CN*, 14 Oct. 1961, 41. Technically "Welfare Plan" emphasized the philosophy of this LDS activity, while "Welfare Program" emphasized its organization and conduct, but the terms were used interchangeably.

[3] *D&C* 49:20.

[4] See also *D&C*, 1981 ed., s.v. "consecration" and "equal" in index; *B*, 15-19.

[5] *Conf*, Oct. 1942, 55.

[6] Lyndon W. Cook, *Joseph Smith and The Law of Consecration* (Provo, UT: Grandin Book, 1985), 8-10; *P*, 22-23.

[7] *B*, 25-26, 366-71; Joseph Smith Jr., et al., 7 vols., *History of the Church of Jesus Christ of Latter-day Saints*, 2d rev., B. H. Roberts, ed. (Salt Lake City: Deseret Book, 1960), 1:365-67.

[8] *P*, 24-27.

[9] *B*, 31-38; *P*, 31, 36.

[10] Jill Mulvay Derr, Janath Russell Cannon, and Maureen Ursenbach Beecher, *Women of Covenant: The Story of Relief Society* (Salt Lake City: Deseret Book, 1992), 1-2, 27-35, quote on 30; also Smith, et al., *History of the Church*, 4:567-68.

[11] *P*, 44.

[12] *J* 11:297 (B. Young/1867); quoted in *B*, 59.

[13] *P*, 55 (first quote), 56 (second quote).

[14] Leonard J. Arrington, *Great Basin Kingdom: An Economic History of the Latter-day Saints, 1830-1900* (Cambridge, MA: Harvard University Press, 1958), 108-334; *B*, 59-61; *P,* 57-71.

[15] *B*, 265-93, 309-10, quote from Orderville minutes on 269; also Arrington, *Great Basin Kingdom,* 330-37 ("four kinds of United Orders" in Utah).

[16] Brigham H. Roberts, *A Comprehensive History of the Church* ... 6 vols. (Salt Lake City: The Church of Jesus Christ of Latter-day Saints, 1930), 5:487.

[17] *Conf,* Oct. 1942, 55; JRC, "Private Ownership under the United Order and the Guarantees of the Constitution," *Improvement Era* 45 (Nov. 1942): 688 (first set of quotes), 689 (second quote).

[18] JRC to Frank W. Wylie, 29 Apr. 1948, fd 13, box 378, JRCP. In addition to Clark's familiarity with the 1930 *Comprehensive History of the Church* description of "communistic" United Orders in Utah, Clarkana has Edward Jones Allen, *The Second United Order among the Mormons* (New York: Columbia University Press; London: P.S. King, 1936).

[19] Leonard J. Arrington and Thomas G. Alexander, *A Dependent Commonwealth: Utah's Economy from Statehood to the Great Depression,* ed. Dean May (Provo, UT: Brigham Young University Press, 1974), esp. 86; Leonard J. Arrington, "Utah and the Depression of the 1890s," *UHQ* 29 (Jan. 1961): 3-18, esp. 6; *P,* 72-73.

[20] James B. Allen and Glen M. Leonard, *The Story of the Latter-day Saints,* 2d ed., rev., enl. (Salt Lake City: Deseret Book, 1992), 455; Bruce D. Blumell, "Welfare before Welfare: Twentieth-century LDS Church Charity before the Great Depression," *JMH* 6 (1980): 90-91; *P,* 77-78.

[21] Blumell, "Welfare before Welfare," 91, 93, 104; *P,* 78, 79, 81, 82-87, 90; Derr, et al., *Women of Covenant,* 251, 254.

[22] *T,* 87 (quote), with full discussion on 82-92.

[23] Arrington and Alexander, *Dependent Commonwealth,* 57-86; *B,* 338; *P,* 94.

[24] *P,* 94 (national rate), 96 (Salt Lake City), 109 (quote).

[25] John F. Bluth and Wayne K. Hinton, "The Great Depression," in Richard D. Poll et al., *Utah's History* (Provo, UT: Brigham Young University Press, 1978), 481-96; Hinton, "The Economics of Ambivalence: Utah's Depression Experience," *UHQ* 54 (Summer 1986): 268-85; John S. McCormick, "The Great Depression," in *U,* 136.

[26] *P,* 125-26.

[27] William E. Leuchtenburg, *Franklin D. Roosevelt and the New Deal, 1932-1940* (New York: Harper and Row, 1963), 125-28, 129, 133-34, 174; Lester V. Chandler, *America's Greatest Depression, 1929-1941* (New York: Harper & Row, 1970), 193-94, 197-98, 202-03, 206-07.

[28] *B,* 341-42; *H,* 93-102; *P,* 106-09; Glen L. Rudd, *Pure Religion: The Story of Church Welfare Since 1930* (Salt Lake City: The Church of Jesus Christ of Latter-day Saints, 1995), 7 (70 percent unemployment), 10-22, 32-33; forthcoming BYU master's thesis on the Welfare Program by Joseph Darowski; also references in Heber J. Grant journal sheets, 1, 16 June 1932, 3 Jan. 1933, LDSA.

[29] *P,* 110-12, 117.

588 • *Notes to Chapter 12*

30 Harold B. Lee, Charles S. Hyde, and Paul C. Child (Pioneer Stake presidency) to Heber J. Grant and Counselors, 23 May 1933, binder 1, box 196, JRCP.

31 Blumell, "Welfare before Welfare," 104; *P,* 90.

32 See previous note 21.

33 *P,* 112.

34 For the term, see "42,000 Salt Lake Mormons on WPA, Despite 'Dole' Fight," *New York Daily News,* 21 June 1938, 8; JRC to Golden R. Buchanan, 8 May 1943; Harold B. Lee diary, 3 Sept. 1957, quoted in *L,* 297.

35 *Conf,* Apr. 1933, 103.

36 JRC office diary, 15 May 1933 (Lee's orientation), 16 May 1933 (proposed statement), JRCP.

37 JRC notes for talk, 19 June 1933, binder 1, box 196, JRCP; summarized in "Annual Chest Meeting Held," *SLT,* 20 June 1933, 16; also Abraham Hoffman, *Unwanted Americans in the Great Depression: Repatriation Pressures, 1929-39* (Tucson: University of Arizona Press, 1974); Francisco E. Balderrama, *Decade of Betrayal: Mexican Repatriation in the 1930s* (Albuquerque: University of New Mexico Press, 1995).

38 JRC office diary, 19 June 1933.

39 JRC office diary, 8 Aug. 1933.

40 JRC office diary, 28 June 1933.

41 JRC office diary, 30 June 1933. There is an illegible word and stray dash in the original, both of which I ignored.

42 JRC draft of "Suggestive Directions," 30 June 1933, and his notation on the printed pamphlet in binder 1, box 196, JRCP, emphasis in original.

43 "Pres. Clark Dedicates New Timpanogos Storehouse," *CN,* 21 Sept. 1957, 4.

44 *P,* 122.

45 JRC remarks to North Utah Welfare Region, 22 June 1944, transcript, box 228, JRCP.

46 Sylvester Q. Cannon diary, annual summary for 31 Dec. 1933, LDSA.

47 JRC, *Some Factors of a Now-Planned Post-War Governmental and Economic Pattern* (Salt Lake City: Deseret News Press, 1943), 5, published in full in *Commercial & Financial Chronicle,* 25 Nov. 1943; also JRC talk for Constitution Day, 17 Sept. 1946, given over LDS radio station KSL, summarized in "Pres. Clark Warns of Plot to Wreck U.S.," *DN,* 18 Sept. 1946, 1 (quoted phrase), published in full in *Commercial & Financial Chronicle,* 3 Oct. 1946, in "Common Law Government in U.S. Endangered," *CN,* 21 Sept. 1946, 2, and JRC, *Inroads upon the Constitution by the Roman Law: A Constitution Day Address by President J. Reuben Clark, Jr. (September 17, 1946)* (Salt Lake City: Deseret News Press, 1946), 5; also *SA,* 143-44, 191, 195, 232-33, 235, 245, 246, 253-54, 488, 491, 522, 543-44.

In 1946 JRC named only one "alphabetical bureau"—the OPA (Office of Price Administration), which President Roosevelt established in 1941. See *EA* 20:649 (OPA); *DA,* 30, 225 ("alphabet agencies"); also "OPA Official Praises Foresight of Church," *CN,* 20 Feb. 1943, 4.

48 Heber J. Grant journal sheets, 20 July 1933.

⁴⁹ JRC draft of "Suggestive Outlines," 15 July 1933, with emendation dated 17 July 1933, in binder 1, box 196, JRCP; cf. JRC draft of "Suggestive Directions," 30 June 1933, emphasis added.

⁵⁰ Marion G. Romney oral history, 1976, typescript, 3, LDSA.

⁵¹ JRC office diary, 8 Aug. 1933.

⁵² JRC memorandum of meeting with Franklin D. Roosevelt, 25 Sept. 1933, fd 2, box 350, JRCP.

⁵³ Heber J. Grant journal sheets, 9 June 1932.

⁵⁴ Heber J. Grant journal sheets, 16 June 1932.

⁵⁵ JRC office diary, 9, 18, 22 Aug. 1933, for preliminary references; also quotes cited in note 57.

⁵⁶ Harold B. Lee, Charles S. Hyde, and Paul C. Child (Pioneer Stake presidency) to Heber J. Grant and Counselors, 23 May 1933, with draft of First Presidency letter, binder 1, box 169, JRCP.

⁵⁷ JRC draft of First Presidency letter, 26 Aug. 1933, with carbons of mailed letter, 28 Aug., all in binder 1, box 169, JRCP. *M* 5:330-36 includes the letter and instructions for the survey but incorrectly dates it as July 1933.

⁵⁸ Sylvester Q. Cannon to Wilford A. Beesley, 4 Oct. 1933, in binder 1, box 196, JRCP.

⁵⁹ Marion G. Romney 1976 oral history, 3, said that publication occurred on 23 Oct. 1933, but two years later, JRC's secretary reported that Deseret News Press records indicated that printing commenced on 27 Oct.; also see VaLois South to JRC, 18 Oct. 1935 and JRC notations on the printed pamphlet, both in binder 1, box 196, JRCP.

⁶⁰ *P,* 122-23.

⁶¹ JRC to Sylvester Q. Cannon, 9 Nov. 1933; also JRC to Heber J. Grant, 9 Nov. 1933, both in binder 1, box 196, JRCP. Regarding the New Deal "seriously undermining our moral and spiritual stamina," Clarkana has F. A. Harper, *Morals and the Welfare State* (Irvington-on-Hudson, NY: Foundation for Economic Education, 1951).

⁶² Minutes of meeting of the Presiding Bishopric with First Presidency, 27 Nov. 1933, quoted in Bruce D. Blumell, "'Remember the Poor': A History of Welfare in the Church of Jesus Christ of Latter-day Saints, 1830-1980," 112 (unpublished paper dated April 1981, Joseph Fielding Smith Institute of Church History, Brigham Young University, Provo, Utah). Curiously *P,* 123, 290n89, made changes in this quote and cited my 1983 book as their source instead of the original citation given by one of the authors.

⁶³ *Care of the Poor* (Salt Lake City: Presiding Bishopric, 1934), 1, 12.

⁶⁴ *Conf,* Oct. 1934, 97, 99.

⁶⁵ JRC to "Brother and Sister Richard M. Robinson," 28 Oct. 1934, fd 1, box 351, JRCP. His best-known published statements about its philosophy are *Church Welfare Plan: A Discussion ... at Estes Park, Colorado, June 20, 1939* (Salt Lake City: General Church Welfare Committee, 1939) and *Fundamentals of the Church Welfare Plan* (Salt Lake City: General Church Welfare Committee, 1944).

⁶⁶ JRC to Golden R. Buchanan, 8 May 1943, fd 1, box 367, JRCP. Clarkana

has Paul L. Poirot, *The Pension Idea* (Irvington-on-Hudson, NY: Foundation for Economic Education, 1950).

[67] *E*, 671 (summary of McKay's lifelong Republican activities); also *DM*, 316, 375.

[68] Blumell, "Remember the Poor," 117. This statement did not appear in the corresponding discussion of *P*, 123-30.

[69] JRC to Heber J. Grant, 1 Mar. 1935, CR 1/48, LDSA; JRC draft of First Presidency's message for 5 Apr. 1935 (marked "not announced"), binder 2, box 196, JRCP.

[70] Heber J. Grant journal sheets, 7 Apr. 1935.

[71] David O. McKay to JRC, 6 May 1935, fd 7, box 353, JRCP.

[72] For general principle, see Robert E. Quinn, "Common Consent," in *EM* 1:297-99; for examples of reversals by general authorities after negative votes by conferences, see *O*, 163; *E*, 768, 793.

[73] JRC to David O. McKay, 11 May 1935, fd 7, box 353, JRCP.

[74] *M* 6:10 (conducting survey); with description of its findings in Leonard J. Arrington and Wayne K. Hinton, "Origin of the Welfare Plan of the Church of Jesus Christ of Latter-day Saints," *BYU Studies* 5 (Winter 1964): 67; *P*, 126.

[75] Special priesthood meeting, 7 Oct. 1935, transcript, binder 2, box 196, JRCP.

[76] VaLois South to JRC, 9 Nov. 1935, binder 2, box 196, JRCP.

[77] Arrington and Hinton, "Origin of the Welfare Plan," 75; *P*, 126-28.

[78] Leonard J. Arrington, *Utah, the New Deal and the Depression of the 1930s* (Ogden, UT: Weber State College Press, 1983), 14.

[79] JRC to Welfare meeting, 2 Oct. 1936, transcript, box 151, JRCP.

[80] JRC to agricultural meeting of Welfare Program, 4 Apr. 1955, transcript, 7, box 151, JRCP; also Marion G. Romney diary, 18 July 1951, private possession; JRC to Central Utah Welfare Regional Meeting, 3 Aug. 1951, quoted in *H*, 147.

[81] Also the quotes in Richard O. Cowan, *The Church in the Twentieth Century* (Salt Lake City: Bookcraft, 1985), 151-52; Rudd, *Pure Religion*, 45-47, 48-50.

[82] "A Conversation with Elder Neal Maxwell," in Hugh Hewett, *Searching for God in America* (Dallas, TX: Word, 1996), 128; "Tactical Revelation," *Sunstone* 19 (Dec. 1996): 80.

[83] David O. McKay office diary, 14 July 1947, LDSA.

[84] JRC to Heber J. Grant and David O. McKay, 5 May 1936, CR 1/48.

[85] *P*, 139; also Allen and Leonard, *The Story of the Latter-day Saints*, 525.

[86] *B*, 349.

[87] JRC to George H. Brimhall, [Jr.], 7 Oct. 1936, fd 1, box 354, JRCP.

[88] JRC to David O. McKay, 17 Jan. 1938, fd 7, box 26, McKay papers, LDSA.

[89] David O. McKay to JRC, 22 Jan. 1938, fd 7, box 26, McKay papers.

[90] JRC to David O. McKay, 27 Jan. 1938, fd 7, box 26, McKay papers.

[91] *Conf*, Apr. 1938, 106-07.

[92] JRC to Mrs. Ula K. Baird, 8 Apr. 1938, box 153, JRCP.

[93] Marion G. Romney diary, 10 Nov. 1942; also JRC, "In These Times," *Improvement Era* 46 (May 1943): 269.

[94] *LDS Church Welfare Handbook of Instructions* (Salt Lake City: General Church Welfare Committee of The Church of Jesus Christ of Latter-day Saints, 1944), 60.

[95] *LDS Church Welfare Handbook of Instructions* (1944), 62, also 60 ("sometimes called pensions" provision of Section 79).

[96] Rowena J. Miller to Mrs. Heber M. Slack, 10 Nov. 1958, fd 12, box 403, JRCP; also William E. Leuchtenburg, *Franklin D. Roosevelt and the New Deal, 1932-1940* (New York: Harper and Row, 1963), 132-33; Chandler, *America's Greatest Depression,* 207-08. Clarkana has I. Amter, *Social Security in a Soviet America* (New York: Workers' Library, 1935); *Explanation of Social Security Law as Amended in 1954* ... (Chicago: Commerce Clearing House, 1954).

[97] *H,* 328-29; *L,* 348, also Lee's quote for note 279.

[98] *SA,* 114 (quote), with similar statements on 194-95, 458-59, 497-98, 549.

[99] Minutes of Welfare Committee with First Presidency, 12 June 1937, CR 255/18, LDSA; *P,* 141-42.

[100] *Conf,* Apr. 1940, 17-18.

[101] Minutes of Welfare Committee with First Presidency, 12 June 1937 (JRC proposal), 18 June 1937 (McKay quote), CR 255/18. For incorporation of Co-operative Security Corporation, see *P,* 141.

[102] *P,* 148-49; minutes of Welfare Committee with First Presidency, 3 June and 1 July 1938, CR 255/18.

[103] "'Father' of Deseret Industries Visit[s] S.L.," *CN,* 1 July 1944, 12; Blumell, "Remember the Poor," 150-51, emphasized Hewlett's son Lester, second of the two who met with Clark.

[104] Rudd, *Pure Religion,* 65-82.

[105] JRC to David O. McKay, 2 Mar. 1936, fd 1, box 355, JRCP.

[106] *Conf,* Oct. 1940, 11.

[107] *Conf,* Apr. 1943, 97; JRC, "In These Times," *Improvement Era* 46 (May 1943): 269.

[108] JRC to Heber J. Grant and David O. McKay, 18 May 1936, fd 1, box 355, JRCP; also CR 1/48.

[109] JRC office diary, 25 Oct. 1941 (quotes); cf. Harold B. Lee's talk in *Conf,* Oct. 1941, 110-16.

[110] *Conf,* Oct. 1942, 57; *SR,* 39.

[111] Harold B. Lee diary, 10 Nov. 1941, private possession.

[112] "Mormons Explain Their Relief Plan," *NYT,* 25 May 1936, 20; "L.D.S. to Take 88,000 from Relief Rolls," *SLT,* 25 May 1936, 18; also "Mormons: Church Set to Take Relief Job Away from Nation," *Newsweek* 7 (6 June 1936): 27; "Mormons off Relief," *Time* 27 (8 June 1936): 32.

[113] *Conf,* Oct. 1936, 114.

[114] Minutes of Welfare Committee with First Presidency, 21 May 1937, CR 255/18, restatement of goal announced at 14 May meeting.

[115] "An Important Message," *DN,* 7 Apr. 1936, 1; *LDS Church Welfare Handbook of Instructions* (1944), 62; *P,* 132, 137-38.

[116] JRC to Reeve Schley, 28 May 1936, fd 2, box 354, JRCP.

[117] JRC, *Our Dwindling Sovereignty* (Salt Lake City: Deseret News Press, 1952), 4-5; *F,* 96-97; *SA,* 200. Clarkana has F. A. Harper, *Morals and the Welfare State* (Irvington-on-Hudson, NY: Foundation for Economic Education, 1951); see also Floyd Melvin Hammond, "Some Political Concepts of J. Reuben Clark, Jr.," M.A. thesis, Brigham Young University, 1962, 40-51 (chapter on "Welfare State").

[118] Minutes of Welfare Committee with First Presidency, 21 July 1939, CR 255/18.

[119] Minutes of Welfare Committee with First Presidency, 7 May 1937 (quote from Campbell M. Brown), 30 Sept., 29 Oct. 1937, 3 June 1938, CR 255/18; *P,* 146.

[120] Minutes of General Welfare Committee, 13 Apr. 1938, CR 255/5, LDSA.

[121] "42,000 Salt Lake Mormons on WPA, Despite 'Dole' Fight," *New York Daily News,* 21 June 1938, 8; "Tithes and Security," *Time* 38 (1 Aug. 1938): 26, with photograph of JRC; also report in *Boston Herald* that "the Church Welfare Program was a failure," discussed in minutes of Welfare Committee with First Presidency, 30 Sept., 15 July 1938, CR 255/18.

[122] Minutes of Welfare Committee with First Presidency, 4 Feb. 1938 (*DN* claim ending up in national *Literary Digest*); also minutes of 18 Feb. 1938 (JRC quote), CR 255/18.

[123] For example, "Mormons Explain Their Relief Plan," *NYT,* 25 May 1936, 20; "Predicts Mormon Gains," *NYT,* 2 Aug. 1937, 21; "Mormons Fearing Famine, Eat Single Meal; Plan Granary to Store Their Bumper Crops," *NYT,* 19 Sept. 1937, sec. II, 1; "125,000 Mormons Fast: Eat Only One Meal in Order to Save for Another Depression," *NYT,* 20 Sept. 1937, 44; "Mormon Speakers Attack Planned Economy and the Child Labor Amendments," *NYT,* 17 Nov. 1938, 37; "Mormon Relief Plan and WPA Contrasted," *NYT,* 21 June 1939, 2.

[124] *B,* 347-48.

[125] *H,* 153.

[126] JRC memorandum, "Church Security Plan," 19 Oct. 1937, fd 1, box 358, JRCP; also Marion G. Romney 1976 oral history, 6; *W,* 84; Blumell, "Remember the Poor," 148-49, softened in *P,* 142-43.

[127] Minutes of Welfare Committee with First Presidency, 30 Sept. 1937, CR 255/18.

[128] *Conf,* Apr. 1938, 95; Wilburn D. Talbot, *The Acts of the Modern Apostles* (Salt Lake City: Randall Book, 1985), 232-33; *Deseret News 1999-2000 Church Almanac* (Salt Lake City: Deseret News, 1998), 60.

[129] This was a result of political differences, not hostility toward the Cannon family. Heber J. Grant's son-in-law was George J. Cannon, brother of Joseph J. and Sylvester Q. See computerized Ancestral File, FHL.

[130] Lucile C. Tate, *LeGrand Richards: Beloved Apostle* (Salt Lake City: Book-craft, 1982), 27, 162, 256 (quote).

[131] Heber J. Grant journal sheets, 6 Apr. 1938.

[132] Sylvester Q. Cannon diary, 6 Apr. 1938; minutes of General Welfare

Committee, May 1937, CR 255/5; Tate, *LeGrand Richards,* 196, describes his choice of Ashton and Wirthlin from a list of prospective counselors during a meeting with President Grant and LeGrand's father, George F. Richards, an apostle; also *E,* 137.

133 Marion G. Romney diary, 30 Jan. 1942, also entry for 23 January. For the tensions between the Welfare Committee and Relief Society, see *P,* 143-44; *W,* 87.

134 Derr, et al., *Women of Covenant,* 244.

135 *H,* 554.

136 LeGrand Richards to Ernest L. Wilkinson, 5 June 1957, fd 1, box 108, Wilkinson papers, HBLL.

137 Marion G. Romney oral history, 1972-73, typescript, 15-16, LDSA.

138 Harold B. Lee diary, 17 Nov. 1954.

139 "Pres. Clark Testifies of Divinity of Church Welfare Program," *CN,* 8 Aug. 1951, 13.

140 JRC office diary, 10 Jan. 1939.

141 Minutes of Welfare Committee with the First Presidency, 8 Sept. 1939, CR 255/18; also *W,* 87-88.

142 *Conf,* Apr. 1944, 113-14; JRC, "The Way of Unity," *Improvement Era* 47 (May 1944): 271.

143 *Conf,* Apr. 1945, 25.

144 JRC to agricultural meeting of Welfare Program, 5 Apr. 1954, transcript, box 151, JRCP.

145 Minutes of Welfare Committee meeting with First Presidency, 6 Jan. 1939, CR 255/18.

146 *P,* 154.

147 *P,* 113 (programs and quotes), 97 (LDS as proportionately higher recipients of federal relief than non-LDS Utahns).

148 Leuchtenburg, *Franklin D. Roosevelt and the New Deal,* 346-47.

149 *P,* 154 (137,166 assisted in 1940 versus 155,460 in 1939).

150 JRC to Welfare meeting, 10 Apr. 1940, transcript, box 151, JRCP.

151 Rudd, *Pure Religion,* 65-82.

152 *P,* 154 (30,822 assisted in 1942 versus 124,599 in 1941).

153 Frank Evans diary, 21 Mar. 1942, LDSA.

154 Frank Evans diary, 30 July, 4 Aug. 1942.

155 Marion G. Romney interview with D. Michael Quinn, 26 Oct. 1977.

156 JRC, "Budget Beginnings," 36, bound volume, box 188, JRCP.

157 JRC to presidencies and superintendents of all LDS auxiliaries, 1 Apr. 1940, transcript in fd labeled "Suggestions to Auxiliaries," box 207, JRCP; also his less detailed reference in *Conf,* Apr. 1940, 14.

158 JRC office diary, 23 Jan. 1939.

159 *Conf,* Apr. 1938, 105-06 (first set of quotes); JRC, "In These Times," *Improvement Era* 46 (May 1943): 269 (second quote).

160 "Financial Report for the Year 1947," 11, CR 1/48; also "Welfare," *DN,* 7 Oct. 1939, 9, for JRC's statement that "the greatest depression in all history" will follow World War II.

[161] Harold B. Lee diary, 31 Aug. 1945.

[162] JRC to Aaronic Priesthood meeting, 6 Oct. 1944, transcript, box 151, JRCP.

[163] JRC to bishops' meeting, 8 Apr. 1944, transcript, box 151, JRCP.

[164] "Financial Report for the Year 1947," 11.

[165] Harold B. Lee diary, 23 Jan. 1948.

[166] JRC, "Against the Time of Need," *Improvement Era* 51 (May 1948): 270; *Conf,* Apr. 1948, 117-18.

[167] Martin Berkeley Hickman, *David Matthew Kennedy: Banker, Statesman, Churchman* (Salt Lake City: Deseret Book; Provo, UT: David M. Kennedy Center for International Studies, Brigham Young University, 1987), 202-03. This incident occurred about 1960, but McKay on 6 May 1962, after Clark's death, dedicated the stake center with its lannon stone (203): "When President McKay saw the beautiful new chapel, he confessed to Edmunds that he was glad the stake president had held out for stone" rather than red brick.

[168] JRC to bishops' meeting, 30 Sept. 1949, transcript (recommended reduction in expenditures), 7 Apr. 1950, transcript (quote), both in box 151, JRCP.

[169] The joint British-American bombing of nonmilitarized Dresden was the most famous example. See David Irving, *The Destruction of Dresden* (London: William Kimber, 1963); "The Bombing of Dresden" section in Garold N. Davis and Norma S. Davis, comps. and trans., *Behind the Iron Curtain: Recollections of Latter-day Saints in East Germany, 1945-1989* (Provo, UT: BYU Studies, 1996), 1-45.

[170] James B. Allen, Jessie L. Embry, and Kahlile B. Mehr, *Hearts Turned to the Fathers: A History of the Genealogical Society of Utah, 1894-1994* (Provo, UT: BYU Studies, 1995), 222.

[171] JRC, "Budget Beginnings," 9; see examples in *O,* 70-71, 76; *E,* 132-36.

[172] JRC, "Budget Beginnings," 9.

[173] Frank Evans diary, 5 Mar., 5 May, 17 July, 4 Aug. 1941.

[174] JRC statement, 8 Apr. 1943, in "Budget Beginnings," 9.

[175] JRC, "Budget Beginnings," 15.

[176] Ibid., 6-8.

[177] Harold B. Lee diary, 8 Apr. 1943, quoted in *L,* 198.

[178] JRC, "Budget Beginnings," 30. For Quorum of Twelve Apostles expressing resentment against being left out of financial oversight by First Presidency and the Presiding Bishopric, see *E,* 134-35, 139; also Lee quote for note 186.

[179] JRC office diary, 8 Apr. 1943; Harold B. Lee diary, 8 Apr. 1943; JRC, "Budget Beginnings," 33-34 (quote on 34).

[180] "General Principles Underlying Church Finances," final draft of 7 May 1943, in "Budget Beginnings," 76-92.

[181] JRC office diary, 28 Apr. 1943; Heber J. Grant journal sheets, 28 Apr. 1943.

[182] Verbatim interchange between JRC and Stephen L Richards in temple meeting of 29 Apr. 1943, "Budget Beginnings," 45.

[183] "Budget Beginnings," 35.

[184] Harold B. Lee diary, 29 Apr. 1943.

[185] *Conf,* Oct. 1943, 12; *M* 5:200; also JRC's explanation in *Conf,* Apr. 1948, 116-17.

[186] Harold B. Lee diary, 13 Oct. 1943; also George Albert Smith quote for note 178.

[187] Marion G. Romney diary, 6 Apr. 1944.

[188] JRC office diary, 3 Apr. 1953.

[189] *E,* 26-27.

[190] JRC to John A. Widtsoe, 1 May 1946, fd 2, box 374, JRCP.

[191] JRC statement to temple meeting of 8 Apr. 1943, "Budget Beginnings," 28.

[192] JRC office diary, 26 May 1943 (quote), also 4 Sept. 1946; Marion G. Romney diary, 27 Aug. 1948.

[193] Although resolved prior to Clark's arrival, a similar conflict of values surrounded the sale of alcohol at the church-owned Saltair resort. See *T,* 260-61.

[194] Brigham Young Hampton journal, 240-42, LDSA. According to his account, he had protested these leases but was brushed off by Brigham Young Trust Company officers. When non-LDS judge Charles S. Zane threatened in 1891 to prosecute the brothel owners, the trust company's officers decided to make Hampton the scapegoat due to his 1885 conviction for running a Mormon spy ring to entrap federal officials with prostitutes (167-68). Hampton was indicted on 15 November 1891 for operating a house of prostitution, but the charges were dropped on 26 March 1892.

As evidence of the truthfulness of Hampton's statements about these operations, the First Presidency and Quorum of Twelve agreed on 14 June 1900 to pay Hampton $3,600 for his previous work in a house of prostitution. See Journal History of the Church of Jesus Christ of Latter-day Saints, 14 June 1900, 1-2, microfilm, JWML. Hampton originally presented his claim for this "detective work" on 7 June 1900, the same day that the First Presidency and apostles discussed the then-current situation of LDS-leased brothels. See Journal History, 7 June 1900, 4; Brigham Young Jr., diary, 7 June 1900, LDSA. For the context of this situation, see D. Michael Quinn, *Same-Sex Dynamics among Nineteenth-Century Americans: A Mormon Example* (Urbana: University of Illinois Press, 1996), 317-22.

[195] Anthon H. Lund diary, 8 Apr. 1897, microfilm, LDSA. The microfilm is available to all researchers at LDSA by stipulation of its donor.

[196] Brigham Young Jr. diary, 7 June 1900; corporation documents and trustee bonds of Brigham Young Trust Company, file 737, Corporation Files, Salt Lake County Clerk, Utah State Archives, Salt Lake City.

[197] "Pages from the History of Zion: Something about the Brigham Young Trust Company and Its Stockholders. Trust Owned Property in Tenderloin of Zion. Buildings of Company Rented by the Officers for Immoral Purposes," *SLT,* 26 Sept. 1908, 14.

[198] "Compelled to Sell," *DN,* 12 Sept. 1908, 11.

[199] Aside from previously quoted statements by Apostles Lund and Young, see John Henry Smith diary, 8 Apr. 1897, in Jean Bickmore White, ed., *Church, State, and Politics: The Diaries of John Henry Smith* (Salt Lake City: Signature

Books/Smith Research Associates, 1990), 369; J. Golden Kimball diary, 7 May 1897, JWML.

[200] Translation of Danish entry in Anthon H. Lund diary, 6 Aug. 1897. His English language entry on 8 April 1897 described Grant's attending a late-night reception at what he thought was a newly opened LDS business, only to discover that he was "in a regular whore-house."

[201] JRC office diary, 10 Mar., 18 Aug. 1941.

[202] Frank Evans diary, 18 Aug. 1941.

[203] Excerpts from the verbatim minutes of KSL board of directors meeting, 25 Oct. 1951, quoted in full in Heber G. Wolsey, "The History of Radio Station KSL from 1922 to Television," Ph.D. diss., Michigan State University, 1967, 224-25.

[204] For the early 1900s as the beginning of strict prohibition on Mormon use of alcohol and tobacco, see Leonard J. Arrington, "An Economic Interpretation of the Word of Wisdom," *BYU Studies* 1 (Winter 1959): 37-49; Lester E. Bush Jr., "The Word of Wisdom in Early Nineteenth-Century Perspective," and Thomas G. Alexander, "The Word of Wisdom: From Principle to Requirement," *Dial* 14 (Autumn 1981): 47-65, 78-88; *T,* 258-71; Joseph Lynn Lyon, "Word of Wisdom," in *EM* 4:1584-85; *E,* 118-19, 121, 145-46, 686, 749, 762-63, 766, 768, 772, 775, 780, 782, 796-97, 800-01, 803, 807-08, 810, 822.

[205] Official KSL announcement, 25 Oct. 1951, box 244, JRCP; Wolsey, "History of Radio Station KSL," 222. Use of "unescapable" rather than "inescapable" identifies the author as JRC, who often used the older spelling.

[206] JRC to general priesthood meeting, 6 Apr. 1935, transcript, box 151, JRCP.

[207] JRC to Lute, 11 Jan. 1936, at end of JRC 1935-36 office diary.

[208] JRC to Henry H. Eyre, 7 Feb. 1941, fd 1, box 363, JRCP.

[209] JRC to Louise Clark Bennion, 24 Apr. 1941, fd 1, box 363, JRCP, emphasis in original.

[210] JRC to Beth Moffett, 29 July 1938, fd 2, box 359, JRCP; JRC office diary, 30 June 1950, 24 Mar. 1952.

[211] JRC to J. H. Gipson, president of Caxton Printers, 9 June 1949, fd 9, box 379, JRCP.

[212] JRC to Hazel Liston, 14 Feb. 1948, fd 15, box 377, JRCP.

[213] JRC office diary, 14 Feb. 1952.

[214] Harold B. Lee diary, 23 June 1945.

[215] When LDS president Joseph Fielding Smith died in 1972, his royalties from Deseret Book Company totaled $9,636 for the previous six-month period. See *E,* 210; Joseph Fielding Smith estate file #59189, Third District Court of Utah, Utah State Archives. Lowell L. Durham Jr. said that Apostle LeGrand Richards was the only general authority who declined to receive royalties during Durham's service as president of church-owned Deseret Book Company (Durham statement after tape-recorded interview with D. Michael Quinn, 1992).

[216] Peggy Petersen Barton, *Mark E. Petersen: A Biography* (Salt Lake City: Deseret Book, 1985), 107, also 75-76 (Petersen as "a protégé" of JRC).

217 Tate, *LeGrand Richards,* 236-37, 255.

218 JRC to David O. McKay, 22 May 1951, fd 19, box 410, JRCP.

219 JRC to Otto Norman Olsen, 21 Sept. 1949, fd 6, box 380, JRCP; also quoted in *E*, 835-36.

220 F. Burton Howard, *Marion G. Romney: His Life and Faith* (Salt Lake City: Bookcraft, 1988), 165.

221 *L*, 148.

222 JRC to Rulon H. Tingey, 14 Dec. 1950 ("5% increase"), fd 14, box 382, JRCP; cf. *M* 6:284 (letter of 18 April 1950: "The living allowances of the General Authorities be increased 30 percent retroactive to January 1, 1950").

223 JRC office diary, 28 Dec. 1950.

224 JRC to J. Rolfe Pratt, 12 Sept. 1931, fd R12, box 38, JRCP.

225 Harold B. Lee diary, 15 Dec. 1950.

226 JRC to William E. Stoker, Orval C. Fox, and E. Stephen Buckmiller (bishopric of South Twentieth Ward), 22 Mar. 1943, fd 3, box 367, JRCP.

227 Minutes of General Welfare Committee, 20 July 1936, CR 255/5.

228 Harold B. Lee diary, 31 May 1955.

229 Reed Smoot diary, 2 Nov. 1926, 13 Dec. 1927, 1 June 1928, in *I*, 634, 634n28, 669, 669n52, 681.

230 JRC to Richard R. Lyman, 2 Sept. 1942, fd 2, box 365, JRCP; also JRC to Welfare meeting, 1 Oct. 1955, transcript, box 151, JRCP.

231 JRC estate file #45114, Third District Court of Utah, Utah State Archives.

232 JRC to Ezra Taft Benson, 8 July 1940, fd 1, box 362, JRCP.

233 Frank Evans diary, 8 Nov. 1945.

234 Harold B. Lee diary, 2 Nov. 1948.

235 Henry D. Moyle diary, 24 Mar. 1953.

236 JRC office diary, 9 Apr., 11 May 1953.

237 JRC to agricultural meeting of Welfare Program, 4 Apr. 1955, transcript, 3, box 151, JRCP. For context and further examples involving Apostle Henry D. Moyle, see Thomas G. Alexander, *The Forest Service and the LDS Church in the Mid-Twentieth Century: Utah National Forests as a Test Case* (Ogden, UT: Weber State College Press, 1988).

238 JRC to special meeting for Welfare Program, 1 Oct. 1955, transcript in fd for October 1955 conference, box 164, JRCP.

239 JRC office diary, 1 July 1957. As an indication of the importance of this conversation with Ezra Taft Benson, JRC also recorded it in a memorandum dated 1 July 1957, fd 4, box 398, JRCP.

240 JRC ranch diary, 11 Oct. 1957, JRCP.

241 Harold B. Lee diary, 17 Oct. 1957; follow-up on 25 October: "I learned from Bill Marriott [J. Willard Marriott, hotel-entrepreneur and LDS stake president] that Ezra Taft Benson took his wife and two daughters, after all, with him on his round the world trip, contrary to the advise [sic] of Pres. Clark."

242 JRC ranch diary, 29 Oct. 1957.

[243] Ezra Taft Benson to David O. McKay, 3 Dec. 1957, with carbon copy of undated letter to JRC (quote), both in fd 1, box 194, McKay papers.

[244] JRC to Karl D. Butler, 4 Dec. 1957, fd 9, box 398, JRCP.

[245] JRC, *Grazing on the National Forests* (Salt Lake City: Utah Cattlemen's Association, [1957]); *SA*, 575-606.

[246] M—— J. R——— to David O. McKay, 17 Dec. 1957, and O—— M. D——— to JRC (copy to McKay), 18 Dec. 1957 ("tyrants" and connected quotes), A. C. H— Jr. to McKay (copy to Ezra Taft Benson), 28 Dec. 1957 ("selfish" and connected quotes), C. N. W—— to McKay, 14 Jan. 1958 ("impassioned" and connected quotes), all in fd 1, box 194, McKay papers.

[247] David O. McKay office diary, 30 Jan. 1958.

[248] Ezra Taft Benson to JRC, undated carbon copy in Benson to David O. McKay, 2 Jan. 1958, fd 1, box 194, McKay papers.

[249] JRC home diary, 12 Feb. 1958, JRCP.

[250] JRC to meeting of Welfare Program, 5 Apr. 1958, transcript, box 151, JRCP.

[251] JRC memorandum, 18 Apr. 1958, unnumbered box, JRCP.

[252] JRC office diary, 4 Dec. 1959; also John A. Widtsoe, "President J. Reuben Clark, Jr., Farmer," *Improvement Era* 45 (Sept. 1942): 556-57, 605, 607.

[253] JRC to agricultural meeting of Welfare Program, 4 Apr. 1960, transcript, 1, box 151, JRCP, parentheses in original.

[254] JRC farm diary, 5 June 1960, JRCP. For two of his talks about the small farmer and rancher, see *SA*, 419-35, 575-606. For a personal view and defense, see Ezra Taft Benson, *Cross Fire: The Eight Years with Eisenhower* (Garden City, NY: Doubleday, 1962).

[255] Alexander, *Forest Service and the LDS Church in the Mid-Twentieth Century*, 10 (first quote), 21 (second quote).

[256] Harold B. Lee diary, 19 Apr. 1950.

[257] William F. Edwards, *Budget Preparation and Control Report to the First Presidency* [printed and spiral-bound] (n.p., 21 Oct. 1955), 6, Stephen L Richards miscellaneous files, CR 1/14, LDSA.

[258] Harold B. Lee diary, 22 Apr. 1955.

[259] JRC memorandum, 21 Sept. 1956, removed from JRCP in 1977 by David H. Yarn because he regarded it as too controversial for other researchers, but given to me by J. Reuben Clark III for my own information and note-taking.

[260] Harold B. Lee diary, 9 Sept. 1955.

[261] *W*, 94.

[262] Marion G. Romney diary, 16 Jan. 1959.

[263] *E*, 218.

[264] David O. McKay office diary, 22 Jan. 1959.

[265] *Conf*, Apr. 1959, 45.

[266] *L*, 288, 295, 297, for Richards as source of the conflict; *H*, 327-29, for less specific "the First Presidency" as source of the conflict.

[267] JRC to temple meeting of First Presidency and Quorum of Twelve

Apostles, 27 Apr. 1961, transcript, box 264, JRCP. I reversed the order of these two quoted sections of his remarks.

[268] JRC report, 6 Feb. 1950, removed from JRCP in 1977 by David H. Yarn, but given to me by J. Reuben Clark III for note-taking; also *E*, 832, for full Clark quote about what should be done with a local bishop who embezzled funds.

[269] JRC memorandum of conversation with William F. Edwards, 22 May 1957, removed from JRCP in 1977 by David H. Yarn, but given to me by J. Reuben Clark III for note-taking.

[270] JRC office diary, 3 Jan. 1945 (with the word "rob"), 3 Feb. 1961; Rowena J. Miller to Max Dean, manager of the Hotel Utah, 23 Feb. 1961, fd 18, box 411, JRCP.

[271] William F. Edwards to the First Presidency, 20 Jan. 1960, Edwards fd, CR 1/48, LDSA.

[272] JRC office diary, 13 Feb. 1960 (first quote), 19 May 1960 (last quote).

[273] Ernest L. Wilkinson diary, 19 Oct. 1960 (with the symbol for "cents," which I spelled out), photocopy, JWML; also Gary James Bergera, "Building Wilkinson's University," *Dial* 30 (Fall 1997): 125-26, 128, 128n98.

Undoubtedly reflecting President Clark's viewpoint, his protégé Harold B. Lee told Reuben III: "Ernest comes in here with the most elaborate set of hogwash that I have ever seen to justify his need for money [at BYU]. And he always gets it because there is no point at which you can attack it; there is no point where you can show that it is wrong; there is no point where you can show a fallacy in his argument. All you can say is that we just do not have it [the money]." See J. Reuben Clark III oral history, 1982, typescript, 7, HBLL.

[274] Spencer W. Kimball interview with D. Michael Quinn, 2 Feb. 1979.

[275] William F. Edwards oral history, 1983, typescript, 8 (business role in New York City), 9 (positions at BYU and salary), 10 (LDS banks and Orval Adams—wrongly identified by the transcriber as "Al Adams"—and conflict at LDS headquarters), HBLL. The transcriber also misspelled the word as "backbitting."

[276] Ernest L. Wilkinson diary, 19 May 1960 (Edwards's resignation, effective 1 July); William F. Edwards oral history, 1983, 11 (Moyle's role in his "release"). President McKay said, "Brother Edwards, we will release you" (oral history, 11), but allowed him to submit a written resignation. Edwards said: "When granted that release, I was fifty-five years of age, in Salt Lake, unemployed. We had used up a considerable part of our meager savings and I had only accumulated one hundred dollars a month of retirement income" (oral history, 11).

[277] Ernest L. Wilkinson diary, 1 Oct. 1960.

[278] Harold B. Lee diary, 4 Mar., 14 May 1952, 31 July 1953, 31 Dec. 1957; Marion G. Romney diary, 25 Mar. 1947; JRC ranch diary, 6 Oct. 1957; *H*, 327-28.

[279] Harold B. Lee diary, 3 Sept. 1957, quoted in *L*, 297; also see "year's supply" in "Glossary" of *EM* 4:1773.

[280] *L*, 341-43.

[281] Minutes of Welfare Committee meeting with First Presidency, 6 Jan. 1939; JRC, "Budget Beginnings," 28; also JRC office diary, 8 Feb. 1947.

[282] Allen and Leonard, *The Story of the Latter-day Saints,* 545–47 (background and preparations for aid); "LDS Donations for Europe Total 85 Cars," *SLT,* 26 Oct. 1947, B-20; *P,* 152 (quote); also Richard Neitzel Holzapfel, "Friends Again: Canadian Grain and the German Saints," *JMH* 23 (Fall 1997): 46–76.

[283] JRC office diary, 22 Sept. 1947.

[284] Minutes of Welfare Committee meeting with First Presidency, 19 June 1953, CR 255/18.

[285] *B,* 353–54.

[286] *H,* 228; also Marion G. Romney diary, 29 Aug. 1951, "Following the General Welfare meeting this morning, went with Elders Harold B. Lee and Henry D. Moyle to Grantsville, where we spent the day with President Clark going over the proposed welfare handbook." Howard, *Marion G. Romney,* 119, says this occurred in 1941, which was a typesetting error.

[287] *P,* 249–52; *E,* 879–80, 883–85, 888, 893.

NOTES TO AFTERWORD

[1] *D&C* 124:96.

[2] Ralph Barton Perry, *Characteristically American* (New York: Knopf, 1949); Henry Steele Commager, *The American Mind: An Interpretation of American Thought and Character Since the 1880s* (New Haven: Yale University Press, 1950), esp. 8–10, 29–31, 45–54; David Riesman, "From Morality to Morale," in Michael McGiffert, ed., *The Character of Americans* (Homewood, IL: Dorsey Press, 1964), 256–57; Helene S. Zahler, *The American Paradox* (New York: E.P. Dutton, 1964), esp. 153–234; John Higham, "The Reorientation of American Culture in the 1890s," in John Weiss, ed., *The Origins of Modern Consciousness* (Detroit, MI: Wayne State University Press, 1965), 34–39; John Morton Blum, *The Promise of America: An Historical Inquiry* (Boston: Houghton Mifflin, 1966), 54–148.

[3] Spencer W. Kimball to JRC, 28 Aug. 1958, fd 7, box 401, JRCP.

[4] D. Arthur Haycock interview by D. Michael Quinn, 3 Aug. 1979.

INDEX

Based on a comprehensive index submitted by the author, the publisher prepared this index which significantly revised the subject headings and deleted the names of many persons mentioned in the biography.

A

Abel, Elijah, 343, 356, 574n190

Adams, Orval W., 63, 269, 270, 271, 422

adultery, 192-93, 245, 251, 253

Affleck, Gordon Burt, viii, ix, xvi, xvii, xviii, 138-39, 162, 174, 176, 177, 191, 270, 473n42, 473n45

African Americans, 264, 325, 339-59, 369, 427, 572n176, 574n187, 574nn189-90, 575n192, 575n199, 576n201, 576nn204-05, 576n211, 577n214, 577n216, 578n231, 579n242, 580n246, 581n265, 584n39

afterlife, 170, 188, 193, 227, 250, 364

alcohol. *See* prohibition

Alexander, Thomas G., xvii, 418

Allen, James B., xvii, 476n87

Allen, Marilyn R., 328, 563n76

America/Americans, xiv-xv, 32, 137, 359, 425, 520n155, 530n278, 569n137, 569n139

America First Committee, 290, 539n90

American Association of Blood Banks, 337, 350

American International Corporation (AIC), 16, 28, 29-30

American Jewish League Against Communism, 327, 562n59

American Legion, 75, 260, 317

American Peace Society, 267, 278-79, 281, 299, 300, 547n182

American Society for Judicial Settlement of International Disputes, 278-79

Anderson, Byron D., 67-68, 71, 72

Anderson, Jack, 264, 266-67

Anderson, Joseph, 89, 100, 104, 141, 149, 268, 474n52

Anderson, Marian, 345, 347, 576n204, 576n211

apostasy/apostates, 83, 189, 190, 209, 226, 228-29, 502n122, 574n190

archaeology, 207-08, 236

Arizona, 80, 114, 253-54, 337, 348, 395, 577n214

art and culture (JRC views on): artistic performers, 371; expressionist caricature, 365; general, 37, 362-76; music/musicians, 37, 367-74, 376, 583n28; opera, 37, 367-68, 376; paintings, 365-66; sculpture/sculptors, 362-63, 374

Articles of Faith, 10, 285

Aryans, 304, 334, 548n199

Ashton, Marvin O., 401, 593n132

Asia, communism in, xi, 282, 314; poverty, 424; religions, 205-06, 209

Asper, Frank W., 49, 370, 372, 373

atheism, viii, 27-28, 135, 202, 206, 207, 208, 230, 233, 426

Austria, 333, 540n99, 557n20

Aztecs, 37, 212

B

455n108, 492n20, 521n156, 521n158, 521nn160-61, 522n167, 522n168, 523n175, 524n181, 550n234, 553n278, 561nn55-56, 563n71, 564n82, 570n145; Marxists, 257-58, 264, 266, 268, 310, 316, 521nn157-58; *Naked Communist,* 268; Russian revolution, 258, 280, 315, 326, 327; war of 1918-20 against Bolsheviks, 259, 280

Community Chest (now United Way), 385, 387

conspiracies/plots, 254, 268, 281, 327, 337, 392, 519n136, 537n60

Constitution (U.S.): adherence to (JRC), 75, 189, 228, 273, 275, 344, 348, 357, 530n278; amendments, 34, 198, 255-56, 340, 346, 451n37; general, 69, 75, 80-81, 95, 203, 228, 254-57, 260, 268, 275, 312-13, 314, 337, 346, 348, 425, 530n278; Mormons saving, 257; restraints, 254-55

Cornwall, J. Spencer, 369-70, 371

Cossacks (singing group), 370, 584n44

Coughlin, Charles E., 75, 455n108

Council of Fifty, 221, 243

counseling LDS members: general, 119-20, 187, 188; JRC personally, 119-20, 180, 184-201, 206-07, 210, 211, 212-13, 221, 238, 249-50, 265, 268, 291-92, 301-02, 309, 311, 324-25, 350, 352

Cowley, Matthew, 138, 272, 473n45

Cowley, Matthias F., 240, 249, 471n8, 513n83, 517n112

CPUSA. *See* Communism

critics/criticism: of JRC (by LDS), viii, xvii, 32, 65, 70, 74, 76, 78, 80, 81-84, 103, 107-08, 119, 186, 203, 234, 266-67, 291, 293, 297, 395, 417-18, 421-22, 458n155, 532n16, 539n91; (by non-LDS), 34, 293, 298, 443n160, 463n248; of JRC proteges, 155-56, 273; JRC view of criticism, xviii, 32, 34, 53, 70, 76, 82-83, 119, 136, 291, 300, 301, 311, 332, 405, 417-18, 421-

22, 463n248; of LDS president, 22-23, 84, 405; of Nazi Germany, 282, 288, 291-92, 332, 333, 335, 557n20; religious "cranks," 186-87

cultists, 223, 268

Cundick, Robert, 370-71

Curtis, Fred E. H., 251, 253, 518n113

Czechoslovakia: foreign policy, 173; general, 88, 294, 292

D

dancing: general, 190-91; JRC, 11; Samoan, 77, 456n118

Dante Alighieri, 48, 62; (quote) 48, 62, 448n235

Dean, Joseph H., 517nn111-12

Dearing, Fred Morris, 30, 83-84, 168, 316

death, "dedicating" to God, 183-84; FDR, 104; friends and relatives, 43, 168-69, 183-84, 185, 323; general, 30, 101-02, 185-86; LDS presidents, 105, 130; spirits of deceased, 113; suicide, 194

democracy, 225, 278, 287, 290, 315-16

Democratic Party, xiv-xv, 2, 15, 22, 46-47, 57-58, 60-61, 62, 66, 71, 73, 82, 95, 100, 257, 259, 268, 269, 271, 272, 273, 278, 279, 329, 330, 331, 383, 386, 400, 402, 454n101, 461n219, 520n155

democratic socialism, 57, 264, 326, 521n157, 522n167

Dennis, William Cullen, 245, 296, 299-300

Depression (1920s in Utah), 17-18, 382; (1930s in U.S.), 57, 132, 142, 332, 382-84, 388, 393, 403-04, 419, 420, 444n173; (post-World War II predicted), 289, 406

Derounian, Arthur, 301, 546n175

Deseret News, 22, 60, 67, 74, 80-82, 94-95, 97, 98, 158, 190, 209-10, 221-22, 254, 255, 260-61, 265, 267, 275, 283-84, 285, 292, 298, 309, 312, 323, 332,

H

ABOUT THE AUTHOR

D. Michael Quinn (Ph.D., history, Yale University), is a former Professor of History, Brigham Young University, and currently an Affiliated Scholar at the Center for Feminist Research, University of Southern California. His accolades include Best Book awards from both the American Historical Association and the Mormon History Association.

He is the author of *Early Mormonism and the Magic World View*, the two-volume *Mormon Hierarchy* series (*Origins of Power, Extensions of Power*), and *Same-Sex Dynamics among Nineteenth-Century Americans: A Mormon Example.* He is also the editor of *The New Mormon History: Revisionist Essays on the Past* and has contributed to *American National Biography*; *Encyclopedia of New York State*; *Fundamentalisms and Society: Reclaiming the Sciences, the Family, and Education*; *New Encyclopedia of the American West*; *Under an Open Sky: Rethinking America's Western Past*; and others.

Quinn's many honors include fellowships and grants from the American Academy of Arts and Sciences, American Council of Learned Societies, the Henry E. Huntington Library, Indiana-Purdue University, and the National Endowment for the Humanities. He has been a keynote speaker at the Center for the Study of Religion and American Culture, the Chicago Humanities Symposium, Claremont Graduate University, University of Paris (France), Washington State Historical Society, and elsewhere, and a consultant for television documentaries carried by the Arts and Entertainment Channel, the Canadian Broadcasting Corporation, the History Channel, and the Public Broadcasting Service (PBS).